Organization and Decision

Translated into English for the first time, Luhmann's modern classic, *Organization and Decision*, explores how organizations work; how they should be designed, steered, and controlled; and how they order and structure society. Luhmann argues that organization is order, yet indeterminate. In this book, he shows how this paradox enables organizations to embed themselves within society without losing autonomy. In developing his autopoietic perspective on organizations, Luhmann applies his general theory of social systems by conceptualizing organizations as self-reproducing systems of decision communications. His innovative and interdisciplinary approach to the material (spanning organization studies, management and sociology) is integral to any study of organizations. This new translation enables researchers and graduate students across the English-speaking world to access Luhmann's ideas more readily.

NIKLAS LUHMANN (1927–1998) ranks as one of the most important German social theorists of the twentieth century. His works have been highly influential in sociology and other social sciences, including organization studies. The significance of organizations for Luhmann can be traced in his biography: at the beginning of his career, he spent almost eight years as a legal expert in public administration, through which he gained professional expertise in the function of organizations. This practice inspired much of his later theoretical work at Harvard's Graduate School for Public Administration, the University for Public Administration at Speyer, the Center for Social Research in Dortmund, where he was head of department, and at the Department of Sociology at Bielefeld University, where he largely refrained from administrative work. This book, which was one of Luhmann's last, can be regarded as his conclusion to over thirty years of research on organized social systems.

RHODES BARRETT is a professional translator. He has previously translated two other books by Niklas Luhmann: *Risk* (1993) and *Theory of Society* (2012).

Organization and Decision

Niklas Luhmann
Rhodes Barrett

CAMBRIDGE
UNIVERSITY PRESS

CAMBRIDGE
UNIVERSITY PRESS

University Printing House, Cambridge CB2 8BS, United Kingdom

One Liberty Plaza, 20th Floor, New York, NY 10006, USA

477 Williamstown Road, Port Melbourne, VIC 3207, Australia

314-321, 3rd Floor, Plot 3, Splendor Forum, Jasola District Centre, New Delhi - 110025, India

79 Anson Road, #06-04/06, Singapore 079906

Cambridge University Press is part of the University of Cambridge.

It furthers the University's mission by disseminating knowledge in the pursuit of education, learning and research at the highest international levels of excellence.

www.cambridge.org
Information on this title: www.cambridge.org/9781108472074
DOI: 10.1017/9781108560672

Translation from the German language edition:
Organisation und Entscheidung
by Niklas Luhmann
VS Verlag für Sozialwissenschaften
Copyright © Springer Fachmedien Wiesbaden GmbH, Wiesbaden 2011
This Springer imprint is published by Springer Nature
The registered company is Springer Fachmedien Wiesbaden GmbH
All Rights Reserved

First published 2018

A catalogue record for this publication is available from the British Library

Library of Congress Cataloging in Publication data
Names: Luhmann, NIklas, author. | Baecker, Dirk, author. | Barrett, Rhodes, author.
Title: Organization and decision / NIklas Luhmann, Dirk Baecker, and Rhodes Barrett.
Description: Cambridge, United Kingdom ; New York, NY: Cambridge University Press, 2018. | Includes bibliographical references and index.
Identifiers: LCCN 2018026131| ISBN 9781108472074 (hbk. : alk. paper) | ISBN 9781108458962 (pbk.)
Subjects: LCSH: Organizational behavior. | Organizational change. | Organizational effectiveness.
Classification: LCC HD58.7 .L855 2018 | DDC 302.3/5–dc23
LC record available at https://lccn.loc.gov/2018026131

ISBN 978-1-108-47207-4 Hardback
ISBN 978-1-108-45896-2 Paperback

Contents

Preface   *page* vii

 1 Organization Theory: The Classical Constructions   1

 2 Organization as an Autopoietic System   26

 3 Membership and Motives   62

 4 The Paradox of Decision-Making   98

 5 Time Relations   122

 6 Uncertainty Absorption   147

 7 Decision Premises   181

 8 Decision Programs   210

 9 Personnel   230

10 The Organization of Organization   250

11 Structural Change: The Poetry of Reform and the Reality
    of Evolution   273

12 Technology   299

13 Organization and Society   316

14 Self-Description   347

15 Rationality   369

    Conclusion: Theory and Practice   393

Index   395

Preface

Organizations deserve more attention than they have hitherto found – above all, a different sort of attention. This may seem a bold assertion given the many ways in which organizations are discussed in everyday communication and in the relevant scientific disciplines. But this is the very reason to concentrate our attention more strongly not on organizations as countable entities but on organization as a process. This is relevant from a theoretical perspective, given that inquiry into the essence of organization seems to have become unproductive (which is typical of questions of essence; indeed of what-questions per se). But a different understanding of organization could prove important for the purposes of practical policy. Precisely because organizations (again in the plural) have become crucial, indispensable to modern life, it could be important to have a better grasp of their "intrinsic logic." Especially if heteronomy – be it subjection to owners or other "masters," to liberal or socialist ideologies, or to representatives of interests that are themselves organized – is increasingly called into question, it could be important to give organizations a conception of themselves that enables them to answer for themselves. There is much talk of decentralization; more flexibility is demanded – for instance in regulating working time or flattening hierarchies, or in eliminating what is superfluous. But fashions in the slogans bandied about by the consulting industry are perhaps also among the external factors that ignore the question, far too complex for the sector, of whether the individual organization is not best able to find out on its own how best to cope. Where "participation" is practiced, the term is no longer used to express the pathos of becoming human or treating human beings as human beings; it addresses how to obtain the best possible results.

This should, however, not be interpreted as a recipe for "individual responsibility," "deregulation," "decentralization," and so forth. And, of course, there is no organization that does not depend heavily and with little freedom of action on its environment – for example, on its market or its sources of finance. But this still leaves unsettled the question of how an organization determines what it can do in the light of such dependence – in other words, how it can build freedoms, alternatives, leeway into its dependence on its environment and into its dependence on its own past. We can reckon with a need for orientation. If this is so, the point of departure would have to be the question of how an organization distinguishes itself from what it is not and does not want to be.

However, such an inquiry takes us far beyond the usual conceptual and theoretical scope of organizational studies. We will have to address it without losing sight of the immediate aim of an organization theory adapted to present-day conditions. All cognitive systems process distinctions. They are the processing of their distinctions. This holds true for organizations – the subject of this study. But it also holds true for descriptions, for texts written about organizations. And it also applies, to quote Friedrich Schlegel, for the "organization of text" about organizations. The question is only how strict the linkage between distinctions turns out to be, how logically the system processes.

Models can be found in Hegel's dialectic. In describing self-organization (of the mind), Hegel treats distinctions as oppositions and oppositions as unstable. Having rejected subject theory as one-sided, he can therefore treat construction only as the cancellation of opposites. The consequences are well known. George Spencer-Brown's calculus of forms offers another example. In the guise of a mathematical calculus, it describes how forms (marked distinctions) come to observe themselves. Whereas Hegelian dialectic ends with the concept having done its job and "coming to itself," the calculus of forms ends by overreaching the scope of its own calculability and attaining a state that can only be described as "unresolvable indeterminacy," which requires further processing of imaginary worlds, time, memory, and leeway for oscillation. The system thus becomes an unpredictable, historical machine with an unforeseeable future.

Organizations are more likely to fit the calculus of forms than dialectal theory – at least if we no longer regard the organization as a goal-attaining (self-terminating) system (which has always been a normative-rational model and never an empirical description). On the other hand, it will hardly be possible to attribute the stringency of self-calculation to it. Organizational sociology will therefore have to go its own way.

Organizations are clearly non-calculable, unpredictable, historical systems each of which assumes a present it has itself generated. They are clearly systems that can observe themselves and others, which thus oscillate between self-reference and other-reference. They clearly owe their stability to a network of loose couplings and not to a "technology" of tight couplings. But this does not exclude writing texts about organizations that organize observations more stringently than do organizations themselves. Such a text will not seek to present a normative model of a rational organization; it promises no gains in rationality let alone lower costs. Nor does it seek to portray reality in the form of a reduced overview – as a map does of a country. It ventures beyond the

classical opposition between normative and descriptive theories in an attempt
to show that a theoretical text can generate more cognitive consistency than is
apparent in the everyday operations of systems. In this sense, the text will seek
to elucidate through its own processing of distinctions – but, of course, by
processing distinctions that distinguish the distinctions of organizations.

The first distinction (of the text) states that organizations are autopoietic
systems, which produce and reproduce themselves through their own operations. This includes the thesis that organizations describe themselves as organizations; for an external observer could otherwise not know whether the
system under observation is an organization or not. An observer can naturally
construct their own "analytical" concepts, but these concepts can help one only
to observe oneself.

We then come to the question of the operation by which an organization
distinguishes itself from other autopoietic systems, thus defining itself as an
organization, making itself into an organization. The answer is by decision.
This raises the question of how decisions are distinguished and how they can be
linked despite, indeed because of, their discreteness. The answer is provided by
the concept of the absorption of uncertainty. This could suggest that by linking
decisions, organizations transform uncertainty into certainty. Although this is
true, it does not suffice to explain the potential of organizations for reflection
and self-change. This can be achieved by distinguishing between decisions and
the premises of decisions, which permits double closure of the system at both
the operational and structural levels; and double closure is in general
a condition for reflection. Finally, the premises for decision-making – differentiated into various types, namely decision-making programs, personnel and
communication channels, responsibilities (division of labor) – are realized in
decision-making contexts.

This crucial element of the theory makes it possible to treat the history of
theory in organizational research in terms of what distinctions gain prominence
and how the transition from one distinction to another can be explained,
keeping in mind that every single distinction produces subcomplex results
and calls up "supplements" (Derrida). Moreover, with the aid of the theoretical
core we can try to estimate what barriers there are to the efforts of the
organization at self-change and self-reflection; in other words, how real organizations differ from ideal conceptions of open changeability and complete
self-transparency. Finally, it can be shown that and why organizations that
generate and close themselves off in this manner differ from the societal system
that makes them possible by enabling communication, that uses them to
coordinate all sorts of communications, and that can nevertheless neither
control nor monitor them.

The final question that arises from the distinction-theoretical approach is
how the unity of a distinction is to be conceived (we have always spoken of

distinctions as if they were unities). The answer is that the unity of the distinction that is used for observation in each case cannot occur within the distinction itself. The unity of the distinction contradicts itself. It is a performative self-contradiction. It is a paradox. But the paradox is the observer himself, who cannot observe himself observing. In this sense, theory is concerned with resolving this paradox of observation – both at the level of its subject matter and at the level of the theory itself, that is to say, both other-referentially and self-referentially. And the link between theory and subject matter lies only in this insight. We thus presuppose neither principles of nature nor of reason, nor a concept of truth that promises some sort of "adequate" linkage of these two components of knowledge. The premise of organization is the unknownness of the future, and the success of organizations lies in the treatment of this uncertainty: its intensification, its specification, and the reduction of its costs.

Whoever has difficulty coming to terms with this and is not curious enough to try it out should read no further.

1 Organization Theory: The Classical Constructions

The concept of organization took on clearer contours only in the second half of the nineteenth century. In the Middle Ages there had been no need for a special concept for what we now call organizations. It would have lacked substance: the stratification of family households and corporations provided for social order, which for the rest was subject to a multiplicity of legal arrangements.[1] Only in the nineteenth century did it become usual to conceptualize the organization as a social formation distinct from other social orders (e.g., communities or social classes). Then the term "organization" found its way into normal, everyday and scientific usage to describe a special type of object. Already frequent in the eighteenth century, it originally referred to the order of organic life as opposed to artifacts and mechanisms.[2] Jean Paul had still regarded the term organization with reference to non-organic matters as a metaphor,[3] but himself wrote about the organization of texts in the sense of actively ordering production.[4] Perhaps the transition to an active, activity-related usage of the term generalized the concept. At any rate, the concept of organization, originally, offered the possibility of referring to both an activity and its effect without addressing this difference.

Because the eighteenth century tended to replace hierarchical distinctions by the distinction between "inside" and "outside," in the semantic field of organization we already find the distinction between internal and external relations. This enabled the disorganization concept to be introduced – separately from any hierarchical architecture of the world and with reference to the internal defects of an organism. At about the same time, biology and demography adopted a new concept relating to the individual: "population," which deprived the old genus/species schema of much of its significance and prepared the way for the evolution theory of the nineteenth century. In explaining internal organization, however, the whole/parts schema persisted, and thus the assumption of a harmony tuned to this schema, almost in the old sense of *ordinata concordia*. The distinction between means and ends could be used, treating the compounding into a whole as the end and the combination of parts as the means. This allowed Kant to introduce fuzzy concepts like "interaction" [Wechselwirkung] between parts and the idea that the whole was its own end.[5] This prepared the conceptual isolation of organized entities in themselves and gave substance to the distinction between inside and outside.

After these first ventures and the quite positive complexion lent to the concept, the nineteenth century came to use organization above all in the theory of society. Modern, post-revolutionary society was in search of a form for itself – partly in distinction to the aristocratic societies of the European tradition, partly in conceptual defense against the unrest generated by the French Revolution. What was at stake was reconstruction on a new basis with promise for the future. Saint-Simon announced his program as follows: "The philosophy of the last century was revolutionary, that of the nineteenth century must be organizational,"[6] and August Comte was to endow the same thought with characteristics like scientificity, positivity, and sociology. Despite the deliberate quest for historical distance and new, reliable objectives, the conceptual elements of attributing parts to a functioning whole were retained. However, the organization concept now exuded strong positive qualities such as "social" and "solidarity"[7] that had a good chance of calling attention to the inadequacy of mere organization; of becoming desiderata, indeed oppositional concepts. It was demanded, as we would now say, that an enterprise ought to keep the social interests of its employees in mind – as if working together was not yet in itself social. While retaining its original characteristics, the organization concept when applied to society now bifurcated. It marked an inadequacy, a dissatisfaction with the typical features of modern society, together with such concepts as commodity, market, exchange, finally money. In 1887, Tönnies's "Community and Society" [Gemeinschaft und Gesellschaft] appeared; it enjoyed little success with its unusual conceptuality, but the dualization it introduced captured and long influenced the spirit of the times. Parsons's "pattern variables" still followed this model.[8]

The first distinction that produced the modern concept of organization was accordingly the distinction between order and organization, both referring to societal phenomena. This was the basis on which general theories of organization were still elaborated in the first decades of the twentieth century, which, however, no longer addressed the societal problems that preoccupy sociology, restricting themselves to special issues of good work organization or the very formal analysis of relations. "Organization," like "management," was now a term that allowed knowledge to be withdrawn from the direct work process and autonomized as institutional and supervisory knowledge. Organizational knowledge and the knowledge of scientific management now claimed to be more than the sum of the working knowledge needed to take action.

Publications by individual authors were primarily involved, who, few in number and widely scattered internationally, could not underpin a discipline grounded in research.[9] Only Taylor's microscopic theory of work organization[10] attracted greater attention, but from the 1920s onward met with increasing opposition from anthropologists and sociologists.[11] Whereas concern about jobs has since muted this "humanistic" critique, the temporal contingency of Taylorism has become more apparent: its dependence on mass markets for standardized products that changed little in the long term. This limitation has changed owing, above all, to the introduction of microelectronics in the production process.[12]

Organizational theories at this level of abstraction have found no successor in the present day. Why is this so? They clearly offer obsolete models, models no longer pursued. On the one hand, faith in the possibility of organizing rationally (in the sense of optimally) on the basis of principle has been lost – both in managerial business theories and in sociological organization research. On the other hand, abundant empirical organization research and lively business consulting – efforts that constantly launch new slogans on the market – generate a complexity that can no longer be dealt with by the old forms of theory. What is more, it no longer suffices, as in older organization theories, to consider only a few types of organization, notably the factory and the public authority. Symphony orchestras, newspaper offices, banks, political parties, sport and recreation clubs, schools, hospitals, and prisons also have to be taken into consideration. How is alcoholism therapy organized? Or libraries? Or container transport, which has drastically changed the organization of ports and shipping? Or waste disposal involving the modern functions of sorting and recycling? If this diversity is to be amenable to a general theory of organized social systems at all, the conceptual tools discussed so far will no longer suffice to produce it. Thinking in wholes and parts has had its day without being replaced by a theory of complex systems. The question is whether this must remain so, or whether quite different theoretical approaches may allow us nevertheless to elaborate a general theory of organization.

II

Since the Second World War, organization research has reached such proportions that no adequate account of trends, results, authors, and publications can be given. We must leave it to the textbooks to report on theory; they often do little else.[13] Our approach is to present distinctions that have played a role in research. When a distinction has exhausted its usefulness, it is replaced by another. This occurs when literature uncovers problems or phenomena that had not been sufficiently taken into account and that require a change of frame.

Our coverage of theory will ignore research that pursues a normative line in quest of rationality, which seeks to establish how certain results can be most effectively achieved with the greatest certainty or at minimal cost, limiting ourselves to approaches that are explicitly or implicitly formulated on the basis of the causality concept. Our theoretical and methodological ambition is to coordinate the distinction between cause and effect with other distinctions, for example, that between means and ends or between command and obedience, or between group formation and motivation. In this sense we are concerned with a sociology intent on explanation and, where possible, prediction; or which is also intent on providing technical, advisory aid for organizational planning. Research in business administration or developments in the theory of the firm are also relevant, but their exploitation in sociology has to this day been hampered by barriers between subjects and disciplines, not to mention the sheer volume of the literature. The way is now paved primarily by analysis of relations between structures and decisions. We will be returning to this.

From the older literature, organizational sociology has taken over, above all, the distinction between command and obedience familiar from the sociology of power, as well as the rationality-related distinction between means and ends. Authority can accordingly be rational if it uses commands in such a way that its ends can be attained through obedience. This is not only the old European myth of order,[14] reaching even into theology, but certainly, after the transition from created nature to value relations and the need for legitimation, also Max Weber's bureaucracy model.[15] According to Weber, the historical condition for this is that workers lose their owner-ship of the means of production and are paid in money. As a result, they come under the pressure of imposed work discipline, and the master (whether a holder of political power or the owner of the plant) can rely on the efficacy of his commands. However, such practice in governance and administration is rational only if it can manage without the enormous cost of communicating instructions individually, and can draw up general rules that subordinates can apply to the concrete state of affairs by logical deduction or in typical cases through appropriate interpretation. The model on which this theory draws is legally elaborated public administration. But according to Weber, "bureaucracy" with its formal rationality has imposed itself throughout the world in modern society; for not only political power but also property is a possible basis for power.

The success of this bureaucracy model is best explained historically. It opposes arbitrariness at all levels of order, concentrating it at the apex, which is assumed to be disciplined by its own value relations and by environ-mental conditions – in the economy by the market and in public administration by politics governed by the rule of law. Bureaucracy also means that large working units can be formed in which many people can work together at the same time and in coordination. And, above all, this allows the order of rank established by society to be replaced by the principle of equality. In both external and internal relations, bureaucracy proceeds on the assumption of equality – *unless the organization itself draws a distinction*. All this, in reality as in theoretical modeling, takes account of the immense complexity of modern society – in a form that we could describe in systems theoretical terms as outdifferentiation [Ausdifferenzierung] *within* society, as outdifferentiation of an autonomous but nevertheless steerable system, adaptable to societal interests, amenable to coordination, "controllable."

There are innumerable objections to the European, if not "Prussian," model of bureaucracy. As far as economic enterprises are concerned, in particular, it is claimed not to do justice to in-house super- and subordination relations.[16] It is asserted that it does not work outside Europe and is not a suitable standard for modernizing developing countries.[17] It is said to ignore the scope for interpretation that goal orientation would necessarily allow.[18] The result is, not least, that collusion between internal and external forces is difficult to discover and difficult to prevent, and can be stamped as corruption only where the law has clearly been broken. The organization, also and particularly in government and municipal administration, connects up at lower levels via negotiations with systems of the environment in order to generate the necessary cooperation.[19] The centralization of control over the means of production (including legal decision-making powers) clearly no longer suffices to ensure the isolation of the system as the object of centralized control.

In economics, the experience that the market offers possibilities for observation but no clear directives on decision-making has produced a theory of organization (often also called hierarchy). This is partly because corporate organization manages with lower transaction costs, partly because the market does not yet determine the decisions of economic participants (the latter point raising the question of how market participants make decisions).[20] This paradigmatic shift[21] clarifies the need for organization but not its internal structures and processes.

Finally, the problem of work motivation has also long been discussed. The more latitude there is for decision-making, the more important motivation becomes to ensure efficiency in the workplace. Barnard's highly regarded management theory had, as regards motivation, postulated a "zone of indifference" within which personnel do not care what they do as long as they are acknowledged to be fulfilling the conditions of their membership.[22] This may well also be true today. But it raises the question of whether such indifference is not harmful to the enterprise, especially if dismissal is difficult due to labor market conditions or for legal reasons. Moreover, recent research on Swedish welfare bureaucracies shows an inverse relationship between rationalization, democratization, and motivation. If plans and rules are made by means of complex rationalization and consensus-finding processes, this so exhausts the organization that, should obstacles or unforeseen difficulties arise, members are unlikely to continue working actively on implementing the solution found.[23] After all, they had failed to garner acceptance for what they themselves considered to be right.

Another proposal that could have been pursued comes from psychiatry, and (for that reason?) was long ignored by organization theory. Only more recent organizational consulting methods have used ideas from this source, stemming from systems therapy and especially family therapy. The basic thought is that every communication that conveys commands and, in so doing, distributes information (even if only information about authority, motives, and good will as the reason for the command) tends to generate paradoxes or, as one now says in semiotics and linguistic text theory, to deconstruct itself.[24] As information, the world is described as it is or should be; and the right to make this description and the expectation that it will be accepted is also communicated. At the same time, however, the fact that this is communicated means that things could be otherwise. Unity and difference, indication and distinction are synthesized in communication. But the fact that this (and not something else) happens produces the opposite of what was intended. This naturally does not mean that nothing more can happen, because every determination is paradoxical and is immediately deconstructed. However, therapists ask what normally prevents the deconstruction and disintegration of communication and motivation, and what in exceptional cases nevertheless unblocks deconstruction, opens Pandora's box, and puts paradoxization into effect.[25] We will be considering this subject at a late stage under the heading of "uncertainty absorption."

All this criticism is now a conspicuous component of every theory in organizational science. But it should not distract attention from the fact that hierarchy, in the sense of chains of command, is indispensable in constructing complex organizations. Vertical integration is still the most important way of handling uncertainty,[26] that is to say, the future. "Alternatives to hierarchies"[27] are hardly to be found. On the other hand, we should avoid using the term hierarchy as more or less synonymous with organization.[28] At any rate, the consequences of hierarchizing social relations have to be registered, and this cannot be done in the form of in-house cost accounting, indeed not at all in the form of "costs." Sociological analysis is needed. It has therefore been clear for some time that the characteristics of Weber's bureaucracy do not necessarily have to do with the criteria of rationality elaborated independently of them.[29] All this obliges us to abandon the notion that organizations *are* hierarchies. Max Weber himself had diluted such statements of essence under the influence of Neo-Kantian theories of knowledge into statements on "ideal types." This was to concede that reality did not necessarily need to correspond to type – for instance, such formulations as "in greater or lesser approximation to the pure type."[30] In this manner, however, what is important, namely the difference between type and (diverging) reality, could not be reflected.[31] A different, both more abstract and more complex organization theory is clearly needed.

III

Another key distinction was not a divergence from Max Weber's bureaucracy model but the result of social science experimentation with Taylorist work organization. The breakthrough in the scientific literature came when the irritating results of the "Hawthorne" experiments became known.[32] The experiments had not been planned as a test of the theory later imputed to them; but they contradicted expectations about the links between working conditions, incentive systems, and performance, so that an explanation had to be sought. The concept of group, which had become fashionable in social psychology, appeared to offer a solution, and the result was formulated in terms of the distinction between formal and informal organization.[33] A structural conflict between individual motives and organizational purposes was presupposed, and it was assumed that the motives of individuals could be better accommodated in groups than in the formal organization.

The formal/informal distinction treats the formal organization as given. One can think in terms of a hierarchy of authority to which members of the organization are subject. The problem with implementing this order is seen on the other side of the distinction, in informal organization. This side of the distinction is therefore marked (in linguistic terminology), because there is something to be done there. For the informal organization can support the goals of the formal organization or run counter to them; it can encourage members to perform or to hold back performance – depending on what the group holds to be right and imposes on the individual. It can adapt organizational changes to local conditions or oppose and forestall them.[34] The question fits the possibilities of empirical social research: it is about the measurable effects of different conditions. Corporate management could accordingly be expected to take a favorable interest in such research.[35] However, the Hawthorne experiments had already shown that the intervening variable "group" makes the formulation of rules governing dependence on conditions and consequences more difficult if not impossible. Using Heinz von Foerster's terminology, we could say that the group is a nontrivial, historical machine that does not operate in accordance with fixed rules (which is precisely what formal organization is supposed to ensure) but is guided by the state in which it happens to be at a given time.[36]

What is gained is therefore a mode of observation and not fixed knowledge – a mode of observation that pays attention to local social conditions of individual behavior and does not prematurely classify behavior in the usual terms of conforming or deviating. Many studies show the beneficial effect deviant behavior can have on work, but also – especially in connection with risk technologies – the danger of noncompliance with rules even if this normally goes well.

The dubious nature of the findings deprived the formal/informal distinction of much of its former importance.[37] The reaction was to extend the understanding of structures to allow the close interaction between formal and informal organization to be addressed. Since the 1960s, organizational sociology has again tended to prefer the concept of formal organization to enable a return to the distinction between formal and informal within this framework.[38] This is not least because the concept of group has remained fuzzy in the context of organizations with respect to membership, boundaries, fluctuations, and tolerance for internal differentiation. But it is striking that the concept of group dynamics has retained its importance in organizational consulting, now going by the name "organizational development." Emerging originally as a practical consequence of the human relations approach, it is now more concerned with the autonomization of functional areas from excessive hierarchical control. This indicates that a socially more sensitive mode of observation is involved, which escapes schematization by formal organization and the management's operational understanding. Advanced consulting concepts also tend to combine organizational development with systems theory and to set their sights on developing the capability of the organization for self-observation and diagnosis.[39] The interest in "informal organization," by contrast, appears to have shifted from groups that management regards as helpful or disruptive to individuals, who, depending on the organization of their work and their individual inclinations, develop greater or lesser interest in elaborated, "helpful" social contacts.[40] Where the formal/informal distinction is still used today, interest has shifted to the question of whether and how formal organization (= bureaucracy) is able to control informal organization.[41]

If the formal/informal distinction no longer divides theories or research preferences, the question can finally be addressed of how organizations themselves deal with this distinction. Research will then investigate when and by what criteria formal or informal communication is chosen. Network analysis could be a good starting point for examining such questions. For the network concept is not defined from the outset in terms of formal organization but rather in terms of a sort of trust grounded in recognizable interests and repeated proof. To demand or initiate formal communication is a way of avoiding tests of trust and gaining greater certainty – not infrequently to the detriment of the network, which is thus treated as superfluous. Vice versa, the choice of informal communication, and the explicit avoidance of formalization (without waiving its possibility), is a move by which the choice between formal and informal can be left open and reproduced. Whereas the official description of the organization will tend to regard the formal structure of responsibilities and official channels as the condition for informal communication also being an option, network analysis might show that informal communication predominates, reserving the ceremonial of formal communication only, as it were, for emergencies and borderline cases. On this point, the official self-description of the system diverges from what anyone working in an organization has to learn.

There are, meanwhile, many indications that the concept of informal organization, along with the group concept, are being replaced by a theory of interaction systems.[42] This draws on ideas developed by Erving Goffmann, and reformulates them with recourse to the general theory of social systems. The advantage is that analysis does not need to answer the question of whether and to what extent groups actually form in organizations. This means that the concept of group, not very amenable to theoretical development, can be replaced by a theory of face-to-face interaction. The problem is then that systems of a different type develop within organizational systems, more or less usurping influence on decision-making.

IV

When rationality was at issue, classical organization theory focused on another distinction, that between means and ends. This goes back to a concept of the rationality of action, and hence to the presupposition that someone imagines being able to attain certain ends by certain means. The classical concept assumed that an organization was managed through actions, and that the apex of the hierarchy identified themselves with the purposes of the organization and imposed them through the exercise of authority, whereas the means envisaged tended to autonomize[43] or even to escape organizational control. In this sense, a package was put together that presupposed the concordance of a multiplicity of distinctions or treated this concordance as a problem of control, namely whole and part, top and bottom, ends and means. The organization could then be understood as a goal-directed system, and the subordination of persons/ roles/positions as the means to an end.[44] But a closer analysis of these various distinctions very soon put paid to such assumptions of harmony.

The distinction between ends and means was limited on both sides by presupposed value judgments (hence by a worth/worthless distinction). It was thus not simply a matter of the causality of effects. Ends are evaluated ends, and, even as means, only ends that do not "cost" much can be considered. It is therefore not difficult to describe the unity of the distinction, namely as a positive (if possible maximal or optimal) return on the relationship between means and ends. What values (= preferences) are to realized can be left open. We can, hence, describe the schema in abstraction from all concrete value judgments provided that they are within the scope of what can be causally realized. Programs for the maximization of spiritual welfare, too, have at times been considered a possible object for organization.[45] There must, of course, be some preferences or other if the system is to operate selectively; but preferences are introduced into the model as external factors, as independent variables.

However, closer analysis and the empirical examination of the demands this schema makes of information processing in organizations brought difficulties to light, indeed inevitable renunciations. Economic enterprises, above all, which have to fix the prices of their products, discovered that (in the absence of "perfect competition") the market does not simply dictate prices. They have to be set in the organization. But how? In more general terms, the environment of organizations does not absorb enough contingency, so that the organization cannot content itself with working out the one and only right decision. Without sufficient knowledge and curtailed information processing, it has to decide for itself. The organization is not subject to the authority of an environment whose will has to be carried out. Both in the economy and in politics it is a turbulent, opaque field in which the organization has to establish its own basis for making decisions. And how good these decisions are will depend, by whatever criteria, on the structures of the system.

The ends/means schema or, to put it more abstractly, the general medium of possible causalities and possible evaluations therefore provides no more than a framework for necessary restrictions, which still have to be decided within the organization. Max Weber, above all, used this schema – firstly to "interpretatively explain" action and, secondly, to limit it through hierarchical rule and command boundedness to a general, ideal type of bureaucracy (however, in Weber it is not clear that the infinite horizons of this schema render such limitation possible and necessary). It was only after the Second World War and especially in the United States that this was to become a guiding principle for specific organizational studies detached from societal theory.[46]

However, what one had assumed to be the inner rationality of the ends/means schema dissolves on closer examination. It is increasingly seen only as a symbol of rationality. A now only symbolic use of the schema nurtures suspicions that it is no more than an ideology in the unchecked pursuit of interests under the guise of a rationality beneficial to society.

Such suspicions cannot be dissipated by distinguishing, with Max Weber, between types of rationality (instrumental rationality [Zweckrationalität], value rationality [Wertrationaliät]), nor, with Jürgen Habermas, by favoring a particular type of rationality, namely understanding-oriented rationality [verständigungsorientierte Rationalität]). Herbert Simon had suggested making do with "bounded rationality."[47] This amounts to drawing a distinction between two levels, one of which sets sufficient conditions as premises for decision-making, leaving the details up to not very far-reaching, but at any rate practicable, decisions. The significance of this concept lies not only in weakening the demands made of rationality. It means, above all, that how a system is organized makes a difference; and, furthermore, that learning can be important, because rationality is not already defined by the relation of the system to the environment (of the enterprise to the market). However, what the sociologist finds to be lacking is consideration of the social limitations to action.

Today it seems obvious to interpret this difference with the aid of cognitivistic concepts such as "schema," "script," and "cognitive map."[48] Other concessions are that unforeseen side-effects are allowed for and reserves are built up to cover the risk of miscalculation. Other modifications are to reverse the direction of ends and means asymmetry and to include the case of an organization seeking ends for a given stock of means (or a useful investment opportunity for capital). We then speak not only of goal-oriented organizations but of goal-seeking organizations.[49] This reversal of perspective shows that the schema has to be considered contingent on both sides and, therefore, serves to implement value judgments that, in the distinction between ends and means, can only take a form that can be described as rational.[50]

If rationality in the strict, classical sense is regarded as unattainable, this does not mean that behavior in organizations is arbitrary. A new distinction looms, that between rational and intelligent behavior.[51] Intelligent behavior can find order even in the ruins of the conditions for rationality, even in the "garbage can."[52] But research on this subject can no longer limit itself to models of the one and only right decision. It must first discover the structures of disorder, the inconsistency of demands, and the limits to cognitive orientation capacity in order to see that those involved nevertheless seek – and find – comprehensible contexts for decision-making.

Even if variation in evaluation is also to be included, whether of means (e.g., ecological re-evaluation or cost increases) or of ends, it seems advisable to introduce – in the sense of older functionalism – the self-preservation of the system as meta-goal[53] guiding all other variations. But this was unfortunately formulated in terms of a resource conservation program. For what are these "resources" if all operations of the system are guided by values and can be re-evaluated, and if there is no strict criterion for identity? It therefore seemed reasonable to criticize this theory of goal variation in the interest of resource conservation (and with it structural functionalism in systems theory) as "conservative." But the principle had already attained the form of scarcely covert paradox with the insight that conservation requires variation and that limits to it cannot be given theoretically. It what follows we will therefore not be adopting the formula, although we will be addressing the problem.

Another criticism of the resource conservation formula is that an organizational system cannot be looked at in isolation, but only in relation to its environment or environments with which it exchanges performance and information. The coincidence of ends/means schema and hierarchy could then be replaced by the coincidence of ends/means schema and system/environment distinction. This could be formulated in terms of the input/output model, with output being formulated within the system as the end and the necessary input as the means of the system. But this brings us to a further distinction, which since the 1960s has, in accordance with developments in general systems theory, begun to assume the function of a lead distinction: the distinction between system and environment.

V

No one will doubt that there is more to the world than organized social systems. The question is what one does with this insight theoretically.

There is also no disputing that every scientific study (like every observation and description) is based on the isolation of specific objects. If we want to indicate something determinate, it must first of all be distinguished from everything else. Every observation begins with a distinction. It must then be asked whether and why certain distinctions are more suitable than others – and for whom.

The distinctions we have discussed so far, hierarchy, formal/informal organization, ends and means, have addressed the internal affairs of the organization. It had perhaps been assumed that, once internal distinctions were clarified, the object concerned would emerge as a matter of course. One would then have to take recourse to assumptions about essentiality, to say, for example, that the essence (or ideal type) of bureaucratic organizations consists in a command hierarchy and can be defined in such terms; or that the essence of industrial organizations is goal orientation (which can be described more precisely). Or a very old distinction can be revamped, that between the whole and its parts.[54] But this is quite obviously a resolved paradox. For in this description, the system occurs twice: at the level of the whole, which cannot be a part of itself, and at the level of the parts, of which none can be the whole. The doubling requires the difference to be creatively attributed to unity with the aid of such concepts as integration, domination, representation, and participation, but which can hardly conceal that there are residual problems that this procedure cannot solve.

Experience in research with such distinctions has raised doubts. And the aging of these classical approaches has shown that their area of research was too strongly limited. What is more, if one recognizes that this reduction is not a matter of theory but has to be achieved by organizations themselves, a new distinction is called for, that between system and environment. The problem is still seen in the system itself, but the main question is now how the system is to be organized in relation to its environment; and all the distinctions to date, between the whole and its parts, the hierarchy, and the ends/means schema now have to be reinterpreted as forms that have to prove their worth in the relationship between system and environment.

The first reaction to the possible relevance of the environment for the development and structuring of organizations had drawn on the theory of open systems. Interest in this theory had arisen from the discussion on thermodynamic laws, which had predicted a tendency toward entropy in closed systems to the detriment of all useful differences. Reversing or at least halting this tendency seemed to require open systems, whose exchange relations with the environment enabled it to produce useful differences, to exploit chance opportunities to build up its own order, and to keep itself "homeostatically" stable in the state attained. This version, formulated partly in terms of the distinction between machines and natural systems,[55] dominated organization theory in the 1960s.[56] The asymmetry between environment and organization was thus accepted, but in one direction only, which could be described as reducing environmental complexity or providing requisite variety, or, finally, as the principle of order from noise. This was convincing where a natural environment was involved. But if the human, societal, and political environments were also taken into account, there was no overlooking that and how the reductions achieved in organizations – from their point of view successfully and rationally – affected their environment. And given the growing interest in ecological issues, the impact of organizational successes on the natural environment was soon to attract attention.[57]

The openness of the system to the environment immediately raises the question of how reductions are to be achieved. Perhaps the most important solution to this problem proffered since the 1950s lay in the distinction between input and output. This distinction differentiated the environmental relations of the system in terms of whether the system received something or gave something. In the theory of the firm, for example, commodity markets, labor markets, and financial markets are distinguished from product and sales markets, and it is assumed that organizations can develop only if these markets can be distinguished (alternatively, that they become distinguishable by developing corresponding organizations).[58] In the state organization political system, the input of information and declaration of interests can be distinguished from the output of collectively binding decisions,[59] and here, too, the primary achievement of the system is that these environments are distinguished at all or are assumed to be distinguishable and do not fuse in the confused interplay of particularistic collusion.

However, this model merely shifts the problem of generating reductions. It now lies in the question of how the link between input and output or the transformation of input into output is to be understood. There are various possibilities, which have led critics to argue that the model is technical if not technocratic. A mathematical transformation function comes to mind, but no real system would render itself superfluous through such a description. Another possibility would be transformation on the pattern of a machine, which, if not in disrepair, always produces the same outputs from identical inputs, thus functioning reliably. The third possibility is to assume that internal processes cannot be observed and to limit observation to external regularities. This version has been labeled the "black box." It has provoked so much curiosity that people finally started to speculate on what happened in the black box or what was to be assumed if the functioning of the machine was not orderly but clearly unpredictable, not reliable but erratic, not trivial but nontrivial. And the assumption that brought us to a quite different sort of systems theory was that self-reference was at work in such a machine or that imaginary numbers, paradoxes, or similar specters played a role in its mathematics.

Apart from these modeling attempts, more strongly abstracted issues had also been addressed since the cybernetics of the 1950s, concerned with the asymmetries in relations between system and environment. Cybernetics addressed the question of requisitive variety, which enables a system to gain or construct information adequate to the environment.[60] In the functionalistic cognitive psychology of the period, but also on the basis of empirical organizational studies, the problem of this difference was seen to lie in a complexity gap. The expression "reduction of complexity" dates from this period and context.[61] Simon had drawn attention to this problem at an early date in the theory of rational decision-making.[62] Early empirical studies in organizational sociology looked into organizational forms that fitted turbulent environments.[63] We can either set out from forms of organization and ask about environmental correlates (e.g., formal/informal, steep/flat hierarchy, delegation of powers, or strict/loose rule-boundedness) or tackle the problem of complexity difference in different ways. If we start with the resources required, it is a question of ensuring access to resources in the face of varying business success, thus a problem of liquidity, of creditworthiness, or of internal elasticity that permits substitutions. Thus, stressing dependence on resources raises the question of the extent to which having the necessary resources at one's disposition gives one external control of dependent organizations.[64] If we see the problem in information, it is a question of coping with uncertainty, of minimizing the cost of processing information or of rationalizing or renouncing further information, and overall, of managing risk. The two questions can largely translate into one another, so that we face the question of what theoretical treatment of the system/environment relationship gives the better results.

Following the work done by Lawrence and Lorsch, so-called contingency theory took the lead in the 1970s.[65] They inquired into the forms and conditions for fit between environments and systems.[66] Complexity, above all of the organizational systems themselves, was, however, underestimated for reasons of empirical methodology. The self-referentially determined unpredictability of systems was also initially ignored, and without paying sufficient attention to this problem, it was assumed that establishing a fit between environment and system was a job for the management of an organization. Organization theory could thus claim to be working very close to the interests of management, helping to adapt the organization to the demands and the possibilities of the environment.

VI

The environment? Theory had hitherto assumed that the environment was the part of the world that did not belong to the organization. The environment was thus seen as given. It was assumed to be objectively given but to burden the system with a scarcity of resources and a surplus of information, and therefore to require the system to reduce its complexity. Since the second half of the 1970s we find critical remarks on the subject, which are, however, not consistently elaborated in the sense of constructivist theories.

Karl Weick goes farthest.[67] He sees the environment as the result of an "enactment" that obeys the logic of internal processes. In his view, it is not a given independent of the organization. It is the result of action by the organization, which, like all action, can be observed only in retrospect. We could say that what one has done can be seen only with the help of the environment concept. And this concept makes externalizations possible, that is to say, it allows causes to be attributed beyond the internal responsibilities of the organization. The environment is accordingly an assumption that holds true even though – indeed because – it cannot be tested.

So far-reaching a conceptual reshuffle has hitherto met with little response in organization research, particularly as systems theory itself had not been prepared for it (the theory of self-referential systems, second-order cybernetics, and constructivist epistemology are only gradually beginning to provide a basis). Instead, the distinction between system and environment merely weakened. Criticism of contingency theory, which had objected to the strictness of the distinction and the lack of societal-theoretical reflection, had led to the so-called "institutional" approach in organization theory[68] – with a corresponding return to the concept of institution in political science, in the theory of science, and in legal theory.[69] Relatively permanent behavioral premises resistant to change are meant on which action can be based and which obviate further analysis. To this extent, taking institutions for granted also marks the limits to the rational classification of preconditions for action. In succession to the fit problem of contingency theory, cultural accord between organizations and their societal environment is investigated. It is rightly stressed that accord between systems and environments is not be explained solely in terms of technical requirements or exchange relations. Conceptual elaboration (as typical in recourse to old theoretical resources, and, for example, related efforts to re-introduce culture or ethics) has not succeeded, and all explanations only make things worse.[70] The institution concept is countered partly by technology, partly by instrumental rationalism, partly by limitation to the perspective of individual actors, and partly by overly strict isolation of the organization from the values and the cultural and semantic constructions of reality in the surrounding society. There seems to be a sort of pendular movement between "disembedding" and "embeddedness."[71] The scholarly situation in which this new institutionalism has developed makes the desire comprehensible, but the inclusion of further phenomena does not justify regarding it as a new theory.

In the American context, recourse to "institution" can also be explained by the view that systems theory has had its day. The concept of institution is used to set accents directly or indirectly, countering assumptions that are, with some justification, attributed to older systems theory, namely inadmissible object isolation, overestimation of technical-mathematical possibilities, rational instrumentalism, and "holistic" mysticism.[72] But the polemic has been unable to secure or even explain its own theoretical foundations. In the meanwhile, systems theory has further developed its own tools by building in self-reference concepts, so that the system/environment distinction now has quite different implications than it did from the 1950s to the 1970s. Applied to social systems in general and organizations in particular, systems theory shows that the difference between system and environment has to be produced and reproduced within the system itself, and that precisely this obliges systems to take their environment into account.

Once this research approach has been adopted, all hitherto prominent distinctions can be subordinated to it. We can say, for example, that the function and legitimation of hierarchical superordination result from better or more important environmental contacts that can be centered at the apex. The boss is the resource procurer, at the level of smaller working units and at the level of highly complex systems. He transforms irritation[73] into information. It is also easy to see that distinctions such as that between formal and informal organization or between ends and means relate to different environments of the system, for example, the environment of markets on the one hand and that of personal motives and willingness to work on the other; or to the environment of resources markets and product markets in the economic system; or, in the case of public administration, to the environment of interested parties and their organizations and political parties. Finally, the distinction between the whole and its parts can be reformulated as a theory of system differentiation, if system differentiation is treated as the repetition of the differentiation of systems and environments in systems. Such systematization could prove the superiority of the systems-theoretical distinction between system and environment if the problem addressed by this distinction can be characterized more exactly.

The distinction between system and environment offers greater scope than others for expression, a greater variety of forms. At least, this appears so in theory, if only because the other distinctions can be attributed to it. On the other hand, it has difficulty indicating the unity of the difference. It is not authority, it is not formal and informal social cooperation, it is not rationality, nor is it integrated wholeness. More so than in other cases, one is therefore discouraged from asking about the unity of the difference between system and environment at all. Of course it is always possible to say that the system and everything else taken together constitute the world. But what would be gained by doing so? From a formal point of view, asking about the "sameness of difference" amounts to a paradox. An organizational system exists only by distinguishing itself from its environment. How can it then reflect on unity and operate on the basis of difference at the same time? Faced with this problem, older societies were able to reflect on a cosmological totality. However, today's holism in the New Age sense or similar notions serve only as self-descriptions of sectarian movements rather than as an answer to a question that can no longer be convincingly posed.[74]

Many theoretical controversies have established themselves within the framework set by the distinction between system and environment (and which alone offers the possibility to describe something as a "system"). This apparently has to do with the endogenous dynamics of the science system, which demands a "critical" attitude toward existing theory design and in the form of critique provides the fastest way to mark out new knowledge. However, this has considerable disadvantages, which have since become apparent and subject to discussion. For one thing, this procedure hardly (or only, as it were, by chance) leads to the accumulation of knowledge. One works with distinctions until a sort of fatigue sets in and innovative approaches turn to other distinctions. Moreover, distinctions that are used for polemical purposes (e.g., system vs. conflict; action vs. structure; micro- vs. macro-) split subject matter that can be understood only where both sides are adequately included.[75] Empirical studies, in particular, which always have to do with mixed relations, can make no theoretical headway.[76]

Controversies of this sort are then nothing other than resolved paradoxes.[77] In the form of a controversy, one can avoid asking about the unity of the distinction that makes the controversy possible. But this soon renders such discussion unproductive.

These considerations bring us to a point where it seems worthwhile to turn to more general theoretical foundations – be it a general theory of social systems or even the basic problems of general systems theory. Systems theory at least has the advantage of being unsuitable for playing off environment against system or system against environment. This need not mean neglecting the peculiarities of organized social systems. But we can recognize the specificity of organization only if we can distinguish organizations from other sorts of system formation; and, where systems theory is involved, if we can determine how organizational systems generate the difference between system and environment.

Notes

1. This was true even of production plants, which we would now set up as organizations. See the example of the Lüneburg saltworks in Egbert Kahle, Die Organisation der Saline Lüneburg vom Mittelalter bis ins 19. Jahrhundert, *Zeitschrift für Unternehmensgeschichte* 1 (1987), 1–22; idem., Interrelations Between Corporate Culture and Municipal Culture: The Lüneburg Saltworks as a Medieval Example, in: Barry A. Turner (ed.), *Organizational Symbolism*, Berlin 1990, 33–41.
2. See, e.g., Pierre-Louis Moreau de Maupertius, *Essai sur la formation des corps organisés*, Berlin 1754; Abbé Joannet, *De la connoissance de l'homme dans son être et dans ses rapport*, 2 vols. Paris 1775, esp. vol. 1, 180 ff. ("organisation du corps humain").
3. Vorschule der Ästhetik, Jean Paul, *Werke*, vol. 5, Munich 1963, 296.
4. "Just organize a volume of epigrams!" – loc. cit. 357. Friedrich Schlegel, too, uses the word organization in all sorts of ways: "the thoroughly organized and organizing work" (Wilhelm Meister), "female organization," "philosopy that has to re-organize and disorganize itself," "Organization of the universe," etc. works in two volumes, Weimar 1980, vol. I, 145 vol. I, 230 vol. II, 113. See also Karl Philipp Moritz, *Schriften zur Ästhetik und Poetik: Kritische Ausgabe*, Tübingen 1962, e.g., 76, 82, who demands that an organization should have so fine a texture that its organ can be "an impression of overall conditions," and "Therefore every higher organization, by its nature, takes up what is subordinated to it and incorporates it into its essence" (p. 82); or Johann Gottlieb Fichte: "I find myself to be an organized product of nature," in: *Das System der Sittenlehre*, Zweites Hauptstück § 9, Werke vol. II, Darmstadt 1962, 516.
5. See in particular § 65 of Critique of Judgment [Kritik der Urteilskraft] under the heading "Things considered as natural purposes are organized beings." In a lengthy remark there is also reference to reform of the body of the state: "In a recent complete transformation of a great people into a state the word organization for the regulation of magistracies, etc., and even of the whole body politic, has often been fitly used.

For in such a whole every member should surely be purpose as well as means, and, whilst all work together towards the possibility of the whole, each should be determined as regards place and function by means of the Idea of the whole" (Kant's Critique of Judgement, translated with Introduction and Notes by J.H. Bernard (2nd ed. revised) (London: Macmillan, 1914)). "Member" clearly refers to human beings, whom moral law does not allow to be reduced to mere means but who must have the opportunity to realize their humanity in relation to a whole.

6. "La philosophie du siècle dernier a été revolutionnaire, celle du XIXe siècle doit être organisatrice," see Claude Henri de Rouvroy, Comte de Saint-Simon, *De la réorganisation de la société européenne*, Paris 1814 Œuvres, Paris 1868 ff, reprint Paris 1986, vol. 1, 153–248 (158).

7. See, e.g., Alfred Fouillée, *La science sociale contemporaine*, Paris 1880; Charles Gide, L'idée de solidarité en tant que programme économique, *Revue internationale de sociologie* 1 (1893), 385–400, and looking back on the history of the concept J.E.S. Hayward, Solidarity: The Social History of an Idea in 19th Century France, *International Review of Social History* 4 (1959), 261–284.

8. See Talcott Parsons, Pattern Variables Revisited, *American Sociological Review* 25 (1960), 467–483.

9. See, e.g., Johannes Plenge, *Drei Vorlesungen über die allgemeine Organisationslehre*, Essen 1919; Henri Fayol, *Administration industrielle et générale*, Paris 1925; A. Bogdanow, *Allgemeine Organisationslehre (Tektologie)*, vol. 1, Berlin 1926; Luther Gulick and Lyndall Urwick (eds.), *Papers on the Science of Administration*, New York 1937; Karl Stefanic-Allmayer, *Allgemeine Organisationslehre: Ein Grundriß*, Vienna 1950.

10. See Frederick Winslow Taylor, *The Principles of Scientific Management*, first Norwood, MA 1911; idem., *Shop Management* (1903), New York 1912.

11. See, with considerable influence on further research, Elton Mayo, *The Human Problems of an Industrial Civilization*, New York 1933. In Germany, e.g., R. Lang and W. Hellpach, *Gruppenfabrikation*, Berlin 1922; Eugen Rosenstock, *Werkstattaussiedlung*, Berlin 1922; Heinrich Nicklisch, *Grundfragen für die Betriebswirtschaft*, Stuttgart 1928; Walter Jost, *Das Sozialleben des industriellen Betriebs: Eine Analyse der sozialen Prozesse im Betrieb*, Berlin 1932, esp. 10 ff. On the persistence of these anti-Taylorist notions based on the community [Gemeinschaft] under the Nazi regime, see Theodor M. Bardmann, *Wenn aus Arbeit Abfall wird: Aufbau und Abbau organisatorischer Realitäten*, Frankfurt 1994, 303 ff.

12. See among others Richard Hyman and Wolfgang Streeck (eds.), *New Technology and Industrial Relation*, Oxford 1988.

13. See, e.g., Charles Perrow, *Complex Organizations: A Critical Essay*, New York 1986, or Alfred Kieser (ed.), *Organisationstheorien*, Stuttgart 1993. For an account explicitly designed as theory history, see also Giuseppe Bonazzi, *Storia del pensiero organizzativo*, 5th ed. Milan 1993.

14. See, e.g., Thomas Aquinas, *Summa Theologiae* I q. 65 a.2.

15. See Max Weber, *Wirtschaft und Gesellschaft*, 5., rev. ed. Tübingen 1972, 125 ff.

16. See Jost loc cit, 55, further to the article by Götz Brief, *Betriebssoziologie*, *Handwörterbuch der Soziologie*, Stuttgart 1931.

17. For many similar studies, see Onofre D. Corpuz, *The Bureaucracy in the Philippines*, n. p. (Institute of Public Administration, University of the Philippines) 1957; Morroe Berger, *Bureaucracy and Society in Modern Egypt: A Study of the Higher Civil Service*, Princeton 1957; Edgar L. Shor, The Thai Bureaucracy, *Administrative Science Quarterly* 5 (1960), 66–68. Ralph Braibanti, Public Administration and Judiciary in Pakistan, in: Joseph LaPalombara (ed.), *Bureaucracy and Political Development*, Princeton, NJ 1963, 360–440; Lloyd A. Fallers, *Bantu Bureaucracy: A Century of Political Evolution among the Basoga of Uganda*, 2nd ed. Chicago 1965; Louis A. Zurcher, Jr. et al., Value Orientation, Role Conflict, and Alienation From Work: A Cross-Cultural Study, *American Sociological Review* 30 (1965), 539–548. At this time much research was undertaken under the heading of "comparative public administration," which sought to clarify the conditions of modernization at the organizational level. See, e.g., Ferrel Heady and Sibyl L. Stokes (ed.), *Papers in Comparative Public Administration*, Ann Arbor, MI 1962. In the late 1960s, such attempts were halted by both severe and sweeping social theoretical critique. More recent discussion has often also objected that this bureaucracy model does not take adequate account of the dependence of all organizations on "human capital" or "social capital." The reference is to traditional attitudes and institutions that could be used with somewhat more adroitness, for example, in development projects. The criticism is clearly directed against theory simply assuming differentiation whereas the very question of differentiation is in reality the problem. In this context, the expression "capital" betrays the persistent underlying "instrumentalistic," goal-directed perspective.

18. Not least, it is a problem of the legal order and its constitutional supervision, and thus also has to do with increasingly purpose-oriented public administration in industrial countries. See for a case study Keith Hawkins, *Environment and Enforcement: Regulation and the Social Definition of Pollution*, Oxford 1984; also Arthur Benz and Wolfgang Seibel (eds.), *Zwischen Kooperation und Korruption: Abweichendes Verhalten in der Verwaltung*, Baden-Baden 1992, and on problems of constitutional law, Dieter Grimm, *Die Zukunft der Verfassung*, Frankfurt 1991.

19. This also strikingly applies for otherwise rigorously managed industrial enterprises, where, for example, the "just-in-time" principle for component supply requires cooperation between various firms at lower levels, with the result that even centralized production planning has now become difficult.

20. See Ronald Coase, The Nature of the Firm, *Economica* 4 (1937), (which initially attracted little attention) 386–403, reprinted in idem., *The Firm, the Market, and the Law*, Chicago 1988, 33–55; also Herbert A. Simon, *Models of Man – Social and Rational: Mathematical Essays on Rational Human Behavior in a Social Setting*, New York 1957; James G. March and Herbert A. Simon, *Organizations*, New York 1958; Oliver E. Williamson, *Markets and Hierarchies: Analysis and Antitrust Implications*, New York 1975.

21. See Brian J. Loasby, *Choice, Complexity and Ignorance: An Enquiry into Economic Theory and the Practice of Decision-Making*, Cambridge 1976, 211.

22. See Chester I. Barnard, *The Functions of the Executive*, Cambridge, MA 1938, ed. 1951, 167 ff.

23. See Nils Brunsson, *The Irrational Organization: Irrationality as a Basis for Organizational Action and Change*, Chichester 1985.

24. See Jürgen Ruesch and Gregory Bateson, *Communication: The Social Matrix of Psychiatry*, New York 1951, using the concepts "command" and "report". On "deconstruction" see, beside Jacques Derrida and Paul de Man, Jonathan Culler, *On Deconstruction: Theory and Criticism After Structuralism*, Ithaca, NY 1982.

25. In the sociological theory of society, the same topic could be dealt with in the context of a theory of symbolically generalized communication media. See Niklas Luhmann, *Die Gesellschaft der Gesellschaft*, Frankfurt am Main 1997, 316 ff.

26. See, e.g., Jay B. Barney and William G. Ouchi (eds.), *Organizational Economics*, San Francisco 1986, Introduction 12.

27. See the title of Ph.G. Herbst, *Alternatives to Hierarchies*, Leiden 1976 – written in connection with the human relations movement of the Tavistock Institute.

28. Thus in the much-discussed opposition of market and hierarchy. On the point of departure for the discussion, see Oliver E. Williamson, *Markets and Hierarchies: Analysis and Antitrust Implications: A Study of the Economics of Internal Organization*, New York 1975.

29. See only Stanley H. Udy, Bureaucracy and Rationality in Weber's Organization Theory, *American Sociological Review* 24 (1959), 791–795.

30. On the misunderstanding that Weber's theory of ideal types is an empirical theory in the usual sociological sense, see Renate Mayntz, Max Webers Idealtypus der Bürokratie und die Organisationssoziologie, *Kölner Zeitschrift für Soziologie und Sozialpsychologie* 17 (1965), 493–502; reprinted in idem., (ed.), Bürokratische Organisation, Köln 1968, 27–35. However, the concept of ideal type can also be empirically defined as marked resistance to blending with other principles. In this sense, bureaucratic hierarchies have survived all attempts to enrich them with other principles such as participation, teamwork, and humanization without abandoning the terrain to reform.

31. It could be conceded that Weber had conceived of typification as an essential condition for understanding, thus of understanding in everyday, organized and organization-related action. But this does not necessarily mean and cannot guarantee that everyday typification coincides with scientifically instrumental idealization – an issue that was to be addressed by Alfred Schütz with reference to Weber and Husserl.

32. The final publication is Fritz J. Roethlisberger and William J. Dickson, *Management and the Worker*, Cambridge, MA 1939. On the ideological concept see Mayo loc. cit. (1933).

33. A better formulation would perhaps be "prescribed framework" and "emergent interactions." See C.R. Hinings and Royston Greenwood, *The Dynamics of Strategic Change*, Oxford 1988, 11 f.

34. See, in particular, Lester Coch and John R.P. French, Jr., Overcoming Resistance to Change, *Human Relations* 1 (1948), 512–532.

35. "Empirical knowledge" is no protection against ideological prejudices or those oriented on power structures. See, with reference to the presupposition of a worker influenceable by conditions, Dana Bramel and Ronald Friend, Hawthorne, the Myth of the Docile Worker, and Class Bias in Psychology, *American Psychologist* 36 (1981), 867–878.

36. See Heinz von Foerster, Principles of Self-Organization – In a Socio-Managerial Context, in: Hans Ulricht and Gilbert J.B. Probst (eds.), *Self-Organization and Management of Social Systems: Insights, Promises, Doubts, and Questions*, Berlin 1984, 2–24; reprinted in: Heinz von Foerster, *Wissen und Gewissen: Versuch einer Brücke*, Frankfurt 1993, 233–268.

37. See, e.g., Martin Irle, *Soziale Systeme: Eine kritische Analyse der Theorie von formalen und informalen Organisationen*, Göttingen 1963. For a good retrospective see Anna Maria Theis, *Organisationskommunikation: Theoretische Grundlagen und empirische Forschungen*, Opladen 1994, 123 ff. See also H. Roy Kaplan and Curt Tausky, Humanism in Organizations: A Critical Appraisal, in: Amitai Etzioni and E. W. Lehman (eds.), *A Sociological Reader on Complex Organisations*, New York 1980, 44–55.

38. As a text for university use, see Peter M. Blau and W. Richard Scott, *Formal Organizations: A Comparative Approach*, San Francisco 1962.

39. See, e.g., Rudolf Wimmer, Organisationsberatung: Eine Wachstumsbranche ohne professionelles Selbstverständnis: Überlegungen zur Weiterführung des OE-Ansatzes in Richtung systemischer Organisationsberatung, in: Michael Hofmann (ed.), *Management Forum*, Heidelberg 1991, 45–136; idem., Was kann Beratung leisten: Zum Interventionsrepertoire und Interventionsverständnis der system-ischen Organisationsberatung, in: idem. (ed.), *Organisationsberatung: Neue Wege und Konzepte*, Wiesbaden 1992, 59–27; idem., Neuere Methoden der Organisationsentwicklung zur Steigerung der Überlebensfähigkeit mittelständischer Unternehmen, in: Dieter Schwiering (ed.), *Mittelständische Unternehmensführung im kulturellen Wandel*, Stuttgart 1996, 182–205.

40. See hierzu Lothar Peter, "Jeder irgendwie für sich allein"? Probleme und Chancen sozialer Interaktion am Arbeitsplatz, *Zeitschrift für Soziologie* 22 (1993), 416–432.

41. See, e.g., Charles Heckscher, Defining the Post-Bureaucratic Type, in: Charles Heckscher and Anne Donnellon (eds.), *The Postbureaucratic Organization: New Perspectives on Organizational Change*, Thousand Oaks, CA 1994, 14–62 (21 f.).

42. See André Kieserling, Interaktion in Organisationen, in: Klaus Dammann, Dieter Grunow, and Klaus P. Japp (eds.), *Die Verwaltung des politischen Systems: Neue systemtheoretische Zugriffe auf ein altes Thema*, Opladen 1994, 168–182; idem., *Kommunikation unter Anwesenden: Studien über Interaktionssysteme*, Frankfurt 1999, 335 ff.

43. A classical account of this problem of the ends-means shift and its description as bureaucracy is given in Robert Michels, Zur *Soziologie des Parteiwesens in der modernen Demokratie*, reprint of the 2nd ed., Stuttgart 1957; also, for example, Peter M. Blau, *Bureaucracy in Modern Society*, New York 1956, 93 ff. or Renate Mayntz, *Soziologie der Organisation*, Reinbek 1963, 78 f.

44. See Barnard loc. cit. 231 ff.; Blau and Scott loc. cit. (1962), 5; or Joseph A. Litterer, *The Analysis of Organizations*, New York 1965, 246 ff.

45. That the means have to be included had provoked the well-known criticism of Jesuit organizational practices.

46. On the beginnings see, e.g., Robert K. Merton, *Bureaucratic Structure and Personality, Social Forces* 18 (1940), 560–568; Philip Selznick, An Approach to a Theory of Bureaucracy, *American Sociological Review* 8 (1943), 47–54; idem.,

Foundations for a Theory of Organizations, *American Sociological Review* 13 (1948), 23–35.

47. See Herbert A. Simon, *Models of Bounded Rationality*, 2 vols., Cambridge, MA 1992.
48. See Giancarlo Provasi, Oltre il modello di "razionalita limitata": Il contribute del cognitivismo, *Rassegna Italiana di Sociologia* 36 (1995), 251–278. On the influence of cognition theory on organization research see also vol. 1–2 (1996) of the *Revue internationale de systemique*.
49. See James G. March and Johan P. Olsen, *Ambiguity and Choice in Organizations*, Bergen, Norwegen 1976.
50. For a detailed treatment of this critique in the 1960s, see Niklas Luhmann, *Zweckbegriff und Systemrationalität (1968)*, Neudruck Frankfurt 1973.
51. See Massimo Warglien and Michael Masuch (eds.), *The Logic of Organizational Disorder*, Berlin 1996.
52. Following Michael D. Cohen, James G. March, and Johan P. Olsen, A Garbage Can Model of Organizational Choice, *Administrative Science Quarterly* 17 (1972), 1–25.
53. See, e.g., Harry M. Johnson, *Sociology*, New York 1960, 284 ff.
54. See still today the "system-oriented management" approach of the Hans Ulrich school (St. Gallen). The core concept of integration is defined as the bringing together of parts to form a whole. See, e.g., the festschrift Hans Ulrich: Gilbert J.B. Probst and Hans Siegwart (eds.), *Integriertes Management: Bausteine des systemorientierten Management*, Bern 1985.
55. For a typical text see Daniel Katz and Robert L. Kahn, *The Social Psychology of Organizations*, New York 1966.
56. An attempt at integration that had at the time attracted a great deal of attention reacted to this distinction: James D. Thompson: *Organizations in Action: Social Science Bases of Administrative Theory*, New York 1967.
57. On this stage of the discussion, see Louis R. Pondy and Ian I. Mitroff, Beyond Open System Models of Organization, *Research in Organizational Behavior* 1 (1979), 3–39. As long ago as 1969, Karl Weick had stressed that organizations "enact their environment" and that criteria for this are needed. See the German translation of the second edition: Karl E. Weick, *Der Prozeß des Organisierens*, Frankfurt 1985.
58. For a relatively late publication of this form of theory see Piero Romei, *La dinamica della organizzazione: Le costanti di comportamento dei sistemi organizzativi aziendali in azione*, 5th ed., Milan 1990.
59. See David Easton, *A Framework for Political Analysis*, Englewood Cliffs, NJ 1965; idem., *A Systems Analysis of Political Life*, New York 1965.
60. See W. Ross Ashby, *An Introduction to Cybernetics*, London 1956, esp. 206 ff.; idem., Requisite Variety and Its implications for the control of complex systems, *Cybernetica* 1 (1958), 83–99.
61. See Herbert A. Simon, *Rational Choice and the Structure of the Environment*, Psychological Review 63 (1956), 129–138.
62. See Tom Bums and G.M. Stalker, *The Management of Innovation*, London 1961. Also F.E. Emery and E.L. Trist, The Causal Texture of Organizational Environments, *Human Relations* 18 (1965), 21–32; idem., *Towards a Social*

Ecology: Contextual Appreciation of the Future in the Present, London 1972; Paul R. Lawrence and Jay W. Lorsch, *Organization and Environment: Managing Differentiation and Integration*, Boston 1967; idem., Differentiation and Integration in Complex Organizations, *Administrative Science Quarterly* 12 (1967), 1–47; Howard E. Aldrich; *Organizations and Environments*, Englewood Cliffs, NJ 1979.

63. See Tom Bums and G.M. Stalker, *The Management of Innovation*, London 1961. Also F.E. Emery and E.L. Trist, The Causal Texture of Organizational Environments, *Human Relations* 18 (1965), 21–32; idem., *Towards a Social Ecology: Contextual Appreciation of the Future in the Present*, London 1972; Paul R. Lawrence and Jay W. Lorsch, *Organization and Environment: Managing Differentiation and Integration*, Boston 1967; idem., Differentiation and Integration in Complex Organizations, *Administrative Science Quarterly* 12 (1967), 1–47; Howard E. Aldrich; *Organizations and Environments*, Englewood Cliffs, NJ 1979.

64. See above all Jeffrey Pfeffer and Gerald R. Salancik, *The External Control of Organizations: A Resource Dependence Perspective*, New York 1978. See also David Jacobs, Dependency and Vulnerability: An Exchange Approach to the Control in Organizations, *Administrative Science Quarterly* 19 (1974), 45–59.

65. On the literature see note 63.

66. See the attempt to cope with the complexity deficit, a (rather vague) type differentiation in Robert Drazin and Andrew H. Van de Ven, Alternative Forms of Fit in Contingency Theory, *Administrative Science Quarterly* 30 (1985), 514–539.

67. See Karl E. Weick, *Der Prozeß des Organisierens*, German transl. of the 2nd ed. Frankfurt 1985, esp. 212 ff.

68. See, e.g., John W. Meyer and Brian Rowan, Institutionalized Organizations: Formal Structure as Myth and as Ceremony, *American Journal of Sociology* 83 (1977), 340–363; John W. Meyer and W. Richard Scott, *Organizational Environments: Ritual and Rationality*, Beverly Hills. CA 1983; Lynne G. Zucker, Institutional Theories of Organization, *Annual Review of Sociology* 13 (1987), 443–464; James G. March and Johan P. Olsen, *Rediscovering Institutions: The Organizational Basis of Politics*, New York 1989; Walter Powell and Paul DiMaggio (eds.), *The New Institutionallsm in Organizational Analysis*, Chicago 1991; W. Richard Scott, *Institutions and Organizations*, London 1995.

69. See only Santi Romano, L'ordinamento giuridico (1918), reprint of the 2nd ed. Florence 1962.

70. See only W. Richard Scott, The Adolescence of Institutional Theory, *Administrative Science Quarterly* 32 (1987), 493–511. The "maturity" of theory is seen in the many contradictory versions that one can choose between in empirical research. The same applies with respect to the complementary concept "culture." See below, chapter 7, note 27.

71. See esp. Marc Granovetter, Economic Institutions as Social Constructions: A Framework for Analysis, *Acta Sociologia* 35 (1992), 3–11.

72. For the theory of science and legal theory we could also add positivism.

73. Used in analogy to the biological sense of to stimulate (an organism, cell, or organ) to produce an active response (translator's note).

74. See Horst Stenger, *Die soziale Konstruktion okkulter Wirklichkeit: Eine Soziologie des "New Age"*, Opladen 1993.
75. See W. Graham Astley and Andrew H. Van de Ven, Central Perspectives and Debates in Organization Theory, *Administrative Science Quarterly* 28 (1983), 246–273.
76. Of course, it also does not help to react with criticism of "grand theories."
77. See Robert E. Quinn and Kim S. Cameron (eds.), *Paradox and Transformation: Toward a Theory of Change in Organization and Management*, Cambridge, MA 1988.

2   Organization as an Autopoietic System

I

If we proceed on the lines of the organization theories presented in the first chapter, we have difficulty coming up with an unambiguous concept of organization. If we set out from the distinctions discussed, the concept of organization would have to indicate the unity of what is differentiated, that is to say, what is the *same* in the relationship between superior and subordinate or between rules and the application of rules, or between formal and informal organization, or between input and output, and so forth. In any case, this would amount to the paradox of sameness, hence to what one nowadays calls performative contradiction: One draws a distinction while at the same time claiming that what one means is given on both sides of the distinction – input *and* output; successful *and* unsuccessful rationality; or even both *and* the relationship pertaining between the two. Apart from this, quite different "and" concepts of organization result depending on the distinction taken as starting point. It is therefore not surprising that a multiplicity of possible organization theories is held to be unavoidable.

This may well be so. But is there one among them that contains all the others?

This poses a methodological problem. How must we proceed if we wish to determine the subject matter of organizational studies?

Old European philosophy would have asked about the essence (essentia) of organization. It had distinguished between species and genera and had assigned an essence of its own to each of them. A definition then had to describe the species and the specific difference. This was to avoid the paradox that the one grouping was another at the same time.[1] Such an architecture can be described as an inclusion hierarchy. In recent decision theory, inclusion hierarchies have been reconstructed on the premise of "near decomposability"[2]; they apply only under certain circumstances – for example, where during a short span of time the influence of the environment on subunits of the system could be ignored.[3] And whether these conditions pertain is to be decided from case to case.

Already Kant had lost interest in such classificatory games; he considered such procedures as no more than a cognitive technique.[4] But it is not easy to find a substitute. Kant preferred the concept of interaction [Wechselwirkung], which anticipates later theories of circular self-reference; but if formulated as a causal concept, this solution hides a paradox, for causality presupposes time and therefore excludes any temporally stable identity of causes and effects with the possibility of retroactive effects of effects on causes. What has remained is the proposal to shift from what-questions to how-questions (in Kant: as the question about the conditions of possibility); however, the transcendental dissolution of the circle of knowledge that has to presuppose itself now finds little acceptance, for it has to prove that what one has to renounce, namely the cosmos of essences and the knowability of the thing-in-itself, is a performance of consciousness.[5]

"Dialectic" was the name Hegel gave to another attempt to break the circle and asymmetricize the self-realization of knowledge. He treated distinctions (the primary focus) as oppositions and oppositions as logically and metaphysically unstable. When they occur, they seek their own unity and find it in their notorious "sublation" [Aufhebung].[6] However, time as historical time and as process or movement has simply to be presupposed, and presupposed in an ontologically paradoxical form, namely as existing and not existing [seiend/nichtseiend].[7] This way of resolving the basic problem of how what is differentiated can be the same or how difference can be identical now also fails to convince. This is not least because time distinctions such as before/after or past/future have to be treated no differently than other distinctions. But the most spectacular failure of the Hegelian dialectic is its inability to demonstrate the process of sublation of oppositions in real history – either as an epiphany of the spirit or as an epiphany of the classless society.

It is no surprise that, after these setbacks in philosophy's efforts to operate free of paradox, it has shown signs of fatigue and concerns itself mainly with analyzing the history of its own texts or linguistic usage. But the question remains of whether paradoxes have to be excluded and why. And how. In historical retrospect, it is striking that, at least since the sixteenth century, rhetoric in particular had been concerned with paradoxes.[8] On the one hand, this was a sideline, a para-doxon; on the other it was the only domain in which communication was reflected upon as communication, namely rhetoric as rhetoric. This can set one thinking. A certain lack of seriousness is understandable; a literature that often lapses into levity.[9] On the other hand, especially after the advent of printing when rhetoric was no longer directed toward training in the spoken word, the intention came to the fore of stimulating thought through communication and the defense of counter-opinions. The aim was clearly to generate a sort of irritation that takes effect even before one decides in binary coding on true or false.[10]

This interest in communicative irritation appears to have spread in the twentieth century after the collapse of metaphysical descriptions of the world. Kenneth Gergen (as social psychologist!) recommends theory generation that proceeds in this fashion.[11] In philosophy we think of Nietzsche, Heidegger, and Derrida, in text theory and "literary criticism" of Paul de Man. Proceeding from psychiatry,[12] family therapy and organizational consulting attempt to resolve the paradoxes that occur in all communication (or: performative contradictions between "report" and "command"); or if there are doubts about this possibility, to replace them by less weighty paradoxes. George Spencer-Brown's mathematical calculus of forms begins and ends with a paradox (not marked as such): the distinction between distinction and indication and the reentry of a distinction into what is distinguished by it.[13]

These suggestions from a wide variety of sources can be combined if we assume that descriptions of the world and society are produced in societies, and only in societies, which employ a mode of operation that they alone have at their disposal, namely communication.[14] We then see that paradoxes must necessarily occur behind all descriptions. On the one hand, all observations and descriptions are obliged to distinguish what they indicate while not being able to occur themselves in the distinction; in brief, this means that they have to make themselves unindicatable in order to indicate something.[15] On the other hand, every communication is a synthesis of information, utterance, and understanding, giving rise to the paradox that the synthesis is also communicated and informs of its right to communicate.[16] One can thus replace the rhetorical concept of paradox by a theoretically grounded concept, resulting in both cases in an autological conclusion: the concept also applies to itself, and one has to accept that self-exemption is prohibited.

If we go along with these reflections, we are obliged to conclude that all descriptions and thus all scientific theories presuppose a paradox, to which they have to turn a blind eye since they cannot introduce it into the description without blocking the descriptive operation. From a methodological point of view, this means that one has to shift from what-questions (questions of essence) to how-questions; and that the first how-question is always about what paradox is unfolded by which distinction, allowing one to work with the distinction and forget the paradox – until someone comes and reparadoxizes the basis for analysis in order to work with another distinction. And in doing so, that person has to accept the same necessity of invisibilizing the paradox of the unity of his or her distinction.[17]

Whatever we may think of this paradox-oriented semantics, it fits the view that the modern world can now only be described polycontexturally and that every operation that observes and describes can be observed and described through other operations in the mode of second-order observation.

II

As we have seen in Chapter 1, organization theory was hived off in the nine-teenth century from the general discussion on order and developed a normative, as well as evolutionary (Darwinist), model of the individual organization for its specific purposes. An organization was to operate rationally and efficiently and, like an individual, be able to decide, and thus to be hierarchically structured from the apex down.[18] This alone was seen as ensuring its survival. But the conversion from evolutionary conditions to a normative model of rationality is not confirmed at the level of real operations; it can be observed only as a myth cultivated in organizations.[19] This insight confronts us with the question of how organizational systems otherwise reproduce their own unity if not thus.

In the theory of self-referential and, in the narrower sense of the term, autopoietic systems, we now have at our disposal a concept that can do justice to the epistemological conditions outlined in the preceding section without sacrificing scientific productivity with its embedding in paradoxical and tauto-logical presuppositions. Autopoiesis, in particular, has been the subject of lively discussion for a number of years now.[20] To quote Jean Paul loosely, light moves faster than sound in the realm of knowledge.[21] Although the term autopoiesis is known, the discussion does not yet evidence an adequate under-standing of the concept. Conversely, however, we also find formulations with the term autopoiesis that mean the same without their implications being fully grasped.[22] We must therefore briefly outline how the conceptual complex self-reference/autopoiesis/operational closure is to be understood in what follows.

The theory of self-referential systems manages without defining its subject matter (in our case organizations) in terms of assumptions about essentiality. Experience teaches that such assumptions lead to unresolvable differences of opinion as soon as various observers define was they hold to be the essence of a matter – whether of law, politics, family, religion, or organization. We therefore begin with a circular definition: an organization is a system that generates itself as organization. We then only have to define how this happens. This next step, however, requires a series of theoretical decisions that could turn out differently if we could offer an alternative at the same level.

The most important of the concretizing, circle-breaking assumptions can be briefly summarized as follows:

(1) The basal unity of an autopoietic system takes the temporal form of an event, thus an occurrence that draws a distinction between "before" and "after"; which can therefore be observed only on the basis of the distinc-tion between before and after. When we are concerned with results, we will also talk of "operation" and, in the case of organizations, of "deci-sion." In comparing theories, it is important to bear this grounding in events (and not in substances) in mind.[23] It follows that the theory

presumes discontinuity – continuous disintegration – and considers continuity (thingness, substance, process) to need explaining.[24] A theory of autopoietic systems construed in this manner is in radical opposition to all sorts of process theories, including dialectical theories. It rejects any sort of essentialism and, on the contrary, demands that every event (or in our field every decision) leave the following one to a subsequent event. Forms of essence are only directives for the repetition of selection. Autopoiesis theory is also to be seen in opposition to action theory. For action theories rely on the ideas (such as intentions, or purposes) of actors for linking up their "unit acts," whereas events such as communications that form autopoietic systems produce a surplus of possibilities, so that something suitable can be chosen in the next step. What is then selected need not be anticipated; the decision is better and more typically made with a preceding event in mind.

(2) A system that generates itself has to observe itself; that is to say, it has to be able to distinguish itself from its environment.[25] This is sometimes denied,[26] but since "organization" cannot be taken to mean the entire world, some criterion or other has to be given for defining what is indicated as an organization. The theoretically decisive question is then whether this demarcation is carried out by the organization itself or, if this is not the case, by whom.

(3) In observing itself, the organization does not observe itself as a fixed object whose properties are recognizable but uses its own identity only to present and abandon ever new determinations.[27] Autopoietic systems can therefore also vary their structures (one speaks of "self-organization"), provided that this is compatible with the continuation of autopoiesis. All reflection on identity that enduring self-descriptions with substantive characteristics propose therefore has to proceed highly selectively, opting for normative assumptions in the process and mostly remaining controversial.

(4) The variability of the self taken in each case as point of reference is guaranteed by the circumstance that the organization observes itself in observation. Even the organizational system itself operates on the level of second-order observation; it constantly diagnoses its own observations (albeit not in every single case). The *theory* of organization must therefore set in at the level of *third*-order observation. It observes a system that is observing itself and can consequently extend its observation to the matters that are inaccessible to self-observation. This brings us to the classical sociological problem of latent structures and functions.[28]

(5) Autopoiesis is accordingly possible only if the system is in a constant state of uncertainty about itself in relation to the environment *and can produce and monitor this uncertainty through self-organization.*

The system cannot convert the built-in (we shall also say self-generated) uncertainty into certainty. The absorption of uncertainty (which we will be dealing with in detail) can only be a transformation of the given, current form of uncertainty in adjustment to changing states of irritation. Reflection or self-description can do nothing to change this state of affairs. Every "transcendental" identity could endanger the further reproduction of the system by itself.

(6) The best possibility for coping with uncertainty is to stick by what has already happened. Organizations therefore clarify the meaning of their action largely in retrospect. This in turn tempts them to pay little attention to the given state of the environment. This outdifferentiation at the operational level must, however, be balanced out at the structural level. The appropriateness of structures (e.g., decision-making programs or the typical time needed for operations is mostly decided with an eye to the environment.

(7) Concepts such as self-reference, self-observation, or self-description presuppose operations that realize what is meant. These operations have to be carried out in the system (where else?). If, at the same time, one takes into account that this is not possible in the form of unconnected, singular events, one comes up against the problem of the recursive interconnection of these operations. To make itself possible, every operation has to presuppose recursion to and anticipation of other operations of the same system. This is the only way in which contexts can be identified and boundaries produced and reproduced in relation to the environment. Regardless of the fact that this state of affairs was first mentioned by a biologist, Humberto Maturana, we therefore also speak of autopoietic systems in our context.[29] When the term was first applied to organizations, it was therefore explicitly marked out as a metaphor.[30] Too broad a concept of cognition and too narrow ties to biochemistry have strongly influenced further discussion and often led it astray.

(8) In view of a complex, often confused debate on the subject, a number of explanatory remarks are called for.

(a) As the term "poíesis" indicates, it is a question of producing a work, of generating the system as its own product. This naturally does not mean that the system itself has all the causes necessary for self-production at its disposal. No causal theory could accept such a concentration of all causes in one system (unless it be God). This is already true of concepts like product, production, and reproduction at the conceptual level. Indeed, only when a system not simply exists but has to reproduce itself out of its own products can it, in precisely this regard, be independent of the environment. But it is important for the system to have causes at its disposal (in an organization, for example, members bound by instructions), so that under normal circumstances it can ensure its own reproduction.

(b) The concept stresses not the regular – let alone unconditional – certainty of production but *reproduction*, that is to say, production from own products. With Heinz von Foerster we can also speak of a "historical machine," in other words, a system that produces further operations from the state in which it has put itself.[31]

(c) Autopoiesis is accordingly formally defined. As concept, it therefore leaves completely open what material operations it performs. They can be biochemical or neurophysiological operations, but also conscious disposal over attention or communications. Neither analogy nor metaphor enters the argument.[32] What is involved are various applications of a general theory.

(d) The simple concept of autopoiesis serves to distinguish and indicate a state of affairs. It has no empirical explanatory value as concept. What it does, above all, is to oblige other concepts to adapt – for example, the concept of evolution or the understanding of the relationship between system and environment. Everything else depends on what operations materialize autopoiesis, and through what structures produced by evolution and learning.

(e) The autopoiesis of the system is realized at the level of *operations*. It is therefore compatible with all structures that permit operation to connect with operation. In this context the concept of structure correlates with autopoiesis, and not as it usually does with the division of work.[33] Through operations, structures are generated and reproduced and possibly varied or simply forgotten for use in operations.[34] We can therefore not infer structural conservatism from the concept of autopoiesis.[35] On the contrary, it is the very closure of the system against the environment that gives it opportunities for structural variation that direct ties would not afford. Autopoietic modes of operation are typically one-off inventions of evolution, which in the course of history tend toward structural diversification. "Autopoiesis" thus refers only to a limit to possible structural variation. But as evolution over long periods and domains teaches us, it is precisely the difference between inside and outside that accelerates change. However, it naturally also teaches us that change does not obey the wishes of particular observers, so that to the observer the systems involved may appear rigid and immobile.

(f) The recursive interconnection of operations follows neither logical nor rational rules. It merely produces connections and the prospect of connectivity. Sales figures, for example, can be treated as proof of the success and quality of the given organizational structures. Information can thus arouse suspicion of interest-specific distortions and encourage further efforts to confirm this suspicion. In international relations between organizations, for instance, ecological criteria for products may be interpreted as trade barriers. Recursions, therefore, ensure the maintenance and reproduction of suppressed paradoxes. Anything particular is always something else at the same time.

(9) Autopoietic systems are operationally closed, and for this very reason they are autonomous systems.[36] The concept of operational closure allows for no gradualization; in other words, it does not allow the system to operate in its environment or the environment to operate in the system. A system cannot be more or less autopoietic,[37] but it can be more or less complex. If only for mathematically demonstrable reasons,[38] operationally closed autopoietic systems cannot be described in terms of input/ output functions. This gives rise to impressions and descriptions like freedom, arbitrariness, and intransparency, which we shall be going into in detail. The concept of operational closure, too, abstracts from causal assumptions, and thus by no means claims (even relative) causal isolation. A system can be operationally closed and, like the brain, rely strongly on the constant input of resources of a very specific sort (in this case blood circulation). Operational closure means only that the system can operate only in the context of its own operations and in so doing has to rely on structures generated by these very operations. In this sense we can speak of self-organization or, as far as operations are concerned, of structural determinedness.

(10) These theoretical propositions have far-reaching consequences for the relationship between system and environment. In this case, operational closure does not mean that an organizational system can have no contact with the intra-societal environment. Society makes intra-societal communication possible across subsystem boundaries. On the other hand, an organization cannot participate in communication without observing itself as participant. As recipients of communications, the organization's own structures control what information the system is irritated by and stimulated to process information itself. As sender of communications, the organization makes decisions about what it wishes to communicate and what not. To this extent, the environment remains for the organization a construction of its own whose reality is naturally not questioned. In this, we agree with Karl Weick.[39] What is observed as environment in the organizational system is always a construct of its own, filling in the other-reference of the system.[40] As it were, the environment validates the decisions of the system by providing the context that allows the system to determine in retrospect what has been decided (Weick speaks of enactment). It allows uncomfortable causes for the system's own

decisions to be externalized, thus "punctuating" its own operations. It is a backup area for problems, which allows the system to ignore the part it plays in generating problems. In sum, it allows the system to relate its own operations to a niche without asking why the world and society in particular contain such niches. This is what the old concept of "milieu" means.

(11) Although biology has given us the concept of autopoiesis, we can very well leave it open whether and how the reproduction of relatively stable large chemical molecules in cells can be understood as autopoietic: perhaps because it is possible only in cells, perhaps because they are highly unstable entities that have to be constantly replaced. In the case of social systems, autopoiesis is much easier to recognize, or at least quite differently structured, for social systems are not entities requiring replication that constantly have to be replaced. Like consciousness systems, they consist only of events, which pass in arising and which have to be succeeded not by the same events but by *others*. The ongoing transition from one element to another – the ongoing reproduction of otherness – can be understood only as autopoiesis, for it presupposes connectivity generated within the system itself. No environment could input anything suitable at the speed required. Only the system itself can stop its own decay, which takes place from moment to moment. And this makes very specific demands on structures; they must not strive for repetition but first of all regulate the transition from one to the other. As we have seen, this requires orientation on highly referential but also determinable *meaning*.[41]

(12) Autopoiesis relies on a system being able to generate internal improbabilities deviating from what is usual. Structurally limited contingencies then take effect in the system as *information* – as information not from the environment, which the system cannot contact, but at best *via* the environment (not in biological systems such as cells, immune systems, brains, but only in systems that can distinguish between themselves and the environment in the medium of meaning). An autopoietic system can thus inform only itself, and in the system information has the function of selectively limiting the options for continuing the system's own operations, with the further function that decisions can be made relatively rapidly through connectivity options.

(13) Closure in this operational sense is a condition for the openness of systems. Older systems theory had, with respect to the law of entropy in thermodynamics, spoken of open systems to explain how order is developed and maintained against the trend. But it failed to ask what enables a system to be open; in other words, what systemic order has to exist for a system to be able to afford openness and possibly even increase the

complexity of the aspects in which it can be open. This question was not put because empirical examples and/or the input/output model had been the orienting factors. Although even older cybernetics had spoken of systems that were closed with regard to information and open with regard to energy, only the more recent theory of self-referential systems clearly states that operational closure is the condition for openness.[42]

(14) The theory of autopoietic systems distinguishes strictly between the continuation of autopoiesis and the maintenance of certain structures that serve to ensure sufficient redundancy and connectivity, and thus make autopoiesis possible in the first place – in one way or another. Structures are thus assumed to be functional, contingent, and differently possible. From the disposition of the theory, this permits understanding for the ambiguity of structural arrangements, the need to interpret them, and their circumventability. We could also say that the theory of autopoietic systems draws the attention of the observer particularly to the circumstance that structures have meaning, and thus have to be constituted in open horizons of reference to other possibilities, whereas autopoiesis itself is not a topic in autopoietic systems. This brings us very close to theories of "symbolic interactionism" or theories of the hermeneutic "interpretation" of reality, without, however, having to take recourse to behaviorist (Mead) or subjectivist assumptions. In what follows, we will repeatedly see that uncertainties have to be reduced and ambiguities clarified in the decision-making process; but also that uncertainty and ambiguity in the processing of meaning are always regenerated, and that the autopoiesis of organizations, in particular, is kept in motion precisely by uncertainty being both reduced and renewed. The impressive gain this complex conceptual maneuver affords is to shift the basic problem in systems theory from *maintaining resources* to that of *maintaining a difference*. This also means that one no longer speaks of "existential" necessities (an organization can exist only if . . .[43]) but of conditions of possibility for observing organizations. If they cannot be distinguished, they cannot be observed. If we describe organizations as autopoietic systems, we are therefore always concerned with the generation and reproduction of a difference (systems-theoretically: between system and environment), and the concept of autopoiesis means that an observer who uses it presupposes that this difference is generated *by the system itself* and reproduced by systemic operations.

The theory of self-referential, autopoietic systems knows that with the switch from unity to difference it uses a paradox, but it avoids including the paradox in the theory because as theoretical figures paradoxes would block observation and description. In other words, it entertains a paradoxical relationship with the paradox that establishes it: it operates on the assumption that the exclusion of the paradox is included. Or in logical terms: the paradox is a *tertium* whose *non datur* has to be taken into account, and therefore has to be "given."

However, otherwise than assumed by logic, this does not remain without consequences for the elaboration of the theory. The paradox remains sovereign – even if captive in the palace and under instruction from advisors. It makes itself felt over and over again at each step of theory elaboration. It changes shape with every distinction that is added. For the unity of the distinction underlying the particular observation always has to remain unobserved. The good conscience that the theory thus gives itself arises from insight into this necessity. The paradox is and remains its principle of sufficient reason, its transcendental principle.

In the case of systems theory, the fundamental difference is the distinction between system and environment. The paradox that has to remain excluded is therefore the unity of this difference, and that is the world. Systems theory accordingly has to renounce conveying knowledge of the world. Instead, with sufficient plausibility it keeps to the rule of relating all observations thematically either to a system or to its environment. In so doing, however, it must first of all decide from the perspective of which system everything else is environment. This requires a statement of system reference. This decision must and can only be contingent. We therefore have to take an equivalent of the creation-theology figure of necessary contingency into account. But it is no serious disadvantage if theory has once accepted not to provide knowledge of the world but only polycontextural descriptions.

III

One of the paradoxes we have to look at more closely is that of time – the paradox of the unity of before and after. It cannot suffice to speak with Hegel of "transition" [Übergang], because precisely this will hide what we wish to keep in mind but disregard as paradox. If autopoietic systems exist as successions of events, how does the system proceed from event to event? To put it in more theoretical and longwinded terms: how does theory indicate the transition, that is to say, the unity of the temporal difference between passing (but still kept in mind) event and subsequent event?

A concept that can do this job and replace the colloquial concept of transition must offer a form with two sides to it. On the outer side, everything that does not come into consideration has to be indicated. It is a matter of negative selectivity. We shall call this side of the process *connectivity*. The inside of the process is concerned with what the passing event means for the coming event, and is thus concerned with positive selection. The well-established concept of information fits the bill. Connectivity is hence attained as information. The success of information also sorts out what is not realized. Or, to put it in systems-theoretical terms, information reproduces the boundaries of the system *and can therefore never cross the boundaries of the system, never pass from outside to inside or from inside to outside.*[44] As far as cognition is concerned, this proposition is identical with the theses of operational constructivism.

The description of organizations as information processing systems is current; its empirical productivity does not need to be justified. Only a suitable concept for it still needs to be supplied. Gregory Bateson provides it: "The technical term 'information' can be succinctly defined as any difference that makes a difference in some later event."[45] The concept covers the two measures needed while ignoring the temporal paradox: the unity of two different points in time. The concept of difference replaces the concept of fact,[46] which is no longer needed thanks to the assumption that systems react only to differences that they make themselves, which therefore do not need to exist "out there" but have to be constructed "inside" (Bateson incidentally understands facts as the infinity of possible differences to which systems can react only by determining what differences make a difference *for it* in deciding its own states).

In the construction and processing of information, the system deviates from the state that would have to be described as entropy, as loss of all usable difference, including that between system and environment. Information processing is the generation of negentropy. But not in the sense that it begins with nothing, produces an origin, thus following the *creatio ex nihilo* model, but in the sense that it reads a difference into something that exists with which it can operate. Even if, in the operations of the system, the question of origin, of the act of founding, were to be put, it would be on the basis of a difference of ad hoc interest, namely the distinction between the act of founding and what precedes it and is therefore not of interest. All operations of the system are information processing. We thus merely repeat that autopoietic systems are operationally closed systems.

In other words, a system has to presuppose itself when it generates and processes information. It must already have limited the arbitrariness of possible surprises, and it must have redundancies at its disposal if it is to obtain information and process it within a limited time span. It has to be able to expect, typify, or guess what could be involved. This applies for perception (this is why the newborn cannot see immediately), and, *a fortiori*, for elaborated communication (for which one needs language, which has its own – phonetic – redundancies). In this context, redundancy does not simply mean "superfluousness" in securing message transmission against disturbances (noise) from outside but the saving of avoidable (and in this sense superfluous) information work.

Another correlate of the closure thesis is that the negative can also take on informational value *if it is distinguished*. No applications are made, a product does not sell, an employee does not turn up at work. The autonomy of the system is also apparent in that it not only reacts to facts but, thanks to its structures, also registers disappointments, that is to say, can assess them as difference and draw information from them. This is one of the many reasons why it is not possible to attribute the operations of the system causally (let alone in terms of causal laws) to the environment. The system causes itself, even if, as an independent observer can easily ascertain, it depends in many regards on its environments.

Moreover, the time element has to be taken into consideration in the information concept. An item of information has to be new, it has to be surprising (however minimally), and therefore always relates to the state of knowledge of the system. This distinguishes between meaning and information. Meaning stays the same even when repeated, and repetition is only to be recognized as repetition if this is so. When information is repeated, by contrast, it loses its informational value; or it changes it completely, so that repetition merely informs that someone considers it necessary or that some breakdown has occurred in the system.

Finally, this concept of information also permits the meaning of forecasts or instructions to be determined, thus the meaning of expectations directed at the future. Whoever makes a forecast or gives instructions may be of the opinion that he can indicate or bring about future states. But what he does, at any rate, manage to do is generate information – be it that expectations are met or that they are disappointed. Setting expectations is the condition for the meeting or disappointment of these very expectations to make a difference, which can then be further processed as information.

It used to be said that cybernetic systems were informationally closed while being open with regard to material and energy. In the light of our investigations, this formula needs to be corrected, for the openness of the system arises only from its irritability, that is to say from its ability to read something as a distinction and to gain information from this – even if only from fluctuations in energy or temperature, the absence of food, etc. The system remains indifferent with regard to energy or material as such, which are as they are. They are *continua*, which do not know the distinction between autopoietic system and environment and which have a destructive impact while, put in the form of distinctions, they can have an immense impact on the system.

IV

Social systems consist of communications. Communication is the autopoietic operation that takes recourse to and anticipates itself, thus generating social systems. There is therefore communication only as social systems and only in social systems. Sociality is not a state of affairs independent of communication (for instance, as a property of the human being).[47]

This can all also be said (if true) of organizations. Theoretical decisions on the subject have to be made at a more abstract level. Communication, in other words, is not only a particularly important aspect that deserves attention in connection with culture in organization research.[48] Through communication every organization thus reproduces not only itself but, like every social system, society as well. To this extent, organization theory can draw on the general theory of social systems, and can accordingly show that organizations are institutions of the societal system that guarantees the conditions for the possibility of communication. An example can illustrate this.

In social systems, which generate information and process information in the form of communication, a distinction has to be drawn between the *topics* and *functions* of communication. The topics of communication differentiate communication substantively, while at the same time structuring it temporally. Every topic differs from other topics and hence distinguishes between the subjects communicated about. One can negotiate about a certain price, about a possible variation in certain products, about relations with a certain client, about the redevelopment of an urban district, about the construction of a new road, etc. The choice of topic creates, *pari passu*, the difference between topics and comments. The topic structure of a communication system presupposes that several different comments on each topic are possible. Otherwise the topic could not be recognized as a topic. Topics therefore have to remain identifiable, even though, indeed because, quite different comments on them are possible. A proposed decision is and remains a topic even if the decision is rejected; and only thus, only as topic, can the decision enter memory and be praised or condemned.

Topics consequently form the memory of the system. Also as a consequence of the operational closure thesis, the memory function never relates to facts of the outer world (although to the system this may seem to be the case) but only to the states of the system itself. In other words, a system can remember only itself. With the form of topics it regulates what it can forget and what it can remember. Topics take part in all operations of the system (one always has to communicate *about something)* in order to generate and represent recursions. The ability to become a topic is practically unlimited. It depends solely on the individual topic history of the system. This holds, for example, for the question whether and under what circumstances "private matters" can become topics. Also unique events– indeed, even the topicalization of a topic – can become a topic. In its unfinished but nevertheless structure-forming mobility, the topic structure represents the world of the system, not in blanket indeterminacy but as the result of the system's history, which is open to the future.

The functions of communication, by contrast, have to do with the autopoiesis of the system, that is to say with the enablement of further communication. Since further communication always depends on recursions, on memory, on structures, this does not exclude but rather includes the assessment of topics. The perspective merely shifts. What is involved from a functional point of view is the distribution of opportunities for participants and for contributions to further communication. Communication observes itself as the past of the then-still-possible future. Agreement has a topic, but at the same time is an element for further communication. One might attempt to develop a topic through contradiction, but the contradiction also has a functional and dysfunctional meaning for further communication. Decisions can be assessed from the point of view of whether they expand or limit the system's scope for decision-making, whether they generate or absorb uncertainty. Risks and responsibilities can thus be at one's disposition without this having to be a topic.

The tacit evaluation of the function of communications appears at first glance to be and remain a purely mental process, precisely when it remains unspoken; and indeed, were there to be such a thing as *esprit de corps* or collective mind, this is where we would look for it. However, closer analysis would soon show that the encapsulation of such calculations in the individual consciousness would have no social consequences of any sort. A contribution to the autopoiesis of contribution can be made only through communication, whatever high demands on the involvement of consciousness are assumed. Social response is to be obtained only where what is at issue is understood. Communication is and remains the controllable vehicle of its own autopoiesis. It processes topicalized and non-topicalized information, manifest and latent aspects of the meaning relevant for it – topics and functions – while also disposing over the topicalization of functions, with dexterity or clumsiness, with or without the assistance of advisers.

V

Autopoiesis, operational closure, event-type elements, connectivity, and information are very general concepts that reach far beyond the subject of our investigations, namely organization. But for special areas of application, general theory offers certain guidelines. If we wish to change such guidelines, for example, the link between closure and information or between event and structure, we have to argue at the level of general theory. But this does not mean that theories dealing with specific areas can be gained by deduction from general theory. Such abstractions are concerned only with exploiting the possible reach of conceptual decisions. For more concrete research on special system types, further decisions are therefore needed, which can be tested, criticized, and possibly modified at their level. This concretization has to take place – on the instruction of general theory! – by indicating the mode of operation whose autopoietic closure generates a system of the type in question; in our case, an organization.

Even and precisely if one renounces assumptions about the nature or essence of organizations, thus leaving it up to them to decide whether they exist and as what, one cannot avoid indicating the operation that generates and reproduces an organization. A *single mode of operation* must be stated, since it could otherwise not be explained (or only by an ominous "and") that a system of a certain type is being generated. The sort of organization theory that this produces depends on this definition of the autopoietic operation – just as the biochemical reproduction of life, when autopoietic closure occurs, generates living systems, and gearing to precisely this operation determines what view of life a theory adopts.[49]

As we have already proposed, we assume that all social systems, including organizations, consist of communications and only of communications. If the concept of communication is broad enough and relates to the world as the domain of possible references, not much meaning (at any rate incommunicable meaning) is lost. The limitation lies at the operational level, not at the semantic level. Communication can relate to non-communicative systems (e.g., to human beings[50]) – *relate* to them but not *generate* them; it cannot *be* a non-communicative system.

Recent developments in organization theory come very close to this emphasis on communication. We read, for example, that communication is "an essential element in the ongoing process of organizing through which social structures are produced, reproduced, and changed."[51] But this means only that without communication no organization could come about or be continued[52] and would thus remain trivial. Formulations such as "essential" also remain indeterminate. One would first have to clarify the essence of essence and state what is required apart from the essence for an organization to come about: further essentials, or only accidentals, which can vary from organization to organization but which in one way or another are indispensable?[53] All this can be avoided if we change the question from essence to production and thus from unity to difference. Communication produces and reproduces a difference, whatever on the system side of the difference between system and environment is asserted to be unity, essence, or necessary structure.

However, this does not yet bring us to the question of what special sort of communication produces *organizations* when recursively interconnected and reproducing itself from its own products. The following reflections seek to show that organizations arise and reproduce themselves when decisions are communicated and the system becomes operationally closed on the basis of this operation. Everything else – goals, hierarchies, opportunities for rationality, members bound by instructions, or whatever else is regarded as a criterion of organization – is secondary in comparison and can be seen as the result of the system's decision-making operations. All decisions of the system can hence be traced back to decisions of the system. This presupposes that the founding of an organization and also acceptance into membership are described as decisions, even where in family businesses members of the family are given preferential treatment.[54] Operational closure does not mean that members have no other roles to play, too, in the environment of the organization, for example, as housewives and mothers or members of a radical party or friends of influential politicians. However, such relationships are treated not as nature-given, but as the outcome of decisions; in other words, not as dangers but as risks.

Of course, physical behavior and manual operations take place in organizations – above all in the production process but also when an office worker moves files from desk to trolley. In other words, it is not worthwhile decomposing certain actions into decisions and communicating them as decisions. Taylorism has its limits. But decisive for concept formation is that these checks on breakdown into decisions are set by the organization itself, and are thus themselves the result of decisions.

Already at this stage it is advisable to point to a problem that, more than anything else, determines the particularity of organized social systems. Decisions can be communicated only if the possibilities that have been rejected are communicated along with them, for otherwise they would not be understood as decisions at all. Research approaches in communication theory very typically face the problem that they cannot treat communications simply as facts[55] because understanding a communication requires knowledge of what could have been said instead. For participants in face-to-face interaction, this knowledge may be implicitly available, but at a greater distance it is difficult to reconstruct. From a distance, one can only react to what is factually communicated. If, however, it is a matter of communicating decisions, it is often clear enough, at any rate easier to recognize, what other decisions a particular decision has excluded. This alone makes it understandable why broader working contexts cannot be organized through communication as such, but only through the communication of decisions. Neither non-communicated decisions (if they exist at all) nor communications that do not show themselves to be decisions suffice.

This routine co-presentation of what is rejected, as we shall see in detail in the chapter on the absorption of uncertainty, combines reducing uncertainty with doubts about whether it is right to do so. Organizational systems, thus, change only the form of uncertainty they have to deal with. They de-ontologize the world, as it were. They fill their memories with information about what has not happened, and have to integrate this other side of their decision-making, as well. They can, therefore, not simply operate as representation of the world as it is but have to rely on presenting their unity as their own achievement, for example, through the semantics of advantage and disadvantage, through member selection, or, as is repeatedly presumed, through the exercise of power.

Decisions mark a difference between past and future that they produce themselves. They thus mark the irreversibility of time. It is striking that this occurs in the form of events, which are themselves bound to points in time and are accordingly neither reversible nor irreversible.

Operational closure on the basis of systemic decisions can be recognized from the circumstance that every decision has to be accepted as the premise of further decisions and as such contributes to the absorption of uncertainty. The organization can also communicate its decisions to the environment and thus create facts others have to observe – for example, it can approve or reject applications, provide statements to the press, or publish advertisements. This possibility is guaranteed by the participation of the organization in societal communication.[56] But for internal purposes of decision-making coordination – which is what operational closure means – every decision takes on a special sort of importance for others, in the double sense of binding effect and responsibility. This does not mean that deviance can be effectively excluded, but it becomes a topic of communication, and recognizable as such.

Since decisions that continue the autopoiesis of the system can be made only within the system (and not in the environment), but as operations also generate a difference between system and environment, then every operation of the system imposes a coupling of self-reference and other-reference – self-reference in the sense of reference to the network of the system's own decisions and other-reference in the sense of the motivation of decisions, which can never be solely that decisions have already been made in the system. In other words, by drawing a boundary and through operational closure, the system obliges itself to oscillate continually between self-reference and other-reference, and the oscillator function is built into the operation of communicating decisions so as to effectively prevent the system from losing itself to itself or to the world. This alone makes it possible to reproduce openness to the environment under the conditions of operational closure.[57] If, however, a distinction is drawn between system and environment, the system has to experience that event sequences (processes) in the environment proceed differently than in the system. And only for this reason does the system have to develop temporal perspectives. A notion of time that goes beyond immediate coming and going becomes necessary only because the course of time in the environment diverges from that in the system and has to be synchronized in the system. And only for this reason does the need arise in the system to communicate ever new decisions – however inconsequentially, however routinely, however rationally or erroneously this occurs.

The advantage of this theoretical disposition, which we initially justify only on the basis of this advantage,[58] is that it can treat all the essential characteristics of organizations so far mentioned as variables and can place them in a more general theoretical framework. But why the *communication* of decisions? And what is the problem if decisions are communicated? Hence, *why* do problems, and *which* ones, have to be resolved in the form of organization?

If decisions are understood in mental terms, thus geared to someone becoming aware when choosing how to behave that he could also behave differently, this is an everyday phenomenon that lies within the range of mentally available attention and varies with it. When someone has opted to behave in a certain way, it is normally socially apparent, even if the person concerned does not immediately realize that a decision has happened to him: he becomes aware of it only owing to the social response. The horizon of alternatives deliberately taken into consideration depends on the importance of the behavior and changes from moment to moment and from person to person. The continuation of individual behavior can therefore not depend on reaching agreement with others that a decision is pending or has been made and what alternatives are available. Given the mutual intransparency of individual consciousness systems, everyday life is sufficiently cushioned by abundant possibilities for thematization, only few of which can be used, often by chance. They can be seen as protective devices that are necessary because psychic systems, too, are operationally closed and are, on this basis, open systems. In the normal course of events, there is not enough time, nor is it so important, to record decisions in socially visible fashion or to make it clear when a decision is made, on what subject and over what other options, and why one behavior is preferred to another.

But if a decision is communicated, almost inevitably along with the decision to communicate it, we are dealing with an event of a different format. A man tells his wife that he is going to the club that evening even though he knows (and she knows that he knows) that she would rather go out with him or stay at home with him. The utterance both informs about the decision (in the double sense of what has been decided and that a decision has been made) and is geared to being understood. In other words, it is a component in a complex communication. It produces the impression of an irrevocable past, which can be renegotiated only in the form of resistance. In other words, communications of this type increase the risk of dissension. Whether deliberately or not, they mark out the limits to power. If agreements can be expected, there is something provocative about them. Above all, in systems sensitive to agreement like primitive hordes or modern families, they are anything but harmless. They tend to outdifferentiate power relations (or to fail in the attempt). If there are sufficiently complex boundary conditions and form typicality is institutionalized, they tend to *outdifferentiate organizations*.

Power relations are structures, not systems. They develop, for example, within families or as patron-client relationships in stratified societies. They are, so to speak, parasites of stability interests in outdifferentiated systems. They asymmetricize the communication of decisions, and one grows accustomed to them because belated resistance would meet with surprise and trigger disadvantageous conflicts.[59] They profit from framework conditions that they have not produced themselves. They legitimate themselves through tradition, through conventionality or, as older nobility theories tell us, through initial successes in the depths of time.

The same problem with the communication of decisions takes another turn when it comes to outdifferentiating organized social systems. The characteristics of operational closure and the specification of the corresponding type of operation are to be added. A master is always more than a mere decision-maker. He is also spouse or father, noble, patron, and involved in other roles of his own in which he does not act as master. When an organization comes into being, a recursive decision-making network comes into being. Everything that happens at all happens as the communication of decisions or with regard to this communication. Although other behaviors can also occur in organizations, for example, gossip[60] (just as in living cells there are also minerals that do not participate in the autopoiesis of the system and nevertheless perform important functions), the continuance of autopoietic reproduction and the resulting reproduction of the difference between system and environment are required to maintain the system as a system (of a given type). Without the basal operation of communicating decisions, there would be no other behavior in the system because there would be no system. Particularly in organizations, moreover, practically all behavior – even machine operation, dealing with enquiries, or coming late to work – can, in the event of problematization, be thematized as decisions. The operational form of communicating decisions is the form in which the system reacts to irritations and reflects on itself.

Even the authorization or duty to take part in the communication of decisions goes back to decisions made in the system, namely to the appointment or dismissal of members of the organization. We will be returning to this point.[61] At the moment we are concerned only with the thesis that we are dealing with an operationally closed system that reproduces itself by operations typical of the system. In order to continue its own operations this system therefore has to relate implicitly or explicitly to decisions – whether past or future – that the system produces itself.

This is why there are no masters in organizations, but only bosses who hold office and exercise responsibilities that go back to decisions of the system or that can be clarified by decisions of the system. They must of course be living persons, and system and environment depend on one another in innumerable ways. We have already said what needs to be said on this subject. But causalities also need to be thematized in the system – for example, to settle the question of whether someone is still able to exercise his office. Or external observations are involved that have no consequences for the system.

In communicating knowledge, news, and thus also gossip, one risks saying something that is already known and therefore has no informational value. The gain in prestige that the gossip network enables and with which it rewards the adepts at this métier consists precisely in the fact that, and how, this danger is avoided and how interesting, possibly useful, and novel news is come by. Efforts must be directed toward getting in first and obtaining news as directly as possible from the source. Decisions, by contrast, have informational value *eo ipso*. It may be a matter of uninteresting trivialities, but that they are new cannot be denied, for they would otherwise not be decisions. This shows why it makes sense to outdifferentiate a system for the communication of decisions, and thus to form organizations. At any rate, organizations supply themselves with information; their elementary operations reproduce information, whatever goals they pursue and whether they attain them or not. These insights, like everything that has to do with autopoiesis, may well be trivial. And this is perhaps why organization theory has so far overlooked them or not paid sufficient attention to them in their theoretical fundamentality.

It remains to be said that, although the autopoiesis of an organizational system comes about only through the communication of decisions, there is, as we have seen, also an abundance of other communications in every organization, for example, enquiries, preparatory discussions, information on circumstances and possibilities that ought to be taken into account, or simply sociable communication on which, however, no value would be placed if both parties were not members of the organization. Just like the chemical circularity of reproducing life in cells, the system's network of reproduction is by no means everything that actually exists in the system. And, of course, communicating decisions is itself a quite concrete, materialized process that changes states of consciousness, whose consequences within the material state of affairs or within consciousness, however, no longer contribute to the autopoiesis of the organizational system.[62]

VI

The conceptual opposition between openness and closure can easily lead to misunderstandings. After everything that has been said, it should be clear that closure is not to be understood as causal isolation or insensitivity.

This insight has also been applied to living systems understood as "subjects": they must (not only can) concern themselves with their environment if they are no longer determined by that environment.[63] With regard to organizations, this is hence not a new version of the old "machine model" of organization, according to which a good organization reacts only to quite specific stimuli and registers all other environmental impacts as disturbances that call for repair or replacement. Such assumptions would guide the theory in a direction that reality and, above all, organizational developments have clearly proved wrong over the past ten to twenty years. Interconnectivity between system and environment is not decreasing but increasing. In industrial production, for instance, this has been the result of technically more complicated products, of economies in storage, and just-in-time component supply; but also of the increasing involvement of customer communications in production planning. Another reason for such interconnectivity lies in the problem of informational asymmetries. The seller knows his product better than the buyer. Trust-building connections of this sort can weaken incentives to exploit such asymmetries, since it could put such valued relations at risk. The same applies in public administration, owing to the increasing political emphasis on programs dependent on cooperation between beneficiaries and disadvantaged parties. This is most apparent in local government authorities strongly differentiated in terms of clientele and professions. In the private sector, these changes tend to be apparent in increasing pressure to innovate (e.g., overcapacity reduction or internal rationalization to ensure fluctuating adaptedness); in public administration it is seen in increasing politicization and more closely interlocking interests. These changes are so well known and have been so widely discussed that we can take them as given.[64]

The theoretical basis for analyzing growing interconnectivity and interdependence lies in the thesis that openness is possible only on the basis of closure, for interdependence can exist only where there are boundaries that can differentiate and regulate expectations.[65] We had already pointed this out when presenting the basics of the general theory of self-referential systems. In the cognitive sciences, too, it is recognized that a system has first of all to be capable of reproducing itself before it can develop cognition, memory, anticipatory reactions, and the like. What then matters is what sort of systems are involved, and this means what sort of operation carries out reproduction. In this connection one cannot argue in terms of analogies, for example, to suggest that, because the principle of opening through operational closure applies for living cells, it also applies for brains, for consciousness systems, or for social systems. It must rather be shown in concrete terms that operational closure also works on the basis of other forms and how this takes place.

This principle of opening through closure proves its worth, if anywhere, in the field of organized social systems. The mode of operation "communication of decisions" and the constant reproduction of decision requirements through decisions ensure the system a sort of self-generated restlessness, and thus high endogenous irritability. It cannot switch off – unless an organization dissolves itself by decision. The decision-making process requires a constant supply of information and reasons, which, however, can be produced only in the system itself. It draws on impulses from the environment; but organizations notoriously also build problems into their environment so that they can decide on them. For example, welfare bureaucracies generate demand for their aid by offering it in the first place, while production organizations first have to develop the market that they then serve with their products. The other side of the system boundary would not be another side, would not be an environment, and would not be a possible other-reference for the operations of the system if the system were not to reproduce itself and its boundaries.

As a result, we will want to know *how* a closed system can open itself to the environment, even though it cannot reach the environment through its own operations because it cannot operate beyond its own boundaries. The answer to this question lies in the concept of self-observation.[66] This has far-reaching consequences for the theory of social systems in general and organized social systems in particular. We must therefore take a brief look at the subject.

Like all observation, self-observation requires a distinction, that between self-reference and other-reference. With this distinction, the difference between system and environment, which the system generates through the autopoiesis of its operations, is copied into the system. In formal terms, it is thus a reentry in the sense of George Spencer-Brown's calculus of forms: the reentry of the distinction into what is distinguished.[67] As Spencer-Brown shows, reentry leads to the indeterminacy of the system that cannot be resolved with the simple observational means of the system (that is to say, by indicating things and events, numbers and variables).[68] This indeterminacy is produced in the system itself. It is not the result of the uncontrollable randomness of environmental impacts.[69] This is clear from the circumstance that the environment, which the system constructs through other-reference, is not necessarily congruent with the environment that an external observer can observe and describe, let alone the world "as it really is," which is accessible to no observer. That this is so can, however, still be observed in the system. The "reentry" indicates the limit values, the beginning and the end of the bivalent calculus that can be carried out.[70] The system can thus itself point to unresolvable indeterminacy. And through suitable semantic expressions it can restore a closed world for itself. Spencer-Brown shows this with the help of the "imaginary space" concept, which expands operationally accessible space, and also by including time, which, however, is likewise operationally inaccessible and has therefore to be thought of as past (memory) or future.[71] In this process (hence always in the context of self-observation), the operation of differentiating indication becomes an always present event, which needs no time, which arises and disappears as it happens, but also constitutes time horizons to shape infinity in finite performance, namely a past that can be remembered or forgotten (Spencer-Brown: memory) and a future in which the system can oscillate in accordance with the two sides of the distinction that it uses in each case, for example, that between self-reference and other-reference or between success and failure in keeping with accepted criteria.[72] This means that the calculus thus extended (giving us a system capable of self-observation) is excluded as a representational description of an external truth. It is rather a matter of intensifying centers of reflection in a world that for this very reason remains unobservable.[73]

Heinz von Foerster constructs the same basic idea with the distinction between trivial and non-trivial machines.[74] Machines that do not observe themselves are trivial, performing functions imposed from outside and, where input remains the same, producing the ever same results. Non-trivial machines, by contrast, are "historical" machines that in all operations first have to consult the state in which their preceding operations have put them. These non-trivial machines, too, are incalculably complex, and therefore have to be treated (by themselves or by other observers) as if they could freely decide. And only this incalculability (affecting every observer) makes it possible to observe decisions.

Organization theory presupposes decisions; it has terms and concepts for them, which are used in the organizations themselves or can be introduced into them. It assumes that there is time, that the past is immutable and that the future still offers elements of indeterminacy and shapability. It assumes that the environment of organizations is too complex to be fully known, let alone for external and internal events to "match" point by point. More far-reaching analysis can confirm these assumptions – while dissolving them as mere assumptions by showing why things are the way they are.

In what follows we shall be keeping to these guidelines but shall attempt to describe with greater precision what happens if operational closure is compensated by self-observation, hence by the distinction between self-reference and other-reference; what happens if this happens in the semantic form of decisions and decision chains, and how on this basis structures develop on which the complexity of the system and hence the differentiation of its sensitivity to information depends.

VII

Among the most important consequences of the theory of autopoietic, operationally closed systems is the switch in semantics from adaptation to learning. In speaking of autopoiesis, we must assume that the system is tolerated by its environment and in this sense is already adapted; otherwise it could not reproduce itself. Operations and the structures they build therefore serve not to better adapt the system to its environment but to continue the autopoiesis of the system. In the structural drift of evolution, this allows the system to enhance its own complexity (as long as the environment tolerates it) and thus expand its irritability. But here, too, irritation serves not to better adapt the system to the environment but to generate intra-systemic problems (probably always problems of consistency with what the system's memory claims) and thus to find solutions to problems – and adapt the system to itself.

The theory of adaptive learning in organizations has made important progress in this direction.[75] The assumption that decisions by the system are closely linked to environmental reactions has to be abandoned. It had led to the conclusion that an organization could learn directly from its own impact on the environment. On the one hand, the environment varies largely independently of the organization; it is turbulent owing to the workings of other autopoietic systems. Moreover, even if (in ecological contexts, for example) an organization believes it knows what impacts it has on the environment, causal attribution remains a problem along with the question of whether a causal constellation can be expected to recur if the organization changes its mode of action or fails to do so.

Furthermore, learning is the general precondition for an organization to distinguish between success and failure. It naturally does not find this distinction in its environment but in itself – for example, in corporate accounts or in the ratio of cured to still ill or dying patients. The components of the distinction may well point to the environment, but the distinction itself, not to mention assessment statistics, are intra-systemic constructions. What is more, it depends on the given state of the system whether and how intensively it is impressed by success and failure. There are indeed organizations, for instance, in the therapy business, that are not discouraged by repeated failure but which can offer professional explanations for their lack of success that are apt to underline the importance of indefatigable effort.

Furthermore, all learning is based on the performance of the system's memory, which recalls some things but forgets a great deal more. An impression of cumulative learning thus arises in the system, together with the possibility of calling on "experience." And, as always, recourse to self-reference produces a non-calculable surplus of possibilities here, too, which impose a highly selective course of action. As psychological research teaches us, such selection can also serve to correct the level of aspiration in relation to the environment. If perfect adaptation is the goal, what then matters is adaptation to non-adaptation.

Operational closure also prevents the system from attributing too great importance to individual irritations. Even if one does not see the problem, as here, in the operational unattainability of the environment but, like James March and others, only in its random fluctuations, its uncontrollable turbulences, and in the "imperfect matching" between system and environment, one can recognize the problem that would be posed by too rapid adaptation to the

environment, thus by random constellations. If a system operates autopoietically, and can accordingly learn only from the resistance of its own operations
to its own operations, the problem of maladaptation for supposedly inescapable
causes is not solved, but it can be seen that and how the system is able to protect
itself through delayed learning and lethargy in internal self-adaptation processes. Rapid learning is not necessarily advisable.

As far as practical conclusions are concerned, it is only a small step from
a theory of an uncertain, noisy, turbulent environment to a theory of operational
closure and autopoietic reproduction. In both cases the consequence is to refer
the organization to itself in its learning efforts and to leave successful adaptation to evolution.[76] The theoretical consequences, by contrast, are considerable.
One can link organization theory more than has hitherto been the case to
interdisciplinary developments and, more than hitherto usual, abandon unanalyzed abstractions. Existing knowledge can then be couched in still unfamiliar
terminology and reformulated. At the same time, it becomes clear how far the
"behavioral theory of the firm"[77] has already distanced itself from the classical
assumptions of rational decision and organization theory.

VIII

Every theory is the construction of an observer, including the theory of
autopoietic systems. Varela concludes that an observer has the choice between
input/output models or operational closure models.[78] But how is one to choose
between the two?

One point of reference could be Heinz von Foerster's distinction between
trivial and non-trivial machines. Input/output models are appropriate only if
relations with the environment are so exactly specified that their transformation
can be described in terms of a mathematical calculus or a machine process.
However, this is not the case with social systems or even organizations.
If organizations are nevertheless described in terms of input/output models,
this means opting for an ideal-typical abstraction (like rational choice theory),
making it necessary to explain deviations. Scientific interest then shifts from
normality to deviation.

Without knowledge of this theoretical apparatus, John Meyer and Brian
Rowan[79] come to similar conclusions, but use them for quite different purposes, namely to recommend a theory that treats organizations as institutions.[80]
Borderline cases are conceivable in which organizations are technically so well
structured that they react to specific market stimuli with specific products.
The formal structure of the system could then be explained in terms of classical
rationality theory. In reality, however, things are different. As soon as organizations begin to operate and develop their own complexity, they convert the strict
coupling of their formal concept into loose couplings. Formal structure thus

assumes the main function of presenting and maintaining legitimacy. It certifies, as it were, how things are to be done. It nurtures the belief that others believe in it, and the system switches its mode of self-organization from technology to good faith and trust – one could also say to "pluralistic ignorance" with regard to actual motives. If a trivial machine transforms itself into a non-trivial machine, or if a trivial model can be realized only in a non-trivial manner, this changes the functional meaning of formal structure even if its formal presentation (positions, decision-making programs, linking rules) remains the same. This broadens the domain of what is relevant in the way of environmental concerns. The organization is also in quest of confirmation in the environment for its organizational culture and for belief in the myth of its own rationality.

In comparison with the classical theory of rational decision-making, the theory of autopoietic systems dissolves a unity that had formerly been taken for granted, namely the unity of practical (let us say intelligent) orientation and prediction of how others will behave. The question is – and research in both systems theory and decision theory[81] appears to impose it – whether behavior prediction is really such an indispensable benchmark or whether one could not just as well, and perhaps more successfully, take other criteria, for example, norms or cognitive routines, which have proved their worth and to which communication can relate.

Whether concepts like institution or culture can make a useful contribution can remain open. What institutional theory at any rate shows is, paradoxically, precisely a consequence of the link between operational closure, self-referential historicization, non-triviality, and intransparency. Even if the myths by which the system solves these problems are projected into the environment, there is no changing the fact that the system cannot operate in its environment, and that, in the longer term, structural drift sets in, deciding whether and for how long the system is on track. In contradiction to institutional theoreticians, one can therefore not assume that the system copies the institutional patterns of its environment correctly. It is not a matter of taking over but of imagination.

IX

Recent research has often stressed that the model of the organization as a limited system has failed or has at least been rendered obsolete by the recent developments in organizations of the economic system. The concept of autopoiesis reacts to this critique, not by denying system boundaries in the face of extensive and intensive crossings but by defining them differently, namely as an expression of operational closure.

Organizations can indeed be characterized by intensive internal conflicts and strong external ties; there are at any rate organizations where this is the case. This has consequences for the concept. System boundaries can then no longer be understood as insurmountable barriers. They are only the consequence of the fact that the system orients itself internally on the distinction between self-reference and other-reference. They are not objectively established matters like the hides or feathers of animals. They arise rather from the recursive interconnection of the system's operations, thus from the system having to recognize itself what past and what future operations are to be treated as "its own."

This is a condition for the continuous crossing of boundaries by causal relations between causes and effects, as well as for the containment of internal conflicts. No political party would get very far if it was unable to distinguish internal conflicts, however violent, from conflicts with other parties. And it also has to be able to attribute its impact on the government apparatus or public opinion to itself, even though such impacts occur in the environment and therefore arise only by crossing the boundaries of the system.

The abstraction of the theory of autopoietic systems serves to include such states of affairs. What ultimately matters is who observes a system, and which one, with the help of the distinction between "inside" and "outside." This does not mean that systems theory is at the mercy of unrestrained relativism. The thesis of autopoietic self-constitution asserts rather that what primarily matters is the self-observation of the given system, thus the distinction between self-reference and other-reference. All other observers have to comply if they cannot otherwise find their object but only follow their imagination or model constructions.

The solution, like all solutions, comes at a cost. It lies in the fact that the unity of the system can be described only as a paradox. It is, according to Yves Barel, an existential paradox.[82] We can speak of unity only in a constructivist context, that is to say, only in distinction to something else. What it excludes has to be included. Exclusion has to be understood as an operation of the system. That organizations are to be understood as an existential paradox is no longer an unusual thought. Other theoretical approaches have also taken this path.[83] The consequences have still largely to be clarified. We shall be going into them in greater detail when we examine the concept of decision.

Notes

1. To avoid precisely the paradox that the *same* genus (génos) is *another* or *another the same*, Plato had called for a art of differentiation (dihairesis). This is stated explicitly in Sophist 253 D. But then one has to presuppose that something or other legitimates the choice of this distinction rather than another (even if it is the recall of ideas). But

if distinguishing distinctions also becomes a problem or if, as Gotthard Günther puts it, it is a question of "polycontextural" conditions, one does not escape so easily. See Gotthard Günther, Life as Polycontexturality, in idem, *Beiträge zur Grundlegung einer operationsfähigen Dialektik* vol. 2, Hamburg 1979, 283–306.

2. See Herbert A. Simon, The Architecture of Complexity, *Proceedings of the American Philosophical Society* 106 (1962), 467–482; also in: *General Systems* 10 (1965), 63–76.

3. See Albert Ando and Franklin Fisher, Near Decomposability, Partition and Aggregation and the Relevance of Stability Discussions, *International Economic Review* 4 (1963), 53–67.

4. In the Critic of the Power of Judgment, Introduction 6, we read: "It is true that we no longer notice any decided pleasure in the comprehensibility of nature, or in the unity of its division into genera and species, without which the empirical concepts, that afford us our knowledge of nature in its particular laws, would not be possible. Still it is certain that the pleasure appeared in due course, and only by reason of the most ordinary experience being impossible without it, has it become gradually fused with simple cognition, and no longer arrests particular attention." *In the translation by* James Creed Meredith, *Critique of Judgement*, Oxford University Press 1952, 2007. In short: a mere knowledge technique that has been misunderstood as ontology.

5. See the criticism by Martin Heidegger, *Die Frage nach dem Ding: Zu Kants Lehre von den transzendentalen Grundsätzen*, Tübingen 1962, Gesamtausgabe vol. 41, Frankfurt 1984.

6. That a play on words comes in lieu of a solution to the problem recalls the heyday of rhetorical paradox management, the sixteenth century. We shall be coming back to this.

7. On the critique see again Martin Heidegger, *this time Sein und Zeit*, 6th ed. Tübingen 1949, 432 note 2.

8. See overview in Rosalie L. Colie, *Paradoxia Epidemica: The Renaissance Tradition of Paradox*, Princeton, NJ 1966.

9. Their communication "deserveth no hard conjecture among the learned, because they are onely but exercise of wit," writes Anthony Mundy, *The Defence of Contraries*, London 1593, reprint Amsterdam 1969, A 3. It is to be noted that this retraction takes place on another textual level, namely in a dedication. Or, in other words, in a cover letter (see John Donne, *Paradoxes and Problems*, ed. Helen Peters, Oxford 1980) or in a counter-publication (see Ortensio Lando, Confutatione del libro de paradossi nuovamente composta, in tre orationi distinta, n.p, n.d.). Rhetoric thus appears to be intent on distributing the paradox of the communication of paradoxes between two different sorts of text, and thus to resolve it. This naturally presupposes writing and in the cases cited the printed word.

10. This uncomfortable state of excitement is traditionally known as admiratio. See René Descartes, Les passions de l'âme Art. 53, *Œuvres et Lettres, éd. de la Pléiade*, Paris 1952, 723 f.

11. See Kenneth J. Gergen, *Toward Transformation in Social Knowledge*, New York 1982, 142: "One may also foster generative theory by searching for an intelligent antithesis to commonly accepted understandings."

12. See Jurgen Ruesch and Gregory Bateson, *Communication: The Social Matrix of Psychiatry*, New York 1951.

13. See Laws of Form (1969), reprint New York 1979. For earlier application of this calculus in organization theory see Philip G. Herbst, *Alternatives to Hierarchies*, Leiden 1976, 84 ff.

14. See Niklas Luhmann, *Theory of Society*. Translated by Rhodes Barrett, Stanford UP, vol. 1 2012, vol 2 2013.

15. See also with reference to the problem of a world that seeks to observe itself, Spencer-Brown loc. cit., 105.

16. On the consequent problems for the theory of the state, see Niklas Luhmann, Metamorphosen des Staates, in idem., *Gesellschaftsstruktur und Semantik* vol. 4, Frankfurt 1995, 101–137.

17. Similarly Nicholas Rescher, *The Strife of Systems: An Essay on the Grounds and Implications of Philosophical Diversity*, Pittsburgh 1985 – albeit in the certainly unjustified hope that this was only a problem of theory and that "methodological pragmatism" could point the way to a solution. But there is no method that does not itself require theoretical assumptions.

18. See Nils Brunsson and Johan P. Olsen, *The Reforming Organization*, London 1993, esp. 60 ff. with the thesis that this view of identity in organizations also serves as never-ending reason for reforms.

19. See, e.g., John W. Meyer and Brian Rowan, Institutionalized Organizations: Formal Structure as Myth and Ceremony, *American Journal of Sociology* 83 (1977), 340–363.

20. For an up-to-date overview see above all John Mingers, *Self-Producing Systems: Implications and Applications of Autopoiesis*, New York 1995. Also Fenton Robb, Cybernetics and Supra Human Autopoietic Systems, *Systems Practice* 2 (1989), 47–74; Hans Rudi Fischer (ed.), *Autopoiesis: Eine Theorie im Brennpunkt der Kritik*, Heidelberg 1991; Roeland J. in't Veld, Linze Schaap, Catrien J.A.M. Termeer, and Mark J.W. van Twist (eds.), *Autopoiesis and Configuration Theory: New Approaches to Societal Steering*, Dordrecht 1991; Theodor M. Bardmann, *Wenn aus Arbeit Abfall wird: Aufbau und Abbau organisatorischer Realitäten*, Frankfurt 1994, passim, esp. 72 ff. and in connection with the discussions on "organizational culture" 365 ff.; Kenneth F. Bailey, *Sociology and the New Systems Theory: Toward a Theoretical Synthesis*, New York 1994, 285 ff. The wealth of essays on the subject is now almost overwhelming. On application to organizations, see, e.g., Werner Kirsch and Dodo zu Knyphausen, Unternehmungen als "autopoietische" Systeme?, in: Wolfgang H. Staehle and Jörg Sydow (eds.), *Managementforschung I*, Berlin 1991, 75–101; Walter J.M. Kickert, Autopoiesis and the Science of (Public) Administration: Essence, Sense and Nonsense, *Organization Studies* 14 (1993), 261–278. Helmut Willke, Systemtheoretische Strategien des Erkennens: Wirklichkeit als interessierte Konstruktion, in: Klaus Götz (ed.), *Theoretische Zumutungen: Vom Nutzen der systemischen Theorie für die Managementpraxis*, Heidelberg 1994, 97–116; Michael Wollnik, Interventionschancen bei autopoietischen Systemen, in: Götz loc. cit. 118–159.

21. Jean Paul, *Clavis Fichtiana seu Leibgeberiana*, Werke vol. 3, München 1961, 1011–1056 (1014): "In the realm of knowledge – unlike in the physical world – *sound* always arrives earlier than light."

22. "Any enterprise's first product is itself," as we read, for example, in Randall Bausor, Entrepreneurial Imagination, Information, and the Evolution of the Firm, in: Richard W. England (ed.), *Evolutionary Concepts in Contemporary Economics*, Ann Arbor, MI 1994, 179–189 (181). There is also talk of "autogenesis"; see Robert Drazin and Lloyd Sanderlands, Autogenesis: A Perspective on the Process of Organizing, *Organization Science* 3 (1992), 230–24. If we go back to the Greek meaning of the word, it is, however, preferable to speak not of "origin" but of "product." For one's own origin is a system only insofar as one's is one's own product. The question of beginnings is one best left to the theologians.

23. For a rather rare conception of this sort, see Floyd H. Allport, An Event-System Theory of Collective Action: With Illustrations From Economic and Political Phenomena and the Production of War, *The Journal of Social Psychology* 11 (1940), 417–445; idem., The Structuring of Events: Outline of a General Theory with Applications to Psychology, *Psychological Review* 61 (1954), 281–303; idem., The Theory of Enestructure (Event-Structure Theory): Report of Progress, *American Psychologist* 22 (1967), 1–24. The links with the cosmology of Alfred North Whitehead are obvious.

24. In Tim Ingold, *Evolution and Social Life*, Cambridge 1986, 24, I found the appropriate formulation: "Process is to event as continuity is to discontinuity."

25. This alone need not lead to a theory of autopoiesis. We find discussions on the subject based on a distinction between matter and symbol. See, e.g., Howard H. Pattee, Cell Psychology: An Evolutionary Approach to the Symbol-Matter Problem, *Cognition and Brain Theory* 5 (1982), 325–341. But these concepts then have to be clarified, especially with regard to the concept of reference.

26. E.g., by Barbara Czarniawska-Joerges, *Exploring Complex Organizations: A Cultural Perspective*, Newbury Park, CA 1992, 32 f.

27. On the self-consciousness of psychic systems, see also Paul M. Churchland, *Matter and Consciousness: A Contemporary Introduction to the Philosophy of Mind*, Cambridge, MA 1984, 73: "[S]elf-consciousness involves the same kind of *continuously updated* knowledge that one enjoys in one's continuous perception of the external world."

28. See summary in Robert K. Merton, *Social Theory and Social Structure*, 2nd ed. Glencoe 111. 1957, 60 ff.

29. See above all Humberto R. Maturana / Francisco J. Varela, *Autopoietic Systems: A Characterization of the Living Organization*, Urbana, IL 1975; Humberto R. Maturana and Francisco Varela G., *El árbol del conocimiento*, Santiago de Chile 1984. Theory development at this stage had been very strongly influenced by epistemological issues, and had, as far as the autopoietic operation itself was concerned, presupposed biochemical processes.

30. See Gareth Morgan, *Images of Organization*, Beverly Hills, CA 1986.

31. See Heinz von Foerster, *Wissen und Gewissen: Versuch einer Brücke*, Frankfurt 1993.

32. It would do no harm but be of little use to confess that it is a metaphor. For this would then apply for all organization theory approaches (see, e.g., Gareth Morgan, Paradigms, Metaphors, and Puzzle Solving in Organization Theory, *Administrative Science Quarterly* 25 (1980), 605–622) and would, since the concept of metaphor (from metapherein) is itself a metaphor, mean nothing more than the demand that

every universalistic theory should point to the necessity of autological self-justification.

33. See, e.g., Henry Mintzberg, *Structure in Fives: Designing Effective Organizations*, Englewood Cliffs, NJ 1983.

34. Here we fully agree with Anthony Giddens's theory of "structuration" – with the sole exception that Giddens rejects a systems-theoretical basis for this concept. See Anthony Giddens, *The Constitution of Society. Outline of the Theory of Structuration*, Berkeley and Los Angeles 1984.

35. Thus, apparently, Kickert loc. cit. (1993) and many others, who associate a conservative ideology with autopoiesis. The consulting sector, too, tends to describe autopoietic systems as structurally conservative in justifying the function, if not the necessity of targeted intervention from outside. See, e.g., Michael Wollnik, Interventionschancen bei autopoietischen Systemen, in: Klaus Götz (ed.), *Theoretische Zumutungen: Vom Nutzen der systemischen Theorie für die Managementpraxis*, Heidelberg 1994, 118–159. The thesis of structural conservatism tells us not about the theory of autopoietic systems but about the person who advances the theory, thus about the autopoiesis of firms and institutions of further education in the consulting sector – or with Maturana loc. cit., 64: nothing about the area described but something about the observer who elaborates and uses such a description.

36. See Francisco J. Varela, *Principles of Biological Autonomy*, New York 1979.

37. This is controversial. The contrary position has been introduced into the discussion above all by Gunter Teubner. See: Hyperzyklus in Recht und Organisation, in: Hans Haferkamp / Michael Schmid (eds.), *Sinn, Kommunikation und soziale Differenzierung: Beiträge zu Luhmanns Theorie sozialer Systeme*, Frankfurt 1987, 89–128; idem., Episodenverknüpfung: Zur Steigerung von Selbstreferenz im Recht, in: Dirk Baecker et al. (eds.), *Theorie als Passion*, Frankfurt 1987, 423–446; and on application in organizations: Kirsch and zu Knyphausen loc. cit. (1991). If one wished to maneuver in this manner in concept formation, however, one would need a concept of the unity of the system that is formed independently of the concept of autopoiesis. This version would in the case of organizations have to abandon the strict link between autopoiesis and decision. "Autopoietic" systems would then be systems in which autopoiesis also takes place, which does not, however, explain the unity of the system. And we should perhaps replace the concept of autopoiesis by the old concept of circular causality. At any rate, from Maturana's point of view, thoughts on "gradualization" lie exclusively in the domain of the structures of systems and precisely not in the domain of autopoiesis itself.

38. On this subject and the justification of a "blind spot," that is to say necessary intransparency of the system to itself, see Heinz von Foerster, Das Gleichnis vom blinden Fleck: Über das Sehen im allgemeinen, in: Gerhard Johann Lischka (ed.), *Der entfesselte Blick: Symposion, Workshops*, Ausstellung, Bern 1993, 15–47 (21 ff.); idem., Für Niklas Luhmann: Wie rekursiv ist Kommunikation?, *Teoria Sociologica* 1/2 (1993), 61–85.

39. See Karl E. Weick, Enactment Processes in Organizations, in: Barry M. Staw and Gerald R. Salancik (eds.), *New Directions in Organizational Behavior*, Chicago 1977, 267–300; idem., *Der Prozeß des Organisierens*, German translation

Frankfurt 1985, esp. 212 ff. See also Linda Smircich, Implications for Management Theory, in: Linda L. Putnam and Michael E. Pacanowsky (eds.), *Communication and Organizations: An Interpretive Approach*, Beverly Hills, CA 1983, 221–241 (229 ff.).

40. "The 'outside' or 'external' world cannot be known," we read in Weick loc. cit. (1977), 273. "The outside is a void, there is only the inside."

41. See Niklas Luhmann, *Soziale Systeme: Grundriß einer allgemeinen Theorie*, Frankfurt 1984, 92 ff.

42. We will be coming back to this in section VI.

43. A great deal too much can then follow. Not only goals or other essential structures ("functional requisites") but also acting persons, fresh air, constant gravitational conditions, etc.

44. It should be added that this naturally depends on the choice of system reference. If the surrounding system of society (or, as many say, everyday speech) is concerned, all social systems can of course exchange information – but in a manner and in forms that only society reproduces and which in subsystems first have to be reconstructed into information they can use. What is more: we can speak meaningfully of information only if we add a system index.

45. Gregory Bateson 1972: Steps to an Ecology of Mind: Collected Essays in Anthropology, Psychiatry, Evolution, and Epistemology, 381.

46. See Bateson, supra note 45. Here we find the most succinct definition of information: "*Information* consists of differences that make a difference."

47. For greater detail see Niklas Luhmann, *Social Systems*, Stanford, CA 1995.

48. See, e.g., Maryan S. Schall, A Communication-Rules Approach to Organizational Culture, *Administrative Science Quarterly* 28 (1983), 557–581. Karl E. Weick, *Sensemaking in Organizations*, Thousand Oaks, CA 1995, 75, rightly remarks: "These outcomes are unsurprising because the communication activity is the organization." But Weick, too, does not base his organization theory, as would have been consistent, on the concept of communication – presumably because the subjectivity of "sensemaking" would then have escaped him.

49. It should be added: excluding any talk of living consciousness, living spirit, or even living society.

50. We will be returning to this in the next chapter.

51. See Wanda J. Orlikowski and JoAnne Yates, Genre Repertoire: The Structuring of Communicative Practices in Organizations, *Administrative Sciences Quarterly* 39 (1994), 541–574 (541), with reference to Giddens and Bourdieu. But Giddens and Bourdieu understand communication in a highly limited sense as action or practice, thus presupposing an actor who would then necessarily have to belong to the organization. Further examples of this sort are easy to find. Anne Donnellon, Language and Communication in Organizations: Bridging Cognition and Behavior, in: Henry P. Sims, Jr., Dennis A. Gioia, et al., *The Thinking Organization*, San Francisco 1986, 136–164, takes the view, for example, that communication in organizations is indispensable as a bridge between cognition and behavior.

52. See also Schall loc. cit., 560, with reference to preceding literature.

53. In a purely academic context, the function of such indeterminacy positions is easy to recognize. They make theoretical innovations and controversies possible, here,

for example, as cultural, symbolic approach, thus enabling scholars to work on their academic repute. But this remains an argument purely for the sociology of science, which leaves theory development to evolution.

54. As far as family recruitment is concerned, as well as forced recruitment, modern organizations differ from similar institutions in traditional societies, *independently of the degree of freedom and motives underlying a decision*. See, e.g., Stanley H. Udy, Jr., Preindustrial Forms of Organized Work, in: Wilbert E. Moore and Arnold S. Feldman (eds.), *Labor Commitment and Social Change in Developing Areas*, New York 1960, 78–91; idem, *Work in Traditional and Modern Society*, Englewood Cliffs, NJ 1970.

55. Even though they do indeed do so for understandable reasons. See Karl E. Weick, Organizational Communication: Toward a Research Agenda, in: Linda L. Putnam and Michael E. Pacanowski (eds.), *Communication and Organizations: An Interpretive Approach*, Beverly Hills, CA 1983, 13–29 (16).

56. We shall be coming back to this in greater detail in Chapter 13 on organization and society.

57. From a formal point of view, this is a consequence of the "reentry" of the distinction between system and environment into the system (and thus into itself). See George Spencer Brown, *Laws of Form*, reprint of the 2nd ed. New York 1979, 56 ff., (60. f.). We will be coming back to this in more detail.

58. A further explanation follows in the coming chapter: With the aid of the concept of decision, we are in a position to include the paradox of the distinction between system and environment in the system and to follow its further unfolding within the system in detail.

59. See Heinrich Popitz, *Prozesse der Machtbildung*, Tübingen 1968; idem, *Phänomene der Macht: Autorität, Herrschaft, Gewalt, Technik*, Tübingen 1986.

60. See Stephan Fuchs, The Stratified Order of Gossip: Informal Communication in Organizations and Science, *Soziale Systeme* 1 (1995), 47–72.

61. See Chapter 9 below.

62. Countering the objection that concept formation in the autopoietic decision-making organization is "abstract" – in, e.g., Albrecht Becker, Willi Küpper, and Günther Ortmann, Revisionen der Rationalität, in: Willi Küpper and Günther Ortmann (eds.), *Mikropolitik: Rationalität, Macht und Spiele in Organisationen*, Opladen 1988, 89–113 (105 f.). But two things must, of course, be said. First, the formation of concepts (including that of action) always addresses only sections of reality (never, for example, the entire human being), and, second, the formation of every system reproduces only sections of reality and never everything that is needed to reproduce it.

63. See Gotthard Günther, Cognition and Volition: A Contribution to a Cybernetic Theory of Subjectivity, in idem, *Beiträge zur Grundlegung einer operationsfähigen Dialektik* vol. 2, Hamburg 1979, 203–240 (212 ff.): "[I]f we assume that the relation between a living system and its environment enters a state in which the environmental world does not positively influence the subjectivity which it harbors, then the subjectivity itself, in order to overcome this indifference, and in order to maintain its characteristics of Life, cannot help but enter into an active role. It is important to say that it *must* assume an active role and not only: it *may* be active. This is a basic criterion that separates inanimate from living matter."

64. On public administration, see, e.g., Karl-Heinz Ladeur, Von der Verwaltungshierarchie zum administrativen Netzwerk: Zur Erhaltung der Eigenständigkeit der Verwaltung unter Komplexitätsbedingungen, *Die Verwaltung* 26 (1993), 137–165.

65. See Edgar Morin, *La Méthode* vol. 1, Paris 1977, 134 f. and passim. See also p. 201: "L'ouvert s'appuie sur le fermé."

66. To what extent one can speak of self-observation when it comes to living cells or even to mathematically highly gifted chemical macromolecules does not needed to be decided here. The question clearly has to do with the degree of abstraction of concepts such as observing, indicating, and distinguishing.

67. See Laws of Form loc. cit. 56 f., 69 ff.

68. Loc. cit., 57: "unresolvable indeterminacy."

69. Or mathematically: it "is not . . . introduced merely by cause of using independent variables" – loc. cit., 57.

70. See Elena Esposito, Ein zweiwertiger nicht-selbständiger Kalkül, in: Dirk Baecker, *Kalkül der Form*, Frankfurt 1993, 96–111.

71. The "bistability" that arises from the distinction between system and environment in the sense that, in deciding about its own operations, the system can either set out from its own preliminary decisions or from the environment, is then interpreted as time-consuming oscillation. On "frequency of its oscillations" see Spencer-Brown, loc. cit., 59. Oscillation can be so fast that a (relatively short) *present* is defined in which system and environment are given *simultaneously* for the system.

72. On the link between reentry and temporalization see also Dirk Baecker, Im Tunnel, in idem. (ed.), *Kalkül der Form*, Frankfurt 1993, 12–37 (28 ff.).

73. See Spencer Brown loc. cit. 105.

74. On application to organizations, see Heinz von Foerster, Prinzipien der Selbstorganisation im sozialen und betriebswirtschaftlichen Bereich, in idem, *Wissen und Gewissen: Versuch einer Brücke*, Frankfurt 1993, 233–268.

75. James G. March, A Model of Adaptive Organizational Search, *Journal of Economic Behavior and Organization* 2 (1981), 307–333; Scott R. Herriott, Daniel Levinthal, and James G. March, Learning From Experience in Organizations, *American Economic Review* 75 (1985), 298–302. See also James G. March and Johan P. Olsen, *Ambiguity and Choice in Organizations*, Bergen 1976; B. Levitt and James G. March, Organizational Learning, *Annual Review of Sociology* 14 (1988), 319–340; James G. March, Exploration and Exploitation in Organizational Learning, *Organization Science* 2 (1991), 71–87.

76. See above all Richard R. Nelson and Sidney G. Winter, *An Evolutionary Theory of Economic Change*, Cambridge, MA 1982. For Nelson and Winter, the structural apparatus of self-reference lies in the "routines" developed and occasionally tested in organizations.

77. As put at the time by Richard M. Cyert and James G. March, *A Behavioral Theory of the Firm*, Englewood Cliffs, NJ 1963 (2nd ed. Cambridge, MA 1992).

78. See Francisco Varela, Two Principles for Self-Organization, in: Hans Ulrich and Gilbert J.B. Probst (eds.), *Self- Organization and Management of Social Systems: Insights, Promises, Doubts, and Questions*, Berlin 1984, 25–32.

79. See Meyer and Rowan loc. cit.. (1977).

80. Further references in Chapter 1 above, note 68.

81. On the latter see James G. March, Bounded Rationality, Ambiguity and the Engineering of Choice, *Bell Journal of Economics* 9 (1978), 587–608.

82. See Yves Barel, *Le paradoxe et le système: Essai sur le fantastique social*, 2nd ed. Grenoble 1989.

83. For example, "cognitivistic" approaches. See Alain Lavallée, Stratégies de Gestion et Complexité: Une Approche Épistémologique et Cognitive, *Revue internationale de systémique* 10 (1996), 57–77.

3   Membership and Motives

I

The theory of social systems that reproduce themselves through their own operations imposes a sharp distinction between psychic and social operations, structures, and systems. Regardless of all the causal interdependencies that an observer could attribute, there can be no overlapping at the operational level. An operation connects either in psychic or in social systems, even if an observer might be inclined to compress both into one event – a conscious communication act. But conscious disposition over one's own attention is not itself already communication, because a communication is completed only when it is understood by another; and the mental preconditions and consequences of disposing over attention are quite different from the social preconditions and consequences.

This theoretical approach draws on empirical, as it were microanalytical, evidence. However, it runs so contrary to customary thinking in the sociological tradition,[1] particularly in action theory, that we need a special chapter to explain it. The main question is what it brings for a theory of organization.

In the sociology of the 1940s and 1950s, the notion of role had been popular as a concept mediating between individual psychological events and social events. Role was defined as social behavior expectations addressed to individuals, and thus not simply as a connection between factually related modes of behavior (e.g., as work process).[2] It was a step toward distinguishing between psychic and social systems that sociology should not reverse. This is often misunderstood when sociology accepts a methodological individualism or a theory of action with the implication that only individuals can act. Although such a concept traces out the requirements of causal attribution that define the concept of action, with a quasi-natural notion, it fails to explain who undertakes the causal attribution: the individual himself, or other individuals, or a social system. It thus throws no light on the relationship between organic or psychic systems and social systems.

But even as interface between individual motivation and social stability,[3] the concept of role has considerable weaknesses. For one thing, not all social action can be attributed to specific social roles expected as a unity. For another, it integrates individual motivation and social stability so strongly that all the endogenous dynamics of the individual consciousness have to be classified in terms of conformity and deviation.[4] Although this makes the return to a theory of individual action that is more open in this regard understandable,[5] this theory, as we have seen, fails to address the relationship between organic-psychic systems and social systems.

From the outset, that is to say since work began on an independent political economy in the seventeenth century, economic theory had assumed uniformity in human motives insofar as participation in exchanges was concerned. The concept of interest allowed much that had previously been regarded as a vice to be reformulated. This assumption alone allowed a special economic theory (today a theory of rational choice) to distinguish itself from concrete reality, namely in the form of strongly reduced suppositions about the nature of human action.[6] This had sufficed to replace the embedding of economic communication in religion by a psychological legitimation of the outdifferentiated system of money-economy transactions. Economic calculation, which led to the making or omission of monetary transactions, was presupposed as an individual psychic event; what is more, it was seen as the normal attitude of the human being in pursuit of his advantage. We now know that "homo oeconomicus" is a social construct that is necessary precisely because *one can never know how individual operations of the consciousness actually proceed from moment to moment.*[7]

First in the theater and from the eighteenth century onward above all in the novel, the development of such motive constructs specific to a given functional system was accompanied by the development of forms of a narrative concretization of individual motives,[8] the plot being initially determined by the profit motive (*Robinson Crusoe, Moll Flanders*), but later more and more by the intimation of latent, incommunicable motives (*Pamela*). In this bifurcation of fictional narrative and scientific theory, it was initially possible to retain the idea that psychic causal factors were involved. Then, in the nineteenth century, an understanding of politics in relation to the state developed that assumed that politics was about solving the conflicts of interest that remained after the economy had done its bit.

In organizational studies, too, the problem of psychologically understood individual motivation was long the focus.[9] This was the case for the group dynamics theory of informal organization, for the human relations movement of the London Tavistock Institute, and for more recent efforts in "organizational development."[10] Insofar as the concept of role is used, the membership role can be understood as an abstraction of motivation potential,[11] as the generation of indifference, which can then be specified in the system through special rules and instructions.[12] What is meant is that the member of an organization can engage in different, externally determined behaviors without losing self-respect and without feeling in conflict with oneself. However, the question is how strong and how resistant such motivation based on indifference can be when difficulties arise in implementation or if more is demanded of the individual than mere obedience.[13] Responsibility, too, is seen as an aspect of the membership role (and not, for example, as logical component of every decision, as absorption of uncertainty). It can therefore scarcely be distinguished from accountability for mistakes. As a member one must avoid being disturbed by oneself.

Above all, leadership theory and theories on innovation and structural change persist in the idea that the impulse comes from individual managers. This is presumably due to decision theories that require a subject to select an alternative. Only in the more recent literature do we read that the individual manager is a fiction,[14] and for all important decisions a leadership team has to be presupposed.[15] Nowadays one accordingly speaks of "control illusions," which allow the individual manager to feel good.[16] If an organizational culture nevertheless insists on attributing decisions to individual managers, as an institutional constraint this produces false descriptions, and a second-order observer will have to correct this.

With abandonment of the authority model and the machine model (input/ output model) of the organization, the notion of organization members also appears to be changing, even though no similarly simple theory to replace it is on the horizon. This may be because society now makes greater but also worse-defined demands of its organizational systems; because the problems no longer appear to be primarily questions of centralization / decentralization; because crises and the pressure to innovate are increasing; and because much of the criticism leveled at modern society basically addresses organizations – witness the criticism of political parties (the "political class") or of the modernization ambitions of "development aid." Since the early 1970s, something in the way of a value change has taken place, also in research promotion programs, bringing a shift in efforts to improve performance by influencing motivation to promote the quality of life and satisfaction with work as values that organizations have to take into account and help to satisfy.[17] Even so, one still counts on general organizational measures being able to shape individual attitudes and motives in a predictable manner, and thus to influence specific psychic systems. But these variants, which change only preferences, not causal-technological premises, have also failed both theoretically and empirically to produce convincing results.[18] Despite far-reaching efforts in this direction, there is no reliable empirical evidence that greater participation correlates with more satisfaction and greater satisfaction with better performance; satisfaction could well be due to having a secure and undemanding job. In response, systems theory will need fundamental changes to its tools if it is to show the heterogeneous operation of organic, psychic, and social systems, and if in relations between individual and organization it is to look not primarily for the conditions (the same for all individuals!) of motivation beneficial to the organization but rather to set out from structural coupling between operationally separate, closed systems.

Moreover, greater account must be taken of the circumstance that organizations rely not only on individuals' motivation for participation but also on their memory. Without memory, even motives are inconceivable. Above all, the possibilities of creating an organizational memory are very limited. Organizational memory requires well-documented facts. However, much information comes into being in highly ambivalent, context-dependent forms, and may be badly "registered." The members of an organization, chiefly managerial staff, can help with their personal memory. But assessment of this memory remains subjective and is consolidated only through communication. What is more, the organization benefits from its members forgetting as well as remembering; and how they do so is difficult to objectivize. One of the most important tasks of management is therefore likely to be to convert personal memory into organizational memory, and, above all, to put it on record. This produces decision-making premises that can then be used in further operations of the system and give direction to them.

Contingency theory (Lawrence / Lorsch) had already sought to relate the problem of the organizational importance of individual attitudes and motives in systems-theoretical terms to the difference between system and environment. But it was a mistake to do so on the basis of the distinction between external and internal environment.[19] The psyche cannot be the internal environment of a social system, because such environments form only when the social system differentiates itself on the basis of its own operations into subsystems (e.g., organizational divisions). We must keep psychic and social system references strictly apart, especially when the two sorts of system distinguish differently between self-reference and other-reference (environment).

Recent cultural and institutional theory rejects recourse to psychic factors even more strongly. What constitutes the unity of an action and how the identity of an actor can be determined through the attribution of actions cannot be discovered by plumbing his internal mental life. Such identification is possible on the basis of cultural demands and reaches consensus only through institutionalization.[20] Organizational science analysis must therefore also keep to accounts and give up the attempt to include psychic realities. And this is no longer merely a methodological problem of unfathomable complexity, but would amount to misapprehending the conditions for constituting social reality. The term "account" tends to evoke defensive presentations concerned with errors and poor performance. However, it is just as important to discover how one can demonstrate competence and find recognition.

The theory of separate autopoietic operations finally invites the conclusion that organizations can continue to exist *without an individual seeing any benefit for himself from this continuance.*[21] Although it is indispensable for communication in the organization to calculate motives for participation and assume the operation of mentally secured memory, as well as coaxing corresponding communication from its personnel environment, the inner state of individuals or what we could call their happiness remains for the organization a non-testable fiction that it reproduces by its own operations.[22]

If we introduce this hypothesis of operational separation with strong structural coupling into organization research, it requires some terminological clarification, which can partly be found in the existing literature but which still needs to be distilled out and whose consequences need explaining. We limit ourselves to four concepts, namely person (3–2), consensus (3–3), motive (3–4), and integration (3–5). When these concepts are coordinated, they contribute to an understanding of the sources of friction between individuals and organized social systems, an understanding that keeps its distance from both efforts to generate motivation beneficial to the organization and the idea that organizations should offer individuals the opportunity for optimum "self-realization." For in *both* directions the organization theory that espouses them tends to take no notice of the individual in his actual and concrete existence as an individual human being.

II

In older societies, people had lived in family households, even though they often had their place of work elsewhere (e.g., in the bazaar). And they died where they had lived. Life and death were thus a "placed" unity of social disposition. In modern organizations people do not die; and if they do, such an incident is subsumed under the concept of accident and processed accordingly. This simple reflection alone shows that the concept of humanity can be of only ideological or compensatory importance in organizational policy. It concerns only a very limited reintroduction of something that is per se excluded. An appropriate theory has to be able to describe this exclusion of humanity and find concepts for it.[23]

In interaction between human beings, the other party is in the first place perceived as a body. But the phenomenology of bodily perception (and now of one's own body and those of others) does not provide the conditions for the autopoietic reproduction of life. It supplies only attributed, interpreted, and constantly updated meanings; it provides only a "text" that gives the basis for making decisions in the course of interaction. Even when bodies touch, contact is limited to the surface; and even if experience and imagination are added (e.g., in dangerous situations), contact beyond phenomenal perception is all the more excluded.

No one will deny this. But in exactly the same way, the consciousness of others is inaccessible and can be plumbed only as a text. This state of affairs calls for a differentiated conceptuality that takes account of the gap between the different ways in which autopoietic systems operate that causes general terminologies (individual, human being, subject) to degenerate in unanalyzable abstraction. In this question it is therefore particularly indispensable to keep system references separate.

The concept of *person* should, with recourse to old usage, serve to indicate author, address, and topic in communication systems.[24] It also serves to indicate a form that has another side to it, namely the vast amount of factual biochemical, neurophysiological, immunological, consciousness operations that remain completely opaque for all conscious and communicative operations, and which can be guessed at only from certain regularities in behavior. As a "black box" of this sort, the individual human being belongs to the environment of society, and hence to the environment of its organizations. But communication can also very well refer to such an environmental complex, give it names, allow it to interpenetrate communication through the use of personal pronouns; that is to say, to presuppose it as a functioning complexity.[25] And it suffices for the continuation of its own operations to assume the unity of individual and person as an operational fiction. A person is therefore treated as a human individual; and a person's identity helps in specifying ignorance about the bodily and mental processes a social system has to rely on in carrying out its own operations. A person is accordingly nothing other than a "token for (eigen-)behaviors" of social systems.[26]

Persons thus come into being through the participation of human beings in communication. They take account of the needs of observation by being attributed consistency in opinions and attitudes, purposefulness in behavior, and self-interest with regard to predictability, etc.[27] They are not alive, they do not think; they are constructions of communication for the purposes of communication. They owe their unity to the autopoiesis of the social system society, whose products they are. However, the presupposed context of reference is that psychic systems can make out identifiable entities in individual human beings (also in themselves); at least it has nowadays become unusual (except in certain circles) to attribute personality to non-perceptible entities. But the use of the identity tag "person" in communication presupposes neither presence nor perception. By means of names one can refer to those absent or reduce perception to a minimum on the telephone without the slightest uncertainty about the identifiability of the person. One can oneself take part in communication without knowing or considering what operations of life and consciousness this requires. Personality mediates between the necessary tempo of always sequential communication and the inevitable opaqueness for oneself and for others of living and experiencing systems.

Moreover, the concept of person presupposes that every person can play many different roles. In every current situation, this allows a glance to be cast over other potential roles of participants and to use the presence of persons to bring up this topic. And, naturally, it makes a difference whether communication is concerned with the other roles of persons who can be addressed on the subject or with the behavior of just anyone.

While we tend to deny personality to unperceivable beings,[28] we are expected to attribute personality even to completely unknown human beings we have never seen. From the point of view of universal history, this, too, is not self-evident, but it is inevitable in a society that brings together known and mutually unknown people in innumerable everyday situations, and it excludes projecting this difference onto a general (e.g., moral) difference. Personality is accordingly nothing other than a symbol for the ability to participate in communication, and "symbol" is used here in the original, strict sense of a marking that brings about the cohesion of something separate.

It is important to look at this point more precisely. At the beginning of this section we had said that a person can be author, address, and topic of a communication. The concept indicates the unity of this trinity, the switching between possible participatory positions, and calls on communication in the one position to take the other into consideration. The three components of every communication, namely utterance, understanding, and information, are thus copied into the entity composing the person. In organizations, too, persons cannot be spoken about, disposed of, or decided about without taking into account that they also take part as addresses and as authors, that they learn about what is happening and can respond.[29] In other words, the system has to operate under conditions of calculated humanity.

III

Although every observer can in his own way imagine what goes on inside someone else's mind, no one can know for certain, no one can know whether other people develop expectable attitudes and how permanent they are. This being so, the relationship between communication and consensus needs to be redefined. The usual view is that communication generates consensus or, otherwise, leads to conflict and differentiation. We need not deny the possibility of generating mental agreement (shared opinions, common memories, etc.), but if this occurs, it is an uncontrollable by-product of communicative operations. How is one to establish whether consensus or dissent exist if not by communication? How can this become apparent and available for further communication if not in the meaning conveyed by communication? Consensus and dissent can gain social relevance only as communicative artifacts, and "gaining social relevance" means being what they claim to be.

As in the case of "person" and "motives," communication has to rely on constructions of its own in the consensus/dissent question. If these constructions work, that is to say, if they can be maintained in further communications without communicated contradiction, they are treated in communication as reality; and communication cannot test the reality of its assumptions except through the contradiction of communication by communication. Communication can always assume that, even in the event of dissent, there is consensus about the fact that dissent has arisen. But this is no more than the precondition for psychic systems to participate in communication if communication itself is not to come to a halt.

The next question can then only be about the forms in which the assumption that individual opinions are congruent is produced and processed in communication. With Ludwig von Bertalanffy and Stafford Beer, we could speak of the equifinality of individual states of consciousness.[30] Whatever they are, they are treated as congruent.

There are then various options for testing and confirming this equifinality. The most important lies in failing to protest, missing the opportunity to contradict, thus ultimately in the scarcity of potential for communication. Along the same lines is the commitment to language, which forms sentences and thus takes the meaning of words as given. Then there is the use of metaphor and ambiguous language, which allow participants to express their own meaning and nevertheless contribute to the autopoiesis of communication. Finally, one should consider the possibility of indicating or provoking emotions without intervening in communication itself.[31] This may serve as a sort of warning, as indirect communication, which does not have to be answered but which indicates that communication is balancing between consensus and dissent. This can encourage self-control in communication.

In this manner, "agreement" is constantly reached which, however, is not rooted in mental commitment but only has to reckon with communicative difficulties if one wishes to retract, reinterpret, or simply forget it. In communication one can agree without being convinced, and, *a fortiori*, without being convinced that one will continue to be convinced.[32] Individuals who feel they were not adequately understood or taken into account may, perhaps, merely be waiting for times to change or for better opportunities – which might never arrive.

IV

The concept of *motive/motivation* needs to be geared to the marked division between psychic and social operations, each with their own structures and system formation. However, psychologists may use it to indicate internal psychic mechanisms, in sociology it is concerned only with the ascription of motives in social communication.[33] Such a proposal is not new; it goes back to renowned authors in the social sciences, perhaps even to Max Weber.[34] Motives are accordingly forms of communication, the explicit or implicit ascription of grounds for certain actions – of grounds or (now increasingly) backgrounds. Simple motive ascription typically takes the form of an intention. Reasons, justifications, precautionary justifications, suspicions, etc. gather around such "intentions" until the domain of incommunicabilia is reached, of the unmentionable, which in communication throws a dark shadow over what is explicitly said. For the cognitive organization of such motive ascriptions, the term "script" has become established.[35]

Like language in general, motives serve to bind time.[36] They generate a system memory, a network of links between interpreted past behavior and expectations directed toward the future. With the aid of motives, the system thus regulates a connection between past and future. But whereas persons develop stable identities to which one can repeatedly refer as being always the same, motives have to be constantly renewed – also a typical characteristic of memory. Persons (not human beings), we shall say, have a character allowing the regulation of what motives can be more or less plausibly ascribed to them.[37] The historical machine of the social system can change the motives ascribed to persons. The person/motive symbolism equips the social system with a combination of continuity and discontinuity, thus with the possibility of limited and controllable change. And this takes place in an organic-psychic environment that remains inaccessible.

Every social system limits the type of motives that can be recognized and acknowledged in the system. To this end, each social system uses typical distinctions – in organizations, for example, the distinction between official and private. Every social system limits motive research or, like forensics, is specialized in motive research (but then in relation to non-members of the organization). This also means that motives (presentable grounds, "accounts") can be distinguished in terms of *for whom* they can be furnished, *to whom* they can be communicated. There are addressees in the organization to whom one is well advised to identify motives with the decision-making programs of the organization (and then to identify oneself with these motives).[38] Vis-à-vis others, this same behavior would indicate a lack of competence, and presentable motives would rather lie in a liberal, aloof stance toward the rules, not excluding deviation from them. This very flexibility in switching between addressee-specific motives characterizes a competent member, and this requires a further dimension of freedom in disposing over motives and, above all, opaqueness in this disposition.

Ultimately, every social system must assume that the conscious/subconscious inner life of psychic systems cannot be examined – and this very circumstance allows regulation within the social system itself of the extent to which one may communicate about motives and what the consequences are of overstepping the discretion threshold.[39] Organizations, too, have their embarrassment thresholds – precisely when communication in the workplace is still experienced as communication within the organizational system and not, for example, in the context of "private" friendship. Typically, the terminology of "motives" tends to explain actions (including excusing them) rather than communicating influence. For "motive" in this sense of the word is something that is to be decided within the actor himself. It shows little understanding of social and psychological realities when managers believe and assert that they wish to "motivate" members of the organization.[40]

Since it has been possible to distinguish between purposes and motives, presumably since the seventeenth century, society has developed a need for tact. Tact requires not offending the self-presentation of others, not infringing its limits, and, if not confirming what is asserted, at least tacitly letting it be. Tact requires that stated or implied motives are not called into question, that a possible difference between purpose and motive is thus not exploited.

Above all, tact is considered a precept and skill in social relations, and the literature on the subject comes essentially from the eighteenth century.[41] It proves useful in interaction that immediate reactions to overstepping limits can be recognized, and that they can also serve as signals, communicating that this is not to be treated as communication. In all this, the object of tactful treatment is expected to cooperate: one is not to show that one feels oneself to be treated with tact; one must not expose the necessary fictions. And when this happens, tact has to be used reflexively in order to heal breaches of tact tactfully.

These insights can apply to organized collaboration only with modifications. On the one hand, such collaboration often involves the enforcement of decisions, so that it is not advisable to reward tactfully implied resistance tactfully; on the contrary, it has to be forced out into the open. Above all, however, the organization provides the level of official communication at which private motives obviously have no place (whatever the individual might think about it privately). An early treatment of this subject therefore recommends "setting a workplace tone" to "involve all employees willingly and essentially in corporate cooperation,"[42] with this fiction thus recognizing the personality of the other and excluding questions about his convictions. Nowadays we would no longer formulate it in these terms; but the fact remains that the level of task-oriented communication makes it possible even without the acrobatics of tact to treat the other as a person without offending. All motives are hence couched in organizationally possible linguistic terms – or left to gossip.

With concepts such as "social sensitivity" or "interpersonal competence," the dominant literature treats the problems discussed as matters of psychological skill, which may need to be trained.[43] We, on the contrary, shift the problem fully to the level of social communication. This naturally does not exclude psychological studies, sensitivity training, and the rest. But the level at which such competence is realized is always that of social communication; only there can the question arise of whether and how communication avoids examining participants' innermost thoughts and feelings and making do with the motives asserted. In other words, it is a matter of the communicative respect of a difference, of a boundary that can possibly be shifted; whoever does this all too skillfully or even with training and is caught in the act may very well seem tactless – a tactless presenter of tact.

This situation is reflected in the treatment of time. Since the environment, including the inner worlds of members, cannot be apprehended or known, one has to switch to the future – which cannot be known anyway. The system uses forward-looking planning in the form of means and ends, now increasingly also in expectation of unexpectable side effects, which could require correction. We will later be dealing with this at length.[44] For the moment we need only note that task orientation (environmental orientation) and time orientation (orientation on the future) are reduced in compensatory relation to the common denominator of ignorance. And this offers the advantage of being able to invoke (good) intentions, will, and trust, and thus the *present* unity of the system with regard to shaping the *future*.

V

Finally, the concept of *integration* has to be placed in this theoretical framework. The usual sociological view of integration as consensus (and thus as good) is dissolving.[45] With respect to the empirical operations of the conscious handling of attention, consensus is nothing other than a construction tested for consistency, and thus not intersubjective in any way. The impression of consensus arises in retrospect if behavior has been successfully coordinated.[46] In the communication system, there is consensus (like motives) as explicitly or implicitly communicated assumption. But this has nothing to do with integration, especially because the communication of (let alone the demand for) consensus is a tried and tested means of bringing dissent to light. See Habermas!

Instead, by "integration" we understand the *mutual limitation of a system's degree of freedom*.[47] The limits to a system's freedom can be measured in terms of what is compatible with systemic autopoiesis, for individuals, the possibility to continue life and consciousness. However, like every recourse to "naked" autopoiesis, this is an empty phrase. This concept of integration can be used only if we add that the limitation of complexity (of what is autopoietically possible) is the precondition for enhancing complexity. For a system can exceed a minimum threshold of internal relationization below which every operational element is linked with every other only if it excludes certain mathematically possible combinations.[48] This requires selection, and at the level of *this* selection, a system can – indeed must – be coordinated with its environment. This is true even though – or rather because – the system can choose to build and demolish structures only internally, only on the basis of its own operations, and in relating to the environment has to rely on its own constructions.

One of the remarkable characteristics of integration in organizations, between organizations, and in relations between organizations and the organic-psychic systems of their members is that it takes time. Thus, not only something in the way of structural compatibility is involved – for example, between requirements and suitabilities – but also delayed integration. Not only the current state of affairs needs to be taken into account: possibilities, including the possibility of continuous stability, as well as that of improvement or deterioration, also have to be considered. But economic theory finds it difficult to include a possible shift in preferences (and in this sense, the future) in its models. The notion thus develops that "mobilization" can serve integration[49]; but individuals are seen only as persons, and insufficient account is taken of how individuals as organic (aging) and psychic systems accept their mobilization. At any rate, "prospects" play an important role, both in motivation (psychic *and* social) and in the assessment and treatment of persons, under the heading "human resources management." As we will be seeing in detail in the next section, career assumes a key function in the integration of individuals and organizations.

Finally, it should be noted that the term integration refers to a variable but not to a state that is to be positively assessed.[50] A high degree of integration (tight coupling) is characteristic of technical system, of conflicts,[51] but also an effect of exclusions in which exclusion (e.g., from school education or monetary income) almost inevitably provokes other exclusions. Overly strong integration prevents the development of complexity within systems, thus preventing learning processes. But this, too, should not immediately be judged negatively or positively, for learning can also have disastrous consequences. Therefore, to treat the concept of integration as a variable means keeping it open for empirical research and for widely differing system contexts.

VI

The only real (= resistance-tested) mode of integration in an age permeated by organizations is accordingly career. This can be said for individuals in relation to modern society, but only because there are organizations in this society that participate in the coming into being of successful or unsuccessful careers. It is not only a matter of careers as professionally employed members in organizations – consider, for example, schools or the reputation careers of artists, entertainers, sportspeople, or scientists.[52] But without the selection mode of organizations, no careers would unfold. Life is possible without career – as exclusion from participation in all functional systems.

In organization theories, which sum up the meaning of organization in concepts such as rationality, efficiency, control, and learning ability, career orientation tends to be seen negatively, to be regarded, so to speak, as a concession to personal ambition that has to be accepted as a reality – and can also be exploited.[53] The theory of informal organization, too, had worried that careers and career-orientation endangered group cohesion.[54] However, this assessment depends on the priority given to a normative description of the meaning of organizations. If, instead, we set out from the paradox of the unity of difference and note that in one's experience principles change more rapidly than realities, proving inconsistent in practice, this throws a different light on career orientation. It suddenly seems to be a stable element that enables both individuals and organizations to bear and use the decision-making contingencies of the organizations. Persons are then assumed to be flexible who do *not* identify with specific ideas, goals, projects, or reforms but only with their own careers; that is to say, persons who will survive all possible ups and downs as members of organizations, persons to whom identification with specific projects is *only ascribed* with the aim of furthering their career or of excluding them. And career as a form for structural coupling is stable precisely because it is nothing other than contingency that has been given form.

The concept of career should not be limited to a person's own ambitions for advancement and moving up the ladder.[55] There are careers that lead downward and there are careers that come to a standstill and perhaps allow this to be enjoyed. Indispensable is only that there are gradations and consequently an experience of time that perceives better and worse possibilities within the horizons of past and future.

But that is not all. The distinguishing characteristics of a career include the interplay between self-selection and other-selection in attaining every position whose totality shapes the career.[56] In stark contrast to the old world, birth is not a characteristic that determines status, and is thus not a characteristic of a career (but naturally a characteristic of its memory; the unborn cannot be remembered). And, because careerists play their part through self-selection, career cannot be imposed, cannot be understood as resulting from the exercise of power. It does, however, retain a certain affinity with the old concept of fate in which the "hero" finally has to admit how very much he has himself contributed – like Oedipus, for instance, in trying to avoid his fate. But whereas in narratives of fate (Jane Austen, Hegel) self-participation is realized only at the end, in the context of career it is geared to the future and is itself a driving motive. Career is, so to speak, fate reflecting itself in itself.

Self-selection means that one has to communicate one's own drive – whether positive (showing interest) or negative. Careers may well be simulated in daydreams, but a person's own interest affects his career only through communication. Other-selection means that how a career develops does not depend solely on self-selection. An external factor plays a part – and practically always, directly or indirectly, an organization. This also means that interpretation of a career remains open to self-ascription and other-ascription; one can attribute success and failure to oneself or to others, and it will be not be unimportant whether success or failure is involved.[57]

The necessary interplay between self-selection and other-selection excludes the calculation and prediction of careers. Careers operate in a space of self-generated uncertainty. Probability calculations (which never have anything to say about isolated cases) are possible. An individual, too, can calculate his prospects if he marginalizes one of two factors: he applies for many jobs but is never invited for an interview; or, vice versa, the labor market is practically swept clean and recruiters have to take anyone who presents himself. Attention to information can then concentrate on the one side or the other. But there are borderline cases showing only that both for the individual's prospects in life and for whoever does the selecting, contingency and uncertainty predominate over the long term in career-dependent integration. The conditions for predictability themselves become unpredictable as soon as the daily horizon broadens.

It should also be remembered that vacant positions and suitable and interested applicants do not meet as a matter of course. Information about positions must first flow to potential applicants and information about potential candidates to the people who decide on whom to hire. This information flow, too, has a social structure; it depends essentially, for example, on personal contact networks, and the informant for his part has to be informed that someone is interested in changing jobs.[58] From the standpoint of the individual case, a career seems therefore to be the result of chance that permits the information flow to reach certain persons/authorities to the exclusion of others.

Such socio-structural analyses show that it is questionable whether and to what extent personal characteristics are good indicators of the cognitive and motivational levels for career success.[59] There may be signs of this in statistical analysis. In practice, however, it will depend above all on differences between the persons who present themselves at the same time for good grades or good positions. Among the consequences of this structurally determined uncertainty is that far too much weight is placed on the beginning of a career and thus on educational performance and qualifications,[60] even though these factors then count for little in careers within the organization. The self-determination of intra-organizational careers is so strong that neither social background nor school and university qualifications are decisive.[61] Nevertheless, initial success is considered important because access to further possibilities in career assessment depends on it. That is to say that the integration mediated by career burdens the young and leads to protraction of the educational phase in life with dramatic experience of success and disappointment. And this in turn has a positive or negative effect on the willingness for self-selection.

Careers are also self-reinforcing insofar as they affect the résumé. A curriculum vitae or résumé is a communication, either oral or written, about the past of a person that, while not determining his future, raises expectations about it. This serves to anchor the always uncertain future in a past constructed especially for it. Individuals therefore have to communicate their résumé, have to be able to present themselves with one. Their mere presence would not provide enough information for the purposes of self- or other-selection. Some stations in a career demand a "complete" résumé. Someone who cannot account for ten years of his life will not have much of a chance. Now and again, the career is thus appreciated as a unity; so to speak, it enters itself as a condition for the direction of its own continuance. This, too, presupposes that there can be mobile and immobile careers, upward and downward career paths.

Such an entry of a career into itself is possible only because there is a relevant factor that does not adapt to the career and its management: the aging of participants.[62] A curriculum vitae has to supply data, has to take account of the aging of its hero, and from this perspective communicate early maturity or belated development. However, the extent to which age itself provides a schema for normality – for example, a normal age for completing school, for marrying, for retiring – is variable and depends on societal tolerance of diversity, which appears to be growing.[63] Regardless of this, society cannot itself prevent aging but can only evaluate it differently;[64] for this reason, a person's age cannot be ignored in reflecting on career contingencies because it necessarily affects what is already or still possible.

In sum, all this shows that a fully and completely difference-oriented principle of integration is involved. There is assessment but no natural télos. The "nature" of career is its self-generated uncertainty. This suggests that this structure affects the construction of persons and motives that are observed on the basis of the schema "career." Thus, careers not only distribute persons (successfully or unsuccessfully) across roles or positions, but also distribute motivation (also ambivalent, partly positive, partly negative motivation).[65] What is more, career suggests a type of individuality in which the individual does not define himself through special, essential characteristics but individualizes himself by observing how he is observed. At this level of second-order observation, self-selection and other-selection can be brought together. On both sides, in the contexts of both self-selection and other-selection, it is necessary to observe how one is "appreciated" – whether one is favorably or unfavorably assessed and whether the distinctions, rewards, positions, etc. on the market are seen as attractive or unattractive. From the standpoint of a third-order observer, who observes observers observing observations, it is a matter of highly flexible constructions of reality that adapt to the structural contingencies of modern society. In this sense, it is a matter of the unity of happiness and unhappiness in a world of self-management that one can no longer simply regard as the best of all possible worlds.

Finally, the interplay between self-selection and other-selection cannot hide the fact that career requires public symbolization. One must be able to express clearly who one is; that is to say, how successful one has been. This can be done by passing examinations or by occupying (titled) positions, but also by signaling one's level of income or through mention in the mass media or gossip. Only through such added value does career contribute to self-development, to consolidating an identity one can hold up to people who are not involved. This means not least of all that careers cannot simply be invented but presuppose societal institutionalization. But, unlike fixed societal ranking, such institutionalization does not determine modes of selection. It guarantees only that success and failure, where they occur, remain communicable.

VII

The theory of individually motivated membership and the idea that entry into systems is accomplished by contracts that induce the member to override his own preferences and bow to the conditions and instructions prevailing in the organization are based on assumptions that need to be examined. The concept went well with both liberal and humanistic societal theory, which assumed that forms had to be found and "institutionalized" to enable individuals to make individuals of themselves through the free choice of profession and employer. The precondition was that the use of freedom was attributed to the individual himself. Fate was self-earned fate.

In societal theory, the concept of the individual developing through the use of freedom had already been controversial in the nineteenth century – not as idea but only in relation to the actual circumstances prevailing in capitalist society. It survived in organization theory until the second half of the twentieth century. Despite considerable differences, controversies of this ideologized sort have never seriously posed the real question let alone answered it, namely *how* the individual actually makes use of his freedom or could do so in a future ("classless") society. Since the individual is opaque anyway and partly disguises, partly betrays himself in communication, and can express what he wants to express only to a limited degree, there were no barriers to attributing him with "free will" – except in cases of obvious coercion.[66] Freedom was consequently defined through the counter-concept of coercion (and not through the cognitive notion of alternatives).

Freedom accordingly served as an empty formula (and, since it was only conceivable as being limited, as a paradox) for determining certain social structures – either to recommend or reject them. The discussion was conducted above all in social policy terms, but in a knee-jerk reaction also at the level of organizations. Thus, from the 1950s to the 1970s the debate was permanently concerned with reforms that would weaken or even completely replace the principle of hierarchy,[67] without taking into account how oppressive groups intended to replace the hierarchy can be. In groups, practically only the monastic combination of melancholy and discipline remains to the individual, whereas he can always keep a boss, if there is only one, in tow.

In recent organization theory with a leaning toward "institutionalism," we find tendencies to supplement – if not replace – classical contractualism by stressing the symbolic components of decisions and their structuring premises. We could then still regard contracts as symbols of decision-making autonomy, but the relationship between individual and organization would no longer be based on freedom, nor on the voluntary renunciation of freedom, but on the interpretation of meaning.[68] What is to be understood by "symbol" is generally not explained. The question would be what distinctions are involved if their unity is symbolized. The resuscitation of the symbol concept in the nineteenth century was particularly concerned with symbolization of the general in the particular (and no longer symbolization of transcendence in immanence). Now, to judge by the way the concept is used, it is more a question of the distinction between individual and society. The provision of symbolic identifications would then be a functional equivalent of careers – or a necessary correlate insofar as the career symbolizes the social recognition of the individual.

However, this brings us only to the further question of whether freedom can also be symbolized, perhaps as indispensable prerequisite for the individual to appear as such. How, we could ask, can an individual interpret situations on the basis of cultural guidelines in such a way that alternatives become visible to him? How, for example, can a present situation be grasped on the basis of detailed experience of the milieu or professional competence in such a way that, although determined by the past and although things are the way they are, choices become apparent. The symbolic processing of the world of experience need not mean that everything has to be observed in terms of the conformity/ deviation schema with the result that individual freedom can be indicated only as deviation.

The "formally free contract," too, could be interpreted as the exercise of freedom to the extent that the parties understand what it is about. And, finally, we could use careers despite the other-selection involved for self-symbolization; after all, many others contribute and doors open or close by chance; but the person who is passing through the career and with whom the individual identifies remains the same.

Such a reformulation of the freedom problem changes views on the relationship between psychic and social systems. In the liberal understanding, freedom had been presupposed as a natural endowment of the human being. In this, one followed Hobbes and Locke. Social factors were accordingly taken into consideration as restrictions on freedom, above all through the law. If, by contrast, we understand freedom as a heuristic construction of alternatives, at least two social influences have to be distinguished. On the one hand, it is a matter of communication and of understanding for the possibility of choice. On the other, a distinction must be drawn between whether a choice and its criteria are approved or not. The institutionalization of the form of contract makes freedom of choice communicable and comprehensible, although it remains open and can be decided ad hoc whether accepting or rejecting the conclusion of a contract (e.g., entry into the organization, recruitment of a member) is approved and how one behaves if one can foresee that the decision will be disapproved.

If the use of freedom has to be attributable to individuals, this limits the range to relatively concrete, local options – for instance, those of a farmer who looks at the weather before he plans his working day, or those of a doctor who examines the patient before operating or postponing the operation. This puts narrow limits on the understanding of freedom. Whoever also wishes to change the premises for decision-making or the rules of the game, or "the system," has only the freedom to communicate, and typically in a manner that presupposes and shows that others should do so. As complexity increases, freedom, at both the societal level and in organizations, is taken as a license to appeal or provoke in communication.[69] The consequences are to be seen in the eagerness with which reforms are discussed.[70]

VIII

The construct of "membership" makes it possible to concentrate heterogeneous motivational assumptions. In the simplest terms, the following components can be distinguished:

(1) a variant of economic utility calculation, which is, however, open and leaves it to the individual to determine what preferences he pursues;

(2) a variant of normative obligation (in this case *qua* contract), but which is open and leaves it to the individual to determine whether his behavior does in fact conform or covertly deviate;

(3) an interest in career, but which is open and leaves it to the individual to decide whether or how he invests in his career (where, however, renunciation or indifference are still observed under the "career" schema).

It is clear that, as far as the individual's actual state of awareness is concerned, these are social constructions that are not apt to do psychological justice to reality. They work only as "communication-maintaining fictions."[71] But they display indeterminacies that mark where psychic systems and organizations irritate one another. In this sense, the role of the member is an overall formula for structural couplings whose irritations are then processed in psychic systems and in organizations in very different, non-integrable, often surprising ways.

If we equate membership with motivation and limit ourselves to the single organization in the choice of system reference, we may miss important changes. We then presuppose a need for money, but only in an abstract sense on the assumption that in a functioning money economy, money is always interesting and everyone who wants to consume has to and will go about securing a corresponding income. If we change our system of reference and set out from the economic system, membership motivation is a variable whose importance depends on how strongly individuals' lifestyles depend on spending and earning money.

Although many consumer goods have long had to be procured and paid for on the market, market dependence seems to be increasing markedly, even in the most private of fields. If the housewife works outside the home, housework becomes a problem – and can to a considerable degree be shifted onto the market: new electrical appliances, precooked and deep-frozen food, babysitters and disposable diapers; not to be forgotten are the costs of divorce and the follow-up costs, which increasingly burden the normal family budget, or, in exceptional cases, the costs of artificial insemination or surrogacy. All in all, the indebtedness of private households is growing and thus also the cost of interest payments and loan repayments. And what is to be done if the car needs replacing?

Such all-round dependence on the market may change the motivational situation in a manner invisible to the organization. The tools of hierarchical authority, instruction, and control become less important in the face of the need to keep one's job or move to a better one. And this holds true not only for the lowest stratum of society, of whom Marx believed that their physical survival depended on accepting factory work under any conditions, but at all levels of the hierarchy and the wage scale. We will have ample opportunity to show that this does not go so far that hierarchy could be abolished. It retains many functions, for example in the field of uncertainty absorption. But we can presume that its function as a motivational tool, in other words as authority that can assert itself against resistance, has decreased, and that it does not need to be so strongly stressed in the self-description of organizations at it was in Max Weber's time. Power in organizations is rather a simplified form of observing the future, of focusing on uncertainty.

IX

After these effort to adapt the concepts of person, consensus, motive, integration, freedom, and career to the theory of operationally closed, autopoietic systems, we return to the concept of membership. There is nothing to be said against continuing to use the term to describe a role that distinguishes members from non-members. But this does not mean to say that this role brings about a semi-fusion of psychic and social operations. From a strictly empirical point of view, this is impossible. We therefore replace the usual *social* interpretation of the concept of role ("social" in the sense of "social integration") by a *factual* and a *temporal* interpretation.

From a factual point of view, membership enables the *double framing* of the system's communicative operations. Externally, the system demarcates itself through the distinction between belonging/not belonging. Non-belongingness marks fundamental indifference, which is converted only exceptionally into relevance in accordance with the endogenous dynamics of the system. Internally, the low specification of membership requirements gives rise to a medium that requires further specification, hence, a medium that needs forms to generate operations; in other words, a medium that makes other internal distinctions possible as frames in which behavior can be determined with a residue of spontaneity but within expectable limits.

Interestingly, a structure is realized in the form of double framing that in a similar manner is typical of works of art.[72] The painting has a frame that sets it off from its environment. Theater performances take place on a special stage (unlike the religious plays of the Middle Ages). Textual works of art are to be found in books. External framing is the prerequisite for a medium to come into being internally, which in the late sixteenth and seventeenth century was described as "schöner Schein" and defended against critical objections. This parallel between organization and the work of art may be surprising,[73] and under no circumstances should it lead overhastily to an aesthetic theory of organization. However, in both the theory of art and organization theory, it directs attention to the phenomenon of self-generated uncertainty – and thus to the time needed to process this uncertainty step by step.

The communicative operations of the social system need time to form a temporal sequence of events (in this case decisions). The simultaneity of different decisions is naturally not excluded, for simultaneity, too, is a temporal modality. What happens at the same time cannot be observed, and thus happens on the other, unmarked side of the form "succession"; but it can be included in a sequence only if what happens simultaneously and thus inaccessible to observation at the given moment is recalled, or it is anticipated that it will be recalled later. In this temporal context, the membership role of the organization serves as part of its memory. Above all, it recalls that the person involved is a member of the system by decision, and that, as long as this decision is not retracted, recourse can be taken to it at any time. It also recalls where the role comes in the positional context of the system, and thus to what division or section it belongs. This works, and so does "role," also regardless of personal acquaintance, and thus also in first encounters in complex systems. To a certain extent, membership can also organize the interactional memory of the system, although, where no written record exists, hardly in a uniform manner for the entire system and mostly not independently of incidents attributable to specific persons. And it also works in the ongoing consistency checks of the system (as in every memory) independently of dating, and hence even when communication cannot remember the date when a member entered the system or the point in time when certain events took place.

The system can use its short-term/long-term memory without the contents being explicitly retrieved and without them passing through a consciousness and being remembered there.[74] This applies above all for negative matters, in this instance for a person not being dismissed, remaining a member with all the assumptions and exigencies that this evokes.

As always, memory allows unimportant details to be deleted, and thus forgotten. After a certain time, one will no longer remember the motive for joining or the competitive situation in which the appointment was decided (but precisely in this regard the psychic memory may diverge from the organizational memory). What is remembered is what is of value for the future and is therefore constantly re-impregnated by subsequent decisions. The difference between forgetting and remembering is constantly updated, for often widely differing reasons. As distinction, it serves to continuously link current past and current future. Given the wide range of topics involved, this is best achieved through an independent identity, and precisely this is ensured by the characteristic of being a member of a system.

X

As long as the willingness to work appeared to be ensured contractually, as long as the organization was conceived of as a system that buys a "zone of indifference" (Barnard) from its members, and as long as supervision and sanctions were the means by which such an agreement gained permanence and was protected against slip-ups, theory and practice appeared to offer a practicable concept. However, it has been obvious for decades that this by no means exhausts the possibilities. The leadership of an organization expects more voluntary engagement. Members hope for more satisfaction and "self-realization" in their work. Organizational research has taken up these desiderata and confirmed them "scientifically." More opportunity for employees to make a contribution of their own, more consensus, more motivation, more integration – why should all this not be possible if one could only discover the organizational conditions under which such expectations can be combined and realized? The example of Japanese production organization, where these expectations seem already to have been met in the form of cultural self-evidences, has intensified this trend. If self-evidences of this sort are entrenched in tradition and culture, however, they do not need to be formulated. They do not need to be translated into a performance program or ideal that gives the organization a yardstick for reform. However, the question is what happens if one formulates such perspectives, if one encourages corresponding attitudes or seeks to impose them through social pressure, or just if one looks for conditions under which they can hopefully be realized. The result is paradoxical, self-deconstructing communication.

The paradox lies not, as a cursory glance might suggest, in a contradiction between individual self-motivation and hierarchical supervision and control.[75] Although these are different variables, they can be combined in different ways with differing results. Witness the innumerable reflections on an appropriate "leadership style" or the advantages of a "communal" organization that accepts leadership as necessary for orientation. The paradox lies rather in the communication itself, in a "performative contradiction" between what it demands and the fact that it demands it. It is a paradox of the sort illustrated by the demand to be natural, to be spontaneous, to do what is expected of one voluntarily.

This paradox occurs not only when one is explicitly exhorted to self-motivation and consensus. That is only the extreme case. It also determines communication if communication is geared to allowing the desideratum to be guessed. This is the case for all reforms, but also in scientific studies that assume that more self-motivation, more consensus, and paying more attention to unused opportunities, disturbances, and deficiencies in quality ("Total Quality Management" by everyone) will produce better results. This is pre-supposed as obvious, and it is marketed as the "truth"; we could say as a "beautiful truth" (in the sense of Baltasar Gracián) but one that needs to be communicated and promoted. But precisely this gives rise to a problem that preoccupied first family therapists and then organizational consultants, the problem of a ruinous contradiction between the information content (report) and the utterance (command) of communication.[76]

As far as the consequences are concerned, we need not immediately reckon with "schizophrenia"[77] or, per postmodern philosophers and literary scholars, with the "deconstruction" of premises. We can be satisfied with considering the sort of paradox resolution chosen by the system to be unpredictable. Perhaps most probable is that the system will begin to oscillate between pursuing the demanding goals and mistrust of those who recommend this course. Or that differing opinions will develop in the system and a gap open between proponents and opponents, zealots and critics that one can live with as long as it does not develop into a permanent conflict. Or that one will react with ambivalence, for instance, confirming success where everyone knows that nothing has changed. And, finally, time helps with the charitable veil of forgetfulness, with the arrival of new problems and new fashionable terminologies (e.g., "culture").

If we ask systems theory why this is so, it could answer that psychic and social systems are formed through different operations and are operationally closed. Communication, which itself only generates social systems, can do nothing to change this. There is no unity of a psychic-social system. Communication is free to address this in the terminology of person/consensus/ motivation/integration, but the content of such communication can be mentally experienced in very different ways and in a manner that cannot be controlled through communication. If this difference, too, is to be described as a unity, then this is possible, but only as a paradox of the unity of difference, the unity of inside and outside, the unity of self-reference and other-reference.

XI

Although the boundary between psychic and social operations can be seen at the operational level as clear, sharp, and insurmountable, it does not prevent this from being reflected upon in the given systems; indeed it provokes such reflection. The baffling difference irritates both psychic and social systems. Leaving aside the psychic problems,[78] we concentrate on the forms that develop in response in communication. They are of considerable formal and informal importance for organized communication, and without the ability to know and judge this state of affairs, one cannot really understand organizations.

Throughout society and also in organizations, the solution to this problem lies in a behavior that, in terms of systems-therapy theory, is referred to as paradoxical communication. In the reformative ambitions we have just mentioned, the problem is resolved by including the future. The organization is at present not yet in a position to exhaust the possibilities of human resources development, consensus, motivation, and integration. This, therefore, has to change. But if one communicates this, paradox finds its way back into communication and deconstructs its goals. But quite apart from major plans of this sort, the problem occurs in everyday communication, too, when it seeks to convince, persuade, or motivate.[79] Such communication shows that it does not (or not completely) correspond to the views consciously involved, but at the same time prevents this discrepancy from itself becoming the subject of communication. It remains "polite."[80] It can give voice to both principal and secondary notes, and it formulates a clear utterance while adding reservations, warnings, or restrictions that contradict the principal meaning and more or less neutralize it.[81] It operates precisely and ambiguously. The addressee may understand how this is meant or may fail to do so; but especially if one understands, one also understands that it is not appropriate to elucidate the contradiction and transform it into an either/or. For the subliminal meaning of such communication is precisely the avoidance of binary logic. Such an attempt would also be in vain, for communication has enough avoidance strategies at its disposal, enough defense mechanisms, and this is also known.

In the older theory of sociable communication, such problems were dealt with under the heading of sincerity/insincerity, and it was implied that sincerity is incommunicable. One can stress, indeed swear to, one's own sincerity, only to raise the suspicion that the opposite is also possible, perhaps even probable. Communication protects itself against the resolution of its paradox and shifts the problem onto a sort of culture of suspicion. Every participant is obliged, both mentally and with social repercussions, to reckon with uncertainty and to go on communicating with this hanging overhead. There thus seems to be a sort of conspiration between psychic and social systems, which leads to communications being equipped with self-protection mechanisms, which individuals may know about or not, which they benefit from or which they suffer under, but which in any case protect them even in their own worlds of thought against exogenous determination.

The consequences include information typically not being taken as it presents itself but having to sustain a second look. It is filtered again from the point of view of whom it comes from. Can it be trusted? What is not said? What is behind it? This is probably one of the reasons why so much oral face-to-face communication takes place in the upper echelons of organizations. Those in doubt seek additional certainty in their own perception of others.

In the extremely formal concepts of Spencer-Brown's calculus of forms,[82] we can recognize in this a reentry of the form into the form (of the distinction into what is distinguished). Communication cannot itself process the muddled thoughts, let alone the perception, of individuals; but it can also not ignore their existence or that they can irritate communication. A communicable form has to be found in communication for the difference, and this is achieved through paradoxical communication, through the communication of non-communication, through the communication of barriers to communication.[83] The reentry is naturally itself a paradox, and, depending on the distinction that reenters itself and is thus the same and not the same, it assumes as paradox various forms that are themselves paradoxical but adapted to the domain of operation. This transformation is fertile because it finds expression in a wide range of forms and can thus make manageable contributions to the autopoiesis of the systems in question.

XII

A final aspect that has so far played little role in the discussion is the function of sensory perception, especially vision and hearing. We seldom realize it, but the theory of operationally closed systems imposes the conclusion that social systems, and thus also organizations, cannot perceive. Sensory perception presupposes close structural coupling between brain and consciousness. The brain carries out complex neurophysiological calculations, both fast and in parallel. The consciousness transfers the internally produced results out into the environment. It assumes that the world outside is how it is perceived and, in order to maintain this fiction, must know nothing about the work of its own brain. This externalization work of the consciousness is only indirectly accessible to social systems, namely only in the form of their own operations, only insofar as they are communicated on the basis of perceptions.

In view of the complexity and constant shift in the perceptual field of a multiplicity of simultaneously experiencing individuals, this conversion of perceptions into impulses for communication is possible only to an extremely small, highly selective degree. This is what gives communication the opportunity to control what products of perception it takes up and equips with effects in further communication. Perception itself cannot decide. Especially characteristic of organizations is that they standardize the perceptual field of individuals, for example, through the written word,[84] hence regulating what perceptions have a chance of being transformed into communication.

The freedom of such structural coupling between perception and communication has two different forms at its disposition and can oscillate between them. Individuals can report on what they perceive, for example, by keeping minutes. But they can also produce perceivable artifacts and make them available for perception by others. Thus already at the level of rendering perception perceivable, sufficient normality and permanent presence is guaranteed, from which the autopoiesis of communication benefits, and without which it would be impossible.

This conversion of perception into the perceivable has achieved an autonomy of its own in the form of works of art.[85] For the rest, however, it remains dependent on continuous linguistic, oral or written, communication. Where else could a perceiving individual who renders this perception perceivable find out what is of interest in communication and what can be understood and how? The result of this link between perception and communication is an evolutionary advance in which the standardization of communication as an excerpt from individuals' possibilities of perception goes along with a high degree of responsibility for the transformation that is attributable to individuals. In the domain of the perceivable, only individuals with brains and consciousness can act; but the selection of a contribution to communication presupposes the recursive network or the self-renewing communications system. This link has encouraged the error that individuals are able not only to perceive but also to communicate. However, if we consider the selectivity of single operations, the discrepancy is unmistakable. No individual can carry out understanding for another individual, and no individual can determine the informational value of his or her contributions to communication. At the level of perception, individuals produce events running parallel to ongoing communication: audible words and legible written characters. What happens with them and, above all, what affirmative or negative reaction they generate in communication can be clarified only by communication itself.

Only if one carefully analyzes the structural couplings between perception and communication with regard to the selectivity of individual operations and their recursion in their own system does one recognize precisely where individual-conscious perception processing and communication are structurally coupled. Individuals free communication, as it were, from the diffuse, spatially complex, temporally restless and "undecided" process of perception, translating only a few selected results into signs that other individuals can perceive as communication. This alone is an evolutionary advance without which communication would not be possible, and luckily an advance that is quite independent of whether individuals think correctly, judge reasonably, and are emotionally willing to seek consensus.

In the occidental tradition, which was oriented on the distinction between human being and animal, thinking is overestimated, and we have to correct this. Thinking typically operates retrospectively; it observes an operation that has already taken place. This can be a conspicuous perception, but above all communication. One often thinks about what one has said or could have said at almost the same time, but at any rate after the topic has been verbally determined. Only subsequently can thinking generate its own confusions and attempt to resolve them (e.g., through equations, metaphors, or recourse to familiar schemata). However, the autopoiesis of communication presupposes that consciousness is operational beforehand, and it has to operate independently of whether individuals succeed or not in their thinking. It depends on the externalization of the perceiving consciousness of individuals, but not on further demands on understanding, reason, or emotion, which receive impetus and criteria only from communication. It is only communication that turns the willingness of individuals to communicate what they perceive or their conclusions on what they perceive into a context for the reproduction of meaning, which in turn influences the selection that individuals have to make if they wish to transform perceptions into communication, in the first place into perceptions for others.

Only this sort of theoretical description shows what a turning point the supplementation and extension of oral communication by written communication must have meant. It permits stronger control of what individuals get to read and at the same time greater freedom in the conversion of written texts into other, either oral or written, communication. Participation in written communication makes greater personalization possible, because it frees one from the pressures imposed by the presence of others.[86] The written working procedures of organizations exploit this advantage and thus generate a combination of discipline and individuality that would otherwise scarcely be attainable. On the same terrain, the proliferation of electronic data processing now poses quite new problems. In comparison with operations performed by machines, what individuals can perceive is so limited that the participation of individuals in the communicative activities of the organization appears to be changing fundamentally. On the one hand, the retrieval of available knowledge for perception on the monitor requires more activity. On the other, precisely this activity is highly standardized; it can be carried out either correctly or incorrectly. Since a great deal more knowledge is accessible than before, one could suppose that freedom in transforming what is perceived into material that is perceivable for others is increasing. On the other hand, the machine has to accept what it is fed. Input into the device, unlike written communication, is independent of the constellation in which input is retrieved and of whether the next user reacts affirmatively or negatively to it. From the input point of view, this can be controlled even less than in written, let alone oral, communication. However, communication comes about only through re-perception. The real problem is accordingly likely to be the question of how this transformation of perceived into perceivable relates to the communication process of the organization.

Already perceivable things largely obviate consensus, or, to put it more precisely, they make it unnecessary to see the difference between consensus and dissent as a problem. This effect will intensify if computers are assumed to be a common reference-reality. The computer is essentially an invisible machine whose states of operation are limited and can be made visible only through very specific commands. If, in this context, one orients oneself on common perceptions, it must be assumed that the invisible machine is adequately represented in the perceptual field. The "virtual reality" of the machine can therefore not be reduced to a question of consensus, although it can be used to outwit others. One must make do with fictions of consensus, and where necessary, look for agreement on questions of where and how these machines are used.[87]

Notes

1. In the recent literature we still read, e.g.: "The business organization consists fundamentally of individuals" (Robert Lee and Peter Lawrence, *Organizational Behaviour: Politics at Work*, London 1985, 52). And this is what students are taught. At the same time, the concessive "fundamentally" shows that the authors are not certain whether they mean what they say, and how they mean it. The paradox that an organization consists of individuals but not only of individuals is discussed, for example, very deliberately in Henry P. Sims, Jr. and Dennis A. Gioia et al., *The Thinking Organization: Dynamics of Organizational Social Cognition*, San

Francisco 1986. But, since the paradox is not resolved, we are left with more or less speculative ideas about what the abundant research in cognitive psychology could contribute to organizational research.

2. Parsons, above all, had repeatedly polemicized against a purely behavioristic definition of the role concept. See also the programmatic "general statement" in Talcott Parsons and Edward A. Shils (eds.), *Toward a General Theory of Action*, Cambridge, MA 1951, 3–44 (19 f.).

3. See early statements by Parsons in a posthumous text: Aktor, *Situation und normative Muster: Ein Essay zur Theorie sozialen Handelns*, German transl. Frankfurt 1986, esp. 174 ff.

4. See the well-known criticism by Dennis Wrong, The Oversocialized Conception of Man in Modern Sociology, *American Sociological Review* 26 (1961), 183–193.

5. See Richard Münch, Über Parsons zu Weber: Von der Theorie der Rationalisierung zur Theorie der Interpenetration, *Zeitschrift für Soziologie* 9 (1980), 18–53; idem, *Theorie des Handelns: Zur Rekonstruktion der Beiträge von Talcott Parsons, Emile Durkheim und Max Weber*, Frankfurt 1982.

6. The notion that economics was a sort of natural science had survived up to Karl Marx. Since his sociology-of-knowledge critique, economics has appeared to be satisfied to ground its claims to being a science in the use of mathematical calculi.

7. Our account contradicts both the psychological and the purely analytical theory of the homo oeconomicus model. See Michael Hutter and Gunther Teubner, Der Gesellschaft fette Beute; homo juridicus und homo oeconomicus als kommunikationserhaltende Fiktionen, in: Peter Fuchs and Andres Göbel (eds.), *Der Mensch – das Medium der Gesellschaft?* Frankfurt 1994, 110–145.

8. See Ian Watt, *The Rise of the Novel*, Berkeley 1959. On the theater see Jean-Christoph Agnew, *Worlds Apart: The Market and the Theater in Anglo-American Thought, 1550–1750*, Cambridge 1986.

9. See, e.g., Victor H. Vroom, *Work and Motivation*, New York 1964; J.G. Hunt and J.W. Hill, The New Look in Motivation Theory for Organizational Research, *Human Organization* 28 (1969), 100–109; Barry M. Staw, Motivation in Organizations: Toward Synthesis and Redirection, in: Barry M. Staw and Gerald R. Salancik (eds.), *New Directions in Organizational Behavior*, Chicago 1977, 55–95; Lee and Lawrence op. cit. (1985), 61 ff., at what is now already classical attribution theory with its attempt to link up cognitive and motivational mechanisms.

10. As we read in Burkard Sievers (ed.), *Organisationsentwicklung als Problem*, Stuttgart 1977, in the introductory chapter by the editor, p. 24: "To this extent a more balanced relationship between the social system of the organization and the personal systems of members needs to be found than can be actualized, comprehended, and influenced as meaning and meaning selections of the organization, while the work situation is organized to permit a maximum level of self-actualization and fulfilment."

11. See Niklas Luhmann, *Funktion und Folgen formaler Organisation*, Berlin 1964, 39 ff.

12. On the "zone of indifference" see Chester I. Barnard, *The Functions of the Executive*, Cambridge, MA 1938, reprinted 1951, 167 ff.; Herbert A. Simon, Das Verwaltungshandeln: Eine Untersuchung der Entscheidungsvorgänge in Behörden

und privaten Unternehmen, also Chris Argyris, *Personality and Organization: The Conflict Between System and the Individual*, New York 1957, 89 ff.

13. This is the topic dealt with by Nils Brunsson, *The Irrational Organization: Irrationality as a Basis for Organizational Action and Change*, Chichester 1985. See also the earlier treatment by Albert O. Hirschman, *Exit, Voice, and Loyalty: Responses to Decline in Firms, Organizations, and States*, Cambridge, MA 1970. See Barry M. Staw, Knee-Deep in the Big Muddy: A Study of Escalating Commitment to a Chosen Course of Action, *Organizational Behavior and Human Performance* 16 (1976), 27–44; Barry M. Staw and Frederick V. Fox, Escalation: The Determinants of Commitment to a Chosen Course of Action, *Human Relations* 30 (1977), 431–450.

14. See Karl E. Weick, Organizational Redesign as Improvisation, in: George T. Huber and William H. Glick (eds.), *Organizational Change and Redesign: Ideas and Insights for Improving Performance*, Oxford 1993, 346–379 (359).

15. See Sidney Finkelstein and Donald C. Hambrick, Top-Management-Team, Tenure and Organizational Outcomes: The Moderating Role of Management Discretion, *Administrative Science Quarterly* 35 (1990), 484–503; Charles A. O'Reilley III, Richard C. Snyder, and Joan N. Boothe, Effects of Executive Team Demography on Organizational Change, in: Huber and Glick op. cit. 147–175. By "demography" variables are summed that facilitate communication.

16. See J. D. Dermer and R. G. Lucas, The Illusion of Managerial Control, *Accounting Organizations and Society* 11 (1986), 471–482.

17. See, e.g., J. Richard Hackman and J.L. Suttle, *Improving Life at Work: Behavioral Science Approaches to Organizational Change*, Santa Monica, CA 1977.

18. See the early critique by Gerald R. Salancik and Jeffrey Pfeffer, An Examination of Need-Satisfaction Models of Job Attitudes, *Administrative Science Quarterly* 22 (1977), 427–456.

19. See Jay W. Lorsch and John J. Morse, *Organizations and Their Members: A Contingency Approach*, New York 1974. The concept "internal environment" is "the individual system's environment" (p. 13), which helps one to adapt oneself to the organization. But, from the perspective of the system reference of the individual, it is a matter of its external environment or sections thereof. From the standpoint of the organization, it cannot be an internal environment, because for the organization the individual himself is not an internal but an external factor.

20. See, e.g., John W. Meyer, John Boli, and George M. Thomas, Ontology and Rationalization in Western Cultural Account, in: George M. Thomas et al., *Institutional Structure: Constituting State, Society, and the Individual*, Newbury Park, CA 1987, 12–40, e.g., 13: "We see action as the enactment of broad institutional scripts rather than as a matter of internally generated and autonomous choice, motivation, and purpose." And p. 23: " … at the institutional level, action also creates the actor."

21. See George A. Akerlof, The Economics of Caste and of the Rat Race and Other Woeful Tales, *Quarterly Journal of Economics* 90 (1976), 599–617.

22. During a visit to the desolate settlements that remain after the cessation of coal mining in Wales, I was told that, although the miners cursed their work and had made every effort to spare their sons such a fate by, for example, having them train

as teachers, they had nevertheless fought doggedly to keep their jobs. See WCCPL & NUM (South Wales Area), *Striking Back*, Cardiff 1984, the special edition of the *Journal of Law and Society* 12/3 (1985). Marx, too, had only a societal theory explanation: exploitation.

23. Lyotard's discourse theory also attempts this by setting out from the sentence (phrase) and, ignoring subjective intentions, concentrating on a concatenation (enchaînement) of these elements. See Jean- François Lyotard, *Le différend*, Paris 1983.

24. This ancient concept of person was combined in the Middle Ages with the concept of human individual, thus lending it soul. The increasingly complex economic and political conditions in early modernity and not least the emergence of the modern theater in the second half of the sixteenth century led once again to a separation. See above all Thomas Hobbes, Leviathan ch. XVI: "So that a *Person*, is the same that an *Actor* is, both on the Stage and in Common conversation; and to *Personate* is to Act, or *Represent* himself, or an other." For greater detail see Niklas Luhmann, Die Form "Person," *Soziale Welt* 42 (1991), 166–175. See also Manfred Fuhrmann, Persona, ein römischer Rollenbegriff, in: Odo Marquard and Karlheinz Stierle (eds.), *Identität, Poetik und Hermeneutik VIII*, Munich 1979, 83–106. Despite the continuity of tradition, there is a break to be noted that emerged in the mid-seventeenth century in Hobbes, but also John Hall or Baltasar Gracian, as a consequence of suspected motives and unmasked appearances. Person is now no longer the representation of a being but presentation of a self, cleverly chosen self-presentation adapted to social conventions and expectations. This already produces the gap that concerns us in this text: the gap between the capacity of a human being to change his appearance and the security requirements of social intercourse. Today objectivistic distinctions are again drawn in reaction to this, for example, between the individual as a biological and psychological system and the person in the sense of social anthropology as point of reference in social relations. See, e.g., Alfred R. Radcliffe-Brown, *Structure and Function in Primitive Society*, Glencoe, IL 1952, 193 f.

25. Interpenetration as used by Niklas Luhmann, *Soziale Systeme: Grundriß einer allgemeinen Theorie*, Frankfurt 1984, 286 ff. Usage has remained controversial.

26. In the sense used by Heinz von Foerster, Objects: Token for (Eigen-) Behaviors, in idem, *Observing Systems*, Seaside, CA 1981, 274–285.

27. A sensitive observation of leading English politicians during the American Civil War (Palmerston, Earl Russell, Gladstone) is to be found in The Education of Henry Adams, Boston 1918 (first ed. 1907), esp. 144 ff. The determination imputed to the politicians in pursuing their goals could not be verified psychologically, and thus served only to give direction to the given political action, which then called for reaction.

28. Among the exceptions is "spiritualism." It teaches that the deceased, too, continue to exist in fully individualized form and can communicate with the aid of mediums. See Allan Kardec, *The Spirits' Book (1857)*, Sao Paulo 1986; idem, *The Medium's Book (1861)*, Sao Paulo 1975. Such assumptions seem less absurd if one accepts that personality is in any case a construction established for one's own purposes in communication.

29. The destruction of precisely this triad of personality in totalitarian regimes is dealt with by Vesela Misheva, Totalitarian Interaction: A Systems Approach, *Sociologia*

Internationalis 31 (1992), 179–196 from the point of view of the reversal of positions between the present and the absent in interaction systems, and thus the elimination of boundaries.

30. See Anne Donnellon, Barbara Gray, and Michel G. Bougon, Communication, Meaning, and Organized Action, *Administrative Science Quarterly* 31 (1986), 43–55. However, the authors attribute the generation of this equifinality to the members themselves ("Communication enables members to create equifinal meaning from which organized action can follow" – p. 43), and that brings us back to the question of how communication can determine the equifinal orientation of members if not through communication.

31. Donnellon et al. op. cit., 50 speak of "affect modulation."

32. See F. Fisher and W. L. Ury, *Getting to Yes: Negotiating Agreement Without Giving In*, Boston 1981. See also Alois Hahn, Verständigung als Strategie, in: Max Haller et al. (eds.), *Kultur und Gesellschaft. Verhandlungen des 24. Deutschen Soziologentages, des 11. Österreichischen Soziologentages und des 8. Kongresses der Schweizerischen Gesellschaft für Soziologie in Zürich 1988*, Frankfurt 1989, 346–359.

33. In contrast, management theories typically opt for the opposing view and look for direct links between management strategies that also offer structural variations and psychological variables. For an overview see Wolfgang H. Staehle, *Management: Eine verhaltenswissenschaftliche Perspektive*, 4th ed. Munich 1989, esp. 750 ff. Even if such links could be established empirically and could be largely isolated from other variables (e.g., economic cycles), it would always have to be presupposed that communication takes place on the subject of motivation. In empirical social research (e.g., Geert Hofstede, *Uncommon Sense About Organizations: Cases, Studies, and Field Observations*, Thousand Oaks, CA 1994, esp. 25 ff., first published 1972), preferences (stated when asked) are also treated as an indicator of motivation.

34. See, e.g., C. Wright Mills, Situated Actions and Vocabulary of Motive, *American Sociological Review* 5 (1940), 904–913; Kenneth Burke, *A Grammar of Motives* (1945) und *A Rhetoric of Motives* (1950), joint edition Cleveland Ohio 1962; Anselm Strauss, *Mirrors and Masks: The Search for Identity*, Glencoe, IL 1959, esp. 45 ff.; Alan F. Blum and Peter McHugh, The Social Ascription of Motives, *American Sociological Review* 36 (1971), 98–109; Andrew J. Weigert, Alfred Schutz on a Theory of Motivation, *Pacific Sociological Review* 18 (1975), 83–102; George K. Zollschan and Michael A. Overington, Reasons of Conduct and the Conduct of Reason; The Eightfold Route to Motivational Ascription, in: George K. Zollschan and Walter Hirsch (eds.), *Social Change: Explorations, Diagnoses, and Conjectures*, New York 1976, 270–317; Jonathan H. Turner, Toward a Sociological Theory of Motivation, *American Sociological Review* 52 (1987), 15–27; Austin Sarat and William L.F. Felstiner, Law and Social Relations: Vocabulary of Motive in Lawyer/Client Interaction, *Law and Society Review* 22 (1988), 737–769. For recourse to Dilthey and Simmel see also Alois Hahn, Verstehen bei Dilthey und Luhmann, *Annali di Sociologia* 8 (1992), 421–430.

35. Scripts are not yet motives, but they do enable understanding, correct placing, and comprehensible communication about motives. See Roger C. Schank and Robert P. Abelson, *Scripts, Plans, Goals and Understanding*, Hillsdale, NJ 1977, esp. 36

ff.; Robert P. Abelson, Psychological Status of the Script Concept, *American Psychologist* 36 (1981), 715–729.

36. See Alfred Korzybski, *Science and Sanity: An Introduction to Non-Aristotelian and General Semantics*, 4th ed. Lakeville 1958.

37. See also Chap. 9–2.

38. See Phillip K. Tompkins and George Cheney, Account Analysis of Organizations: Decision Making and Identification, in: Linda L. Putnam and Michael E. Pacanowsky (eds.), *Communication and Organizations: An Interpretive Approach*, Beverly Hills, CA 1983, 123–146 esp. 131.

39. This is likely to apply even in intimate relationships, even in marriage. See Alois Hahn, Konsensfiktionen in Kleingruppen: Dargestellt am Beispiel von jungen Ehen, in: Friedhelm Neidhardt (ed.), *Gruppensoziologie: Perspektiven und Materialien, Sonderheft 25, Kölner Zeitschrift für Soziologie und Sozialpsychologie*, Opladen 1983, 210–233.

40. See Michel Crozier, *L'Entreprise à l'écoute: Apprendre le management postindustriel*, Paris 1989, 99: "Dans notre société libérale avancée, on ne 'motive' pas les gens, pas plus qu'on ne les 'mobilise', on leur offre des occasions, des possibilités de *se mobiliser* et on les laisse *se motiver* eux-mêmes." But precisely this version of sociality presupposes insightful second-order observation on both sides. One can create and offer conditions for self-motivation only if they give expression to an assessment of the other that this other (as one believes) can accept.

41. We read, for example, "avoid to make anyone uneasy in communication," in John Locke, *Some Thoughts Concerning Education § 143*, Works vol. IX, London 1823, reprint Aalen 1963 – to cite only one instance. On the more recent debate see almost all publications by Erving Goffman; also Tom Burns, Friends, Enemies, and the Polite Fiction, *American Sociological Review* 18 (1953), 654–662; Edward Gross and Gregory P. Stone, Embarrassment and the Analysis of Role Requirements, *American Journal of Sociology* 70 (1964), 1–15.

42. See Walter Jost op. cit. (1932), p. 66.

43. From the comprehensive literature see, e.g.: J. Richard Suchman, Social Sensitivity in the Small, Task-Oriented Group, *Journal of Abnormal and Social Psychology* 52 (1956), 75–83; Chris Argyris, *Interpersonal Competence and Organizational Effectiveness*, Homewood, IL 1962; Abraham Saleznik, Managerial Behavior and Interpersonal Competence, *Behavioral Science* 9 (1964), 156–166.

44. See Chapter 4 (Time Relations) and Chapter 8 (section on purpose programming)

45. This dissolution begins already with the distinction between social integration and system integration, which David Lockwood sees as lacking in Parsons. See: Social Integration and System Integration, in: Zollschan and Hirsch op. cit. (1976), 370–383. But "system integration" is a superfluous concept and "social integration" needs explaining. Anthony Giddens, *The Constitution of Society: Outline of the Theory of Structuration*, Berkeley 1984, p. 28 seeks a way out that has nothing more to do with the original intention of the distinction: "Social integration means systemness on the level of face-to-face interaction. System integration refers to those who are physically absent in time or space." But this distinction fails to answer the question of societal integration, for the societal system would require both sorts of integration – as system integration!

46. "Consensus was created by playing the game," as we read in Barbara Czarniawska-Joerges, *Exploring Complex Organizations: A Cultural Perspective*, Newbury Park, CA 1992, 148.

47. Similarly, but without further theoretical elaboration, Robert Anderson, Reduction of Variants as a Measure of Cultural Integration, in: Gertrude E. Dole and Robert L. Carneiro (eds.), *Essays in the Science of Culture in Honor of Leslie A. White*, New York 1960, 50–62. This would be compatible with a definition that Walter L. Bühl, *Ökologische Knappheit: Gesellschaftliche und technologische Bedingungen ihrer Bewältigung*, Göttingen 1981, 85 proposes: "'Integration' means the degree of functional cohesion of the differentiated parts or components, so that the one component cannot be effective without the other." However, this definition still presupposes as framework the part/whole schema and does not distinguish clearly between components (operations?) and parts (subsystems?).

48. See Niklas Luhmann, *Complessita sociale, Enciclopedia delle scienze sociali*, Rome 1992, 126–134; idem, Haltlose Komplexität, in idem, *Soziologische Aufklärung* vol. 5, Opladen 1990, 59–76.

49. See at the level of societal theory Edmund Dahlström, Development Direction and Welfare Goals: Some Comments on Functionalistic Evolutionary Theory about Highly Developed Societies, *Acta Sociologica* 17 (1974), 3–21 (9 f.).

50. For example, this excludes Karl W. Deutsch, who would like to assess integration in terms of the degree of need satisfaction and sees "government" as the authority that ultimately decides, but then has to set off the costs of integration. See: The Price of Integration, in: Philip E. Jacob and James V. Toscano (eds.), *The Integration of Political Communities*, Philadelphia 1964, 143–178.

51. See Niklas Luhmann, *Soziale Systeme: Grundriß einer allgemeinen Theorie*, Frankfurt 1984, 488 ff.

52. Suggestions for a general concept of career addressing the social conditions of self-development came above all from the Sociological School of Chicago. For a range of variants see Norman H. Martin and Anselm L. Strauss, Patterns of Mobility within Industrial Organizations, *Journal of Business* 29 (1956), 101–110; Everett C. Hughes, *Men and Their Work*, Glencoe, IL 1958; Anselm Strauss, *Mirrors and Masks: The Search for Identity*, Glencoe, IL 1959; Howard S. Becker, *Outsiders: Studies in the Sociology of Deviance*, New York 1963; Julius A. Roth, *Timetables: Structuring the Passage of Time in the Hospital Treatment and Other Careers*, New York 1963; Wilbert E. Moore, *Man, Time and Society*, New York 1963, 61 ff.

53. "Exploitation" includes particularly the calculation that career prospects can encourage someone to stay with the organization, since a change of employer would require starting from scratch. See also the comparison of "career versus organizational roles" in Harvey Leibenstein, *Economic Theory and Organizational Analysis*, New York 1960, 276 ff.

54. See, representative of many, Robert Dubin, Stability of Human Organization, in: Mason Haire (ed.), *Modern Organization Theory*, New York 1959, 218–253 (233 ff., 243 f.). However, it should also be taken into account that in more strongly career-oriented administrative organizations there is also less informal group cohesion than in production organizations.

55. On an extended concept see Jeff Hearn, Toward a Concept of Non-Career, *Sociological Review* 25 (1977), 273–288; Niklas Luhmann and Karl Eberhard Schorr,

Reflexionsprobleme im Erziehungssystem, 2nd ed. Frankfurt 1988; 277 ff.;
Giancarlo Corsi, Die dunkle Seite der Karriere, in: Dirk Baecker (ed.), *Probleme der
Form*, Frankfurt 1993, 252–265.

56. For an empirical study that operates with this distinction see Niklas Luhmann and
    Renate Mayntz, *Personal im öffentlichen Dienst: Eintritt und Karrieren
    (Studienkommission für die Reform des öffentlichen Dienstrechts vol. 7)*, Baden-
    Baden 1973, 119 ff.

57. On this and other factors see Luhmann and Mayntz op. cit. (1973), esp. 239 ff., and
    in greater detail Niklas Luhmann, Zurechnung von Beförderungen im öffentlichen
    Dienst, *Zeitschrift für Soziologie* 2 (1973), 326–351.

58. On the importance of personal contacts compared with formal employment
    agencies, advertisements, etc. see Mark S. Granovetter, *Getting A Job:
    A Study of Contacts and Careers*, Cambridge, MA 1974. However, the study
    covers only cases of moving between organizations. With respect to careers
    within organizations, as well as political careers in relations between parties,
    parliaments, and public administration, closer links between information and
    promotion are likely.

59. See the relatively small difference in Luhmann and Mayntz op. cit. 164 ff. If one
    combines cognitive and motivational characteristics, the results are better. See
    Charles O'Reilly III and Jennifer A. Chatman, Working Smarter and Harder:
    A Longitudinal Study of Managerial Success, *Administrative Science Quarterly*
    39 (1994), 603–627. On the other hand, this result is trivial because it is likely to be
    obvious even without empirical investigation that intelligence without motivation is
    just as unhelpful as motivation without intelligence.

60. At the beginning of a wave of reforms in the education system, this was pointed out
    particularly by Helmut Schelsky, *Schule und Erziehung in der industriellen
    Gesellschaft*, Würzburg 1957.

61. There is at least some empirical evidence to this effect. For top position holders in
    the German public service see Luhmann and Mayntz op. cit. (1973), 140 ff.; also
    Wolfgang Pippke, *Karrieredeterminanten in der öffentlichen Verwaltung:
    Hierarchiebedingte Arbeitsanforderungen und Beförderungspraxis im höheren
    Dienst*, Baden-Baden 1975, 97 ff., 110 ff., 140. On the declining importance of
    origins (in relatively short-term research perspectives) see also James Q. Wilson,
    Generational and Ethnic Differences Among Career Police Officials, *American
    Journal of Sociology* 69 (1964), 522–528; Christopher Otley, The Social Origins
    of British Army Officers, *Sociological Review* 18 (1970), 213–239; Maurice
    A. Garnier, Changing Recruitment Patterns and Organizational Ideology:
    The Case of a British Military Academy, *Administrative Science Quarterly* 17
    (1972), 499–507; Gerald Bernbaum, Headmasters and Schools: Some
    Preliminary Findings, *Sociological Review* 21 (1973), 463–484.

62. On this "other side" of the form "career" see Corsi op. cit. (1993), 260 ff.

63. The Federal Labor Court has even ruled (Aktenzeichen 7 AZR 135/93) that reaching
    the retirement age of 65 is no reason for the employer to terminate employment if the
    employee is interested in further employment (self-selection!) – to the horror of all
    organizations with an interest in predictability, including the employers and trade
    unions; see the report in the Frankfurter Allgemeine Zeitung, 29 October 1993, p. 5.

64. See Keith Thomas, *Vergangenheit, Zukunft, Lebensalter: Zeitvorstellungen im England der frühen Neuzeit,* German translation Berlin 1988.

65. On this "double function" of careers (but with a psychological motivation concept) see Renate Mayntz, Die Funktionen des Beförderungssystems im öffentlichen Dienst, *Die öffentliche Verwaltung* 26 (1973), 149–153; reprinted in: Andreas Remer (ed.), *Verwaltungsführung: Beiträge zu Organisation, Kooperationsstil und Personalarbeit in der öffentlichen Verwaltung,* Berlin 1982, 375–383.

66. See Larry M. Preston, *Freedom and the Organizational Republic,* Berlin 1992.

67. See the work done by the Tavistock Institute, London, e.g. Philip G. Herbst, *Alternatives to Hierarchies,* Leiden 1976.

68. See, e.g., Martha S. Feldman and James G. March, Information in Organizations as Signal and as Symbol, *Administrative Science Quarterly* 26 (1981), 171–186; James G. March and Guje Sevon, Information, and Decision Making, in: Lee Sproull and J. Patrick Crecine (eds.), *Advances in Information Processing in Organizations* 1 (1984), 95–107.

69. As Preston op. cit., p. 31 puts it: "our freedom has been reduced to pointing behavior."

70. See Chapter. 11.

71. See Hutter and Teubner op. cit. (1994).

72. See David Roberts, Die Paradoxie der Form in der Literatur, in: Dirk Baecker (ed.), *Probleme der Form,* Frankfurt 1993, 22–44.

73. In the literature, one tends rather to find comparisons between the market system of the economy and the modern understanding of fictional art. See above all Jean-Christoph Agnew, *Worlds Apart: The Market and the Theater in Anglo-American Thought,* Cambridge 1986.

74. For a conversation-analytical example concerning modes of expression to which one can react in communication without noticing, see Peter Fuchs, *Moderne Kommunikation: Zur Theorie des operativen Displacements,* Frankfurt 1993, 48 ff.

75. See, however, Janice A. Klein, The Paradox of Quality Management: Commitment, Ownership, and Control, in: Charles Heckscher and Anne Donnellon (eds.), *The Post-Bureaucratic Organization: New Perspectives on Organizational Change,* Thousand Oaks, CA 1994, 178–194

76. See Jurgen Ruesch and Gregory Bateson, *Communication: The Social Matrix of Psychiatry,* New York 1951, new edition New York 1968, as well as the associated therapy schools of Palo Alto and Milano.

77. See Gregory Bateson, Don D. Jackson, Jay Haley, and John Weakland, Toward a Theory of Schizophrenia, *Behavioral Science* 1 (1956), 251–264.

78. One could consider further treatment on the basis of Freudian concepts, for example, that of repression into the unconscious. But this would contradict the manifest finesse shown in dealing with this problem. A concept such as focused inattention could be more useful. The individual keeps to protective routines. He "internalizes" social precepts of politeness and respect for the self-defense of others.

79. Incidentally, we recognize in this the advantage of the pure exercise of power under the master/servant schema. The order "do this" can be communicated free of any paradox. Only the servant who has to give the impression of consenting and will

carry out the order as his own action communicates politely, that is to say, paradoxically.

80. See Niklas Luhmann, Takt und Zensur im Erziehungssystem, in: Niklas Luhmann and Karl Eberhard Schorr (eds.), *Zwischen System und Umwelt: Fragen an die Pädagogik*, Frankfurt 1996, 279–294.

81. Chris Argyris, Crafting a Theory of Practice: The Case of Organizational Paradoxes, in: Robert E. Quinn and Kim S. Cameron (eds.), *Paradox and Transformation: Toward a Theory of Change in Organization and Management*, Cambridge, MA 1988, 255–278 (258) provides examples: "You are running the show, however ... "; You make the decision, but clear with ... "; "That's an interesting idea, but be careful ... ". Argyris's term is "designed inconsistency." See in detail Chris Argyris, *Strategy, Change, and Defensive Routines*, Boston 1985.

82. See George Spencer Brown, *Laws of Form*, reprint New York 1979.

83. Another, functionally equivalent but telltale solution to this problem lies in the form of the *secret*.

84. Apart from writing there are of course also acoustic signals, noises, and smells. They serve above all as alarm signals that trigger attention or also as agreed signals to set off pre-programmed action.

85. See Niklas Luhmann, *Die Kunst der Gesellschaft*, Frankfurt 1995, esp. chap. 1.

86. This naturally holds true above all for the reading of printed texts. See Elena Esposito, Interaktion, Interaktivität und Personalisierung der Massenmedien, *Soziale Systeme* 1 (1995), 225–260.

87. See also Günther Ortmann, *Formen der Produktion: Organisation und Rekursivität*, Opladen 1995, 132.

4   The Paradox of Decision-Making

I

In pursuing the idea that an organization consists operationally of (the communication of) decisions,[1] much will depend on what is meant by "decision." At this point, one would think, theory development can still be controlled, before rapidly becoming too complex to control itself.

The literature on decision-making tells us at best that it is a matter of choice.[2] This sounds very harmless, almost tautological, but possibly contains theoretical dispositions that ought to be examined.

Choice is probably conceived of as an action that someone carries out. Choice does not happen: someone chooses. The theoretical option for action thus deals with the problem of attribution. The act of choosing is attributed to the actor. Like a magnet, action attracts the attention of the observer interested in causality. It offers a clear and certain link between cause and effect: the will of the actor causes the action. No will, no action. However, this obviously doubles the state of affairs, and is thus a fiction; for the will is nothing other than the action itself. We can look for further causes and effects, but soon face the infinite problems of causal attribution. If the actor gives us a firm footing on which to build, we can always go on to consider what influences the action or what unforeseen side effects the action produces; but the elementary causality of this action gives us a point of reference that limits any further search for causes and effects. This was perhaps why, in matters of attribution, such methodologically cautious authors as Max Weber finally came up with the concept of meaningful social action. But what do we let ourselves in for if we accept this reduction as a concession to methodological problems?

The action concept is thus associated with reduced modes of attribution, and this raises the question of who does the attributing. In more general terms: Who observes and describes an action as action, a decision as decision? For action theory the obvious answer is the actor himself. After all, he cannot act without will and consciousness. This excludes anyone else describing a behavior as an action or even as a decision that is not seen as such by the person to whom it is attributed. But who, in the network of social communication operations, can ascertain the state of the actor at the time of acting? Are we not necessarily obliged to rely on social attributions and thus on conventions, because anything else would not work at all? Is this perhaps why action theory moves on so rapidly and without further theoretical reflection to institutional theory? And would one not also have to say that only the social response to an action makes the actor aware that it is attributed to him; and that he is then well advised to take this into account through anticipatory adaptation, keeping appropriate explanations such as motives at the ready?[3] But then we have to admit that the person who is treated as actor does the acting.

The relationship between taking action and making decisions is also not easy to establish and therefore remains unclear or at least controversial. Action is often defined in terms of freedom of choice, as it was in ethics from time immemorial. Then every action is a decision, and if we want a special concept of decision, we have to add a special characteristic – for instance, the difficulty of choice (decision-making is work!), decision-making in uncertainty, or lack of routine or programming. Critique of the all-too-rationalistic premises of older decision theory has so far limited itself to these assumptions, seeking to modify them in the direction of uncertainty, information load, preference change, etc.[4] We shall leave these complications aside for the moment, because, where need be, they can easily be reconstructed within decision theory, turning rather to the question of what makes an action (possibly all actions) into a decision.

If we limit ourselves to the concept of decision, defining it as choice gets us nowhere. It remains tautological. We then supplement this definition by the information that choice has to be oriented on an alternative. This reduces the complexity of the world to a few possible variants, but provides no answer to the interesting question of what a choice is, merely shifting the problem to the question of what constitutes the alternativity of the alternative, and what it could mean for the future if one believes one has found an alternative as outcome of the past; and an answer to these questions again presupposes the concept of choice (or decision). Above all, we now face the problem of what possibilities are *included* in the alternative and which are *excluded* from it. Is this question, as could be assumed, predetermined by the logical or cosmological order of the world or do we have to presuppose an observer who decides? And if this is the case, does the exclusion of other possibilities belong to the logical structure of the alternative? In other words, does this exclusion have to be included? Looking back, was this perhaps why Kant wished to speak of freedom only on condition that it could dealt with reasonably?

We are thus turning in circles. There is an alternative, if the possibility of making a decision is confronted by one or more other possibilities on the condition that only one of them can be realized: choice means waiving the others. It therefore requires careful thought and may provoke objection or cause subsequent regret. Linguistic usage is characteristically ambivalent. Sometimes the majority of possibilities are indicated as alternative, sometimes only one among the multitude of possibilities that cannot be realized at the same time; and it often remains unclear which of these two mutually exclusive meanings is intended. This ambivalence in linguistic usage suggests that we are dealing with a paradox, which is not, however, to be admitted. It has to be concealed, because at the same time (again!) making a decision requires caution if not rationality.

Above all, however, the relationship between decision and alternative has to be clarified. The alternative does not decide itself. Not even dialectical theories based on "opposites" would have claimed that opposites cancel themselves out. Another factor is needed: concept or mind or revolution. But if we then need a decision (or even a decision-maker capable of acting) in order to choose among alternative possibilities, what is this decision, who is this decision-maker?

II

To help us make headway, we propose an abstracting concept. We replace action by observation as ultimate concept. There is always observation where a distinction is made to indicate one side of the distinction (and not the other).[5] Every psychic experience, which has to focus its perception and thinking, is accordingly observation, as is every action that seeks to achieve one thing and not another, and finally every communication that selects an item of information in order to pass it on. It is a more elementary concept than, for instance, thing, event, symbol, action, or decision, which always presuppose distinctions, whereas observation indicates the indicating distinguishing itself, and thus includes itself in its conceptual scope. The concept must be kept correspondingly abstract it if is to encompass various forms of materializing the operation of observing, and has the advantage of being able to concentrate on a specific problem, namely on how something determinate can be indicated while leaving everything else out of consideration. And how do we get from there to a specific distinction of the sort needed in deciding this rather than that? And this alternative and no other?

Already in analyzing the conditions of the possibility of observing, we come up against a problem that will reoccur in analyzing decision-making. How is it possible to use a distinction, but only one of its sides, and thus not to indicate the distinction itself? We can naturally also indicate distinctions, but then we have to distinguish the distinction to be indicated from other distinctions – and face the same problem of a presupposed but not indicated distinction. We can naturally form a concept of the distinction as we have just attempted to do, but then we have to distinguish this concept from others, for instance, from those that only try to give things a name (and with this distinction we would establish a good point of departure for the distinction [once again distinction!] between modern, differentialist, and old European theory). There is, therefore, no avoiding the realization that something becomes unobservable where something is observed,[6] and that in any case the world remains unobservable, whether it is taken to be the totality of things (*universitas rerum*) or the totality of distinctions.[7]

We thus face a fundamental paradox: every observation generates things that are observed and things that are not observed. But what is paradoxical about this? It does not block the operation of observing. On the contrary, it makes it possible in the first place. And we can shift the focus of observation and proceed from the one to the other. We can know, and by the "one after another" method can accumulate action-caused changes in state. The only problem is that we can never produce world knowledge and better worlds in this fashion, and can therefore never experience and act on a well-founded basis but only in relation to differences. The consequence of the form-dependence of all observing is that, in selecting one side of a form, the other has to be left free. But if we also take time into account, this can only mean that it has to be left free for reselection. This also applies "autologically" for distinctions such as subject/ object, self-reference/other-reference, observer/observed. Unity can then be conceived of only as crossing the boundary, as oscillation. This presupposes memory; for what has been left free has to remain available for reselection if it is not to dissolve into an indeterminable concept of world.

But what have we gained if we say the *unity* of objects of all sorts (subjects, decisions, etc., included) *is this oscillation*? One could at least say, the circumstance that every resolution of the paradox requires unity of the form time, and, indeed, that it has to occur not only in time but above all with the aid of time, with the aid of the temporal distinction between future and past. But this merely shifts the problem to the question of how a system memory can operate so as to produce the illusion of the unity of objects from the necessity of sequential selections in which the other side is left unindicated. This also holds true, again "autologically," for the question of how an observer can distinguish himself from what he observes.[8]

The paradox of the form as unity of what is distinguished is accordingly a problem of memory. It becomes a fundamental problem only if and insofar as one insists on recognizing the unity that includes observation itself, and thus the world – but also the observing system! For here, too, we have the problem of self-observation, which seeks at the same time to observe the self that is observing. Not only observation, but also the observer, remains unobservable. This can naturally be remedied by substituting another distinction. The observer distinguishes himself as system from his environment and thus from other observers in his environment. For the observer himself (and indeed for every observer), this will even be the first distinction on which all others depend.[9] Above all, the self-distinction of the observer (= system/environment, inside/outside, or self-reference/other-reference) prevents the observer from constantly confusing himself with others. It makes attribution possible. But it does not exempt from the iron law that in every shift, *"différance"* in Derrida's sense, observation – and thus the observer, too – remains inaccessible to himself. We cannot even say the observer is there and thus metaphysically present. For this would merely raise the question of who is distinguishing between present and absent. In other words, an observer cannot, as Descartes and Fichte had assumed, recognize or "posit" himself with any self-assurance. He can only distinguish himself. And the meaning of this distinction lies not in its selective or "subjective" certainty but in its connectivity – in what this observer or another who distinguishes him can make of it.

If we ask how the problem of the paradox of observation is handled, it is to be assumed that it cannot be "resolved" in the sense that it afterwards no longer exists. That would also mean that we discontinue observation and pass into a state of entropy or nirvana. But what can still be done is to unfold the paradox, to displace the paradox by a distinction that operates with identities that can be relatively convincingly communicated without anyone (or perhaps only a philosopher) coming up with the idea of asking about the unity of the distinction. Three of these unfoldings deserve particular attention:

(1) The now classical and linguistic solution is to distinguish between logical levels, in this case between the level of deciding and the level of deciding how to decide. However (a meanwhile current objection), this gets us no further, in the first place because distinguishing between levels is already a distinction drawn by an observer for which the problem of the blind spot repeats itself.[10] What is more, a decision at the meta-level, thus a decision between deciding and not deciding, is – if it is to be a decision – burdened with our problem: it is not a component of its alternative. As was pointed out at an early date,[11] the economy of the observational operation speaks against any such resolution. For the operation of observing has to use fast simplifications, for example, gestalt perception and its indication or the observation of what others "mean." And while observation is going on, it cannot dissolve such complex identifications any further.

(2) Moreover, under the lasting impression of Marx and Freud, we can distinguish between latent and manifest structures. This requires second-order observation. A second observer observes (distinguishes!) a first (direct) observer in the interest (again a distinction!) of seeing what this observer does not see and, owing to the focus of his observation schemata, cannot see.[12] The background may be a therapeutic interest that extends to entire societies, to organizations, to families, or to individuals who have problems

with themselves. In times of general uncertainty, this interest in therapy appears to be particularly great, so that the distinction latent/manifest can be plausibly communicated, and no one asks whether the therapists, above all (who are out to see something that others do not see), do not need therapy, as well. Were this question to arise, we would have to shift to another form of paradox unfolding, namely:

(3) The reentry of the distinction into what it distinguishes.[13] If one has once grasped this figure, it is easy to find, and in many unexpected places,[14] for example, in law and in morality. The right/wrong distinction or that between good and evil are subject to reentry when one takes the view that it is right or good to so distinguish. But then one has to find for this right or this good another wrong or another evil – for example, in natural law or ethics, at any rate in a "more elevated" domain – so that the problem is resolved in a hierarchy of levels, as long as this is convincing; or in the relation of the observer to what he indicates through his observation. But then one has to accept a structurally irreducible infinity and, for example, dissolve it in time; observation then has to be understood as an operation that, although it requires no time because it is only an event, takes place between the infinite horizons of past and future, which have to be distinguished and synchronized by it.

The tricks mentioned cannot eliminate the paradox. One might well wish to be rid of it, but it can be eliminated neither ethically nor logically, neither normatively or cognitively. It is also to be found (in the form of a reentry!) in the distinction between paradox and paradox unfolding. Logic is also no help. It might well try to exclude the paradox, but then faces it in the form of including its exclusion. Regardless of what distinction under-lies a paradox, by its form it poses an insoluble problem. But this does not mean that one has to lose heart and accept that "anything goes." The question is only under what conditions paradoxes can effectively be unfolded. And this question is to be addressed to a historical system, to a non-trivial machine, always in a self-determined state, which it finds out in carrying on with its operations.

The form of the paradox is thus the form by which observation blocks itself in order to tell itself that it cannot observe the world. At this level, we could say with Spencer-Brown that the world and observation cannot be distinguished – precisely because a distinction would be necessary for the purpose.[15] With the observation of a paradox, of an infinity in finite form, the observing system attains the height of irritation. And this can be assumed if a world is to be generated, because a "universe comes into being when a space is severed or taken apart," a "world where, in the first place, the boundaries can be drawn anywhere we please."[16]

III

If we are to draw conclusions about the paradox of decision-making, we need only copy the analyses of the preceding section and add a few particularities.

To begin with, we give a new version of the paradox relating to decisions. Decision-making paradoxes are undecidable because every decision contains its opposite. But undecidabilities in Gödel's sense are, at the same time, the precondition for the possibility of deciding; they can be brought on only by decisions. "Only *those* questions that are in principle undecidable, *we* can decide."[17] At first glance, this looks like a play on words, but we have to use language to establish that every decision presupposes that it has not yet been possible to decide. Behind the modal formulation of "undecidability" we find a temporal problem if we understand time in radical enough terms. And Gödel's undecidability theorem, too, allows a decision to be made externally (or in the future?).

For anyone who asks about a decision, its unity is accordingly a paradox – in various regards, depending on what distinctions are used (means and ends, before and after the decision, alternativity, self-generated uncertainty). This, it should be noted, holds for every decision of whatever format. Incidentally, this rules out the view that only outstanding performance takes this special form of paradox.[18] It may well be that top performance can only be explained by such phrases as "you have to be lucky,"[19] or excellence can be permitted to explain itself as a paradox even in public. But this would soon become an ideology that excludes others. Closer examination shows that every decision that describes itself as a decision runs into a paradox.

Decisions are observations. They observe with the help of sub-decisions, which we had called alternatives. The form "alternative" is thus the form that makes an observation into a decision. The decision indicates the side of the alternative that it prefers. This and nothing else is the specific mode of its (autopoietic) operation. For this reason, clarifying the alternative situation is much more important for a decision (and faster to attain) than going into all the consequences of a given option.

Alternatives are special sorts of distinction. Like all distinctions, they provide for two sides, but presuppose that *both sides of the distinction are accessible, that both sides can be indicated*. This is a remarkable particularity (which, however, we also find elsewhere, for example, in the logic of species and genera, in the distinction between colors, animals, etc.). Spencer-Brown's mathematical theory only presupposes that something is distinguished, and distinguished from everything else. Observation thus marks and generates a non-marked state of the world – behind its back, so to speak.[20] Since every observation requires marking, one can cross the boundary to the unmarked state but cannot mark anything there because one would then be using another distinction with another unmarked state. Merely crossing the boundary at best confirms that boundary. If the operation of indicating is repeated, identity comes into being on the inside of the boundary. If the system reaches across the boundary, it finds no basis for operating there and has to cross back, with the result that everything is as if nothing had happened.[21]

This condition changes when two indicatable sides are involved. For we then have a distinction that can be determined on both sides, and thus a *distinguishable distinction*. This does not void the basic rule that every distinction generates an inaccessible, unmarked state of the world. It does mean that now one has to distinguish two distinctions and relate them to one another: the constitutive distinction, which distinguishes itself from the unmarked world, and the distinction that can be distinguished within this distinction. The construction of an alternative creates "surroundings" [Umgebung] for itself, as Eva Meyer puts it.[22] In other words, we find neither distinctions within a species nor alternatives if we do not at the same time distinguish the type or the alternative from all others. Within the type or within the alternative, a unity can then still be found and indicated, albeit with considerable loss of information. Colors are then involved (and not women or pots or heads) or various ways of solving a problem or attaining a goal are at issue (and not other problems or other goals).[23] But a domain of mutually exclusive markings always first has to be produced, and produced by the observer himself. Thus, specifying a distinction domain does not eliminate the paradox of the unity of the distinction – but it makes it easier to ignore this paradox.

Whoever has followed this analysis so far will have to admit that these two distinctions cannot be combined into one. But this is precisely what typically happens. This means that the contrast within the alternative is exaggerated (for instance, the contrast between adjacent colors), while ignoring the fact that the alternative itself is paradoxically constructed, being based on the choice of precisely this schema of observation not also being observed. In order to avoid uncertainty, the diversity of the mutually exclusive possibilities is stressed. One can then decide because one has to decide. And *only afterwards* are preferences generated and possibly values generalized in order to give direction and justification to the decision.[24]

These considerations bring to a head the question of how the decision relates to the alternative within which it has indicated one of the possibilities. We now see that the description of the decision as a "choice" is only a tautological paraphrase of the problem. If we do not leave it at that, we notice that the decision itself does not occur at all in the decision. The decision is not one of the possibilities among which one chooses (and this is naturally also true when deciding between whether to decide or not to decide; now or later or not at all). But without an alternative there would be no decision; only the alternative makes the decision a decision. The decision thus appears to be the included excluded third; or the observation that uses the distinction but in so doing cannot indicate itself; or, in the terminology of Charles S. Peirce's semiotics, the "interpretant," which has to be involved if the distinction between sign and signified can be put in a new state.[25] Each of these versions, which basically say the same thing, indicate that the decision, whatever it is as operation (e.g., communication) occurs at the point where we assume there is a paradox, that of the unobservability of the operation of observing, and thus of the observer.

This explains why decision theory operates with the concept of choice, which, like that of selection, explains nothing but merely marks the spot where something needs to be explained.[26] That a choice has taken place can be recognized only in retrospect, only in its result.[27] The event itself remains unexplained and, worse still, ununderstood. The result is the frequent resort to *mystification* in describing decisions – not only within organizations but also in theory. After all, it cannot be admitted that a decision cannot decide itself (just as fire cannot burn itself). A description therefore has to be chosen that avoids this impression and proposes meaning that is more convincing.

Perhaps the commonest solution is to attribute an element of *arbitrariness* to the decision. But this information remains indeterminate; it serves only to demarcate what one considers to be the essence of the decision from attributable influences. The need for explanation is only postponed. For the next question is immediately: How is arbitrariness "operationalized," how does it become information? The way out is to shift the problem to the *decision-maker*. It is he who decides. Instead of the paradox we thus have a tautology: the decision-maker decides. This tautology is more amenable to further handling. One has to know him if one wants to predict decisions; although one knows that, if he knows that one wants to know how he will decide, he will be sorely tempted to decide differently. The problem is accordingly shifted from diagnosing a situation to diagnosing a system. More complexity comes into play, more redundancy, and more variety. One has more pointers for suppositions and for subsequent explanations. One can more easily make a mistake and discover it less easily.

The assumption that it is the decision-maker who decides engenders myths that arise partly from expectations, partly from explanations and justifications. The most important are that, at least from the point of view of intention, decisions are rational, that they are in line with the long-term interest of the organizers; for example, the profitability of business enterprises or the objectivity of decisions made by public authorities as opposed to short-term political pressures. They seek to regain a lost balance. Closer observation of the decision-making paradox will reveal considerable discrepancies between myth and reality.[28] We will be coming back to this in Chapters 5 and 14.

Even if the link between decision and decision-maker is an attribution construct, this does not mean that it is merely a fiction that collapses when seen through. We could rather speak of an "eigenvalue" of the organization that is repeatedly confirmed in the recursive practice of organized decision-making. This is due not least to the fact that not only observers but also the decision-makers themselves do the attributing, thus developing emotional ties with "their" decisions and their principles. At the same time, this means that caution is called for in the communicative handling of decisions. Criticism can be hurtful, and very often decisions are accepted because one wishes to spare the decision-maker.

With a metaphor introduced by Michel Serres,[29] we can therefore say that the decision-maker is the parasite of his deciding. He benefits from the decision being based on an alternative. The decision passes, he remains. The decision can at best be the topic of further communication; one can ask the decision-maker (and thus acknowledge him).

But the decision-maker is and remains the construction of an observer, who can be the decision-maker himself. Investigation of the real reality can never be permitted in the system, because it would bring things permanently to a halt. What counts as reality is only the resistance of observations to observation. For everything that is to function as reality, an operationally closed system has to be assumed, because only in a system does such resistance to itself occur. It is therefore easy to say that the organizational system itself is the system that observes its decisions and its decision-makers and in so doing generates reality in the form of resistance to itself. The unfolded tautology of decision/decision-maker provokes the organization (and naturally all the psychic systems involved) so strongly that resistance is sought – and found.

There are clearly individuals who can project themselves into the mystery of deciding better than others. With Max Weber, we then speak of charisma.[30] This is based on a secularized understanding of the religious concept. What it involves is therefore not a bestowed gift but a sort of self-inspiration. Belief in this, not least on the part of the person endowed with charisma, can be taken as a fact or described as a phenomenon. But the explanation is that one would otherwise have to face the paradox of decision-making oneself, and hence accept the blocking of observation. One is released from this by the ascription of charisma, which, we could say, phenomenalizes the problem. We may assume that the mystery of decision-making stimulates reflection on leadership qualities, and does so on the level of both first- and second-order observation.[31] There can be no "leadership theories" independent of this (that are not concerned with resolving the decision-making paradox).

Since a decision has to be attributed, errors in attribution can occur. A decision is not necessarily made by the person who is nominally responsible and puts his name to the communication of it. This is known and taken into account. But even if one sees through the attribution error, one does not necessarily learn who has "really" made the decision; or, to be more precise, where to start if one wishes to influence a pending decision or correct one that has already been made.

If decision theories take no account of the attribution problem and regard the decision-maker, so to speak, as an ontological locus of decision-making, a resolution of the paradox presents itself in relation him. The problem then shifts to the limitations to the capacity of the human mind, to its limited scope for information processing, and to the discrepancy between optimal and factually possible calculation. Both organization research (following Simon) and psychology now agree on this.[32] In the theory of autopoietic decision-making, this means that the paradox of decision-making is resolved through a certain distinction, that between optimal and limited rationality. This has greatly stimulated research – on condition, however, that the concept of decision itself is not defined, or only tautologically.

Probably the most important consequence of attributing decisions to decision-makers is that the importance of decision-makers increases with the importance of decisions – and vice-versa. Regardless of all actual influence lines and all "informal organization," the decision-making system tends to develop a hierarchy. The important decisions then have to be made higher up, the most important at the very top. But, in the other direction, too: what comes down from the top has to be considered so important that ignoring it must be disguised.

In similar and complementary fashion, it is assumed that the need to accept decisions increases with their importance, and that with the need for acceptance, opportunities also increase for obstruction, for delay, for building in obstacles for the next decision-maker. The need for acceptance means that the acceptance of decisions has to be decided on. Important decisions have to be drawn up as written texts and "co-signed." The result is a tendency for clauses and conditions, concessions and compensations to proliferate, making decisions so complex that, at least for insiders, the decision-maker can no longer be pinpointed. The paradox is concealed under complexity.

It can be assumed that a balance is typically found. The demand for consensus can lead to standstill, stagnation, and omission, whereas hierarchization can produce energy and innovation. But, we could almost say, this is an aesthetic impression.[33] When an organization overdoes the hierarchy, this can be compensated for by seeking consensus – and vice versa. With these two possibilities at its disposal, the system can react to perceived environmental situations, crises, and other temporal conditions with more leadership or more consensus, more clear commands or more spontaneous order formation.

However, the mystery is resolved, whether through personalization or consensus building, further procedure makes use of the one-sided attribution of causes and effects. Causal assumptions with which the system can work are brought into play without giving them further thought. If difficulties arise, great individuals or consensus are sought, excellence or agreement – only because they are seen as factors that can offer solutions to problems. Processes of "superstitious learning" develop.[34] But no objection can be raised as long as it cannot be shown how the paradox of decision-making could otherwise be resolved.

This is not the place to take these reflections any farther. It should, nevertheless, be noted that in this way the participating individuals are also given a sense of their own importance (or unimportance). Within the limits set, they can unfold not only the paradox but also themselves; they can find a niche, aspire to greater importance, or simply take an interest in other persons and "their" decisions, and spread rumors.

IV

The conundrum of how decisions emerge from a sort of decision-making chemistry is thus not solved through the concepts of choice and subject, but only distributed between two concepts. This raises the question of whether we can form a concept of decision that avoids this dead end. We shall attempt to do so by relating the problem of decision-making to the time dimension.

Every decision presupposes world time, which continuously moves the distinction between past and future into a different, a new present. Only rough simplification allows us to understand this as a movement or process. In fact, every present is burdened with the problems of redescribing its past and reprojecting its future. However, time allows little time to do so. Reflections of this sort can therefore only be highly selective and undertaken only for special reasons.

This problem is, as it were, copied in the decision. It establishes a past that is relevant *for it*, and therefore requires a memory that helps it to understand problems, alternatives, and resources as aspects of its present. Moreover, a decision can occur only if those involved understand that it makes a difference. If the decision is made, the world will look different from what it would if it were not made. The projection of a difference is therefore an integral part of decision-making. A decision constructs a different context of past and future than that which otherwise exists in world time. But this happens in the world, and hence in world time, for example, at a datable point in time. What occurs is a "reentry"[35] of time into time, or, more precisely, of the distinction between past and future into the distinction between past and future.

A reentry gives the system so many possibilities (so much meaning) that it becomes incalculable for itself. It cannot work out its own possibilities; it cannot attain its own unity operationally. It has to rely on imagination.

Precisely this is experienced in operational performance as freedom of choice. If operations can be communicated as decisions, this secures the possibility of making decisions. But what does this possibility and its successful implementation depend on?

A decision, it appears, has to be based on a contingency schema that also limits what has to be taken into account. In the present of the decision, the past makes resources available that could also be used elsewhere. And, although it is what it is, it leaves alternatives open. The future, too, although it is and remains unknown, appears as a horizon in which other possibilities can be introduced. If, for example, a capital increase is at issue, the survival of the business can and must be assumed to be ensured by a certain level of capitalization, and any projection of the future will be concerned with costs and benefits. From the classical perspective, one now inquires about the subject that makes the decision and is answerable for it. This may well facilitate foresight and explain events for an observer. In the theory we propose, which also explains the emergence of imagination and the freedom of decision-making, however, attention would be directed rather to the contingency schema. It is then not so much a matter of limiting the discretion of the subject but of what variant can be associated with a proposed topic.

V

Whatever decisions "are," within organizational systems, they can come about only as communication.[36] For us, a decision is accordingly a communicative event and not something that happens in the mind of an individual.[37] We therefore have to ask how the paradox of decision-making can be communicated. Clearly not as paradox, for this would mean communicating the abandonment of connectivity. Nor as arbitrariness, for this would mean arbitrary acceptance or rejection. The paradox therefore has to be wrapped up and sealed in communication. But how does one then prevent the seal from breaking and the wrappings being gleefully removed to let everyone see there is nothing inside but pure arbitrariness?

The question can be put in more concrete terms: wow can decisions be communicated together with their alternatives and in relation to them? Communication produces itself as a unified operation, as a unity of information, utterance, and understanding. But how can this unity communicate an alternative, not only as information about a multiplicity of possibilities but as decided alternative? The decision has to inform about itself, but also about the alternative, thus about the paradox that the alternative is an alternative (for otherwise the decision would not be a decision) and at the same time not an alternative (for otherwise the decision would not be a decision). Does not every decision communicate criticism of itself, because it also communicates that it could have been different? The decision could, we could say, communicate meta-information, too, to the effect that the decision-maker has the right or the authority or good cause to decide the way he does. But is not this meta-information constantly disavowed by the fact that communicating the decision includes communicating the fact that one could have decided differently? In the terminology of linguistics, does not every communication of a decision contain a performative self-contradiction? And if this is so, is it not a constant invitation to "deconstruct"?

Following the older literature,[38] we can distinguish in communication a "report" aspect and a "command" aspect, in other words, constative and performative functions. On the one hand, a decision communicates a certain meaning, which it establishes; on the other, it communicates the expectation that this established meaning will be taken over in follow-up communication, that it will be believed and considered correct or suitable. In this context, too, a law of the tempo and economy of communication applies. The report aspect and the command aspect can thus not be kept apart, not isolated from one another; indeed, in practice not even analytically distinguished from one another, because this would only reveal the paradox and raise the question of why the decision is being communicated at all. The components of a communication, namely information, utterance, and understanding, mutually presuppose one another in acceptance or rejection; they are thus circularly linked, so that none of these components has primacy. The primary concern is neither the truth value of information, nor the conception or will of a subject (an actor), nor, finally, conditions for consent and dissent. From one situation to the next, there is a shift in the components that are retained in order to problematize others.[39]

This dissolves many tacit assumptions that we find in the literature, for example, that "information" is to be understood strictly as a surprise and thus as a component of other psychic or communicative operations. Like all events, information disappears as soon as it arrives. It cannot be understood both as surprise and an atom-like something. It cannot be introduced into a system from outside (which would run contrary to the concept of autopoiesis). Information is immobile, since it disintegrates on occurrence and loses its quality as information on becoming known. It can only be put in the form of knowledge. It thus takes on another form, so that, although one can gain knowledge unexpectedly, one cannot "know it away" again. The transformation of information into knowledge is a process that takes time, a process that involves memory; this means that information in the form of knowledge is no longer what it was when it surprised one as information. The quality of surprise cannot be repeated, and therefore, strictly speaking, cannot be remembered either. It occurs in memory only as a paradox, as a contradiction of what one now knows.

That decisions gain social reality only as communication also means that there is a latent possibility of psychiatrization, which can be used if the additional distinction between normal and pathological can be introduced. This means nothing other than that every communication of a decision undergoes a normality test, that is to say, contains a self-correction mechanism, which sorts out the imprecise and the all too peculiar. This problem is, finally, the point of departure for deconstructivism, which is concerned rather with long-term developments in the self-dissolution of credibility. The alternative is not immediately deconstructed, although this is also possible through recourse to its unmarked environment, and does occur. What is deconstructed, if it comes to it, is the unity of the communicative operation. Its components, information and utterance, are separated; one takes the alternative as information, but does not accept the decision as utterance that the one side of the alternative and not the other is indicated. And precisely because one has to set out from an alternative, this deconstruction is almost imposed. The communication of the decision will tend to undermine its own preconditions.

In "deconstructivism"[40] we find a theory of society concealed in a critique of metaphysics. The more a society must, for whatever reason, rely on decisions to generate a future out of its past, the more it will tend to deconstruct the semantics it draws on for this purpose. The more one tries to reestablish what is necessary, valuable, ethical, and so forth, the more the contingency of precisely these operations becomes apparent. This is shown by the legal system having to replace natural law by a constitution; by ethics having to convert from a theory of naturally perfect habitus to a theory justifying moral judgments; by metaphysics confronting the divisions of being (categories, species, genera) with the question of the conditions of its own possibility; by belief in God being replaced by the question of the meaning and importance of religion, and by theological theories – for instance, the *immediacy* of the sense of per se dependence – requiring arguments; or succinctly formulated in Lyotardian terms, by the circumstance that credible meta-reports are no longer accepted.

We leave it open whether and how one can react at the level of societal descriptions of the world and society to the deconstructability of all meaning proposals. Our question is whether safety nets can now be spread at the level of organizational systems and how this happens. Thus, how do organizations prevent the constant deconstruction of their own decision communication, which imposes itself so strongly? The answer to this question lies in the concept of autopoiesis. Precisely because organizations are social systems that consist only of decisions and are reproduced only through the reproduction of decisions, they survive thanks to the prevention of their own deconstruction. However this happens, they can secure acceptance of decisions through decisions. To this end, they form the necessary structures. If the performative self-contradiction of decision communication infects every operation, and thus also those that actualize it, this is a condition that prevents its actualization. For this, too, can take place in the system only through the communication of a decision.

In itself, this statement has little explanatory value – as does an isolated concept of the format of autopoiesis. But it opens the way to further theory development. One can now put "how" questions, notably: how is a return to paradox prevented? How is the constant deconstruction of decision communication prevented or at least sufficiently discouraged? And these are variants of the question: what self-organization at the structural level enables the autopoiesis of the communication of decisions in organizations?

Given these considerations, we can assume that structures develop in every organization that do not derive from the decisions of the system, although they come into being only if the system works autopoietically, and can accordingly reproduce itself through decisions. We shall call such non-decided premises for decision-making "organizational culture." This approach explains that organizational cultures are, on the one hand, contingent with respect to how they come into being; for, like all structures, they arise only in specific, concrete systems and only on the basis of operations of the system that uses them as structures. On the other hand, they are not treated as contingent in the system but regarded as self-evidences that are understood and accepted by everyone who has experience with the system and is familiar with it.[41]

VI

Modern organizations appear to have a sort of problem awareness that Michel Crozier has described as follows: "Paradoxalement, nous nous sentons beaucoup plus responsable qu'auparavant du futur que nous contribuons à créer, mais nous sommes beaucoup moins capables d'en préciser la configuration."[42] Precisely this problem can be reconstructed with the concept of the autopoiesis of decision-making. The paradox it contains can be resolved only through reproduction, and this makes the reproduction of the system highly probable. If everything that happens has to be put in the form of decision-making, and decisions are always only current, can always be made only in the present, this uncertainty with regard to time has to be expected. Decisions are only possible because the future is uncertain, and therefore unknown. And this constitutes what we normally call responsibility.

We have revealed the paradox that organizations have to reckon with and resolve not at the structural level but at the operational level. In this, our concept differs from theories that set out from structural contradictions, for example, the notions of latent or more or less open structural contradictions in Karl Marx or Robert Merton. This switch has to do with the transition from structuralistic to operational systems theory. The result is that all structural contradictions that confront behavior with a dilemma and stimulate the search

for solutions have to be understood as deriving from more deep-seated paradoxes, which can thus be derived theoretically.

The prevailing treatment of system paradoxes – meanwhile a widespread
topic of discussion – is still to be found at the structural level, for example, the
paradox of the second violin in the string quartet, which, while having to follow
the first violin, is, as the weakest link in the chain, decisive for the success of the
quartet.[43] If, as in systems therapy, one shifts to the operational level, one often
comes across the notion, going back to now obsolete logical and linguistic
theory, that paradoxical communication is an inadmissible mixture of logical
types or linguistic levels that should (and could?) be avoided. However, the two
problem presentations do not reach down to the level at which system paradoxes arise and then make transformation, unfolding, and resolution necessary
to avoid observation blocking autopoiesis.

To recapitulate: even communication itself generates a contradiction
between the selectivity of information and the selectivity of utterance (or, in
the usual terminology, between the constative and performative aspects of
communication), which can be "understood" at any time and can thus come
out into the open. Why, if information is a selection, can a certain selection be
uttered to the exclusion of other possibilities? What bestows the right to do so,
what sources of truth or authority that cannot be questioned because they would
require endless communication after communication (and thus environment-
less communication)? If communication were allowed to observe itself strictly,
grounds for self-destruction or deconstruction are thus built in, in the classical
definition: a self-reference involving negation and which would produce
a vicious circle – if it were not prevented from doing so through creatively
introduced distinctions that take over the paradox and make it invisible.

If this applies for communication as such, it also applies for every communication of a decision. And does so in both intensified and modified form. One
resolves the paradox, if decision-making is involved, by indicating the decision-maker. The decision-maker to whom the decision is to be attributed is then
to be distinguished from other decision-makers. And the organization helps in
this, above all through its differentiation of positions and responsibilities, but
also because who has made and communicated the decision is made apparent.
The organization forgets itself, as it were; it employs a highly selective memory
that records what condensates from information processing are to continue in
use. Were this to fail, the system would be unable to carry out its own
autopoiesis independent of observation. It would disappear in the infinite
unmarked space of what has not come into being. In other words, autopoiesis
is tied to the successful, at least occasionally convincing unfolding of this
fundamental paradox of decision communication. And structural contradictions or behavioral burdens are only a distant derivative of this fundamental
(we could say contingent) necessity on which everything else depends.

VII

With the abstraction process, which replaces the action concept by the concept of observation and which in the concept of communication includes not only "communicative action" (utterance) but also information and understanding, and, finally, with the notion of decision as resolution of a paradox, we face a problem that deserves particular attention. The analytics of organizations may well benefit from such abstract concepts, but the question is now one of practice. Even if the organization follows the conditions imposed, it has to offer something perceivable on which people can orient themselves. In other words, it needs symbiotic mechanisms that ensure relations with psychic systems are not interrupted.[44] It needs "design." With Parsons we could also ask about "real assets," which guarantee that, despite extravagant generalizations, the system keeps its feet on the ground. What is involved is not the structural coupling of communication and consciousness in general but the question of how organizations make themselves perceivable.

This is not the place to discuss how, with regard to psychic systems, perception relates to other operations of the consciousness, for example, thought. However, we reverse the classical notion of a hierarchy of psychic abilities, which had assigned sensory perception a subordinate role because human beings share it with animals. Instead, it must be assumed that only perception provides the consciousness with an external world, and does so even though the brain, as an operationally closed system, generates all perceptions internally. The consciousness may then well simulate perceptions, may well occupy itself with the imagination and build in reflexive controls; but without perception it would unable to accept a world in which it can distinguish between self-reference and other-reference. This means that all communications – and those of organizations are no exception – have to offer a perceivable external surface, acoustically in the form of language, optically in the form of the written word. Nor can we go into what can be inferred from such external surfaces about the depths – in old traditions this was the function of divination and ornament.[45] We are concerned only to point out the indispensability and considerable effects of such symbiotic mechanisms, which ensure that human beings and social systems can live together.

Above all, this would involve visible, bodily action, action whose meaning is directly perceivable and already understandable through perception. In this sense, Lanzara, for example, speaks of *attivita osservabili*.[46] Action theory, in particular, does not take sufficient account of this special aspect, submerging it unnoticed under the excessive demands made on the action concept. Moreover, for example, organizations have to be located in space, have to be recognizably tied to buildings if members are to be expected to turn up for work in the morning. Communication, too, finds its limits in perception, at least in a negative sense. One cannot claim not to be somewhere where one can be seen, or that a text says something else than what one can read in it. The perceivable world guarantees that others can perceive the same. It thus imposes itself, and we have to interpret it if we wish to loosen the bonds and return communication to its "real" meaning. In itself, directly understandable perception leaves too many connectivity options open and generates and absorbs too little uncertainty.

The more the system steers itself by memory and decision-making premises, the less it will have to rely on direct understandability. Just as in the field of societal communication media a kind of generalized trust marginalizes "real assets," such as the coverage of bank deposits or the availability of police prone to violence, a complex organization can also fall far short of coverage by understandable perception. One then normally operates on the secondary level of signs for signs. This separates what is understandable for members from what is understandable for outsiders. We could thus also speak of the problems of an inflation that relies too much on indirectness and loses direct motivational capacity. In the case of structures and of necessary innovation, it will then not be easy to return to the level of perceivable understandability. Tangible symbols are then called for, but the loss of directness is hardly to be regained by reacting to a deficiency. One sees through the proffered surface and recognizes the intention.

VIII

In the normal operations of organizations, we find two schemata with which the paradox of decision-making is rendered invisible: the schema of *problems* and the schema of *interests*. The problem schema soon comes up against the metaproblem of the unclearly defined problem.[47] The schema of interest finds itself in situations where one interest can be promoted only at the cost of other interests. Depending on which metaphor we choose, we thus end up with quite different situation definitions.

The two schemata do not exclude but interpret one another. Under the problem schema one can always ask what interests are behind the problem and being concealed by seemingly objective definitions of it. And the promotion of interests in turn becomes a problem, especially because in detailed planning the number of opposing interests that suffer increases. Nevertheless, and precisely because of this mutual infiltration, it is important to observe which of the schemata the analysis of a decision or a decision-making process sets out from.

Problem analysis suggests possible consensus and a sort of objective diagnosis. One gets caught up in the usually formidable difficulty of finding an unambiguous problem definition. Seemingly, one proceeds rationally. Giving priority to interests, by contrast, signals a standpoint that is clearly particular-istic from the start and will take no account of other, opposing interests. The argument then typically seeks to show that the particular interest is the general interest or can at least cover very many other interests, as well.

This can be further elaborated. At this point, however, the most interesting question is why this dichotomy of schemata arises and why one therefore feels obliged to choose between the two in setting out to analyze decisions. The answer could be that this dichotomy renders the paradox of decision-making invisible, leaving only the question of whether one wants to solve problems or promote interests. One can then attempt, by choosing between these points of departure, to initiate decision analysis and decision-making processes while ignoring the existence of the other possibility. That it is relatively easy to ignore this question (and thus the question of the unity and function of the distinction between problem and interest) is explained by the circumstance that one would otherwise have to endure the paralyzing sight of the paradox.

Notes

1. In what follows, we put "communication" in brackets to avoid the need to constantly repeat that communications are at issue and not consciousness events. This simpli-fication naturally does not change the theoretical premises.
2. Typically, the *concept* of deciding is then not seen as a problem. In a textbook on decision-making (Irving L. Janis and Leon Mann, *Decision Making: A Psychological Analysis of Conflict, Choice, and Commitment*, New York 1977), we find no defini-tion of the concept but merely the casual formulation, "When people are required to choose among alternative courses of action . . . " (p. 21). Who demands this? How do alternatives arise? What is "choice"?
3. See far-reaching research drawing partly on Max Weber, partly on Alfred Schütz. Reference Chapter 3 n34.
4. See, e.g., the brief overview in the epilogue to the 2nd ed. of Richard M. Cyert and James G. March, *A Behavioral Theory of the Firm*, Oxford 1992, 226 ff. with further references.
5. This version of the concept comes not from psychology but from cybernetics. But it can also be interpreted in psychological terms. On the general concept see, e.g., Heinz von Foerster, *Observing Systems*, Seaside, CA 1981; Niklas Luhmann et al., *Beobachter: Konvergenz der Erkenntnistheorien?*, Munich 1990; Niklas Luhmann, *Die Wissenschaft der Gesellschaft*, Frankfurt 1990, 68 ff. See also Francesco Pardi, *L'osservabilita dell'agire sociale*, Milano 1985, including older literature.
6. See Heinz von Foerster, Das Gleichnis vom blinden Fleck: Über das Sehen im allgemeinen, in: Gerhard Johann Lischka (ed.), *Der entfesselte Blick: Symposion, Workshops Ausstellung*, Bern 1993, 15–47; but also the much older theory going back to Leonardo da Vinci of the "perspectiva de'perdimenti," which had stressed that something disappears despite focussing and increasing distance. See Ernst H. Gombrich, *Ornament und Kunst: Schmucktrieb und Ordnungssinn in der*

Psychologie des dekorativen Schaffens, German transl. Stuttgart 1982, 107 ff. It will also not have been considered an accident that precisely the theory of artistic production, which seeks to *generate* possibilities for observation, came upon this problem. It serves as both insurmountable difficulty – and exoneration.

7. In this sense for a world that wanted to set itself up for self-observation, also George Spencer-Brown, *Laws of Form*, reprint New York 1979, 105.

8. See Ranulph Glanville, *Was ist und wie kann ein Gedächtnis sich erinnern, was es ist?, German transl.* in Glanville, *Objekte*, Berlin 1988, 19–46, as an attempt to solve the problem through a concept of "object" that understands self-observation as a precondition for being an object.

9. On the implications of such a "primary distinction," which generates all others, including the axioms needed for a calculus, see again Spencer-Brown, op. cit. Ultimately this leads to the abolition even of ontology in the traditional sense. *For the distinction between inside and outside is now more fundamental than the being/non-being distinction.*

10. The "blind spot" here is naturally the pure intention of avoiding paradoxes.

11. See, e.g., Jurgen Ruesch and Gregory Bateson, *Communication: The Social Matrix of Psychiatry*, New York 1951, 2nd ed. 1968, 192 ff.

12. See Niklas Luhmann, Wie lassen sich latente Strukturen beobachten? in: Paul Watzlawick and Peter Krieg (eds.), *Das Auge des Betrachters – Beiträge zum Konstruktivismus: Festschrift Heinz von Foerster*, München 1991, 61–74.

13. Following Spencer-Brown op. cit. (1979), 69 ff. See also Louis H. Kauffman, Self-reference and Recursive Forms, *Journal of Social and Biological Structures* 10 (1987), 53–72 (56 f.). See also above, p. . . . (Chapter 2, section 4).

14. See Niklas Luhmann, Observing Re-entries, *Graduate Faculty Philosophy Journal* 16 (1993), 485–498. Reprinted in *Protosoziologie* 6 (1994), 4–13.

15. See A Note on the Mathematical Approach, in: Laws of Form op. cit., XXIX.

16. Spencer Brown op. cit., XXIX. The formulation is easily misread. This is of course not a matter or arbitrariness, for there is no arbitrariness in the world. We are dealing only with an equivalent of the realization that the mathematical calculus has itself to introduce all the assumptions on which it is based. In other words, we are dealing with a formulation of the operational closure of systems capable of observing. Spencer-Brown himself also mentions "motives" as a requirement to introduce distinctions. But the distinguishing of such "motives" or the distinguishing of the distinctions by which the world is split, and hence produced, must be left to a later place in the theoretical architecture because the operation of reentry has to be presupposed for this purpose.

17. Heinz von Foerster, Ethics and Second-order Cybernetics, *Cybernetics & Human Knowing* 1/1 (1992), 9–19 (14).

18. See, as answer to the problems that the search for excellence and distinct leadership qualities had caused, Robert E. Quinn, *Beyond Rational Management: Mastering the Paradoxes and Competing Demands of High Performance*, San Francisco 1989.

19. Quinn, op. cit., p. 23.

20. We therefore do not presuppose chaos, an entropic primeval state of the world from which order comes into being through Creation or through change and evolution; even the first difference between marked and unmarked is produced by an observer – by whatever distinction. See also Philip G. Herbst, *Alternatives to*

Hierarchies, Leiden 1976, 104 f.: " ... the original state is not originally the original state but only becomes this *after* a primary distinction has been made." The concept of autopoiesis means the same. An autopoietic system too, cannot observe its own beginning, but only, with the aid of the before/after distinction, its already-having-begun.

21. See axiom 2: "The value of a crossing made again is not the value of the crossing." And: "For any boundary, to recross is not to cross" (op. cit. 2). See also 5: the form of cancellation.

22. See Eva Meyer, Der Unterschied, der eine Umgebung schafft, in: ars electronica (ed.), *Im Netz der Systeme*, Berlin 1990, 110–122, following Gotthard Günther's attempts to distance himself from simple logical decisions.

23. Here we allow species logic and problem logic (or substance logic and functional logic) to run in parallel, because in this context we are concerned only with commonalities. But it also seems logical to apply this insight into similarity historically so that we can better understand why it has been possible in recent times to shift from genus to problem, from substance to function. See the still readable monograph by Ernst Cassirer, *Substanzbegriff und Funktionsbegriff*, Berlin 1910.

24. This obviously goes against the thesis, current in around 1900, that values apply a priori, and are thus final, unsurpassable points of reference.

25. The interpretant is the sign that guarantees that the same is meant in the difference between sign and signified. But the concept also points to the necessity of developing a triad out of a dyad. However, in principle it is still conceived in identity-theory terms and not as paradoxical.

26. This is not to suggest that there are finally valid explanations at all. The argument is directed only against pseudo-explanations and proposes a return to the paradox to find a point of departure for further analysis.

27. Lloyd E. Sandelands and Robert Drazin, On the Language of Organization Theory, *Organization Studies* 10 (1989), 457–478 (459 f.) and Robert Drazin and Lloyd Sandelands, Autogenesis: A Perspective on the Process of Organizing, *Organization Science* 3 (1992), 230–249 (231) therefore speak of "achievement verbs," which explain nothing. But in returning to concepts like action or interaction, one would only be turning in circles, for they implicitly also subsume the concept of decision and are similarly recognizable only in retrospect as specifying something (rather than something else).

28. On managing bodies in business see Gordon Donaldson and Jay W. Lorsch, *Decision Making at the Top: The Shaping of Strategic Direction*, New York 1983, summary 6 ff.

29. See Michel Serres, Le Parasite, Paris 1980.

30. However, this interpretation owes nothing to Weber. For Weber, charismatic authority was a counter-concept to bureaucratic authority; in the charismatic filling of the decision mystery we see, on the contrary, a final figure that protects an operation against its paradox. We therefore have to water down Weber's emphasis on the (ideal-typical!) non-everydayness of charisma, without losing sight of the circumstance that there are exceptional cases of charismatic personality that give no cause to raise the question of how a decision comes about.

31. See Bobby J. Calder, An Attribution Theory of Leadership, in: Barry M. Staw and Gerald R. Salancik (eds.), *New Directions in Organizational Behavior*, Chicago 1977, 179–204.

32. See only Janis and Mann op. cit. (1977).

33. If "leanness" is currently in vogue for organizations, it is not by chance that reformers cite an aesthetic criterion to justify their goals. Organizations in need of consensus would then have to be described as fat and sluggish. However, it should not be overlooked that what is always at issue is how the importance of decisions is distributed among decision-makers.

34. See James G. March, Eine Chronik der Überlegungen über Entscheidungsprozesse in Organisationen, in idem. (ed.), *Entscheidung und Organisation, German translation* Wiesbaden 1990, 1–23 (15) with further references.

35. In the sense of George Spencer Brown, *Laws of Form*, reprint of the 2nd ed. New York 1979, 56 ff., 69. ff.

36. Research into communication in organizations typically assigns communication a secondary status – as if it were possible to "make" decisions first and then to communicate them. Any strict connection between decision and communication is generally also lacking. We can communicate all sorts of things: information, opinions, desires, etc. But then it becomes difficult to distinguish between communications within (the autopoietic context of) organizations and communications outside (e.g., private communications during work). For a comprehensive overview of theories, see Anna Maria Theis, *Organisationskommunikation: Theoretische Grundlagen und empirische Forschungen*, Opladen 1994.

37. In this we differ from other attempts to integrate decision theory and communication theory, which regard the individual as a node in a network of information processing. See, e.g., Terry Connolly, Information Processing and Decision Making in Organizations, in: Barry M. Staw and Gerald R. Salancik (eds.), *New Directions in Organizational Behavior*, Chicago 1977, 205–234.

38. See Ruesch and Bateson loc. cit. (1951), 179 ff., 186, 191 ff.

39. Projected onto metaphysical positions, this means that we can assume neither an objectively given world (which can be described only as true or false) nor a subject theory or an action theory; nor can we claim that there is a presupposed norm that tells us it is reasonable to seek understanding and consensus. For a comparable analysis, which, however, resolves the concept of the linguistic proposition somewhat differently, see Gilles Deleuze, *Logique du sens*, Paris 1969, 22 f. Here, too, the result is that the concept of meaning is a paradoxical concept.

40. For a still useful overview see Jonathan Culler, *On Deconstruction: Theory and Criticism After Structuralism*, Ithaca, NY 1982.

41. For further treatment see Chapter 7 – 6

42. See Michel Crozier, *L'Entreprise à l'écoute: Apprendre le management post-industriel*, Paris 1989, 201.

43. See J. Keith Murnighan and Donald E. Conlon, The Dynamics of Intense Work Groups: A Study of British String Quartets, *Administrative Science Quarterly* 36 (1991), 165–186, in connection to Kenwyn Smith and David Berg, *Paradoxes of Group Life*, San Francisco 1987.

44. On the subject of macro-societal communication media see Niklas Luhmann, Symbiotische Mechanismen, in idem, *Soziologische Aufklärung* vol. 3, Opladen 1981, 228–244.

45. Now, above all, Gilles Deleuze subscribes to a theory that localizes meaning on the surface of phenomena. See *Logique du sens*, Paris 1969.

46. See Giovan Francesco Lanzara, *Capacità negativa: Competenza progettuale e modelli di intervento nelle organizzazioni*, Bologna 1993, 173 f. See also idem, Ephemeral Organizations in Extreme Environments: Emergence, Strategy, Extinction, *Journal of Management Studies* 20 (1983), 71–95. Lanzara shows above all that nascent organizations and ephemeral organizations (after a disaster) have to rely particularly strongly on this direct intelligibility guaranteed by perceivable meaning.

47. There is an abundant literature on the subject under the heading of problem definition. See, e.g., Walter R. Reitman, Heuristic Decision Procedures, Open Constraints, and the Structure of Ill-Defined Problems, in: W. M. Shelley and G. L. Bryan (eds.), *Human Judgments and Optimality*, New York 1964, 282–315; W. F. Pounds, The Process of Problem Finding, *Industrial Management Review* 11 (1969), 1–19. Also in: Louis R. Pondy, Richard J. Boland, Jr., and Howard Thomas (eds.), *Managing Ambiguity and Change*, Chichester 1988.

5   Time Relations

A theory positing that social systems in general and organizations in particular do not consist of fixed particles (let alone individuals), but only of events that disappear as soon as they come into being, places unusual importance on the time dimension. The consequences are far-reaching. To a considerable degree, they contradict what we think of as time with regard to things, changes, and movements, seduced by the perceptual apparatus of the consciousness. We must therefore be very cautious in clarifying how systems that consist only of events, and that therefore have to produce other events from moment to moment, deal with time. Only when we have sufficiently elucidated these modalities of realizing time can we recognize how the paradox of decision communication is resolved in organizations, namely distributed among different points in time with different pasts and futures.

The question of what time *is* in essence has repeatedly proved unanswerable, and is probably the wrong question. We shall therefore not pursue it any further, but ask instead how time is calculated – by psychic systems or by social systems. This perspective is blocked by a sort of ban on aggregation. Points in time cannot be added up, even if they can be dated or otherwise indicated. There is no such calculation along the lines of (Tuesday between Monday and Wednesday) + (Wednesday between Tuesday and Thursday) = x. And it is not only that x cannot be resolved. The whole calculation seems somehow wrong. In other words, there is no total today.

The aggregation ban points to the irreducible meaning of points in time, which, unlike points in space, cannot be summed to form greater territories. This might have to do with the fact that the relations between places and objects are differently ordered in time than in space. Whereas in space objects can leave their positions and we can follow their movement, in time positions leave their objects, *something that we can neither see nor remember.* And even if nothing moves, "flows" (though this is the wrong metaphor), time and the world grow older. And time itself does not move. If we represent its "passing" as movement, this is no more than a visualization aid and a technique for measuring time.

For a theory of organization, these are certainly unusually abstract, far-fetched considerations. We mention them merely so that in what follows they can be taken as given in two regards. They are important in understanding the dependence of all events and all operations on given points in time. Points in time disappear of their own accord, even if one does nothing, and they cannot be marked as such but only with the help of a difference, that between past and future. But this schema can be used only when one expects something new of the future. The unknownness of the future, as has repeatedly been pointed out, is an indispensable condition for the possibility of making decisions.[1] The future is not only different from the past: it promises novelty as surprise, as information. Being different could be preserved in transition to the past, but novelty disappears as soon as it becomes present and thus known. To be exact, one cannot even recall novelty. Memory does not admit it. At best, one can reconstruct that what has passed today once had a then-unknown future.

This theory of time calculation is accordingly important for a theory of memory.[2] That points in time and, with them, the surprise value of information constantly disappear – leaving not even a trace – explains how memory deals with time. The task of memory is not, or only exceptionally, to occasionally re-actualize past states of affairs.[3] The memory accompanies every operation of information processing, regulating what is to be recalled and what can be forgotten. Time itself is one of the conditions for the possibility of forgetting, against which the memory then constructs schemata enabling the selective reuse of what is irretrievably past.

In general, the memory of an organization does not retain *why* a decision was made the way it was. This has to do not least with the ambivalence of the "why" question. In this regard, the organization must accordingly rely on the individual memory of participants, and this will often produce widely differing output. It will therefore often prove expedient to proceed on the basis of the situation created by the decision without asking why. One then takes uncertainty absorption for granted.

Another likely advantage of the individual memory is that it can work with analogies. This, too, endangers social accord, for the choice of analogy cannot be controlled in communication, or only with great effort and delay. And this brings us to assume that an organization normally operates with its own memory, resorting to the richer but more uncertain memory of individuals only on occasion.

II

Societal communication calculates its time (as does the consciousness in a different way) on the basis of a brief, event-determined, immediately elapsing present.[4] Time is always actual, but only in the sense that its actuality is exposed to non-actual time horizons: the given past and the given future.

The present is accordingly not a brief interval between past and future. It is nothing other than the difference between past and future and only as difference (and not as momentary absence of being) does it have actuality. It *is* only in that it *is no longer and not yet*. It has no place in the world. To use an old expression, it is the *átopon*. If, in keeping with a tradition stretching back to antiquity, we describe time as movement (but what except the clock obliges us to do so?), we would have to say the given unity of actuality and non-actuality moves from non-actuality into non-actuality. For every description, whether as immobile or mobile, is operationally made or read only in the given actual present, but has to include the given non-actual time horizons, because otherwise neither the immobile nor the mobile can be described as identical. Only thus can something fixed in the system serve for something that is indicated as not fixed. Only thus can a system relate its eigentime and hence the ordering of its self-mobility, its progression from event to event to an environment that, although surrounding it, is inaccessible. And it can then remain open whether the time of the environment, if there is such a thing, exists on the basis of "repeatedly actual" as enduring actuality (e.g., of God), or whether it is the non-actuality that is only divided into past and future by the momentary present.[5]

In observational operations, the necessity to proceed on the basis of distinctions and to indicate only one of the two sides corresponds to this time dependence. As we have already noted,[6] the marking of the one side requires the other to be free for later re-marking. Every fixing of unity, including that of decisions, therefore has to be based on the possibility of oscillation between the two sides of all the distinctions used, and has to have a memory at its disposal that enables unmarking and reuse for something identical. To this extent, unity is always constituted counterfactually by skipping the need to separate release and reuse purely operationally. Unity is the contraction of a time difference, and only for this reason does it make sense to distinguish identities as structures from the events and processes that they generate and use as memory to regulate oscillation.

This applies in general and also when observation takes no note of time differences. In time-related observation, the environment of the system appears to be simultaneously actual, simultaneous with the currently actualized operations of the system. Similarly, organizations themselves are simultaneously occupied all the time with various matters, and this also applies for the coordination of activities. The typical description of organized decisions as a sequence of operations is thus highly misleading. For even if decisions come to be linked up, attention in the system remains diffuse and the information taken into account or left out of account, as well as the excluded alternatives, are not also coordinated. All those involved in deciding communicate at the same time against the background of differing opinions.

What exists simultaneously, however, is unobservable and cannot be causally influenced; one needs time to observe and to produce effects. Simultaneity is consequently a temporal expression of the operational inaccessibility of the environment; in other words, an expression of the necessity of constructing the environment, its resistance, its identities and structures, within the system itself. And only experience of the system with itself, experience that is retained by the system memory and can be re-actualized, can show the system which assumptions about the environment hold good and which do not. The same is true, and is repeated, for intra-systemic system/environment relations generated through differentiation. If the system describes itself as a sequence of events, as process, permanently staggered simultaneity is always included. And in this sense, the simultaneity of the other is the other side, the included excluded side of the form of succession.

As pure difference, the present is in itself undetermined. This is the basis for the possibility of decision-making. In other words, the present is at every moment new, at every moment the start of a new story, and it therefore has to become information and decision so that, through the indication of its past and its future, it can gain form for itself. Determination must therefore take place either through recourse to the past or through anticipation of a future, thus always through extension into non-actual times (or times that can be actualized only as "horizon"). This requires memory – for both time horizons.[7] From this point of view, memory is the blind spot in the distinction between past and future. It enables their separation because it enables their reconnection by exploiting the circumstance that both past and future can be "presented" only through selection. Thanks to its memory, the system can oscillate between self-determination through the past and through the future,[8] but only on condition that the present can determine itself only self-referentially and only through recursive excursions into the non-actual: only by decision.

The result of systems defining the actuality of their operations in observation as present is not least that they always find themselves in the midst of time, as if they were players in a game that has already begun.[9] This has a twofold consequence: on the one hand, the necessary retrospect and outlook of currently non-actual time horizons show that the course of the game cannot be calculated but that decisions have instead to be made. And, on the other hand, the observational frame (we shall say the decision-making premises) for concrete decisions also determines the uniqueness of the system that it demarcates. Every marking carries out and also confirms the difference between the marked and unmarked domain of the system in an observed environment and of the world.

From this point of view, the present and the decision are concurrent. The two paradoxes explain each other mutually. The decision copies the time paradox by duplicating it in itself. The past is reconstructed as alternative, the future as difference. The past is deprived of its determinacy, the future of its indeterminacy. The alternative that "arises" from the past in the present situation organizes remembering and forgetting. The difference that is placed in the future as purpose organizes foresight. Thus the decision has to accept itself as paradox in order to provide itself with the resource "memory." In order to gain time, it must hence construct itself as indeterminate, as "to be decided."

All more precise analysis of the memory function will confirm the need to make risky decisions. After all, memory is not a resource that is only occasionally used, activated when past occurrences are to be recalled. The memory serves rather to discriminate constantly between forgetting and remembering, between releasing operational capacities and constructing identities for repeated use. In this sorting function, the memory is used in every observational operation and is at the same time re-actualized. It confirms, as it were, the state from which the operation sets out; it re-actualizes the world in the mode of knownness. Only from this perspective can irritations, unusualness, surprises, information, and plans for innovation be recognized as deviations. Not only is forgetting forgotten but also the sorting function itself; for the memory would sabotage itself if it wished constantly to recall that it had distinguished between what was to be forgotten and what was to be remembered. Consequently, the system has to include the risk of forgetting something in the decision, and understand it as a risk of decision-making – of making decisions in an unknown world with infinite possibilities of further information.

Contrary to the commonly accepted view that the function of memory is to retrieve the past and make it accessible as far as possible, our investigations show that memory invisibilizes the past, stamping it as concluded because nothing can be changed. It puts itself in the place of the past. What is retained is only what can be used in the present and what relieves the burden on information processing through redundancy. And if the memory looks back over the dated past (which can occur only in exceptional cases), it constructs itself a present past under the implicit condition that the past itself remains inaccessible.

These are conceptual dispositions with far-reaching implications. They no longer permit the future to be seen as amenable to rational planning and control. The concept of "rational expectations" now appears to be paradoxical. Instead, they justify regarding organizations as autopoietic systems. For if a system observes the present of its operating as decision, it constitutes from within itself an internal indeterminacy with which it can occupy itself in the form of information processing. Indeterminacy is accordingly not the result of dependence on independent variables and thus on the environment. As with second-order equations in Spencer-Brown's calculus,[10] it is rather a self-generated, autonomously produced indeterminacy, which is available for independent uncertainty absorption – insofar that the system has a memory.

Decision and memory thus determine one another. As a present relating to itself, the decision can come about only on the basis of recursions that presuppose memory. On the other hand, the memory of organizations presupposes constant reimpregnation by decisions in order to discriminate between forgetting and remembering. This circumstance explains the constitutive importance and not only the technical usefulness of the written word for organizations.

First of all, writing (or now the functionally equivalent computer) selects what is to be forgotten, what remembered. And here, as in the neurophysiological network of the brain, forgetting is the normal process and remembering the exception.[11] Despite the use of the written word, the decision remains a time-bound event, which can, however, distribute itself in space and time – can, so to speak, break itself down into sub-events. For information can only surprise once and never again; the utterance of the written decision cannot be repeated as action (although it can be corrected), and understanding is also a one-off event, even if it can be remembered. Although writing gives considerable range to the decision-making event, so that it is advisable to date decisions, every breakdown of this decision-making event forces all components into the form of single events, which for their part have to rely on remembering the decision and its date.

But writing itself is only the physical substratum of memory and not memory itself. Just as the consciousness does not remember the neurophysiology of its brain, its memory being based precisely on the repression of corresponding information, in written communication it is not the writing that is recalled but the text that has functioned as communication. In this regard, too, the system is accordingly autopoietically autonomous – and at the same time dependent on external support. This naturally does not exclude, is indeed a condition for, the outdifferentiation of a special administration for the written residues of operating, thus the establishment of registers and archives and the protection of material against mice and decay. One also knows that a not inconsiderable proportion of subordinate activities of the system consists in looking for and transporting files.

The phenomenology of files could give the impression that the system is lethargic under the weight of its history. However, this would be to overlook the fact that records "organize" not only remembering but also forgetting. And that, reread as texts, they can motivate both conformity and deviation. The communication of decisions on a written basis generates its own time, a time for self-mobility, for dynamic stability; and the empirically undeniable obstacles to innovation may have quite different grounds, for instance, "organizational culture" not recorded in the files.[12]

III

For organizations, the structures of their own constitution of time are binding, since organizations generate themselves as social systems in society; on the other hand, they are weakened by societal time regulation, above all the measurement of time. The paradox of time, its unity of actuality and non-actuality, need not disquiet organizations. Instead, they keep to time as domesticated by society, to given time semantics, and to the usual measurement of time. For organizations, measured time therefore runs at the same pace in the system and in the environment. If this is Tuesday, it is Tuesday everywhere, and if clocks do not agree, they are either fast or slow. For more than a century now there has even been a regulatory world time. The world ages in step, and if a decision is made at a given point in time, it is made everywhere and for everyone at this point in time. We are no longer even astonished at this significant civilizational achievement.

This societal domestication of time does not mean that the paradox of time, namely the unity of actuality and non-actuality, has disappeared. The question is rather about the form in which it returns, or how it becomes a problem.

Probably the most important precondition is the simultaneity of system and environment; we could also say the unity of world time. This means that everything that happens at the same time.[13] While the organization is occupied with its present, nothing can already happen in its future; nor can the organization hurry ahead of society into the future and make decisions there that are not made for its environment but are still to come in the mode of uncertainty. These are radical simplifications, which, however, have their cost, namely that what happens simultaneously cannot be controlled, either informationally or causally, either through knowledge or through action. The system can try to compensate for this loss of control. We could speak of problems of synchronization. What is at issue is not the production of the fundamental simultaneity of all actual events in system and environment but the coordination of these events, in organizations, decisions, with what has happened in the system and in the environment in the past and what will happen there in the future. As we see, the repressed time paradox takes its vengeance by setting a task that cannot be fulfilled.

For the synchronization demanded can only take place in the system and always only in the short moment of actualizing time.[14] It uses a recursive network of memories and anticipation under conditions that shift from moment to moment. To this end, identities relatively fixed in time have to be formed and updated from moment to moment. The system therefore has to have a highly selective memory at its disposal, mostly in the form of written reports, documents, files that record not only information but above all the system's own decisions. For every decision, its suitability as future past thus has to be planned, as well. The organization is constantly at work writing its own memoirs without being able to foresee what elements will be needed again. Experience shows that this anticipatory memory management absorbs a great deal of capacity and, moreover, sets the synchronization of the system on a course in which self-reference is favored over other-reference. This allows the system to operate essentially from within itself. Changes then have to take the form of innovation, and innovation has to take the form of a disturbance of experience and routine. When under pressure to select, the system prefers to synchronize itself with itself, but can do so in forms that are more or less sensitive to the environment, so that irritation and hence information is produced. What counts as environment is only what can be shaped by the organization.[15]

This might well sound like a reproach, which is how it would be meant in the usual complaints about "bureaucracy." But the contrary is the case. Before judging, the basis on which judgment is to be made has to be established and one has to recognize how improbable innovation is and how doubly improbable innovation based on the interpretation of environmental events is. "The human situation (permits) invention only under conditions of considerable effort."[16] We will see that a system that reproduces itself through the autopoiesis of decision-making synchronizes itself far more than is otherwise usual and possible, also with respect to the future, and consequently operates in the mode of "what would be if ..." More than is possible in other systems, decision-making is seen as what makes a difference (= generates information) in relations between past and future. What allows all present to be experienced as the separating difference between past and future is projected as difference into the future.

For if one has to decide, the future is thought of as a difference – a difference between what is to be achieved through the decision and what would be the case without it. This difference is usually referred to as "purposes."[17] A purpose can be understood as an actual problem and a decision as an actually communicated solution to the problem, which with its communication becomes past, whatever happens afterward. At the same time, however, the purpose projects itself into the future as difference between the state aspired to and the state that would otherwise pertain. It can thus, because it is understood in the mode of non-actuality – in the mode of the "not yet" – be treated as a relatively stable identity, as a form, almost as a thing, and kept available for recursive intervention. As a difference that is at present non-actual, the purpose must have a value that is already convincing in the present.[18] And if the purpose aspired to is projected into the future, one has time. It is possible to differentiate the purpose itself, to distinguish between means and ends, to outdifferentiate means as sub-purposes, to distinguish between important and less important aspects of the intended state. In brief, it permits one to fill out the future – at present unknown and remaining unknown – with a network of identities, which for their part can be remembered and where needful actualized.

But purpose is only a special case of difference. It focuses the future on a difference generated by decision between attaining and not attaining the purpose. If we wish to include other possibilities for giving form to the future, it is advisable to translate the conceptuality of purpose into more general terms. We therefore speak of distinctions (necessary for observation) that make it possible to oscillate between the two sides of the distinction. This allows us to include such distinctions as useful/harmful, good/bad, friend/enemy, even marked/unmarked.[19] The future is then determined by the choice of distinction with which one observes at present, and at the same time remains indeterminate because which side of the distinction will be actualized in future presents and under what conditions remains open.

If a future susceptible to oscillation is postulated, however, the past is also not what it was. It is only selectively recalled in recursions, which are always to be carried out in the present, and is thus also selectively forgotten.[20] In view of an unknown future, it could therefore be useful to read "trends" into the past. One has survived, and that suffices.[21] The past can thus be constantly adapted to what transpires from oscillation. In the process of divorce, the spouse is no longer but nevertheless the person one had married. For the analysis of decision-based organizations, all "genealogical" theories are therefore inadequate that proceed on the assumption of an origin or a founding and assume that the foundation in some sense dominates what has been founded.[22] The operation of observing, which takes place in the present and de-actualizes its time horizons, has primacy in any case – the primacy of facticity. Whatever mishaps might occur, what is important for the continuation of the system's autopoiesis is only finding a follow-on operation. To this end, however, the generation of a common past and a common future is likely to be useful, indeed indispensable. And both time horizons can be kept stable, because they are both non-actual.

Decisions can always be made only in actuality and always only at the same time with everything that is otherwise actually happening. But this actuality is nothing other than the difference between past and future, and to actualize this difference, the system needs to know how past and future differ – apart from the purely formal distinction that a decision can no longer be made in the past and cannot yet be made in the future. This separation and linking of time horizons serves the identities on which the system orients itself recursively. Past and future, thus memory and oscillation, mirror one another: the past had determined itself with regard to the then future, and the future is taken into consideration on the basis of purposes that, in this way or another, one had always wanted to attain. Through such recursions, the present eliminates the need always to determine everything anew from its own nothing. And only thus is it conceivable at all for an organization to use its decisions to separate and connect pasts and futures from moment to moment.

Purposes are accordingly not motivating factors that, in the sense of Max Weber, permit action to be "interpretively explained" [*verstehend erklärt*]. It is rather the difficulties shifted to the future that allow decision chains to be added and, even if the decisions are long past, repeatedly to refer to them. They are structuring elements of a system memory enabling past and future to be synchronized in the present.[23] James March's proposal to describe organizations as systems in search of purposes is therefore well considered.[24]

IV

In a fast-moving society with innumerable simultaneous structural changes and many overlapping causal chains producing unexpected effects, with mass media geared to information, and thus to novelty, and with rapid changes in technological possibilities and their consequences, organizations, even if they contribute to all this, appear to be slow, sluggish, if not conservative. The hectic pace at which they now commit themselves to "innovation" without considering how its effects can be controlled supports this diagnosis.[25] The tempo required might then well be due to the effects of innovation rather than to their internal logic. But this impression could be deceptive. In a further analysis, which again proceeds on the assumption that organizations are concerned with the autopoiesis of decisions, we shall therefore examine and revise this impression.

The normal notion of time sees the past as concluded and unchangeable and the future as open to change, which one partly can bring about intentionally, and partly has to let happen and to accept against expectations. This hardly contestable relationship between past and future, however, tends to be reversed by decisions, or at least corrected by an opposing principle. Decision-making is possible owing to an exchange of temporal determination. The past remains irreversibly determinate and the future indeterminate, but the decision postulates that it is not determined by the past and for this reason must determine the future. But how is this reversal carried out?

On the one hand, ties to the past are loosened owing to the reconstruction of what has resulted from history as an open alternative, as a choice. This generates the impression that a new story begins with the decision. In order to commit oneself by making decisions, what the "historical machine" system – which always sets out from its own states – has determined needs to be set aside, but naturally not to such an extent that the system can no longer ascertain its own identity. On the other hand, the possibilities of the future that are relevant for making decisions need to be limited, very typically by defining purposes, but also, for example, through the notion of limited risks or certain dangers. The future therefore has to be introduced into the past, and the past into the future. Only thus is extended time and not only present time understood as a medium of possible decisions, and only thus can the decision be understood as a form of "time binding."[26]

With Shackle we can resume this analysis in noting that a new story begins with every decision[27] – a story, however, that consists of decisions, and which will thus generate new stories, which then have to rely on uncoupling themselves from a past that determines them. With decisions, indeterminacy is accordingly introduced into the story, always selective, always actual. What has already been decided has become past and is therefore definite. At any rate this is what one thinks. At the same time, however, every decision still to be made searches its past, to which past decisions also belong, for information and alternatives. The terrain is continually being replowed; but in a way that cannot be described as a linear process (or only in extremely rough simplification). The next decision hence distinguished another past and another future, even with the same purposes in mind. It cannot undo what has happened, but it can correct it.

The common denominator of the autopoiesis of decision-making is therefore uncertainty, uncertainty with the prospect of uncertainty. In what follows we shall therefore also be speaking of uncertainty absorption – not only in the sense that uncertainty is more and more reduced but also in the sense that uncertainty is built up at the same time, and thus renewed. We could also say that organization is the (self-continuing) autopoiesis of the *form* of certainty – that is to say, a two-sided form with uncertainty on the one side.

Thus, by fixing the result of its past as alternative, a decision generates an uncertain future. By presenting a multiplicity of possibilities as simultaneously given, it generates ignorance about how things are to continue.[28] The lack of knowledge is, after all, a necessary complement to the notion of possibilities. The decision thus also generates the disturbability of the course it intends. Without decisions there would be no forecastable future, and therefore no disappointments and no planning of behavior to deal with possible disappointments, and thus no norms either. "Angels can still fall and the devils can multiply," according to Jean Paul, who continues, "no finite being can prophesy his will and say he will do and want this or that in the week to come. For if he also fulfils his prophecy, he does so not with his previous will but with that of the moment."[29]

If this is so, it means that ignorance about the future cannot be changed. In this regard it makes no difference how knowledge is distributed socially and whether someone has better knowledge at his disposal than someone else. The search for further information also concerns only the past. To this extent, we need to correct the widespread view that more information gives us a better grip on the future.[30] The uncertainty that information removes is not uncertainty about the future but uncertainty about the choice to be made in a domain of selection. However, a decision-maker with an enriched memory can see more possibilities, use more differentiated schemata, and, to put it in somewhat old-fashioned terms, can decide more wisely. This is the sole advantage that milieu knowledge and expertise offer.[31] But this means only that the decision-maker has more complex structures at his disposal, which differentiate ignorance about the future but do not eliminate it: through schemata, scripts, cognitive maps, implicit theories – all concepts that are concerned with memory and not with the future. It is therefore hardly surprising that the unknownness of the future cannot influence the efficiency of organizations.[32]

With every effort to gain a better basis for making decisions, for gaining more knowledge or new information, the difference between past and future remains, as does the transience of the given actual present, which constitutes its past and its future as a difference. This raises the question of how, under these conditions, a decision can be observed and described at all. There must be semantic forms that allow such durable observation of past decisions as well as the observation (which means the distinguishing and indicating) of expected future decisions. How, for example, is the identity of a decision constituted as an object of observation (which is itself possible only as event)? There is no doubt that the observation of past and future events is also possible: yesterday one met a friend, agreed for him to call, and is now waiting for him to do so. Events can thus be durably identified and can thus be repeatedly referred to. This is also the case for decisions, insofar that they are events – but also insofar that they are decisions? To the extent that they reverse temporal determination and, we might say, de-determine themselves with regard to the past in order to gain the possibility of limiting the future?

We often read that one can only know how one has decided after the decision has been made.[33] At any rate, only the decision makes it possible to include reactions to it in its meaning. But even then the identity of a decision remains a construction, which calls on memory, and thus on forgetting, and establishes itself as the form of an event, as "this and nothing other" only with the aid of recursion. But this is also true when one considers how future decisions can be identified on the lines of "what would be if." Incidentally, this retrospective relationship with oneself is difficult to achieve in computers. They always need programming ex ante, even if on this basis they are supposed to be capable of learning. Psychic and social systems, by contrast, can learn purely on the basis of memory through schemata confronted with new situations. In other words, in learning they can let the future be. They work with a schematized past, whereas the computer requires a schematized future.

It is therefore worthwhile inquiring into the time relations of decision-making in so complicated a fashion. We then see that computerized decision-making processes owe their certainty only to the circumstance that the unknownness of the future is replaced by a program, whereas organizational decision-making communication normally sets out from a continually revised past (whatever justification is offered at the secondary level). Certainty is not to be gained from observing and describing decisions, either. This is precisely what the concept of risk expresses. Risks have no ontological locus in the world; the concept (in contrast to the concept of danger) describes a form of observing decisions.[34] The function of this form becomes clear when we consider the disastrous consequences that would occur if the future were known or if this were to be believed. Every decision would then prove unnecessary, because what is foreseen would happen anyway. Risk awareness is therefore a functionally equivalent attitude toward the future that makes deciding possible in the first place; in practice, an antidote is then needed, a more or less unrealistic reduction of risk awareness.

After all is said and done, decisions are not predicatable objects but difference-generating operations. Such a complex state of affairs cannot be "identified," or at least only symbolically. The solution is nevertheless relatively simple (and only its description is complicated): one observes the alternative to be decided differently depending on whether one focuses on the time before the decision or on the time after the decision.[35] In both perspectives the components of the alternative are observed as contingent. With regard to the decision, its realization is neither necessary nor impossible, and thus contingent,[36] for otherwise there would be nothing to decide. But the point in time when a decision is made changes the form of contingency. Before the decision, contingency is open, the choice of every possibility is still conceivable. After the decision, contingency is closed, a different decision is no longer possible and at best one can correct course by a new decision. But alternativity and with it contingency remain. They are not eliminated by the decision nor are they transformed into a different modality of necessity or impossibility. Otherwise one could neither criticize nor regret a decision, one could neither make it an object of reproach nor a topic of responsibility. Precisely the observation and registration of a decision as decision records the alternative in the system memory, hence facilitating re-actualization. The excluded possibilities are retained as possibilities. Disregarded interests can make their presence felt again, the opportunities not taken up are lost and for that very reason become more important.

This alone explains why one can fear decisions, why one shuns risks because subsequent changes in assessment and even in assessment criteria are to be expected.[37] Especially in organizational situation assessment, open contingency often seems less problematic than closed contingency, which can give cause for reproach. However, the organization is not free to choose the transition from open to closed contingency at will. For even the decision not yet to decide about a certain matter is a decision that closes the contingency of its alternative, and to this extent must, under certain circumstances, be regretted. Since all events are bound to points in time, one cannot decide later to have decided earlier.

The decision before the decision accordingly differs from that after the decision, and during the decision (at the same time) one cannot observe it at all. The decision (if someone asks what it "is") is thus a paradox: the same and not the same. Furthermore it is a reentry of time into time, namely a reentry of the difference between past and future that is experienced in the present into itself – with all the consequences that Spencer-Brown mentions for his calculus of form. For, on the one hand, time in the operational mode is present in the form of transition from what is already elapsing to that which is just beginning to be actual. This holds true for all conscious perception and thought,[38] but also for current communication, which, like the operations of the consciousness, needs time, while at the same time letting something become irrevocably past by continuing the operation with what has not yet been uttered and through passive realization. If, by contrast, a decision is made, the difference between past and future, between memory and oscillation, is marked in a certain way. It re-occurs in time in that the decision articulates itself in time as decision with the aid of the time difference. One does not allow time simply to come and go; for the future one generates a difference from what would occur without a decision from the past.

This reentry (like every reentry) is a form of paradox unfolding. Time in time is the same time and also not the same time. This means that the decision generates an operationally not determined situation in which it can act as decision and by decision can resolve indeterminacy into determinate performance. In this sense, every decision is new. Every decision begins a new story. But the decision owes this possibility only to the reentry that it carries out of time into time. Decision-making is therefore the resolution of a self-generated indeterminacy. And only for this reason can a decision be differently observed but nevertheless as the same, depending on whether the observer localizes it in his future or in his past.

However, precisely this is not a bad thing, since in organizations one generally knows or can find out whether a decision has already been made or not. We again confront the paradox – in unfolded form, distributed across two distinguishable distinctions. What we learn theoretically from our somewhat complicated analysis is that time is required to resolve the basic paradox. But also that the practical situations and concerns typical of organized work in particular can be better understood in this way.

V

A decision divides "its" time into past and future. Past is given in the mode of immutability and future in the mode of the not-yet-determinate. From the two currently non-actual time horizons, the decision finds orientation for its own actual realization. It integrates its past and its future. Only thus can it determine itself; only thus does it come about as an event that is determined neither by the past nor by the future.

Here we need to probe a little deeper and show how this happens. Clearly not in the sense of causal determination (even though an observer can attribute causes). But the usual conception that it is oneself that makes one's (what? whose?) choice is not satisfying, for it leads us astray into the mystery of unfathomable judgments or "will" formation. But we do not want to know how the decision is explained in order to withstand critical scrutiny in a supposedly rational organization and, where necessary, to elicit decisions on responsibility for the decision. We want to know how the decision is made.

All that helps is more precise analysis of the recursions typically activated in such cases. As we shall see in the chapter on programming, orientational focus can be anchored in the past or shifted to the future. It is then provided by conditional programs or purposive programs. The decision can either be restricted if not imposed by conditions set in the past, or shift a purpose to the future that indicates a difference from what would otherwise occur. Both forms of using non-actual time horizons have the function of shifting responsibility in accordance with requirements onto programmers; and along with this, a shift in responsibility to provide a mode of rational justification. In this manner, rationality is coupled with discharge from responsibility. Rationality is a form with which one can excuse oneself. In this sense it is a "motive" as presentable explanation. The range of responsibility for decisions can then in crises be so reduced that the criticized decision can be presented as imposed by programs and circumstances.

We can understand the attractiveness of such a combination of rationality and responsibility shift, and also the basis on which classical theory associated hierarchy with rationality. But it is also clear that this does not exhaust the temporal recursions with which the decision determines itself. Apart from this official consideration of time, it is taken into unofficial account: the manifest treatment is attended by a more latent consideration: repetition. From this perspective, past decisions are relevant if they have been received without complaint, and can thus be presumed to be acceptable. Whoever holds a different view has to bear the risk of the innovation, has to argue, has to take the onus of proof on himself. The future is accordingly brought into play from the point of view of the precedent effect of decisions. The decision-maker and the parties that accept the decision also have to keep in mind that similar cases will be dealt with in future on the same pattern; or at least that a pending decision will raise expectations in this direction. If everyday routine has once set in, countermeasures come as a surprise – and too late. Greater effort will foreseeably be required. It is therefore preferable to form an appropriate habit right away.

Anyone who knows organizations from within knows the care with which these problems of repetition are handled and which induce retrospection and forethought. They are among the most important causes of probably unnecessary conflicts that nonetheless make preventive sense (the same naturally applies in marriages and families, where a great deal of everyday "stress" is due to the inability to turn a blind eye). The forbearance of one-off cooperation cannot be made permanent. What is particularly serious is that what can be "repeated" in the way of decisions is by no means self-evident but has to be constructed. Identities are not given, they have to be selectively extracted from the material; they have to be condensed. Experience helps, and thus a person's length of service. But psychic factors are also likely to have an effect on this organization-determined variable: some may fear repetition more than others; some rely more on formulas while others are confident they will come up with something should the need arise. Precisely because repetition, recognizability, and identity are not nature-given phenomena but constructions, structural couplings can be effective; above all there is no guarantee that such constructions will remain unchanged over time or that everyone involved will see them in the same way. This is why access to what is meant is difficult in this domain, and the extent to which decisions can work with unformulated premises of this sort could be a matter of organizational culture.

At this point we cannot go into such details. It should be noted that, apart from programmed recursions, there are also these non-programmed recursions, and that the recognition of repetitions does not necessarily depend on program requirements. Nor is there any guarantee that a more detailed program will reduce or even obviate informal precedent effects. The opposite is even more probable: that the fine filters of defined programs will capture all the more case-related identifications not provided for by the program.

VI

If single decisions require and order time because they generate a difference relating to them between past and future, this is all the more true for a plurality of decisions; at least when such decisions are to be made in the same system. In relation to the environment, an organization, however much forethought it might exercise, will have to tolerate a great deal of chance. Internally, however, greater demands are made on the synchronization of decisions; for this alone allows the system to temporalize its own complexity and to enhance it as sequential order. Dates and deadlines serve this end.

Dates and deadlines provide additional marking for decisions. We speak of dates where the decision has to be presented at a specific point in time and of deadlines where it has to be presented within a certain period of time. Setting a date always has the effect of setting a deadline. To simplify things, we shall therefore be referring only to deadlines while not forgetting that deadlines run only from the occurrence of a specific event (e.g., the receipt of an application), so that they cannot be coordinated from the perspective of a dated end.

Deadlines are additional markings because decisions with a deadline involve an additional distinction: they can be kept or missed. Experience shows that deadlines can considerably influence the quality of a decision: only the amount of work possible within the deadline can be devoted to the decision.[39]

Deadlines are required to produce decision-making contexts, which we shall call *relays*.[40] In such relays there are points in time when the results of prior decisions have to be available as precondition for further decisions. Relays make it possible to combine the advantages of simultaneous parallel work with linear structures. Deadlines are particularly important where there is regional or some other sort of segmentary differentiation that has to be centrally managed. Annual budget planning is naturally subject to deadlines. But also sequential arrangements for various tasks often require dates and deadlines to be set. For instance, a patient has to be prepared for an operation prior to the operation and must therefore be available in the hospital at an early enough date. The tighter time planning is and the shorter deadlines are, the more susceptible the system is to disturbance.[41] This means that time reserves for unforeseeable events are likely to be planned, or reliance is put on everyday routine, which can if necessary be converted into time resources.[42]

Setting deadlines makes time scarce, and does so not evenly but unevenly.[43] Some decision-making sequences have to be considerably accelerated to meet the deadline, and the deadlines set for the decisions that contribute to this become shorter and shorter. In other cases, one has a great deal of time because the deadline is far off or the decision does not require much work. This is often the impression students have when it comes to preparing for examinations. There are meanwhile sophisticated time planning methods by which one can try to rationalize these differences away, so that the time load in the system is more or less evenly distributed and no one can sit around and relax while others have to keep their noses to the grindstone. We must leave this to the specialized literature. By contrast, particular attention needs to be paid to the considerable strain that time pressure can put on attention, which affects the quality of decisions.

Under the pressure of time, easily obtainable information is favored over information that is harder to come by. Quickly produced decision components are favored over those that take more time. In the event of conflict and competition, the first sufficiently elaborated proposals on hand therefore tend to be taken up.[44] A considerable role is played by textualization, reading facilitation, plausible probabilities, and, above all, recourse to experience, to what is already known, to what has been tried and tested. Moreover, time pressure discourages repetition and re-examination. One relies on existing information processing, especially if accountability for any mistakes lies with others.[45] We know from studies on the failure of safety technology how willingly any growing but uncomfortable suspicions are dismissed, even when no decision-making process with a deadline is involved, just the desire to avoid time-consuming investigations.[46]

Whereas these consequences of time scarcity tend to inhabit the cognitive field, there are also consequences for the preference structure of organized decision-making. Work with a deadline is done first. What does not have a deadline and could be done the following day is postponed. Deadlines are therefore not value-neutral. Whatever the program and official ideology of an organization proclaim, operationally effective preferences are steered by dates and deadlines. This is all the more so because the respect of time rules is easier to monitor, because it is subject to a simple yes/no schematism. The cognitive quality of information processing, by contrast, and its conformity with the preferences of the system are much more difficult to monitor; even if they can be checked on, this is not possible in a perceivable way in the workplace (or only in the form of regular top-down exhortations to be courteous or thrifty, to obey regulations, etc.). Universities, to give a particularly drastic example, confront the double task of teaching and research. But since only teaching is governed by dates and can to this extent be monitored (once again, not in its quality but only as to whether it takes place at all), activity tends in practice to shift toward teaching. Whoever does not teach inevitably attracts attention and has to expect sanctions. Whoever does not engage in research can lean back in his chair unchallenged. As far as research is concerned, the organization therefore depends on incentives not at its disposition and affecting only the individual (such as reputation and career), which the science system provides as a non-organized functional system of society. Although this imbalance is compensated for organizationally by the circumstance that the quality of teaching plays hardly any role in appointment decisions because it can hardly be established in a relevant manner, whereas the results of a candidate's past research can be assessed from publications, this constellation can easily lead to a combination of punctual but poorly qualified teaching with flagging zeal in research. Politicians who become aware of this situation but understand nothing about the subject then react with operationally unsuitable solutions such as the introduction of "competition" or regular evaluation rituals.

Another, famous effect of dates and deadlines is the tendency of public authorities to disburse unspent funds at the end of the budgetary year (under whatever pretext) because it would otherwise become apparent that more had been allocated than was needed. Sufficient knowledge of a milieu will provide many such examples. Also clearly apparent is the helplessness of organizations in the face of these effects of deadlines and supervision. One cannot give up structuring time – whether to increase task complexity or to avoid wasting insufficiently exploited time. Finally, the repressed paradox takes its vengeance – now in the relatively harmless form of unwanted effects of unavoidable structures and of countermeasures that do not achieve much because they do not go far enough.

VII

Causality clearly has something to do with time; at least if we assume that causes have to exist before their effects can occur. At most, we abstract *subsequently* from time when we speak of "interaction" or of "circular causality," or in cybernetics of "feedback." But even then, in a realistic perspective that considers not only structures but also operations, we can and have to add time again. Elementary causality in the sense of bringing about effects through causes is thus an occurrence that always takes time and bridges time differences. The switch in time conceptuality from process to the given actual distinction therefore has considerable implications for our understanding of causality.

We assume that causality requires effects to be attributed to causes, thus selection from an infinite horizon of possible causes and a second infinite horizon of possible effects. As we know, such causal attribution can be carried out in very different ways.[47] If we want to know how causality is constructed, we therefore have to observe the observer. At the same time, this second-order observation has to be causally neutralized; otherwise the attributer or the attributer of attribution would be the real cause, the prime cause of all causal events. We can therefore conceive of the causal schema as a special medium that offers possibilities of form formation, which then picks out a convincing context of specific causes and specific effects while ignoring the circumstance that innumerable other causes and innumerable other effects could be considered important in the same causal constellation. There are a number of criteria for the plausibility of such a selection, for example, temporal and possibly spatial proximity (contiguity), repeatability, interventive action. We touch on all this only in brief, bringing us to the question of what really makes causality causality; in other words, what constitutes the unity of the difference between cause and effect. And this brings us to the relationship between causality and time.

For the unity of the difference is clearly not a further cause that has to be added if causality is to come into effect. This would only put off our question. It seems that the choice of the causality observation schema obliges us to assume a "bringing about" in the sense of a coupling of causes (infinitely many) and effects (again infinitely many). The linking of causes and effects (of infinitely many past causes and infinitely many future effects) can take place only in the present, albeit secondarily also in a past or future present projected from the present into a past or the future. Causality accordingly appears to be nothing other than time schematized in a certain manner, as is the case in a different manner for space.

But how is it then possible to establish a causal connection between the currently non-actual causes and effects? How is it possible, without bringing in a further cause (namely the attributer as cause) to lend causality/effectiveness to currently non-actual causes and effects, and thus to carry out an operation without which they would remain ineffective or uncaused? Obviously this is again a trace of the mysterious third that never shows itself because it has to be systematically excluded and can be included only as excluded; or another form of the paradox of decision-making.[48] Causality is evidently neither a cause nor an effect and nevertheless, or for this very reason, a complete, a universal description of the world.

Causality is therefore to be understood as a schema of an observer, that is to say as a medium in which an observer forms. The medium is formed by the possible causal factors (always both causes and effects); the forms come into being through an observer distinguishing between causes and effects, picking out and concretely coupling the causes and effects that interest him. The medium is reproduced by the use of form formation; the forms are determined case by case and lose their relevance when the observer turns to other constellations.

From among the possibilities provided by the medium, the observer must accordingly select those needed for form formation, thus actualizing the non-actual. This would explain why deciding on actions plays such a big role in causal constellations. As it were, the decision materializes the illusory components of causality. It is and remains a personified mystery, but can also be read as an infinite need for "rationalization." Or, per Herbert Simon, as an unrealizable need for more information. The connection between past and future, between worlds of causes and worlds of effects, has to be brought about operationally, thus always now. In other words, there is no causality already offered by the world into which human beings would have to worm their way cunningly (in the old sense of *mechane, machinatio*, mechanically) – which had split the concept of rationality into *logos* and *metis*.[49] The point of departure for all observation of causality and of time is rather the paradox of the observation schema, which can be actualized only as unity but is capable of connection only as difference.

VIII

Setting out from the concept of decision and from the single decision, we had described a decision as a projection of its own time into the world time constituted by society. We now come back to the definition of organizational systems as the autopoiesis of decision-making. The characteristics of the single communication of a decision thus become system characteristics; and since the autopoiesis of decision-making, if it takes place, opens a perspective on the future of the system (that can, however, never be "sure"), we must seek to understand the system with respect to time and especially with regard to the future that it envisages for itself.

As far as the future is concerned, autopoiesis means that no decision generates an ultimate state of the system, a state of repose, but every decision sees a future full of further decisions ahead of it (probably we should rather say behind it; for the decision extricates itself from the past and operates with its back to the future). But like the future itself, future decisions are unknown in the present. The still required or possible decisions articulate, as it were, the unknownness of the future; they fill it with still unknown events. Only for this reason can we speak of an autopoietic *system*.

If we project this onto system variables, it follows that organizations generate their own decision-making capacity, and that the maintenance and improvement of this capacity (instead of rationality) are the real criteria for effective organization. The projection of decision-making time onto world time can be seen as a reentry of time into time. As a result of such reentry, the system finds itself in a state in which it can no longer determine itself through its own operations (in this case decisions) as unity or as a "whole." We could also say that the system finds itself in a state of non-computability.[50] A surplus of possibilities arises, which, while guaranteeing the necessary selection scope for decisions, cannot be itself the subject of a decision. The organizational system cannot by decision guarantee or cancel its own possibility of deciding. It can extend it (e.g., by raising capital) or restrict it (for instance, through contract), but it cannot produce it purposively by means of decisions. If autopoiesis comes about at all at the operational level of decision-making, it generates the conditions of its possibility itself.

The theory of the autopoietic organization can no longer be combined with neoclassical economic theory. For mathematical reasons, there is no room in this theory for open decision-making situations and selective decisions, and certainly no place for an open future reproduced in this fashion. We are thus in line with a frequent criticism of neoclassical theory, which, however, mostly focuses not on the concept of organization but on that of evolution.[51] Further thought needs to be spent on possible combinations of organization theory and evolution theory.

Notes

1. See only Brian J. Loasby, *Choice, Complexity and Ignorance: An Enquiry into Economic Theory and the Practice of Decision-Making*, Cambridge 1976, 2 f., 4 ff.

2. See Castoriadis Bernard Ancori, Apprentissage, temps historique et évolution économique, *Revue internationale de systémique* 7 (1993), 593–612.

3. This is probably the predominant view, which can draw on lexical definitions. See, e.g., James P. Walsh and Gerardo Rivera Ungson, Organizational Memory, *The Academy of Management Review* 16 (1991), 57–91.

4. In decision theory, too, this is noted, although rather with regard to outsiders. "[T]he notion of *the present*, the moment of which, alone, we have direct knowledge, the moment-in-being, the moment of actuality embracing all that is. All that is, is the present," remarks G. L. S. Shackle, Imagination, Formalism, and Choice, in: Mario J. Rizzo (ed.), *Time, Uncertainty, and Disequilibrium: Explorations of Austrian Themes*, Lexington Mass. 1979a, 19–31 (20, see also 25). For greater detail, see G. L. S. Shackle, *Imagination and the Nature of Choice*, Edinburgh 1979b.

5. And we still remember that the old European semantics for a temporally complete description of the world therefore provided a difference for this purpose, that between *aeternitas* and *tempus*.

6. See Chapter 4 . . . (4–2).

7. On this Janus-faced function of memory, see also Heinz von Foerster, Was ist Gedächtnis, daß es Rückschau und Vorschau ermöglicht?, in: Heinz von Foerster, *Wissen und Gewissen: Versuch einer Brücke*, Frankfurt 1993, 299–236. See also the role of the "memory function" with reference to imagined values of the present "in relation with itself" in George Spencer-Brown, *Laws of Form*, reprint New York 1979, 61.

8. See in this regard the distinction between conditional programs and purposive programs in Chapter 8.

9. See also Adam in Milton's Paradise Lost. But the archangel Raphael came to his aid to explain to him the meaning of creation in the form of a text in the text, which at the same time is the text itself. On the mathematical problems of observation, which with its own distinctions also distinguishes observation itself (or with the game that is being played, continues the meta-game of this game), see Louis H. Kauffman, Ways of the Game – Play and Position Play, *Cyberneticces & Human Knowing* 2/3 (1994), 17–34.

10. Ibid., 54 ff.

11. As Heinz von Foerster has shown, a theory of memory therefore requires a mathematics of the prevention of forgetting relating to the smallest units in processing the operations of the system. See Heinz Förster, *Das Gedächtnis*, Wien 1948; Heinz von Foerster, Quantum Mechanical Theory of Memory, in: Heinz von Foerster (ed.), *Cybernetics: Circular Causal, and Feedback Mechanisms in Biological and Social Systems. Transactions of the Sixth Conference 1949*, New York 1950, 112–134. We will be coming back to this under . . .

12. See also Chapters 6–7.

13. For greater detail, cf. Niklas Luhmann, Gleichzeitigkeit und Synchronisation, in: Niklas Luhmann, *Soziologische Aufklärung* vol. 5, Opladen 1990, 95–130.

14. We clearly find this state of affairs in Fichte, as well – albeit with regard to the
I relying on itself. The I arbitrarily sets the present, too, as the point in time
when it becomes involved in a relationship with its non-I. The consequence is:
"For us there is no *past* at all except to the extent that it is conceived of in the
present." What was yesterday ... *is not*; it is only to the extent that at the
present moment I think that it was yesterday." (*Grundriß des Eigentümlichen
der Wissenschaftslehre in Rücksicht auf das theoretische Vermögen* (1795),
Ausgewählte Werke in sechs Bänden vol. 1, Darmstadt 1962, 601). While
according to Fichte such statements can be formulated only transcendentally,
we reempiricize them by reference to the actual and empirically observable
operation of self-referential systems.

15. Karl E. Weick, Organizational Redesign as Improvisation, in: George P. Huber and
William H. Glick (eds.), *Organizational Change and Redesign: Ideas and Insights
for Improving Performance*, Oxford 1993, 346–379 (372 f.) speaks of "enacted
environments." See also Karl E. Weick, *Der Prozeß des Organisierens*, German
translation Frankfurt 1983, 212 ff.

16. See George Kubler, *Die Form der Zeit: Anmerkungen zur Geschichte der Dinge*,
German translation Frankfurt 1982, 117.

17. However, it should be noted that a long tradition has made "teleological" semantics
extremely fuzzy. By purpose, for example, one also understands a goal that can be
attained or not, or a teleological idea or value, where the important thing is the
degree of approximation. Thus distinctions are always in play, whose antonyms
can, however, be variously determined and confusingly exchanged. In the text and
in what follows, we define "purpose" [Zweck] as a future-related difference program and speak of "goal" [Ziel] only when the attain/miss distinction is involved.
A purpose can accordingly very well be a goal when what is at issue is attaining or
not attaining it.

18. This formulation was already possible in the eighteenth century. See, e.g., Karl
Heinrich Heydenreich, *System der Aesthetik*, Leipzig 1790, reprint Hildesheim
1978, 181: "Was ist der Zweck selbst werth?"

19. In this sense, Spencer-Brown, *Laws of Form* (1979), 60 f. speaks of the "oscillator
function," which he considers indispensable as soon as a system carries out
a reentry of the distinction into what is distinguished, thus going beyond the
scope of the usual arithmetic and algebra.

20. Even if the consciousness can still remember, it could be better for communication
not to take up certain things again.

21. See Armen A. Alchian, Uncertainty, Evolution, and Economic Theory, *Journal of
Political Economy* 58 (1950), 211–221; also in Armen A. Alchian, *Economic
Forces at Work*, Indianapolis 1977, 73–110.

22. From the point of view of logic, we are thus venturing onto the difficult terrain of
a transclassical or polycontextural logic that includes calculation in calculation.
On the "elimination of any genealogy" and on the "deconstruction of the ground" as
the main problem and real achievement of these logics, see Rudolf Kaehr,
Disseminatorik: Zur Logik der "Second Order Cybernetics": Von den "Laws of
Form" zur Logik der Reflexionsform, in: Dirk Baecker (ed.), *Kalkül der Form*,
Frankfurt 1993, 152–196 (170 ff.). Empirically, it is likely to be comforting that we
have no choice anyway.

23. See von Foerster, Was ist Gedächtnis, daß es Rückschau *und* Vorschau ermöglicht?.

24. See James G. March and Johan P. Olsen, *Ambiguity and Choice in Organizations*, Bergen, Norwegen 1976.

25. See Ralph Grossmann, Ewald E. Krainz, and Margit Oswald (eds.), *Veränderung in Organisationen: Management und Beratung*, Wiesbaden 1995, with reports from praxis.

26. The concept comes from Alfred Korzybsky, *Science and Sanity: An Introduction to Non-Aristotelian Systems and General Semantics* (1933), reprint of the 4th edn. Lakeville Conn. 1958. Korzybsky applies this concept to language, thus to communication per se. But this presupposes a second-order observer, because binding time through communication is, after all, not communicated, and does not become a topic of communication. But precisely this changes when a decision is communicated.

27. "Engenderment of history" Rizzo (ed.), *Time, Uncertainty, and Disequilibrium*, 27.

28. See also Shackle, Imagination and the Nature of Choice, 27: "Plural possibilities entertained by the chooser imply unknowledge in some degree."

29. See Jean Paul, *Traum eines bösen Geistes vor seinem Abfalle, Jean Pauls Werke: Auswahl in zwei Bänden*, Stuttgart 1924, 269–273 (269).

30. See, e.g., Arthur L. Stinchcombe, *Information and Organizations*, Berkeley 1990.

31. See, e.g., Daniel J. Isenberg, The Structure and Process of Understanding: Implications for Managerial Action, in: Henry P. Sims, Jr. and Dennis A. Gioia et al. (eds.), *The Thinking Organization: Dynamics of Organizational Social Cognition*, San Francisco 1986, 238–262.

32. See Ellen Earle Chaffee and Jack Y. Krakower, The Impact of Resource Predictability and Management Strategy on Performance, in: Louis R. Pondy, Richard J. Boland Jr. and Howard Thomas (eds.), *Managing Ambiguity and Change*, Chichester 1988, 157–176.

33. "Only after action has taken place is the administrator able to give a historical account of what has happened, and the psychiatrist is very much in the same position," we read in Jurgen Ruesch and Gregory Bateson, *Communication: The Social Matrix of Psychiatry*, New York 1951, 2nd edn. 1968, 59. For Karl E. Weick, *Sensemaking in Organizations*, Thousand Oaks Cal. 1995, too, sensemaking is a retrospective activity and the manager accordingly a historian. See, esp., 184 f.: "What is crucial about this is that a decision is an act of interpretation rather than an act of choice."

34. Greater detail in Niklas Luhmann, Risiko und Gefahr, in Niklas Luhmann, *Soziologische Aufklärung* vol. 5, Opladen 1990, 131–169; Niklas Luhmann, *Risk: A Sociological Theory*. Translated by Rhodes Barrett, Berlin 1993.

35. Incidentally, this before/after is independent of the point in time of observation. Even before a decision is made, one can distinguish between the time before and the time after the event, as one can after the decision has been made. However, it is very likely that *evaluating* observation will differ depending on whether it takes place in knowledge of the decision or prior to it.

36. Here (and throughout) we use the modal logical concept of contingency, which is gained through negation of necessity and through negation of impossibility.

37. See J. Richard Harrison and James G. March, Decision Making and Postdecision Surprises, *Administrative Science Quarterly* 29 (1984), 26–42, and the ensuing discussion. See also Niklas Luhmann, *Risk: A Sociological Study*. Translated by Rhodes Barrett, Berlin 1993 p.

38. Thinking is "transience," the unity of the coming and passing of thought, according, for example, to Shackle op. cit. (1979b), 1, 46, 93 f., 144. See also Husserl's well-known analyses of the inner sense of time.

39. One could think that this problem occurs principally in administrative organizations. But here and elsewhere we must keep all sorts of organizations in mind. Production organizations, for instance, whether in the form of assembly lines or not, are geared minutely to deadlines often calculated in fractions of minutes. And for this reason keeping to the deadline can be more important than quality or error-free decisions, so that quality control has to be carried out afterward as a separate step in production.

40. We also find this concept in such contexts as environmental adaptation, power structuring, and uncertainty reduction in Michel Crozier / Erhard Friedberg, *L'acteur et le système: Les contraintes de l'action collective*, Paris 1977, 141 ff.

41. See, e.g., Eliot D. Chapple / Leonard R. Sayles, *The Measure of Management*, New York 1961, 38 ff. On the "irregular" ordering of time in organizations, see also Peter Clark, Chronological Codes and Organizational Analysis, in: John Hassard / Denis Pym (ed.), *The Theory and Philosophy of Organisations*, London 1990, 137–163.

42. See Richard M. Cyert / James G. March, Organizational Factors in the Theory of Obligopoly, *Quarterly Journal of Economics* 70 (1956), 44–64 (53 ff.); idem, *A Behavioral Theory of the Firm*, Englewood Cliffs N.J. 1963, esp. 36 ff. and passim; Anthony Downs, *Inside Bureaucracy*, Boston 1967, 136 ff. We can naturally ask how realistic it is to expect everyday routine to be transformed into usable time resources in times of crisis.

43. See, also on what follows, Niklas Luhmann, Die Knappheit der Zeit und die Vordringlichkeit des Befristeten, in idem, *Politische Planung: Aufsätze zur Soziologie von Politik und Verwaltung*, Opladen 1971, 143–164.

44. For a case study, see Herbert A. Simon, The Birth of an Organization: The Economic Cooperation Administration, *Public Administration Review* 13 (1953), 227–236.

45. We shall be returning to this in detail in the chapter on uncertainty absorption.

46. Furthermore, empirical studies show that employees tend to "outwit" safety regulations if keeping to them "leads to disproportionately long interruptions of processes." See Ulrich Pröll, *Arbeitsschutz und neue Technologien: Handlungsstrukturen und Modernisierungsbedarf im institutionalisierten Arbeitsschutz*, Opladen 1991, 37.

47. See, also on what follows, Niklas Luhmann, Das Risiko der Kausalität, *Zeitschrift für Wissenschaftsforschung* 9/10 (1995), 107–119; also in Najib Harabi (ed.), *Kreativität, Wirtschaft, Recht*, Zürich 1996, 1–23.

48. See, e.g., Shackle op. cit. (1979b), 50: "There is a seeming paradox. Without uncause there can be no freedom; without freedom there can be no beginning; without beginning there can be no cause; without cause there can be no effectiveness of choice."

49. Still in early modernity. See Gerhart Schröder, *Logos und List: Zur Entwicklung der Ästhetik in der frühen Neuzeit*, Königstein/Ts. 1985.

50. See Roger Penrose, *The Emperor's New Mind: Concerning Computers, Minds, and the Laws of Physics*, Oxford 1989, 170 ff. and passim.

51. See, e.g., Geoffrey M. Hodgson, *Economics and Evolution: Bringing Life Back into Economics*, Ann Arbor Mich. 1993.

6   Uncertainty Absorption

I

If we are to decide between alternatives, to indicate one variant rather than another, we need information. In addition to the alternative, something else is therefore needed: a choice between a marked and unmarked domain of possibilities – a difference that makes a difference, that helps decide the decision. The reverse is also true: a decision generates the element of surprise that can be communicated as information.[1] The decision is then itself communicated as information, which can prompt further decisions. In this sense, we can describe the autopoietic interlinkage of decisions as information processing.

But what is the purpose of transforming information into information? And how does a system that undertakes such processing relate to the environment?

Classical organization theory would have answered this question with the concept of purposive or means-end rationality.[2] Purposes, on the one hand, and limited resources, on the other, are seen as providing the system with interpretational guidelines for information processing and reducing the complexity of the environment for intrasystemic operations to an extent that allows them to be organized. We shall be discussing this from the point of view of purposive programming.[3] But reference to means-end or purposive orientation is no adequate answer to the very general question of how in organizations decisions are transformed into decisions, and thus how information is transformed into information. Firstly, for many organizations it does not apply (or only if we define the purpose of the organization almost tautologically – by saying, for example, that the purpose of courts is to administer justice); and, secondly, the asymmetry of the relationship between ends and means and the relative insensitivity of ends to a choice of means are in turn only introduced by decisions and monitored by decisions. A theory that understands organizations as operationally closed systems reproduced only through the communication of decisions has to explain the connection between decisions in more general and different terms.

We therefore replace the concept of means-end orientation by that of uncertainty absorption. March and Simon introduced this concept into organizational studies – albeit originally to describe one variable among many, with the result that the theoretical potential of the concept was not fully exploited.[4]

Uncertainty arises where knowledge and ignorance occur at the same time; it is due to this difference. Both knowledge and ignorance are social constructions,[5] produced in the system that uses them. In the case of social systems, we are thus dealing with communicated meaning produced by communication for communication. In the case of organized social systems, uncertainty arises because decisions serve to call up decisions.

To a certain extent, uncertainty absorption can be attributed to persons.[6] But it mainly takes place in social relations, namely always when a decision orients itself on another.[7] It is only putting it differently if we describe organizations as systems in which decisions observe other decisions.[8] In other words, the term uncertainty absorption describes the succession of decisions, the decision process. The absorption of uncertainty is thus built into the decision process itself; it is nothing other than a requirement of its sequentiality. The decision itself is a compact communication, which at least implicitly also communicates its reasons, its justification, and the effort involved. But in the ongoing communication process, it can be treated only as a decision in a specified context of alternatives: as a decision for this and against that.

The autopoiesis of organizational systems thus operates through uncertainty absorption. Uncertainty absorption is accordingly only another term for the intrasystemic generation of information, and, as we have seen,[9] information not about the environment (not as intrasystemic copying of environmental states of affairs) but about the improbability of systemic restrictions on the scope of other possibilities.

In keeping with organizational research, we can thus explain that it is not possible to eliminate the paradox of observation and the paradox of communication, and why not. On the one hand, uncertainty can be absorbed only through the constative components of communication. After all, something determinate has to be said, even though a great deal of indeterminacy might hide under the ambivalences and in the "gestalt" reference of communication. On the other hand, it cannot be denied that this happens in order to direct follow-up communication. In the ordinary course of events, this makes sense. In individual cases it may be delayed through psychiatrization, deconstruction, or simply through queries that address, in particular, the constative or performative aspects of communication; but this, too, can take place only in forms that repeat the problem, which in turn absorb uncertainty autopoietically.

Uncertainty absorption presupposes knowledge as the context of its own mode of operation, knowledge that is available to the organization itself regardless of what individuals know.[10] The knowledge of the organization naturally also includes knowledge about what people who could be questioned could know. For this very reason, however, organizational knowledge cannot be reduced to personal sources. It is stored as the result of learning processes within the organization itself and can be presupposed upon the activation of communication (otherwise intimate knowledge about other people would be needed to judge what they can understand).

If we apply the concept of uncertainty to the difference between knowledge and ignorance (and thus to the form of knowledge), this also makes clear that it is not to be understood, as in the colloquial meaning of the term, to be a dysfunctional state to be remedied as far as possible. On the contrary, enduring and repeatedly generated uncertainty is the most important resource for the autopoiesis of the system.[11] Without uncertainty, there would be nothing left to decide; the organization would come to an end in a state of complete self-determination and would cease to exist for lack of activity.

Since ignorance can be produced and combated only with the aid of knowledge, all organizations, indeed all cognitive systems as such, orient themselves on what they have already achieved. "An organization can never know what it thinks or wants until it sees what it does."[12] This also means that a want of knowledge cannot be reduced by knowledge but only by decisions, which for their part can naturally concern the direction and method of seeking for knowledge. Only by means of decisions can a forecastable future be produced.[13] Uncertainty absorption is a decision process.

But if the absorption of uncertainty is a decision process, this means that the process also has to include the prospect of future decisions, thus regenerating the uncertainty that it eliminates. In more abstract terms, we also see that it is only with the aid of a memory function (Spencer-Brown) that a reentry can be generated, or that a non-trivial machine (von Foerster) comes into being only by the output of the system being reintroduced into the system as input. A linear concept of time would suggest that a certain measure of experience is necessary to structure the future and to maintain one's composure in the face of uncertainties. But this is a highly simplistic way of seeing things. The theory of self-referential, recursively operating systems also draws attention to the circumstance that the *difference* between certainty and uncertainty or between knowledge and ignorance is produced only by recursivity; this means, not least of all, that its production and reproduction are specific to the system.

In fact, the difference between knowledge and ignorance is also reproduced *as a difference* in everything that happens. The absorption of uncertainty merely lends the difference between knowledge and ignorance a different, less disturbing form. But, particularly in organizations, we often note that ignorance is deliberately generated or maintained at other places, and that precisely this serves to absorb uncertainty, because in the knowledge of others' want of knowledge one can put forward communications of one's own that one would otherwise not have ventured. Similarly, one can also be interested in one's own ignorance because it can also later serve as proof of innocence (not having been informed is among politicians' most frequent excuses). Cooperation in organizations requires a highly developed, well-considered art of ignoring; here, too, the rules of calculation apply in the mode of "would happen if. . ." One has to know what consequences knowledge would entail to be able not to know it. Apart from this special case of produced ignorance, the experience or the suspicion that manipulated information is involved is standard knowledge at all higher levels of the hierarchy.[14] In general, managers do not seem to think much of normative models of rational decision-making; at any rate they do not apply them but immediately look for solutions in a terrain familiar to them, taking into consideration only alternatives that appear to be easy to accept or reject.[15] And, finally, it should be noted that the generation of optimism about unattainable or contradictory goals can be a precondition of political consensus without which nothing can be achieved.[16]

In somewhat more usual terms, we can say that no decision can be based on complete information. The burden of a lack of information is the condition for wanting to decide. If one has complete information, no decision can show itself to be a decision.

This has nothing to do with the mental disposition of those involved, nothing to do with felt or recognized uncertainty.[17] The fact that uncertainty is absorbed without it being noticed contributes a great deal to the functioning of organized work, to avoiding stress, and to establishing a psychological "illusion of control,"[18] which, however, is not unproblematic from a risk point of view. Since the absorption of uncertainty in organizations is a social process in which external presentation and internal dependencies need to be taken into consideration, certainty is pretended if only because constant insistence on uncertainty would make work more difficult for others.[19] Whether those involved participate mentally – or as so often, take a rather distanced or cynical attitude toward their work in order to relieve the strain on themselves[20]   what is communicated is confidence in the information processing capacity of the system. The system lives from overestimating itself, indeed, often from fictions that prove useful, and which, uncontrollable in origin, are passed on[21] – for instance, the fiction that an expert is competent, that corporate advice provides a sufficient basis for making decisions,[22] or that consensus is attained if a decision is approved. And good information that confirms expectations and the chosen course is passed on more willingly than bad news.[23] Such self-overestimation may in some cases produce a need for correction, but it persists if only because it is constantly renewed. If doubts arise, they are mitigated by reduction to particular situations and possibly persons. If something goes wrong, mistakes will be sought – and found.

Organizational uncertainty absorption necessarily arises from one decision informing another, and is hence taken to be a difference that makes a difference.

Vice versa, every communication of information is a decision, for resolving to communicate this information has to be decided above all with due considera- tion of what would happen were it not to be communicated. This shows what decision-making performance is involved in, for example, aggregating data, bookkeeping, or corporate accounting systems, and what problems result from the information thus prepared "forgetting" too much and very often coming too late.[24] The issue also arises of how and to what extent it can be ensured that irritations are not only experienced and forgotten, that they do not "seep away" mentally, but are transformed into communicated information without the system being overloaded with warnings and follow-up responsibilities. We need think only of the written records in big medical institutions that might contribute to diagnosis, where the individual doctor's memory of parti- cular cases can no longer be consulted.

Through the autopoiesis of the system, all this becomes decision and hence contributes to the absorption of uncertainty, which, as we will see, can also increase uncertainty. Even if a decision has to be formally iterated – for instance, when it is rejected by a superior or set aside by a higher court – it is never a question of copying; the decision to annul informs us that repetition is required, and the repeated decision, because it is experienced as iteration, is never the same as that which is to be iterated. Only what has been forgotten could purely by chance be repeated in the strictest sense; but this will be a rare and unnoticed occurrence.

It is correspondingly normal for the information processing that has led to the preceding decision not to be repeated. In this respect, however, practice can vary from case to case. A person subsequently dealing with the matter may, for example, be obliged (or feel himself to be obliged) to draw attention to conspicuous mistakes and to steer things in the opposing direction. But then uncertainty absorption itself runs counter to the expected process. The decision to do this and to suggest further examination (have you considered that a powerful group is behind this application?) itself absorbs uncertainty, and it can obviously be practiced only in exceptional cases and only with reasons being stated, for otherwise the process would become circular and grind to a halt. And there is no time for this.

And even if uncertainty absorption cannot be avoided, its occurrence can be anticipated – for example, in the form of observing communication difficulties and the need for simplification, without which communication would not function. "The truth could not ordinarily be conveyed by stating it exactly," states one author with a great deal of experience in administration.[25] This is why, in administrative organizations with highly developed decision aware- ness, we find much attention being paid to language and much effort being invested in smoothing communication by omitting incidental remarks, unne- cessary details, and unconfirmed but crucial conjectures. "Hence, the speaker must often be dishonest in statement from his own point of view in order to achieve honesty of result, although he ceases to be aware of it."[26]

Such reflections have meanwhile been elaborated into a special field of research that draws on sociolinguistic, semiotic, and rhetorical sources.[27] Detailed linguistic analysis has shown that and how communication protects itself against ubiquitous uncertainty without renouncing the possibility of indicating uncertainties *specifically* when it is felt to be necessary. It operates with standardized labeling, with repetitions of what is already known in changed situations, with metaphors, with trivialities, in an effort to skate over possible doubts. It generates a genuine appearance of definiteness to prevent questions being asked; or in order to keep control over what is useful in the way of further communication. Otherwise than the tradition of rhetoric would lead us to assume, it is not a matter of tricks occasionally employed but a necessity lying in language itself, a continuous protection against irritation with the proviso of self-provocation.

Only against this backdrop of everyday self-evidences can deliberate or also communicatively negotiated maneuvering with language occur, up to and including ironic adaptation to what we nowadays call "political correctness." But irony is also chosen as a form for absorbing uncertainty. It reveals double meanings together with the indication that they should not be gone into.[28] In this context we find the not infrequent decision not to communicate a decidable decision, thus a decision not to decide, because the inevitable absorption of uncertainty this would involve would strengthen suspicions or existing conflict lines through contradictory interpretations of the "real intention" behind the decision.

II

Uncertainty absorption connects decisions with decisions, but does not connect every decision with every other decision of the system. Organizations are thus complex: they cannot link up every element with every other element; they can only establish selective connections.[29] We can also understand this necessary selectivity as the need for a system memory.

By "memory" we mean that the system has to discriminate between forgetting and remembering, and, whether in the short or longer term, has primarily to sort out what it can forget in order to regain capacities for processing information.[30] The main achievement of memory is therefore forgetting, and remembering takes place only indirectly through the inhibition of forgetting. A theory of memory must hence explain that and how the inhibition of forgetting is conditioned.

This happens always in the present, and normally as comprehension of the current state of the system as known and familiar, and thus apt to continue without any problem. Only exceptionally (once again: exceptionally) are meaning components required that are dated or in some other way provided with an indication of their "pastness." This is particularly important when inconsistencies would otherwise occur in the present. A certain decision has been made in the past; if one felt that it had to be made now, this would bring confusion to what is to be done at present. In relation to time (and to space), the memory thus serves to iron out inconsistencies that, given the high complexity of information processing, would bring the system to a halt or radically reduce the capacity for processing. Time-indexed memory can in turn (for another observer) provide correct or incorrect recall. For their part, correct memories are only an exception to an exception to an exception that inhibits forgetting.

In any case, the system memory is not a special capacity, not an outdifferentiated competence for only occasional use, for instance, to eliminate doubts (just as there are no special "memory cells" in the brain in which matters past are stored). The memory participates in all operations (in this context: decisions) of the system; otherwise these operations would be quite unable to recognize that they are decisions, nor would they be able to assign themselves to one specific system (and not another). Like the God of the theologians, memory works everywhere and nowhere in a specific fashion in all operations of the system.[31]

So much can be said in general terms. As far as organizational systems are concerned, the memory connects to the absorption of uncertainty that links decisions with decisions. It forgets the uncertainty on which everything is based to the extent that it does not feed into the decision itself as doubt or as proviso for change. But it also forgets the innumerable lead-up decisions (the invitation to the meeting, the unsuccessful attempts to get certain matters accepted); it therefore suppresses most of what contributes to the autopoiesis of the system.[32] On the whole (leaving aside private memories), it recalls only what has been taken into account as premise for making further decisions. Through decisions, the system gives a form to environmental influences that can be remembered in the system without also having to recall the underlying environmental situation. A good example is double-entry accounting in business, which does what no mental memory (including that of the individual businessman) could ever do, while on the other hand forgetting what is retained as particularly striking in the individual memory. Uncertainty absorption and the ongoing reshaping of decisions into decision premises are two sides of the same process: and in both regards subsequent decisions decide whether memory is to be used and reproduced.[33] This is why all recording systems, such as registers and electronic databases, operate with the proviso that they be actually used, which becomes more and more unlikely as complexity grows. Only continuous reimpregnation produces what performs the function of a memory, accompanying and inspiring all operations and providing them with identification.

Above all, remembering decisions is facilitated, if not enabled, by the organization's ability to remember the positions and, via these positions, the persons who did the deciding. If the course of uncertainty absorption cannot be traced in terms of positions and persons, the memory typically chooses to forget. In this sense, the organization primarily has a memory for people, nurtured by gossip and rumor. This may prove fatal for the individuals involved as persons; but for this very reason this structure of memory is also a motive to keep working on the memory of the system, to develop a "policy" of discriminating between forgetting and remembering, which is often borne by individual awareness and communicative forbearance. In other words, the memory itself remembers. Only against this backdrop can we understand what is recorded and filed, what can – if need be – be denied, and what is not put on record at all, but respects the future in the sense that it is assigned no place in the past but forgotten.

On the other hand, the memory of the organization, even if it is oriented on the identity of persons and imputes consistent behavior to them, remains a social memory. It has to be guaranteed by reiterating the frame of reference of communication, and what must be prevented is that too much material worth remembering is available only in the mind. The social memory would then dissolve, disintegrate, and be available only mentally. Although it could be retrieved in communicative procedures with a great deal of effort, there would be no guarantee that different individuals would remember the same thing. The past can be reconstructed on the basis of individuals' awareness only in very exceptional cases, only with respect to special problems, and not in the form of organizational memory that participates in all decisions.

Since memory is used in ever new situations and develops continuously, it must be understood as an *inventive* mechanism. Even recognition and iteration is in new situations a new operation, and whether it is chosen or not is determined not by the past alone but also through the involvement of memory. We could say that everything that happens with the participation of memory modifies what is familiar and known. Since the memory can forget, it affords all the necessary freedoms for this modification.

We now see somewhat more precisely *how* an organization is able to generate system-specific time by separating past and future and, in one and the same selection process, connecting them as different time horizons.[34] Only with the help of its memory can the organization read alternatives into its past and structure its future by setting differences without being hampered too much by "truth values."[35] At the same time, the organization can clearly use the marking of decisions to secure its memory doubly against forgetting. This happens firstly through a narrower concept of decision, whose other side is consigned to oblivion as routine behavior. But it happens above all through the selection of a special sort of decision premise, which, although put into effect by individual decisions, is intended as a rule for an indeterminate number of further decisions. Since regulatory decision premises often have hierarchical connotations and regulate the system top-down, the system, thanks to the form in which its memory is re-impregnated, also calls itself to mind as a hierarchy without having to justify doing so.

III

We have assumed that uncertainty is absorbed when decisions are linked to decisions. This starting point needs to be modified, not calling it into question but supplementing it. In every organization (as in everyday life), situations, operations, and complexes of operations are typified in many ways. Examples of this typification are the conference, the request for information, the submission of a draft proposal for co-signing, setting homework for schoolchildren, obtaining peer reviews before deciding to publish an article, admitting new patients to a hospital, returning a defective product for repair, or completing a form. Rhetoric has recently begun to call such typifications "genres."[36] Cognitive psychology speaks of "schema," "script," "cognitive map"; and in economics we find the concept "indicator."[37] What we are dealing with are varying restrictions on behavior that are appropriate within a particular type. In selecting a type, we therefore choose a framework that is limiting but does not determine what decisions are made when using the type, for example, when completing a form.

The choice of type can be normatively prescribed, for instance, a court hearing or staff council participation in certain decisions; but it can also be left open and then more or less impose itself for practical reasons. When decision processes are more or less routine, they therefore take place as a succession of type choices and not simply as a chain of individual decisions. They are, as it were, two-track occurrences, in which framing by type already creates sufficient certainty and dedramatizes the deciding. Those involved gain a certain distance from the content, they proceed in the normal run of things and rarely take recourse to the corresponding figures.

Moreover, most complex types – for instance, the conference, the surgical operation, the school lesson – can, where necessary, be broken down into subtypes until the type practically merges with the decision and leaves only marginal uncertainties. The certainty that the type provides lies in its repeatability with varying content. One can and must learn the types that come into question in order to know what mobility they offer and what risks one runs of making the wrong impression – for instance, when a candidate in an oral examination begins to read a prepared text and has to be put off his stride through the normal question and answer game.

Types of this sort work only because and as long as everyone involved knows them. Deviations from what is usual can creep in and themselves become usual – for example, when an examination begins with "statements" by the candidate on previously agreed topics. However, one of the main sources for the development of new types and the disappearance of older rituals is likely to lie in technological developments. Working with computers, with medical engineering, or with educational films in schools automatically leads to new standardizations.[38] At this level, too, there is therefore organizational "learning"; it is an empirical question, to be answered differently from case to case, whether new types expand or reduce the decision-making repertoire.

Finally, it should be noted that such types are initially not officially introduced decision premises but can be stipulated as such. This then amounts to regulation of the decision-making *procedure*, opening up other possibilities for learning, namely those that do not "creep in" but have to be introduced by decision.

IV

The contribution a decision makes to absorbing uncertainty can be described as its *responsibility*.[39] In this sense, responsibility is something that is happening all the time and that can be attributed as a mistake at best only secondarily to a decision-maker. Only where this is the case and where it can be expected does it make sense to speak of accountability. Accountability always has to be tailor-made for persons, for decisions themselves do not last. Nor can bodies, groups, or teams that decide by a majority be made accountable (which could explain the popularity of these forms of organization). This person-related customizing of accountability means that it always encompasses too much and too little – too much because a person functioning repeatedly and in the long term as decision premise[40] is always more than a single contribution to decision-making; too little because the information processing network cannot be exhaustively described in terms of single persons.

The difference between responsibility and accountability draws attention to the limits to organizational self-regulation; and to the possibilities (and again limits) of organizational learning. Mishaps can teach an organization to transform responsibility into accountability – albeit at notoriously high cost, because information processing now also, if not primarily, focuses on the factors that could prompt the updating of accountability.

If we could manage to measure information in keeping with the standard guidelines of information theory regarding the possibilities they exclude, we could also measure responsibility. Responsibility would be the information value of a decision. In the practice of organized collaboration, however, this at best points to the problems of the context that determines the possibilities information chooses among. A great deal of effort – of latent, only implicitly communicated and often opaque endeavor – lies in the definition of this framework, in the alternatives still open. On the one hand, a decision can stake out its own discretionary power by reference to binding previous decisions: that only a given sum of money was earmarked, or that the law excluded certain attractive solutions to problems, diminishes the information value of the decision. Such limitations often lead to the decision-maker expressing and communicating the decision in terms of dissatisfaction with himself. On the other hand, possibilities overlooked in the course of the decision process can be discovered, suppressed possibilities brought to light, or, finally, further possibilities invented to expand the decision-making framework and increase the weight of decision attribution. In the "micropolitics" of organizations,[41] differences of opinion about such frameworks and their social and temporal instability play a considerable role. Even if the decision clearly communicates its option, its information value, or its meaning, the responsibility for it can remain controversial. This selection accompanies the decision like a shadow, just as the hero in antique tragedy shapes his fate through his actions; and future decisions can be influenced by the fact that, although the decision is accepted, its assessment depends on the framework conditions.

In short, from a "micropolitical" point of view, information is interesting as a form, that is to say as a difference that has another side to it. It excludes this other side but, in so doing, includes it in the decision, and passes it on with the decision. At the level of explicit communication, uncertainty is absorbed by the decision opting for *this* and not that. One can make do with this, and normally does so. But the "*and not that*" can endure for some time in the meaning horizon of the decision process. The form of closed contingency remains contingent. In other words, there are possibilities that are constructed and introduced into the system memory only because consideration of them is excluded in the decision process. To a certain extent, the organization thus remains sensitive to what it has excluded or omitted. And in the course of events there may be occasion to come back to it.

Normally, however, the possibilities selected are favored. They serve as points of departure for further decisions. In the process, they can be corrected, can be developed through learning in the organization, can, for instance, be further processed in terms of the rule/exception schema, thus gaining complexity. By contrast, rejected possibilities remain unchanged; they gradually become abstract, at any rate not complex. We could even say that the rejected possibilities bind the system much more strongly precisely because they can no longer be corrected, can no longer be changed in the process of learning.[42] They determine the "structural drift" (Maturana) of the system much more strongly than the possibilities accepted, which can be modified by subsequent decisions. From this point of view, it is a useful maxim always to decide in such a way that the decision enlarges the system's scope for decision-making.

V

What is described as uncertainty absorption in the theory of operationally closed organizational systems is often treated in the literature under the heading "power."[43] At first glance, the two expressions seem to mean the same thing; but they point in different directions. Uncertainty absorption stresses the processual aspect. This concept also fits better into a systems theory that sets out from constructivist assumptions and stresses that the relationship of a system with its environment can be only referential and not operational. The power concept, by contrast, focuses attention on a definitive, determining cause that is to be assumed and can be localized in the system or in the environment.[44] What is involved is the attribution of responsibility, thus also the discharge from responsibility or finally the determination of the position that has to be worked upon if one wishes to influence the decisions of the system.

If we choose the power-theoretical description, everything depends on proposing a sufficiently discriminating and differentiating concept of power. If, because the system is in a certain state, one is satisfied to conclude that this must have been brought about by power (or "symbolic force," or what have you), all one can offer is a double description of the phenomena. From the point of view of conceptual economy, we can manage without such a concept of power.[45] It covers only ascribed power as one of the possibilities for those involved to explain the state of the system.[46] Its sole merit could be that it points to the contingency of all factual states of affairs under the motto: other power holders, other conditions. If we seek limitations and hope to find them with reference to the system's formal hierarchy of positions, the same applies. Such a power concept is simply superfluous. Or we would have to distinguish it from the exercise of formal powers, but the theory would then soon prove empirically untenable. For, however we now define power, anyone familiar with the internal milieu of an organization – like any sociologist versed in the subject matter – well knows that the power profile of an organization does not coincide with the formal super- and subordination of positions.

One way out could be to take a narrower view of power and define power potential as the possibility to threaten overtly or covertly with negative sanctions.[47] This also makes the classical political and legal objections to the unregulated exercise of power comprehensible. For power as the power to threaten extends to areas of activity that have nothing to do with the context to which this power owes its existence. Thus, the threat of physical violence or dismissal or the disclosure of unpleasant information can be used to push through all sorts of "extraneous" wishes. But it is to be assumed that "threat power" in this sense plays only a small role in organizations. In a complex, circularly networked, self-referential system, too much reciprocity is involved to allow threat power to be exercised without harm to whoever exercises it. The power of the superior to assign work under the threat of dismissal in the event of disobedience confronts the power of the subordinate to deny coopera-tion in cases where the superior has to rely on it. What accrues in the way of power resources, which is likely to be considerable, can therefore hardly be deployed openly and for precise, verifiable purposes. The system disciplines, indeed suppresses the open use of power and reduces the power game to attempts to cushion contacts through mutual consideration and to avoid friction that could provoke reactions. Within organizations, but also in relations between organizations, it then seems advisable to suspend the use of power and to transform mutual dependencies into islands of cooperation in good faith, whose resilience, however, is limited.[48] For this very reason, we have to return to the level of "micropolitics" if we wish to examine where and how the exercise of power comes up against limits in the prospect of self-damage.

However, this diagnosis – valid under normal circumstances – does not hold true in situations that can be defined as crises and that thus call for exceptional measures. Then one can show where the power lies. But experience also shows that the deployment of power can change at best marginal zones of the system, whereas in-depth effects in almost all system structures are prevented by resistance or are left to slow processes of adaptation, in which initially latent countervailing power diverts the impulse for change into channels acceptable to it.[49]

These brief reflections show that taking the "power" perspective tempts one to address wide ranging topics such as uncertainty absorption and structural change, or to explain decisions in terms of decision premises, without really guiding experience and research accumulated in this field by a single concept. This is not to deny that identifying power relations and exercising sufficient circumspection about what can be afforded or risked can, from a situational point of view, prove very helpful strategically. But it must also be said that this game requires insider knowledge difficult to capture in sociological studies. We shall, therefore, stick to the concept of uncertainty absorption without trying to replace it by assumptions about power and the distribution of power in the system.

VI

The fact that uncertainty absorption happens always and everywhere in the system, because decisions could otherwise not be linked to decisions, does not spare us the question of how it is distributed within that system. That the measurement of information in the system has to reckon with a socially and temporally unstable framework does not yet explain whether there can be conventions that allow us to infer that some decisions absorb more uncertainty than others. But even if this is so, we cannot assume that the distribution of contributions to uncertainty absorption in the system is random or purely ad hoc; we can rather expect or perhaps even conclude that the distribution (e.g., in the sense of a hierarchical order) is itself used as a resource in the self-organization of the system.

In the autopoietic system, such conventions are also products of the system, thus "autological" rules, which are ultimately sustained by being themselves due to uncertainty absorption. The assignment of information differences can therefore be handled seriously only with irony, and conventions are designed to include their own infringement or what it is that they exclude.[50] We could also say that the framework of the possible is constructed, deconstructed, and reconstructed within the framework.[51] Nevertheless, the system does not rely only on current uncertainty absorption but also on differences in the information value, importance, and responsibility for decisions thus constructed, if only because the system does not have the time to constantly call the distinctions it uses into question.

In a traditional sense, differences in the process of uncertainty absorption are described as differences of *authority*. By taking recourse to authority, the communication process refers back to itself. It is supposed that, if queried, the decision can be so well justified by reference to its sources of information that it appears reasonable; but for this very reason one can spare oneself the query and replace it by credit, that is to say, by authority.[52] By authority we thus mean not a special ability of a charismatic or articulate personality, but an assumption abbreviating the communication process, which can be made for a wide variety of reasons.

In past times, especially in the organizations of the nineteenth century, one had to reckon with social stratum components, which were gradually replaced by certified academic competence. Then, however, selection for higher schooling and university studies was strongly influenced by a person's social stratum, a tendency that began to weaken only in the second half of the twentieth century. Especially in the public service, personnel are recruited and paid in terms of grades, so that the claim to competence in judgment, however long one's experience in the job, is visibly reproduced. The possibilities of promotion within the system therefore come up against clear obstacles in entry and pay level ceilings. To some extent, this model is also copied in the private sector – albeit with less need for university graduates, greater stress on intra-systemic training, and better career opportunities, accompanied by greater uncertainty about the duration of membership in the organization. Conditions vary so strongly from country to country and from organization type to organization type (police, schools, newspaper offices, local authorities, etc.) that we cannot go into any detail at this point. What is of interest is, first, whether this support for authority from correlation with stratification and with school and university education (which is now freeing itself from dependence on social origins) is decreasing, and second, what the consequences are for easy uncertainty absorption.

Traditionally, authority was seen as resting on two coordinated pillars, and was therefore also able to take presumption relatively far. Firstly, a great deal could be explained and communication could be kept more succinct than is usual today; and, secondly, queries were discouraged (except in the form of zealous indications of things that might have been overlooked) where class and educational barriers had to be overcome. Where personal relations were relatively stable, informal cooperation could nevertheless develop – in administrative organizations, however, not so much in the form of clearly defined working groups but rather in hierarchical position structures.

If we assume that authority in organizations could always rely on this sort of societal subsidization without it becoming a subject of debate, it would seem that drastic changes have taken place. Whoever now invokes authority puts it at risk. Changes concern firstly the disciplining of communication through stratification, then the relevance of education for jobs, and finally a factor that we could call the expiration date (or "half-life") of experience.[53] The possibilities of invoking experience in communication and thus saving oneself further argument have considerably diminished, for example, for parents with their children, and thus between generations, but also for loan officers or financial consultants in banks or sales representatives in relation to their markets, or government officials in relation to their political environment. The turnaround time of knowledge, and of ignorance, is shortening without our being able to assume that the world is better known. Only the onus in communication is shifting – at the cost of seniority values such as authority and experience.

But the pure facticity of uncertainty absorption remains, and with it the need for the recognizable ordering of contributions and responsibilities. The network itself absorbs uncertainty. As ethnomethodologists have repeatedly pointed out, this happens already in everyday culture and, *a fortiori*, in specific milieus such as organizations through tacitly accepted rules that limit queries. Without having to refer to clearly formulated directives, one knows what would be "too much." There are narrow limits to what can reasonably be expected, and in this context differences in rank come to bear, as do such distinctions as oral/written. Nevertheless, time-consuming forms of negotiation on outcomes can ensue.[54] In the process, ignorance is translated into freedom, namely into the freedom conceded to the partner to accept or reject, because he has the best access to the relevant knowledge. However, this, too, requires points of departure in distributed competencies and responsibilities. The ordering of competence may then replace authority and at the same time impose an individual and place-related style of uncertainty absorption – at the cost of commitment to the overall interest of the organization, the firm, or the state. As complexity and intransparency increase, one keeps oneself to oneself and accepts the decisions made elsewhere.

Where consensus is required, it is requested and granted in the form of explicitly communicated consent – with or without modifications to the proposed decision. In the communication process, *agreements* thus come about and are documented; however, they do not presuppose that anyone abandons his convictions or is willing to stand up for implementation of the decision against resistance or in the face of unexpected difficulties.[55] Agreements, therefore, serve more or less to give form to conflicts, which can then be resumed under new premises and for new reasons. To a certain extent, they replace the preceding past through new historical points of departure and can thus facilitate changes to the decisions made, if they do not prove successful and no one is in favor of retaining the solution found; if they are only temporary arrangements, made until further notice, this also makes it easier to consent. They require neither changes in the opinions expressed during negotiations nor reasonable insight. No one can or has to be expected to behave either reasonably or unreasonably. It suffices to take account of a still uncertain future in which, should the need arise, different decisions can be made.

Finally, agreements mark the boundaries of systems and the boundaries of subsystems. They connect and separate from those with whom agreements are considered unnecessary or impossible. In this sense, agreements follow the lines of system differentiation. But if we were to examine the limits to the need for agreement and the practice of reaching agreement, we would presumably also discover subsystem differentiations that are not provided for in the organizational plan.

In the light of these reflections, it is advisable to look for a structure concept that corresponds to the process concept of uncertainty absorption, and that is at the same time broader than the concept of hierarchy. For this purpose, Herbst proposes the biological concept of "directive correlation."[56] One arrangement "directs" others when it facilitates and supports the fulfillment of tasks by other positions, thus relieving them of the burden of information processing and, hence, responsibility. From a structural point of view, such directive correlations exist in more or less standardized, expectable form, but we find them in both vertical and horizontal communication channels and both top-down and bottom-up in the hierarchy. They give uncertainty absorption a typical form; one does not then need to re-invent it from case to case, but can stick to "procedure" that is then protected even if expectations are disappointed in particular instances. And because of the structure of the overall system, which provides only the communication channels (positions, addresses), what uncertainty absorption relies on in individual cases can be left open.

Even if organizations describe themselves as hierarchies, one can assume that directive correlations come to bear de facto. It can be useful not only to accept this fact as a deviation or as "informal organization," but also to recognize that the real work of the organization is done in this manner. Instead of observing only deviations, we would also have to assume officially that the structure of the organization consists in these directive correlations and that the hierarchy with its emergency powers of formally binding decision-making fulfills only an auxiliary function. Such weakening of hierarchy would, if recognized, also serve to admit more diverse irritation in the system.

VII

In the forms of responsibility and accountability, the system directs its own attention to the problem of uncertainty absorption. Typically and continuously, reflexive processes unfold processes of second-order observation. In practice, this happens not simply in the form of certainty and uncertainty being generated in relation to certainty and uncertainty. Little would be gained if certainty that uncertainty exists were to be established in the decision process, or if constant doubt were to be cast on assumptions believed certain. In practice, the problem tends to be tackled in terms of disposition over knowledge and ignorance.

On the one hand, there is a widespread practice of generating uncertainty in others – notably by supervisory positions, but also when a preferred variant is to be established as the only sensible one and communication about alternatives suppressed. The choice between alternatives is typically made on the basis of information density rather than rational comparison. What is known and can clearly be imagined deserves preference – unless one wishes to delay decisions and therefore wants more information.

However, just as noteworthy is the other case where the decision-maker keeps himself uninformed in critical regards to avoid having responsibility ascribed to him. Already in the old reason of state theory, the advice to dissimulate knowledge played a considerable role. Under certain circumstances, knowledge generates an undesirable obligation to decide. In this context, too, the state of consciousness naturally plays no role. On the contrary, only whoever knows or suspects what is to be known can avoid taking cognizance of it. In this instance, too, the problem is fully on the level of communication. As a counter-strategy, attempts may, under certain circumstances, be made to force unwelcome knowledge on the decision-maker and thus maneuver him into a situation he would rather avoid. Zeal and circumspection are among the possibilities for gaining unpopularity, even if the decision-maker who has been put under pressure cannot take revenge ad hoc. In manipulating one's own and others' knowledge and ignorance, one therefore runs a special sort of risk. Whoever fails to recognize this, in other words, whoever is unable to act at the second-order observation level in the "what would be if. . ." mode, can hardly be said to have the qualities needed for taking part in intricate processes of uncertainty absorption.

VIII

That a system can dispose only over its own operations follows from the requirement of operational closure. The system (the system itself!) can do nothing to change this. But this does not mean that the system can observe only itself. On the contrary, in the principle of operational closure lies an irresistible impulse to base observation by the system on the difference between system and environment, which means to structure the observations of the system primarily through the distinction between self-reference and other-reference. As we have seen, this is why the closure of the system is the precondition for its openness; not only in the sense that this system *can* observe its environment but that it *must* observe it if it is to establish a relationship with itself.[57]

But how can the system observe an environment that cannot be accessed through its own operations? To a considerable degree, the system manages to do so by assuming against the facts that during a longer process of uncertainty absorption the environment remains constant, if information to the contrary does not impose itself. In other words, a sort of temporal *"ceteris paribus"* clause applies on the assumption that the world itself naturally always stays the same. Furthermore, the inaccessibility of the environment appears to be the source of all internal uncertainty, and if this is so, observation of the environment by the system is likely to play a major role in intrasystemic uncertainty absorption. For the system, disregarding the fact that certainty/uncertainty are constructions of the system, the environment is seen as the main source of all uncertainty,[58] whereas its own contribution is taken rather to be the risk of error and fallacy. This, in turn, affects the process of uncertainty absorption. The ability to present environment successfully in the system is likely to be a first-class source of authority, however uncertainty is absorbed via the environment at the boundary positions[59] of the system. This also means that these boundary positions are often in close interactional contact with systems of the environment. They represent and inform in two directions and in this function can only to a limited degree be controlled by their own organization. What they offer their system as excuse, as it were, is interactionally negotiated uncertainty absorption.

In the classical model of the organization, the function of uncertainty absorption is assigned to the hierarchical apex of the organization. The owner of the business is seen as able to learn the right prices from the market owing to (more or less) perfect competition, as able to accept any risks as capital risks,[60] and accordingly able to manage the business successfully. And one could just as easily imagine that the apex of the political apparatus had power because it disposes over the means of force or generates it in processes of political negotiation under the conditions of electoral democracy and then, with due regard for the law, formulates the program according to which it is to be exercised. In both cases, the apex guarantees for its apparatus or administrative staff (*Verwaltungsstab*, as Max Weber put it) the conditions for their reproduction in an environment that it does not need to know but only to shape. A residue of unresolved malfunctions may remain, which have to be reported to the top so that they can be analyzed for information. But this is true for every machine. Management, risk assumption, and uncertainty absorption coincide.

For a good thirty years now this machine model has been criticized by organizational sociology.[61] Neither does it match the empirical findings of organizational research nor are the assumptions of such a centralist organization theory about the environment realistic.[62] However, this must raise the question of how uncertainty in relation to environmental conditions is absorbed *instead*. A great deal of uncertainty absorption has been discovered in horizontal relations, together with the supposition that less arbitrariness prevails in horizontal communication than in vertical communication or that expertise or milieu knowledge come to bear more effectively.[63] There is no denying that organizations continue to be hierarchically structured and that binding instructions are issued and obeyed; but the problem has shifted to the question: What instructions? Modern production planning of the complex sort has, for example, to take account of so many different environments – sales markets, financial markets, technical possibilities, supplier efficiency, fashion, and what competitors are planning – that the centralization of the necessary knowledge and thus the centralization of uncertainty absorption are excluded, and other ways to plan coordination have to be considered, such as the simultaneous and step-by-step concretization of planning in different divisions of the organization, which observe the various environments but have to be ready to reach agreement internally. Such conditions exclude the adoption of plans on the basis of central assumptions about the environment, to be subsequently carried out with minor, ad hoc corrections. And the question is then whether a hierarchy suitable for the up-down conveyance of binding instructions is also suitable for conveying the necessary environmental knowledge (whatever its quality as "knowledge") bottom-up in the same channel.

Such situations, increasingly typical, make it appear advisable to take recourse to more abstract concepts like boundary position[64] or uncertainty absorption or directive correlation. But this also makes it difficult to abide by assumptions still widespread in organizational sociology, for example, that uncertainty absorption correlates with power in the system.[65] This is not a matter of course and does not result from the requirement of uncertainty absorption as such. We can therefore argue only conversely that power can develop only where a decision-maker can dispose over *others'* uncertainty about their decisions. Even if power continues to be hierarchically ordered, this does not mean that uncertainty is concentratedly absorbed at the top, nor does it mean that power is withdrawn from the power holder through diffusion of uncertainty in the system and at its boundaries. One may retain power, but not know how and to what ends one should use it.

It can accordingly be assumed that, with the diffusion of uncertainty in the system, the power organized in the formal hierarchy is not obsolete but that how it is practiced changes. It is neutralized neither by power from below nor by power working on it horizontally: it merely becomes a special source of uncertainty with which one has to come to terms. If agreements are to become effective, one has to gain the support of the competent superior at the appropriate level. And precisely when no one, superior included, can know what the one and only right decision is, the superior, too, has discretionary leeway to adequately fulfill supervisory duties. The organization needs someone who can ascertain the facts and legitimate this ascertainment.[66]

Parallel to these analyses, which set out from the social structures of the distribution of authority and power, psychological studies have shown that uncertainty absorption does not proceed in obedience to the directives that theories of rational behavior would propound. It neither follows the rules of statistics, nor does it seek to ensure the greatest possible utility subjectively expected. In everyday life, one overestimates, for example, the importance of particularly striking information or information that is known or easier to obtain than that which can be gained only at great effort and cost.[67] We could say that, in absorbing uncertainty, in assessing uncertainty, probability, and risk, one does the best one can. The possibility of constructing causal links between available data or the possibility of gaining a narratable story seem to be more important that the reliable reconstruction of probabilities. Both causal relations and stories provide forms of communication that clarify something by withholding their premises, which could contradict it. Causal relations are based on a preliminary selection of matching causes and effects, which could also be differently sorted. And stories are "interesting," because in the form of singularity and uniqueness they convey a generalizable message.[68] We thus have to do with paradox-resolving forms of communication, and this explains their contribution to the given case of uncertainty absorption.[69]

The framework for decisions is accordingly constructed with an affinity for decision-making from the outset. The organization guides itself, as it were, by the problem of uncertainty absorption, and constructs knowledge and ignorance, uncertainties and risks *under the guidance of this problem.*

IX

That communication alone is available for the functions of uncertainty absorption is an implication of our theoretical approach. Individuals may well eliminate their uncertainty through perception and on-the-spot inspection; but this has no social relevance if the information they gain is not communicated. However, this does not yet tell us what forms of communication are particularly suitable for tackling the various problems of uncertainty absorption.

In Max Weber's bureaucracy model, the written word was held to be the predominant form of communication. This may well be true when it comes to drawing up programs and providing a uniform draft as a basis for decision-making. In the financial system, too, writing is the predominant means of uncertainty absorption: not the calculation but only the balance is communicated, and this includes possibilities for auditing. If, by contrast, we look at how executives spend their time, we have the opposite impression. Their communication is mainly interactional, that is oral, and this seems to be the case with both intrasystemic and external communication.[70] More than is generally believed, the culture of organizations is an oral one. Face-to-face interaction with "turn-taking" and the possibility, as well as the obligation, for immediate reaction clearly offers considerable advantages for ongoing uncertainty absorption – for establishing both consensus and dissent. That the results are put down in writing is not excluded, but minutes typically contain only the outcome, not the process of absorbing uncertainty.

From case to case there can be very different reasons for preferring the spoken word. Communication may be too illegal to risk a written record. Or there may be reasons for keeping the authorship of an idea anonymous. Or one would first like to test how a proposal is accepted before admitting to it. For these and other reasons, it is important for the system to have the *difference* between oral and written communication at its disposition, and to be able to choose which form to use within this difference.

On the other hand, interaction is naturally time-consuming. To a limited degree, this is offset by the fact that disposition over and the duration of interaction varies with social status, so that superiors can decide whether, for whom, and how long they are available for such interaction. Nevertheless, the demands on time are considerable and little time is left for personal reflection. It could be assumed that this is compensated by a sort of condensed experiential knowledge, which can be neither recorded in writing nor explained, but which contributes to reproducing the mystery of authority and decision-making competence.

Finally, it should be noted that there are also communications that are suitable for neither writing nor speech but have to use non-linguistic forms of perception, and in this context acoustic rather than optical channels. This is typically the case for alarm signals, which, depending on the sort of organization involved, can be sent on more or less probable grounds: fire, disaster, enemy attack, etc. Alarm signals are of use only if they trigger special programs whose implementation requires no or little communication. They have to be highly standardized and well prepared, and their rare occurrence must not lead to their meaning and programs being forgotten.

X

The concept of uncertainty absorption describes organizations as social systems, which, in a world that is opaque to them, transform uncertainty into certainty. The organization thus settles for a world that it has itself constructed and in which it believes because it is the outcome of its own decision-making history. But this is only the one side of the coin. The other is that this happens through decisions, which guarantees the constant regeneration of uncertainty. A decision reverses the direction in which time is determined. It turns an already unalterable past in which nothing more can happen into an open alternative that still has to be decided on; and in return it sets a difference by which the future is to be observed and introduced into the decision in structured form. To the extent that the organization risks losing its way in self-deception, it also enhances its sensitivity to new irritations. But does this self-sensitization suffice? And from what perspectives could an external observer (for instance, organizational sociology) address and answer this question?

For a start, it should be remembered that the social system organization can be produced and reproduced only in a society, thus only within an all-inclusive social system, which for its part has always generated and updated a reality construction.[71] This commitment to constructive guidelines from society is now stressed by the so-called institutional theory of the organization.[72] However, within this general world construction (which, incidentally, cannot be expected to find consensus or even dubious reinsurance in a "life world"), organizations generate special operational correlates, special semantics, and special distinctions with the aid of which they observe the world. We could speak of a concentrated and specific capacity for reflection, which further breaks down the usual world data (e.g., on people's known needs or peculiarities), thus increasing uncertainty on the state of affairs, so that decisions – that is, decisions by the given organization – become necessary. Consider, for instance, how military organizations imagine future wars, or how schools assess the performance of students, or how manufacturing and service organizations sound out their special markets, or political parties probe the willingness of the electorate to reward political platforms with votes – although all this is neither given nor can be ascertained. Regardless of all societal (or as one now also says, cultural) conditions, organizations thus act at their own risk with regard to their own reality constructions.

In the realm of increase that organizations construct as their world, the problem of transforming uncertainty into certainty thus remains, and hence the problem of whether the irritability of the organization suffices to control their world construction – to control it not against the real world but against the resistance of operations of its own to operations of its own. After all, the results of uncertainty absorption can be combated only through decisions, thus only through the absorption of other uncertainties; and historical situations continuously arise in which one questions one's own achievements without ever being able go back and start over again. Much criticism of bureaucracy seems to relate to the fact that organizations abide by their own assumptions about the world more strongly and more enduringly than the external observer can comprehend. We can develop this assumption into the hypothesis that organizations trust their self-made certainties particularly when high uncertainties have to be coped with and they cannot see what could be done beyond what has been done.

This holds particularly true for two sorts of case, which can also coincide and reinforce one another:

(1) when the organization has to reckon with typical *opponents* or *competitors* and has set its sights fully on winning or losing within this framework; or

(2) when high *risks* have to be dealt with and this is managed through specific strategies without the feared disasters materializing. The question is then whether organizations with their decision-making network can register changes in the parameters of hitherto successful uncertainty absorption and abandon self-made certainties without being able to replace these certainties with anything else but uncertainties. Various types of case are conceivable. One could ask what happens with the certainty that one had about an opponent if the opponent bows out or if defining him as an opponent becomes increasingly contrived and costly. The difficulties facing politics after the end of the Cold War, with the associated uncertainties about a new international order or disorder and the parallel problems in the internal affairs of state organizations, offer ample illustrations. Another question that arises when difficulties or other negative experiences occur is whether efforts to carry out the original project are stepped up because it at least offered certainty as an accepted undertaking, or whether it is abandoned. The quite usual overstepping of initial budgets suggests that the uncertainties of a change in course are willingly avoided, but the question would require more precise studies on case types.[73]

The solutions proposed typically point to the necessity of leadership.[74] This often happens with regard to the problem of innovation. But innovation is only a nice-sounding name for the problems we are discussing.[75] Whoever calls for innovation can act rhetorically even if he meets with resistance. In fact, however, it is a matter of replacing certainty by uncertainty; and leadership is required insofar as a sort of substitute certainty can be found in leader personalities until uncertainty absorption gets back on its feet and delivers reliable results. But whatever role increasingly strong leadership plays, the organization needs time to regain lost certainties in the wake of far-reaching structural changes.[76] From the point of view of uncertainty absorption and from the standpoint of manager careers, innovation has to be judged a pretty foolish undertaking – unless a tried and tested solution is already at hand and the problem to be solved is defined accordingly; or during the process of innovation the organization is allowed to discover what this means.[77]

There are certainly organizations that have more to do with opponents and risks than others. On the assumptions we have just outlined, the problem in such organizations of the instability of uncertainty absorption and the fictionality of the reality constructions that result would come to a head. On the one hand, this can mean that the characteristic qualities of the system type organization come to bear more conspicuously and with greater effect on the environment.[78] On the other, it could lead to such organizations having a greater need than others for a "philosophy of uncertainty absorption" and thus having to set up second-order self-observation. A term with a long tradition for this is "critique." But, like "innovation," this might be too strongly tied to expectations of improvement and then all too easily made subject to proof. The theory of operationally closed systems, with its derivatives such as cognitive constructivism and uncertainty absorption, does not go as far as this. But it tries to secure an analytical level from which to investigate whether and how organizations can reflexively apply uncertainty absorption to themselves.

Given this view of the problem and its theoretical construction, it could be advisable to replace the unreserved endorsement of innovation (in a positive sense) by the recommendation, in view of the uncertainty absorption that is operating anyway, to maintain and cultivate the irritability of the organization. On the one hand, this is a paradoxical principle, for irritation is the renewal of uncertainty. On the other hand, paradoxes also fall under this recommendation, for the communication of paradoxes is precisely. in this sense, irritation. This does not in any way exclude innovativeness. And it does not mean that a preliminary decision on its extent and radicalness has been made. Irritation means only the regeneration of uncertainty for special reasons, thus renewing a mix of orientation on structurally determined expectations of the system and perception of new types of requirement, hence a mix of self-reference and other-reference grounded in given situations. Irritation first has to be processed within the system as information: a difference that makes a difference. Only then can decisions be made about innovative structural changes and their extent, or about radical innovations. But irritation pays off not only in the form of innovation but especially because it compels decisions and leads to tested and rejected innovations ("for which the time is not yet ripe") being stored in the system memory.

XI

If the variables uncertainty absorption and power correlate, because power makes uncertainty absorption possible or because uncertainty absorption generates power, we can assume that the power structure of a system provides the opportunity to observe this process. To put this in more precise terms, the power structure of a system gives the system the opportunity to observe uncertainty and, thus, its own future. At any rate, the concrete contours and interest contexts of power distribution provide indications of how power will be exercised, and this will determine how the system prepares itself for a still indeterminate future. The less indication the environment of the system gives of the future of the system, the more important this possibility becomes.

The classical theory of the organization had assumed that both in the economy and in politics organizations are governed by their particular environment – through politically consolidated rule, or through the owners' interest in making a profit. But it is difficult to see how such direction from *outside the organization* could develop. The systems-theoretical analysis of societal functional systems such as the economy and politics tend to give the impression that surplus possibilities and corresponding uncertainties are generated there. This is, at any rate, to be expected if the formation of such systems presupposes decoupling from the environment, outdifferentiation, operational closure, and self-referential operation. In the economy, for example, this is true for self-regulation through the fluctuation of money prices and currency rates. In politics this is the case for electoral democracy and for the projection of the binary schema "right" and "left," which proposes the future in the form of oscillation. Politics tied to ends necessarily becomes despotism. Organizations that form in these functional systems can therefore not be understood as means or "staffs" (Max Weber) for an externally formed will. On the contrary, they are necessary because this is lacking; and because the immense surplus of possibilities that arise through the outdifferentiation and autonomy, as well as the operational closure and self-referential operation, of the functional systems have somehow to be put into shape. For this and only for this reason, organizations have to adopt a hierarchical structure because this is the best way of coping with the uncertainties of the environment.[79]

If a systems-theoretical analysis of the societal functional systems gives cause to switch from "governance" to "uncertainty," the analysis of organizations will have to follow suit. Max Weber's insight that organizations have become the inescapable fate of modern society remains. Only the explanation changes. Organizations are accordingly concerned not so much with equipping a will and the corresponding interests assumed to be extraneous to it; the problem is rather how to cope with the uncertainty in orientation that is continuously reproduced in the functional systems outdifferentiated in society. This, and only this, is why an organization needs a hierarchical order for its internal power relations.

Notes

1. We must therefore distinguish between knowledge and information and, accordingly, between a knowledge society and an information society. A society can only be described as an information society if it constantly surprises itself through decisions. See Niklas Luhmann, Entscheidungen in der "Informationsgesellschaft," Ms. 1996.
2. See Niklas Luhmann, Zweckbegriff und Systemrationalität: Über die Funktion von Zwecken in sozialen Systemen *(1968)*, Frankfurt 1973.
3. See Chapter 8 below.
4. For the original formulation see James G. March and Herbert A. Simon, *Organizations*, New York 1958, 165: "Uncertainty absorption takes place when inferences are drawn from a body of evidence and the inferences, instead of the evidence itself, are then communicated." March and Simon stress above all the link between this variable and influence and power in organizations. Cicourel provides very similar analyses with regard to protocols, registration, and documentation in organizations. See Aaron V. Cicourel, *The Social Organization of Juvenile Justice*, New York 1968; idem et al., *Language Use and School Performance*, New York 1974, 300 ff.; idem, Notes on the Integration of Micro- and Macro-Levels of Analysis, in: Karin Knorr-Cetina and Aaron V. Wildavsky (eds.), *Toward an Integration of Micro- and Macro-Sociologies*, Boston 1981, 51–80. The concept of reduction of ambiguities in organizing is seen as crucially important by Karl E. Weick, *Der Prozeß des Organisierens*, Frankfurt 1985.
5. See Michael Smithson, *Ignorance and Uncertainty: Emerging Paradigms*, New York 1989.
6. Arthur L. Stinchcombe, *Information and Organizations*, Berkeley 1990, esp. 32 ff. defines uncertainty absorption as a "skill."
7. If we set out not from decisions but from permanent positions, the process of uncertainty absorption could also be described as the transformation of input into output. See Federico Butera, *Il castello e la rete: Impresa, organizzazioni e professioni nell' Europa degli anni '90*, 2nd ed, Milan 1991, 155 ff. for the special case of research and development divisions.
8. See, e.g., Michael Masuch and Perry LaPotin, The Disorder of Organizational Logic – Makework Among Members of Bureaucratic Organizations, in:

Massimo Warglien and Michael Masuch (eds.), *The Logic of Organizational Discorder*, Berlin 1996, 163–182 (164).

9. See Chapters 2–3, p.

10. See Helmut Willke, Dimensionen des Wissensmanagements – Zum Zusammenhang von gesellschaftlicher und organisationaler Wissensbasierung, *Managementforschung* 6 (1996), 263–304.

11. In a similar vein, G.L.S. Shackle, *Imagination and the Nature of Choice*, Edinburgh 1979, sees psychic processes ("thought") – decision-making – as "exploitation of unknowledge" (74, 140). Without ignorance of the future, one could not envisage any alternatives ("rival choosables").

12. See Karl E. Weick, Re-Punctuating the Problem, in: Paul S. Goodman and Johannes M. Pennings et al. (eds.), *New Perspectives on Organizational Effectiveness*, San Francisco 1977, 193–225 (195).

13. See also Shackle op. cit., e.g. 15 f.

14. James G. March goes so far as to assume that this is why managers do not apply theories of rational decision-making that leave this factor out of account (and could they do so?). See: Eine Chronik der Überlegungen über Entscheidungsprozesse in Organisationen, in: James G. March (ed.), *Entscheidung und Organisation*, German translation. Wiesbaden 1990, 1–23 (7 f.). Recent developments in electronic information technologies also appear not to have changed anything in this regard. See, e.g., Dirk Hoppen, *Organisation und Informationstechnologie: Grundlagen für ein Konzept zur Organisationsgestaltung*, Hamburg 1992.

15. See Paul C. Nutt, Types of Organizational Decision Processes, *Administrative Science Quarterly* 29 (1984), 414–450. From this, Nutt infers that innovation is not very probable. We could perhaps also conclude that the uncertainty thus absorbed will quickly turn up again.

16. For a case study see, e.g., Leon H. Mayhew, *Law and Equal Opportunity: A Study of the Massachusetts Commission Against Discrimination*, Cambridge, MA 1968. See also Vicki E. Baier, James G. March, and Harald Saetren, Implementation and Ambiguity, *Scandinavian Journal of Management* 2 (1986), 197–212 with further references.

17. The opposite view is more common. See, e.g., Robert B. Duncan, Characteristics of Organizational Environments and Perceived Environmental Uncertainty, *Administrative Science Quarterly* 17 (1972), 313–327.

18. See Ellen J. Langer, The Illusion of Control, *Journal of Personality and Social Psychology* 32 (1975), 311–328; idem, The Psychology of Chance, *Journal for the Theory of Social Behaviour* 7 (1977), 185–207; Lyn Y. Abramson and Lauren B. Alloy, Judgment of Contingency: Errors and Their Implications, in: Andrew Baum and Jerome E. Singer (eds.), *Advances in Environmental Psychology* vol. 2, *Applications of Personal Control*, Hillsdale 1980, 111–130 (115 ff.); Shelley S. Taylor, Adjustment to Threatening Events: A Theory of Cognitive Adaptation, *American Psychologist* 38 (1983), 1161–1173.

19. See Joanne Linneroth, The Political Processing of Uncertainty, *Acta Psychologica* 56 (1984), 219–231, with the warning to make more uncertainty public.

20. See Klaus A. Ziegert, Courts and the Self-concept of Law: The Mapping of the Environment by Courts of First Instance, *Sydney Law Review* 14 (1992), 196–229.

21. Vgl. Chester I. Barnard, The Functions of the Executive (1938), quoted from the Cambridge edition 1951, 314 ff., or Robert Dubin, *Human Relations in Administration*, 2nd ed. Englewood Cliffs, NJ 1961, 433 f.

22. See Günter Ortmann et al., *Computer und Macht in Organisationen: Mikropolitische Analysen*, Opladen 1990.

23. See Abraham Tesser and Sidney Rosen, The Reluctance to Transmit Bad News, in: Leonard Berkowitz (ed.), *Advances in Experimental Social Psychology* 8 (1975), 193–232.

24. This raises highly topical organizational issues about the more concrete and simultaneous meshing of corporate accounting with business transactions and the relevant decisions. After all, the information must not necessarily wait for sums to be done, let alone balance sheets prepared, before it is taken into account.

25. See Chester I. Barnard, *The Functions of the Executive* (1938), Cambridge, MA 1951, 319, quoting an "expert in publicity."

26. Barnard op. cit., 319. And Barnard explicitly stresses that this has nothing to do with moral insincerity, and thus not with any infringement of a personal code of sincerity, but arises from, as it were, the technical conditions of efficient communication. Anyone who enjoys older literature can find all this in Baltasar Gracián, as well.

27. For a brief overview, see Barbara Czarniawska-Joerges and Bernward Joerges, How to Control Things with Words: Organizational Talk and Control, *Management Communication Quarterly* 2 (1988), 170–193.

28. On the age of this concept within a specific rhetorical traditions, see Norman Knox, The Word Irony and Its Context 1500–1755, Durham 1961. It was not until the eighteenth century that, in parallel to the decline of training in rhetoric, the concept and thus the form of irony took on a more general meaning. The Romantics lauded the "logical beauty" of its form (Friedrich Schlegel, *Kritische Fragmente 42, Werke in zwei Bänden*, Berlin 1980, vol. 1, 172), while in the everyday practice of communication, irony tended to be irritating and its innocence doubted.

29. See also Niklas Luhmann, *Haltlose Komplexität, in idem Soziologische Aufklärung* vol. 5, Opladen 1990, 59–76.

30. For neurophysiological systems, see Heinz Förster, *Das Gedächtnis: Eine quantenphysikalische Untersuchung*, Vienna 1949.

31. "Of course we know that this memory is *everywhere*, that it is realized in the structure of the interconnection schema and in the operational modalities of all nodes of this network," as Heinz von Foerster puts it in Gedächtnis ohne Aufzeichnung, in idem, *Sicht und Einsicht: Versuche zu einer operativen Erkenntnistheorie*, Braunschweig 1985, 133–172 (168 f.).

32. However, it should be noted that much of what is omitted from the decision-making memory in this fashion is preserved "undated," as "organizational culture," and hence, even in the way memory operates, limits how and what can be communicated in future presents. We shall be coming back to this.

33. See Heinz Förster op. cit. See also idem., Quantum Mechanical Theory of Memory, in: idem (ed.), *Cybernetics: Transactions of the Sixth Conference*, New York 1950, 112–145.

34. This takes up what has already been said. See above 140 ff. (4/IV.).

35. See also Heinz von Foerster, What Is Memory that It May Have Hindsight and Foresight as Well? in: Samuel Bogoch (ed.), *The Future of the Brain Sciences.*

Proceedings of a Conference held at the New York Academy of Medicine, New York 1969, 19–64; German translation in Heinz von Foerster, *Wissen und Gewissen: Versuch einer Brücke*, Frankfurt 1993, 299–336.

36. See Carolyn R. Miller, Genre as Social Action, *Quarterly Journal of Speech* 70 (1984), 151–167; JoAnne Yates I Wanda J. Orlikowski, Genres of Organizational Communication: A Structurational Approach to Studying Communication and Media, *Academy of Management Review* 17 (1992), 299–326; Carol Berkenkotter I Thomas N. Huckin, Rethinking Genre from a Sociocognitive Perspective, *Written Communication* 10 (1993), 475–509.

37. On the literature see Roger Schank I Robert P. Abelson, *Scripts, Plans, Goals, and Understanding: An Inquiry into Human Knowledge Structures*, Jillsdale, NJ 1977; George A. Akerlof, The Economics of Caste and of the Rat Race and Other Woeful Tales, *Quarterly Journal of Economics* 90 (1976), 599–617.

38. See the example of electronic mail in Wanda J. Orlikowski and JoAnne Yates, Genre Repertoire: The Structuring of Communicative Practices in Organizations, *Administrative Science Quarterly* 39 (1994), 541–574.

39. On this and on older literature, see Niklas Luhmann, *Funktion und Folgen formaler Organisation*, Berlin 1964, 172 ff.

40. See Chapter 7 below.

41. In the sense of Tom Burns, Micropolitics: Mechanisms of Institutional Change: *Administrative Science Quarterly* 6 (1961), 257–281. See also Horst Bosetzky, Machiavellismus, Machtkumulation und Mikropolitik, *Zeitschrift für Organisation* 46 (1977); Henry Mintzberg, *Power In and Around Organizations*, Englewood Cliffs, NJ 1983, esp. 171 ff.; Willi Küpper and Günther Ortmann (eds.), *Mikropolitik: Rationalität, Macht und Spiele in Organisationen*, Opladen 1988; Günther Ortmann, *Formen der Produktion: Organisation und Rekursivität*, Opladen 1995.

42. This is indeed the view taken by Philip G. Herbst, *Alternatives to Hierarchies*, Leiden 1976, 81 note 1.

43. To put it in very broad terms, uncertainty absorption is power because it determines the state of systems. More precisely, we could say that uncertainty absorption *bestows* power because other positions in the system are dependent on how uncertainty is handled. See, e.g., Michel Crozier, *Le phénomène bureaucratique*, Paris 1963; David J. HIckson et al., A Strategic Contingencies Theory of Intraorganizational Power, *Administrative Science Quarterly* 16 (1971), 216–229; C.R. Hinings et al., Structural Conditions of Intraorganizational Power, *Administrative Science Quarterly* 19 (1974), 22–44; Michel Crozier and Erhard Friedberg, *L'acteur et le système: Les contraintes de l'action collective*, Paris 1977, 20 f. Even if this theory can explain how (ascribed) power comes about, the really interesting question remains unanswered, namely what power that has arisen in this way can be brought to. Does it lead to anything more that particular politeness in dealing with those who can decide about uncertainty?

44. See, e.g., Mintzberg, op. cit. Power is defined in correspondingly vague terms as "the capacity to effect (or affect) organizational outcomes" (p. 4), and the attribution problem (the power of attributing!) is not addressed.

45. This same is true if we replace the concept of power by that of interest. For not fully comprehensible reasons, James March sees differences; in explanation

through power but not in explanation through interest he sees a "tautological expression of the unexplained variance in a decision-making situation" – op. cit. (1990), p. 7.

46. The relevant literature then practically delegates responsibility for the power concept to respondents, and takes this to be empirical research. See, e.g., Mayer N. Zald (ed.), *Power in Organizations*, Nashville Tenn. 1970; Gerald R. Salancik and Jeffrey Pfeffer, The Bases and Use of Power in Organizational Decision Making: The Case of a University, *Administrative Science Quarterly* 19 (1994), 453–473; idem, Who Gets Power – and How They Hold on to It: A Strategic-Contingency Model of Power, *Organizational Dynamics* 6 (1977), 3–21.

47. See Niklas Luhmann, *Macht*, 2nd ed. Stuttgart 1988

48. For a case study see Martin Gangiulo, Two-step Leverage: Managing Constraint in Organizational Politics, *Administrative Science Quarterly* 38 (1993), 1–19.

49. See, e.g., Jitendra V. Singh and Robert J. House and David J. Tucker, Organizational Change and Organizational Mortality, *Administrative Science Quarterly* 31 (1986), 587–611, with the distinction between "core changes" and "periphery changes." See also Jacques Delacroix and Anand Swaminanthan, Cosmetic, Speculative and Adaptive Organizational Change in the Wine Industry: A Longitudinal Study, *Administrative Science Quarterly* 36 (1991), 631–661. For more detail on the problem of structural change, see Chapter 11 below.

50. See Jean-Pierre Dupuy, Zur Selbst-Dekonstruktion von Konventionen, in: Paul Watzlawick and Peter Krieg (eds.), *Das Auge des Betrachters: Beiträge zum Konstruktivismus: Festschrift Heinz von Foerster*, München 1991, 85–100, or, in somewhat different vein, idem, Les paradoxes de l'ordre conventionnel, in: Michel Amiot et al. (eds.), *Système et paradoxe: Autour de la pensée d'Yves Barel*, Paris 1993, 107–123. Karl-Heinz Ladeur, Von der Verwaltungshierarchie zum administrativen Netzwerk? Zur Erhaltung der Eigenständigkeit der Verwaltung unter Komplexitätsbedingungen, *Die Verwaltung* 26 (1993), 137–165 (142 f.) suggests understanding this conventionalization as self-fulfilling prophecy and to use the concept in the analysis of modern public administration.

51. Crozier and Friedberg op. cit. (1977), 147, speaks of "*colonisation de l'organisation par ses relais.*"

52. See the definition of authority as "capacity fuɩ reasoned elaboration" in Carl J. Friedrich, Authority, Reason, and Discretion, in: idem (ed.), Authority (Nomos I), New York 1958. See also Herbert A. Simon and Donald W. Smithburg and Victor A. Thompson, *Public Administration*, New York 1950, 189 ff. on the "authority of confidence" and how it relates to hierarchy. See also T. Heller, Changing Authority Patterns: A Cultural Perspective, *Academy of Management Review* 10 (1985), 488–495.

53. Criticism of obsolescent experience is, however, not particularly new. It is already to be found as criticism of the authority of the old in the sixteenth century in the light of numerous technical and agricultural innovations, better schooling, and the spread of printed books. See Keith Thomas, *Vergangenheit, Zukunft, Lebensalter: Zeitvorstellungen im England der frühen Neuzeit*, German translation Berlin 1988. Berlin 1988, p. 65.

54. See Crozier and Friedberg op. cit. 143 f.

55. See already Chapter 3–3 on overestimation of the need for "consensus." See also Nils Brunsson, *The Irrational Organization: Irrationality as a Basis for Organizational Action and Change*, Chichester 1985; idem, *The Organization of Hypocrisy: Talk, Decisions and Actions in Organizations*, Chichester 1989, with the thesis that highly motivated willingness to act can be achieved in "irrational" organizations. On conventional agreements see Alois Hahn, Verständigung als Strategie, in: Max Haller et al. (eds.), *Kultur und Gesellschaft. Verhandlungen des 24. Deutschen Soziologentages, des 11. Österreichischen Soziologentages und des 8. Kongresses der Schweizerischen Gesellschaft für Soziologie in Zürich 1988*, Frankfurt 1989, 346–359 (with basis in empirical studies on modern families). On workable agreements, which do have necessarily mean consensus, see George J. McCall and J.L. Simmons, *Identities and Interactions*, New York 1966, esp. 140 ff.

56. See Philip G. Herbst, *Alternatives to Hierarchies*, Leiden 1976, 32 ff. with reference to Gerd Sommerhoff, *Analytical Biology*, London 1950. See also idem, *Logic of the Living Brain*, London 1974, 73 ff.

57. See Gotthard Günther, *Cognition and Volition: A Contribution to a Cybernetic Theory of Subjectivity*, in idem, *Beiträge zur Grundlegung einer operationsfähigen Dialektik vol. 2*, Hamburg 1979, 203–240 (212): the distinction of living subjects from their environment *forces* them to assume an active role in relation to this environment.

58. Organizational sociology long shared this view. See, e.g., Tom Bums and G.M. Stalker, *The Management of Innovation*, London 1961; Richard M. Cyert and James G. March, *A Behavioral Theory of the Firm*, Englewood Cliffs, NJ 1963; F.E. Emery and E. L. Trist, The Causal Texture of Organizational Environments, *Human Relations* 18 (1965), 21–32; Shirley Terreberry, The Evolution of Organizational Environments, *Administrative Science Quarterly* 12 (1968), 590–612; Robert B. Duncan, Characteristics of Organizational Environments and Perceived Environmental Uncertainty, *Administrative Science Quarterly* 17 (1972), 313–327; Husseyin Leblebici and Gerald R. Salancik, Effects of Environmental Uncertainty on Information and Decision Processes in Banks, *Administrative Science Quarterly* 26 (1981), 578–596 (already taking stronger account of self-generated uncertainty). For early emphasis on self-generated uncertainty, see James D. Thompson and Arthur Tuden, Strategies, Structures, and Processes of Organizational Decision, in James D. Thompson et al. (ed.), *Comparative Studies in Administration*, Pittsburgh 1959, 195–216.

59. On this concept see Niklas Luhmann, *Funktion und Folgen formaler Organisation*, Berlin 1964, 220 ff. For the American discussion see Howard Aldrich and Diane Herker, Boundary Spanning Roles and Organization Structure, Academy of Management, *Journal* 2 (1977), 217–230. Typically, discussion on the subject treats this concept as concerned with subordinate roles and does not take sufficient account of the fact that top positions in particular are typically boundary positions and often spend most of their working hours on external contacts.

60. Still often cited: Frank H. Knight, *Risk, Uncertainty and Profit (1921)*, 7th reprint Boston 1948.

61. See Chapter 1–2 above.

62. On the political system see Renate Mayntz and Fritz Scharpf, *Policy-Making in the Federal Bureaucracy*, Amsterdam 1975; Renate Mayntz, *Soziologie der öffentlichen Verwaltung*, Karlsruhe 1978, esp. 60 ff. Much research on the possibilities of politically controlling the administration, on problems of "implementation" and "implementation deficits," has its point of departure in the inadequacies of the classical model. See Renate Mayntz, Regulative Politik in der Krise? in: Joachim Matthes (ed.), *Sozialer Wandel in Westeuropa: Verhandlungen des 19. Deutschen Soziologentags Berlin*, Frankfurt 1979, 55–81; idem. (ed.), *Implementation politischer Programme*, Königstein 1980; idem. (ed.), *Implementation politischer Programme Teil II*, Opladen 1982.

63. See Henry A. Landsberger, The Horizontal Dimension in Bureaucracy, *Administrative Science Quarterly* 6 (1961), 299–332 (308 ff.) with the then-fashionable recommendation of "management by exception." See also George Strauss, Tactics of Lateral Relationship: The Purchasing Agent, *Administrative Science Quarterly* 7 (1962), 161–186.

64. The literature on this concept takes account of both position-immanent conflict and role stress, and of influence through the channeling of information, but it pays too little attention to beneficial uncertainty absorption. See, in addition to the literature listed in note 4 above, int.al. William Foote Whyte, The Social Structure of the Restaurant, *American Journal of Sociology* 54 (1949), 302–310; Ross Adair, The Indian Health Worker, *Human Organization* 19 (1960), 59–63. Robert E. Spekman, Influence and Information: An Exploratory Investigation of the Boundary Role Person's Basis of Power, *Academy of Management Journal* 22 (1979), 104–117; Robert A. Friedman and Joel Podolny, Differentiation of Boundary Spanning Roles: Labor Negotiation and Implications for Role Conflict, *Administrative Science Quarterly* 37 (1992), 28–47.

65. See March and Simon op. cit. 165, who, however, also point out: "Both the amount and the locus of uncertainty absorption affect the ... influence structure of the organization". See also Crozier and Friedberg op. cit. (1977), 20 f. For more detail, see section 5 above.

66. This, too, is one of the variables identified by March and Simon. See op. cit. 166.

67. See Amos Tversky and Daniel Kahneman, Availability: A Heuristic for Judging Frequency and Probability, *Cognitive Psychology* 5 (1973), 207–232; Daniel Kahneman and Paul Slovic and Amos Tversky (eds.), *Judgment under Uncertainty: Heuristics and Biases*, Cambridge 1982. See also R.E. Nisbet and L. Ross, *Human Inference: Strategies and Shortcomings of Social Judgments*, Englewood Cliffs, NJ 1980.

68. We also offer this reflection as background analysis of the modern semantics of "interesting." On the paradox concealed behind this, see also Joanna Martin et al., The Uniqueness Paradox in Organizational Stories, *Administrative Science Quarterly* 28 (1983), 438–453. In modern literary criticism, the distinction between interesting and uninteresting arose in the eighteenth century in connection with the modern novel written for commercial exploitation (and no longer under the conditions of patronage). Here, too, the point of departure of this code is that the story suggests unique events that nevertheless allow the reader to draw inferences with regard to one's own life. See, e.g., Gerhard Plumpe, *Ästhetische Kommunikation der Moderne* vol. 1, Opladen 1993, 22 f., 156 ff.

69. See Nancy Pennington and Reid Hastie, Evidence Evaluation in Complex Decision Making, *Journal of Personality and Social Psychology* 51 (1986), 242–258; idem, Explanation-Based Decision Making: Effects of Memory Structure on Judgment, *Journal of Experimental Psychology: Learning, Memory, and Cognition* 14 (1988), 521–533.

70. See Henry Mintzberg, *The Nature of Managerial Work*, New York 1973, oder Warren J. Keegan, Multinational Scanning: A Study of the Information Sources Utilized by Headquarters Executives in Multinational Companies, *Administrative Science Quarterly* 19 (1974), 411–421. According to Keegan, sources of information in "general management" are 71% "human" and only 18% "documentary." In finance the figures are 44% and 66%. See also H.E. Dale, *The Higher Civil Service of Great Britain*, Oxford 1941, 157 ff.; Fritz Morstein *Marx: Amerikanische Verwaltung: Hauptgesichtspunkte und Probleme*, Berlin 1963, 126 ff.

71. Now a classical treatment: Peter L. Berger and Thomas Luckmann, *The Social Construction of Reality*, New York 1967.

72. It is not very clear that a special theory is required, and it can be explained only in history of science terms, namely the overly strong isolation of the field of research the organizational sciences address. See Chapter 1–6.

73. See, e.g.,. Barry M. Staw, Knee-Deep in the Muddy: A Study of Escalating Commitment to a Chosen Course of Action, *Organizational Behavior and Human Performance* 16 (1976), 27–44 – a simulated decision game (investment) with the result that accountability requires keeping to the original goals at greater expense (bad for all problems with cost overruns). But see also Barry M. Staw and Frederick V. Fox, Escalation: The Determinant of Commitment to a Chosen Course of Action, *Human Relations* 30 (1977), 431–450 with doubts about the lastingness of such escalation.

74. See, for one example of many, Philip Selznick, *Leadership in Administration: A Sociological Interpretation*, Evanston, IL 1957.

75. Under this label, the topic has long preoccupied organizational science on the assumption that innovations are a necessity and that this is a matter that should be furthered. See, e.g., Chris Argyris, *Organization and Innovation*, Homewood, IL 1965; Victor A. Thompson, *Bureaucracy and Innovation*, University of Alabama 1969; Gerald Zaltman et al., *Innovations and Organizations*, New York 1973; George W. Downs, Jr., Bureaucracy, *Innovation, and Public Policy*, Lexington, MA 1976. Some of the theoretical problems are transferred to methodological problems with the aim of discovering the special characteristics of particularly innovative organizations through comparative empirical studies. See, e.g., George W. Downs and Lawrence B. Mohr, Conceptual Issues in the Study of Innovation, *Administrative Science Quarterly* 21 (1976), 700–714.

76. Nowadays this is more discussed than in the past under the heading of "disruptive change." See Terry L. Amburgey et al., Resetting the Clock, The Dynamics of Organizational Change and Failure, *Administrative Science Quarterly* 38 (1993), 51–73.

77. See James G. March, Footnotes to Organizational Change, *Administrative Science Quarterly* 26 (1981), 563577; Paul C. Nutt, Types of Organizational Decision Processes, *Administrative Science Quarterly* 29 (1984), 414–450 (445 f.).

78. For an analysis of political parties from these points of view, see Niklas Luhmann, Die Unbeliebtheit der politischen Parteien, in: Siegfried Unseld (ed.), *Politik ohne Projekt? Nachdenken über Deutschland*, Frankfurt 1993, 43–53.
79. Economists, in particular, are aware of this. See, e.g., Jay B. Barney and William G. Ouchi (eds.), *Organizational Economics*, San Francisco 1986, 12: "Whenever any environmental uncertainty faced a firm, the firm would adopt some form of vertical integration."

7   Decision Premises

The function of uncertainty absorption is not only to reduce uncertainty. As everywhere, for example, in the evolution of language or the development of a transport network, reducing complexity for this purpose can also facilitate the development of secondary complexity. Basically, this is the principle of forming systems through operational closure: the environment is excluded so that, through this reduction of complexity, the system can develop its own complexity. The operationally produced external boundary is then marked internally by the distinction between self-reference and other-reference.

Naturally, this cannot happen "just anyhow" but only in a very specific, evolutionarily successful manner. Organizations make it possible for themselves to produce internal complexity that still requires determination by deciding on decision premises for further decisions.[1] By "premise" we mean a precondition that can no longer be checked when used; or rather that, although its relevance for the problem at hand plays a role, its truth does not. It should also be noted that the relation of premise to decision is neither logical nor causal. The decision cannot be deduced from its premises nor are the premises the cause of a decision – which would allow the system to be causally derived by ascertaining its premises. For this reason, it has now become usual to describe the relationship between premise and decision, and, in dependence on this, the relationship between decisions, as "loose coupling."[2] In other words, decisions on decision premises can help save decision costs, but decisions that are not fully specified have to be accepted in exchange.

The concept of decision premise can be very broadly defined to include everything that has to be taken as given when making a decision. But this would make the concept superfluous. A useful narrowing of the definition for the purposes of organization theory could be to accept only decisions as decision premises. The concept would then coincide with that of uncertainty absorption and include all, even very concrete prior decisions – for example, that an expenditure that has been ordered is actually made or that the file on a completed case is closed. In this sense, decision premises are the outcome of absorbed uncertainty,[3] or, in other words, the form in which the organization remembers uncertainty absorption. The concept becomes fruitful only through a second (also paradoxical) limitation: there are decisions that set the decision premises for a still undetermined multitude of other decisions.[4] In such cases, the reach of decisions is *extended by limitation*; or, as we have seen, complexity is produced by reduction.

Decision premises enable decision-making processes to be doubly monitored: at the level of observable behavior and its products and at the level of the premises, which are possibly the cause of undesirable results.[5] They intensify intrasystemic uncertainties and put them in a form that can be further processed in the system.[6] The issue may now be interpreting programs or predicting how present employees will behave – intrasystemic variables are always concerned that also hide any external opacity.

Decision premises therefore serve the system only as oscillators. They do not yet determine future decisions; they cannot already decide in the future. But they focus communication on the differences set in the premises, and this makes it likely that future decisions will be observed with reference to the given premises from the point of view of compliance or noncompliance, of conformity or deviation, instead of once again going into the full complexity of the situations involved. This is naturally to simplify things considerably, but the compensation is that the other side of the form is not excluded but kept in mind.

Because decision premises go back to decisions made in the same system, they are automatically valid only within this system. There may well be similar premises (such as similar production programs or other hierarchies) in the environment, too; but from the perspective of the system, this can be seen only as an opportunity, as a non-binding accident. The same can be attained by other means, by assuming the existence of an organizational culture specific to the given system. And it is taken for granted that such an orientation distinguishes the system from systems of its environment and endows it with a distinct individuality. We shall be coming back to this case of undecidable but distinguishing ("identifying") decision premises at a later point (7–6). We are primarily interested in decision premises that are introduced by decision in order to limit the scope for a multitude of decisions in the same direction.

To begin with, we could think of a rule laid down for more than one decision. For example, there can be a rule for a warehouseman to reorder articles when stocks fall below a certain level; or a rule in a bank that a higher authority is to be consulted if loans over a certain sum are requested. Without a doubt, these are examples of decision premises that go back to a decision. We shall call such regulatory conditions for making the right (or, as the case may be, wrong) decision, *decision programs*. But there are also quite different types of decision premise that serve to complement or even replace detailed programming. Decision premises can also stipulate the communication channel that has to be followed if the decision is to be acknowledged as one made by the organization. What counts is the authority set by decision premise: above all, the right to issue binding instructions, but also the right to be heard. This aspect of self-regulation in an organizational system is often called formal organization. We think above all of "official channels," of the involvement of higher posts or cooperation between posts on various levels. Who can order the deployment of a repair crew when a machine breaks down? Or who decides when several demands come at the same time? Or who is authorized to communicate a decision as a binding one to the outside world, however the preceding uncertainty absorption has run? Finally, the regulation of personnel deployment – be it ad hoc, be it in the form of assigning people to functions or posts – also falls under the concept of deciding on decision premises. For, at least according to the official self-presentation of the organization, people are not selected because they are loved or because they buy their way in or because of family ties or friendship, but because they are considered to be suitable for certain tasks. That is to say that, like programs, they are chosen as decision premises for decisions.

Although it is often believed that programs culminating in the organizational objective are more important than other decision premises (after all, what has an organization been founded for?),[7] in actually operating organizations there is no such primacy, hence no hierarchical/transitive relationship between decision premises but, on the contrary, a constant change in primacy; for good reason. Although there are programs for selecting people (recruitment, transfer, promotion), these programs have in turn to be realized by decisions that are made by persons-in-posts. Although there are programs for regulating competences and communication channels (for instance, preferences for delegation, for certain ranges of the "span of control"), these programs can be determined only by certain posts in the communication network. These sorts of decision premise can also be mutually substituted or mitigate one another. If a task cannot be programmed in detail, the demands increase on the person of the decision-maker. If he does not have all the abilities necessary, the involvement of other posts has to be stipulated. Or hierarchical supervision could be increased.[8] For the very reason that these various sorts of decision premise are relatively permanent and, therefore, have to be changed explicitly should the need arise, structures can be put in place making them mutually dependent, thus taking the complexity of the system into account.

We shall be coming back to these types of decision premise in greater detail. At the moment, listing them in addition to the all-too-formal definition of decision premise serves only to show their range.

The concept of decision premise thus breaks with the notion that rationality can be attained by applying rules along the lines of a logical procedure, or one that can at least be controlled for error. This does not have to be excluded, and organized controlling for error can still be sought. But if the organization chooses its premises from the standpoint that no errors should be made, this reveals a not very convincing idea of rationality. Given the need for continuous uncertainty absorption and given the advantages offered by self-made uncertainty, what is more important is that there should be possibilities to limit the horizon, to be chosen depending on the situation in which the decision is to be made. The advantageousness, indeed indispensability, of determining decision premises has to do with the consequences of reentry, which we introduced in Chapter 2. This means that they involve the "unresolvable indeterminacy"[9] that arises when the distinction between system and environment is reintroduced into the system, thus making the system bistable, having continuously to oscillate between self-referential and other-referential indications.[10] It is this basic condition that is, so to speak, defused by the temporary, experimental, revisable introduction of premises for still indeterminable decisions. Decision premises then act as redundancies that reduce the information load to an affordable format. They thus lower decision costs. The already redundant indeterminability (always the same!) is converted into redundant, namely repeatedly applicable limitations. Although the system remains indeterminable for itself, every decision framed by decision premises manages with a lower information load; and each does so on condition that the same redundancies are re-used in the system – or changed.

The problem of bistability and indeterminability is thus transmuted into a time problem, into the difference between definite past and indefinite future and the prospect of follow-up decisions. The switch in the conceptuality of organization theory to decision/decision premise is a reaction to a new understanding of time; at the same time, it overcomes classical controversies about rationalism and structuralism. Although the determination of rationality through maximum values in the end/means schema had provided for a two-sided variation of ends (effects) and means (causes) and had considered preferences to be only parameters or conditions for handling the schema, it had simple presupposed causality or treated it only as a problem of knowledge and not of attribution. Structural analysis had not failed to recognize that structures, too, are changeable and that their relation to time remains open; but it had tied the identity of the system to maintenance of the structure and thus earned the reputation of being "conservative." In neither case was the question raised of who the observer was, because it had already been answered: science in all its self-responsibility and seriousness.

The decision/decision premise terminology takes the dissolution already initiated in these two traditions a step further and completes it. It is geared to reality being given only in the present of decisions, that all time pointing beyond this has to be constructed; and that in this case science observes an observer who observes himself and can make no decision without distinguishing between himself and his environment (self-reference and other-reference), although the environment is operationally inaccessible to him because he cannot decide in the environment. For the concept of decision premise, this means that it is only a premise (referring back to another decision) if in the decision process it is *actually used as such*, be it conforming, cooperative, sabotaging, or tacit, be it "on record" with consent or contradiction.

II

Decisions on decision premises also have to be concretely decided, have to be decisions made in the recursive network of the system's own operations. The system knows no other way of operating. There are, of course, cognitions by which a decision relates to something that it does not itself decide. For example, in preparing a decision, information is gone through, texts are read, people are questioned and listened to. Operations always oscillate between self-reference and other-reference. But the mode of operation that produces and reproduces the historical state of the system is always and only the decision. Without decisions, nothing changes.

This is why, at the level of deciding on decision premises, the condition of operational closure is also repeated. The production of decision premises is also reproduction, that is, production from products of the system. It, too, can be regulated through decision premises; for this purpose, too, there are responsibilities and persons-in-posts, and possibly meta-programs. But if such premises for premise decisions are lacking (and in reality there is no infinite regress), the decision can help itself; it can come up with something and take responsibility for it.

We can also describe this self-sufficient regulation of regulation, this coordination of coordination, as a guarantee of reflexivity. Heinz von Foerster has referred to the same state of affairs in the case of the brain as "double closure."[11] The system accordingly operates on two or more levels at the same time, *but which it distinguishes and keeps separate*. The coordination of coordination is also a product of the system and subject to all the conditions that we have identified in general for the mode of operation: the unfolding of paradox, temporal recursivity, uncertainty absorption, and so forth. Structures and processes are therefore not, as the colloquial use of the terms suggests, various sorts of quality of being comprising the system (whose unity in this case would be the "and" of structures and processes). On the contrary, the unity of the mode of operation *imposes* autonomy *if* at least two levels can be successfully separated and self-organization thus enabled.

If an organization were unable to decide about decision premises, it would remain a mere extension of its environment. At the level of the elementary concatenation of operations, one would not see how something could be done differently if there were no signals from outside. Only if the coordination of decisions, too, can be decided and alternatives thus presented does self-organization take effect and outdifferentiate the system. And only then are decisions also made to the effect that decisions have to be made on whether the expectations produced within the system itself are to be pursued – or not; and whether they are then to be changed or simply ignored and forgotten.[12]

Dependence on decision premises, which have themselves been put in place by decisions, means that orientation on a reality taken for granted carries less weight in organizations than in the everyday life of its environment.[13] This makes it easier to problematize the reality that is presupposed. If a decision on the subject has already been made, it is easy to imagine that a different decision could also be made. Decision premises therefore function as a virtual potential for irritation, which waits only for appropriate circumstances to arise to be reintroduced into the decision process. Compared with the environment, the basis of daily behavior is much more obviously contingent.

III

In the recursive network of autopoiesis, decisions always orient themselves on other decisions and mostly reflect their own orientation value for other decisions. In the concrete course of the decision process, this requires a sort of neighborly relationship that can be appraised without considerable expenditure of time and knowledge. Decision premises, by contrast, orient themselves on other decision premises at a more abstract level of organizational coordination. A person is appointed for a specific job, and it is assumed that he is up to the task. In this sense, decision premises can be coordinated with one another, and there can be programs and persons who are responsible for this.

The test for decision premises then ultimately lies in the question of what the concrete decisions made under the regime of given premises achieve. In other words, there is no abstract guarantee of rationality, for instance, in the form of principles that are laid down and could be translated into decisions via premises.[14] Organizations are historical machines, non-trivial systems, which constantly put themselves in a particular, concrete state to which they have to refer in deciding how to proceed. This point of reference of operational self-reference, the state that is realized, cannot be anticipated (or at best in rough outline and subject to error). This had been the point of the semantic invention of "time," and especially "future": to introduce indeterminability into the present. Nevertheless, it is possible and necessary to coordinate decision premises; but such coordination is only a sort of compensation for the inability to foresee and determine the concrete historical states of the system by which the given, concrete decision process will be guided.

We shall call the decision on decision premises *planning*. Planning decisions are decisions like any others. The organization has only a single mode of operation at its disposal, which it has to use for everything that is to be done. Everything that has been said about decisions, therefore, also applies to planning decisions. They, too, are concrete events that orient themselves self-referentially on the historical state of the system as they find it. They, too, when observed, are grounded in paradox. And they absorb uncertainty. And they transform open contingency into closed contingency. They, too, can be judged differently in retrospect and provided with other alternatives than those considered at the time of deciding. One would assume that they normally have a greater impact than other decisions but this, too, is uncertain; witness concrete errors in the normal decision process that have scandalous effects. Planning decisions accordingly have no other essence, no other nature than decisions in general. The system may place them high up in the hierarchy, but that does not give them a different quality, especially since this says nothing about what decisions influence planning decisions. As in computing, there is thus only a single type of operation by which the system has to determine structures and carry out operations.

"Planning" usually suggests the anticipatory shaping of the future. But even when planned out, the future is and remains unknown. In the complexity of planning, a sort of certainty is sought that the future cannot offer. It should also be kept in mind that, as far as programs, personnel, and communication channels are concerned, decision premises are always already fixed and can only be changed. Planning is, therefore, rather to be seen as a description of a state that could possibly be changed; a state that has been more or less improvised and can only in retrospect be described as order.[15] Only in this way can planning attain the certainty that allows it to overcome the unknown-ness of the future.

What distinguishes planning decisions, however, is the obligation to coordinate different sorts of decision premise. This obligation is structural and therefore inescapable, however good or bad coordination turns out to be. The tool that makes the need for coordination credibly apparent and practically inevitable can described as "post." The construct "post" symbolizes that the replacement of decision premises is consistent with the persistence, with the autopoiesis of the system. The term is used more in public authorities than in private business organizations, because in the public service it is defined in terms of a long tradition of officialdom and in terms of the budget. The public sector is also more accustomed than the private sector to counting on the continuity of posts, whereas the private sector tends to plan more with an eye to the human resources needed. Despite these differences, which have a marked impact on the mentality and elasticity of planning decisions, one should not underestimate the similarity of requirements.

In both the public and private sector it can be assumed that posts are symbolized by an amount of money earmarked for wage or salary payments, and which is continuously renewed. To this extent the organizational post structure confirms the view that modern organizations depend on the money economy and not, for instance, on the assumption that, through the work a member owes the organization, he generates his own income.[16] This order enables the outdifferentiation of organizations in all functional systems, not only in the economy itself, under the very general and not specifically determinative condition that society maintains a functioning money economy.

However important this symbolization of posts by amounts of money is, it does not tell us enough about the function of post as an organizational principle. For the function of such posts in organizations is naturally not to regulate the distribution of money.[17] In the organizational system, posts serve rather to produce consistency in relations between decision premises. In any case, the decision premises program, personnel, and communication channels have to be coordinated. When people are taken on, they are assigned specific tasks, and this also requires their assignment to particular departments and particular levels of the hierarchy. A nurse is employed to perform a specific task in a specific department of a specific hospital. The same is true of the head of a youth welfare office, of foundry workers, and for chairs of supervisory boards in big companies. One can hardly imagine recruiting people without assigning specific activities to them, any more than one would undertake a certain task without determining who was to carry out the relevant activities.

If the notion of post is seen in the context of this need for coordination, it has the advantage of abstract symbolization. The post, whether or not registered in some budget or organization chart or other, is merely an empty identity with exchangeable components. The working capacity of a person as limited by time defines a post's scope (there can naturally also be "half-time" posts for part-time workers), but who is to fill it is left open. The person must be charged with a specific task, but this task can change or be defined in such broad terms that it has to be fulfilled through personal decisions of the post holder. Finally, a post is assigned to a specific communication network, but does not lose its identity when communication channels change or the post is assigned to another section of the organization.[18]

Being an abstract identity, the post remains without information; we could say it does not exist. On paper it may exist as a node in an organization chart, or as a sum of money earmarked for paying someone a salary. But this alone tells us nothing about the functional meaning of posts, only something about organization charts or budgeted funds. The meaning of a post lies in the mutual limitation of decision premises. When and only when a task is defined as a decision program can one decide whom to appoint to the post; or more precisely, who among a number of candidates is best suited. But also conversely: if a particularly well qualified person is available, a post with an appropriate task can be created. Thus, in earlier times, chairs were set up at universities for outstanding scholars, whereas nowadays failures who cannot be dismissed have to have posts created for them where they can do no harm. Integration in communication channels also presupposes that the tasks involved, and sometimes the people involved, are already known. And here, too, one finds that powerful organization departments invent tasks in order to garner posts in which they can employ people they want to fix up with a job or to promote, reward, or shunt off.

Posts have to be understood as vacant posts, as "kenograms."[19] This is fully in keeping with the conditions we have outlined: the simultaneous use of different distinctions in the same system and the heterarchical "change in leadership" in determining decision premises, which then reflect the given historical state and the system's scope for deciding as restricted by this state. Under these conditions, a "proemial" order[20] must be constructively given in which equal (= empty) posts can nevertheless be distinguished from one another, thus also equality from identity[21] – even though at this level the system is by no means operational, so that no pointers for decisions are to be found.

For this purpose, posts must in one way or another be impregnated by what is to be concretely treated as past. In other words, posts have to be already partially defined if they are to offer indications for supplementation by further decision premises. And there is no weighting among decision premises, no essential primacy. Rationalists or rationalizers will, in general, prefer decision programs as a guiding factor in their search for suitable persons and the useful organizational allocation of tasks. In practice, the opposite case could prove more frequent: that one "has" people and is looking for work for them to do. Or that the number of posts is presented as a symbol of the size and importance of an organizational entity, and these empty posts are then filled with tasks and persons.

We could therefore describe posts as mobile redundancies in which decision premises of various types can be incorporated and from which they can be removed. In principle, the whole content of a post can be changed, but not all at once. If a post were to be completely empty for a moment and no more than a framework for possible decisions about possible decision premises, it would lack the element of continuity indispensable to its identity. The old post could then not be distinguished from a new one. In other words, a post needs given decision premises that cannot be disposed over at the moment in order to provide the redundancy that is prerequisite for meaningful supplementation. In this sense, posts are historical entities that, although identified in abstraction from time, cannot be handled in abstraction from time.

At the more abstract level of the theory of self-referential, autopoietic systems, we have seen that such systems have to compensate for their operational closure by reentry of the difference between system and environment into the system; and, moreover, that, in relation to the operations of the system, an indeterminability arises that is triggered by the generation of time. The indeterminability that results from oscillation between self-reference and other-reference is relocated to the non-actual time horizons past and future, which then have to be synchronized. The concept of decision has clarified how this happens at the level of operations – namely by the past being de-determined as alternative and the future being provided with structure as desired difference. Analysis of post identity shows that the same form of temporalization is also to be found at the level of the decision premises that are used as structures in the system. Here, too, the system achieves an order that can be understood as that of a historical machine. Here, too, past and future have to be synchronized through decisions on the basis of shifting self-determinations. The post order enables the continuous integration and removal of coordinated decision premises – but only so that the given historical state has to be presupposed and incorporated in the decision, because it would otherwise be impossible to make any connectivity apparent.

IV

The concept post is normally understood in a structural sense: an organization has a precisely ascertainable number of posts or it does not have them. They exist or they do not exist. The size of an organizational system can be defined in terms of the inventory of posts. Posts are often lacking; they then have to be approved. This could give the impression that posts are decided about in abstraction, even before the decision premises that give the post a concrete meaning come to bear. But this is clearly not the case – either in the public service or elsewhere. The public service knows established posts, shown in the budget and defined in terms of available salaries. They can be approved or cut. But even then a program, at least the notion of a program, has to exist to motivate the decision. Here more than elsewhere, posts, like fixed identities, can be moved from one department to another in the system. Here more than elsewhere, posts are abstractly discussed, negotiated, and decided. Here, above all, organizations are quasi-immortal in their inventory of posts – for reasons of public service law, but naturally also because posts can be defended with respect to the tasks assigned to them.

But none of this alters the fact that for functional entities, contingency regulations are involved that serve to coordinate decision premises. The inventory of posts may well symbolize the size of an organization; but one could just as easily take the current workforce or the costs it entails. One should not be taken in by the merely strategic significance of the structural illusion that posts have, as it were, the right to exist. As a schema for the coordination of interdependence between decision premises, a post makes sense only if there are actually such decision premises.

Above all in the private sector, organizations and, especially in recent times, organization boundaries have been dissolving. Whole business segments have been hived off into the environment even though the organization continues to rely on their services. And, vice versa, elements are acquired and incorporated. Should a brewery own a glass factory, merely because it needs bottles? Widely varying forms of organization can be chosen in this context; operational, managerial, and market considerations, which can be subject to fast-changing conditions, are likely to prove decisive. A publishing house can be happy to have its own printing works, which allows it to bring out small editions in keeping with its own timetable, while external printers calculate in such a manner that only large editions are worth their while. Under such circumstances, calculating on the basis of fixed post inventories makes little sense as a value in itself. If posts are to be shifted across organization boundaries, their organization-specific identity has to be annulled, and recourse must instead be taken to the finance needed to establish posts. But this does not change the fact that the boundaries of what belongs to the organization are a basis for calculation because they determine whether "hierarchy" or "market" regulates the conditions for (always internal) conditions.[22] And, *a fortiori*, the referential problem of the function of posts remains: indication of the need to coordinate the decision premises program, personnel, and communication channels.

V

What are decision premises needed for?

If an organizational system were a strictly sequential machine, which at any point in time (however brief, however transient) could draw only one distinction, and thus make only one decision, it would suffice if it oriented itself on the historical state that it had attained and from which it had to proceed. If, in addition, as in Spencer-Brown's calculus of forms, bivalence was ensured with each distinction having only two sides to it, a marked one and an unmarked one, the system could operate in the form of a calculus. The reality of living systems, of social systems, and also of formally organized social systems is a different one. They have both successive and simultaneous possibilities at their disposal for drawing distinctions. This alone allows them to combine tempo with complexity. But simultaneous distinctions/decisions cannot monitor each other. There are not only predecessors that one knows and successors that one can influence, but also a mass of simultaneous occurrences to which *neither* applies. While something is happening something else is always also happening; not only in the inaccessible environment of the system, but within it. A strictly serial machine would be able only to calculate the simultaneity of diversity back to the sole state possible in each case. It would have to take note of it as a paradox, the sameness of difference. This would amount to self-obstruction, or to hiving off simultaneously different distinctions. But if simultaneously different distinctions are admitted, and we know empirically that this is possible, indeed normal, how is chaotic confusion to be prevented?

Although confusion is not prevented in organized social systems, it is mitigated;[23] this is achieved by deciding on decision premises. Setting decision premises can, above all, determine which decisions are to count as decisions of the system and which not. Roughly, this results already from the recruitment of people for posts, but also through reference to the programs of the system and the integration of communication in recognized competences and communication channels. This does not exclude doubts,[24] nor does it exclude errors being attributed to the organization, for instance, a pilot's navigational errors or violations of the law by a public authority. On the whole, however, setting and continuously adjusting decision premises produces a framework within which an organization can construct its world, process information, and transform ever new uncertainty into certainty.

For the organization lacks what in the functional systems of society is provided by the binary code, the orientation on a single positive/negative distinction such as have/have-not, true/false, right/wrong.[25] Of course, organizations, to the extent that they act in specific functional systems, are bound by the codes of these systems, for otherwise it would not be clear whether they were business enterprises, research institutes, courts, or political parties. But this alone does not yet mark the boundaries of specific organizational systems, the boundaries of a labor court with jurisdiction over a given district or of a political party with a certain platform nor, above all, of organizations that have a specific number of members to the exclusion of everyone else. At the level of organizational systems, decision premises are accordingly the functional equivalent of the coding of functional systems. Decision premises, too, are conglomerates of ultimately binary distinctions: this person and no other, this competence and no other. But, unlike the codes of functional systems, they can be changed, if only in constant, self-referential adjustment to what is not currently at the disposition of the organization.

The external boundaries of the system, which mark what is attributed to it and what not, have a rejective function externally. Everything that is outside remains an "unmarked space" for the operations of the system, even though other-referential observation is undertaken in the system. For example, the system imagines that it has "customers," although the people thus designated would hardly describe themselves as customers of a specific enterprise or even allow themselves to be addressed as such (with the possible exception of Porsche drivers). But the boundaries cannot be operationally crossed with observations, distinctions, or indications. Even their external side remains inaccessible. The inner side of the boundary, by contrast, is articulated by decision premises and is dissolved into a multiplicity of interpretative perspectives. Metaphorically, it is a mirror in which the system recognizes itself and the structural conditions for the continuation of its own operations.

This is far from guaranteeing the smooth, frictionless coordination of the system's operations. This is impossible, if only because time is involved and the temporal stability of individual decision premises and their reaction to irritations differ. Organizations therefore have the lasting task (or "supertask") of constantly recoordinating themselves and decision premises, which appear to change of their own accord. In so doing, the system can, however inadequately, react on a higher level to the problem of a simultaneous mode of operation, namely to the circumstance that simultaneous operations are inaccessible to one another. One can then ensure at least a double requirement: that a multiplicity of decisions (1) orient themselves on the same decision premises and (2) reckon with other decisions orienting themselves on other decision premises.

VI

So far, we have been talking about *decidable* decision premises. Decision premises, too, can be put in place or revoked by decision. But this clearly does not apply for all decision premises. Charles Perrow has therefore postulated a third control level, that of "premise control."[26] But it is not clear what factors are to be attributed to this third sort of control, and the diffuse meaning of the term "control" apparently prevents this from being seen as a problem. There are certainly ever more premises of premises, but who or what "controls" their use?

We shall therefore replace the concept of "premise control" by the question whether, apart from decidable decision premises, there are also undecidable ones. The question would be uninteresting if nothing more was meant than the facticity of the world that always has to be presupposed. But it is more important when organization-specific but nevertheless undecidable decision premises are at issue, which brings us to a topic much in vogue: organizational culture.[27]

In retrospect, the emphasis placed on organizational culture has clearly been a reaction to organizational developments often described as postmodern, or at any rate as the loss (or abandonment) of central control, a preference for informal contacts, soft divisions and categorizations, loose couplings, network formation, greater dependence on trust, more work at and with the computer, greater structural flexibility, much faster organizational change, and an increase in uncertainty about jobs and tasks. Compared with classical notions of organization, this may well be disturbing; and just-in-time is now the concept of the moment in organizational culture, which, like a fetish, can serve to strength the belief in an order that nevertheless still exists.[28]

This is not to say that organizational culture exists only in the imaginations of top management and organizational consultants. Dario Rodriguez has suggested defining the concept of organizational culture as a complex of undecidable decision premises.[29] This has the double advantage of giving a precise definition to the often and vaguely used concept of organizational culture[30] while introducing the distinction between decidable and undecidable decision premises. In other words, what is concerned is the marking of the difference between decidable and undecidable decision premises, the inner side being where problems can arise and be resolved: decidable decision premises. This makes it understandable that organizational cultures develop where problems arise that cannot be resolved by directives, for example, with regard to the need for uniform presentation of the organization to the outside world when there are internal differences of opinion. The organizational culture regulates how to put a face on it without obliging members to believe in it.

We thus deprive the concept of culture (as we shall be doing with the concepts of institution and value) of its positive connotations. It was a sign of organizational culture when, after the 1980 earthquake in southern Italy, the government's first reaction was to send in the military with guns and ammunition.[31] It is part of the culture to know how reproaches are to be formulated and blame attributed. Moreover, the concept of undecidable decision premises frees us from the insinuation that can easily creep in when the concept of organizational culture is, as usual, used in the singular, that *one* organization has *only one* organizational culture and that this culture can be handled more or less consistently. In this regard, it is better to set out from a variable in order to keep the question of the degree of integration of the organizational culture open to empirical investigation. If we set out from the concept of undecidable decision premises, this prejudges neither unity nor consistency in organizational culture.

Undecidable decision premises are, of course, also produced in the organization, and, of course, this also happens with regard to decisions – or rather on the grounds of decisions. How could a structure otherwise come into being? But they are not attributed to specific decisions, nor is it their aim to prepare or carry out specific decisions. One therefore cannot mark how they come into being. They apply because they have always applied (if we can speak of "applying" at all in this context). They therefore lack positivity and, hence, the rule that everything that is introduced by decision can also be changed by decision.

With this concept of organizational culture, we depart from the usual use of the term without, however, contradicting the intended meaning. It is only a question of greater precision. Organizational culture is usually defined with reference to the concept of symbol, and the given system is then described as *differentia specifica.*[32] But this is to replace a vague name by another vague name. The concept of symbol is overloaded with demands on the evolution of emotions, on the stimulation of action, and on the generation of responsive motives. How this is to happen at the operational level is not clear. One thinks of values, not of causalities or scripts. We shall, therefore, replace the conceptual substitution of unity for unity by the statement of a difference (or form) whose one side, namely the undecidability of organization-specific decision premises, gives us the concept of organizational culture.

An organizational culture develops of its own accord. The communications generating it are to be attributed rather to the domain of gossip and conversation.[33] It is formally redundant communication, in Greek not *poiesis* but *práxis*; not the production of a work but an activity that is enjoyed as such. Its results are produced anonymously, and only anthropologists or sociologists discover the latent function of this sort of communication, namely to give expression to a sense of belonging together and its moral demands, without this being directly addressed by communication and thus subject to acceptance or rejection.[34]

The result is that, given the force of habit and what is taken for granted, any query and any request for explanation would be taken as a provocation or a joke, and accordingly discouraged. Furthermore, it is not easy to justify such questions: special pointers in the given situation are required. The doubt thus expressed has to find a reason and has to be specified; otherwise it will disconcert and be attributed to the person expressing it. As ethnomethodology has shown, the forces are strong that keep everyday communication on track and, in the form of intimacy, condense premises, which are not put to the yes/no test but are accepted without being expressed in words.

The topics of organizational culture have the advantage of ambiguity.[35] One can refer to them explicitly or implicitly without already committing oneself. In this way, belongingness and consent can be symbolized without losing maneuverability. In order to eliminate doubts and create certainty, one has to take part in interactions (without this interaction being intended to clarify the organizational culture). Past and future can thus be connected without one being forced to repeat the past. Among the advantages of this ambiguity is that its limits are imprecise. The question is, then, what is still accepted as communication.

Reduced to its ultimate components, organizations' cultures are to be found in the form of *values,*[36] accompanied and supported by the history of the system. Values are pointers in communication that are not directly communicated.[37] To make them the subject (information) of an utterance would make sense only if one wished the utterance to cause surprise and to emphasize that the utterer sees reason to communicate his evaluation, thus anticipating dissent. In other words, the explicit communication of a value exposes it to acceptance or rejection, *and this is precisely the sense of the communication*. For this reason, the validity of values is typically presupposed and assumed in communication. For instance, if one says, "this proposal contradicts the traditions of our firm," the value of tradition does not enter the argument. One does not call the tradition into question but whether the proposal contradicts it or not, and one is at best prepared to accept that the content of the tradition be interpreted. The same applies, of course, when innovation is demanded. Here, as elsewhere, the communicative effectiveness of culture does not depend on individuals sharing opinions and note being taken of this fact; it depends on acting in communication as if this were the case.[38]

Values permeate all societal communication. With respect to form and largely also to content, decision communication in organizations therefore always presupposes society, and not only as environment but in the direct use of societal value assumptions – for instance, when there is talk of "unhealthy" working conditions. The particularity of the specific culture of a specific organization finds expression in explicit or implicit reference to the system's own history. Whoever demands deviation from the organizational culture can accordingly be accused of acting inconsistently with his own prior behavior, indeed in contradiction to it. As always, innovation and deviation come together – and the question is then whether communication is to be stylized and understood as more than (highly welcome) innovation or as deviation. The plausibility of the currently actual situation is likely to be the decisive factor.

Value relations are to be distinguished from typical, unquestioningly accepted causal attributions. Typically, they coordinate cognitive and motivational aspects. Knowledge about remedies and corresponding error diagnosis may be involved; but also forms of attributing blame and the acceptability of excuses. In this connection, probably all organizational cultures overestimate the contribution made by persons and individual acts (we have already discussed that the mystification of decision as an internal mental occurrence serves to dissolve the paradoxical structure of decisions). Organizational cultures consequently both simplify and exaggerate; they concentrate attention and prevent or hamper at least the communication of experience that runs counter to the established picture.

Historically stabilized organizational cultures do not exclude change, but change can be introduced neither as alteration nor by decree.[39] The organizational culture is not a component of the system's statutes. Nowadays, it is regarded as the most important obstacle to planned innovation, for only whoever acts in keeping with what has hitherto been usual can expect to find consensus (a case of self-fulfilling prophecy).[40] Even efforts to get members to participate more strongly in planning and rationalization can fail for the same reason.[41] A change in organizational culture is often induced by a change in societal values. But cases are conceivable in which deviating behavior prevails, with the result that awareness and organizational culture fall in with what is happening anyway because stressful inconsistencies would otherwise occur. Organizational culture is anyway too soft to offer resistance to established behavior. The decline of an organization may be explained by the system paying too much attention to its own organizational culture and too little to changes in the environment.[42]

For the purposes of internal communication, the organizational culture remains invisible, and it would be inexpedient, indeed suspicious, to want to put it in words.[43] A management that cultivates the organizational culture, even if only to inject a bit of color into things, would arouse mistrust, on the lines, for example, that organizational culture serves the self-presentation of top management or that it is a means of generating unpaid motivation.[44] By contrast, organizational culture can be stressed when it is a matter of comparison with systems of the environment or of emphasizing the specificity of "our" organization. But there is no justification at all to speak of culture. This concept came into use toward the end of the eighteenth century to permit explicit comparison of European culture (there was no European state) with one's own history and with other cultures.[45] Culture is therefore nothing other than a double evaluation of what exists and is usual anyway, with the function of making comparison possible and thus of making self- and other-reference for definable entities – initially above all nations – communicable within a society already moving in the direction of world society.

The concept of organizational culture presented here is likely to be suitable, above all, for explaining certain inertial effects that occur when far-reaching organizational changes take place, especially in the privatization now in vogue of enterprises managed by government bureaucracies (which often means party bureaucracies); also in the event of company takeovers, international mergers between businesses with "local" cultures, and similar, currently frequent measures undertaken mainly for technical financial reasons. A privatized state-owned enterprise can be snowed under by new directives; but the habits and self-evidences that govern internal communication cannot be converted in this manner. It is more probable that these circumstances bring them to awareness and transform them into a sort of opposition culture.[46] This may lead to the more strongly explicit communication of hitherto tacit decision premises, hence provoking conflict and change; but this alone will not guarantee that changes are in line with the wishes of the new power holders. In such cases, organizational culture can function as a memory that preserves and recalls one's own hurt and oppression. In the sense of Schiller, organizational culture is then no longer naive but sentimental poetry, admiring or pitying oneself.[47]

If an organizational culture cannot be formulated without revealing intentions, interests, and conflicts, it can nevertheless – "when the time is ripe" – be violated in spectacular manner. As in religion, innovations come about through breaches of taboo. A breach of taboo produces the founder of a new religion. And so, in organizations too, great personalities occasionally arise who introduce a new era, revitalize the organization, or bring traditional habits to the light of day by breaking with them. Such a breach saves, as it were, legitimation; the past is replaced by the future. The breach is made visible only as decision and is endowed with a personality that is for the moment believed capable of achieving the goal set. Causal attribution is reversed with the aid of the paradox of deciding: not the breach produces the personality, the personality produces the breach.

This can naturally happen only within single organizations, just as organizational cultures, which also develop without decision, differ from system to system. To this extent, the concept of organizational culture calls attention to the limits of the generalizability of what organizational science has to say. Dependence on its own history individualizes the system. Even within organizational systems there can be different organizational cultures, which react differently to measures.[48] In other words, the evolution of organizations leads not only to a diversification of species but also to a diversification of exemplars – to a diversity of species and individuals, which, as the result of evolution, are themselves open to further evolution. In this state of affairs, rationalization interests can no longer be condensed to principles.[49] They have to refer back to an evolving population, which can ultimately be understood as a whole only from the perspective of a theory of society.

Among the most important innovations associated with the concept of organizational culture (which are, however, not fixed in the concept itself but owe their existence to its very fuzziness) is therefore the emphasis on the local character of such cultures, differing from enterprise to enterprise even under like environmental conditions. This could, on the one hand, explain why it is possible for individuals to change an organizational culture through conspicuous behavior without wanting to do so. It also explains the current resistance to centralized regulation through agreements between management and labor organizations. In all, organizational culture is no recipe for success, but perhaps a contribution to a theory of the evolution of organizations that shows where variations can set in when selection and restabilization are to take place.

The concept of organizational culture thus matches exactly what systems theory, following Heinz von Foerster,[50] would describe as a non-trivial machine. At the level of decidable decision premises, an effort might be made toward intentional-rational provision for the future. That this can and does happen is not to be denied, and produces, so to speak, the meaning material to which the development of an organizational culture can connect. But this considerably modifies rationality assumptions. It orients deciding on inevitably inconsistent values in order to avoid the problem of the uncertainty of future preferences. In other words, it counts on made decisions being reintroduced into the system as memory and on this recursion possibly, perhaps even regularly, changing preferences. It gives the currently actual present priority in orientation over the uncertain future. The system orients itself self-referentially on itself as it finds itself and not on a future that will arise from the complex interdependencies between system and environment. What is more, the operation "decision" takes account of the circumstance that the system, precisely because it consists of decisions, cannot work itself out in this mode of operation, although – indeed because – it reproduces itself autopoietically in this way. In decision theory, models of "adaptive, selective, and posterior rationality"[51] are therefore postulated even without systems-theoretical elaboration.

VII

The decision-making premises we have been discussing so far have been aspects of the *self-reference* of the system. This applies even when the binding force of decision premises is itself derived from decisions of the system, and even when one sees them only as a peculiarity of the system, only as organizational culture; for both cases have to do with perspectives that distinguish the system from its environment. It must not be excluded that similar things can apply in both system and environment; but for the system that accepts these premises *for itself*, this is purely by chance.

But these self-referentially articulated perspectives do not exhaust the subject of decision premises. There are also decision premises that are relocated into the environment, which are thus constructed from an *other-referential* perspective. We shall call them cognitive routines.[52]

What is concerned here, too, is not the world that has to be accepted as such nor the assumption that every meaning noted updates references, which if pursued would yield determinable meaning. And it is quite certainly not a matter of everything that is perceived by the people involved in the organization. The organization itself cannot perceive. By "cognitive routines" we mean rather identifications stored in communications for multiple use, which can be retrieved when needed. Examples include the names and addresses of customers with whom one has regular contact and the conditions under which they can be contacted; or the normal time needed to receive supplies from the environment or to send them; or assumptions about the typical quality of things (such as machines, raw materials, modes of transport) with which the organization regularly has to do.

Cognitive routines develop with the decision practices of the system and continue to depend on them. They are forgotten when no longer needed. They develop in constant oscillation between self-reference and other-reference, and thus through the reentry of the difference between system and environment into the system. Typically, we can also assume that normal expectations are concerned, which are not invalidated by occasional failures or disturbances but are concentrated in an error-friendly or robust manner. A broken machine is still a machine. Identity takes account of disappointment due to details in advance. This is the basis for the stability of the connection between past and future, and thus of the iteration of the routine. There are of course exceptions, where a unique disappointment leads to the collapse of the entire expectation complex and thus to the destruction of the cognitive routine. A typical case is the blatant disappointment of trust. But such cases are rare, in general and in this particular instance. If the entire cognitive apparatus were so constructed that disappointments destroyed routines, the system would overtax itself. It would have to busy itself constantly with eventualities and would be unable to produce what cognitive routines ensure, namely, an unburdened relationship with the environment, which permits attention to concentrate on the self-referential aspects of the decision situation.

Cognitive routines are themselves the result of uncertainty absorption processes,[53] but the system treats them not as self-constructed artifacts but, so to speak, grants them reality credit. They would otherwise never be able to fulfill their disburdening function but would have to be borne as internal contributions without backing in the environment. The system calculates its environment, as it were, on the basis of the repeated application of the same routines, and in so doing overlooks the fact that iteration in ever new situations is the paradoxical form of a systemic observational operation.[54]

All self-referentially constituted decision premises are embedded in a context of cognitive routines.[55] No definition of a situation would be possible without them, nor any causal attribution, nor definable alternatives – and thus, no decision autonomy.[56] And the system could neither interpret conditions nor ascribe the suitability of means to ends if there were no possibility to condense identities and call them up as routines when needed. This dependence has to replace the certainty that the consciousness has in its also self-constructed but then externalized perceptions. Communication, as we have pointed out, cannot perceive. It is all the more dependent on providing what it speaks about with a self-generated reality index. It can still sufficiently control its memory – partly by registering iteration as proof of worth, and partly through individual corrections on the basis of disappointments, thus through learning.

But, above all, the construction of cognitive routines serves to generate decision possibilities that would otherwise be quite inconceivable. If we could not recognize the transport system, we would not have the freedom to choose among routes and modes of transport; and whoever relies on carpets for air travel would presumable soon find themselves in the care of organizations specialized in the treatment of such cases. Only cognitive routines, therefore, generate the scope for deciding that can then be limited by normative premises. As a condition for the possibility of freedom, cognition is not experienced as a limitation of freedom. For this reason, the stylization of topics as cognition (e.g., in advertising) can also be used to mark the scope in which norms and preferences lead to a decision.

Classical-rationalistic organization theory would treat cognitive routines (if it noticed them at all and did not simply consider them to be a reflection of reality itself) as secondary phenomena, as auxiliary functions of the hierarchy and the goal structure of organizations. From a genetic point of view, this may well be true, for without self-reference there is no other-reference, without the founding of an organization no choice of cognitive relevance. But this does not allow us to conclude that cognitive routines are of secondary importance for the survival, for the autopoiesis of the organization. On the contrary, their importance increases to the extent that organizations are sensitive to error in their operations; we could also say, to the extent that efficiency criteria are less important for organizations than criteria of error avoidance, of risk management, of disaster avoidance.[57] In organizations that work with high-risk technologies, the main problem is to avoid situations with unclear, cognitively indefinable, and, above all, not rapidly definable problems.[58] For such cases, and for organizations in which such risks constitute the chief problem, having complex and seldom (hopefully never) used cognitive routines at their disposal is the critical variable. One cannot rely on the hierarchy – on the assumption that the people at the top will provide better knowledge and responsibility; nor can the system protect itself through normative programming, because it is clear anyway that disaster must be avoided. The problem is rather one of cognitive capacity: one has to be able to recall something that has so far never taken place.

VIII

The unity of the posts that coordinate different decision premises necessarily means that every change has to take account of decision premises that are already set and cannot be changed at the moment; it would otherwise find no hold in the given organization. But this does not tell us whether there can be new planning by an organization that affects all decision premises. The need is obvious – especially when we consider that organizational changes typically no longer take place through almost self-evident adaptation to the environment (the market, for example) but require intervention by management. This can take place ad hoc, and probably does so in most cases. But with formulations like "organizational design," a more demanding concept is often posited. To explain this, one has spoken of archetypes and considered whether and how it is possible to transform an organization from one archetype into another.[59] However, this does not bring much, if not a distinction between ordinary and extraordinary changes. Perhaps more important is the insight that every change has to set out from the organization as it is and therefore has to work with a new description of the organization. This can happen, for instance, with the question of what problem it really wants to solve. The problem is invented, perhaps fabricated to fit the established problem solution, in order to propose other solutions by varying the definition of the problem. The question is then what depth of field problem definitions make possible and plausible. Resistance will then be typically based on interests rather than on problems, or present the protection of interests as a problem.

However one proceeds, the redescription of the organization has to be formulated. Decision premises may well be communicable without difficulty. The decision program is given the form of a text, a person is indicated by name, the communication channels of an organization and, above all, subordination relations are traced out in the form of an organization chart. But as soon as the premises are brought into relation with situations and applied, their meaning and also the meaning of the situations become ambiguous. This ambiguity is an everyday problem for every organization,[60] and ways of dealing with it accordingly develop, such as formulating compromises or putting off decisions.

When ambiguity becomes a problem, oral communication in face-to-face interaction systems is particularly advisable. This does not necessarily mean that interaction serves to transform ambiguity into unambiguity. It appears rather to help it successfully ignore ambiguity and reach agreement on decisions that create a new situation. The demands on precision can (and must) be kept variable. They could, after all, be controlled only by introducing more and more new metaphors, ambiguities, or postponements. The theory of autopoietic decision-making would say that what matters is transforming given, ambiguously described situations into others for which the same will apply for the foreseeable future.

These reflections show that, however much information needs might grow and despite the increasing use of sophisticated communication technologies, oral communication will remain indispensable;[61] they also confirm the observation that, especially at the management level, decisions are made on the basis of selected contacts and not on the basis of complex, elaborate drafts produced by information processing.

IX

With regard to decision premises, we can speak not only of planning but also of self-organization. We can accept this concept more easily. Whereas planning can (and some would say almost inevitably will) produce unwanted results, self-organization describes only a factual state of affairs for which no author needs to be found to blame if things go wrong. What is meant is simply that decision premises cannot be set without a side glance at others, not without a side glance at what already exists; otherwise they would stand in no recognizable relation to an ascertainable system. Self-organization requires no prior calculation and no author in charge. But we still have to ask how self-organization is possible, what it requires, and how it comes about.

We shall be examining this question with the aid of the concept of microdiversity.[62] We find microdiversity in the masses of face-to-face interactions, which, as Erving Goffmann has shown, obey their own order of mutual adjustment of representation and consequently cannot be derived from organizational objectives and organizational structures.[63] Without these interactions, self-organization would lack the material to which it can refer.[64]

With the distinction between self-organization and microdiversity, we can free ourselves from the theoretically unproductive distinction between macro and micro. It is not a matter of an alternative but of necessary interplay. What is decisive is the diversity of forms in which social systems are created. Thus, the special typicality of interaction systems gains a function in its own right that cannot be reduced to a contribution, provided for in the organization, to the objectives of the organization. Self-organization and microdiversity are complementary. They make each other possible. This naturally does not exclude that interactions have to adapt to organizations and that there are limits to mutual compossibility.

Notes

1. The concept of decision premises was introduced by Herbert A. Simon with reference to the aspect of "roles" relevant in organizations. See: Models of Man, *Social and Rational: Mathematical Essays on Rational Human Behavior in a Social Setting*, New York 1957, 201: "The crucial point is that we define roles in terms of *decision premises* rather than in terms of the decisions compounded from such premises. If we take the decision premise – rather than the more global concepts like the decision or the role – as our unit for the description of human choice, then it is easy to place the rational and the nonrational aspects of behavior in proper relation to each other." In earlier publications Simon had also spoken of "behavior premises." See Herbert A. Simon, Donald W. Smithburg, and Victor A. Thompson, *Public Administration*, New York 1950, 57 ff. The limitation to "roles," the fashionable concept of the 1950s, does not do full justice to the systematic yield of the concept (nor to Simon's own use of it).
2. See Karl E. Weick, *Der Prozeß des Organisierens*, Frankfurt 1985, 163 ff.; Massimo Warglien and Michael Masuch, The Logic of Organizational Disorder: An Introduction, in idem (eds.), *The Logic of Organizational Disorder*, Berlin 1996, 1–34 (14 ff.).

3. See Richard M. Cyert and James G. March, A Behavioral Theory of Organizational Objectives, in: Mason Haire (ed.), *Modern Organization Theory*, New York 1979, 76–90. For strategic decisions see also E. Eugene Carter, The Behavioral Theory of the Firm and Top-Level Corporate Decisions, *Administrative Science Quarterly* 16 (1971), 413–428.

4. A broader concept of strategic decisions could be compared with this, as used, for example, by David Hickson et al., *Top Decisions – Strategic Decision Making in Organizations*, San Francisco 1986. "Strategic" indicates a proviso of correction in the event of failure. See also, stressing *deviating* responses to institutional requirements, Christine Oliver, Strategic Responses to Institutional Process, *Academy of Management Review* 16 (1991), 145–179. See also C. R. Hinings and Royston Greenward, *The Dynamics of Strategic Change*, Oxford 1988.

5. On this distinction – "from Behavior and Output Control to Premise Control" – see Karl E. Weick, Technology as Equivoque: Sensemaking in New Technologies, in: Paul S. Goodman and Lee S. Sproull et al., *Technology and Organizations*, San Francisco 1990, 1–44 (34 ff.).

6. See, e.g., Fred H. Goldner, The Division of Labor: Process and Power, in: Mayer N. Zald (ed.), *Power in Organizations*, Nashville, TN 1970, 97–143 (97 f.) on uncertainties *as a consequence of the division of labor*. See also Erhard Friedberg, The Relativization of Formal Organization, in: Massimo Warglien and Michael Masuch (eds.), *The Logic of Organizational Disorder*, Berlin 1996, 107–125 (111): "The structure and formal rules generate in turn problems, i.e. uncertainties, which arise from the difficulties encountered in applying its [sic] prescriptions on a day-to-day basis."

7. Even sociologists can be mentioned. Talcott Parsons, for example, defines organization in terms of a "primacy of orientation to the attainment of a specific goal." See: A Sociological Approach to the Theory of Organizations, quoted from: Talcott Parsons, *Structure and Process in Modern Societies*, New York 1960, 16–58 (17).

8. Just as, vice versa, the standardization of decision programs can permit a downward shift of authority, a decentralization. See Peter M. Blau, Decentralization in Bureaucracies, in: Mayer N. Zald (ed.), *Power in Organizations*, Nashville, TN 1970, 150–174.

9. Spencer-Brown op. cit., p. 57.

10. As the older cybernetics terminology had put it, one's own output has to be reused as input, in other words, using the distinction between input and output for reentry.

11. See On Constructing a Reality, in: Heinz von Foerster, *Observing Systems*, Seaside, CA 1981, 288–309 (304 ff.).

12. For a detailed treatment see Niklas Luhmann, Soziologische Aspekte des Entscheidungsverhaltens, *Die Betriebswirtschaft* 44 (1984), 591–603.

13. See also Barbara Czarniawska-Joerges, *Exploring Complex Organizations: A Cultural Perspective*, Newbury Park, CA 1992, 120 ff.

14. As we know, this was the assumption of older organization theories with the word "principle" in their titles. It must be understood as an attempt to insist on the rationality of the organization despite all unsavoriness, corruption, interests, and lethargy.

15. See Karl E. Weick, Organizational Redesign as Improvisation, in: George T. Huber and William H. Glick (eds.), *Organizational Change and Redesign: Ideas and Insights for Improving Performance*, Oxford 1993, 346–379 (359).
16. Where cases, once quite common, still occur, they are described as "corruption."
17. More precise analysis would have to differentiate between system references. The overall societal and, especially, economic function of posts may very well be to relate income to work and to distribute it by the division of labor. In society, work is therefore esteemed and unemployment lamented, whereas in organizations the opposite tends to be the case: people complain about their workload.
18. Far-reaching switches of this sort are known above all in government, where the distribution of responsibilities among departments is the subject of coalition agreements between political parties; science and education are separated or brought together again, or the office of the prime minister duplicates the responsibility structure of departments, making coordination necessary at a subordinate level where political parties may or may not be able to bring their influence to bear. And all this depends on there being posts or on the possibility of creating posts, which can then be dealt with in this manner.
19. In referring to the concept of Gotthard Günther, it should be noted that stricter requirements apply in kenogrammatic logic. There is, however, a parallel in that this logic also serves to organize distribution, which in simpler systems would appear to be paradoxical.
20. Also "proemial" in the sense of Gotthard Günther. See, with reference to the conditions of a "heterarchy" (McCulloch), Gotthard Günther, *Cognition and Volition: A Contribution to a Cybernetic Theory of Subjectivity, in idem, Beiträge zur Grundlegung einer operationsfähigen Dialektik* vol. 2, Hamburg 1979, 203–240 (228 f.).
21. The necessity of differentiating in this manner also explains the need for special visualization – for instance, in organization charts or budgets.
22. Whether analysis of or intuition about transaction costs actually play a role would for sociologists be an empirical question. The subject has been discussed since Oliver Williamson, *Markets and Hierarchies: Analysis and Antitrust Implications: A Study in the Economics of Internal Organization*, New York 1975.
23. See, e.g., Michael D. Cohen, James G. March, and Johan P. Olsen, A Garbage Can Model of Organizational Choice, *Administrative Science Quarterly* 17 (1972), 1–25; James G. March and Johan P. Olsen, *Ambiguity and Choice in Organizations*, Bergen 1976; Karl E. Weick, Educational Organizations as Loosely Coupled Systems, *Administrative Science Quarterly* 21 (1976), 1–19.
24. How would one judge a case, for example, of a judge finding a court attendant guilty of contempt of court for serving her with cold coffee? Such decisions are classified as "*ultra vires.*"
25. See Niklas Luhmann, *Die Wirtschaft der Gesellschaft*, Frankfurt 1988, 85 ff.; idem, *Die Wissenschaft der Gesellschaft*, Frankfurt 1990, 194 ff.; idem, *Das Recht der Gesellschaft*, Frankfurt 1993, 165 ff.
26. So Charles Perrow, *Complex Organizations*, 3rd. ed. New York 1987, 128 ff.
27. A "trendy" topic: in the first place this suggests a very short-lived phenomenon, especially when "culture" with its positive connotations is brought into play. Organization research had previously tended to describe such phenomena

negatively, or at least critically. See, e.g., William F. Whyte, *The Organization Man*, New York 1956. For a clinically interesting study oriented on the Tavistock Program, see Elliott Jacques, *The Changing Culture of a Factory*, London 1951. This fashion broke out toward the end of the 1970s. By the mid-1980s some were already declaring it over. Since then, adherents have been attempting to reframe it. See, e.g., Peter J. Frost et al. (eds.), *Reframing Organizational Culture*, Newbury Park, CA 1991. The likely fate will be dissolution of the topic in widely ranging linguistic, rhetorical, and anthropological research approaches that cannot be held together merely by the word "culture."

28. Similarly, but less critically formulated, Wolf V. Heydebrand, New Organizational Forms, *Work and Occupation* 16 (1989), 323–357. Heydebrand speaks of "propagation of corporate culture to counteract the centrifugal and deconstructive tendencies of structural flexibility."

29. See Dario Rodriguez Mansilla, *Gestion Organizacional: Elementos para su estudio, Santiago de Chile* 1991, 140 f. This had been preceded by the better known definition of organizational culture as the presumed "basic assumptions" that elude direct enquiry and analysis. See Edgar H. Schein, Coming to a New Awareness of Organizational Culture, *Sloan Management Review* 25 (1984), 3–16; idem, *Organizational Culture and Leadership: A Dynamic View*, San Francisco 1985, 2nd ed. 1992 and idem, What Is Culture?, in: Frost op. cit. (1991), 243–253. Similar, but not clearly distinguishable formulations are "shared core values," "coherent set of beliefs," or definitions that work with the symbol concept.

30. All overviews of the literature show how differently the concept of organizational culture is understood and used. See, e.g., Linda Smircich, Concepts of Culture and Organizational Analysis, *Administrative Science Quarterly* 28 (1983), 339–358, as well as the other contributions to this volume; also, with the formulation "umbrella concept," Barbara Czarniawska-Joerges, *Exploring Complex Organizations: A Cultural Perspektive*, Newbury Park, CA 1992, 159 ff.; or Christian Drepper, *Unternehmenskultur: Selbstbeobachtung und Selbstbeschreibung im Kommunikationssystem „Unternehmung"*, Frankfurt 1992, 11–86.

31. See Giovan Francesco Lanzara, *Capacita negativa: Competenza progettuale e modelli di intervento nelle organizzazioni*, Bologna 1993, 9 ff, 143 ff. The counterpart in the field of local institutions is to be found in the efforts of locals to set up an espresso bar in the open air and use it as a place to meet.

32. See, e.g., Andrew M. Pettigrew, On Studying Organizational Cultures, *Administrative Science Quarterly* 24 (1979), 570–581 (574 f.), which prompted the recent debate. What is meant by "symbol" remains unclear, and this uncertainty is even greeted as cognitively fruitful. See, e.g., Barry A. Turner (ed.), *Organizational Symbolism*, Berlin 1990, Introduction 1 f.

33. See James G. March and Guje Sevón, Gossip, Information, and Decision Making, in: Lee S. Sproull and J. Patrick Crecine (ed.), *Advances in Information Processing on Organizations* vol. 1, Greenwich, CT 1984, 93–107; Stephan Fuchs, The Stratified Order of Gossip: Informal Communication in Organizations and Science, *Soziale Systeme* 1 (1995), 47–72. See also Jörg R. Bergmann, Klatsch: Zur Sozialform der diskreten Indiskretion, Berlin 1987. It should be added that leadership decisions are likely to depend more on gossip than on carefully prepared

information. See Henry Mintzberg, *The Nature of Managerial Work*, New York 1973.

34. See Max Gluckman, Gossip and Scandal, *Current Anthropology* 4 (1963), 307–316.
35. See Joanne Martin and Debra Meyerson, Organizational Cultures and the Denial, Channeling and Acknowledgement of Ambiguity, in: Louis R. Pondy, Richard J. Boland Jr., and Howard Thomas (eds.), *Managing Ambiguity and Change*, Chichester 1988, 93–125.
36. A plea for retaining a sociological theory of values is to be found in Loredana Sciolla, Valori e identita sociale: Perché e ancora importante per la sociologia studiare i valori e i loro mutamenti, *Rassegna Italiana di Sociologia* 34 (1993), 341–359. Sciolla takes the view that one cannot understand values from the action perspective because communicating them would lead to fragmentation and tolerated ghettoization. (But why not?) Values can still be understood as social identity symbols. But one would then have to explain how these identity symbols function in communication; otherwise we end up with the ontification of values.
37. More detail in Niklas Luhmann, Complexity, Structural Contingencies and Value Conflicts, in: Paul Heelas, Scott Lash, and Paul Morris (eds.), *Detraditionalization*, Oxford 1996, 59–71.
38. See Howard S. Becker, Culture: A Sociological View, *Yale Review* 71 (1982), 513–527.
39. See Rodriguez op. cit., 141.
40. See now above all Nils Brunsson and Johan P. Olsen, *The Reforming Organization*, London 1993 – albeit under the guiding concept institution, which is understood, however, as almost synonymous with culture. See also Michel Crozier, *L'Entreprise à l'écoute: Apprendre le management post-industriel*, Paris 1989, 71 ff. For a relevant case study, see, e.g., Ellis Finkelstein, Culture and Crisis Management in an English Prison, in: Barry A. Turner (ed.), *Organizational Symbolism*, Berlin 1990, 67–79.
41. See Anthony Chelte et al., Corporate Culture as an Impediment to Employee Involvement: When You Can't Get There From Here, *Work and Occupations* 16 (1989), 153–164.
42. The findings of Richard A. D'Aveni and Ian C. MacMillan, Crisis and the Content of Managerial Communications: A Study of the Focus of Attention of Top Managers in Surviving and Failing Firms, *Administrative Science Quarterly* 35 (1990), 634–657 point in this direction. For a general theory of rigidity increasing in decline and accelerating decline, see Barry M. Staw et al., Threat-Rigidity Effects in Organizational Behavior: A Multilevel Analysis, *Administrative Science Quarterly* 26 (1981), 501–524.
43. See Anna Maria Theis, *Organisationskommunikation: Theoretische Grundlagen und empirische Forschungen*, Opladen 1994, 102, and Theis adds: "For the analysis of organizational culture this means that the object changes with its investigation."
44. This suspicion is supported by a both naive and widespread literature. The impulse was given in bestseller mode by Thomas J. Peters and Robert H. Waterman, *In Search of Excellence*, New York 1982. See also Terrence E. Deal and Allan A. Kennedy, *Corporate Cultures*, Reading, MA 1982. For more recent literature recommending culture see Christian Scholz and Wolfgang Hofbauer, Organisationskultur: Die vier Erfolgsprinzipien, Wiesbaden 1990, with further

references. This sort of literature gives the impression that one is in search of new management tools after "groups" and "informal organization" have lost their popularity.

45. See Niklas Luhmann, Kultur als historischer Begriff, in idem, *Gesellschaftsstruktur und Semantik* vol. 4, Frankfurt 1995, 31–54.

46. Cases of this sort are also known on the occasion of "political" takeovers of the public service by a radically differently oriented political party.

47. See Friedrich Schiller, *Über naive und sentimentalische* Dichtung (1795/96, 1800).

48. The now current view. See, e.g., various contributions in: Peter J. Frost et al. (ed.), *Reframing Organizational Culture*, Newbury Park, CA 1991, or Sonja A. Sackmann, Culture and Subcultures: An Analysis of Organizational Knowledge, *Administrative Science Quarterly* 37 (1992), 140–161. See also K.L. Gregory, Native-view Paradigms: Multiple Cultures and Culture Conflicts in Organizations, *Administrative Science Quarterly* 28 (1983), 359–376; Barbara Gray, Michel G. Bougon, and Anne Donellon, Organizations as Constructions and Destructions of Meaning, *Journal of Management* 11 (1985), 83–98; Stephen R. Barley et al., Cultures of Culture: Academics, Practitioners and the Pragmatics of Normative Control, *Administrative Science Quarterly* 25 (1988), 24–60.

49. See Richard R. Nelson and Sidney G. Winter, *An Evolutionary Theory of Economic Change*, Cambridge, MA 1982.

50. See above 73 f.

51. See James G. March, Bounded Rationality, Ambiguity, and the Engineering of Choices, *Bell Journal of Economics* 9 (1978), 587–608.

52. This is often also called "culture" and used more or less as a starting point for clarifying this concept. See, e.g., Howard S. Becker, Culture: A Sociological View, *Yale Review* 71 (1982), 513–527. But then culture is everything that has become a habit in dealing with things and people.

53. See March and Simon op. cit. (1958), 155. Also the formulation "stipulated facts."

54. It is a paradox because *different* events have to be involved, which, so to speak, bear witness to the *sameness* of what is repeated.

55. See, e.g., Richard Whitley, The Social Constructions of Organizations and Markets: The Comparative Analysis of Business Recipes, in: Michael Reed and Michael Hughes (eds.), *Rethinking Organization: New Directions In Organization Theory and Analysis*, London 1992, 120–143.

56. On the dependence of cognition of decision autonomy see Larry M. Preston, *Freedom and the Organizational Republic*, Berlin 1992.

57. See Karl E. Weick and Karlene H. Roberts, Collective Mind in Organizations: Heedful Interrelations on Flight Desks, *Administrative Science Quarterly* 38 (1993), 357–381. See also Gene I. Rochlin, Informal Organizational Networking as a Crisis-Avoiding Strategy: U.S. Naval Flight Operations as a Case Study, *Industrial Crisis Quarterly* 3 (1989), 159–176.

58. See in detail Charles Perrow, *Normal Accidents*, New York 1984.

59. See, but with reference to the transformation process itself, Danny Miller and Peter Friesen, Archetypes of Organizational Transition, *Administrative Science Quarterly* 25 (1980), 268–299. See also C.R. Hinings and Royston Greenwood, *The Dynamics of Strategic Change*, Oxford 1988.

60. In recent literature this has been pointed out above all by Karl E. Weick. See *Der Prozeß des Organisierens*, German translation Frankfurt 1985, esp. 257 ff., 312 ff. See also Louis R. Pondy, Richard J. Boland Jr., and Howard Thomas (eds.), *Managing Ambiguity and Change*, Chichester 1988.

61. We find "low technology and high touch" in Richard L. Daft, Kenneth R. Bettenhausen, and Beverly B. Tyler, Implications of Top Managers' Communication Choices for Strategic Decisions, in: George P. Huber and William H. Glick (eds.), *Organizational Change and Redesign: Ideas and Insights for Improving Performance*, Oxford 1993, 112–146 (117).

62. See Stéphane Ngo Mai and Alain Raybaut, Microdiversity and Macro-order: Toward a Self-Organization Approach, *Revue internationale de systémique* 10 (1996), 223–239.

63. See André Kieserling, Interaktion in Organisationen, in: Klaus Dammann, Dieter Grunow, and Klaus P. Japp (eds.), *Die Verwaltung des politischen Systems: Neuere systemtheoretische Zugriffe auf ein altes Thema*, Opladen 1994, 168–182; idem, *Kommunikation unter Anwesenden: Studien über Interaktionssysteme*, Frankfurt 1999, 335 ff.

64. We assume that this cannot be action in the sense of a product of an individual, for then both individuals and acts would have to be understood to be natural products, and social dependencies would have to be introduced externally.

8   Decision Programs

I

Among the decision premises high on the list in the classical concept of organization are decision programs.[1] In a long tradition, they are also called tasks. In politics and in political science one still speaks of the "tasks of government."[2] In the private sector of the economy, too, this way of putting things is to be found alongside talk of purposes, objectives or goals, but rather in the overall sense over and beyond the production of saleable goods, for instance, when talking about supplying the population with the relevant goods or services.[3] Or the concept of task is reduced to goal, purpose, or objective and applied to planning requirements (task analysis), purposes that can be derived from the general corporate purpose. It is then retained as sub-goal (in the sense of task), pointing to a subsection of the corporate purpose.[4] The result of task analysis and its practical implementation is then called organizational culture, and the system itself is referred to as an enterprise.[5] In this understanding, tasks are set top-down, and thus presuppose a directive hierarchy governing communication channels. The term task indicates, as it were, the permissive, the sent-ahead aspect of the premise, but not the need for decision prevailing at this level: the givenness of the premise through environment or internal directive but not the consequent uncertainty absorption.

All this seems to suggest that we can do without the concept of task and replace it with that of decision program, backed by the concepts decision premise and decision. Decision programs define the conditions for the factual rightness of decisions. This does not (or only in borderline cases) mean that decisions can be made through logical deduction. Even if conditional programs in the sense we shall be defining are involved, indeterminate concepts that need to be interpreted in the given situation often play a role. What is more, programmed deciding is typically guided by contextual memories, enabling the original sense of the program to be drawn on if deviation appears to be called for. Despite such ambivalence, indeed thanks to the elasticity it provides, the objective reference to programs in organizations also normally fosters social acceptance. A decision program may well be accompanied by

210

instructions to report anything out of the ordinary or suspicious that could speak against the program; but this amounts almost to paradoxical programming – it may be right or not – and generally has little effect.[6]

At the management level, decision programs initially take the form of criteria for judging complex projects. The uncertainty to be absorbed is reformulated and put in the form of multiple criteria, not all of which can be optimally met at the same time.[7] They thus announce further decision requirements and are often passed down already in this form. However, decision programs in the strictest sense presuppose that compliance or non-compliance can be ascertained. If this general precondition is respected, however, they can be kept variable between indeterminacy to determinacy. "Do something to reduce drug consumption" could be a sensible program. Mere interpretation will already tell us that neither tobacco nor alcohol consumption is meant. Formalization is to be understood as a variable, not as a directive or an inexorable trend.[8] The program concept thus presupposes no determinacy threshold beyond which we are no longer dealing with a decision program. It relates to the factual dimension of the sense of decisions and can, for this very reason, not be strictly limited in this dimension. But, in the course of an organization's history, all too indeterminate programs tend to concretize, even if only as routinized habits, so that innovations then have to be explicitly introduced, with the consequence that they become apparent as program components. In the example cited, the question is likely to be raised at some stage of whether distributing substitute drugs is or is not an acceptable means for combating drug addiction.

Like all decisions in organizations, decision premises, too, have reality only as communications. This imposes simplification and excludes doing justice to application situations in advance. This also brings things to a head in the structure, leading the system to oscillate between utilization/non-utilization or right/wrong use. Where rightness conditions have been formulated, the forms found therefore have another, a dark side to them. On the other side errors loom. What is not right is wrong. There may well be areas in which it is still possible to negotiate on whether an error has been made or an innovation introduced. But such borderline cases call for explicit decisions, which can in turn be altered only by decision. Long deviating practices may show that certain safety rules are simply superfluous; but once these practices have been discovered, a decision has to be made; and if it is not made, this can also be considered a decision.

As in the genesis of norms, it is often error that first shows what should have been regulated.[9] In open situations and under untested working conditions, immanent risks impose a choice: from case to case it has to be decided whether the decision made was the right one or whether a mistake has been made. Consider the activities of doctors or police field work. The double-edged problem of rightness thus acts as a probe introduced into unknown terrain to test working conditions, tending to result in more detailed programming. Any errors that occur have to be concealed if possible. The police know how to write reports.

In the literature, especially from the time of the theory of informal organization and the human relations movement, we find an inclination to regard errors as a leadership problem. This is partly because programming problems occur that have to be decided at a higher level, but also partly because of the "expressive" content of accusations and because of their socio-emotional consequences.[10] Put in more abstract terms, this means that crossing the boundary from right to erroneous also activates another type of decision premise, namely the domain of communication channels and competences. This could be taken as evidence that the individual sorts of decision premise do not take effect separately but are to be seen as acting in conjunction to preform decisions, offering possibilities for load balancing.

On the whole, organizational science has taken the view that a certain number of errors is normal and that it would be inefficient to pursue a policy of absolute fail-safety.[11] After all, nature, too, is "error-friendly." What is therefore more important is to make organizations so robust that they can survive mistakes. In many administrative authorities under the rule of law, the habit has therefore developed in large-scale operations to issue administrative notices schematically while permitting objections, and then examining the matter more closely only when an objection is raised. In the light of problems with high-risk technologies, however, this recommendation is also problematic; and the question is now whether "normal accidents"[12] are the result of a rational error-acceptance policy and permissive leadership at all, or whether they are not produced in all programming as the other side of the form.

II

The social reality of organizational systems cannot be adequately captured if they are described as functions or machines that transform input into output. As soon as they are seen as self-referential, non-trivial systems, it becomes clear that a majority of inputs (for instance, from commodity markets, supplier markets, the financial market) and a majority of possible outputs (to sales markets, which still have to be decided on) would lead to incalculable complexity. Input/output modeling may well be theoretically suitable for clarifying certain things; and it may well contribute to bringing easily overlooked dependencies into the theory (and thus to increasing complexity). But it is not enough for the systems-theoretical analysis of actually operating organizational systems (we refer back to what has been said above[13]).

Nevertheless, and perhaps for this very reason, it makes sense at the decision programming level to distinguish between the system's input boundaries and output boundaries. For the operations of the system (or of the subsystems of the system), these boundaries also distinguish past and future. Despite all the freedoms that the system grants itself in self-referential reference to the given decision situation, no decision can ignore the *difference* between the time horizons past and future. It can therefore also use the flexibility and thus the contingency that it finds within itself because it has to decide, to determine whether it wants to orient its programs more on inputs or more on outputs; thus whether in establishing the right decisions it wishes to proceed on the basis of given conditions or on that of differences to be produced or differences to be reduced. As the concept of the decision program tells us, in both cases we are concerned with the artificial reinforcement of a framework that has to be introduced and that can be changed in the system. In both cases we are dealing with a sort of early, generalized uncertainty absorption. Nevertheless, programs differ considerably, depending on whether they take the input boundary or the output boundary as point of reference.[14]

We shall call primarily input-oriented programs *conditional programs* and primarily output-oriented programs *purposive programs*. Both programs are concerned with introducing an artificial distinction that is not given but has to be constructed and made binding by decision in the system itself. Conditional programs distinguish between conditions and consequences, purposive programs between means and ends. But why are differences produced that are without reference to nature or even to the environment of the system?

This question has to be answered in two steps. First, the distinction – in both cases – enables and requires cognition.[15] Programs of this type are useful only if the world is already known and communication can depend on this being the case. But then the given distinction structures what gives occasion to treat knowledge of the world as doubtful and to elaborate it in the light of specified doubts – for instance, in the professional competence of a semi-skilled worker, a lawyer, an economist. Only if and only to the extent that this happens does the system produce decision autonomy, for example, to examine whether a case can be subsumed under this or that rule; or to decide whether certain means are suitable for attaining a certain end; and whether the end is worth the effort; whether other means should be sought, or whether the end should be abandoned or modified to make it easier to attain. It would therefore be premature to regard programs as patterns for ready-made decisions without taking account of the cognitions they call up. They rather generate the possibility of a decision that is always situation-related. The freedom to decide in different ways arises only through programming. Only for this reason does it make sense to distinguish between decision programs and decisions. Without programming, the only possibility would be to let one's imagination wander or to encourage communication in the search for a topic.

Only when a decision option is cognitively constructed and only when, in relation to it, competences develop that can broaden or restrict its latitude as the need may be can decisions be made and, mostly subsequently, be assessed. All this has to be presupposed before discussing whether a decision is the right one let alone the only right one, whether it is tenable, or whether, under the given circumstances, it is nevertheless excusable; or whether it can be branded an avoidable error. And in relation to this, a secondary competence develops to criticize, explain, and defend planned decisions or decisions already made; very typically, the cognitive framework that had constituted the scope of decision autonomy is also scrutinized.

The directive generation of freedom through cognition accordingly makes a program into a decision premise. Program forms differ depending on how they construct decision possibilities and what sort of competence they allow to develop. Such great demands are made of cognitive competence that difficulties of understanding can result; for instance, when lawyers have no insight into their incompetence in handling issues of purposiveness (for them the problem is one of interpreting conditional programs), while, vice versa, economists have difficulty accepting nonpurposive, conditional programs solely because of the value of a regulated order; they desperately search for an optimizable purpose to give the rule a sense as means.

All this has also to be taken into consideration when observing that both forms of program gain the status of normative validity. But this means only that they are put in place by decision and apply until altered. Furthermore, in handling this distinction it should be remembered that *every* decision that has to be made in the organization has to reckon with the past and with the future – from both a self-referential and an other-referential, environment-related perspective. The distinction between program forms can therefore not go so far as to allow no purposes at all to be taken into account in conditional programs or to construct purposive programs without any consideration of the conditions under which they are to be handled. Type differentiation is due firstly to the programming itself, that is to say, to the points of reference for the decision on whether a decision is right or erroneous. Mixed programs are possible, for instance, the rule that a machine is to be repaired only when it has already broken down (and not as a precautionary measure), but that repairs then have to be carried out to the purpose. Or that a lawsuit comes before the court only if a suit has been filed, but that conciliation has to be attempted, and only if this fails is the court to bring down a decision, again strictly conditionally in accordance with the law – and the conditions can contain reference to purposes.

But if we wish to learn about more complicated combinations of conditional programs and purposive programs, we first need to consider the distinctness of programmatic arrangements.

III

Conditional programs[16] take the general "if/then" form. Usually this means "only if/then," which means what is not allowed – what is initiated by the condition named – is forbidden. It would make no sense to stipulate that a particular medicine may be made available only on medical prescription or without prescription. Both sides of the relationship can be positive or negative; in general, however, reversal is taken for granted.

The condition for actuating a conditional program lies, relative to the operation actuated, in the past, even if the program is concerned with a future present and thus also has to presuppose the trigger signal in the future perfect tense. In comparison with purposive programs, this has the advantage that the conditions can (but not must) be unequivocally set. In borderline cases, the conditional program can therefore be carried out on the basis of inference or by machine. At the time of programming, only the time of performance and possibly the frequency of relevant cases are not yet determined.

Conditional programs can be sequentially interconnected in that the carrying out of one program is the signal actuating the next. This can dissolve complex programs into chains, into chains with built-in, automatic synchronization. This allows different competences and decision levels to be integrated through one position taking action when another has taken action.

The precision achieved in this program form does not, however, exclude indeterminacies from being built in again.[17] And then, as long as the "if/then" form is maintained, the programs are still conditional programs, but their regulatory value and the predictability of effects can decrease to a point where a distinction can no longer be perceived between right and erroneous.

Indeterminacy can be provided for in both if-clause and then-clause. If in the if-clause, we have a problem of interpretation with which lawyers are well acquainted. If in the then-clause, the decision to be made has not been unequivocally settled. For instance, the directive might be that when stocks reach a certain level they have to be replenished; but from which supplier and at what price are not stipulated. This indeterminacy is often to be understood as a pointer to additional criteria, such as suitability for given purposes or cost effectiveness. If programs containing indeterminacies have been long in use, typical fulfillment norms will develop (such as those found in legal commentaries and the like), and a decision-maker will typically be held accountable if he deviates from normal informal practice.

We have another well-known case of organizational learning when the program remains relatively precise but is supplemented by a rule/exception schema. The primary distinction of the conditional program is then once again differentiated, supra-conditionalized as it were, with the clause that it is to be used only if the explicitly mentioned conditions for an exception do not pertain.

In this context, the rule/exception schema is the functional equivalent of what in the case of purposive programs would be the search for alternatives.[18] We may prefer the search for alternatives; but this implies a switch of program form or betrays an orientation that assumes that conditional programs can be justified only in the context of purposive programs.

The rule/exception schema makes it possible to keep both the rule program and the exception program in mind and to avoid the initially obvious assumption that the exception destroys or weakens the rule. To achieve this, however, certain formalities are important; not simply routinized but defective deviations, "patterned evasions"[19] are required. If exceptions are permitted, the assessment situation rapidly becomes more complex, and exceptions therefore have to announce themselves pretty drastically and urgently if they are to attract attention.

In both procedures, filling in indeterminacies and adding exception rules, a conditionally programmed system tends to complicate its regulatory framework and make demands on attention that absorb a great deal of decision time. This can lead to the stronger break-down of positions, and thus to internally induced growth (the counterpart for purposive programs would be the end/means shift still to be discussed). Unlike living beings, organizations therefore appear to grow as they age. On the other side of this development, we find a permanent desire for simplification, for innovation, we could almost say, for shredding the files. And a tendency to tackle new problems by setting up new organizations.

IV

In principle, purposive programs are differently constructed, even if they have an admixture of conditionalization, especially with regard to "means." To begin with, it must be understood that purposes/ends are always "programs," that is to say, constructions, which could also be put together differently. As we have known since Kant, there are no ontologically given, natural ends, and certainly not in the domain of human action. The design of ends, in Kantian terms, is an achievement of reflective judgment, which interprets its object *as if it were purposive*. This can happen with descriptive intent, but also with pragmatic, prescriptive intent. But there is no ontological (teleological) commitment of action to ends.

This rearrangement within traditional teleology has to do with the modern notion of time, with the introduction into time of a not yet determinate future, one that requires decisions. Purposes, too, still have to be decided about, and the decision needs legitimation, which cannot for its part evoke (natural) purposes. Purposive programs are therefore purely future programs The causal relationship between means and ends that underlies them can easily be misleading; but means, from the point of view of programmed deciding, are also and always future means. On the other hand, purposive programs (like conditional programs) are also to be put into practice in the present of the decision operation. They can therefore be used with just as much certainty as conditional programs. Their problem is that an always uncertain, always unknown future has to be treated in the present as if it were already certain.

Orientation on the future leads to a radical distinction between purposive programs and conditional programs. For conditional programs, what is not allowed is forbidden; for the detachment of the decision from the past that determines the situation can proceed only with care; the basic alternative is therefore to follow (interpret, apply) the program, right or wrong. For purposive programs, by contrast, the indeterminacy of the future requires elasticity. For this reason, restrictions that in this context always concern the choice of means must be explicit. This means that what is not forbidden is allowed.[20]

If the future is uncertain, one could think – as does the classical theory of rational decision – that preferences, at least, would provide clear guidance, marking what can be taken into consideration. This may be more or less true of the individual decision. By contrast, organizational systems that conduct their own autopoiesis develop their preferences themselves. Preferences and decisions mutually prove each other's worth, and only what proves worthwhile is retained in the memory of the system to serve as a precondition for further learning. It is therefore advisable not to introduce the purpose concept in value-theoretical terms as if were self-evident (which may indeed be the case for the individual decision).

Purposes are differences; they are to be distinguished from what would otherwise occur. A means is also a difference; it indicates what is required to attain an end and hence to prevent what would otherwise occur from occurring. In order to present such concepts of the future as a present decision program, they have to be evaluated. The structure of a purposive program is therefore based on the differential evaluation of ends and means: ends positive, means negative. Positing value thus holds the program together: through the difference between future and present, through the difference between purposively produced states and states occurring otherwise, and through the difference between ends and means. And for this very reason evaluation has to present a resolved paradox: positive and negative evaluation of the program.

Suppressing the paradox, this is usually formulated as a program for optimizing the relationship between ends and means.

The main problem of all purposive programming is the unknownness and inaccessibility of all future. Whatever happens from decision to decision, the future remains future and means remain means. Although in every present one's own expectations can be checked and corrected in the light of experience with past experience, neither past nor future decisions can be made. Purposive programs can be corrected as far as their causal assumptions and value judgments are concerned, and hitherto overlooked aspects can be included. For example, one can take note that products are not selling as hoped, or that planned investments are becoming more expensive. Where programs for iterative decisions are concerned (for instance, surgical operations, the fight against crime, staff training, waste separation), one can learn. But experience is always condensed in uncertainty about whether past conditions will also be found in the future. Although purposive programming is designed to produce differences, it assumes that the break between past and future is not too drastic.

The causal relationship between ends and means allows alternatives to be constructed. Because every causal attribution, all causal determination, has to be selective. From the point of view of effects, causal horizons are per se infinite horizons. Each cause depends on innumerable other causes, each effect has innumerable further effects, not only sequentially but also in cascade form. Moreover, the total constellation shifts depending on the primary causal relationship. One can apply educational or therapeutic programs to prisoners, but the causes and the means vary depending on the type of concept. It can be a matter of language training aimed at ensuring that conflicts are fought out verbally rather than physically; or a matter of preparing convicts for employment after release to ensure that they can earn their own living. But the program always presupposes that causality is observed in excerpt, and the limitation also provides the possibility to think about alternatives that might offer greater probability of success or a more favorable value constellation. From a divine perspective there can be no alternatives. Everything would be right or everything would be wrong, with no possibility of distinguishing between these two possibilities.

With, and only with causal plans can antennas for the unexpected also be extended. This can to a certain degree diminish the risk of selection, but again only selectively and only in relation to what had been planned. Just as all forecasts also define the regards in which they could be incorrect and might have to be corrected, causal plans include observation of their failure. Without the attempt to demarcate a strictly limited form, "everything else" would also remain undefined. However, observation of the unexpected leads first of all only to the "unmarked space" of the medium of causal possibilities. This does not yet establish what is behind it. Things change when causal relations are "technicalized" to a certain degree, in other words, with a relatively fixed, normally functioning coupling of causes and effects sufficiently insulated against outside influences.[21] To this extent, purposive programs and conditional programs alike have degrees of determinacy; but the form of determination also varies with the program form. Whereas conditional programs would tend to be concerned with the hermeneutic limitation of the scope for interpreting trigger signals, purposive programs are more concerned with insulating the course of causal events against external interference.

Purposive programming builds on these general structures of purpose-directed deciding. They withhold components of this orientation from the positions that have to carry out the program. Garbage collectors are not at liberty to adapt their vehicle for the sale of bottled beer. But what is exactly laid down in the program and what is left to be filled in individual cases?

Typically it sets the ends itself and delimits the choice of possible means. That is at any rate the standard format. But what secondary purposes one also wishes to fulfill with the choice of suitable alternatives is left open. The greater the range of choices that satisfy the program setter, the more additional objectives can be accommodated. When attending conferences, scholars often go sight-seeing on the side: in service, diplomats collect anecdotes to tell at receptions in future postings. Secondary purposes can often also be taken into account – such as local amenities in choosing locations for conferences – but they are typically not included in the program.[22] It is likely that some programs tacitly take account of the enrichment capacity of purposes, for instance, the political bonus governing parties gain with welfare programs. Primary and secondary purposes are on occasion virtually interchangeable. But everything still remains in the framework of the general structure: if no purpose is set there is no purposive program.

Means that are in themselves suitable are typically excluded if, for instance, they are illegal. Despite all their special powers, the police have to respect the law when they pursue criminals or restore public peace and order. But a purpose-directed administration soon finds itself in a twilight zone of half legality if it can achieve its ends only by cooperating with interested parties who are not committed to making concessions.[23] Also in dealing with budgeted funds, situations can arise in which one has to act either contrary to the set purposes or with tricks.

The causal nexus of ends and means seems to make it advisable to declare the means to be ends and then to look for the means to attain the means. Such an ends/means shift has the major advantage of enabling concatenation. One can provide for means that are not available, and only then set out to obtain them. For example, production is planned in a plant that does not yet exist. In this manner, the program departs from the reality given at the time of the programming decision. Moreover, the ends/means shift allows purposes to be so strongly generalized that attaining the end loses all reference to points in time and can be neither positively ascertained nor negatively confirmed as unattainable. Purposes then become confounded with the values that serve to justify the difference sought. The army serves to "maintain the peace"; but then arms have to be procured, barracks constructed, soldiers trained; and the necessary means, once set as sub-purposes, engender requirements for further means. This has permitted organizational science to define even organizations as goal-attaining systems, or allowed the older structural functionalism to regard the preservation of the system as its highest goal. But autopoiesis is not a goal but the mode of operation itself.

In the older organizational sociology literature, the ends/means shift has essentially been seen negatively, if not criticized as pathological.[24] Such an assessment is obvious if the organization as a system is equated with the unity of its goal. If, by contrast, we set out from the concept of purposive programming, we come to a more balanced conclusion. It is inconceivable that all decisions of an organization are guided by a single, overall purpose; and it is also unrealistic to imagine that such an overall purpose could play a part in all decisions as a sort of control criterion. This would charge all decisions in the making too strongly with complexity. The point of speaking about "programming" is to direct attention to the differentiation and distribution of decision-making premises adequate to complexity. Only through programming and, in the case of purposive programs, only through the shift in ends and means can the complexity of the system be enhanced beyond the immediately plausible short-term goal. The ends/means shift enables correlation of purposive programs with the hierarchization of communication channels and competences. It enables more imagination. It makes it possible to make what is not yet realized depend on what is not yet realized. It should naturally not be overlooked that this leads to the autonomization of decisions on means. But this is not a pathological development in the wrong direction that can and should be cured. Improbable advances in general and organized absorption of uncertainty in particular typically have this "other side" to their form: that the improbability turns up again, but now in a much more specific form. It is therefore part of the task of programming positions constantly to monitor the ends/means shift for side effects and, where necessary, to react to unintended developments by changes or supplements to the program.

V

The concept "decision program" normally suggests rules that can apply to more than one case without a time limit. Time then becomes relevant in the form of a proviso for change. The programs are valid once they have been put in force until they are altered or cancelled. They constitute the "positive law" of the organization. But there are also other forms of temporal reference, each with its specific problems.

As actuating factors, conditional programs can stipulate extremely rare events, and events that one hopes will never happen. This is the case for mobilization programs in the event of war and for disaster programs (alert programs, evacuation programs, damage mitigation programs, and so forth). The main problem with such programs is memory. They have to be capable of being remembered and, where need be, updated, even if they are never used. This runs contrary to the typical memory-related organization of remembering and forgetting, namely the ongoing re-impregnation of released capacities as the need arises. The memory adapts itself through release/re-impregnation to the environment it cannot control. What does not occur is forgotten. But in this sort of warning program, this must be prevented through drills or through constant reminders—receipt to be confirmed in writing. A second-order memory has to be built into the memory, a memory that overrides one's own tendency to forget what never happens.

Another problem is the false alarm with its own disastrous, irreversible repercussions. The problem is the need for fast decisions. Nuclear missiles must not be allowed to be launched when no attack is intended but only signs misinterpreted. The problem then has to be "factorized," broken down into signs for the control of signs to allow self-control or such dangerous programs. But this merely repeats the basic problem and decomposes the alternative false alarm and false prevention of the alarm. And this may well be one of the points where the organization has to rely after all on circumspection and insight coinciding in a single individual.[25]

We find quite different states of affairs with purposive programs. In this case, highly complex programs can be elaborated for one-off execution. We then speak of "projects." Consider large-scale projects such as the Channel Tunnel, the construction of major hydroelectric dams, seawater desalination plants and irrigation systems, offshore oil drilling, and, in all these cases, the numerous auxiliary facilities (storage and transport, settlement programs, etc.) that are necessary if the primary facilities are to be used. Characteristic of these one-off projects are temporal limitations and the consequent time planning, where care has to be taken that for cost reasons no segment is completed too early or too late, and that time reserves are nevertheless available to allow delays difficult to avoid to be absorbed by individual segments. The paradox is therefore to save time while providing a time buffer, all on the condition that where and when delays will occur is unpredictable. The onlooker then typically has the impression that the project will be completed later than planned and will cost more than originally estimated.

Whereas many organization usually, indeed necessarily cooperate in this sort of project planning, and "hierarchy" is accordingly excluded as a form of overall coordination (if only because it would not be worthwhile to create a unique organization for a single project instead of involving existing, viable organizations), there are other cases in which the work of an organization comprises sequences of projects. Consider research institutes, business consulting firms, or film studios. The organization, and that is the problem, survives its projects. On the one hand, this raises the question of how new projects are to be acquired in order to keep employees in work, and of how easily the organization can react to the fluctuating project workload by adjusting staffing levels. What is more: how can experience with projects be remembered and made fruitful for further projects? Organizations that engage in project work pay the great variety of tasks with high rates of forgetting. Once completed, projects are forgotten, even though they could continue to yield useful experiential knowledge. The raw data that is produced while researching project commissions and that suffice for the final report are not further analyzed because the staff is occupied with other projects. If this is so, what can be done to rectify it? Is there a "narrative culture" in the system by which personnel convey their experience to one another and to new members of staff? Or, which is likely to be difficult and rare, is there a generalized conceptual system of analysis by means of which "added value" from projects is siphoned off and held ready for other projects? Or are existing personnel involved in initiating and deciding on new projects in a manner that brings "personalized" habits and experience (rather than programs) to bear in accepting or rejecting projects – at the cost of narrowing the range of projects undertaken?

A borderline case of time reference in programming currently attracting a great deal of attention is *risk*.[26] In contrast to danger, the concept of risk covers only consequences attributable to decisions, and which would hence not have materialized if the decision had not been made. From the point of view of the programs, and this is all we are interested in at the moment, risks are the other side of programmed time. They are to be found on the uncontrolled outside of the form. Although one knows that they exist, and do so at all times, one also knows that they cannot be controlled.

In conditional programs a structural indifference to the future, and thus to risk, must be assumed. If one wishes to endow conditional programs with "responsibility for consequences," a purposive program would have to be imposed on them to determine what consequences are wanted and what subsequent events the program would disavow. The risk perspective is thus a boundary perspective of future programs, of purposive programs. In this context, risks are to be distinguished from costs: they cannot, or at best fictitiously, be planned into the purpose decision, so to speak as warning.[27] An end must be worth the cost of the means for achieving it, otherwise no attempt would be made. The associated risks are another matter. One has to decide whether one wishes to take the risk or not. It is possible to shift matters from the domain of risk to that of costs. That is the business of insurance companies. But not all risks can be insured, and, anyway, this solution, too, merely converts the form of risk into the risk of having taken out insurance in vain if nothing at all happens.[28]

In all cases of programming, time problems in carrying out the program must thus be increasingly expected, and not only in the general form that (working) time is money. It is above all a matter of memory, especially self-correction in the normal performance of memory, namely adjusting to the environment by remembering and forgetting. But other time problems are also becoming increasingly important; in large-scale projects, for instance, constantly rethinking the progress achieved, the historical situation of the project, to ensure timely modification of planning should the need arise. Reflection loops have to be built in – partly to correct the normal functioning of the system memory, partly to carry out the project as a non-trivial, self-reflexive machine, and to ensure a thoroughgoing and constantly updated information flow. However, all this does not mean that the demands made on decision programming have to be reduced with regard to time dependence. The contrary is the case: it has to be reflexively developed so that problems consequent on simple programming can for their part be controlled.

VI

Structured decision programs, both conditional programs and purposive programs, are the *memory* of the system. For memory formation they have the indispensable advantage of being well documented. They decide what is to be remembered and what can be forgotten of the cases the system has handled.

The orientation-memory retains the aspects of decisions that can be used as decision premises, and forgets all the rest. It therefore prefers events on which records have been kept or at least events that can be kept on record. People's interactional experience is also important as social memory. It is relied on, for example, when in dangerous situations[29] a decision has to be made on what is to be communicated in writing and what only orally. Difficult to document experience that cannot without further ado be integrated in the course of business is retained primarily in the memory of managerial staff. It is scarcely controllable, "evolved" memory that distinguishes old members from new ones. It is lost when members leave the organization. Decision programs, by contrast, can determine what is to be remembered and what can be forgotten. The system will deviate from these rules and develop a narrative culture and warning practices of its own on the basis of concrete examples. But decision programs are indispensable as the rough structure for discriminating between remembering and forgetting – above all if one has to reckon with continual changes in membership.

The function of a memory is accordingly not to preserve as many "data" from the past[30] as possible but to reduce complexity through continuous forgetting, which in exceptional cases can, however, be interrupted. The Greek word for truth "*aletheia*," meaning the prevention of forgetting, thus describes our problem exactly. The memory always operates in the present, and in forgetting as in remembering refers only to the states of the system itself. Forgetting keeps the orientation capacities of the system free to process new information. At the same time, however, current events are tested for iteration. They are already largely known; only certain aspects, such as the time of their occurrence, are new and surprising. Thus, on condition that identities can be condensed and recognized in different situations, recognition serves to constantly update the system memory and thus to sort out aspects of the environment that are presumed to be important *because they occur repeatedly*. But in the environment itself there is no iteration; the environment is as it happens to be. The system memory therefore has to construct the environment in such a way that it can recognize and remember iterations.[31]

The memory also does not presuppose localization of what is remembered in the past. Who could date the many words they can remember (and those that they have possibly forgotten)? Knowing suffices. For this reason, a memory participating in all operations does not presuppose the intentional deployment of attention. It works unobtrusively, so that communication can maintain its distance from consciousness and generate its own redundancies. As we have seen, this does not mean that consciousness and the individual memory do not play their part. But if the organization wishes to draw on them, this requires communicatively extraordinarily elaborate reconstruction, almost "forensic" procedures. We therefore renounce the widespread notion that an organizational memory consists in a similarity of purpose, a sharing of individual memories.[32] If there were such a thing, it could not be determined through communication (or only in very rare cases).

In addition, however much identities are condensed, the ease and rapidity of recognition have to be ensured. If the demands on interpretation are too great, the decision process cannot attain the necessary speed, and, what is more, such demands would increase the possibility of dissent and misunderstanding. These, too, are internal requirements that can be presupposed for no environmental correlates. It would, after all, be absurd if one had to check out the environment for whether and why meaning is easy to identify and fast to process.

Thanks to programming through decisions, this memory function is available in the system. Conditional programs determine which trigger events are to be given particular attention, even if they occur at different times and in different contexts, for example, filing quite different applications that nevertheless have to be processed in the same way (in the light of this, it is easy to recognize that the call for "impersonal" decision practices makes heavy demands on the system memory and brings the temptation to concentrate more concretely on the particularities of the situation). With purposive programs, too, routines can develop in the coupling of ends and means (or problems and solutions) that are recalled and repeatedly used. Such routines limit the scope of functional equivalences; and even if "innovation" is demanded and rewarded, one generally takes recourse to remembered routines or to the experience of other organizations, and defines the problem at issue in such a way that already known solutions are applicable – or would seem to be so.[33]

The programmed system memory has to be adapted to the decision capacities, thus to the communication capacities of the system. If the system is overtaxed by its own programming, natural "defenses" set in. The discrimination between forgetting and remembering needed to reduce complexity is applied to the decision programs themselves. The system forgets its programs; or it develops a second memory that determines when the books have to be consulted. The decision programs of the legal system of society have long since been practicable only at this level of second memory.

These reflections on memory functions and memory limitations teach us above all how inappropriate it would be to understand organizations as executive institutions of a central will to power, and thus as directive hierarchies. A directive backed by power and authority has no effect if it is not remembered; or if it is remembered together with so many other directives that confusion and thus decision autonomy results. The system memory can of course be influenced and reshaped by programming, but this has in turn to take effect as memory. The system memory controls all volition and operates with the mechanism of inhibition and disinhibition: if something is to be remembered, most of the rest has to be forgotten.

VII

Both conditional programs and purposive programs enlarge the repertoire of their organizational system's causal possibilities. They supplement the natural causality of events through structural causality and through negative causality, namely through a causality of errors and omissions. These causalities, too, are triggered by actually occurring operations, but in the cases mentioned we are dealing with operations that would not take place at all if the structures and the negative facts on which they are oriented did not exist. A program is used or not used, used appropriately or wrongly – and *both* have consequences in the system. The planning and analysis of relations between causes and effects can therefore include structurally stabilized expectations, and this is true both if they are met and if they are disappointed.

With the construction of its own causality, the system attains the independence from the environment that enables operational closure and the development of its own complexity. Intrasystemic causality gives the system a multitude of flexible causes that do not have to be taken from the environment. With their help, the system can vary its own orientation toward the environment and decide which environmental facts (e.g., events or structures) it wishes to endow with causal effect. This does not exclude unexpected irritations from the environment: the AIDS virus has been found in conserved blood. But how these irritations are defined in the system and transformed into information depends in turn on what programs are involved.

Autopoiesis is only production and never overall control over all the required causes. This is already implied in the concept of production. The medium causality always covers the system and its environment, if only because the system would not exist without the environment. As we have seen, autopoiesis can therefore not be understood as causal isolation but only as reproduction from own products. For this very reason autopoietic systems have to obtain sufficient causality of their own if they are to be equipped to deal with causal dependency on their environment and to be able to tackle them selectively and compensatively. In the case of organizational systems, this is achieved through programming.

Notes

1. The literature on the subject (leaving aside computer programming) is extremely compendious. Usually no clear difference is drawn between binding rightness conditions and the various dimensions of position descriptions. For an overview see Andreas Remer, *Organisationslehre: Eine Einführung*, Berlin 1989, 43 ff.
2. See Thomas Ellwein, *Das Regierungssystem der Bundesrepublik Deutschland*, 3. Aufl., Opladen 1973, esp. 74 ff.; Dieter Grimm, *Staatsaufgaben*, Baden-Baden 1994.
3. Or, recently, to take account of ecological circumstances. Karl E. Weick, *The Social Psychology of Organizing (Der Prozeß des Organisierens, German translation*, Frankfurt 1985, 369), gives the following definition, for instance: "A task is a connection between enactment and ecological change. . ."
4. "By task, organization theory in business administration understands an action goal to be attained, a target to be reached by physical or intellectual activities" as we read in the *Handwörterbuch der Organisation*, 2nd ed. Stuttgart 1980 col. 200. See under Aufgabe Also with older literature; see also, e.g., Remer op. cit. 264 ff. Also James G. March and Herbert A. Simon, *Organizations*, New York 1958, 23: "A set of activities S, is a *task* if it can be performed by a person in a certain specified time, T (say 8 hours)."
5. Incidentally, evidence that this terminology can be used only in the discipline of business administration while serving to isolate it from general organization studies oriented on the social sciences.

6. On the "importance of doubt" see Weick op. cit. 320 ff. and passim. However, traditionally (Milton) doubt is the work of the Devil.

7. See E. Eugene Carter, The Behavioral Theory of the Firm and Top-Level Corporate Decisions, *Administrative Science Quarterly* 16 (1971), 413–428; Gordon Donaldson and Jay W. Lorsch, *Decision Making at the Top: The Shaping of Strategic Direction*, New York 1983.

8. This naturally waters down the classical concept of bureaucracy.

9. We recall Arnold Gehlen's concept of the "primacy of the pathological in practical cognition." See: Die Seele im technischen Zeitalter, Hamburg 1957, 85 with noteworthy reference to the consequent distortions. The proverb "nothing ventured, nothing gained" sounds less stern. What has been said here is also a comment on the subject of uncertainty absorption.

10. A quote will show this: "When things go wrong, the dependence-anxiety, aggressiveness, fears of attack, rivalry, and guilt all are stirred up. The way in which mistakes are dealt with is the real testing ground for the quality of executive leadership and the soundness of follower relationship in the T-group." Elliott Jaques, *The Changing Culture of a Factory*, London 1951, 288. It then seems obvious for practical leadership reasons to recommend generosity and orientation on the future in dealing with mistakes. See, e.g., Daniel Katz, Human Interrelationships and Organizational Behavior, in: Sidney Mailick and Edward H. Van Ness (eds.), *Concepts and Issues in Administrative Behavior*, Englewood Cliffs, NJ 1962, 166–186 (173). See also Everett C. Hughes, Mistakes at Work, in: idem, *Men and Their Work*, Glencoe, IL 1958, 88–101.

11. See from the perspective of older cybernetics Stafford Beer, *Kybernetik und Management, German translation*, Frankfurt 1962, 123 ff.

12. In the sense of Charles Perrow, *Normale Katastrophen: Die unvermeidbaren Risiken der Großtechnik, German translation*, Frankfurt 1987.

13. See Chapter 2.

14. For a detailed treatment see Niklas Luhmann, *Zweckbegriff und Systemrationalität: Über die Funktion von Zwecken in sozialen Systemen*, reprint Frankfurt 1973.

15. Without further argument, we presuppose that freedom of choice is not an innate ability of human beings who need only to be directed toward what is good, but that meaning needs first to be communicatively constituted to show what one can decide for or against.

16. See James G. March and Herbert A. Simon, *Organizations*, New York 1958, 142 ff. on "performance programs."

17. See, e.g., William J. Gore, *Administrative Decision-Making: A Heuristic Model*, New York 1964, 51 ff.; or, more formally, on "degree of programming" Remer op. cit. 52 ff., 66 f.

18. See, e.g., David Braybrooke and Charles Lindblom, *A Strategy of Decision: Policy Evaluation as a Social Process*, New York 1963, 158 ff. in one of the few explicit comparisons between "investigating alternatives" and "investigating exceptions."

19. The term "patterned evasions" is from Robin Williams, Jr., *American Society: A Sociological Interpretation*, New York 1960, 379. On its use in organizational contexts, see, e.g., Dean Harper and Frederick Emmert, Work Behavior in a Service

Industry, *Social Forces* 42 (1963), 216–225, on self-introduced labor-saving by mailmen, or Louis A. Zurcher, The Sailor Aboard Ship: A Study of Role Behavior in a Total Institution, *Social Forces* 43 (1965), 389–400 on corresponding experience on warships, or Earl Rubington, Organizational Strains and Key Roles, *Administrative Science Quarterly* 9 (1965), 350–369, on a home for the rehabilitation of alcoholics. There may be a number of reasons for choosing covert deviation – probably in the first place that conditions for exemption cannot be precisely defined or that they would detract from the seriousness (practicality) of the normal rule; or quite simply that the public permitted to know about it is too diverse.

20. If we dissociate these two principles from the level of the organization and its programs and transfer them to the legal system, whether the primacy of prohibition or the primacy of permission should be proclaimed becomes undecidable and ultimately an ideological issue. Taken together, the two possibilities constitute a paradox that can be unfolded only through programming.

21. See on a typical case in which this assumption cannot be realized, Niklas Luhmann and Karl Eberhard Schorr, Das Technologiedefizit der Erziehung und die Pädagogik, in idem (eds.), *Zwischen Technologie und Selbstreferenz: Fragen an die Pädagogik*, Frankfurt 1982, 11–40, and comments on this in the same volume.

22. Still, the author has been offered accommodation in a "first-class hotel" on being invited to conferences. Such blunders happen.

23. See Keith Hawkins, *Environment and Enforcement: Regulation and the Social Definition of Pollution*, Oxford 1984; Arthur Benz and Wolfgang Seibel (eds.), *Zwischen Kooperation und Korruption: Abweichendes Verhalten in der Verwaltung*, Baden-Baden 1992.

24. See, e.g., Robert Michels, *Zur Soziologie des Parteiwesens in der modernen Demokratie*, reprint of the 2nd. ed, Stuttgart 1957; Philip Selznick, An Approach to a Theory of Bureaucracy, *American Sociological Review* 8 (1943), 47–54; Peter M. Blau, *Bureaucracy in Modern Society*, New York 1956, 93 ff.; David L. Sills, *The Volunteers*, Glencoe, IL 1957, 62 ff.

25. On the importance of cooperatively schooled circumspection ("heed") for organizations with fast and risky decisions (aircraft carriers) see Karl E. Weick and Karlene H. Roberts, Collective Mind in Organizations: Heedful Interrelating on Flight Decks, *Administrative Science Quarterly* 38 (1993), 357–381. However, we are dealing with cases in which this cooperative socialization does not occur owing to the infrequency, indeed absence, of such situations.

26. See also Niklas Luhmann, *Risk: A Sociological Study.* Translated by Rhodes Barrett, Berlin 1993.

27. A typical case of the anticipatory risk management is to avoid risks, for example, in investing, that would threaten the liquidity of the firm if they materialized.

28. See Niklas Luhmann, Das Risiko der Versicherung gegen Gefahren, *Soziale Welt* 47 (1996), 273–283.

29. See also Weick and Roberts op. cit.

30. This is, however, the strongly predominant view, oriented on the memory of the consciousness. See, e.g., James P. Walsh and Gerardo Rivera Ungson, Organizational Memory, *Academy of Management Review* 16 (1991), 57–91, with a quote from the

American Heritage Dictionary 1969: "Memory is 'the faculty of retaining and recalling things past'."

31. See also Heinz Förster, *Das Gedächtnis: Eine quantenphysikalische Untersuchung*, Wien 1948; Heinz von Foerster, Qauntum Mechanical Theory of Memory, in idem (ed.), *Cybernetics: Circular Causal, and Feedback Mechanisms in Biological and Social Systems, Transactions of the Sixth Conference*, March 24–25, 1949, New York 1950, 112–134.
32. See Walsch and Ungson op. cit. 61.
33. We will be coming back to this in the chapter on structural change.

9   Personnel

I

Questions of personnel management have long been overshadowed by other forms of decision premise. The organization was identified in terms of its goals (and thus largely in terms of purposive programs), and rationalization considerations were therefore concerned primarily with the hierarchical structure of the organization, and thus with responsibilities and communication channels. The issues were centralization or decentralization, steep or flat hierarchies, the relationship between staff and line organization, the inclusion of the group principle in all too individualistic job descriptions (criticism of "Taylorism"), and the like.[1] The selection of personnel had presupposed the relevant decisions about the other components of the position.[2] It had to comply as best it could with the principles of rational decision-making. Personnel management was regarded as a special responsibility – both in description of the tasks to be performed and in the organizational endowment with decision-making authority. The guiding principle was "the right man in the right place."[3] The principle of its rationality was thus the correlation between two unknown variables, and the principle of its practice was consequently oscillation between stipulations on the one hand and, on the other, between staff assessments and job descriptions. And because people are difficult to move and difficult to change, it could never be put into practice fast enough to satisfy the hopes set in rationality under constantly changing conditions.

Moreover, these maxims do not take the factual expectations of an individual into consideration. Such expectations are formed by the individual's assessment of the possibilities for and obstacles to a career. But superiors had to reckon with such expectations; they could play with them. For as soon as chances of promotion come to play a role, the relevant decision-making powers are difficult to separate from the superior's general powers. The authority to appoint and dismiss is (and naturally remains) an important tool of power, especially where subordinates can be left in the dark about how it is wielded. Group participation in personnel selection as demanded by the human relations movement has always been a contentious issue.[4]

The secondary importance accorded personnel questions has nurtured illusions about the propensity of organizations for change. Organization charts and job descriptions can be modified with a stroke of the pen, so to speak. By contrast, the conglomerate of an individual's own expectations and those of others that is identified as a "person" is difficult to adjust, if at all. This is due not least to the circular interplay between one's own and others' expectations. Even if the individual were willing to change, he sees himself defined by the social expectations he daily faces; and, similarly, changing demands are made of the same person, who has to preserve his identity for many social contacts. Personal and social memories are so closely interwoven that plans for change have difficulty discovering the asymmetry required to tackle the task. It therefore seemed an obvious course to set about change not in this domain but through organization charts and job descriptions – on the assumption that persons as individuals would somehow fall in with the changed realities. The problem of personnel decision premises was accordingly underestimated.

In recent times, this traditional view of personnel management appears to be changing.[5] Tasks are defined in more complex terms, and greater attention is paid to how the willingness and the ability to work relate to the tasks set and where they are located in the system.[6] This engenders new expectations and hence new chances for the subjectivity of those involved, for their utilization as "system regulators."[7] For the public service it has been noted, for example, that greater demands are made on executive officers by more and more complex decision problems, and, in particular, by the shift in focus from conditional programs to purposive programs, with the result that their differing personal characteristics and decision-making styles have a stronger impact.[8] But it is also less self-evident than in the past that white-collar and blue-collar workers perform their tasks properly and can, when necessary, be constrained to do so by directives and controls. This is not to say that directives and controls could be replaced by self-discipline. This, too, is less true than ever before. But the problem of bridging the system difference between individuals and organizations is attracting increasing attention as a component of "general management" that is difficult to hive off,[9] which can probably also be said of the willingness to take risks. But, above all, the focus is shifting to cooperative problem-solving and thus to the question of how the expertise, experience, and contacts distributed in the system can best be used.[10]

Such changes – initially manifest only as desiderata and not with respect to existing personnel – are likely to have repercussions for what at all levels of the hierarchical classification we could term the core competence of personnel. Old virtues like commitment to organizational goals, discipline, and putting aside private interests may well be still important, but a sort of upstream competence could be more and more necessary, which would have to consist in the recognition of opportunities and in an extension of alternatives that is perhaps only temporary, and therefore cannot be prescribed. The system would have to oscillate at all levels of its personnel structure between taking and not taking opportunities (opportunities are not in themselves necessarily positive), and would bring rationality considerations and communication with other positions into play only if decision problems arise at the level of this primary oscillation. But it is immediately apparent that this would produce far-reaching (and perhaps insoluble) problems for the organization of training and the labor market. In any case, it would be difficult to cover such primary competence with the usual certificates or job titles by which the educational and training systems and labor market job offers have hitherto prestructured recruitment possibilities.

Such changes probably have to do with growing willingness to engage in personal communication.[11] More than in the past, one now says what one feels, prefers, considers to be right with reference to one's own judgment, and thus with reference to oneself as premise of one's own deciding. And the authority for uncertainty absorption is weaker than in the organizations of the past that were still determined by stratification, or by education plus stratification. Circumstances change more rapidly than they used to, with the result that more voluntary, unenforceable adjustment to change has to be demanded. The limits of the "zone of indifference" (Barnard[12]) are now likely to be more blurred and more difficult to determine than in the past, and all this makes one less confident about which assumptions find consensus in the system and which do not. All this points to the need for open communication, to use a term much bandied about. And finally, the vogue for corporate culture, organizational symbolism, and corporate identity and the like draws its strength and popularity from this extended interest in persons.[13] The hope is that culture will deliver more or less reliable inferences about motives.

This gives personnel management a great deal more to do. The classical tasks of requirements planning and suitable selection naturally remain, but they are supplemented by tasks of a more caring if not therapeutic nature. This includes a tolerable measure of agreement on mutual expectations; job specification that takes the working human being and not only performance into account[14]; the provision of help for personal problems (with alcohol, for example); the planning of familiarization periods for new arrivals and of cooling-off times for failures or the victims of job cuts; and the scrutiny of all positions with regard to the career opportunities they offer, including planning for new blood that offers prospects of promotion within the system and provision against poaching from outside. This includes providing people without prospects of advancement with substitute satisfaction, up to and including pseudo hierarchies that offer possibilities of promotion without there being any corresponding need at the competence level. In short, everything there is in the system would have to be re-examined with regard to effects on people and their decisions.

However, such high-flying expectations come up against the unpredictability of individuals. The capacity of the individual for rational decision-making despite all limitations is also still overestimated (as if one could recruit better decision-making).[15] Concepts of such broad responsibility for personnel therefore generate a reality that does not correspond to the one they seek to generate. This is not least because people are involved as individuals, because they observe how they themselves and others are treated, and because all personnel planning operates as self-fulfilling/self-defeating prophecy. It is observed that counseling is offered for alcohol problems, but also that there is nothing beyond the counseling; it is also noted whether the relevant programs are used in the upper echelons of the system or not. The intensive interest in persons, further fueled by official attention, sets off an abundance of causal attributions. If someone is promoted or, as a lateral entrant, attains a higher position, there must be reasons that do not necessarily have anything to do with the reasons stated (best possible choice). In this field more than in any other, the system writes its own history, and this organizational-culture forming effect is difficult to anticipate and take into account or correct in personnel planning.

In view of these difficulties, we have to seek a better explanation for the increasing and ever more complex interest in persons that take such problems into account. It is provided by analysis of the autopoiesis of decision-making. All decisions are confronted by an unknown future, by the leeway for oscillation that also points them in a certain direction and accordingly reproduces them. The unknownness of the future is the most important and the lasting, constantly renewed resource of decision processes. Persons, therefore, serve as tangible symbols for the unknownness of the future. It should therefore not come as a surprise if the official and informal interest in persons increases as the dependence of the system on decisions becomes a topic of communication, and as the change in decision premises comes to be included in daily routines. In persons one finds, as it were, a compromise between past and future (they are as they are, but one cannot know with any certainty how they will act) that the organization has to implement through decisions.

This then also applies all the more strongly for personnel decisions themselves. Realistically, we therefore have to assume that there are cognitive limits and technical decision-making limits to all personnel management. We therefore abide by the distinction introduced in Chapter 3 between individual human beings and organizations as social systems, and hence by the assumption that human beings in organizations gain operational relevance only insofar as they are indicated in communication.

II

This chapter about personnel therefore deals only with persons, not with individual "full human beings" in the performance of their living and mental autopoiesis.[16] Persons are special forms of observing the coherence of situations; they are thus ordering patterns with highly selective properties. A person's name stands for a set of situations (inconceivable individually). Moreover, we limit ourselves to the treatment of persons as decision premises, and to this extent we follow the directives of Chapter 7 on decision premises. By decision premises we mean two things: premises that are communicated as personal in every decision communication, and premises that are anticipated in personnel decisions as premises for future decisions by certain persons.

At the level of operational uncertainty absorption, decisions are to a greater or lesser degree always attributed to persons, and (with considerable divergence) by both the decision-makers themselves and those who have to deal with their decisions, who await them, who seek to influence or explain them, in order to be prepared for the decision-maker's preferences and style in future dealings with him. Attribution to persons is possible only, but then obviously, if one expects that other persons would decide otherwise. This might well remain an implicit premise that is activated only when the issue of whether someone is to be involved in decisions or not comes up, or if personnel decisions are on the agenda.

Despite all legends about "impersonal" bureaucracy, it must be said that the orientation on persons within organizations is of considerable importance. The way in which the decision paradox is resolved by attribution to persons even suggests that the personal contribution to the decision-making process tends in practice to be overestimated rather than underestimated. How and in what forms persons are communicated about should therefore be examined more closely. Only then can insight be gained into the context into which personnel decisions, however made, have to be inserted and on which these decisions meeting either with understanding or disapproval depends.

As soon as persons become known, narratives are constructed about them that, in written documents, only to a very small degree are fixed – for example, in official staff assessments. These accounts operate above all with the distinction between constant and variable characteristics. They appearm on the one hand as characters, on the other as motives. The observation schema also applies, incidentally, for the modern novel and has thus probably made its way into everyday experience. The character is treated as given, as a constant that can be relied on. Jean Paul advises novelists that "the character as such cannot be motivated."[17]

In the novel as in everyday communication about persons, the distinction between constant and variable, between characters and motives is also an artifact without any basis in the bodily and mental reality of human beings. The construct simplifies communication about persons and leaves it to the success of communication whether and what motives are attributed and thus exposed to influence or reproach. Empirically verifiable speculation could furthermore posit that, upon closer acquaintance, the character condenses, so to speak, and motivatability decreases because more and more experience is registered as iteration of characteristics that have often been registered. Aging organizations, like aging marriages, can then suffer from a loss of hope that motives can be isolated and influenced. Far-reaching restructuring can then fail owing to the strength-of-character artifact developed in communication, and the realization of hopes can consequently be sought by recruiting fresh blood or by founding a new organization.

III

We shall speak of personnel decisions when talking about membership of the system or about filling vacancies. This is the case for decisions concerning entering (appointment) and leaving (dismissal) and for decisions about redeployment within the system with or without promotion. A positive choice requires assumptions about the match between the expectations of the organization defined in terms of positions and what a person offers in the way of skills and attitudes. Such expectations may arise from investigations during the process of deciding on appointment, or as a condensate of experience in dealing with the person, which is occasionally fixed in the form of written "employee assessments." But, since judgments about persons are not very reliable and, moreover, depend in considerable measure on whoever is doing the judging, a great deal of weight in personnel decisions is placed on the possibility of later correction.

Personal decision premises differ from decision programs in an essential regard: they cannot be broken down any further. We can distinguish analytically between the knowledge, skills, preferences, environmental contacts, ages, genders, cooperativeness, and rates of work, etc. of specific persons – important variables for every formulated employee appraisal. But these and other variables are applied compactly to one person at a time, are identified with them, and cannot (or rarely) be changed separately, to the disappointment of everyone who has to do with "personnel development." To the extent that this holds true, personnel planning has to concentrate on movement processes in the system, and this means above all operating with selective (rather than merely reward) promotions.

If the individuality of persons is so emphasized in recognition of the fact that each is different from all others, one could conclude that persons then also have to be treated individually. What stands in the way of this is that individuals observe how other individuals are assessed and treated, and draw conclusions for their own situation from their observations. A dense network of gossip, of handing on information about personnel decisions and the overt or covert reasons for them, links up all information, recalls cases (however much in the short term), and compares. Condensing this information, the result is a demand for equal treatment, disclosure of the "real" reasons and, on top of it all, strong pressure on the decision process, which cushions it by schematization. Gossip produces the schematism of justice and hence the conditions for its own continuation in the event of supposed deviations; it also produces the expectation of common indignation and in this sense solidarity.[18] The schematization this imposes explains marked preferences for seniority as the basis for promotion, for internal job advertisements, and for long-winded consultations, often in bodies, to prepare important decisions. Much of this is symbolic work on a decision that has long been made or as good as made. This imposed "objectivity" results in a certain formalism in the presentation of the decision, and banality in the expectations communicated, in criteria and explanations, and in the dubious manipulation of requirements with regard to the favored candidate. The impression has to be given that the decision has been made in favor of one individual over another both fairly and more or less by chance, be it only in order to obviate or at least deflect any suspicion of unobjective motives being in play. If the decision is presented as carefully considered, appropriate, and free from ulterior motives, the process of uncertainty absorption is reason enough to favor it; and the suspicion that ulterior motives are involved can then be aired only as an affront that has to be proved.

IV

Personnel decisions decide how vacancies are filled and thus decision premises. The contribution a person makes to decisions is hence also due to a decision. There are no principles for this decision and no guarantees for its correctness, no matter what communication within the organization has to say about it. What it produces is solely the decisions that the premise "person" enables and differentially pre-controls. Only on the assumption that different persons will decide differently does it make any sense at all to decide on personnel issues in the form of appointments. Since attribution to a person is difficult and will remain controversial, it is hardly possible to keep a record of success and failure, except in borderline cases. Later recognition of a choice as good or bad presupposes relatively clear deviation from normal expectations. The person is surprising – in a positive or negative sense. Only in such cases do the underlying personnel decisions attract the attention that leads to praise or blame. That a sort of belated surprise is necessary for this[19] merely confirms that success or failure in the form of total results of the decision-maker cannot be forecast – despite all the good reasons that can be mobilized for a particular choice. One must therefore be thankful if nothing untoward happens.

The most important distinction in this domain is that between recruitment decisions and redeployment decisions. Bernhard and Simon have proposed a general theory in the shape of a theory of balance between inducements and contributions in which non-members on whom the organization depends (thus its markets) can also be included.[20] The problems are hence broken down behavioristically into behavioral problems and then declared to be problems of maintaining a balance. However, this makes excessive demands on the concept of balance. If we understand this concept as the willingness to identify disturbances, it skips the level of programming,[21] which provides the structures against which the organization can gauge disturbances. For the rest, this theory confronts the empiricist (whom it addresses) with the question of whether and how he can ascertain behavior except in relation to the organization and its contingencies (degrees of freedom). In what follows, we shall therefore leave aside this demanding concept of the order of relations between the organizational system and (personal) environments and set out from the difference between system and environment.

In the field of personnel decisions, this places the focus of theory on the difference between recruitment decisions and redeployment decisions, and with an opposing set of problems in relations between individual and person. The problem in recruitment decisions is that the person (as an individual) is unknown. In the case of redeployment decisions, the problem is that the person (as an individual) is known. And for objectivity-focused personnel management, both can prove fatal.

The problem with unknown persons is how to assess their suitability as decision premise despite their being unknown. Many tools have been developed for this purpose, notably the résumé, the reference, the external audit, the recommendation; then there is the job interview and the qualifying examination; finally there is the probationary period preceding longer term employment. In all these cases, the recruiter faces a mix of purposeful self-presentations and background information (e.g., about the authors of references or about the quality of examinations). In view of the uncertainty involved, selection tends to shift toward comparison between different applicants. A general preliminary qualification filter is applied before making a decision by comparing short-listed candidates. For important recruitment decisions, selection thus runs through a two-stage procedure for uncertainty absorption; conditions have to be kept variable depending on the candidate situation (depending on the self-selection of candidates).

This general problem is compounded by another variable, the indeterminacy of future requirements. We can exclude the borderline case of completely unknown persons being recruited to perform completely indeterminate tasks.

The organization always has experience – be it with its own requirements, be it with certain sorts of person, for instance, with lawyers or high school graduates in not very demanding activities. Decision situations without any guidelines are not to be expected. But it still makes a big difference whether recruitment is for positions or careers and what requirements profile the decision has to address. Recruiting a woman for the assembly line offers less of a risk than adding another member to the executive board.

External recruitment for higher positions can be avoided by advancement within the organization. But, as comparison of the functional equivalents of entry and advancement shows, this also poses problems. If a personnel system is geared to advancement, which is very much the case in most fields of government administration up to the point where political appointments come into play, corresponding expectations rapidly develop and, given the job hierarchy, corresponding disappointments. In order to keep the disappointment rate low, the system may well construct a functionally unnecessary stairway up which one advances in small steps.[22]

This is joined by the general problems of internal redeployment decisions with or without promotion. They arise from the involvement of known persons who expect their own expectations to be honored.

V

Another division has only to do with recruited persons. It distinguishes between changing persons and moving them within the system from position to position. If the intention to change persons is concerned with individuals in the sense of organic and psychic systems, experience with training programs to this end is not very encouraging. After all, of interest is only what communication an individual triggers, which depends essentially on the social context in which communication is expected, received, and understood. There might be cognitive training ("further education programs") in which specific expertise, such as language skills, legal knowledge, police tactics, computer skills, is taught. But this makes sense only if these accomplishments can be immediately used; otherwise they rapidly go to waste.

The lesson from such experience, which we cannot document here in greater detail, is likely to be that an organization's personnel policy has to be oriented above all on positions defined in terms of premises, and that the wherewithal is to be found less in the practically hopeless endeavor to change (adult) human beings than in the selection of persons for positions, and thus in movement processes. But this, too, is difficult enough.

In abstract terms we can postulate that what matters is a match between job description and personnel assessment. The appraisal of a person must show him or her to be suitable to perform the tasks of a given position; and if the position is attractive and there are many candidates, the person favored should be better suited than the others. In practice, however, at least three serious problems arise.

(1) Non-formalized criteria always play a role in the process of filling a vacancy. Under certain circumstances, the candidacy of a person focuses attention on aspects that had hitherto been ignored or not taken into account in the job description – and the effects of such criteria can be both negative and positive. The decision premises a person represents are also a factor in defining the position. When the incumbent changes, a position takes on a different character; and why should this be left out of account in the selection process as a matter of principle? But this leads to not unproblematic ad hoc variation in the expectations associated with positions – to the advantage or disadvantage of the candidates under consideration. One therefore has to reckon with such ad hoc variation being perceived as unobjective bias in favor of certain persons, and hence as difficult to communicate. While decision-making positions may have the best of intentions for the organization, they can nevertheless find themselves under suspicion. And the more formalized the whole procedure is, the more this will be the case.

(2) Redeployment and promotion processes within the system presuppose that proving oneself in a position provides sufficient indication of the likelihood of being able to prove oneself in another position. But this is more than questionable, especially when assessment criteria are tailored to the position that a person holds. There are two sides to this problem, too. It could be that proving oneself in one position gives the delusion of having prospects that cannot be realized in other positions. Whoever is judged to be good need not necessarily be suitable for promotion. But there is also the converse, perhaps more tragic case, which comes to light less easily because it leads to the prevention of promotion. Someone might prove unsuitable in all positions because he or she can unfold his potential only at the apex of the system. Selection processes in political parties certainly produce a great deal of miscasting; but they are likely to suffer most from their failure to further the advancement of persons suitable only for top positions (and who are perhaps themselves unaware of this).

(3) Since individuals identified as persons are highly complex systems and since positions, too, represent systemic complexity, (forms for) personnel assessment and job description have to be multi-dimensional in design. This means that they do not produce unequivocal decisions: the one applicant will be better in some regards, another in others. This perhaps allows obvious nonstarters to be excluded, but does not lead to objective, well-founded decisions being made between several capable but not in every respect excellent candidates. The dimensions must rather be

reassessed ad hoc in relation to one another. This can easily give the impression of an arbitrary decision in favor of certain persons preferred for reasons impossible to explain. This can be avoided by quantifying the weighting of dimensions (for instance, qualifications 50%, cooperativeness 30%, intelligence 10%). But this shifts the arbitrariness to quantification, under certain circumstances singling out a person who would never have been chosen on the basis of direct impressions or experience in dealing with people. Such calculative procedures therefore tend rather to be used for commission decisions, since they obviate internal disputes. Schematizations are accordingly likely to serve principally to localize arbitrariness (alias decision paradox) and to conceal it in communicating the decision.

The more the selection process is driven by criteria, the greater is the danger of these problems being underestimated; this is especially true when criteria are conceived of as programming personnel selection[23] and their dysfunctionality perceived not as violations, not as errors in the handling of personnel affairs. This can be taken into account in certain measure in the formulation of standpoints (questions) for personnel assessment and in job descriptions. If personnel selection is programmed by criteria, decisions on individual cases can be delegated – and this demonstrates once again the close links between all sorts of decision premise. This need not necessarily lead to more rigid selection with losses of opportunity in individual cases.[24] Nevertheless, it can hardly be denied that the procedure itself has side effects because it has exclusion effects. It would therefore have to be ensured that the system evaluates its descriptions and learns from wrong decisions. And even automatisms of this sort must not be allowed to divert attention from the fact that there are problems that lie in rationalization and objectivization themselves. What had been designed to exclude arbitrariness ultimately has only the effect of relocating and restructuring arbitrariness.

Not least of all, efforts to rationalize attribution depend on the possibility of positions becoming vacant or new positions being established. This, too, means that personnel policy depends on factors like the death of members or the growth of the system that are not amenable to systematic planning. What is more, positions that become vacant have to be filled as quickly as possible if their superfluousness is not to become too obvious. Even a sort of static rationality is hardly attainable under such conditions.[25] All in all, such objections confirm the suspicion that appeals to rationality at the level of the overall system serve rather to launch reform initiatives than to improve conditions – which does not mean that in particular cases better or worse decisions could be made.

VI

As soon as decisions are made about personnel deployment (recruitment, redeployment, promotion, dismissal) they are also observed and attributed. Attributed – to what? Even if personnel decisions are programmed in the system, they are not unequivocally determined by programs. Attribution therefore ends up not at the criteria but at the persons who decide about personnel. This is also the case when criteria have been objectively applied, since a margin of discretion is assumed. And this is all the more so when criteria are actively interpreted to adapt them to the persons favored – not least of all when in effect it makes no difference whether they are applied or not because they exist only on paper. In every case and in all organizations a patronage network is superimposed on "rational" personnel management. How decisions really come about cannot be established. Conjecture therefore counts and comes into play. Everyone is thus well advised to act as if there were patronage, and if situations are defined in this manner, then it is so.

Whoever disposes over personnel decisions *ex officio* can accordingly expect that others will expect that he has influence or can exert influence if he wishes. It may be a matter of mythology, of the products of gossip, and, above all, of provision for a future hidden in the unknown. It could be that investing in advantageous opinions pays off, and if not, the same mythology offers an explanation. It is confirmed by positive and negative experience.

Everything else is a matter of the form the variable patronage takes and the attitude of the system toward it. In extreme cases, which are, however, very typical for stratified societies and present-day so-called developing countries, personnel selection is guided largely by relations between patrons and clients external to the organization.[26] In Vatican terminology, we could speak of nepotism. It may be a question of family relations, extended families and their circle of clients, but also of ethnic and religious solidarity. Characteristic of this order is that external relations establish a sort of claim to preferential treatment and support, and that accepting it is no cause for embarrassment. Only modern judges see corruption in this. It should also be noted that the organization is thus provided with sources of solidarity that it could not itself tap in the given society. Another characteristic of this order is that it relies in large measure on mediation roles: on sponsors with good access to sponsors, so that favors can be asked not directly but "for others who deserve them." The system works altruistically and, to this extent, impeccably from a moral point of view, although on the basis of a particularistic morality, which is, however, usual in the society in question.

There is no clear-cut dividing line between such systems and the modern organizational system with universalistic decision criteria. One of the most important differences is that the possibility to practice patronage derives from positions internal to the organization and not from an external societal status.[27]

The advantages of supporting persons then flow back into the organization itself. The concomitant gain in power can be re-invested in the system itself and only there, and does not flow back into the general societal networks of sponsorship, aid, and gratitude (just as under the conditions of an outdifferentiated money economy, capital gains have to be re-invested in the economy itself). Expectations of patronage can, above all, motivate unenforceable performance. For this reason, it is difficult to relocate personnel decisions away from the managerial positions of the system.[28] The party political spoils system also serves to consolidate career expectations in politics, which in turn makes service in political parties attractive for people aspiring to a career.[29]

The double observation of personnel decisions is accordingly unavoidable, from formal and informal standpoints, programmable and non-programmable perspectives. By contrast, it remains an open question – contingent on the societal context – how far informal elasticity helps increase power within an organization and can be used as a leadership resource, or whether it serves to coordinate organizations with the systems of its societal environment: powerful family clans, the military, political parties, business enterprises, or, within the economy, with banks, for instance. Moreover, it makes a difference whether using margins of discretion in personnel decisions for external coordination is approved in the system or disapproved and decried as corruption.[30] From a sociological point of view, there appear to be narrow limits to rationalizing personnel decisions by setting criteria. It therefore has to be expected that potential for decision-making will be diverted for patronage purposes. This is not to be condemned already as a principle; one has to watch how the state of affairs is observed in the system and what effects this observation has.

VII

Under whatever criteria personnel decisions are made, as soon as positions are differentially evaluated, careers will develop. We have already dealt with careers[31] in detail from the perspective of the now predominant form of integrating individuals and society. Here we turn to the topic once again to examine the importance of the intentional or unintentional development of careers for the personnel decisions of the system.

Career is a form of observation that sets out from the identity of a person (with which the individuals engaged in the career can identify themselves) and enumerates the positions that the person has held or has prospects of holding. The career form thus requires fixed and evaluated positions (or, at school: grades, levels of schooling, ranked types of school), which can be held by individuals or distributed among individuals, and which thus serve as indicators of success or failure. Since these conditions are institutionally entrenched in schools and organizations, one often does not realize what far-reaching consequences they have. For they couple incentive and reward techniques with the form of career and leave little room to operate with incentives and motives independently of the ranking of positions. What remains are largely vain attempts to honor outstanding achievements at least symbolically by adding awards, prizes, or performance bonuses. Here, too, the difficult problem of individually attributing special merits cannot be avoided, particularly when special value is placed on "teamwork." In consequence, attention will be diverted from merit to attribution and the problem is then seen and treated in "political" terms.

This sort of experience suggests the wisdom of regulating incentives essentially through careers, thus tying them to the position structures of the system. At the same time, however, what is needed to order careers in the way of a rigid schema is not very motivating, because one soon becomes accustomed to any position attained and has difficulty adapting to the situation-dependent demand for special skills or special performance.[32]

The construction of every career sets out from the position held at the moment and is divided from this perspective into past and future – past achievements relevant to the career and positions whose attainment is probable or at least possible on the basis of the person's career biography. Positions already attained are entered in the career account as achievements;[33] holding these positions is treated as a merit justifying claims to consideration or at least rendering them communicable. The extent to which such claims to consideration are institutionalized depends on the organizational culture[34]; and it also depends on whether they can be asserted personally or whether an advocate has to be mandated to do so. Although, especially in the public service, the conviction is widespread that one has a right to a career simply by existing, this can at best have to do with titles and pay scales and not with shifting from one position to another.

Career is thus a form in which the past, and hence the present as future past, counts for the future. A career is a sort of capital formation, albeit of uncertain utility. For every station in a career depends both on self-selection and on other-selection – on applications, interest shown, and performance delivered, as well as on the occurrence of vacancies and the selection decisions of others. Careers are only possible if self-appointment is excluded.[35] Success and failure in a career can therefore always be attributed to two things: merit and fate. Future prospects can accordingly be divided into one's own efforts, good behavior, and performance, thus provisioning the career fund, and hopes that this will be honored. All of this can be oriented on the position structure of the system, which, owing to its hierarchical nature and due to the horizontal differentiation between better and worse jobs, keeps career opportunities scarce. Especially in the top echelons, careers depend in strong measure on chance – for example, on death or an opportune scandal providing the desired opening. It could be said that career hopes form a reservoir of talent governed by chance.

An objective reality therefore underlies careers: the number and quality of positions available and the programs and practices of personnel decisions – for example, compelling selection conditions that are to be ignored only at the risk of illegality, or the option of recruiting both internally and externally. This sets the limits of the observation form "career." But the effects of this observation form do not consist in vacancies actually being filled. In other words, they do not lie in the current operations of personnel decisions, which take place only in the present. Their point of departure is an observation encompassing past and future that is oriented on the identity of persons and on the assessment of positions.[36] Since this applies to both the personal career of individuals involved as persons and, inseparably bound up with this, to the careers of other persons, we can speak of ongoing self-observation of the organizational system on the basis of the highly complex schema "career." The system regards itself as an ordering of career enablement.

To the extent that this form of self-observation is used (which depends not least on adequate reference to reality, thus also on sufficient mobility in relation to persons and positions), further variables are added to the observation schema. Thus the relative weight of professional culture and organizational culture could shift in favor of the latter if the organization offers career opportunities, while the profession tends to be built on equality among colleagues (all lawyers, all doctors, all nurses, or other professions defined in terms of educational qualifications). Above all, however, orientation on careers considerably deforms the official rationality-focused self-description of the system. Decision premises are subjected to secondary assessment, firstly as to whether they are objectively well-founded and secondly as to their career value. Tasks serve to draw attention to the person who performs them well or less well. Status hierarchies establish career opportunities and are elaborated with a view to this function.[37] Possible influence on personnel decisions is taken into account in advance. The communication network of gossip is concerned with persons, with regard, among other things, to deserved or undeserved careers. And every reform improves or worsens career opportunities, thus finding the corresponding proponents and critics. With all this, careers generate motives – also in the psychological sense but above all in the sense of a perceptive attribution of behavior to conditions.

The personnel management of an organizational system can attempt to develop criteria for assigning persons to positions, to refine these criteria through ongoing evaluation, and thus to control personnel movements in the system rationally. There is nothing to be said against trying. But there is no preventing the result from being observed in the career schema and producing corresponding reactions. And it must be doubted whether the rationality of personnel management efforts to give due consideration to the tasks to be performed can go so far as to include direct and indirect effects on self-observation of the system in the career schema. And even if this happens, unplanned effects may well occur.[38]

There are typical, widespread conditions under which career expectations amount to random forecasts. This is particularly true when jobs are scarce and suitable candidates are numerous. Under these conditions, even more careful regulation of selection would not counteract an impression of random choice. On the contrary, it would heighten it.[39] From the point of view of the individual, this very situation would make career forecasting (for himself and for others) a fascinating occupation. And this encourages communication, as if one could combat chance by exchanging ideas. Under these circumstances, regulation can produce only "perverse effects." The more systematic the planned intervention is, the greater will be the incentive to convert the resulting randomness into cognitions and motives through local speculation about chances and obstacles.

Career is accordingly the form that integrates individuals and organizations; by integrate we mean mutually limit. Every single position has to be so defined that it can be held by different "suitable" persons. From the point of view of positions, all individuals have doppelgängers. It is thus not the position, but only the career, that gives persons – and consequently the individuals who involve themselves as persons – an individual profile. This insight may help correct the questionable reputation of careers and careerism for the better.

Notes

1. References Chapter 1 n11.
2. For a classical statement against giving priority to orientation on persons, see Lyndall F. Urwick, *The Elements of Administration*, New York 1943, 38: "It is wasteful [to orient oneself on the particularities of persons] because unless jobs are clearly put together along lines of functional specialization it is impossible to train new men to succeed to positions as the incumbents are promoted, resign or retire. A man cannot be trained to take over another's special personal experience: and yet if jobs are fitted to men rather than men to jobs that is precisely what the employer must try to do. . . . It is difficult enough to find suitable individuals to fill positions of responsibility when one half of the equation is 'given,' that is, when the job is defined. When both the job and the man are uncertain, unknown quantities, hours and days are likely to be expended in fruitless discussion and indecision."
3. This formulation is to be found in Walter Jost, *Das Sozialleben des industriellen Betriebs: Eine Analyse der sozialen Prozesse im Betrieb*, Berlin 1932, 6.
4. The opposing principle is to prevent the formation of cliques. See report on experience in the firm Bahlsen, Kurt Pentzlin, *Rationale Produktion: Methodik, Grundregeln und praktische Beispiele*, 2nd ed. Kassel 1950, 92 f.
5. See the suggestion by Herbert A. Simon et al., *Centralization vs. Decentralization in Organizing the Controller's Department*, New York 1954, 95 ff., always to take the

training and career value of positions into consideration when thinking about organizations.

6. For textbook-like business administration overview, see Wolfgang H. Staehle, *Management: Eine verhaltenswissenschaftliche Perspektive*, 4th ed. Munich 1989, 718–828. On changes see idem, The Changing Face of Personnel Management, in: G. Dlugos et al. (ed.), *Management under Differing Labour Market and Employment Systems*, Berlin 1988, 323–333. See also M. Kolb, Flexibilisierung und Individualisierung als neue personalwirtschaftliche Gestaltungsprinzipien, Zeitschrift für Personal … (1992), 37–48; Dieter Wagner, *Personalfunktion in der Unternehmensleitung: Grundlagen, Empirische Analyse, Perspektiven*, Wiesbaden 1994, esp. 293 ff. Overall, however, one has the impression that business administration in the sense of German "Betriebswirtschaftswissenschaft" cannot yet adequately capture the changes in enterprises themselves with its conceptual apparatus and analytical schemata. Nevertheless, it is at present difficult to judge the extent to which changes take place only at the rhetorical level, and the extent to which they affect actual behavior and the organization and programming of personnel management.

7. See Martin Baethge, Arbeit, Vergesellschaftung, Identität – Zur zunehmenden normativen Subjektivierung der Arbeit, in: Wolfgang Zapf (ed.), *Die Modernisierung moderner Gesellschaften: Verhandlungen des 25. Deutschen Soziologentages in Frankfurt am Main 1990*, Frankfurt 1991, 260–278.

8. See Rainer Koch, Entscheidungsverhalten und Entscheidungsunterstützung höherer Verwaltungsbediensteter: Zur Weiterentwicklung des Führungs- und Entscheidungsinstrumentariums öffentlicher Verwaltungen, *Verwaltungsarchiv* 83 (1992), 26–52; idem, Entscheidungsstile und Entscheidungsverhalten von Führungskräften öffentlicher Verwaltungen, *Verwaltung und Fortbildung* 21 (1993), 179–197.

9. See Rudolf Wimmer, Wozu brauchen wir ein General Management, *Hernsteiner* 6/3 (1993), 4–12 (11 f.).

10. See Michel Crozier, *L'Entreprise à l'écoute: Apprendre le management post-industriel*, Paris 1989, 201.

11. On this and the following points of view, see Emil Küng, Gesellschaftlicher Wandel und Unternehmensführung, in: Gilbert J. B. Probst and Hans Siegwart (eds.), *Integriertes Management: Bausteine des systemorientierten Management. Festschrift Hans Ulrich*, Bern 1985, 445–453; Theodor M. Bardmann and Reiner Franzpötter, Unternehmenskultur: Ein postmodernes Organisationskonzept?, *Soziale Welt* 41 (1990), 424–440; Theodor M. Bardmann, *Wenn aus Arbeit Abfall wird: Aufbau und Abbau organisatorischer Realitäten*, Frankfurt 1994, esp. 339 ff.

12. See Chapter 3, note 12.

13. See especially Mats Alvesson and Per Olof Berg, *Corporate Culture and Organizational Symbolism: an Overview*, Berlin 1992, esp. 35 ff.

14. See specifically Charles Perrow, The Organizational Context of Human Factors Engineering, *Administrative Science Quarterly* 28 (1983), 521–541, and Greg R. Oldham and Nancy L. Rochford, Relationships between Office Characteristics and Employee Reactions: A Study of the Physical Environment, *Administrative Science Quarterly* 28 (1983), 542–556.

15. This is likely to apply quite generally and as overestimation is, as it were, institutionalized. "The extraordinary modern built-in faith in the capacities of the self as decision maker is still amazing, and little justified by any experience," remarks John W. Meyer, Self and Life Course: Institutionalization and Its Effects, in: George M. Thomas et al., Institutional Structure: Constituting State, Society, and the Individual, *Newbury Park* 1987, 242–260 (248).

16. And it should be noted that this distinction is, for its part, a reaction in theory to excessive demands that would otherwise be made on personnel management. For as insight into the complex empirical individuality of individuals increases and society provides and approves communicational forms of expression for precisely this purpose, we have to abandon the notion that individuals are, in broad terms, dependent variables in a planning and administrative process.

17. See Jean Paul, *Vorschule der Ästhetik, Werke* vol. 5, Munich 1963, 245.

18. This is particularly striking in societies that produce little information and therefore concentrate communication on the generation of solidarity. See, e.g., Max Gluckman, Gossip and Scandal, *Current Anthropology* 4 (1963), 307–316. But see also the critique directed more at individual strategies, prestige interests, and information management by Robert Paine, What Is Gossip About? An Alternative Hypothesis, *Man* 2 (1967), 278–285.

19. See J. Richard Harrison and James G. March, Decision Making and Postdecision Surprises, *Administrative Science Quarterly* 29 (1984), 26–42.

20. See Chester I. Barnard, *The Functions of the Executive*, Cambridge, MA 1938, reprint 1951, esp. 139 ff.; Herbert A. Simon, Donald W. Smithburg, and Victor A. Thompson, *Public Administration*, New York 1950, 381 ff.; James G. March and Herbert A. Simon, *Organizations*, New York 1958, 84 ff.

21. Which, incidentally, applies only for this concept and not for the entire theory of Barnard and Simon. But programming then has to be introduced as an additional variable.

22. This is also the case, indeed particularly so, in private sector enterprises. Business consultants then find that they come across hierarchical levels for which they can discover no job description. They have to construct a sense for them or, in times of crisis, propose cutting such levels.

23. A program designed for use in the organization naturally differs from the results of the scholarly investigation of corresponding correlations. Scientifically demonstrated connections are unlikely to lower the practical risk of programming.

24. See Peter M. Blau, Decentralization in Bureaucracies, in: Mayer N. Zald (ed.), *Power in Organizations*, Nashville, TN 1970, 150–174. See also Peter M. Blau and Richard A. Schoenherr, *The Structure of Organizations*, New York 1971, 115 ff.

25. "Rational control is very difficult, even to plan; large systems of men and jobs evolve in complex paths responsive mainly to inputs of new jobs and deaths of men," as Harrison C. White sums it up in: Control and Evolution of Aggregate Personnel: Flows of Men and Jobs, *Administrative Science Quarterly* 14 (1969), 4–11.

26. See, e.g., Fred W. Riggs, *The Ecology of Public Administration*, London 1961.

27. See, e.g., Morris Janowitz, *The Professional Soldier*, Glencoe Ill. 1960, esp. 145 ff.; Peter G. Richards, *Patronage in the British Government*, London 1964 (with a very vague concept of patronage).

28. For German public administration, see Thomas Ellwein, *Das Regierungssystem der Bundesrepublik Deutschland*, 3rd ed. Opladen 1973, 397 ff.

29. See, e.g., Daniel P. Moynihan and James Q. Wilson, *Patronage in New York State 1955–1959, American Political Science Review* 58 (1964), 286–301; Rudolf Wildenmann, *Macht und Konsens als Problem der Innen- und Außenpolitik*, 2nd ed. Frankfurt 1967, 146 ff.; Wolfgang Runge, *Politik und Beamtentum im Parteienstaat: Die Demokratisierung der politischen Beamten in Preußen zwischen 1918 und 1933*, Stuttgart 1965.

30. For the political appointment of civil servants in Germany, see the strikingly high rejection rates in the data of Luhmann and Mayntz op. cit. (1973), 255 ff. Rejection predominates in the literature, too, because the influence of political parties on appointments is mostly regarded as a matter of "personal relations" (overlooking the extent to which this is also true with internal patronage). See, e.g., Peter Hubler, *Probleme der Rekrutierung und der Selektion von Bewerbern für den öffentlichen Dienst, in: Studienkommission für die Reform des öffentlichen Dienstrechts* vol. 10, Baden-Baden 1973, 155 f. with further references; Wolfgang Pippke, *Karrieredeterminanten in der öffentlichen Verwaltung: Hierarchiebedingte Arbeitsanforderungen und Beförderungspraxis im höheren Dienst*, Baden-Baden 1975, 138 f. One then frequently speaks of "extra-functional" selection or selection without regard to suitability, without being able to point to any empirical suitability comparison. For an external observer, these judgments reveal a piece of the historically determined organizational culture of the German public service.

31. See Chapter 3–6

32. See Anne Donnellon and Maureen Scully, Teams, Performance, and Rewards: Will the Post-Bureaucratic Organization Be a Post-Meritocratic Organizations?, in: Charles Heckscher and Anne Donnellon (eds.), *The Post- Bureaucratic Organization: New Perspectives on Organizational Change*, Thousands Oaks, CA 1994, 63–90.

33. Not only the positions attained at the given moment count but also and in particular positions with which a career begins, especially, of course, educational qualifications, as well as entry positions. "Indeed, mobility in the earliest stage of one's career bears an unequivocal relationship with one's later career," as James E. Rosenbaum, Tournament Mobility: Career Patterns in a Corporation, *Administrative Science Quarterly* 24 (1979), 220–241 (220), puts it. This means that young people, in particular, come under career pressure because what they miss out on at the beginning is difficult to catch up on later.

34. According to press reports in January 1994, the mass promotion of several thousand civil servants in North Rhine-Westphalia before a promotion freeze took effect was defended on the grounds that the civil servants concerned would otherwise have had to wait for over a year to be promoted! What was at issue was naturally not transfer to other posts but promotion to higher ranks with higher salaries.

35. There are clearly many parallels for this prevention of self-gratification – for instance, in the symbolically generalized communication media truth, love, money, and power. In all these cases, blocking self-gratification is the precondition for the development of more exacting social structures.

36. This distinction between operation and observation is not taken into account if, in keeping with the prevalent structuralistic orientation, one asks only about the

complex factors that influence careers. See, e.g., James N. Baron, Alison Davis-Blake, and William T. Bielby, The Structure of Opportunity: How Promotion Ladders Vary within and among Organizations, *Administrative Science Quarterly* 31 (1986), 248–273. Although an external observer is presupposed, namely the investigator, the distorting effects of self-observation of the system are not taken into account.

37. This can also be seen in title differences. See James N. Baron and William T. Bielby, The Proliferation of Job Titles in Organizations, *Administrative Science Quarterly* 31 (1986), 561–586.

38. See for the case of using fixed-term contracts to improve the career opportunities of permanent employees: William P. Barnett and Anne S. Miner, Standing on the Shoulders of Others: Career Interdependence in Job Mobility, *Administrative Science Quarterly* 37 (1992), 262–281. And, conversely, on the use of project work and fixed-term contracts as springboards for careers: Robert R. Faulkner and Andy B. Anderson, Short Term Projects and Emergent Careers: Evidence From Hollywood, *American Journal of Sociology* 92 (1987), 879–909.

39. See the empirical study of top careers in the American school system: James C. March and James G. March, Almost Random Careers: The Wisconsin School Superintendency, 1940–1972, *Administrative Science Quarterly* 22 (1977), 377–409. On page 379 we read: " ... if one believes a social system is closely regulated, one should generally be more surprised by large deviations from a chance model than by small ones."

10   The Organization of Organization

I

In classical, rational-instrumental organization theory the concept of organization was used in a broad and a narrow sense. By organization it understood firstly systems that seek to attain specific goals in a rational and efficient manner, and secondly the endowment with the competence (in the double sense of capability and authority/responsibility R.B.) and communication channels necessary for the purpose. Organization was thus not conceived of as a natural system; it was not simply there, but had to be organized. This ambiguous use of the term organization to describe the system and the structure of the system seems to have to do with the circumstance that business studies ("Betriebswirtschaftswissenschaft"), as we have seen, describes the organizations in which it is interested as "enterprises" ("Betriebe") thus reserving the term organization to describe the distribution of tasks among positions. Reflection on improving organization thus took these instruments for networking positions as its point of departure. The issues addressed included the size required for certain tasks (number of positions); the distribution of competences in the form of super- and subordination, and thus the unity and controllability of the system that this ensures; furthermore, in applying this principle, it addressed issues of centralization or decentralization; of the "span of control" for superordinate positions not to be exceeded in the interests of system manageability; of auxiliary functions (staff functions), their extent and their conflicts with the line responsibilities of the hierarchy; finally, once again extending the same point of departure, the question whether cooperation/ collusion among subordinates through "group formation" is to be encouraged or combated as "clique formation." Despite all modifications and supplementation, classical theory concentrated on the principle of hierarchy, understood not as a hierarchy that includes parts in a greater whole but as a top-down chain of command. The duty to comply with instructions was intended to ensure the unity of the system, which was to be able to make decisions like an individual, and to do so at the top. Among other things, this led to overestimation of the frequency with which hierarchical communication channels are actually used.

This distinction between horizontal and vertical differentiation (division of labor/hierarchy) could encourage problems in organizing positions to be treated as division of labor problems and thus as coordination problems, and to leave them to the hierarchy to resolve (although the hierarchy itself then has to be structured on a division-of-labor principle).[1] By distinguishing different sorts of decision premise, we arrive indirectly at a more complex description. We then see that classical organization theory expects too much of the hierarchy, above all in resolving the problems it entails. With the distinction between formal organization and informal organization, this had already been seen but not adequately addressed in so far as the two were treated only as management tools. Thanks not least to the "upgrading" of personnel management and career planning problems, a more complex analysis has become unavoidable. It naturally does not suffice to settle for criticizing or diluting the principle of hierarchical organization. The tasks of management seem rather to have become greater and more difficult, but at any rate more problematic than in the past.

In fully elaborated form, this theory of hierarchical organization left an impression of an unfolded paradox. Opposites were defined, with – depending on the circumstances – one side or the other appearing worth fostering:[2] both line and staff, both centralization and decentralization, both group and clique, and, finally, both formal and informal organization. As in rhetoric, there were good and bad names for all "principles," so that one could choose labels in function of what one wanted to achieve. But how was one to know what one wanted?

Typically, the unfolding of the paradox amounted to temporalization and historicization of the basis for decision-making. The principle of efficient rationality proved to be a perpetual incentive for reform.[3] Measured against this principle, every state realized could be perceived as inadequate. Orientation of the given historical state of the system was sufficient cause for further reforms, which, however, could only oscillate within the schema of the opposites (which need not exclude new opposites being invented to reformulate the original paradox). In the line, one could discover "cross-sectional functions" (staff functions) that were not sufficiently attended to; the need for decentralization where centralization was too strong; indications of clique formation in the groups hitherto favored; informal organization in formal organization – and vice versa. Just as provided for in Spencer-Brown's calculus of forms, the paradox was set in oscillation and endowed with memory functions for the given reform-triggering historical state.[4] A total description would then have had to present the system as *bistable* in principle. But such a description would have required a reflection loop, which was not provided for in the system itself. It was possible only as external observation. Counseling by rationalization experts was intended only to facilitate the step from past, sedimented reforms to new reforms. An essential function of business consulting thus lay in the function opposite to remembering: in forgetting that the principle now on the agenda had long ago been tried out, had been the basis for long past reforms.[5]

If classical theory is now to be seen from an already historical perspective, this changes the situation both for research and for organization planning itself. We have dealt with some of the theoretical adjustments in preceding chapters, notably:

(1) the switch in perspective from the application of (rationality) principles to the unfolding of paradoxes with a necessarily contingent choice of form;
(2) the treatment of system unity as autopoiesis and the (theoretical and practical) construction of the system with a single mode of operation, in this case decision, which is responsible both for the continuation of operations and for the generation of the necessary structures, and for which there is no alternative in the system (operational closure);
(3) the treatment of the link-up between a number of decisions as uncertainty absorption, both for the simple transition from decision to decision and for the structural gains from decision (always only concretely possible) via decision premises.

On the other hand, the change in theory and terminology this indicates should not be overestimated. One speaks less of "hierarchy" and more of "structural" organization – as if the system had to be "structured" bottom-up, "built up." "Exercise of power" is frowned upon, "decision" is in vogue. But since positions still have to be held by persons and since the concept of decision, as we have seen,[6] points to persons as decision-makers, it is doubtful whether this changes much with regard to structural issues. "In the ultimate importance of the *personnel dimension* the power model and the decision model meet."[7]

At any rate, one can emphasize the autonomy of position-linking problems by relating them not to persons but to responsibilities that are exercised only in the network itself. In consequence, we can ask ourselves what this means for the organization of organization, for the planning of the third sort of decision premise that lies at the heart of the classical theory. It is clearly insufficient to demand a "balance" or on-going coordination of tasks and persons, of decision programs and individual suitability. This would amount to an equation with two uncertain variables,[8] in which certainties have to be introduced in the form of historically successive self-determination. This is precisely what is meant by the thesis that an autopoietic system orients itself self-referentially on the given present state in which it had placed itself through its own operations. We know that such a non-trivial machine (Heinz von Foerster) operates unpredictably, both for itself and for external observers. However, this need not exclude meaningful "self-organization" capable of drawing distinctions. On the contrary, this very state of affairs explains that organization has to be organized if the system is to be able to give itself the framework conditions that enable it to decide about decision premises, and thus to plan organization.

If the rationalistic notions about the function of organizing competence and communication channels now seem unrealistic and unrealizable, what then is the function of organizing, in other words, what is the problem this task is concerned with? The following reflections proceed on the assumption that the problem is complexity. From the decision program perspective, it can be advisable to break down the task schema more strongly on a division of labor basis. People are unlikely to oppose such impetus for growth if they benefit from it. Objecting that management has to control such a development is no answer to the question of how this is to be done and what lateral information is needed for the purpose. Pleading a scarcity of financial resources is also insufficient; at least in large government or business organizations, there might well be enough money to finance useful advances. Calling for "reflection loops" to be built in again raises the problem of the necessary criteria and information. It therefore makes sense to assume that control of an organization's own complexity requires specialized tools, however little this formulation of the problem betrays how "adequate complexity" is to be adequately defined.

However, complexity is only a paradox, a formula for the unity of diversity. But a step toward resolving this paradox could be first to define this obviously multi-dimensional concept more precisely and then to identify planning tools, namely the special decision premises that make the complexity of a system, if not rationally controllable, at least observable and describable. At the structural level we shall use the concept of competence and at the operational level the concept of (actually used) communication channels. To begin with, it should be noted that the point of departure for every analysis of the complexity of the system is the size of that system; only from a certain (very small) size does a system become complex in the sense that it can no longer connect every operation with all operations of the system. And only this produces a selection constraint that lends the individual operations of the system diversity (that is to say, quality).[9]

II

Among the fundamental decisions to be taken in building up or dismantling an organization are decisions about the size of the system, in other words, about the number of positions to be established. This determines what complexity the organization can attain in the sense of diversity of positions, which in turn determines what complexity reduction problems have to be resolved through the networking of positions. Classical and neoclassical economic theory provides many arguments in favor of large organizations. They can operate more economically, and above all make more rational use of overheads; they can provide for more specialization, and, especially in recent years, they can afford technologies unavailable to smaller organizations on cost and capacity utilization grounds. This has led to the development of gigantic organizations in manufacturing, transport, and telecommunications. Attempts to counter this trend politically have failed. The conversion of the economy in the new states of East Germany to market conditions has not, as had been hoped, taken place at the SME level but in the form of takeovers by large organizations. In the public service itself, especially in the German local and county reforms of the 1970s, the "economies of scale" argument has played an important role.[10] On the other hand, the economy has long since begun to react at the level of network-like links between large and small organizations,[11] and sociological studies of the problems caused by organization size give cause for skepticism.[12]

Classical organization theory had sought to solve the problem of optimum system size.[13] However, this did not go beyond very formal wishful thinking. Problematic side effects of growth in size were listed intuitively and on the basis of practical experience,[14] but how inevitable they were remained open. The main finding, which we owe chiefly to extensive research at the University of Aston,[15] was that there were links between the variables of size and bureaucratization in the sense of specialization, standardization, formalization, centralization, and concatenation. The explanatory value of these results remained controversial.[16] Much could be attributed to another variable, namely technological requirements, which can be met only when the system is sufficiently big. When the number of variables to be taken into account increases, the difficulties of attribution and the inconsistency of findings also grow.[17] The reason is probably that, for methodological reasons, such studies cover too few variables; or that the concept of size is too broadly defined, thus offering too many combinations;[18] or, finally, that decisions on size are guided too little by real conditions. A plausible hypothesis (but one that can be formulated only if consciousness of every sort is treated as system environment)[19] is that large organizations can be less influenced by non-members (and this means also by other organizations) but are more exposed to the accidents of their own members' consciousness events and have to take structural precautions to protect themselves against such events. A recent analysis of the state of research shows that, although large organizations are more productive (perhaps because that have better possibilities for internal structuring), they are not more efficient (i.e., in the exploitation of economies of scale), and thus also not ahead in the rationality by which input/output relations are regulated.[20] This research suggests that redefining the problem is likely to be worthwhile and, instead of looking for abstract correlations, we should go in search of correct correlations, setting out from the question of what possibilities are available to an organization of a given size in a given historical situation.

Organizational systems tend to handle their size without reflecting, i.e., they change size for cogent reasons. Two examples, probably the most important, show this.

Organizations constantly need vacancies, positions that have to be filled, if they are to undertake reforms or other innovations. But people do not age or die fast enough. New positions therefore have to be established, new departments set up, new organizations founded. A national airline founds subsidiaries for secondary routes. New tasks such as environmental auditing or the advancement of women lead to new departments, at least to new permanent posts in the public service. The school system appears to support children from the lower classes or late developers insufficiently, so that more suitable schools have to be set up. It is obvious that perfectly sensible objectives are involved, but they are introduced into communication as normative values and not as results. They can thus retain their persuasiveness without being put to the test. The difficulty of communicating not intentions but results suffices to make organizations grow.

While this problem appears to originate internally, there are also market-determined problems of short-term variation in size, above all for economic-system organizations. If demand increases, capacities have to be expanded; if it declines, the problems are resolved by cutting jobs. And since low turnover suffices to drive a firm into the red, size varies rapidly depending on environmental conditions, which in turn result from the efforts of organizations to take advantage of market opportunities or to maintain if not increase their share of the market.[21] But would it not make sense to arrange for an organization to grow and shrink within a certain range of normal market fluctuation?

Since growth in size has hitherto largely been a byproduct of efforts to improve performance, theories are lacking that can explain that shrinkage, too, can improve performance.[22] In general, downsizing is a reaction to financial bottlenecks, and takes the form of shedding staff. But what needs to be clarified is whether downsizing also offers advantages even when the financial situation does not impose it. This is possibly particularly true of the public service.

Especially in economic organizations, the experience of the past two decades has shown that economies of scale are to be sought no longer in size alone but also in the time dimension. This is true for the acceleration of production and changes in products; but above all for the adjustment of production to individual customer requirements and to changes in important environmental variables such as demand, competition, and technology.[23] The solution is accordingly "flexibility." It is likely that similar adjustments will find their way into other organizational domains, above all government authorities after local government reform – such as the school reforms of the 1970s – had still put its trust fully in size.

In the new, temporal perspective, we also see that system size is one of the easiest variables to change. The boundaries of a system can very easily be shifted by buying and incorporating other enterprises or hiving off parts of an enterprise. In the latter case, fixed contractual ties and structural couplings, for instance, dependence in production planning, serve as functional equivalents of formal mergers within a system. But it should be noted that this flexibility in size variation is not a general characteristic of organizations. It is not to be found in public administration, or in the court system, or in organizations of the educational system. For it depends on entrepreneurial calculation, which enables it to compare various solutions involving internal or external ties from the point of view of costs and risk spreading.

III

Problems of this sort (and perhaps others) can help us to get away from the abstract search for the right size or for the equally abstract necessity of finding job requirements and personal suitability ("the right person in the right place"). But how further analysis or planning can be specified is still not clear. The number of positions as a purely quantitative variable must, therefore, first be supplemented by a concept that takes account of the diversity of positions. The number and diversity of jobs together give a measure of the complexity of the system.[24] The two variables of complexity determine one another, since diversity can develop only where units of reference (in this case positions) are available. Division of labor theory generally posits that the potential degree of specialization increases in proportion to the size of the system. If the organization is big enough, the diversity of demands made on the individual position, and thus the need for the incumbent to constantly switch attention, can be reduced; diversity shifts to relations between jobs. But this has its price; as the number of positions entrusted with different tasks increases, so do the load on communication channels and the information losses that have to be expected in these channels. The counterprogram to specialization, namely "job enlargement," is therefore also to be found (mostly from a human relations point of view).

The lead distinction that develops the complexity of the system on the basis of suitable size is that between professional competence and hierarchical competence. With professional competence, the educational and vocational spectrum of society is largely copied into the system. In hospitals there have to be doctors, in television stations there have to be lighting technicians. But there is also competence acquired subsequently on the job within the organization, from experience, and through specialization. A factory that mass produces plastic windows has to have people who can deal with customer complaints and adjust or repair windows in situ.

The second sort of competence, the hierarchical authority to issue instructions, is an internal construct. Career climbers or lawyers often find employment in this function. Management of a hospital might be entrusted to a doctor; university officials are former professors. The research divisions of big pharmaceutical firms are headed by specialists no longer engaged in research themselves. The "tragedy" of such careers has been much discussed in the literature. Advancement brings a loss of competence in comparison to subordinate colleagues, which makes the job of management more difficult.

The principle of hierarchy is now regarded as a feature of a classical but obsolete organization theory whose factual, structural importance has diminished.[25] In practice, hierarchical communication channels are used less frequently than had been assumed, and there are many other forms of uncertainty absorption.[26] Recent organizational developments also point in this direction, above all the replacement of elaborated hierarchies by more autonomy in the workplace. But why is this a substitute for hierarchy? It should be realized that the function of hierarchy formation had always been *horizontal* coordination, the extension of coordination possibilities beyond what top management can do itself. The chain of issuing instructions, obeying instructions, and reporting back was not an end in itself but only a condition for the horizontal outreach of subordinate positions. This also explains that this coordination function can, as it were, be localized through the autonomization of jobs. There may well be environmental conditions and, above all, tempo requirements under which this makes sense. But whether this is so will differ from case to case. It is not a question of the "right principle." In principle, one can only assume that the problem of horizontal coordination (which includes outreach into the environment) can be solved in different, functionally equivalent ways.

While this correction to the classical picture of hierarchy still insists that hierarchy is about the implementation of knowledge formed at the center, this, too, is now called into question, namely by the thesis that hierarchies prove their worth as forms of dealing with uncertainty.[27] This fits in well with a theory of functional systems in society that are geared not to governance but to the intrasystemic generation of uncertainty. Functional systems have to be equipped with organizations – not to carry out a will from within (but where?) but to absorb the uncertainty they generate.

If we distinguish professional from hierarchical competence (or specialists from generalists) on the basis of hierarchy formation, we also see that complexity is developed with a both other-referential and self-referential orientation. Professional competence is recruited with the person or imparted through training; but expectations and demands are guided by what the educational and training systems and the market offer. Hierarchical competence, by contrast, is produced and assigned internally. And only the interplay between the two develops both the quantitative and the qualitative complexity of the system.

According to old cybernetic rules, internal complexity (the number and variety of elements) is the form in which a system reproduces the environment within itself without being able to achieve the requisite variety.[28] Point-for-point correspondence is not possible, nor does the system seek or find for its units equal units (also eyes, also positions) in the environment.[29] System complexity is thus not an adequate – with some reservations – representation of the environment within the system, but a reconstruction of the operationally unattainable environment the system requires. Where are we then to find indicators of what could be called adequate complexity?

Organizations develop tools for testing opportunities offered by the environment. They can – but this is a question of definition – distinguish between requirements and chances. A business enterprise sets prices for its products in order to observe how it is observed by market participants. Public service organizations use policy as a procedure for testing whether decision initiatives find support or not. Actions are filed before a court, patients are admitted to hospital; and the type and frequency of such events allow conclusions to be drawn on whether it is worthwhile to set up a special division for building land matters or a special emergency ward. Both functional differentiation and segmentary differentiation – for example, the number of hospitals, schools, courts, and fire stations needed for a given area – arise from such multiplication of opportunities for action seen within the system.

Such procedures for developing one's own organization as a dependent variable are not only compatible with operational closure; they are the obvious course to take because the system operates as a closed system and relies on developing itself. But if the organization provides its own performance, it also produces the corresponding demand. Social work helps produce the problems it has to deal with. (This is naturally not to deny that that the world is in a bad state. World pessimism is the generalized precondition for organization. But the question is how and in what forms this triggers communication.) The operational inaccessibility of the environment (in other words, the boundary of the system) is itself a precondition for induced growth, for increasing complexity. Increases in complexity seem almost necessarily to occur under two conditions, namely when society enables communication and when it builds system boundaries into communication, so that everything that happens outside the boundary can be interpreted as an occasion for growth.

With Maturana we could therefore describe the consequences of this operational closure as "structural drift." In the first place, this is a phenomenon of evolution, the transformation of the improbability of occurrence into the probability of maintenance, of the generation of diversity through cuts in what exists. If the reduction of complexity takes the form of system boundaries with insulation of an operative area, complexity develops in this area. The question posed by the organization of organization can therefore only be whether one has to accept this or should also demand it for one's own system (under the heading "competition"); or whether something in the way of *prevention ration-ality* is possible.

In more recent organizational developments, it seems that the internal costs of complexity are attracting more attention. At any rate, more complex cross-linking between system and environment is accepted. Organizations do not attempt to incorporate everything that they know their operations depend on in the system, nor can systems be accurately defined in terms of internal inter-dependencies being greater than those between system and environment. The question whether operational units are incorporated in the system and thus hierarchically controlled, or whether they are left in the environment or even hived off into the environment to be influenced only by market mechan-isms, is the subject of constant examination and decision-making. It can often be assumed that the market absorbs more uncertainty than decision chains within the organization. In other cases the opposite is true. The ongoing observation of the distinction between inside and outside is therefore consid-ered an important dimension of general management.[30] From time to time, privatization or lean management may come into vogue – but probably only in reaction to an epoch that had favored the counter-strategy of establishing the greatest possible hierarchical control and avoiding external dependencies. What can, in the long run, be recommended for an organization is not to take this direction or that but to take its boundary, too, into consideration. But only if this boundary can be fixed and varied, and only if this can be done by internal decisions.

IV

Now we come to the real topic of the chapter: organizational decision premises. They consist in the establishment of communication channels that connect decisions with decisions and thus make the autopoietic production of decisions possible in the first place. Positions are required that serve as addresses for communication. Job descriptions also indicate what positions are involved in what processes. This might be spelled out in detail in rules of procedure as is usual in administrative organizations, but it may also be self-evident – for instance, that the appropriate medical specialist participates in operations requiring an anesthetic; that repair crews have to be called in if machines break down; or that finished products have to undergo quality control or be warehoused. We can speak of decision premises only if regulation is general. But even if decisions about who is to take part are made only in individual cases[31] (for instance, deciding who has to co-sign a draft decision before it is submitted to the superior for signing), this presupposes recognizable responsibilities. Here, too, mistakes can be made and admonished – for example, if the leading position overlooks the fact that expenditures are involved and that the position responsible for managing the budget therefore has be consulted.

In this sense, communication channels develop from the responsibilities invested in positions – be it from exclusive responsibility for making decisions binding, typically a question of the hierarchical order, be it on the basis of technical responsibilities, ignoring which would be judged a procedural mistake. From the point of view of accountability and the division of labor, however, when considering this order of responsibilities it is easy to overlook the problems to be found, particularly in the ongoing communication of decisions. Organization charts are structural plans; they give a static impression and stay the way they are until changed. But the dynamics of the organization lie in the process of communicating decisions, in which decisions are produced from decisions. Here, and only here, is uncertainty absorbed and thus transformed into self-guaranteed, constructed certainty. This is where the necessary information losses are processed. This is where things are remembered and forgotten. Finally, this is where it is decided what operational and not only structural complexity the system attains.

Structural diversification not only enhances the system's performance to the extent that – and so long as – a certain scale is needed for this purpose and that corresponding demand can be expected, it also increases self-generated uncertainty. Since each position handles its own speciality, it is difficult for others to pose questions, to criticize, to propose better solutions, or even to repeat the line of reflection pursued in other positions. This is particularly true for superiors in relation to their subordinates, but also for subordinates in relation to their superiors. But horizontal communication, too, has to accept this reduction in complexity. The surgeon has to rely on the anesthetic being adequate, on the instruments handed to him being sterilized, and the pre-operative tests having accurately diagnosed the state of affairs. A certain overlap of attention remains possible, especially attention to critical values, to the unusual, to danger signals. But in principle, the division of labor leads to capability being transformed into communication. This is why organizations are set up.

With the increase in substantive complexity, the ability to construct and process information increases, in other words, the ability to transform stimulus into information. Through decisions constantly updated in communication, the system stimulates itself – always at another point. There is always something to do when others have done something. But this also organizes enormous information losses into the system. Seeking to avoid this would lead to duplication of work and ultimately to the collapse of complexity. This system accordingly needs a memory that can recall and forget, thus linking past and future. What is achieved is enhanced selectivity.

This contradicts classical rationality requirements. Neither better adaptation to the environment nor the realization of principles is concerned. The rationality of the system consists rather in copying the uncertainty (not the states or events) of the environment into the system. The "unmarked space" of the environment becomes the "unmarked space" of the system – a dark side accompanying all operations. What rationality can then be is nothing other than a reentry of the difference between system and environment into the system. This might suggest above all a more strongly situation-specific mode of operation, which is less limited by instructions, conditional programs, and supervision than in the past but "systemically integrated" with the aid of data processing. The demand for precautionary determination is reduced, the demand for immediate transparency and corresponding correctives is increased.

If one proceeds on these assumptions, it is understandable that reform efforts do not change much but serve rather to establish the conditions for further efforts at reform.[32] But it is also apparent that organizations are not completely at the mercy of this oscillation between remembering and forgetting but develop facilities that enable it *to observe itself in precisely this regard*. This is helped above all by adding another distinction, that between the normal course of events and signs of danger.

Every memory that has practice in normality and impregnates it anew when it recurs has to rely on additional arrangements for triggering attention. March and Simon accordingly distinguish between "evoked set" and "evoking" as a special function of the memory of organizations.[33] The system protects itself, as it were, with "double closure"[34] in that, while communicating decisions, it also keeps an alarm system in operation that reacts to anything unusual. In other words, expectation of the unexpected has to be provided for. We are familiar with this in the monitoring of high-risk technologies and know how difficult organizations find it to deroutinize themselves when routines are functioning. However, this is not a special problem but one found in all uncertainty absorption: that one must both let things ride and monitor events. Every brain can do this without attaining ultimate certainty for always appropriate arrangements. Families notoriously find it hard to judge the behavior of a member "abnormal" in a way that could require psychiatric help precisely because they know him so well personally. Similar problems arise in the case of organizations at the level of decision communication. But if they do not succeed in providing for attention and communicability, this could be taken at the level of the organization as a danger signal. The organization is then perhaps too large and too complex, or also simply too blind to the paradox of deciding to which it owes its operational capability.

This being the case, it makes sense to place competences where they are most needed in the decision process. Whether determined in general form or established case by case, communication channels are meaningful only for the conveyance of competences (typically with heavy losses and disturbance from "noise"). The organizational goal should then be to shorten communication channels while using existing (or stimulatable) competences to better effect. This is true of all types of responsibility; also, for example, of competence that can vouch locally for the approval required higher up. In the organization of industrial production processes, such an objective currently results in cutbacks in intermediary, middle management stages.[35] But dovetailing accounting more strongly with daily decision practices should also be considered, involving it more closely in transactions instead of limiting it to bookkeeping and to the *posteriori* observance of results (which should naturally not be excluded); for in this separate form it can serve only as information for the managerial level, and, in a fast-living age, such information, let alone its conversion into new instructions, often comes too late. The organization of the system memory is only one, albeit the most important, facet of the link between competence and communication. It should, however, always be taken into account. For even if the pressure for change exerted by the environment is great, it can be perceived and tested only with the aid of a memory.

V

The classical concept of division of labor had assumed that the advantage of organizing in this manner lay in focusing attention on the tasks assigned to a particular position and in developing the necessary skills. The other side of this form was a sort of ban on interference. The work assigned to *other* positions need not, and indeed should not, attract interest. This principle was compensated for by installing a hierarchy that established greater responsibility on higher levels and endowed the apex of the system with a sort of overall competence. The assumption was that people at the top of the hierarchy could perform their functions in the form of decision-making and that rationality criteria could be set for this purpose. Nowadays it is generally conceded that this overtaxes the hierarchy and notably the people at the top. A second point of criticism is the failure to fully exploit capacities and information that, perhaps quite by chance, may be available at lower positions, but that are blocked by the ban on interference. This criticism led to the demand for these shackles to be loosened, for more interaction, more dialogue, more mutual stimulation and participation, and more team work at lower levels.[36] At first glance this sounds convincing, but in practice this stimulus appears to have been, if at all, only hesitant. What thus seems to be at issue is not replacing a worse type of organization by a better one, a rigid type by a more flexible variety, for this would merely substitute a positive description for a negative one. What is the problem?

From the point of view of communications theory, the concept of competence in both the technical/professional and hierarchical sense obviously performs two quite different functions, which have to be distinguished at least analytically. In the first place it is concerned with skills, with ascribed cognitive and motivational capabilities, realized more or less well in the person of the position holder. This includes the capability – more in demand in the upper echelons of the hierarchy – to make decisions even without adequate information or technical knowledge. However, competence in the social system of communication also has the function of an address. It cannot come to bear if no one knows about it; or if locating it is time-consuming and frustrating; and competence in this sense can hardly come to bear if communication notices it purely by chance. The wisdom of classical theory apparently lay in making no distinction between capability and address and making do with the fiction that the position indicated as address, and only this position, was able to do what was expected of it.

If we abandon or water down this both practical and unsatisfactory solution, we face two problems. The first is how addresses can be equipped with capability. This is essentially a matter for personnel management in the broader sense that includes personnel development. Jobs have to be designed in such a way that the capabilities of the position holder do not shrink to the format of the job; and personnel assessment must provide information on people's usefulness in other, also higher ranking positions. This is complemented by another problem: How can available capabilities be provided with addresses if they are not registered by personnel management and not marked by positions? To go by the position-related organization chart, this is a negligible factor, an invisible potential, involving widely differing sorts of ability. It can be a matter of vocational/professional training and experience, of access to certain sectors of the environment, of occasional information, or of purely personal capabilities, which tend to develop in some positions more than in others. It is usually seen as a personnel problem, a problem of finding and furthering appropriately gifted people. But this soon leads to bottlenecks in bringing people and jobs together, raising the question of whether one would not soon lose one's capabilities (e.g., environmental contacts) in another position. The problem of how to provide capabilities with addresses can, therefore, not be reduced to a problem of personnel management. It is presumably the fundamental problem in organizing organization, that is to say, in organizing communication chains to absorb and regain decision-making uncertainty.

With the distinction between capabilities for addresses and addresses for capabilities, we also distinguish problems of personnel management from problems of organizational planning. In both fields, further-going analysis will come across imponderables in which the different approaches once again merge. Personnel planning cannot know for certain whether and how persons will prove their mettle in positions in which they have not yet not worked. Organization planning will be concerned, above all, with making communication as mobile as possible to enable it to investigate and discover where and how it can activate capabilities. This will require a great deal of time and often vain effort. Moreover, making use of nonproven capabilities raises the question of risk and responsibility that can no longer be answered simply by reference to the competent position or superior. Furthermore, if such far-reaching organizational planning is to be really effective, wage and salary structures have to be adjusted; they could no longer reflect only the rank of positions and would thus lose the criterion that in the traditional understanding provides objectivity. Not least, new sorts of problem would arise for the memory of the system. If capabilities are discovered and registered outside the position chart, who will learn of it and how does one prevent this from being treated as a special situation, a rare exception, or an accident, and hence destined to fall into immediate oblivion?

Current recommendations to strengthen project groups, team work, dialog, and the search for consensus without intervention from above would have to take these questions into account.

VI

These considerations do not invite the conclusion that doing without hierarchical super- and subordination could be rational; no complex organization completely replaces hierarchy by other, for instance, merely situational forms of uncertainty absorption. We are merely talking about a more abstract conception of autopoietic organization problems; hierarchizing communication channels is one contribution among others to resolving them: a contribution toward shifting problems, a contribution toward transforming problems into other problems.

Even the recursive interconnection of decisions requires sufficiently clear "punctuation." Hierarchical differentiation is also likely to be indispensable for episode formation and in freeing capacities for new departures.

Nevertheless, the understanding of hierarchy in the practice of interconnecting decisions to absorb uncertainty and in organizational consulting appears to have fundamentally changed – perhaps owing to the loss of societal subsidization of authority through origins or education, or variation in determining what is important and what is unimportant. These changes can be summed up under three headings, discussed below.

A differentiation of competence levels is retained. It is indispensable not least as a mechanism for conflict regulation and for varying the conditions of organizational membership. But the assessment of what is important and what is less important can be shifted between these differentiated levels – top-down or bottom-up. Although a sort of task logic continues to be sought in order to determine what has to be decided farther up the hierarchy and what can be delegated, such considerations presuppose that the formal differentiation of levels provides corresponding powers. The extent to which changes in the distribution of weight are appropriate is then an empirical or practical question. At any rate, alternating between more centralization and more decentralization – and leaving it at that – is unlikely to offer a realistic solution to current problems.

If we see hierarchy not only as a mode of distributing competence but also as a management structure, this provides insight into another change. The old asymmetry of the master and servant logic no longer applies. Not only does the servant have to observe how the master (alias God) observes him or her. The master has to observe how he or she is observed by the servant. The relationship is fully adapted to second-order observation. And at this level it is symmetrical. This could be recommendable as a more humane arrangement for organizational systems, and its humaneness could be found in the mutual respect among participants as subjects, that is to say as observers. However, such counsel should not divert our attention from the tactical (Habermas would perhaps say strategic) aspects of everyday calculation. The difference in competence is not abolished, it remains as an element of mutual calculation. But the card is not played until called for. And if directives are then issued contrary to ideas that have already been intimated, perhaps communicated, this is understood to signal a conflict. The instruction might then be carried out to the extent that this can be monitored; but the more serious consequence is that the conflict is remembered as a conflict.

If we wish to decipher the communication to be observed in such an order, we have to apply a "what if" calculation. This is also true for the planning of shifts in weight within the levels hierarchy that, even before being prescribed, is observed as planning, and, because it is planning, can no longer be defended in terms of natural standards or self-evident practices. It also notably applies for constant preliminary reflection on the consequences of second-order observation. It thus appears to be characteristic of the organization of organization that more and more decisions are attributed to precursory decisions. Even if this is accepted as a commendable aim for reform, it is most likely to result from the societal outdifferentiation of autopoietic organizational systems, which have themselves to organize all the restrictions to which they are subject.

It would thus seem to change the demands made of managerial functions, already a much discussed development. The gesture of superiority based on stratification, better education and training, and better information has less and less impact. This does not necessarily mean that persons (and thus personnel selection) are less important. On the contrary, if such resources for pretending to authority fail, greater demands are made of the personality exposed to observation. The superior will have to engage more strongly in communication. However, the problem is not one of "tone" or of management "style." What is at issue is the congruence between personal capabilities and the requirements of the position held. These requirements appear to be shifting toward a general competence for situation management, with "situations" arising not least from the constant contradictions between useful desiderata and from the corresponding "micro-political" conflicts between specialists.

In this context, research that examines how decisions are actually made at the top in organizations deserves attention.[37] The old exception of a predominant orientation on the environment remains. It is due not least to the extent to which those at the top dispose over the decision premises of the organization (to which they also belong). To this must be added the highly ambivalent definition of situations, which make it advisable to seek guidance more in interactional contacts than in formally supplied information. The information not laid down in documents plays a considerable role, along with rumors and gossip. The tasks of management thus include recording information in such a way that it can be used in the course of business. Also striking is the high degree to which everyday working practices are fragmented, leaving little time for reflection or general planning. Moreover, it is not simply a matter of solving problems but also, and primarily, of selecting (or inventing) the problems that deserve attention. If this is taken into account, it is clear that the decisions made at the top of the organization are also strongly "programmed";[38] it is just that the pressure at the top differs from that in the lower echelons of the organization.

Ultimately, hierarchical communication channels also perform the function of every decision chain: they absorb uncertainty. And they do this in both directions: top-down and bottom-up. Of course superiors inform their subordinates of their decisions in the form of instructions or in the form of communications that point to a possible instruction while obviating explicit formulation. But bottom-up communication, too, takes the form of decisions, for example, the form of a decision to request a decision; or the form of a decision to provide information that, once provided, shifts risk and responsibility upward. In all cases and in both directions, uncertainty absorption is to be linked with information processing, or, in other words, with updating the memory of the system and deciding what is to be remembered and what forgotten.

Here, too, the background question arises of how competence distribution affects the decision process. However, this cannot be known with certainty in organizing organization. The decisions that have to be made here, too, have to absorb uncertainty. The lesson to be learned can only be that there is no one and only right decision, and that decisions about decision premises have to reckon with their effects being observed and possibly revised.

Whether and to what extent the organization's communication channels are used to obtain decisions on clarifying consensus and dissent can depend partly on the type and complexity of decision programs and partly on the characteristics of the persons involved. This mode of uncertainty absorption requires a great deal of informal preparation, as well as a command of the distinction between formal and informal. It is a question of what Tom Burns calls "micropolitics."[39] Generalists are likely to prefer this form of uncertainty absorption while specialists or experts will favor improved information processing under the relevant decision program. In the event of failure, generalists will tend to shift loyalties whereas specialists will react with frustration or cynicism. If this hypothesis holds true,[40] it would point to links between personnel and organizational decision premises.

These reflections show that the formal organization of competences and communication channels is a problem not only of structural determination, not only of organization charts and the corresponding implementation directives. Even if all this has to be taken into account and followed, the problem, from the standpoint of the system's operations, lies rather in preparing these practices and obtaining access to decisions that cannot be directly attributed to given positions. Whoever wishes to get certain decisions made or to prevent them cannot simply leave it up to the usual channels; this applies equally for superiors, subordinates, and colleagues. Things have to be sounded out, proposals made, feelers put out, half-truths spread; and expectations and goals have to be modified in the event of rumblings.

The visibility of formal organization is extremely helpful in enabling the opposite, as well: the circumvention or evasion of its requirements. The organizational determination of competences that are undisputed also makes it possible to keep one's distance and to establish a second level of communication for communicating about what can be left up to the formal network and what not. This second level also serves for smuggling real intentions past supervision. We could again call this informal organization, but would have to excise the group principle from this concept. More important is another insight. The official image of the organization gives the impression that reflexiveness of operations – decision-making about decisions – is tied to the hierarchy because setting decision premises is typically reserved to the higher echelons. In fact, however, there is permanent reflexiveness about what information, what knowledge, and what decisions can, should, and must be fed into the formal (and thus tangible) network. And the hierarchy is helpless against this sort of controlling reflection, because it is itself monitored in the same fashion.

VII

The title of this chapter, "The Organization of Organization," points to the function of reflection on organization in the organization. This function shows itself only if one sets no organizational principles and, if not abandons, then at least questions such classical dichotomies as centralization/decentralization, vertical/horizontal communication, and division of labor/integration. As formulations of problems they are quite obviously nothing more than paradoxes, ambivalent expressions for an always correct "both the one and the other."

We could, on the contrary, assume that the organization of communicative interconnection in the system is nothing other than the structural complement to the autopoiesis of the system. The structure of the system includes everything that defines positions, and thus also the programs that have to be carried out there and the personnel that hold positions there. But positions are not units that operate in isolation. Only their interconnection through communication determines and varies the demands to be met. This is not simply a matter of joining up units that exist by themselves. Positions are given their particular profile only by what happens elsewhere. A static description, for instance, the popular cartographic representation of the organogram, may well ignore this. But organizations are dynamic systems, and constant monitoring of what needs to be changed in other positions if job descriptions or position holders change is therefore indispensable – monitoring of what has to be changed elsewhere if, for whatever reason, positions do not function as expected.

From the perspective of the communication channels available to an organization, other forms of setting decision premises look like variables. This is particularly true for decision programs. Whether purposive or conditional programming is chosen, and however narrowly decision-making behavior keeps to the provisions of the program, or, in other words, how much variability for continuously changing situations is permitted, has to be determined by the given organizational context, and can change as the context changes. Similarly, personnel deployment can be utilized, not least deployment for managerial tasks. What qualities are required is determined by the organizational contexts in which these qualities can take effect or, if they are lacking, can lead to considerable irritation. In these regards, the organization of organization is the superordinate question, which can, however, never be answered in abstract terms but only with the historical state of the given system in mind.

If we have to assume that positions define each other mutually, and do so under continuously changing conditions, self-observation of the system has to be geared to this circumstance. It will be able to use the concept of competence to mark what is expected of particular positions. The practical problem lies in the speed with which changes are registered and exploited for changes in the structure of the organization. Electronic data processing opens up new per-spectives. As we will be seeing, it provides a fast-working memory that participates in the operations it records, and analyzes what has happened to discover what still has to be decided.[41] Such a development would, inciden-tally, apply to itself; it, too, would be a change that sets in somewhere and whose consequences for other positions need to be assessed. For this reason, too, attempts to introduce electronic data processing in businesses is a test case for the thesis that organizational interconnectivity can serve to reflect on the system in the system.[42]

However, this is only part of the answer to the question of how reflection loops can be established in organizations to replace the old command and control schema. The first question is what units of measurement can be used to record and observe operations in terms of past/future differences. In this the organizations of the economic system have a clear advantage because they have an elaborated cost accounting system at their disposal, which can be supple-mented by translatable parameters. Research on the subject has accordingly been concerned mainly with business administration. Differently oriented organizations, because their success or failure cannot be fed into the system in the form of market data, have to operate with estimates, and for them it is always a "political" question when these estimates are to be revised in the light of experience. Simply translating cuts in resource allocations into cuts else-where, now the usual practice, shows only that convincing reflection on organization in the organization is lacking.

Notes

1. See the classical presentation by Luther Gulick, Notes on the Theory of Organization, in: Luther Gulick and L. Urwick (eds.), *Papers on the Science of Administration*, New York 1937, 1–45. On criticism with reference to other problems, esp. career problems, see Fred H. Goldner, Division of Labor: Process and Power, in Mayer N. Zald (ed.), *Power in Organizations*, Nashville, TN 1970, 97–143, and the following commentary by Richard A. Peterson.
2. See Herbert A. Simon, The Proverbs of Administration, *Public Administration Review* 6 (1946), 53–67.
3. See Nils Brunsson and Johan P. Olsen, *The Reforming Organization*, London 1993.
4. See George Spencer-Brown, *Laws of Form*, reprint New York 1979, 54 ff. on second-order equations.
5. On "organizational forgetfulness" as a resource for reform efforts and on the role of business consultants as aid to forgetting see Brunsson and Olsen op. cit. 41 ff.
6. Chapter 2.
7. See Michael Behr, Martin Heidenreich, Gert Schmidt, and Hans-Alexander *Graf von Schwerin, Neue Technologien in der Industrieverwaltung: Optionen veränderten Arbeitskräfteeinsatzes*, Opladen 1991, 50.
8. See the warning by Urwick cited above, chapter 9n2.

9. For greater detail, see Niklas Luhmann, *Haltlose Komplexität, in idem Soziologische Aufklärung* vol. 5, Opladen 1990, 59–76.

10. The warning from experienced local government civil servants (as I recall from discussions) that this made a further hierarchical level necessary because municipal or county CEOs were no longer personally acquainted with the members of their administrative staff was ignored. The organizational advantage seemed to be obvious, and the problem was seen exclusively in the relationship between administration and public. The same can be said of local government reforms in England, for the conversions of professional systems (horizontally strongly sub-divided) into corporative systems. See C. R. Hinings and Royston Greenwood, *The Dynamics of Strategic Change*, Oxford 1988.

11. We shall be coming back to this in Chapter 13–9.

12. On the advantages of the medium-sized enterprise see Gianfranco Dioguardi, *Organizzazione come strategia*, 4th ed. Torino 1992.

13. See, e.g., Marshall E. Dimock, *Administrative Vitality*, New York 1959, 255 ff.; John M. Pfiffner and Frank P. Sherwood, *Administrative Organization*, Englewood Cliffs, NJ 1960, 445 f.

14. See, e.g.,. Eugen Schmalenbach, *Über Dienststellengliederung im Großbetriebe*, Köln – Opladen 1959, 42: "Clearest are the phenomena that have to do with growing size of the enterprise and which manifest themselves in a not only absolute but also relative enlargement of the clerical and accounting work, controlling, the suppression of entrepreneurship in favor of a civil service mentality, the decline in thrift, the greater emphasis placed on representative needs, etc."

15. See D. S. Pugh and D. J. Hickson, *Organizational Structure in Its Context: The Aston Programme I*, Aldershot 1976; D. S. Pugh and C. R. Hinings (eds.), *Organizational Structure – Extensions and Replications: The Aston Programme II*, Aldershot 1976; D. S. Pugh and R. L. Payne eds.), *Organizational Behaviour in Its Context: The Aston Programme III.*, Aldershot 1977; D. H. Hickson and C. McMillan (eds.), *Organization and Nation: The Aston Programme IV*, Aldershot 1981.

16. This is confirmed by ethnological research. The relations between system size, division of labor, hierarchization, and ritualalization are concerned. See Gregory A. Johnson, Organizational Structure and Scaler Stress, in: Colin Renfrew, Michael J. Rowlands, and Barbara Abbott Segraves (eds.), *Theory and Explanation in Archaeology*, New York 1982, 389–421.

17. See Sergio Talacchi, Organization Size, Individual Attitudes and Behavior: An Empirical Study, *Administrative Science Quarterly* 5 (1960), 398–420; Bernard P. Indik, Some Effects of Organization Size on Member Attitudes and Behavior, *Human Relations* 16 (1963), 369–384; idem, The Relationship Between Organizational Size and Supervision Ratio, *Administrative Science Quarterly* 9 (1964), 301–312; Richard H. Hall, J. Eugene Haas, and Norman J. Johnson, Organizational Size, Complexity, and Formalization, *American Sociological Review* 32 (1967), 903–912; Organizational Size, Complexity, and the Administrative Component in Occupational Associations, *The Sociological Quarterly* 11 (1970), 435–451; Grant W. Childers, Bruce H. Mayhew, Jr., and Louis N. Gray, System Size and Structural Differentiation in Military Organizations: Testing a Baseline Model of the Division of Labor, *American*

Journal of Sociology 76 (1971), 813–831; Bruce H. Mayhew, System Size and Ruling Elites, *American Sociological Review* 38 (1973), 468–475; and for a review of research to date, see John R. Kimberly, Organizational Size and the Structuralist Perspective: A Review, Critique, and Proposal, *Administrative Science Quarterly* 21 (1976), 571–597.

18. See, e.g., Kimberly op. cit.
19. To quote Jean Paul on the theater: "The more collaborators there are in a *single* event, the less dependent it is on a single character, the more ways remain open for the intervention of outside, mechanical world forces. The machine god has suddenly become many people at the same time." See Vorschule der Ästhetik, *Werke* vol. 5, Munich 1963, 239.
20. See Richard Z. Gooding and John A. Wagner III, A Meta-Analytical Review of the Relationship between Size and Performance: The Productivity and Efficiency of Organizations and Their Subunits, *Administrative Science Quarterly* 30 (1985), 462–481.
21. We find notable exceptions in micro-enterprises in the craft industries. Given very high wages and nonwage labor costs, as well as labor law problems, there is now a tendency to keep businesses small and constant, thus renouncing exploitation of less lucrative market opportunities. As a result, demand in this important sector can no longer be met or only by the black economy.
22. See Kim S. Cameron, Sarah J. Freeman, and Aneil K. Michra, Downsizing and Redesigning Organizations, in: George P. Huber and William H. Glick (eds.), *Organizational Change and Redesign: Ideas and Insights for Improving Performance*, Oxford 1993, 19–65.
23. See, e.g., the distinction between standardization, variety, and reactivity models in Arman Avadikyan, Patrick Cohendet, and Patrick Llerena, Coherence, Diversity of Assets and Networks: Towards an Evolutionary Approach, *Revue internationale de systemique* 7 (1993), 505–531.
24. This is the usual definition of structural complexity, which still takes no account of the time aspect (diversity in the succession of reference units). See, e.g., Todd R. La Porte, Organized Social Complexity: Explication of a Concept, in: idem (ed.), *Organized Social Complexity: Challenge to Politics and Policy*, Princeton, NJ 1975, 3–39.
25. See only Rosabeth Moss Kanter, The Future of Bureaucracy and Hierarchy in Organizational Theory: A Report from the Field, in: Pierre Bourdieu and James S. Coleman (eds.), *Social Theory for a Changing Society*, Boulder – New York 1991, 63–87.
26. See Arthur L. Stinchcombe, *Information and Organizations*, Berkeley 1990, 74 f.
27. See Jay B. Barney and William G. Ouchi (eds.), *Organizational Economics*, San Francisco 1986, 12.
28. See W. Ross Ashby, *Design for a Brain: The Origin of Adaptive Behaviour*, 2nd ed. London 1954; idem, *An Introduction to Cybernetics*, London 1956; idem, Requisite Variety and Its Implications for the Control of Complex Systems, *Cybernetica* 1 (1958), 83–99.
29. That this remains possible is naturally not to be denied. Consider, for example, lovers' "eye language" or the precondition that the telephone also works at the other end of the line.

30. See Rudolf Wimmer, Wozu brauchen wir ein General Management, *Hernsteiner* 6/ 3 (1993), 4–12 (8 f.).

31. Following a suggestion by Henry Mintzberg such an order can be referred to as "adhocracy." See Henry Mintzberg, *Structures in Fives: Designing Effective Organizations*, Englewood Cliffs, NJ 1983, 253 ff.

32. See Brunsson and Olsen op. cit. (1993).

33. See James G. March and Herbert A. Simon, *Organizations*, New York 1958, 10 f.

34. Following Heinz von Foerster, we had already used this term to describe the invention of decision premises (see Chapter 7) and not come to a further level of normalization of attention for the non-normal.

35. See Michel Crozier, *L'Entreprise a l'écoute: Apprendre le management post-industriel*, Paris 1989.

36. See, e.g., Charles Heckscher, Defining the Post-Bureaucratic Type, in: Charles Heckscher and Anne Donnellon (eds.), *The Post-Bureaucratic Organization: New Perspectives on Organizational Change*, Thousand Oaks, CA 1994, 14–62.

37. See, e.g., Henry Mintzberg, *The Nature of Managerial Work*, New York 1973.

38. See Minzberg op. cit., 135.

39. See Tom Burns, Friends, Enemies, and the Polite Fiction, *American Sociological Review* 18 (1953), 654–662; idem, The Direction of Activity and Communication in a Departmental Executive Group, *Human Relations* 7 (1954), 73–97; idem, The Reference of Conduct in Small Groups: Cliques and Cabals in Occupational Milieux, *Human Relations* 8 (1955), 467–486; idem, Micropolitics: Mechanisms of Institutional Change, *Administrative Science Quarterly* 6 (1961), 257–281; idem, Des fins et des moyens dans la direction des entreprises: Politique intérieur et pathologie de l'organisation, *Sociologie du Travail* 4 (1962), 209–229. On the present discussion see, e.g., Willi Küpper and Günther Ortmann (eds.), *Mikropolitik: Rationalität, Macht und Spiele in Organisationen*, Opladen 1988.

40. See the findings in Rainer Koch, Entscheidungsstile und Entscheidungsverhalten von Führungskräften öffentlicher Verwaltungen, *Verwaltung und Fortbildung* 21 (1993), 179–197.

41. See also Chapter 12–1.

42. There is now a great deal of literature on the subject. See, e.g., Michael Behr et al., *Neue Technologien in der Industrieverwaltung. Optionen eines veränderten Arbeitskräfteeinsatzes*, Opladen 1991.

11 Structural Change: The Poetry of Reform and the Reality of Evolution

I

In some regards, the concept of change is usefully vague. Now it is probably generally accepted that change cannot be understood as a return to an (old or new) equilibrium. But this leaves open whether change is brought about deliberately or whether it simply happens. If intentional, it is also unclear whether it meets the intentions or not; and, if not planned, whether it is noticed before occurring, during occurrence, or only afterwards. With the distinction between formal and informal organization in mind, broad research into transformation in organizations has concluded that transformation succeeds if it manages to overcome resistance to change and gain acceptance.[1] But this does little more than translate a paradox into a tautology. The transformation paradox (the organization is the same in different states) is reformulated as a tautology: it succeeds if it succeeds. Such a reformulation is useful only if it provides access to conditions for acceptance, thus proposing and verifying conditioning. Also inadequate are purely "biographical" solutions, which assert that things differ from case to case and depend on the history or culture of the given system.[2]

This sort of solution is a reaction to the inadequate specification of problems, which fails to define the concept of change precisely enough. It is likely to be all the more important to keep in mind two reservations that have arisen from our analysis. The concept of organizational learning is always and exclusively concerned with the structures of the system, never with its operations, and thus never with the level at which the dynamics of the system are realized. For operations (in this case decisions) are always events that cannot change themselves but that pass as they come into being. The dynamics of the system are, as it were, existentially guaranteed, but they appear only in the form of structural change. And organizational change is always observed change.[3] Observation may take place after the fact and it may consist of a conclusion drawn from an abundance of detailed observations. But unobserved change is not change, because the system cannot react to it. Observation is necessary, because change cannot otherwise be worked into the autopoiesis of the system and therefore has no consequences.

In organizations, structures take the form of decision premises. Each decision itself presupposes the continued existence of the world. From this point of view, everything that exists could be regarded as a decision premise, including mere events that are recalled and can prove relevant for further decisions in one regard or another. However, we had given a narrower sense to this concept, and we abide by it. Such premises have to be important for more than one decision; they must therefore be regulatory in nature and used to distinguish one concrete organizational system from others. This may find expression in the attribution of decision premises to decisions of this system; or in their being presupposed as "organizational culture." For both reasons, the system can assume that the same premises do not also apply in the environment, or if they do, it is merely by chance.

The consequence is that differential variation can be assumed. Structural changes in the system and in the environment of the system do not occur in coordination, and if their occurrence is coordinated, this requires corresponding causalities to be provided for ad hoc. The boundaries of the system prevent systematic co-variation, even if they do not in many cases exclude this being specifically sought or even corresponding rules being drawn up (e.g., the pensioning off of members when they reach a certain age). Only where systematic co-variation is interrupted can we speak of systemic structural changes at all. And this holds true not only for planned changes but also, and in particular as a condition, for the possibility of evolution.

II

We begin our investigations with structural changes, which are usually referred to as innovations or reforms. The literature addresses the subject under the heading of "organizational change."[4] With its empirical assumptions, the classical theory of rational organization had almost automatically overestimated the possibilities of reform. This was due firstly to the assumption that the intentions of management that set reform in motion were unequivocally formulated or at least could be unequivocally formulated.[5] Descriptions of managers' everyday working practices[6] could have a sobering effect. Secondly, the couplings in the system – couplings between decisions, between decisions and decision premises, between problems and solutions, etc. – had been seen as sufficiently tight and therefore amenable to accurate change; in reality, in all these regards, the stability of the system depends rather on loose couplings,[7] so that operations not subject to direct intervention can survive reform without being affected, leading to considerable conflict and frictional loss. On the basis of the classical assumptions, reforms could be regarded as linear processes running from planning and decision-making to implementation. Things are different in reality.[8] As soon as the intention to reform becomes known, the situation becomes complicated. Opinions for or against reform are advanced, along with wide-ranging modifications, stipulations, and anticipations. Delays occur, as well as oscillation between old and new ideas, and the intentions of a reform have to be described over and over again in adaptation to changing situations. Carrying out reforms then requires strategic behavior in ever new situations.

Reforms are prompted by proposals to change existing structures. They assume that reality is socially constructed and observe this reality on the basis of the distinction between deficiencies and possible improvements. What has to be decided is then whether to change things or not (often in more than one regard). The observation of inconsistencies gives a binary perspective. But such a simply formulated alternative leaves little room for rational decision-making. And the risk of reforms lies not in the relations between choices offered within the alternative but in the question of how the intended reform can be integrated into the given system. From this point of view, it is only the reform that appears to be risky. The risk of retaining the "tried and tested" structures is often not seen or is underestimated.

There is no unanimous opinion on the reasons for the difficulty of implementing reforms, and cases certainly differ so much that the problems, too, vary from case to case. On the basis of studies on French industry, Michel Crozier identifies miscalculations at the managerial level, deficient communication, and a failure to exploit opportunities for cooperation as major causes.[9] Resistance among middle management is also often cited as causing implementation difficulties.[10] As far as remedies are concerned, others are less optimistic, even taking the view that any proposal for innovation almost necessarily creates conflict, which then has to be endured. There will always be losers. At the level of simple, easily communicable quasi-theory, two alternating theories are advanced in reaction.[11] The one says that it is creativity that counts; the other that the human mind has only a limited capacity for grasping complex states of affairs. The paradox of failure in the search for success is attributed to the generalized individual and dissolved in a distinction between theories. Or it is unfolded over time: first exaggeration, then disappointment.[12]

To quote Gregory Bateson, we could also speak of schismogenesis.[13] Concrete reform initiatives easily demonstrate that one project comes into conflict with other projects, or at any rate with the status quo – if attention focuses on mutually exclusive conditions. Skillful reform management would then involve avoiding or postponing schismogenesis and formulating proposals not in either/or terms but in terms of "this as well as that."

Experience with failed reforms or with unexpected results (often unanalyzed) has ultimately led to sociologists taking a rather skeptical view of the possibilities of reform[14] (while the literature on management elaborates ever new strategies for planning innovation). To some extent, reform returns organizations to the founding situation, burdening them with problems that Stinchcombe calls the "liability of newness"[15] and that raise the question of whether it would not be better to found new organizations instead. Reformers themselves speak of the need to find or create unoccupied social spaces into which their reforms can be built and from which they can then be diffused.[16] Moreover, we now see more clearly that all reforms have both constructive and destructive effects[17] and that they leave it up to the observer to concentrate more on the constructive or on the destructive impacts. While the status quo can be considered, so to speak, as a pacification formula for wide-ranging interests – history has made it what it is – reform projects put an end to this multi-interest peace and revitalize differences. Whatever the intention, the initial result is the difference between protagonists and affected parties, and what actually happens depends on how the system to be reformed deals with this difference. As always, producing a bifurcation means producing system history. In brief, centralized competence suffices to rouse the system but not to reform it.

Apart from these lessons of experience, a theoretical consideration gives ground for skepticism: if setting rules has any function at all, it cannot make sense to recommend changing them under well-sounding headings such as reform or innovation.[18] Such positive evaluation merely conceals the underlying paradox: that both changing and retaining rules can make sense depending on the circumstances, about which nothing certain can be known. Naturally, the same applies for the opposite case: resistance to changing rules is not justified simply because, when in doubt, it is better to follow local experience. Corresponding ambivalence in dealing with rules is to be found at a level that is not formulated as a preference for change but can affect the organizational culture in a running battle between the organization and itself.[19] However, in some cases this may also develop into a push for reform.

Reforms can be marketed under different, indeed opposing labels: as better adjustment to ideas (e.g., more humane working conditions) or as better adjustment to realities (e.g., shrinking markets). Where reforms are driven by ideas, the simplification necessary to get them going comes from the ideas concerned; where reforms are motivated by deficiencies, it is provided by the assumption that there is a link between various complaints and disappointments. In both cases, one does not set out from an overall construction but from inconsistencies, from "misfits" in the given conditions; otherwise the complexity of the task would prove too great to handle.[20]

In the event of stepped up changes in the environment or in the system, one is more likely to react only to one's own states. The practical difference as far as resistance, feasibility, strategic flexibility, etc. are concerned is unlikely to be very great. Even well-meant reforms prompted by ideas (e.g., more participation, more democracy, humanization of work) meet with resistance because they involve elaborated goals poorly coordinated with the actual attitudes of those affected.[21] Which description is chosen will therefore depend essentially on the plausibility attainable at the given moment. Typically, the favored description will then be decked out with secondary goals or with additional arguments that pay tribute to the opposing principle at the intersection between idea and reality.

In theory and in practice, the skeptical to pessimistic view of reform naturally depends on whether one feels that reforms ought either to succeed or not be ventured upon at all. This premise depends, in turn, on whether organizations are assumed to be systems of rational problem-solving. If we abandon this assumption, the function of reforms could then be to bring differences between interests to light that would otherwise have remained latent, thus contributing to controversial self-descriptions of the system; and hence to produce resistance by the system to the system, enabling a better understanding of reality than the problem/solution schema can offer.

Both ideas and descriptions of reality, and naturally also the prospect of results, require persuasion, rhetoric, information management, concessions, and support from more or less indifferent bystanders; in brief, a degree of communication that leads reformers themselves to believe in their reforms. The communication activity of reforming does not fail to affect its mental environment; its endogenous dynamics "alienates" itself, shaping its environment with the aid of the disjunction between support and resistance.

Reforms are concerned with decisions about decision premises, with the intention of improving the overall state of the system or at least braking or preventing deterioration. Quite similar projects are pursued when it comes to changing the managerial personnel of an organization. Since, for whatever reason, this does not go by the name of reform, we shall leave aside this intervention in the decision premises of a system, and merely note that changes in management are also structural changes in the system and clearly a functional equivalent of reforms. An organization or a society that no longer ventures to reform, for which there may be good reasons, will tend all the more to tackle problems by changing the people at the top. We can perhaps even postulate that at times when the force for reform is lacking, the susceptibility to scandal increases. Even trifling matters are then blown up into scandals in order to at least enable top management to be ousted, offering career opportunities for the upcoming generation.

In usual parlance, the term reform refers to the organization of competences and communication channels or to the decision programs of the system. This includes the organization and programming of personnel decisions. Hardly anyone would now claim that there are principles for this that derive directly from concepts of rationality. The aim is rather to improve the overall quality of the system's decisions. Whatever drives proceedings, the shift from principles to results brings into play the complexity of the system, as well as the time gap between the initiation of reform and its success or failure. For all reforms, explanations for failure are thus built in from the outset.

Reforms are clicked into place between past and future. They use the circumstance that the past is known but the future unknown. However, the past is known only because what is forgotten remains unknown. In this respect, discreet forgetting, namely forgetting why earlier reforms had failed, is one of reformers' most important resources. It allows them to claim that their project is new. The future seen from the present, by contrast, is unknown. At the present moment it is still indeterminate; this is what gives the present the chance to determine the future. But the future survives, so to speak, every attempt to determine it. Time turns all attempts to determine the future into past, which in later presents one can look back on with a better knowledge of things. All that can be done is to keep putting the future off as indeterminable. Taking a phrase of Yeats, Lanzara calls this negative capability.[22] Reforms, then, are articulated time paradoxes that treat the indeterminable as determined by them, and thus as a past that can be observed. In the time context, reforms are accordingly nothing other than an expression of a structural dynamic, and they serve not to attain their goals but to maintain this dynamic.

The good intentions behind reforms are therefore difficult to refute because the acid test is still to come. Objections, therefore, have to operate with uncertain assumptions about the future. And then assessment of the organization's present situation may decide the issue. Like forgetting the reasons why reforms have failed in the past, the unknownness of the future is a condition for the possibility of reform. Shackel calls this the "exploitation of unknowledge"[23] and concludes that "... one aim of policy is to attain a new platform from which policy itself can be re-formed."[24] One result that can be expected of reforms is, therefore, the generation of new possibilities for observation, which one would not have had without making decisions of one's own.

Reform projects certify themselves with an often detailed semantic apparatus consisting of principles, norms, evaluative standards, statistics, audits – thus not only with value judgments but also with statements of facts. The poetry of reform is geared fully to consensual constructions, such as one finds in the formulation of values and in the construction of facts. But the description of the future aspired to often remains rather vague, and reform presents itself primarily as a means and a procedure. It is often admitted that the results cannot be predicted at all and that carrying out reforms is a strategic process of constant learning[25] (which certainly does not include forgetting the real intention).

In extreme cases, it may limit itself to describing its own implementation and holding out the prospect of good results.

This problem of the unknownness of the future is often defused by the fact that similar reforms have already been undertaken in other organizations, so that one is following a pattern and can benefit from the experience of others. The future of the organization is then the present of other organizations. This facilitates the proposition and may explain why certain sorts of reform project spread like fashions through diffusion.[26]

If there is no possibility to project one's own future by copying, its uncertainty must, so to speak, be semantically accepted and built into the reform proposal. For this reason reforms are often described as "experiments," for example, in organizations of the education system. This gives the impression that nothing has been settled and everything is open and reversible depending on the results of the experiment.[27] Nevertheless, and despite assertions to the contrary, scientific experiments are not involved in which only a few controlled variables are likely to be changed. Reform experiments serve rather to accommodate the zeal of reformers while shielding normal operations against the effects of the undertaking. Reform schools or reform universities with certain characteristics then often also find their place in the overall organized implementation of societal functions, and it is then practically impossible to evaluate let alone abolish them. Reform schools survive as schools. They are merely standardized through more or less bureaucratic regulation.

Motivating reforms through desired results does not mean that guiding principles are superfluous. They are already presupposed in diagnosing a state of affairs that needs to be reformed. Reforms are elaborated and launched only in systems that burden themselves with ideas against which actual behavior can be measured and recognized as unsatisfactory. This alone suggests that the main result of reforms could be to ascertain the need for further reforms.[28] *Ecclesia reformata semper reformanda.*

Among the most important resources of reform are, therefore, to omit evaluation of their results and to forget that similar attempts have been made in the past. This may be why organizations employ successive firms or teams of business consultants who withdraw before reforms have been fully implemented; this makes it easier to forget previous attempts and facilitates the new start.[29]

Not much else is to be expected, since organizations can operate only through concrete decisions, also in initiating and carrying out reforms. This, too, must actually take place sometime and somewhere – and must do so with a usually high level of uncertainty and uncertainty absorption; and also typically in situations in which conflicts, differences in the impact of reform, and lines of resistance are already emerging. Moreover, the loose coupling required for the system's stability and operational integrity has to be kept in mind, especially the loose coupling between decision premises and decisions. Organizations are not trivial machines, not technical artifacts in which one can calculate the consequences of changes in single factors. They always orient their operations on themselves, too, that is to say, on the state in which they find themselves at the given moment thanks to previous operations.[30] And to a limited extent they have a memory of their own. They remember and know why something is the way it is. If reform impulses are imparted to such a nontrivial machine, it immediately defines its own state as one in which a reform can take place. It is difficult to calculate how the system will react to such self-observation, precisely because this information puts it in a different state than before; indeed, makes it a different non-trivial machine with different possibilities.[31]

The difficulty, if not impossibility, of keeping reforms on course for the intended effects and attaining the goals set does not mean they have no effect. On the one hand, decision premises can naturally be changed. Responsibilities can be changed, competence can be strengthened or weakened. Programs can be added or abandoned or hived off into the environment. Analysis of management strategies for change largely sticks to this possibility of introducing impulses for reform by changing decision premises – nowadays probably without pretensions to being thus able to determine the future state of the system.[32] All this has an impact on the further decision practices of the system. Only in the intention of changing the decision-making practices of the system in this way, of making them more rational, more efficient, more economic, more democratic or humane, or whatever, will one be disappointed. Decision premises and decisions, too, are loosely coupled. This does not exclude reforms in the system from being considered successful; but probably only if, in the course of implementation, they have been able to adapt to existing practices to such a degree that things do not turn out as badly as had been feared and that the reconciliation of reason with reality can be celebrated. "As a consequence, there is a blurring between 'success' and 'failure' as results become interpreted against varying personal perspectives and frames of reference."[33] Or in other words: "Achieving success is much more difficult than claiming success."[34]

Primarily, reforms are therefore descriptions of deficiencies against the background of the assumption that things could be improved. The sense of reforms is ultimately a paradox, which Gille Deleuze[35] has carefully analyzed: the past is disparaged so that the future can be better. But the past, when it was still the present, was not as bad as it had to be for the purposes of reform; and the future, once it becomes the present, will not be as good as the reformers had thought. Deleuze sees two series at work – a deterioration and an improvement – that are construed as a single series "from worse to better" running parallel to the course of time.[36] But the concrete event of meaningfully communicating reform proposals is always an element in both series. Nothing can be construed as better without something else being construed as worse. Such communication benefits from being able to distribute – and thus distinguish – negative and positive assessment to two time horizons; time horizons that are at the moment non-actual but separated by the event that actualizes itself as the present.

Thus in the 1960s the school and university system in the Federal Republic of Germany suddenly came under suspicion of not sufficiently exploiting the "educational reserves" available in the population. This led to reforms that improved access to tertiary education for working-class children and gave late developers a better chance of obtaining a more advanced education and catching up on what they had missed.[37] Long before then there had been experiments with reform schools. In the 1960s, the awareness of deficiencies, and thus the goals of reform, shifted from strictly educational ideas to the socio-political domain. However, the mutual specification of deficiency definition and reform measures is apparent in both cases, and in both cases reforms use the possibility to change the decision premises of the organizations involved. Finally, what triggers reforms in both cases is the burdening of the system with ideas, and in both cases the reforms implemented generate the need for further reform.

Similar experience was gained with moves to reform public service law in the Federal Republic of Germany. At the outset, in the late 1960s, the problem had been politically defined as an interest in abolishing the division between civil service law (regulated by legislation) and employment and labor law (negotiated with the unions). It was clear from the start that this abolition was politically impossible. A commission was accordingly set up. In search of a way out of this dilemma, it redefined the issue as one of rational personnel planning, that is to say planning staff change procedures on the basis of job description and personnel appraisal criteria.[38] But this redefinition was rejected by the political system (already at the ministerial level).[39] The preferred solution was apparently to adopt a symbolic policy of "bringing up the topic" of reform now and again as an insoluble problem.

Reform is still spoken of, but any hope of improvement has much diminished. In the context of research on organizational culture, appreciation of resistance to change, and thus of inertia effects, has spread[40]; there are likely to be good reasons for this, too.[41] For example, an organization has to take stable expectations in the environment into account; it should not lose its recognition value by too rapid or too frequent changes. Guiding principles have changed accordingly. They are increasingly no more than reactions to problems that impose themselves in relations between system and environment or within systems themselves. Today's reformers are, to use a distinction coined by Odo Marquard,[42] no longer intent on attaining goals but on eluding defects (Zielstreber/Defektflüchter).[43] Business enterprises currently favor a "lean management" concept, or they are at least advised to do so. Everything not needed is cut or hived off; profit margins are apparently now so narrow and the ratio of equity capital to debt kept so small that even minor changes in the environment or normal macroeconomic fluctuations can threaten a company's survival. However, no methodology for improving performance through downsizing is in evidence.[44] In public administration one is beginning to react to the excessive political demands made by the welfare state. Privatization or market orientation are recommended to find out what demand there actually is for services outside the imagination of politicians. Here, too, mythological descriptions of the past are helpful, for instance, that the administration has not been thrifty or efficient.

That reforms are welcomed or at least considered a necessary exercise is not only a calculated invention of organizations to divert attention from recurrent problems. This view has taken root in the societal system itself. This has to do with the modern revision of our understanding of history. As early as the seventeenth century, history had ceased to be merely a quantity (*copia*) of rhetorical forms – of narratives, object lessons, striking characters or events, emblems or symbols for identifying an old family. Moreover, history no longer provides "origins" for legitimating present pretensions. It is seen rather as in temporal continuity with the present. This means firstly that it constantly ages, vanishing into a past that lies farther and farther back, less and less relevant for the present – such as the rights and wrongs of the Norman invasion for the validity of common law.[45] Secondly it has to be presented as a sequential development of complexity bringing benefits and problems. It is this detachment from thoughts of origin and this shift to historical complexity that suggests that both problems and alternatives can be seen in a present determined by history. On the basis of historical studies and material, *De origine iuris germanici: Commentarius Historicus*,[46] the work by Hermann Conring that is regarded as founding German history of law, questions whether the validity of Roman civil law had been established in Germany by an imperial law and advances proposals for improving law in the German Empire.

In correlation, how history is addressed in society therefore seems to demand the possibility of and willingness for reform. But can this persist if one has to accept that reforms in their field of reference and their instrumentation require organizations, and that experience at this level has not been exactly favorable? One can attempt to judge reform projects in organizations themselves more discriminately. But, the notion that shifting from anticipation of a better future to crisis management can better solve the internal problems of implementing changes is not obvious. Reformers can at least cite crises – and not only ideas.

Reformers claim, and it is expected of them, that a connection can be made between ideas, deficiencies, and measures. This suggests strict coupling between causes and effects. However, as social systems, organizations have to rely on loose coupling,[47] and they are self-referential systems, all of whose operations are guided by the historical state they have attained through their own operations. This self-determination also means that reformers come into play who consider the organization to need reforming. What then happens is no longer only a question of implementing the reform plan more or less well (although events can also be described in this manner), but of the evolution of the system.

III

When innovations are initiated under the heading of reform, the inevitable side effect is public visibility. Reforms have to be decided explicitly and high up if not at the top. The guiding principles are communicated as good, the changes as intended. This effect can hardly be attenuated, but has consequences in its turn, because every explicit communication can be reacted to with acceptance or rejection. The reaction may be to stress good intentions, to point out the poor state of the system, or to cite material and statistics. But this can only intensify the effects of bifurcation; and it obliges the affected parties to state their views. They can no longer remain silent or turn a blind eye to what is happening. Further communication need not concentrate on acceptance or rejection of the package as a whole. It may be concerned with modifications or with saving as many habits as possible. But the focus on the future that is now to be decided always intensifies conflicts. Especially when there is no certainty about how things will go, it is important to uphold – or to invent – positions.

Experience with reform shows a very one-sided underlying understanding of the time dimension of societal reproduction. The future had seemed to offer scope for realizing projects – even in the face of resistance, even with unforeseen side effects. A different reading of the story shows it as a field in which intended effects slip out of control, where they disappear under the mounting mass of new information. Things do not run as planned; in the course of time they lose their plannedness. The arrival of new information blurs the distinction between intended and unintended effects; not only because the world "in itself" (as nature) is too complex but because certain systems constantly intervene in it through planning, thus producing confusion – confusion not least in the sense of confounding "planned" and "unplanned." In the light of such experience, modern society, in continuing and strengthening its efforts to establish rationally planned order, gears itself to supplementary mechanisms of "incompetence compensation competence" (Odo Marquard), symbolization, and communicated protest; thus it tends to translate substantive problems into communication problems. What comes of this is decided by evolution.

Evolution, it should be noted in advance, is not a method for solving problems. It provides no answer to urgent questions that arise when an organization seeks to improve things or reacts to deterioration. Reform can therefore not be abandoned in favor of evolution. Given the time horizons in which problems unfold, evolution is much too slow, even though it can produce structural breaks with rapidly developing consequences. Evolution is not a linear process nor is it a process that offers prospects of a good conclusion, a better state. The decline of organizations also takes the form of evolution.

This may be one of the reasons why evolution has scarcely been discussed in the context of efforts by organizational systems to control their own development.[48] There are evolution theories for firm populations.[49] But the evolving entity they address is not the individual organization but the "population," in our present case subsystems of the economic system as a subsystem of the societal system.[50] There are then two possibilities. One (daring to presuppose assessment criteria), we see the diversity of the organizations that survive in the population as evidence that high-powered (innovative, assertive) organizations could also be included and, because of their better chances of survival, could increasingly determine the nature of the organization. Or two, we do without such criteria for success and limit ourselves to seeing the variety within the population itself as a chance for further evolution under still unforeseeable circumstances. Because it presupposes criteria, the first variant is still close to theories of rational decision-making. Only the second variant follows evolution-theoretical design with all its consequences, because it leaves all criteria to evolution and, for example, leaves it quite open whether more information has a favorable effect or steers developments into an evolutionary dead end.

In any case, these theories are concerned with the evolution of populations, not with the evolution of single organizations (theories on this subject are rather to be found under the heading of organizational learning and are again limited by the assumption that more learning is better than less learning). The progress made by population theories over older theories that had operated with generic characteristics (hierarchy, goal orientation, etc.) is that the individuality of population members and not their typicality is stressed. The unity of the population is then defined in terms of relations with the environment (e.g., a certain task, a certain market, a certain technology) and not in terms of invariant structural characteristics. This has reawakened interest in Lamarck, who had focused on irritability and not on structural invariance.[51] However, all this does not change the fact that population theory does not even ask whether a single organization can evolve.

This theoretical deficiency is due to planned changes playing too great a part in thinking about structural changes in organizations. But this does not suffice, even if one does not deny that planning takes place or underestimate its effects. In other words, evolution is determined by the shortcomings of methods for the rational planning of change. The opposite state of affairs is also worth noting: one can provide for the possibility of evolution – but only in forms that planners would classify as non-rational. This is the case, for example, when organizational procrastination is planned as a reserve for unforeseen emergencies.[52] Ambiguity in sense-making is also often cited as a point of departure for innovation.[53] To put it more precisely in evolution-theoretical terms, we could say that ambiguity offers an opportunity to introduce variation. This possibility is, as it were, concentrated if the system itself offers the occasion and variation can be presented as clarifying a state of affairs that has already been accepted. Karl Weick argues along similar lines that an organization has to be quarrelsome, sluggish, superstitious, hyper-critical, monstrous, etc. in order to increase the possibilities of variation.[54] More abstractly, we could also speak of the "generation of variability."[55] However, this should not be interpreted as a recommendation for planning, for this would amount to saying that a rationality that embraces and includes evolution is possible.

A theory of evolution that addresses single organizations would have to treat the organization as a population of decisions, which, although always new as decisions, offer a variation of structures only under special conditions. Decisions that accept or reject the suggestion could then follow. This could have the advantage of allowing one to proceed from something visible and not necessarily having to begin with a negative assessment of prevailing conditions.

Such ideas about unplannable evolution give rise to discussion on whether changes and survival in a population of firms are matters of adaptation, as management theories claim, or questions of selection through internal and external moments of inertia, which can also reward "high fidelity reproduction of structure" because this better fits both the low information processing capacities of the system and external expectations.[56] This is at best a useful correction to the inflated expectations of management theories; but an elaborated evolution-theoretical treatment is not in evidence. However, a lack of clarity about what evolution actually means in the case of social systems and how it comes about is likely to prove a hindrance. We must therefore first turn to this question.

Following biological genetics, population ecology sees the problem largely in the transmission of cultural goods across breaks in generations or across changes in members in organizations.[57] Essentially, however, these are questions of the autopoiesis of the systems in question, whereas evolution theory is primarily interested in the conditions under which divergent transmission that changes structures can nevertheless succeed.

With the concepts autopoiesis (Chapter 2) and decision (Chapter 4), we have also changed the point of departure for a theory of the evolution of organizational systems. Autopoiesis means evolution without guidance by improved adaptation. And if decisions are always understood as new, as the beginning of new narratives, this means that futures are generated that contain new starting points and therefore, being dependent on decisions, cannot be foreseen. Reform projects do not need to be discouraged, but they have to accept that what future decisions make of them is and remains unknown. In other words, reforms produce a characteristic oscillation between success and failure in attaining goals, and even between their own and other preferences. Evolution is, as it were, the overall concept for the unpredictability of future decisions.

The outstanding characteristic of evolution theories (as opposed to development theories) is that they explain structural changes caused by the interplay – not coordinated by the system – of various evolutionary functions.[58] Masses of variations have to occur, which undergo a positive/negative selection process, producing in turn results that can be restabilized in the system. The theory then has to explain how these different evolutionary functions can be distributed among different mechanisms in such a way that their interplay in the system cannot be predicted and cannot be planned but has to be treated as random.[59] One typically speaks of evolution where doubts about the rational self-regulation of development processes arise – in the evolution of life and in the evolution of science or the economy or law.

In social systems, the distribution of evolutionary functions cannot, as in living systems, be guaranteed by different levels of system formation – not in the form of genetic mutation, or survival of the individual organism, or even up to and including the reproduction and stabilization of genetically changed populations in an ecological environment. How can it then be achieved?

We assume that variation has to do with operations in the nature of events, selection with the structure-forming value of these operations, and restabilization with the system in its environment.[60] Variations occur, if this is the case, at the level of everyday decisions. They have to address different situations, to modify them in accordance with decision premises, and to activate human resources for understanding the situation and context-specific requirements. But initially they remain one-off events. However, all decisions can be suitable premises for other decisions; they can develop a pattern, can enter into the narrative culture of the system, can serve in recognizing similar cases, and can thus both condense, as well as generalize and refine their purpose. Decisions can be remembered and forgotten; and if they are remembered, it is as worthy of emulation or as a warning, as success or failure. Initial massive variation generally has no consequences. The system finds relief in forgetting. But it can sometimes also be the occasion for positive or negative selection. This changes the structures of the system without a decision on introducing new decision premises being needed. This, too, is not excluded – be it in the form of reform projects or in the form of changes decided ad hoc. But planned changes are always embedded in an evolutionary process that takes them up, we may say, in a deformed state. For decisions on decision premises are also decisions that are observed in the system and accepted with modifications or forgotten.

For good reason, these considerations contradict the assumption obvious for theories of management and planning that bad business results or "crises" draw the attention of management to problems in relations with the environment and then trigger innovative measures. This may well be the case, but innovations are risky interventions, which organizations with serious survival problems can hardly afford. It is also a risk whether the environment accepts changes or upholds its habitual expectations; also risky is the question of whether and how changes can be carried out within the system if they concern not only single subsystems or only marginal variables.[61] It is therefore hardly surprising that business consultants tend to be commissioned by flourishing firms that would like to do things better, and that bad results in enterprises that undertake innovations often accelerate the departure of such advisers. Evolution requires the capacity to wait for opportunities.

Moreover, if we remember that decisions are always communicated as information, as differences that make a difference, it is also clear that only what has been decided is normally remembered and not what has been decided against. This means that the alternatives, or the memory of what would have happened if no decision had been made, fade more rapidly than the memory of what the decision contained. This is due not least to the linguistic recording of decisions, but above all to the need to absorb uncertainty. The system memory hence operates with strong simplification, with meaning specification, not with specified contexts; with descriptions, not with distinctions/differences. If variations are available for selection, they are no longer what they were as decisions. This, too, leads to variation and selection necessarily going their own ways and eluding every planning effort to integrate them into the system.

Separate evolutionary mechanisms for variation and for selection accordingly require the logical, mathematical, and technical cohesion between decisions and decision premises to be broken. Decisions are not automatically suitable as premises for further decisions (e.g., as models to be emulated), nor can decisions that are made on the basis of (let alone with disregard for) these premises be automatically inferred from them. Consider, for instance, the need of interpretation for decision programs and their susceptibility to deformation, the often serious effects people can have on decisions, and, not least, that the system can constantly decide whether it wishes to call on the formal competencies of the hierarchy or not.

The controversy between planning theories and evolution theories is thus ultimately decided on the terrain of systems theory. If tight coupling could be established between decisions and decision premises to enable intervention in the decision-making process by changing a few structural variables, planning could be implemented with a degree of certainty as to the results. But crucial variables in such a system would be extremely responsive to the environment. Instead, one has to proceed on the assumption of loose coupling, for precisely this is a condition for amenability to evolution. How the system reacts to planning is then not a question of intention and leverage but a question of evolution.

The relationship between variation and selection guarantees neither variation nor even the continuance of the system. Nowadays, one hardly ever assumes that selection (whether "natural selection" by the environment or selection within the system) leads to an "optimal fit" between system and environment that would then guarantee the continuance of the system until the next change in the environment.[62] The outcome of evolutionary changes is decided only by processes of restabilization, which bring the system into a new balance with its environment. Even organizations that do not understand their selection of structures as adaptation to their environment (or misconstrue it) can survive in the long term. At this point, evolution theory as the comprehensive theory can call on "population ecology" research, which had anyway limited itself to investigating the entry of systems into a population capable of reproduction and their exit from it. In single organizations, processes of self-observation, accounts control, and risk management typically come to bear, which can in turn prompt planned (and nonetheless evolutionary) structural changes. In any case, the system does not have to rely on taking rational action with regard to itself, for this would overburden it. But it can develop and improve a network of parameters on the basis of which it can observe and, where needful, correct what has come about through evolution. In the process, however, it not seldom finds that the information provided by the system's cost accounting arrives with considerable delay and often too late to permit timely intervention.

So far, we have localized all evolutionary functions – variation, selection, and restabilization – in the evolving system. This is in keeping with the theory of autopoietic systems and diverges radically from classical evolution theory, which had expected surviving exemplars to adapt optimally to their environment through external selection (natural selection). But what role does the environment then play in the evolution of organizations?

At the level of overall societal evolution, it might well suffice to see the environment as "noise," as regular or fine-grained, swirling chaos, from which the system extracts the structures necessary for autopoiesis. For organizations, this view of things cannot be upheld, because their environment is too strongly ordered in advance by society itself (e.g., through market formation by the economy). At least one environment-related distinction suggests itself, and has attracted increasing attention in recent organization research "population ecology," namely the distinction between gradual (incremental, scarcely noticeable) and abrupt changes in the environment of organizational systems.[63] Both forms of change in the conditions of structural coupling with specific environmental conditions put organizations under very different forms

of pressure, not least time pressure, to change. Whether this distinction correlates clearly with a greater willingness to take risks in planning or also with
a rapid decline in hitherto unquestioned organizational cultures would be an
important field of investigation for the time to come. But whatever planning
contributes – whether survival is assured or succeeds only with the help of
external symbiosis (for instance, government aid) – is ultimately settled in the
course of system evolution.

If the theoretical controversy between planning and evolution is resolved in
favor of evolution theory, this naturally does not mean that planning should be
abandoned and reliance placed on evolution. System leaders would be ill
advised to retire into the role of observers of the evolution of their system.
The planned selection of structures (decision premises) and the observation of
the system with an eye to emerging possibilities for restructuring remain
important. But planning should not primarily be judged by whether it attains
its goals, regardless of whether it is prompted by reform ideas or crises.
Planning is a component in the evolution of the system. A planning system
has to be able to observe itself in evolution, and for this purpose systems-
theoretical analysis is particularly helpful.

The question whether consensus is to be found for planning or at least an
understanding reached also remains important; but it is no longer a tragic one.
What defuses the implications is that evolution and the observation of evolution
will establish how conditions change and what attitudes are taken to developments. One of the most important advantages of an evolution theoretical
approach to structural change – which also affects research methodology –
could be that it assumes from the outset that there are differences generated by
evolution itself in the points of departure for evolution – in brief, that there is
differentiation into types and species.[64] Whereas management philosophies
tend to generalize their recipes as broadly as possible, barriers to generalization
are built into evolution theory. Of course evolution theory itself remains
a general theory. But if we wish to study how variation, selection, and restabilization interact in concrete cases, we have to reckon with far-reaching differences – in the case of organizations, with differences in the breadth of variation
for possible operations or with differences in the extent to which the environment expects structural stability in the system.

IV

Venturing an evolution-theoretical description of structural change in organizations inevitably raises an old and key problem of evolution theory: evolution
leads to specified adaptation to a given environment, which can then prove
a hindrance to further evolution.[65] This has also impressed organizational
sociology.[66] Successful organizations, for instance, ones that grow to meet

increasing demand, are particularly endangered in the next round. The problem has attracted an abundance of unhelpful advice. At the psychological level some have called for "creativity," at the level of social structures others have advised "flexibility." But these are merely different names for the same problem. The current tendency is to point out that inertia in adapting to opportunities has its advantages, and that adapting too fast to ephemeral changes in the environment should at any rate be avoided.[67] Past success also leads to delays in adaptation, but whether this sort of inertia offers potential for development remains a moot point.

Just as unspecific is Weick's suggestion to create complexity (clumsiness), or to allow it to grow in the hope that such a system would be sensitive enough to discover opportunities for restructuring within itself; at any rate, complexity would mean that the system has more possibilities for changing and not changing structures at the same time. The unspecific nature of such proposals, fully in keeping with the diagnosis that danger lies in specification, can be ensured if a random factor is built in from the outset but not identified as such. For example, one could construct a large building with long corridors, relatively spacious elevators, and only a few restrooms, increasing the likelihood of staff encountering and recognizing one another, and thus encouraging contact outside the formal structures of the organization; or one could devise an organization that so obstructs itself and is so impractical that the fine art of improvisation has to come to the rescue.[68] The superstition that organizational consultants or even academics know better could be mentioned in this connection. It can at least serve as a useful functional equivalent for other random generators without being labeled as such.

Another possibility is to use the surplus meaning of the semantics to deceive others and, on occasion, oneself. We now know that structural inertia does not exclude changes but simply does not mark them as such; similarly, reforming zeal that comes up against persistent resistance may lead to states of affairs hardly distinguishable from the situation preceding reform but which are nevertheless described as such. Rhetoric can therefore be employed to conceal desired innovations in the old state of affairs, presenting them, for example, as restoration or as the elimination of abuses that had taken hold; or, vice versa, things that serve above all to save what can be saved can be declared innovations.[69]

These and many similar pointers could suffice when it comes to explaining how organizations manage to cancel their own structural specification as an obstacle to further evolution. In sum, the other side of the specification, the unspecifiedness it excludes, has to be preserved, reproduced, and when necessary reactivated. In the terminology of Yves Barel, it is a question of "potentialization."[70] What is excluded through specification is by this very exclusion shown to be possible. But the system's memory prefers to take the result of selection as tangible present and acts against what is excluded. Second-order observation (which can also be provided for in the system) is therefore needed if one wishes to keep both in mind: the unity of included and excluded.

In this area we thus typically find explanatory concepts that cannot be translated into recipes or demands – for example, in the form of advice to be creative, to be flexible, to be guided by chance, and to be insincere. Such demands can be said to contain a communicative paradox, some would say a self-destructive, performative contradiction. If meant seriously and not used to elude the problem, they would return the system for a moment to the state of paradoxical self-observation. No information is to be gained from this. *"On doit et on ne peut choisir. C'est la quintessence du paradoxe."*[71] One can take up the first idea that occurs to one or prefer the program that is submitted first or by the strongest party. But this means merely leaving things to evolution once again.

V

The recent literature on economic system organizations regularly points out that conditions have fundamentally changed over the past two or three decades and calls for more structural change than ever before. This situation is claimed to be due to the globalization of markets and to ground-breaking technological developments, as well as to changes in communication and transport systems. There is already talk of "hyperturbulence."[72] Company management is called upon to take account of these changes in the structures of their businesses. One may well agree with this diagnosis, but what does it mean for internal organizational changes?

We will scarcely assume that this all amounts to a shift toward evolution, for evolution is too slow and too unpredictable. On the other hand, reform has always been difficult enough. It may be that it is easier to justify under the given circumstances because there is clearer evidence of disadaptation. For this reason, downsizing has come under discussion not as an expedient but as a method.[73] Above all, however, it is the situation of successful organizations that is likely to change. Whereas success had in the past weakened any incentive for organizations to learn – they were satisfied with results and saw no reason to put them at risk through innovation – nowadays it is successful organizations that are particularly at risk because they do not learn quickly enough that they, too, have to learn and adapt.[74] This means that the description of the successful organization would have to change. It would have to rely not on the figures that evidence its success; it would have to stress context and contingency. Only thus can one sound out the environment for changes and at the same time recognize what would consequently have to change in the organization.

Nevertheless, it would be grossly simplifying things to declare innovation, creativity, and learning to be positive factors (as usually happens). A great deal can also go amiss when changes are undertaken, and the risk of organizational change may well be too high when the environment is in turbulence.

Notes

1. The literature on "organizational development" provides information about the origins of this approach from the human relations movement and research into "group dynamics." See, e.g., Burkhard Sievers (ed.), *Organisationsentwicklung als Problem*, Stuttgart 1977. Further references see chap. 1n39.
2. See, e.g., John R. Kimberly, Reframing the Problem of Organizational Change, in: Robert E. Quinn and Kim S. Cameron (eds.), *Paradox and Transformation: Toward a Theory of Change in Organization and Management*, Cambridge, MA 1988, 163–168.
3. See also the definition by Andrew H. Van de Ven and Marshall Scott Poole, Paradoxical Requirements for a Theory of Organizational Change, in: Robert E. Quinn and Kim S. Cameron (eds.), *Paradox and Transformation: Toward a Theory of Change in Organization and Management*, Cambridge, MA 1988, 19–63 (36): "Organizational change is an empirical observation of differences in time of a social system."
4. The rules of sociological methodology are typically followed, with the frequency of structural change being treated as a variable to be correlated with other variables. See, e.g., George P. Huber, Kathleen M. Sutcliffe, C. Chet Miller, and William H. Glick, Understanding and Predicting Organizational Change, in: George P. Huber and William H. Glick (ed.), *Organizational Change and Redesign: Ideas and Insights for Improving Performance*, Oxford 1993, 214–265.
5. See Vicki E. Baier, James G. March, and Harald Saetren, Implementation and Ambiguity, *Scandinavian Journal of Management* 2 (1986), 197–212.
6. See above all Henry Mintzberg, *The Nature of Managerial Work*, New York 1973. No time for "general planning" – op. cit. 37.
7. See especially Michael D. Cohen, James G. March, and Johan P. Olsen, A Garbage Can Model of Organizational Choice, *Administrative Science Quarterly* 17 (1972), 1–25.
8. See especially Andrew H. van de Ven, Managing the Process of Organizational Innovation, in: Huber and Glick op. cit. 269–294.
9. See: *L'Entreprise á l'écoute: Apprendre le management post-industriel*, Paris 1989.
10. Apparently especially in Germany. See the article concerned with improving the exploitation of existing (?) motivation by Rüdiger Soltwedel, Im Dialog zum besseren Betriebsergebnis. Paradigmenwechsel in der Unternehmensführung: Die Mitarbeiter stärker in die Verantwortung nehmen, *Frankfurter Allgemeine* Zeitung No. 72, 25 March 1995, 13. This article shows how important it is for reformers to forget that such things have often been attempted in the past.
11. This can be compared with the rhetoric of proverbs. See Herbert A. Simon, The Proverbs of Administration, *Public Administration Review* 6 (1946), 53–67.

12. On this values paradox see also Karl E. Weick, Technology as Equivoque: Sensemaking in New Technologies, in: Paul S. Goodman and Lee S. Sproull et al., *Technology and Organizations*, San Francisco 1990, 1–44 (39), addressing the case of technological innovation.

13. See Gregory Bateson, *Ökologie des Geistes: Anthropologische, psychologische, biologische und epistemologische Untersuchungen*, German translation Frankfurt 1981, 156 ff. On the application for structural changes in organizations see also Robert E. Quinn, *Beyond Rational Management: Mastering the Paradoxes and Competing Demands of High Performance*, San Francisco 1989, 26 ff., 58 ff.

14. "By far the largest number of efforts fail," as we read in Charles Heckscher and Russell A. Eisenstat and Thomas A. Rice, Transformational Processes, in: Charles Heckscher and Anne Donnellon (eds.), *The Post-Bureaucratic Organization: New Perspectives on Organizational Change*, Thousand Oaks, CA 1994, 129–177 (132), with reference to debureaucratization efforts, and the few instances of success "have generally worked by splitting off into a new 'greenfield' organization rather than by transforming from within."

15. See Arthur L. Stinchcombe, Social Structure and Organizations, in: James G. March (ed.), *Handbook of Organizations*, Chicago 1965, 142–193.

16. " . . . to create or to utilize previously unrecognized empty social spaces," as we read in Philip G. Herbst, *Alternatives to Hierarchies*, Leiden 1976, 48. But what follows shows clearly that only formally unregulated fields are meant. The question is therefore whether there are any such empty spaces at all in the totality of social expectation structures and whether reform intentions do not draw attention to the fact that the space they are targeting is already occupied.

17. See Nicole Woolsey Biggart, The Creative-Destructive Process of Organizational Change: The Case of the Post Office, *Administrative Science Quarterly* 22 (1977), 410–426.

18. See G. Brennan and J.M. Buchannan, *The Reason of Rules*, Cambridge 1985.

19. For an example from the field of well-meaning, helpful organizations see Michael Patak and Ruth Simsa, Paradoxien in Nonprofit-Organisationen, *Managerie* 2 (1993), 242–249.

20. See Christopher Alexander, *Notes on the Synthesis of Form*, Cambridge, MA 1964. "Misfits" is an indefinable concept (p. 101).

21. On this discrepancy between intellectuals, professional reformers, and this for whom that take action, see Geert Hofstede, Humanization of Work: A Matter of Values (1979), quoted from idem., *Uncommon Sense About Organizations: Cases, Studies, and Field Observations*, Thousand Oaks, CA 1994, 37–50. See also G. Hespe and T. Wall, The Demand for Participation Among Employees, *Human Relations* 29 (1976), 411–428; as well as Crozier op. cit. (1989).

22. See Giovan Francesco Lanzara, *Capacità negativa: Competenza progettuale e modelli di intervento nelle organizzazioni*, Bologna 1993.

23. See G.L.S. Shackle, *Imagination and the Nature of Choice*, Edinburgh 1979, 74, 140.

24. Op. cit., 142. A similar view is to be found in Lanzara. op. cit., esp. 138. Instead of prepared plans being realized, situations arising from one's own action are continuously modified. Reforms therefore put a strain on the system with certain obligations to ensure consistency in new situations under unexpected circumstances.

25. See Herbst op. cit., 57 ff. following E. Thorsrud, Policy Making as a Learning Process, in: A.B. Cherns et al. (eds.), *Social Science and Government Policies and Problems*, London 1972. However, the concession of having to "learn" from reality is still completely geared to the ideas and mentalities of the reformers. It does not mean that resistance is accepted as well founded.

26. See for the example of American municipal administration reforms Pamela S. Tolbert and Lynne G. Zucker, Institutional Sources of Change in the Formal Structure of Organizations: The Diffusion of Civil Service Reform 1880–1935, *Administrative Science Quarterly* 28 (1983), 22–39. Reforms required by individual state laws differ from reforms prompted by problems in cities and from those in which latecomers follow a reform movement that is no longer problematic. The same is to be seen in the Italian cities of the Middle Ages, where the issue was to resolve disputes between noble families by engaging a city manager.

27. See Giancarlo Corsi, *Reform als Syndrom: Organisatorischer Wandel im deutschen Erziehungswesen 1965–1975*, Diss. Bielefeld 1995, Ms. 83.

28. This is shown not least by studies in organization from the private business sector and the public sector. See Nils Brunsson and Johan P. Olsen, *The Reforming Organization*, London 1993. Similar results are presented by Terry L. Amburgey and Dawn Kelly and William P. Barnett, Resetting the Clock: The Dynamics of Organizational Change and Failure, *Administrative Science Quarterly* 38 (1993), 51–73, who show that organizational changes either bring a risk of failure or provoke further changes. See also Lanzara op. cit. (1993), esp. 103 ff.

29. See Brunsson and Olsen op. cit., 41 f.

30. On the dependence of successful or unsuccessful reforms on the history of the organization, especially the age of the organization and any preceding changes, see also Amburgey et al. op. cit.(1993).

31. See Heinz von Foerster, Principles of Self-Organization – In a Socio-Managerial Context, in: Hans Ulrich and Gilbert J.B. Probst (eds.), *Self-Organization and Management of Social Systems: Insights, Promises, Doubts, and Questions*, Berlin 1984, 2–24.

32. See. e.g., Rainer Frericks, Peter Hauptmanns, and Josef Schmid, Die Funktion von Managementstrategien und – entscheidungen bei der Modernisierung des Produktionsapparats, *Zeitschrift für Soziologie* 22 (1993), 339–415. One then finds, however, again at the management level, a preference for relatively easily calculable reforms. Or one defines the problem in such a way that already known, tried, and trusted solutions to the problem fit – solutions that have, for example, been tried out elsewhere.

33. Van de Ven op. cit. (1993), 282.

34. Gerald E. Caiden, *Administrative Reform Comes of Age*, Berlin 1991, 42.

35. See Gilles Deleuze, *Logique du sens*, Paris 1969, esp. 9 ff.

36. Slightly corrected. Deleuze is concerned with growing/downsizing, which one could also apply directly to reforms that (probably like all reforms) seek to attain an increase in certain values.

37. See Niklas Luhmann and Karl Eberhard Schorr, Strukturelle Bedingungen von Reformpädagogik: Soziologische Analysen zur Pädagogik der Moderne, *Zeitschrift für Pädagogik* 14 (1988), 463–488. See also Ladislav Cerych and

Paul Sabatier, Great Expectations and Mixed Performance: The Implementation of Higher Education Reforms in Europe, *Stoke-on-Trent* 1986.

38. See Bericht der Studienkommission für die Reform des öffentlichen Dienstrechts, Baden-Baden 1973. See also Niklas Luhmann, *Reform des öffentlichen Dienstes: Ein Beispiel für Schwierigkeiten der Verwaltungsreform. Vorträge der Hessischen Hochschulwoche* vol. 76, Bad Homburg 1974, 23–39; reprinted in: Andreas Remer (ed.), *Verwaltungsführung*, Berlin 1982, 319–339.

39. One can only speculate about why this is so. One of the standpoints could have been that too much rationality built into decision-making processes had weakened the power that personnel decisions gave ministers.

40. See Chapter 7–6 above.

41. See Danny Miller and Peter H. Friesen, Innovation in Conservative and Entrepreneurial Firms: Two Models of Strategic Momentum, *Strategic Management Journal* 3 (1982), 1–15; Michael T. Hannan and John H. Freeman, Structural Inertia and Organizational Change, *American Sociological Review* 49 (1984), 149–164; and Danny Miller and Ming-Jer Chen, Sources and Consequences of Competitive Inertia: A Study of the US Airline Industry, *Administrative Science Quarterly* 39 (1994), 1–23.

42. See Odo Marquard, *Kompensation – Überlegungen zu einer Verlaufsfigur geschichtlicher Prozesse, reprinted in:* Odo Marquard, Aesthetica und Anaesthetica: Philosophische Überlegungen, Paderborn 1989, Anm. 11 (150 f.).

43. For a typical case study (a success story despite resistance) see Crozier op. cit. (1989), 133 ff.

44. See Kim S. Cameron, Sarah J. Freeman, and Aneil K. Mishra, *Downsizing and Redesigning Organizations*, in: Huber and Glick op. cit. (1993), 19–65.

45. See Matthew Hale, *A History of the Common Law (1713)*, 3rd revised ed. Chicago 1971.

46. Helmstedt 1643, German translation Frankfurt 1994

47. For the example of education-system organizations, see Karl E. Weick, Educational Organizations as Loosely Coupled Systems, *Administrative Science Quarterly* 21 (1976), 1–19.

48. There are also certain examples that go even beyond this. See Robert A. Burgelman, Strategy-Making and Organizational Ecology: A Conceptual Integration, in: Jitendra V. Singh (ed.), *Organizational Evolution: New Directions*, Newbury Park, CA 1990, 165–181, who even sees strategic management of an organization as subject to intraorganizational ("ecological") evolution.

49. See Richard R. Nelson and Sidney G. Winter, *An Evolutionary Theory of Economic Change*, Cambridge, MA 1982; Michael T. Hannan and John Freeman, *Organizational Ecology*, Cambridge, MA 1989; Singh op. cit. 21142; Joel Baum and Jitendra Singh (eds.), *Evolutionary Dynamics of Organizations*, New York 1994, as well as far-reaching studies published in journals.

50. Within economics, evolution theories live by polemics against neoclassical theories that rely on the rationality of balances. See, e.g., Richard W. England (ed.), *Evolutionary Concepts in Contemporary Economics*, Ann Arbor, MI 1994.

51. Too much so, as biologists are now convinced. See Jean-Baptiste Pierre Antoine de Monet de Lamarck, *Philosophie zoologique*, Paris 1809, reprinted Weinheim 1960. On irritability as the most general property of all organisms esp. vol. 1, 82 ff. On the

revival of discussion on Lamarck in systems theory see no. 5 (1993) of the Revue internationale de systemique.

52. See Richard M. Cyert and James G. March, *A Behavioral Theory of the Firm*, Englewood Cliffs, NJ 1963, e.g., 36 ff., 2nd ed. Cambridge, MA 1992, 41 ff.; Curtis L. Mann and James C. March, Financial Adversity, Internal Competition, and Curriculum Change in a University, *Administrative Science Quarterly* 23 (1978), 541–552.

53. See Louis R. Pondy, Richard J. Boland Jr., and Howard Thomas (eds.), *Managing Ambiguity and Change*, Chichester 1988.

54. See Karl E. Weick, Re-Punctuating the Problem, in: Paul S. Goodman and Johannes M. Pennings (eds.), *New Perspectives on Organizational Effectiveness*, San Francisco 1977, 193–225.

55. See Thomas Dietz, Tom R. Burns, and Frederick H. Buttel, Evolutionary Theory in Sociology: An Examination of Current Thinking, *Sociological Forum* 5 (1990), 155–171 (164). See also Tom R. Burns and Thomas Dietz, Cultural Evolution: Social Rule Systems, Selection and Human Agency, *International Sociology* 7 (1992), 259–283 (263 ff.).

56. See Hannan and Freeman op. cit. (1989), 66 ff. See also idem, Structural Inertia and Organizational Change, *American Sociological Review* 49 (1984), 149–164; idem, The Population Ecology of Organizations, *American Journal of Sociology* 82 (1977), 929–964. See also W. Graham Astley and Andrew Van de Ven, Central Perspectives and Debates in Organization Theory, *Administrative Science Quarterly* 28 (1983), 245–273; Lawrence G. Hrebiniak and William F. Joyce, Organizational Adaptation: Strategic Choice and Environmental Determinism, *Administrative Science Quarterly* 30 (1985), 336–349; Jitendra V. Singh, Robert J. House, and David J. Tucker, Organizational Change and Organizational Mortality, *Administrative Science Quarterly* 31 (1986), 587–611; Jacques Delacroix and Anand Swaminthan, Cosmetic, Speculative and Adaptive Organizational Change in the Wine Industry: A Longitudinal Study, *Administrative Science Quarterly* 36 (1991), 631–661. Further references under "inertia" (See n41 above). Something else may well hold true, namely chances for planned changes, if the impetus comes from drastic changes in the environment; then it is not a matter of reform but of conservation if not survival. Given the changes in the economy (globalization, stronger competition) in the 1990s, these conditions appear to apply for many business organizations. For such a case see Heather A. Haverman, Between a Rock and a Hard Place: Organizational Change under Conditions of Fundamental Environmental Transformation, *Administrative Science Quarterly* 37 (1992), 48–75.

57. See Luca Cavalli-Sforza and Marcus Feldman, *Cultural Transmission and Evolution*, Princeton 1981; Robert Boyd and Peter J. Richerson, *Culture and the Evolutionary Process*, Chicago 1985, and specifically for organizational "routines" see Nelson and Winter op. cit. (1982) or Sidney G. Winter, Survival, Selection, and Inheritance in Evolutionary Theories of Organization, in Singh op. cit (1990), 269–297. See also J. Richard Harrison and Glen E. Carroll, Keeping the Faith: A Model of Cultural Transmission in Formal Organizations, *Administrative Science Quarterly* 36 (1991), 552–582.

58. Following Donald T. Campbell, Variation and Selective Retention in Socio-Cultural Evolution, *General Systems* 14 (1969), 69–85, the term "blind" variation is often

used. Donald T. Campbell, Unjustified Variation and Selective Retention in Scientific Discovery, in: Francisco Ayala and Theodosius Dobzhansky (eds.), *Studies in the Philosophy of Biology*, New York 1974, 139–161, later corrected through "unjustified" variation. Both remain imprecise. For variation can very well be observed and be understandable and acceptable as individual event. With Weick op. cit. (1977) we can also stress that variation itself has to be stable enough to await selection. Descriptions such as "blind" or "unjustified" do not necessarily apply to variation but to the lack of coordination (or chance interlocking) of individual evolutionary functions.

59. Another version of this dependence of variation and selection on chance in stabilization is to be found in remarks that firms whose decisions have been crowned with success have been lucky. See Daniel A. Levinthal, Organizational Adaptation, Environmental Selection, and Random Walks, in: Singh op. cit. (1990), 201–223 (212).

60. For the case of the societal system, see Niklas Luhmann, *Die Gesellschaft der Gesellschaft*, Frankfurt am Main 1997, 451 ff.; Engl. translation Rhodes Barrett, *Theory of Society*, Stanford 2013.

61. See James G. March, Footnotes to Organizational Change, *Administrative Science Quarterly* 26 (1981), 563–577; Daniel A. Levinthal, Organizational Adaptation and Environmental Selection: Interrelated Processes of Change, *Organization Science* 2 (1991), 140–145.

62. See Hannan and Freeman op. cit. (1989), 21 ff.

63. An example for abrupt environmental changes are radical innovations in the field of economically utilizable technology. See Michael L. Tushman and Philip Anderson, Technological Discontinuities and Organizational Environments, *Administrative Science Quarterly* 31 (1986), 439–465; Philip Anderson and Michael L. Tushman, Technological Discontinuities and Dominant Designs: A Cyclical Model of Technological Change, *Administrative Science Quarterly* 35 (1990), 604–633. One could similarly think of far-reaching political changes, globalization of markets, changing customer demands, or the rise of technically competitive low-wage countries.

64. See Bill McKelvey and Howard Aldrich, Populations, Natural Selection, and Applied Science, *Administrative Science Quarterly* 28 (1983), 101–128.

65. See, E.D. Cope, *The Primary Factors of Organic Evolution*, Chicago 1896, S. 172 ff.; Elman R. Service, The Law of Evolutionary Potential, in: Marshall D. Sahlins and Elman R. Service (eds.), *Evolution and Culture*, Ann Arbor, MI 1960, 93 ff. It is now undisputed that "Cope's rule" does not apply unconditionally. There are also evolutionary specifications that serve to develop greater complexity. See, e.g., G. Ledyard Stebbin, *The Basis of Progressive Evolution*, Chapel Hill, NC 1969, esp. 120 ff. But very rare evolutionary inventions are involved, whereas normal evolution operates with the development and destruction of systems. The system type organization with its potential for evolution is itself likely to be such an evolutionary invention. But it is more likely to be a matter of the emergence of a new form of autopoiesis and not of the normal learning/forgetting of structures in organizations we are looking at in the present context.

66. See, e.g., Weick op. cit. (1977), 199 ff.

67. See, e.g., Miller and Friesen op. cit., (1994).

68. See Karl E. Weick, Organizational Redesign as Improvisation, in: George T. Huber and William H. Glick (eds.), *Organizational Change and Redesign: Ideas and Insights for Improving Performance*, Oxford 1993, 346–379 (359).

69. Somewhat drastically, Weick op. cit. (1977), 207 ff. calls this "hypocrisy." In practice, however, it will frequently prove almost impossible to ascertain whether communication deceives itself or others.

70. See Yves Barel, *Le paradoxe et le système: Essai sur le fantastique social*, 2nd ed. Grenoble 1989, 71 f.

71. Barel op. cit. 282.

72. See Alan D. Meyer et al., Organizations Reacting to Hyperturbulence, in: George P. Huber and William H. Glick (eds.), *Organizational Change and Redesign: Ideas and Insights for Improving Performance*, Oxford 1993, 66–111.

73. See p. 344 above.

74. See Karl E. Weick, Organizational Redesign as Improvisation, in: Huber and Glick op. cit., 346–379 (369 f.).

12 Technology

I

Organization is certainly a form of social cooperation, but it could nevertheless be considered closely akin to technology. We speak of organizational technology. We now leave much of what used to be done through social interaction to computers. They can do the job just as well if not better. Classical organizational sociology also appears to have had this parallel in mind when it described the organization as an apparatus of power or even as a machine that performs set tasks. The analogy rests on the assumption that organizations can fairly reliably repeat the same work processes, and that if something does not work, the defect can be looked for and found.

Max Weber and "Taylorist" work organization had operated with such notions, pointing to the need for a general theory of organization. A political ruler, it was claimed, relied on an administrative staff programmed through rules that spared him from having to make decisions in individual cases and, nevertheless, ensured that such decisions were consistently made in accordance with the rules. Taylorist work organization sets itself the task of breaking down the working process to allow the best combination of steps in that process to be worked out. Both forms of organization could be framed by an end/means schema to ensure that the ends could be met reliably and at predictable cost. If this did not happen, the machine had to be repaired or parts had to be replaced by functionally equivalent elements.

As a result of its own empirical research, however, organizational sociology has gradually distanced itself these notions without quite abandoning them at the management theory level. A first step in this direction was the theory of "socio-technical systems."[1] It had developed in parallel to interest in "informal organization" and "human relations," and its aim had been to determine the links between technology, work organization, and social relations in the workplace in order to establish a scientific basis for efforts to "democratize" and "humanize" the working world. This was an advance over older studies of technology-driven work processes[2] because it differentiated and linked up different areas of the system, introducing difference-oriented systematization.

The connections between technology and organization did not permit the one to be introduced without taking account of the other. It was implicitly presupposed that changes in technology were neither frequent nor rapid.

Further developments pointed to a stronger interest in the problems of managing technological innovations and their implementation in a smoothly running organization of work. This may have been prompted by technological developments themselves (such as computer technology or jet propulsion in aviation) and by other market requirements (for instance, more strongly differentiated products, or such with small production runs or even made to order[3]), but also by experience with resistance to the introduction of innovations.[4] The focus of research thus shifted from systematic contexts to perspectives for planning changes. This shows once again that technical innovations cannot be understood as the application of scientific knowledge available to all and sundry but that "implicit," firm-specific if not product-specific knowledge plays a role, knowledge that emerges when needed.[5] At the slogan level we find the "humanization of work" being replaced by "socially compatible technology design." "Socially compatible/responsible" appears to amount to decentralization and user participation in the planning, introduction, and recurrent modification of the system.

A current manifestation of the old concept of socio-technical systems could be the insight that introducing new devices or technologies has structural consequences for a given system.[6] This is still called "contingency theory" (even though such a trivial insight hardly deserves the title of theory).[7] Whether planned in advance or not, the new couplings bind other work processes, and this means that old habits have to be jettisoned and new ones developed. In Giddens' terminology, such a process intervenes in the mutual determination of structures and actions; but it does not necessarily decide which structures are to be forgotten and what new ones have to be formed; for this is likely to depend not least on the historical particularity of the systems in question.

The identity of the term "technology," defined as the fixed coupling of causal elements, cannot hide the fact that widely ranging matters are involved in how it impacts organizations. Above all, the operational basis for realizing a technology has to be identified; in other words, the operations that have to be coupled: physical, chemical, biological, or social. Technical apparatus is accordingly a factor of the environment of the communication system or a form with which communication itself limits acceptable connections. And the organization accordingly has to deal with the problem of adapting to apparatus if failure is to be avoided, or handle restrictive expectations very easy to deviate from. Technicizing communication itself thus requires error control, supervision, and social sanctions.

Furthermore, a distinction can be made between whether innovation is prompted primarily by science or inventions in the technology itself, as with the internal combustion engine or in electronics, or whether it is rooted in or has to do with organizational advantages, as with container transport. This is intersected by the distinction between whether innovation renders old knowledge and old forms of organization obsolete or whether it gradually improves and refines the initial invention, in either product type or production process.[8] Depending on how radical the break is, management will have to adapt, or opportunities will emerge for starting up new firms. Large organizations are more likely to have the necessary resources for introducing improvements while small firms set up to exploit technological innovations will have a better chance of realizing such innovations. However the line of intersection might run, it is at any rate a clear argument against the notion of organizational forms being determined by technology. A distinction has at least to be drawn in terms of the sort of break with old habits required. Container transport revolutionized shipbuilding, the organization of shipping and ports, including the associated transport systems. But the changes had to be made within the context of existing shipyards, shipping companies, and port organizations. In the automotive industry, the invention of the automobile gave ample opportunity to set up new companies; only later as the product was improved and manufacturing rationalized did the number of enterprises on the market decline, leaving only a few big companies and a trend toward further shrinkage to only a few enterprises offering mobility as a service. In the case of telephone networks, both possibilities were tried out side by side from the very outset in both the United States and Europe.

While discussion on the "socio-technical" approach has subsided, the impact of technology at all levels of the organization has increased, namely through the use of computers. This development has clearly changed communication channels and decision-making competencies. At least in the field of automation, the notion that social systems are determined by technology had to be abandoned; the use and organizational embedding of the use of the computer in office and production had to be understood as a matter of more or less risky, more or less successful decisions[9] that offered greater or lesser justification for introducing changes on the basis of experience.[10] Moreover, it is questionable whether the optimum use of new technology can be a goal in itself. In the first place, it is only a matter of a shift in the means and ends typical of the organization. The question is, therefore, what general notions are to guide the introduction of computerized information production in organizations: more controllable information processing (also to monitor the day-by-day performance of employees?) or uncertainty absorption?

The mechanical engineering of the nineteenth and twentieth centuries had understood the human body as energy = work. Its peculiar humanity had been to save energy and gain time, to save labor and accelerate the transport of things and bodies. In the second half of the nineteenth century, this had led to the mass production of goods and the development of correspondingly big organizations. It was a question of tangible machines and tangible products. The computer realizes a completely different concept. Here we have to do with an invisible machine that can transform itself into another machine from one moment to the next in the course of utilization. Its switching processes are invisible, its speed of operation requires clear coupling; but results are accessible only via commands that render selected aspects of machine states visible. Inquiries permit unambiguity to be transformed back into ambiguity (purposefulness) of the use context. But the relation of surface (monitor, printout) to depth will change the possibility of problem presentation and argument. The time problem no longer lies in speeding up work processes (although this is still being worked on) but in the sequence of inquiries. Saving body energy reaches a point where, with extremely reduced use of the senses and bodily movement, it becomes dysfunctional. What is gained is the almost unlimited technicization of work processes. Developments seem to be moving from more peripheral areas toward key questions of organized decision making, but technology itself offers no concept for this. How much loose coupling, how much dependence on chance can be saved? And how can the impacts of failures be prevented from cascading? Through redundant parallel arrangements, thus through technical precautions against problems entailed by technology alone?

This is not the place to engage in this discussion with detailed analysis. But one more problem needs to be mentioned. Computer technology leads to the spatial fixing of work, not only at the level of the machine production of material goods but also at all levels of management. This is not to say that planned conferences or other face-to-face interaction are excluded. Inquiry facilities can be installed in conference rooms or printouts can be brought along. But little attention is given to the question of whether chance contacts among people circulating in space are not reduced.[11] Will this lead to a clearer dividing line between work and socializing? And what are the consequences if this deprives the organization of an important source of chance stimulus?

Other sorts of problem arise when technical couplings become more complex, that is to say, come to consist of many, diverse elements that make varying demands on time. Time then becomes scarce, especially time for reacting to surprises. For from the temporal point of view, the tight coupling of technologically determined operations means immediate coupling. The system then has to reckon with malfunctions without having enough time in reserve to detect and correct them.[12] The problem occurs independently of the magnitude of the damage or loss that such malfunctions can cause; but it becomes particularly serious in the field of high-risk technologies, where disasters can and have already occurred.[13]

At issue, against the political backdrop of such technology being banned, was to find some sort of encasement that would ensure that nothing happens and that, if disaster nevertheless threatens, the threat is registered and defused in time. In extremely threatening and unclear situations where highly urgent decisions have to be made, otherwise functioning divisions between systems can tend to collapse. For comprehensible neurobiological reasons, emotions mount and mental control of perception is reduced, making the situation even more complex than it already is.[14] How others will react can no longer be foreseen, and there is no time to find agreement on how to define the situation. Such desiderata as humanization or social compatibility are completely out of place. Quite the opposite is required: safety technology must not be adapted to human beings with their weaknesses. It has to work with complete reliability, even more reliably than the risky core technology that is to be prevented from getting out of control. The malfunctions involved will be unexpected and very rare; but because this is so, the organization has to work reliably. It would therefore have to be more strongly technological in operation than the technology itself.

One problem clearly lies in the relation of controlling authorities to operational units.[15] From a technical point of view, the computer offers the possibility of providing for both greater centralization and greater decentralization; indeed, even give ground for calling the sense of this distinction into question. But this does not mean that such possibilities can be realized in existing, still hierarchical organizations. The more elaborate control requirements become, the more attractive labor-saving circumventions, informal understandings, and restrictions on the flow of information will appear. Control is probably never realized to the degree that is technically possible,[16] and the possibilities for socially acceptable follow-up measures would probably also be lacking. It is at any rate a negotiable, if not power-political issue.

Another problem is how to deal on the spot with poorly defined problems. The causes of an emerging disaster cannot be discerned clearly enough and, above all, not fast enough. Moreover, the implications of small problems are not always apparent, since they are likely to give rise to disasters only under rare and complex ("chance") secondary conditions. Although post-disaster inquiries may well pinpoint causes, this transforms a poorly defined problem into a clearly defined problem, whereas the typical and recurring difficulty had been precisely in the relation between lack of clarity and workload, thus in the economy of attention, or in the unrecognized misinterpretation of communication or other signals.[17,18]

To be essentially distinguished from risky technologies are so-called large technical systems (LTSs) – transport systems, power supply, telecommunications, extensively networked information provision – which provide the technical infrastructure for a wide range of other systems. In such systems, the risk of partial failure can be cushioned by redundant capacities, and only blackouts of considerable magnitude make themselves felt. The overall impression is that malfunctions caused by technology itself are on the increase without the system being capable of switching to manual operation or coordinating orally. More than in the past, the organization now needs the competence to ride out situational difficulties; but where is this competence to come from if everything is geared to computers and the capacity to intervene at other points in the system is lacking?[19] The core technology may well be relatively simple, but its connections and resulting dependencies make the overall context confusingly complex – all the more so because it cannot be controlled by a single (however vast) organizational system. Since dependencies are highly complex and access has to be safeguarded, a sort of political responsibility for such systems is difficult to avoid, even though organizational problems differ strongly from those that are typically handled by public administration. Hybrid structures have thus developed, which dissolve the strict separation of public and private and, regardless of their technological infrastructure, have in recent years attracted a great deal of attention also as social systems.[20] Where the basic product of an organization is highly uniform (energy, mobility, information), it will have to obey technological imperatives far more strongly than otherwise. It consequently does not make much sense to construct an umbrella concept for service organizations that also cover social work, therapy, education, and the like.

In the light of such heterogeneous demands on technology in general, research approaches have become more complex in the course of this development. The literature on management is now too vast for comfort. Research on safety engineering has not produced satisfying findings but rather disquieting results; there is even talk of "normal" disasters that have be reckoned with.[21] But concern about the disasters caused by technology that the mass media daily report conceal a much more profound problem, namely the irreversible dependence of society on technology and thus on the technically possible production of energy. It is therefore high time to re-examine the foundations for theory. What do we wish to understand by "technology"?

II

Technology can be very formally defined as the tight coupling of causal elements, no matter what the material basis for this coupling.[22] The concept includes human conduct insofar as it takes place automatically and is not interrupted by decisions. For example, the development of unproblematic readability (to be distinguished from textual comprehension) is part of the technology of the printing press and was developed as its correlate. The same can be said of the ability to drive a car (again: to be distinguished from decisions on direction or conduct in critical situations), and of other cases of machine operation. The range covered by technology cannot therefore be construed from the "materiality" of the coupled operations. In other words,[23] technology can form functioning networks from quite heterogeneous elements as long as tight coupling succeeds. Technicization includes human perception and motoricity, and precisely this is the problem – not (to take the example of reading) because it is somehow non-human, but because it raises the problem of whether, when, and how one sees alternatives in the technicized process and consequently assumes responsibility for decisions.

Where technical coupling can be set up, a given cause (or a given complex of causes) A is always followed by an effect B: or a given item of information A (e.g., an advertisement or an application to a public authority) is always followed by a decision B.[24] The reliability of such coupling can always be treated as a variable; we then have to do with various degrees of the process technicization. However, here, too, we would start from the boundary concept of non-variable tight coupling.

We can speak of tight coupling in both mechanical and electronic machines, and in so-called "software technologies" – for instance, timetables, airline reservation systems, or merchandise price marking. A typical advantage of such technologies is their very specific and rapid adjustment to unpredictable customer demands. It always has to do with tying down resources that can then no longer be transferred or only at great effort and cost. The advantages are thus not only in the length of the chain that can still be controlled by initial impulse. They lie also in network-like relationization with optional access to connections chosen ad hoc, where one cannot simply assume without further checks whether they are practicable in the system.

The concept of tight coupling clearly shows the advantages of a technical arrangement. Tight coupling enables considerable simplification in dealing with technology. Within the computer, in its "invisible machine," it enables a speed of operation beyond the grasp and control of the mind. Above all, technology reduces the need for consensus. That it works can itself be taken for granted, and taken for granted in such a way that others can be assumed to take it for granted, as well.[25] It makes artificial objects available, which also serve as a substitute for consensus. Technology divides consensus issues into problems of ends and problems of means, thus enabling relational rationalization that seeks to establish a favorable (possibly "optimal") relation between ends and means. Advantages are also to be found in practical application: to start a technical process, one need only know what sets it off.[26] To use technology, one does not even need to know the theories required for a scientific understanding and explanation of technical processes.[27] This characteristic of technology offers organizations considerable advantages. Operation can be left to semi-skilled personnel, professional competence being reserved for questions of constructing technical processes or diagnosing malfunctions.

Another advantage of technical processes is that the resources they require can be calculated. This also means that the dependence of technology on environmental resources can be determined. Energy requirements depend on the extent to which the technology is utilized. This includes human work performance insofar as it is itself technicized or required as annex to technical processes.[28]

Finally, a technical substratum makes it possible to detect irregularities. Malfunctions literally attract attention automatically, and, albeit with more effort in diagnosis and knowledge, one can discover how to eliminate them. This has to do with the fact that technology facilitates learning. Frequent malfunctions allow vulnerable elements to be identified and defined as problems, and better solutions to be sought. What is more, technology makes its own conditions for utilization transparent. What problem it was designed to solve is known or can be determined, and on this basis functional equivalents can sought. This also works the other way round: one knows the process and in one way or another can look for the problem it can solve, and which could be rethought.

In sum, these various advantages of technology constitute the condition of the possibility for forming hierarchies. Work processes, such as teaching in school and preaching in church, which cannot be technicized, also resist hierarchical supervision, calculated resource allocation, and learning in the system of the organization.[29] They oblige the organization to outsource the conditions for its success to face-to-face interaction, and leave their fulfillment to events supervision cannot follow. This does not exclude such interaction being influenced through resource allocation – when, for example, the educational system allots more time to certain subjects.[30] But it is practically impossible to foresee the effect of differences in allocation on differences in operational results. The battle for resources is therefore always a struggle for the symbolic recognition of the importance of the recipient organizations. The hierarchy can react only to social noises, to complaints and protests, and it can perform its supervisory function at best in more or less ceremonial forms (inspection, visits, circulars).

This shows how strongly classical organization research has focused on the relation between a core technology and rational hierarchical control. If "informal organization" was also taken into account or the environment included through the question of resource dependence, this did not mean the basis conception was abandoned; it was merely modified. There is, indeed, a significant link between core technology and hierarchy formation. So the classical theory is by no means disproved. But it throws light only on a subphenomenon and does not convey an adequate idea of how an organization reproduces itself as system.

The use of causal technologies does not necessarily mean that the system as a whole or at the top is fully aware of what is going on within it or can at least ascertain what state it is in. The more complex technical couplings and variability in the temporal use of factors become, the less this can be said. The theorem of self-generated uncertainty then comes to bear. In virtually geometrical progression, uncertainty increases, especially under the impression of unforeseen surprises, malfunctions, or opportunities. The simple means of tight coupling and hierarchy are then, so to speak, exhausted, and the system has to react ad hoc, fast, competently, and professionally.

Continuing to reproduce under complex conditions requires loose coupling.[31] This is true for the relation between motives (intentions) and performance and between decision premises and decisions. The need to take uncertainty absorption into account in linking decisions also points to (more or less) loose coupling. All tight and therefore vulnerable coupling of core technologies and all hierarchical concentration and control based on such coupling must therefore be embedded in a system that is based on other, more robust conditions for reproduction. Where technology does work, it works reliably, but reliability should not be confused with robustness. It is based on a high degree of indifference, but for this very reason is risky. Conditions shift on the other side of the form "technology." Technology can register malfunctions if they occur within itself. It can react by repairs or by substitute performance. But tight coupling also means that diagnosis and learning requirements are limited. What is an advantage in the sense of a condition for specific reactions to occur is a disadvantage if the problem cannot be resolved by replacement or repair. Meticulous and detailed accounts usually provide no information on how to help an enterprise in difficulty.

Organizations that technicize work processes will accordingly have to provide for tight and loose couplings side by side and in conjunction. This can rightly be seen as a paradoxical requirement.[32] At the same time, this distinction, if its unity is dissolved in the sense of the asserted difference, also points the way to resolving the paradox through decisions about concrete problems. One can decide in favor of a technology and then, looking at the problems it entails, be better able to discover the network of loose couplings in which it has to be embedded. For there are always two sides to a paradox. They reveal themselves when one pays attention to the unity of a distinction; but they also give widely ranging indications about deparadoxization in practice, depending on the type of distinction at issue.

This strict concept of technology raises doubts about the extent to which the automation of processes in offices and factories can be understood as "new technology." Computers themselves are, of course, technical in conception. They have to work reliably. They cannot be allowed to be temperamental. They generate copious new information and combinatorial evaluations of information about their given area of operations, including, if hierarchical supervision is maintained, new possibilities for supervising and monitoring work.[33] In the not too distant future, cars can be expected to tell their drivers how they are misbehaving. Computers thus expand the memory performance of the system – also for non-automatic follow-up decisions. They generate new possibilities for seeing alternatives. They lead to new self-descriptions of the system with unpredictable (needing a decision) connectivity options. "Il sistema sembra autoricognoscersi," according to Butera[34] with reference to Maturana und Varela's theory of autopoietic organisms. The conclusion can only be that the automation of decisions at the operational level leads to more decisions having to be made at other levels. In the work process, less manual skill is required and more attention – which should not too hastily be interpreted as higher qualifications with a claim to better pay.

From the technology perspective, too, it is accordingly appropriate if not necessary to see organizations no longer as relations between more or less disciplined people but as the transformation of decisions into decisions under the conditions of autopoietic closure.

III

Technical systems can be described as allopoietic systems, which are exogenously controlled and which cease to operate when impulses cease. But they are obviously constructed to reduce the workload of autopoietic systems, if not to replace them. Since the invention of the computer, these possibilities of providing relief and substitution have multiplied, and in many organizations computers are now so integrated that their failure would cause serious disruption if not irreparable losses.

There are many facets to the consequent problems whose presentation would require specific studies. Provision has to be made for risks, redundancies have to be built in, backup has to be ensured, all at a cost that far exceeds the price of the computers themselves and their programs. Another problem has hitherto attracted little attention or been relegated to the background by well-established assumptions. The question is what autopoietic systems are actually replaced by the computer and superseded in the workplace.

As the example of artificial intelligence shows, studies of this sort usually set out from human consciousness, which is defined in terms of cognitive competence, ratio, intelligence, or similar traditional concepts.[35] What tradition saw as distinguishing humans from animals is now and for the future to distinguish them from electronic machines. This at any rate is the hope of humanists – the vanishing point at which they hope to free the "human being" from the embrace of technology. At this point we could already consider whether the particularity of human consciousness, which the computer is likely to have difficulty attaining, does not lie in perception, and – in contrast to animals – in perception that is strongly language-dependent, directed and differentiated by language.

Be that as it may, a quite different question that arises is the relation between electronic data processing and communication. As the euphoria about artificial intelligence reaches its limits, the problem of substitution and improvement in relations between computer and communication appears to be shifting. For communication takes place under the conditions of mutual intransparency, which includes the intransparency of systems for themselves. One does not know a great deal about oneself or others, and so one talks, writes, prints, and transmits. For the computer, the operational and structural inaccessibility of what has been developed so far in the history of "human beings" is therefore likely to be due to the specific nature of social systems and not to the particularity of psychic systems. Humanists would then take refuge not in the consciousness or subjectness of the human being but in the autopoiesis of communication, or, to put it in terms more to their taste, in culture.

Computer systems can naturally be networked with one another and exchange the results of their work in the form of data. But precisely this is not the real achievement of communication. Communication produces a synthesis of information, utterance, and understanding on the basis of constructing a meaning that suppresses uncertainty, whose lack of grounding in physical, chemical, and organic realities can be compensated by the fact that every communication, if understood, can be answered in the affirmative or negative, and thus accepted or rejected in accordance with the means of persuasion that can be activated in the social system itself.[36]

This is also likely to be the case for organizations. However, the problems caused by making communication in organizations dependent on electronic data processing are all the more a matter of concern. And here we face the general problem that society is making itself dependent on technology even in the simplest of operations, and therefore has to ensure the permanent, efficient functioning of technical devices with their tight couplings.

IV

Modern society, more than any society before, is dependent on technology.[37] Malfunctions can have consequences that can spread like an avalanche. If energy supplies and thus technology were to fail, this would cost most people their lives; it would accordingly not only affect societal communication but also have a massive impact on its environment: people would no longer talk, they would die. And the problem is by no means one of sensational one-off disasters alone, however many deaths they might cause, but also a problem of keeping things running at a normal level. Quite concretely and specifically this means the problem of energy supply.

The extent of technology dependence, which no one sought and which has come about through evolution, makes it understandable how much hope is, at least implicitly, placed on organization. This includes monitoring and controlling all core technologies, but also supplementing them by secondary technologies in the organization of human work through conditional programming. It also includes reducing the probability of disasters to rare exceptions, and to finding alternatives in the event of failures (e.g., in the supply of oil) in good time or at least fast enough. But is this hope justified?

The question is certainly too simplistic. It cannot be answered by a yes or a no. Our analysis of organizations as autopoietic systems of a particular type raises certain doubts. It poses the question whether modern society has not maneuvered itself into a double dependency, on technology and on organization, without being in a position to control the one with the aid of the other. Who then is in control? What organization?

Questions of this ilk belong in a theory of society; we can do no more than touch on them here. A sociology of technology would have to address the question of how many tight couplings a society can afford. This is a problem of smooth running at high risk, which is not only, not even primarily, a problem of disasters triggered by technology but above all one of maintaining the supply of energy, which has in turn to be technically produced. Organizational sociology, by contrast, would have a useful theory of organized social systems to offer a theory of society. This is the key issue of how the classical link between core technology and hierarchical control can be built into a more comprehensive concept of organization. For this purpose, it is not enough to supplement formal aspects by informal ones or to address the organization/machine analogy in terms of the organization/organism analogy.[38] An organization is neither a trivial machine nor is it an organism. Unlike a technical system, it cannot tightly couple the totality of its operations. It is an autopoietic system of a specific type – a self-referential system, intransparent to itself and therefore also an unreliable but robust system that establishes itself in society without serving it. The concluding question must therefore be how a societal system can evolve that affords itself organizations, that is indeed dependent on them in almost[39] all functional systems, but that cannot control them – except through organizations.

Technology and organization thus have at least one thing in common: they depend on themselves in fatal loops and are therefore unable to control their own evolution. Technology generates an energy supply problem that can be solved only by technology. The organization generates a control problem that can be solved only by organization. The social system of society provides the framework conditions for this evolution, the explosive mixture of order and chance on which all evolution depends in society. But society can react to what happens only at the level of technical developments and at the level of organization.

Notes

1. The landmark publication was E. L. Trist and K. W. Bramforth, Social and Psychological Consequences of the Longwall Method of Coal-Getting, *Human Relations* 4 (1951), 3–38. It was concerned with the social consequences of reorganizing work in coal mining. See also Charles R. Walker and Robert H. Guest, *The Man on the Assembly Line*, Cambridge, MA 1952. For an elaborated version of the theory of socio-technical systems see Joan Woodward, *Management and Technology*, London 1958; idem, *Industrial Organization: Theory and Practice*, London 1965; also P. G. Herbst, *Socio-technical Design: Strategies in Multidisciplinary Research*, London 1974. For a critical treatment (little link between technology and social structure) see David J. Hickson, D. S. Pugh, and Diana C. Pheysey, Operations Technology and Organization Structure: An Empirical Reappraisal, *Administrative Science Quarterly* 14 (1969), 378–397; Lawrence B. Mohr, Organizational Technology and Organizational Structure, *Administrative Science Quarterly* 16 (1971), 444–459; John Child and Roger Mansfield, Technology, Size, and Organization Structure, *Sociology* 6 (1972), 369–393. For a retrospective appreciation see Howard E. Aldrich, Technology and Organizational Structure: A Reexamination of the Finding of the Aston Group, in: Amitai Etzioni and E. W. Lehman (eds.), *A Sociological Reader on Complex Organizations*, New York 1980, 233–250.

2. See, e.g., Fred W. Cottrell, *The Railroader*, Stanford, CA 1940.

3. This development invites re-examination of older studies on links between technologically imposed mass production and organizational structures (e.g., Pradip N. Khandwalla, Mass Output Orientation of Operations Technology and Organizational Structure, *Administrative Science Quarterly* 19 (1974), 74–97)

4. See, e.g., Hartmut Hirsch-Kreinsen and Harald Wolf, Neue Produktionstechniken und Arbeitsorganisation: Interessen und Strategien betrieblicher Akteure, *Soziale Welt* 38 (1987), 181–196; Gert Schmidt, Die "Neuen Technologien" – Herausforderung für ein verändertes Technikverständnis der Industriesoziologie, in: Peter Weingart (ed.), *Technik als sozialer Prozeß*, Frankfurt 1989, 231–255; Ray Loveridge and Martyn Pitt (eds.), *The Strategic Management of Technological Innovation*, Somerset, NJ 1990; Michael Behr, Martin Heidenreich, Gert Schmidt, and Hans-Alexander Graf von Schwerin, *Neue Technologien in der Industrieverwaltung: Optionen veränderten Arbeitskräfteeinsatzes*, Opladen 1991; Rainer Frericks, Peter Hauptmanns, and Josef Schmid, Die Funktion von Managementstrategien und -entscheidungen bei der Modernisierung des Produktionsapparats (Apparats!, N.L.), *Zeitschrift für Soziologie* 22 (1993), 399–415.

5. See Michael Gibbons and John S. Metcalfe, Technology, Variety and Competition, in: Ilya Prigogine and Michèle Sanglier (eds.), *Laws of Nature and Human Conduct*,

Brüssels 1987, 253–266, with the consequence that technological innovations can both increase and reduce variety in the economic system in the connection with competition.

6. Using the term "structuration" (Anthony Giddens), Stephen R. Barley, Technology as an Occasion for Structuring: Evidence from Observations or CT Scanners and the Social Order of Radiology Departments, *Administrative Science Quarterly* 31 (1986), 78–108.

7. For an up-to-date overview and defense of the concept against critics, see W. Richard Scott, Technology and Structure: An Organizational Level Approach, in: Paul S. Goodman, Lee S. Sproull et al., *Technology and Organizations*, San Francisco 1990, 109–143.

8. On this distinction between competence destroying and competence enhancing technological breakthroughs see Michael L. Tushman and Philip Anderson, Technological Discontinuities and Organizational Environments, *Administrative Science Quarterly* 31 (1986), 439–465. For an evolution theory of technological developments (variation/selection/retention) see Philip Anderson and Michael L. Tushman, Technological Discontinuities and Dominant Designs: A Cyclical Model of Technological Change, *Administrative Science Quarterly* 35 (1990), 604–633.

9. To this extent, the original "socio-technical" approach of the Tavistock Institute is confirmed, indeed expanded, now no longer addressing only human relations but also functioning work organization per se. See, e.g., Arndt Sorge and Wolfgang Streeck, Industrial Relations and Technical Change: The Case for an Extended Perspective, in: Richard Hyman and Wolfgang Streeck (eds.), *New Technology and Industrial Relations*, Oxford 1988, 19–47 (23 ff.). See also Walter W. Powell, Review Essay: Explaining Technological Change, *American Journal of Sociology* 93 (1987), 185–197; Behr et al. op cit. (1991). Above all, the requirements of the market under the conditions of competition are included.

10. We ignore the circumstance that most of the literature is more concerned with the societal effects of automation, above all with the impact on the quantity and quality of the labor on offer.

11. With regard to the distance from places of work, first studies suggest that the possibilities of telecommunications by no means compensate for the advantages of proximity. As in the past, contact frequency diminishes with distance, even though the logic of the tasks in hand would suggest otherwise. See, David Krackhardt, Constraints on the Interactive Organization as an Ideal Type, in: Charles Heckscher, Defining the Post-Bureaucratic Type, in: Charles Heckscher and Anne Donnellon (eds.), *The Post-Bureaucratic Organization: New Perspectives on Organizational Change*, Thousand Oaks, CA 1994, 211–222 (213 f.). This argument naturally holds true only if mobility is presupposed.

12. See Gene I. Rochlin, Informal Organizational Networking as Crisis-Avoidance Strategy: U.S. Naval Flight Operations as a Case Study, *Industrial Crisis Quarterly* 3 (1989), 159–176.

13. See, e.g., Jost Halfmann and Klaus-Peter Japp (eds.), *Riskante Entscheidungen und Katastrophenpotentiale: Elemente einer soziologischen Risikoforschung*, Opladen 1990.

14. See Karl E. Weick, Technology as Equivoque: Sensemaking in New Technologies, in: Paul S. Goodman, Lee S. Sproull et al., *Technology and Organizations*, San Francisco 1990, 1–44.

15. See Diane Vaughan, Autonomy, Interdependence, and Social Control: NASA and the Space Shuttle Challenger, *Administrative Science Quarterly* 35 (1990), 225–257. See also Rochlin op. cit. (1989) with the thesis that under these conditions a system can take recourse more strongly to local, informal networks (we would say cognitive routines).

16. See, e.g., Behr et al. (1991), esp. 35 ff., 88 ff.

17. See the case study by Karl E. Weick, The Vulnerable System: An Analysis of the Tenerife Air Disaster, *Journal of Management* 16 (1990), 571–593, reprinted in: Peter J. Frost et al. (eds.), *Reframing Organizational Culture*, Newbury Park, CA 1991, 117–130.

18. See Barry A. Turner, The Organizational and Interorganizational Development of Disasters, *Administrative Science Quarterly* 21 (1976), 378–397.

19. Examples from the author's experience: Fiumicino Airport, Rome. The ladies at the check-in desks sit staring at their computers. Immobile. One passenger is processed every 20 minutes. People get nervous. The flight has to wait. Düsseldorf Airport: the shuttle is cancelled on grounds of "interruption of service." The aircraft can be reached only because it arrives late anyway and departure is delayed. Rosenheim train station: The connecting train come three quarters of an hour late due to "interruption of service." Another intercity express makes an irregular stop to take the stranded passengers to Munich central. With a bit of skill, a system of integrated delays could perhaps be established if enough local imagination, knowledge about alternatives, and enforcement competence can be activated. That under these circumstances people (the person, the "subject") would again be more important – as claimed by Behr et al. (1991), 143 on the basis of examples from another area – is hardly to be believed let alone hoped for. At any rate, it is not reassurance.

20. See Thomas P. Hughes, *Networks of Power: Electrification in Western Society 1880–1930*, Baltimore 1983; Renate Mayntz and Thomas P. Hughes (eds.), *The Development of Large Technical Systems*, Frankfurt 1988; Todd R. La Porte (eds.), *Social Responses to Large Technical Systems*, Dordrecht 1991; Renate Mayntz, Große technische Systeme und ihre gesellschaftstheoretische Bedeutung, *Kölner Zeitschrift für Soziologie und Sozialpsychologie* 45 (1993), 97–108; Jane Summerton (ed.), *Changing Large Technical Systems*, Boulder 1994. A critical examination of terminologies and the largely untheoretical concepts employed in research to date is to be found in Bernward Joerges, *Reden über große Technik, in: Festschrift Renate Mayntz*, Baden-Baden 1994, 453–490.

21. See Charles Perrow, *Normale Katastrophen: Die unvermeidbaren Risiken der Großtechnik*, German translation, Frankfurt 1987. The original English title is less provocative: Normal Accidents.

22. On the broad debate about the concepts technique/technology see, e.g., Kelvin W. Willoughby, *Technological Choice: A Critique of the Appropriate Technology Movement*, Boulder – London 1990, 25 ff.

23. In the terminology of Michel Callon, Society in the Making: The Study of Technology as a Tool for Sociological Analysis, in: Wiebe E. Bijker et al. (eds.),

The Social Construction of Technological Systems: New Directions in the Sociology and History of Technology, Cambridge, MA 1987, 83–103. See also John Law, Technology and Heterogeneous Engineering: The Cases of Portuguese Expansion, in: Bijker et al. 110–134.

24. This suggests that the legal system can be treated as a highly technicized system. The sociological objection is that only a minimal proportion of legal problems or legally relevant incidents actually take the form of requests for decisions. We can therefore speak of technicization at best within public authorities that deal with legal matters.

25. That this involves a "risk" that can be variously assessed is a late, only recently discussed discovery. See Gerald Wagner, Vertrauen in Technik, *Zeitschrift für Soziologie* 23 (1994), 145–157.

26. This had induced Husserl to raise objections to "the loss of meaning in the mathematical natural sciences in 'technicization'" and to insist that concrete subjective sensemaking be taken into account. See Edmund Husserl, *Die Krisis der europäischen Wissenschaften und die transzendentale Phänomenologie, Husserliana* vol. VI, The Hague 1954, esp. 20 ff. But all this ultimately means is that the form of technology has another side to it, on which everything is to be found, and is to be found in the world, that excludes it as form.

27. Already with regard to technique for constructing the central perspective in making works of art, this possibility of incomprehension was seen – and lamented. See Giulio Trolli, *Paradossi per pratticare la prospettiva senza saperla (1672)*, Bologna 1683.

28. Thus only in this case. Without reference to a core technology of the organization, the relation between pay and performance cannot be determined and obeys the normal systemic conditions of loose coupling.

29. See Niklas Luhmann and Karl Eberhard Schorr, Das Technologiedefizit der Erziehung und die Pädagogik, in idem (eds.), *Zwischen Technologie und Selbstreferenz: Fragen an die Pädagogik*, Frankfurt 1982, 11–40.

30. See Adam Gamoran and Robert Dreeben, Coupling and Control in Educational Organizations, *Administrative Science Quarterly* 31 (1986), 612–632.

31. On living systems see Robert B. Glassman, Persistence and Loose Coupling in Living Systems, *Behavioral Science* 18 (1973), 83–98; on organizations, e.g., Herbert A. Simon, The Organization of Complex Systems, in: Howard H. Pattee (ed.), *Hierarchy Theory: The Challenge of Complex Systems*, New York 1973, 3–27 (15 ff.); Karl E. Weick, *Der Prozeß des Organisierens, German translation*, Frankfurt 1985, esp. 163 ff. Further literature is to be found under headings such as "resilience," "robustness," "error friendliness," "ultrastability."

32. See Kim S. Cameron and Robert E. Quinn, Organizational Paradox and Transformation, Robert E. Quinn and Kim S. Cameron (eds.), *Paradox and Transformation: Toward a Theory of Change in Organization and Management*, Cambridge, MA 1988, 1–18 (7).

33. On changes in the forms of control and overcoming the limitation to *direct* observation of things and behaviors, see Beverly H. Burris, *Technocracy at Work*, Albany, NY 1993. Also L. Winner, *Autonomous Technology*, Cambridge, MA 1977; idem, *The Whale and the Reactor: A Search for Limits in an Age of High Technology*, Chicago 1986.

34. See Federico Butera, *Il castello e la rete: Impresa, organizzazioni e professioni nell'
    Europa degli anni '90*, 2nd ed, Milan 1991, 196.
35. Attempts have also been made to model planning processes in organizations on
    "artificial intelligence." See, e.g., B. Roger I. Hall, Building an Artificial
    Intelligence Model of Management Policy Making: A Tool for Exploring
    Organizational Issues, in: Michael Masuch (eds.), *Organization, Management,
    and Expert Systems: Models of Automated Reasoning*, Berlin 1990, 105–121, and
    other contributions in this volume. The common point of reference for artificial
    intelligence and organizational planning is then the cognitive faculties of human
    consciousness.
36. See Niklas Luhmann, *Soziale Systeme: Grundriß einer allgemeinen Theorie*,
    Frankfurt 1984, 191 ff.
37. This clearly requires no proof. But on the ambivalence of this dependence see
    Alain Gras, *Grandeur et dépendence: Sociologie des macro-systèmes techniques*,
    Paris 1993.
38. At this level James D. Thompson, *Organizations in Action: Social Science Bases of
    Administrative Theory*, New York 1967, has sought to mediate.
39. The main exception is the family, which, however, in the shape of the modern core
    family assumes organization-like characteristics (entry/exit, accountability and
    responsibility for overall conduct, second-order observation as the normal form
    of communication).

13   Organization and Society

Organizations have not always existed; they came into being only in the course of societal evolution. We cannot go into their history in detail, but for every description of the relation between organizational systems and societal systems it is important at least to note that societal conditions must have been responsible for the emergence and proliferation of organizations.

Work is an initial concept that allows us to examine this issue. The term describes performance appreciated because of its result, but which has to be specially motivated, because the worker will presumably not engage in such activity on his own initiative or for its own sake (prâxis). People have worked since the dawn of time. In primitive societies, work is structured and motivated above all by the need for physical survival, and thus by conditions external to society. The product of the activity directly determines what has to be done. This changes with the development of more complex societies, which have to determine what work is needed more and more in social terms because its purposes are no longer directly relevant for the survival of the workers themselves.[1]

Social determination enables role differentiation. It can take widely varying forms, from the domestic division of labor by gender, age, and master/servant differentiation to the politico-legal division of work, above all slavery and other types of forced subordination, notably debt bondage. Moreover, there are many ways of organizing work by groups, for instance, young adults or guilds, that mediate between needs and those willing to work without having to depend on a labor market. However, the potential for developing this social determination of employment relations is limited. Their social embedding limits the specification of individual roles and flexibility in adapting to external and to internal conditions.

There is no way back to direct external determination. The evolution of the organization as a form of system involves the social and thus societal determination of employment relationships. But their outdifferentiation permits the decoupling of societal objectives and motives. While social determination is limited to what an organization can carry out, precisely this opens up new possibilities. The establishment of organizations is based on developments in the economic system and the education system. The outdifferentiation of these functional systems provides the precondition for the outdifferentiation of organizations, even if they work for other functional systems (political administration, medical care, mass media, science, etc.).

The economic system makes money attractive, making it possible to pay money for work (regardless of whether it is organized work or individual contract work). Furthermore, money, in contrast to structurally bound social motives, makes it possible to differentiate pay quantitatively, thus providing for differences in performance and, above all, for hierarchies with different levels of pay within the organization. With whatever limitations, this allows the organization to control personnel movements and also to give symbolic expression to differences in rank. Hierarchies would be difficult to imagine with equal remuneration.

The requirements of the education system have a similar function. Training can be differentiated in accordance with the work that has to be done and adapted when organizations develop that create jobs requiring the corresponding specialized skills. Above all, however, the training provided by schools and universities increasingly dissolves the link between professional qualifications and families. Organizations can then recruit on the basis of skills and not only on that of social status. The socially determined motivation attributable to family origins thus no longer comes to bear in organizations. The long-standing, still highly effective statistical correlation between social status and education is disappointing for proponents of equal opportunities and social justice; but the link is not strong enough to allow motivation, standing, acceptability, and their limits as determined by family origins to influence organizations.[2]

In sum, we can posit that the large-scale formation of organizations begins when society makes it possible to recruit individuals without all the ballast of origin, group membership, social stratification, etc. that had limited the extent to which working behavior could be influenced. The consequence is that social status is determined by careers and particularly by the allocation of rank in organizations, in contrast to the situation in earlier societies, where the work to be performed was determined by social status. Within the system, the scope for action thus provided can be understood as an opportunity for selective decision-making, and the decisions made label themselves "rational"; how could they otherwise justify their selectivity enabled/imposed by the system form?

II

For classical organization theory, the societal justification of organization lay in its rationality. As long as organizations work rationally, it was claimed, this was also good for society. What else could one ask for? Action theory defined rationality in terms of ends and means, systems theory in terms of input and output. Research could concentrate on the conditions for rationality in organizations, that is to say, on organizations as objects, and manage without any theory of society. Organizations might admittedly have secondary purposes (for instance, profit maximization or the provision of members with income) but the societal function lay not in such particular interests but in performance, in what organizations produced. At the societal level, the "market economy" could then be affirmed as a condition for the rationality of organizations and possibly even copied on the basis of the competition principle into other areas of society (e.g., competitive democracy or even reputational competition among scholars). The weakness of this argument for societal theory is that it presupposes that action and system rationalities can be socially aggregated. Nowadays this is hardly convincing as organization theory because there is too much doubt about whether the end/means schema and the notion of a mathematical or technical transformation of inputs into outputs adequately describes the reality of organizations.[3]

In the following examination of relations between organization and society we shall therefore leave aside the question of rationality. In other words, we switch from analyzing principles (of comprehensive rationality) to analyzing differences. This puts the focus on how it is possible and with what consequences for a societal system to draw a boundary within itself with, on the one side, increasingly complex organizations and, on the other, what organizations can treat as their "environment " – despite the fact that this environment, too, is societally ordered and articulates societal interests!

If society is understood as the overall system of all meaningful communications, organizations can exist only within the societal system. Individual organizational systems have a double relationship with society. On the one hand, they realize society with each of their communications; on the other, there is communication in the environments of organizational systems, and hence there is society there, too. The distinction between system and environment, which arises with the formation of organization, engraves itself, so to speak, into society. There is society on both sides of the system boundary. The system boundary of the organization can therefore, unlike the external boundary of the societal system, be crossed through communication, even if the organizational system itself is operationally closed on the basis of its own decisions. An organization, thus, always finds society in a double sense: within itself and in its environment. What is special about organizations is how they organize this difference.

Organization theories, even when they take account of the environment as the other side of the organization boundary, have hitherto systematically neglected the problems that arise – so much so that it is not even clear what constitutes this neglect. This is the case both for theories of the firm proposed by economics (e.g., in transaction cost analysis) and for sociological and, particularly, for systems-theoretical approaches. Even recent institutional-theory approaches are no exception; they consider not only formal particularities of the environment to be relevant for the organization but also linguistic, cultural, and normative peculiarities.[4] Concepts such as culture or institution are then used in defining commonalities or dependencies between system and environment. But not everything that distinguishes an organizational system from its environment is culture or institution. We need only recall the old problems of the cognitive reduction of complexity or the establishment of indifference toward institutionalized interests such as private life, families, religious affiliation.

This problem of the unity of difference or the paradox of the two-sided form "boundary" could perhaps be held to be the constitutive "blind spot" that organizations themselves have to banish from their observational possibilities if they are to observe at all, and which organization theories, too, could include in their second- or third-order observation at best as blind spot, at best in the form of a paradox. But this would be a fallacy. It is not the constitutive difference between a system capable of self-observation and the unmarked space from which it has to exclude itself in order to indicate itself and distinguish between self- and other-reference. It has to do with a very specific distinction, that between organizational systems and the societal system, and with the special problem of including organizational systems in what happens for them both internally and externally, namely communication. The difficulty is, hence, not an epistemological or logical impossibility, but that two system references have to be distinguished and kept in mind: organization and society.

No one will deny that modern society with all its advantages is directly or indirectly dependent on organization. The same applies for technology. Until it has been established which organizations can be expected to contribute to society and which not, the tendency to raise organizational effects to the level of the societal system will remain and increase. This can lead only to inadequate descriptions of society, to ideologically prescribed treatments, or to lamentation and resignation. The best examples are to be found in the field of socialist experiments. One instance is Marx's depiction of the obvious problems of factory organization in the nineteenth century as the expression of a class society. And the attempt to revolutionize the whole of society under the leadership of one (and only one) organization proved a notable failure.[5] Overestimation of the organizational capacity of "unity parties" and under-estimation of the problems of operational closure and dependence on self-constructed information[6] led to the bifurcation of societal problems. What was needed to preserve power and the role of the unity party found themselves more and more in conflict with the (also important) necessity of gaining and retaining the acceptance of the population; and the expansion of planning and control techniques came into conflict with the requirements of economic development, which they were intended to serve. The intellectual grandiloquence of Marxism alone was unable to keep the system running. There was no dialectical cancellation of contradictions by a disaster that was evolutionary, in other words, set off by unpredictable accidents.[7] The gigantic experiment of the Soviet Empire foundered on the contradiction between it and a world society that was already functionally differentiated.[8]

A quite different and nevertheless surprisingly parallel example is to be found in Italy. An increasingly effective *diminishing* of organizations' capabilities grounded in tradition had led in almost all fields to a need for networks that enabled the various organizations to cultivate contacts on all levels. Such networks, currently a favorite topic of research, operate on the basis of trust, but trust that can rely on interests easy to assess.[9] In any case these networks presuppose functioning (or at least exploitable) organizations. We could, therefore, say that they function as parasites[10] that live off organizations and are nourished by them without allowing themselves to be controlled.

More precise examination that takes account of the legal situation can distinguish between legal and illegal variants. On the legal side we find the now typical horizontal links between organizations in industrial production; we also find, somewhat less reputable, the "lobby" organizations that develop around centers of political power. Quite illegal variants develop if trust is strongly personalized and organizational performance is to be achieved only or almost only through personal contacts. In some countries, this has produced useful contact networks and intermediary services that rely on personal contacts, which prove indispensable if anything at all is to get off the ground or be achieved. But these networks, which operate with their own inclusion/exclusion rules, are no longer reinsured by estate-based patron-client relationships; they instead draw their influence from organizational positions, which at the same time they ruin by their own effectiveness.[11] Here, too, chance events or the initiative of a public prosecutor's office can then trigger disaster; and here, too, without control over the causes and without responsibility for the consequences. And we also find a diagnosis of conditions in the political system of society: corruption of the political class. But that does not get us any further if the problem lies in the insufficiency of the organizations in question.

Similar criticism of the political class is to be found elsewhere. In Germany, for example, an interview given by the federal president triggered such critique.[12] The concern that has fired discussion is understandable. It is about the increasing disaffection with politics in this country and the paradoxical shift of voters to parties that do not even try to demonstrate their fitness to govern in the form of a universal political program. Here, too, no attempt is made to establish what can really be expected of political parties as organizations –

organizations that have to deal with almost random contingencies and condense decision premises for collectively binding decisions. This is true for both programmatic and personnel decision premises. If conflicts arise within parties under these circumstances and if career finally becomes the sole stable guiding factor, precisely because it processes contingencies,[13] this is a clear sign that political parties are seeking to provide the uncertainty absorption society expects them to provide. To find in this a topic for polemic is only possible if one has no adequate notion of the relation between society and organization.

There are many more examples that could be cited. We could ask whether the idea of Europe has been ruined by the Brussels administration. Or have the many setbacks suffered by organized development projects led to a loss of faith in "modernization"? In these cases, too, experience with organization provokes a conclusion formulated at the level of the societal system or its subsystems. We cannot go into detail here. But we should ask ourselves whether such a shift in attribution from organizations to society could be avoided or at least better controlled. Have we perhaps already reached what can be attained in the way of rationality and are now simply suffering only from the burden of ideas that do not correspond to what is attainable? That may sound all too appeasing, but this objection brings us no closer to satisfying the need for a better balanced basis for judgment.

Activating the organization theory outlined in the preceding chapters, we would first have to ask how it is possible to form organizations within the societal system and even within its functional systems, and to do so in the form of self-referential, non-trivial, and complex social systems that are intransparent to themselves and unpredictable for external observers. If this is to happen, does not society have to overburden its organizations with highly contradictory requirements – for instance, with the demand for structural inertia as a precondition for reliable observability, on the one hand, and with the demand for innovation and planned adaptation to a turbulent reality as a precondition for rationality, on the other? And how do organizations evolve if they face these paradoxical conditions for their intra-societal reproduction?

These would be long-term perspectives for future research in the context of a double system reference, namely the societal system and organizational systems. What could already be said about such research is that it would have to establish what expectations and what problems are involved in the formation of organizations in modern society.

III

All social systems consist of communications. Communications are the operations by which they can reproduce themselves autopoietically with the help of their own products. But this does not guarantee that social systems themselves can communicate: on their own behalf and, as it were, as collective persons. Societies cannot do this if only because their communication cannot leave the system. Beyond the bounds of society there are no addressees for communication. And the functional systems of society cannot operate as collective persons that can assume responsibility for the totality of their operations. If we leave organizations aside, there is no dialogue between the economy and science, politics and the law, families and religion. Interaction systems are also not capable of communication. As micro-systems, they may occasionally be able to achieve consensus sufficient to present a unified front to the outside world. Lovers announce their engagement, protest demonstrations hold up their banners and whoever joins the march confirms, as it were, the common communication. But these are communications difficult to come back to; unless there are fixed social stereotypizations (for instance engagements) or there is an existing or emerging organization to which one can later turn to recall what had been said. If the outwardly directed communication of social entities is to be perpetuated and fitted into systems of retrieval and anticipation, organizations have to be formed.

Organizations are capable of communicating on their own behalf because they can still decide about such communication and put such decisions into force as decision premises for further decisions. This does not yet say anything about whether the legal system will treat such communications, for instance, in the form of contracts, as binding. For such purposes, organizations can be endowed with "legal personality" in the legal system (which, incidentally, would be possible for neither interaction systems nor societal functional systems). Even without legally binding effect, communications are recognized by organizations as *their* communications. Trade unions protest against legislation planned by the government, and it is understood that they thus wish to signal their willingness to negotiate. The Association of the Chemical Industry places large advertisements in the daily press to inform the public that chemical production is indispensable and ecologically under control. Through the appropriate institutions, governments comment continuously on what is happening politically, and their outwardly directed communication is at the same time weighed up in domestic policy terms. A firm makes an order, a supermarket displays goods for sale, a museum announces an exhibition. Without organized communication, modern life would be unthinkable.

System boundaries are also important because they prevent checks in the environment on how communication is decided internally. Members are likely to be internally under obligation of loyalty and restraint with regard to differences of opinion. But it is more important that, if differences are made public, if a party official distances himself from party conference resolutions or a bishop distances himself from the official line of his church, this is treated as a personal escapade for which personal motives are sought and found. There are also cases in which such loyalty is not demanded or cannot be imposed – in faculty matters professors are deemed unamenable to discipline. But even then, there is no doubt that the organization has expressed itself through decided and communicated texts and is the appropriate addressee for queries or requests for reconsideration.

For society itself, this possibility of organizationally aggregated communication is only a medium, that is, a quantity of elementary communications that are loosely coupled (= diverse but not combinable at will). Society can rest assured that this possibility of condensing information exists and that the communications produced can be understood and, more or less, consequentially treated. But society itself cannot decide what forms are chosen in this medium, what specific communications are realized, and thus how tight couplings come about and are ended. This can be decided only in society by organization systems, and this ensures a sufficient measure of non-coordination, of organized anarchy. The special medium of organized communication thus has no tendency to funnel into consensus. The opposite seems to be true. In a thoroughly organized society, the statements of individual organizations typically provoke counter statements from other organizations. If religious instruction in schools is restricted, the churches are under obligation to state their opinions. If the university demands a public transport connection, the city will react with empty promises. Organized communication acts in society, as it were, as agonal mass, which puts all organizations under pressure to concern themselves with external communication. The medium generates its own perpetually nervous activation in society. And this is a problem of modern society, whereas the organizations involved will have their own problems – depending on how well-established their own institutionalization is or how strongly they feel obliged to conceal institutionalization weaknesses through comments on current events.

IV

Organizations can communicate in their own name only because they recruit members by decision, and, if membership is accepted, they place these members under obligation to accept the decisions of the organization. This means that the entire population is excluded from membership of every specific organization with the exception of the included members. It may well be the case that all individuals are members of some organization or other, above all of organizations that provide them with work and an income; but this does not change the fact that all individuals are non-members in relation to almost all organizations. Exclusion is therefore normal, inclusion the exception.

For the system of society, the contrary is true. In the societal system admittance to communication is normal, and thus inclusion with the recognized status of person is normal. Although there is greater or lesser exclusion on the margins of the system, what is involved ranges essentially from restriction of opportunities for communication to the borderline case of the complete cognitive and moral irrelevance of what someone has to say. But the problem of such exclusions shows that however many people are affected – now untold millions – they have to be treated as exceptions in the self-description of the societal system.

In older societies, inclusion/exclusion was regulated through family households[14] and also through corporations such as temples, monasteries, orders, universities, guilds, and military units. Only those who found no place in this order, thus gaining rank and status, were treated as excluded and had to eke out a miserable existence as vagrants, objects of charity, beggars.

In modern society, there are no longer any macro-societal forms of inclusion/exclusion. Even social control has switched from exclusion to inclusion.[15] Society now recognizes only human beings and all human beings as persons. In fact, however, the decision on inclusion/exclusion has been delegated to functional systems. Here, too, it is dominated by the principle of including everyone. Everyone has legal capacity. Everyone can submit knowledge to scientific examination, even if he or she observes UFOs or has seen a martyr's statue bleed. Everyone is included in the economic system through money, and everyone has to attend school in youth. Everyone has the right to vote and stand for election, as long as minimal competence is guaranteed; and everyone can practice the religion of his or her choice or leave it be.

The basic rights of freedom and equality symbolize this form of the societal inclusion of all individuals as individuals. However, this symbolization is paradoxical because there is no freedom without the restriction of freedom and no equality without inequality. Functional systems resolve this paradox through historicization: what concrete rights one has and what level of education one has attained, how one is politically involved or what knowledge one has gained, is a question of the individual career in functional systems; it is thus a matter of selection history, in which individuals and social systems work together. But the inclusion mechanisms of functional systems are not coordinated, or at best through loose coupling that does not allow individual fate to be predicted. Only complete or almost complete exclusion from functional systems results in fixed coupling: without work and without money, without education, without papers, without the legal right to marry, without a permanent place of residence, without police protection, indeed often without access to the language spoken by the public authorities – one exclusion leads to another in the sense of a negative integration that leaves the individual with little more than one's own body and the problem of surviving from day to day.

Vast numbers of people live under such conditions of exclusion. No organization is needed. The functional systems of society produce and reproduce what they do not need: exclusion. In the field of positive and loose couplings, by contrast, selection is organized in the form of careers (in the broadest sense, including all sorts of cumulative acquisition of, for instance, rights, money, or reputation). Selection cannot be left to mere wishes; it requires agreement (e.g., contracts) and, for control purposes, organizations. The same is true for social control, which has switched from exclusion to inclusion (e.g., prisons, psychiatric institutions, therapeutic organizations of all sorts). And it holds for the entire field of follow-up work that has to do with exclusion or the threat of exclusion, above all social work and development aid.

The interplay between functional systems and organizations is so constructed that the paradoxes of the principles of freedom and equality can be resolved, that is to say, distributed among different entities. The functional systems set out from inclusions and, so to speak, merely let exclusions happen. With organizations the contrary is the case. Everyone is excluded; there is no natural right to membership because inclusion has to be highly selective. We now see the logic of the overall arrangement, which culminates in a specific paradox and its unfolding. By the very nature of the distinction there is necessarily inclusion *and* exclusion, because the form of inclusion would not be possible if there were no exclusion, and vice versa. What resolves the paradoxical unity of the difference is that society opts in its functional systems for the inclusion of all, while organizations opt for the exclusion of all. Society considers exclusion to be degrading and functionally useless without being able to prevent it. Organizations set out from exclusion to allow them to gain control over decisions on membership and thus to establish their own autonomy. Nevertheless, organizations put society in society into effect.

The reverse relationship between inclusion and exclusion also explains why the so-called critical theory fails when applied to organizations. Its aim had been to impose general societal values such as freedom, equality, emancipation, participation, and opportunities for self-realization in organizations, too. But this harmonizes poorly with the special status of members and the exclusion of everyone else. If one wishes to realize general human rights in the organization on the basis of its structures, there is no reason to exclude others from them. This does not necessarily mean that the legal order does not apply within organizations and can be replaced by the organization's own structures. Nor does it amount to silent submission to prevailing power relations. But the exclusion of non-members is justified only if the restrictions are accepted that enable the autopoiesis of decision-making.

The intrinsic logic of the autopoietic organization also explains why we find organizations that are quite differently structured at the level of their decision programs than one would have expected from their function in society and their output. Particularly striking examples in the field of the mass media are offered by the editorial offices of newspapers and broadcasting corporations.

The selection criteria here are novelty, conflict, sensation, local relevance, morality, violation of norms, and everything negative. Organization programs, by contrast, are the exact opposite in every regard: routine programs, columns, and templates geared to repetition, as well as random factors such as free space or program time.[16] The organization would be unable to function if it always had to decide sensationally, conflictually, morally, with a penchant for violating norms, and, above all, always anew. Work is marked rather by unexpectedly great redundancy. Similar reverse relations are to be found in decision-making by courts or in research at scientific institutes. Here, too, the predominant preferences are to be found less in the value of the decisions taken than in the need to get through the work in a limited period of time.

Through its organizations, society is endowed with a capacity for discrimination. It treats everyone equally and each differently. Society processes communications on the basis of universal principles while keeping an eye on the given historical situation. All have legal capacity, but not everyone obtains satisfaction before the courts. The equality principle is, in other words, not yet a conditional program.[17] All are citizens, but not everyone is a member of parliament or a public servant. Everyone capable of learning is required to attend school, but the school decides by internal criteria how successful one's attendance is. With the help of its organizations, society allows the principles of freedom and equality, which it cannot negate, to fail. It transforms them into principles of openness to the future not limited by clauses attached to the principles themselves but only by the current state of affairs, which is the point of departure for determining what is still possible.

V

Another function of organization formation within the societal system is to establish *interruptions of interdependence*. In the terminology of old cybernetics, we could also speak of step functions or of ultrastability.[18] This prevents everything from varying with everything else within the rough societal differentiation into functional systems: the price of skin cream being guided by the price of bottled beer, hotel accommodation, aircraft, or newspapers. At the same time, this builds a device for intercepting risks into society: if a company goes bankrupt, this causes few other bankruptcies, just as one divorce does not automatically entail a cascade of others. Only under this condition, which we nowadays call loose coupling, can complex systems increase their own irritability and nevertheless attain sufficient stability.

But why is such far-reaching interdependence to be expected in societies?

It is likely to be due to the open meaning-horizons of linguistic communication and, in more developed societies, also to the generalization of symbolic communication media.

Although communication proceeds in a relatively orderly fashion as long as it is thematically organized and a communication, once begun, cannot be continued all too erratically, or at least not arbitrarily, there ought to be no doubts about the seriousness of contributions. But this alone is not a sufficient limitation. A communication about beer can be continued as a communication about women as long as the participants go along with it. The institutionalization of symbolically generalized communication media, too, is open; otherwise they could not be used to outdifferentiate systems. If no further precautions are taken, one could expect that every price will be influenced by every other price, that physical truths will come to bear in sociology and vice versa, and that every use of power will jeopardize the use of power per se. Incidentally, phenomena such as inflation or deflation, which occur not only in the financial context but in all symbolically generalized communication media,[19] show that, despite the differentiation of markets and firms, parties and government coalitions, scientific disciplines, faculties, universities, and research institutes, this original interdependence looms in the background and can at any time trigger unwanted intervention in the general utility of the given medium.

Organizations are the essential vehicles of interdependence interruption. This is shown not least by the theory of autopoietic systems, whereas input-transformation-output models easily direct attention to chain-like interconnections. But organizations are also systems that link self-reference and other-reference in their operations, and therefore always place the interruption of interdependence in their environment, too. In the economy, for instance, there are different markets. There are political topic areas in politics and scientific topic areas in science to which organizations relate. While the economy forms relatively stable distinctions between markets, and politics by contrast is concerned with temporally unstable fields which, if topical, have to be addressed by all parties (but not by all government departments), scientific organizations are differentiated for educational reasons into disciplines, and within disciplines there are fashionable, fast changing preferences for topics that research groups keen to be at the cutting edge prefer to address. Relations between organizations and the niches of their environment with which they choose to identify can thus prove very varied, but it is practically unthinkable for there to be environmental differentiations that reproduce of their own accord if differences, barriers, temporal stabilities, or fluctuations are not borne by appropriate organizations.

Without interrupting interdependence, no society can develop structural complexity, but only in modern society do organizations appear to have been necessary for this purpose. Tribal societies managed with their principle of the pyramidal structure of segmentary differentiation. Also, societies differentiated in terms of social stratification and/or center/periphery were able to manage with their own differentiation principle and provide for further differentiation by household, or for more highly developed division of labor within their centers. In all these cases and as long as family economies formed the basic structure of societal differentiation, space-related symbolizations, boundary markings, and the designation of places (e.g., as sacred or as marketplace) were able to solve the problem of regulating interdependence and the necessary crossing of boundaries – such as Hermes being the competent god of merchants and thieves, with his seat on Olympus and in Hades.

Gradually, this function was taken over by law and the civil rights categories of property and contract. However, only modern, functionally differentiated society reaches a degree of complexity at which a quite different type of system formation has to assume the function of interrupting interdependence. Functional differentiation intensifies the mutual independence and dependence of functional systems *together* and thus *at the same time*; every functional system is autonomous in performing its own function, but it is also dependent on other functional systems adequately performing *their* functions. The margins for mutually passing on and substituting problems are very narrow in relation to the level of structural complexity. Politics cannot ignore even small economic fluctuations; the economy has to take up scientific discoveries that can be profitably exploited, whatever this might mean for older invest-ments; and although it can organize private security services, it cannot replace the police. This shows that functional differentiation cannot itself provide the necessary interruption of interdependence; for obvious reasons, it is structu-rally not in a position to do so. If we project the effects onto the overall system of society, it is therefore precisely the operational closure and autonomy of functional systems that enhance endogenous dynamics and mutual involve-ment, interdependence and dependence. For this very reason, society must go beyond functional differentiation and use another principle of system forma-tion to provide itself with ultrastability and with sufficient local capacity to absorb irritations: *the principle of organization*.

VI

Very similar states of affairs can be analyzed with the aid of the *structural coupling* concept. It was introduced by Humberto Maturana[20] and addresses relations ("interactions" to use Maturana's term) between system and environ-ment that, although they do not intervene in the system in a way that determines its structure and that are thus compatible with autopoiesis, do in the long term influence structures produced in the system itself, provoking "structural drift"; an example is regulating how many muscles a species of animal develops to enable it to move, given its body weight and the gravitational conditions. We stress the two-sidedness of structural couplings more strongly than Maturana. They include what can "perturb" the system and exclude what can have only a destructive effect. In the case of the societal system, structural coupling with consciousness systems is produced through language. What is not mediated through language or the language-like use of signs, for example, a physical or chemical change, can have only a destructive effect – on the consciousness and on the communication system society.[21]

Within the societal system, this means that different conditions apply for coupling its subsystems. In aristocratic societies, for instance, the different social strata are coupled through households because they can establish communicative contact in households. Under the regime of functional differentiation, depending on the sort of systems involved, a wide range of structural couplings can occur, so that no standard mechanism is to be found. Science and the economy find themselves coupled through the technical and economic usefulness of new knowledge; the economic system and the health care system through the issuing of sick leave certificates by doctors; the legal system and the economic system are coupled by the mutual use of property and contract; the legal and political systems through the institution of the constitution.

The extent to which organizations are involved in these structural couplings has to be examined from case to case. Large law firms, particularly in the United States, provide their clients with political and economic contacts with legal advice playing only a subordinate role.[22] Some organizations differentiate interaction-intensive contact circles, which, depending very much on the given situation, concern themselves especially with specific structural couplings.[23] In other cases, relatively large and powerful organizations are formed, such as trade unions or employer or industrial associations, to mediate between politics and the economy.[24] And the board members of large business enterprises spend a great deal of time in various capital cities without being missed at head office. Overall we can say only that, in precise adaptation to the special conditions of such structural couplings, a multitude of forms has developed partly at the interaction level, partly at the organization level that would never have been possible without recourse to organizations capable of communicating.

Finally, special, so to speak extravagant organizations deserve attention, where the problem of structural coupling finds expression in concentrated form. The organizations in question are constitutional courts and central banks – both subject to the precondition of political independence. These organizations have no divided loyalties; they are not Janus-faced in their operations. They are also not conceived of as pressure-balancing devices, with first one functional system and then the other gaining the upper hand. Each, rather, constitutes the top organization of one of the coupled systems, namely the legal system and the economic system. This in turn presupposes that these functional systems are ordered on the center/periphery pattern, each forming a central hierarchy – the court system and the banking system – from where other areas of the functional system can be treated as periphery.[25]

Under this precondition, the apex of the hierarchical central system, namely the constitutional court or the central bank, operates as the top organization of the functional system without being able to issue instructions, and thus without being able to govern.

These organizations are then endowed with "autocompetence." They are self-referential and, since negative decisions play a role, they are paradoxically constituted. As far as constitutional courts are concerned, these problems have been known since the late eighteenth century, at least since the famous *Marbury v. Madison* case.[26] Constitutional courts are explicitly or implicitly mentioned in the constitution. Their task of interpreting and applying the text therefore also has to do with the extent of their own competence, especially with whether they can declare even politically endorsed, "democratically" adopted laws to be unconstitutional and thus void. The political repercussions must, of course, be kept in mind, even if political questions are not formally excluded.[27] A constitutional court will, in particular, hardly be able to afford pursuing its own logic so far as to void unconstitutional laws retroactively, thus provoking chaos in reinstating the status *quo ante*. It therefore has to be able to accept the validity of unconstitutional laws – at least for a certain time and often for quite some time.

Similar problems arise in a quite different functional system: in central bank policy. The formal task of maintaining a range of variables, notably inflation, money supply, and the external value of the currency, in balance cannot be fulfilled without keeping a eye on the political consequences, for example, on the level of money creation through government debt. Here, too, we find an organization in the paradoxical position of seeking to limit the money supply with which it operates economically itself.

What these organizations, which are both marginal and central to the system, demonstrate is that – and how – problems of structural coupling are translated into problems of self-reference and then, through the decision policy of these organizations (which must not be political, i.e., democratic policy), are unfolded. The consequence is that the temporal dimension gains particular importance – either in the sense of structural drift by the legal system toward dissolving fixed jurisprudential forms in the interests of judicial control of political development toward the welfare state,[28] or in the sense of historical central bank policy drawing on the latest information, which seeks to moderate its own unpredictability as non-trivial machine through proclaimed goals and effective communication of its decisions shored up by a great deal of informed guesswork.

Structural couplings are consequences of the functional differentiation of society. They develop because, with this form of differentiation, both the dependence and independence of functional systems in relation to one another increase. They are located at the level of the societal system and are hence not a function of organizations. But they would scarcely be possible at the necessary level of complexity and differentiation if there were not organizations able to gather and bundle communications and thus ensure that the continuous irritation of the functional systems generated through structural couplings can be translated into connective communication.

VII

System formation through operational closure and autopoietic reproduction is a highly improbable evolutionary advance, like life, like linguistically communicating society, and like all other instances of autopoiesis in society. When it happens, it can no longer be controlled by the conditions of its possibility. It serves no "higher purpose," it simply is and functions, after evolution has transformed improbability into probability as the point of departure for further evolution.

This typical process repeats itself when organizational systems form in society once society has attained a sufficient degree of complexity. Organizations, too, serve no higher purpose, they are not concentration points of societal rationality; they use the possibility of drawing boundaries and reproducing, they become creative, they proliferate, and for this very reason find themselves exposed to further evolutionary selection.

With respect to modern society, the consequent difficulties are discussed under the heading of problems of control.[29] If functional systems are differentiated out as autopoietic systems, this alone means that they do not determine one another but can only irritate one another to varying degrees through structural couplings.[30] As we have seen when introducing the concept of autopoiesis,[31] social systems can be influenced from outside only because inside they have yes/no options, because with regard to a not-yet-settled future they oscillate. On the other hand, this means that their state cannot be determined from outside; even if external intervention were able to fix a given variable, this would merely set off further yes/no oscillations – for instance, compliance or non-compliance with valid norms. This means that, under such circumstances, only trigger causality comes into question and not intervention causality. Whether setting trigger causes in the observed system has any effect, and what effect this is, is determined essentially by the state of the system at the time and not by a *causa aequat effectum* – a law. What is more, only organizational systems and not functional systems can themselves act communicatively.[32] There are no communications "of" the political system that could be addressed to "the" economic system, but there are naturally decisions by government to safeguard jobs by subsidizing industries unable to sell their products on the market. And there is also abundant control communication from one organization to another.[33] In other words, there are indeed decisions by organizations that change system variables – in our example, decisions that increase the ratio of unproductive spending to productive spending. However, what state this puts the economic system in and what the political consequences are depend on the continuation of the autopoiesis of these systems and the associated activation/deactivation of structures.

For understandable reasons, the discussion about control has limited itself to relations between the political system and the economic system, and judicial control is often the issue. Limitation to this slice of reality has the advantage that, on the debit side of control, government constitutes an organization that is easy to observe. A theory of society, however, is interested mainly in the limited nature of this issue. Should one not also recall (and no less "legitimately") that the economy controls the political system – as one example, through the influence the development of interest rates has on the national debt and via this interim variable on a multitude of policy programs? It should also be noted that influence by organizations of the economic system, although certainly successful here and there (at the policy level), is unlikely to be replicable in the political system or, for example, political elections.[34] Another topic is whether good cooperation between press officers or public relations departments and journalists or editorial offices manages to control what is produced in the way of "public opinion" in the interest of certain organizations. As the slice of reality changes, so does the attitude toward control projects. And the much-lamented pessimism about control often turns into optimism: one hopes that it will not succeed, or at least not lastingly.[35]

These reflections have consequences for the concept of control – for both external and internal control. The problem that control theory needs to discuss thus lies not in the concept of autopoiesis but in that of control; and the concept of autopoiesis provokes at best more precise consideration of what is actually meant by control. Control cannot mean that the system determines its own state, for the concept would then merge with that of autopoiesis and exclude external control. We therefore abide by intentional communication as a characteristic.[36] At the same time, however, as with every intention, this raises the problem of complexity. If we wish to retain the concept of control, we can therefore not relate it to systems but only to specific differences. Setting an objective, after all, means introducing a difference in relation to what would otherwise be the case. No one will deny that this is possible (however successfully). Otherwise there would have long since been no purposes; evolution would have eliminated them long age. Differences can be intensified or weakened through control (for instance, a greater share of the market for one's own products, lower unemployment figures). In any case, attempts to control a system observe it on the basis of a specific distinction. In the process, however, the system is not seen as a compact entity differentiated from the environment. It is not seen as a system at all, but only as the context of specific differences; one could say as the infinite context of the distinction of distinctions, with the proviso that changes in one difference may or may not affect what happens with the differences in other distinctions.

Since this very rapidly becomes unpredictable (owing not least to the necessity of taking account of the other sides of distinctions, and thus alternative contingencies), control intentions fast turn into problems of time. To quote Napoleon, "*on s'engage, puis on voit.*" The necessity of control is thus its own product. Once you start, you have to keep on correcting things however you regard the purpose. In this sense, control accelerates itself – and has to rely all the more on the structural inertia of organizations and on their fixation on known problems, known opponents, known risks, and current forms of uncertainty absorption.

What is gained by this can hardly be described as system rationality. We could not even say that control increases the internal control of systems – internal control understood as congruence between intended and attained states where assessment remains constant. But what is achieved is a high measure of sensitivity to turbulence, due partly to the effects of control itself and partly to changes in its context, which in turn are likely to be the consequences of other instances of control.[37] Society itself, even in its functional systems, appears to be robust (= resilient, = error-friendly) enough to bear this; but at the same time it generates resistance to this mode of continuously changing the course of control. This is apparent in alternative movements, which take to the field against the organized distinctions of the system with bodies and campaigns. It is apparent in novel religious or quasi-religious fundamentalisms. We see it in the semantic careers of fashionable concepts like "identity." The sense of protest and dissidence lies essentially in refusal. It generates its own illusory reality, whose function could be to enable observation of the real reality that does not depend on theory. But this is possible only in society, only in the operational mode of communication.

VIII

Organizations are placed in society largely (if not exclusively) through functional differentiation. The goals of most organizations, such as banks, hospitals, schools, armies, or political parties, are guided by the functions of given functional systems. Cutting across this is the fact that all organizations cost money. They have to pay their members and refinance their expenditure. To this extent, all organizations operate in the economic system. Here, too, there are two sides to be taken into consideration: first, organizations cost money, which has to be earned in the economy. Second, the economy provides jobs for refinancing consumption expenditure. Without the money earned through work in organizations, the markets for consumer goods would collapse, although "independent" work and other sources of income continue to exist to some extent. The relation between work and wages or salaries is rationalized by labor markets – subject, however, to strong political and legal constraints. But this alone does not yet justify treating job creation and hedging the corresponding financing on the same pattern as in a market transaction. Such states of affairs cannot be understood on the pattern of an exchange, although the interdependence between work and money is obvious. It is therefore not by chance that politics takes up this problem and promises to create jobs even though such a promise is completely unsecured, since only the economy has the relevant options at its disposition.

It is consequently a problem of societal structure, which arises when society uses organizations in all functional systems even though only the organizations of the economic system can earn their own money.[38] At present, a "market economy" solution to the problem is advised, but in all cases in which there is no market, such recommendations are clearly duplicitous. One is then working with estimates and not with data.[39]

We must leave aside the social theory problems; as we have seen, they cannot be solved through organized control but at most retrospectively by correcting effects. What is interesting at the level of organization theory, by contrast, is whether something in the way of internal control by all organizations oriented on the financial framework is possible.

For business enterprises, this seems to be conceivable with regard to equity and outside capital, which determine the reach of the organization's own operations and which have to be reproduced by these operations. And even if one no longer believes in a unified theory of rational decision-making in the style of Gutenberg,[40] empirical studies have shown that strategic entrepreneurial decisions are determined by the financial framework and affect it in turn.[41] Not least of all, this limits the willingness to take risks. Moreover, capital in this context is a clear expression for the autonomy of internal control, especially for relative independence from fluctuations in the markets in which the enterprise participates. Corporate accounts provide relatively concrete indications for this, even though the decisions themselves do not follow from the data but are also determined by experience and maxims that management "believes in." For this reason, enterprises differ considerably in their strategic planning, which is now often attributed to differences in "corporate culture."

Such capital calculation can scarcely be expected of organizations whose core competence lies outside the economic system. They will tend, rather, to see their financial requirements as a limit to their possibilities and to have the negative experience that the level of financing justified – indeed demanded – by their function is not provided. In this fashion, they indicate that they primarily belong to other, non-economic functional systems. An adult education center or a church educational establishment may be so skillfully managed that they can cover their costs thanks to the attractiveness of what they offer; but they would be wrongly managed if, in a sort of reversal of ends and means, they came to see this as their main goal. Like a business enterprise, they may at best see in this a certain guarantee of autonomy vis-à-vis financial backers or the capital market. In business enterprises, a contrary ends/means shift is more likely: "that the means to financial ends often become ends in themselves," that is to say, "that the ends of serving the product market and the organization are legitimate and must be met if the company is to survive."[42]

IX

If we have to assume that turbulence in the environment of organizations is largely produced by other organizations because no one else can communicate so concentratedly, what consequences are to be expected, what consequences are already apparent?

Since the 1960s, interorganizational relations have attracted a great deal of attention in the literature. It has also been noted that large organizational systems have increasingly broken up and been recombined, as if group systems were becoming more important, leading to the conclusion that system boundaries are becoming less important. Attention has also focused on networks providing mutual support and preferential treatment,[43] which do not take the form of independent organizations (e.g., cartels) because they seldom cross the line of legality[44] or otherwise subject organization members to the pressure of double loyalties, which cannot be translated into formal rules.

Networks develop on the basis of *conditioned trustworthiness*.[45] They thus replace the security that an organizational system finds in the membership of its members. They can condense into social systems of their own if they produce clear boundaries and generate their own history that can be used recursively as a basis for the trust typical of networks. But trust can be based on other things – and only this justifies a special concept – for example, on personnel. Relative constancy is required for this, and not too frequent changes in personnel.[46] Furthermore, the importance of a concentrated institutional environment is underlined. In developing countries, as in countries that have long since crossed the threshold to industrialization (Mexico, for example, or Taiwan), families appear to play an important role in keeping empires of widely varying organizations together. In other cases (e.g., Japan), government bureaucracy provides for preferential treatment, mediation, and balance. A group of companies often comes into being strictly economically through mutual capital participation. In other cases, one counts on stable customer relationships, for example, in investment decisions. But not only organizations in the economic system are concerned. Many organizations and other functional systems (education, social work, medical care) depend on government funding and find their public partners in the relevant government departments. In government departments, owing not least to long years of patronage, there is networking between public authorities and political parties, which cushions the effects of political changes at the top, but which can also be used by the new bosses to remain in contact with political opponents and if necessary to end political blockade. It is difficult to find a single formula for such varied states of affairs. Research has reacted with concepts such as institution or culture, or has attempted to withdraw the well-known thesis of "disembedding" to once again stress the "embeddedness" of economic organizations (but surely not of the economy itself?).[47] But these notions remain analytically vague.

If, however, we assume that the point of departure for such hybrid formations is to be found in environmental turbulence caused by other organizations, it is understandable that organizations seek a symbiotic relationship with other organizations in order to put the relevant environment into manageable shape. In other words, one seeks to concentrate interdependencies and convert them into "social capital" to which one can take recourse if the otherwise uncontrollable environment changes. But this limits the exploitability of informational asymmetries. In this context, personal relations, well-established trust, and also reputation in the environment, which sabotage could only endanger, are likely to play a role, and a sufficient degree of mutual control will be indispensable.[48] Networks do not ensure a quiet life, but they do keep challenges within manageable bounds.

Such relations have a certain resistance to change; they limit the incentives for learning in the networked systems.[49] On the other hand, changing them has a considerable impact on the continued existence of individual organizations. If, as has happened in Italy, broadcasting stations or state banks "belong" to certain political parties and in other cases influence-sharing has been agreed, a collapse of the party system would have major repercussions for other, formally unpolitical organizations. A vast number of non-professional "politicians" in practically all organizations also find themselves suddenly confronted by fundamentally changed conditions for behavior. If, as in Germany, the federal government extends its influence by allocating finance far beyond what is provided for under the constitution, changes in the system of mixed financing have considerable effects, above all on local government. Symbiosis is thus not without its dangers. Although it makes the system ultrastable by immunizing it against minor changes, it concentrates sensitivity to changes that skip the step function and then have far-reaching effects that go beyond the concrete circumstances. The conditions for stability always define what can destabilize, as well.

Organizations that operate like this in networks are difficult to observe, let alone plan and control from headquarters. The knowledge and intuitions for operating the network are to be found much farther down. This is mainly because it has to do with assessing possibilities, exigencies, trust – and not only with developments that can be read in balance sheets, incoming applications, or orders. The flexibility of such networks – their ability to react to unforeseen events – is praised, thus their local learning capacity and the increasing proportion of unplanned decisions.[50] In the participating organizations, however, this would require a memory completely different from conventional accounting – or would otherwise amount to giving up control and drifting along with societal developments. That could hardly be justified by trust in "market economic principles" and would scarcely be compatible in organizations dependent on politics with (representative) democracy and the rule of law. One would therefore have to reckon with repercussions at the level of societal functional systems. All this might well lead to reservations about the classical model of hierarchically structured organizations, but not about the systems-theoretical description of organization. On the contrary, if planning becomes more difficult, one has to know what belongs to one's own system and what does not. That is the least that can be expected! And if transaction cost analysis or corresponding intuitions lead under changing conditions to the integration or hiving off of sectors, how are such calculations to function if conditions on one of the sides – organization or market – cannot be taken as given? The growing attention paid to networks arises from the acceleration and increasing depth of focus on the possibilities of structural change within one's own and other systems. More than ever before, one sees what had always been the case, that "the environment" is not only "the market" or "public opinion" but consists of distinguishable systems, which act as such and are to be assessed as such. The system/environment distinction is to be complemented but not replaced by the system/system distinction.

The official explanation for abandoning hierarchical control and allowing more autonomy at lower levels or in hived-off operational areas is that hierarchical distance is detrimental to planning and control and that operations have to be planned and controlled where the best relevant knowledge is to be found. However, behind this are far-reaching societal changes in how uncertainty is dealt with. The idea that satisfactory performance is to be had only under strict supervision can be said to scupper itself. Instead, interest in work is presupposed, fast detection of deviations in the informatively observed production process, and, on this basis, tried and tested trust. This is referred to as social embeddedness.[51] It is obvious that this does not solve the problems posed by the horizontal integration of the working process (any more than does a hierarchy).[52]

Underlying the new ways of handling uncertainty are thus societal changes, especially the manifestation of shared interests between "capital and labor." But corresponding changes are also apparent at the level of the societal system.[53] Nowadays it is obviously inappropriate to describe society using traditional theoretical means, for example, in terms of the schema of differentiation and integration or Durkheim's division of labor and (organic) solidarity schema. Yet the problem would be solely to regain unity or the symbolization of the unity of society despite progressive differentiation – partly of functional systems, partly with regard to the differentiation of the societal system, organizational systems, and face-to-face interaction. Instead of focusing on unity as the problem, attention could be turned to difference, that is to say, to maintaining and reproducing the outdifferentiation of systems at all levels of societal reality. We would then also see that drawing system boundaries presupposes overarching networks, that systems do indeed exist as distinct entities that reproduce themselves.

These reflections, like all observations on interdependencies, do not speak against the thesis that organizations are autopoietic systems.[54] Repeated talk about the blurring of organizational boundaries,[55] about boundaryless organizations and so forth, is incidentally easy to test empirically – and to refute. Whoever has doubts should simply try to enter the premises of some organization and start with some work or other – say, behind a desk, on the shop floor, in a school, in a hospital ward. He or she would not get far. On the contrary, organizations are obliged more than ever to presuppose themselves in their operations. How could we otherwise explain that there are thresholds for holding back effects, the crossing of which can have unpredictable impacts? This is not to deny that much may well have changed in the question of what decisions are primarily taken into account in organizations. It could be that partnerships with organizations from the environment have gained in importance and that hierarchical leadership and control have diminished within one's own organization. A system that is based on trigger causality can no longer be controlled by means of intervention causality. This also means that one cannot reckon with adaptive skills in the individual organization[56] – or if so, then only as one reckons with chance events. The right system of reference for this problem is hence not the individual organization but society, which uses organizations to absorb ongoing turbulence, to form step functions, and thus to attain ultrastability – at the risk of dissipative structural changes that systems clearly cannot avoid, which stabilize their own order far from any equilibrium.

Whether the trend is now for more inclusion in large organizations or, on the contrary, for more outsourcing, the entities involved are in any case organizations. Only liquidations and start-ups are accelerated. It is easier to break with one's own past. It is, therefore, no surprise that there is now more and more talk about the opposite: about organizational culture.

X

We should, thus, return to the cultural or institutional approach of more recent organization theory that we have already discussed.[57] It addresses the problem of the relationship between organizations and society (and not only between organization and environment!) and thus falls within the scope of this chapter. But it merely simulates a solution, because neither are the concepts "culture" and "institution" precisely defined, establishing what they exclude, nor can the analysis rely on a clear definition of the problem. Although it is rightly stressed that the social environment does not have to do simply with wild turbulence and chance events, and that the societal system has to be taken into account as a regulatory factor – by organizations themselves and by organization theory – one immediately moves on to empirical case studies that refer back to the institutional theory of the organization only terminologically and no longer conceptually.

We go a step further if we realize that the concepts of culture and institution refer explicitly or implicitly to values. Values are taken as fixed points to guide action, of which nothing more is to be said except that they "apply." They may well be imbued with assumptions about reality, for example, about what is a reasonable ratio of equity capital to loan capital, and thus differ from organization to organization. Even then, they are not subjected to any reality test but at best modified under pressure. The absoluteness of value validity (which is, however, treated as such only in communication) compensates for the fact that all reality is constructed.[58] But there are many values that, in the guise of saints of the system, are responsible for different interests and needs. Everyone can cite values for everything they want to achieve. In communication this happens in the form of assuming that consensus can be attained. The validity of a value is claimed not in the form of a proposal that can be accepted or rejected. But this has its price, namely that conflicts between different values are not settled but left to the situation, i.e., to a decision to manage.

This transforms the solution that institutionalism had offered back into a problem. The question remains of how systems can handle the fact that for all open decisions opposing values can also be mobilized. This is all the more true because what we could call transversal values – such as "environment" or "women" – come to be institutionalized, becoming values that assume a sort of cross-sectional function in the value cosmos and that virtually seek conflict, as well as association, with many other values. Empirical surveys have inciden-tally shown long since (and not only since the spectacular Brent Spar campaign and the retreat of Shell[59]) that the management of an organization places the greatest value on the public image of its organization and in practice often puts more weight on this aspect than on profit maximization, which is anyway difficult to calculate.[60] But this shifts our problem to the question of how management forms an opinion about what public opinion is. This probably happens on the basis of scandals (e.g., environmental damage, bribery, specta-cular errors of judgment, prison breakouts, murder in a psychiatric institution) that catch attention, and which one wishes to avoid in future. But this does not provide adequate guidance for business policy.

Once again, we face the question with which the chapter began: how can the bewilderingly strong interdependence between society and organizations be reduced and the infinite information load be transformed into a finite one? One of the answers may be that the basic problem is always the same, for the differentiation of societal system from organizational system means that solutions to problems can vary from organization to organization. The now usual reference to culture, institutions, and values merely conceals the fact that the question of how the organization relates to society remains unanswered. We shall, therefore, attempt to do so by reformulating the problem.

The classical theory of bureaucratic organization (e.g., Max Weber) had assumed that all organizations serve an exogenous will. This was rendered plausible by reference to political authority or to property. If one abstracts from organization, however, this exogenous will proves impossible to find. It can effectively develop only within organizations, possibly within other organizations. The proprietor is dispossessed by the so-called "managerial revolution." Or rather, he can bring himself to bear only in the form of management. The classical theory has clearly worked with a fiction, ultimately attributable to the circumstance that society was still conceived of as a hierarchical distribution of resources.

If, by contrast, we turn to a systems-theoretical analysis of the major functional systems, we discover that these systems produce not power or rule but a surplus of possibilities and corresponding indeterminacy; or, we could also say, future. The system of the mass media is expected to communicate news every day. Science is expected to constantly present new hypotheses and then to occupy itself with their falsification. Politics limits its future not through fixed purposes whose attainment would mean that the system has performed its task; it oscillates within the framework of a large number of "values," promoting one of which makes the others all the more urgent.

The economy has to reckon with fluctuating prices and currency rates. The medical care system can rely on new patients seeking treatment every day. The outdifferentiation of these functional systems means that external criteria (such as birth status, stratification), which could limit the range of possibilities, do not apply. Even art no longer accepts that clients determine how a work of art is to look. It is clear in all these cases that the outdifferentiation of systems, their operational closure, and their self-referential operation produce surplus possibilities, which are experienced as structural indeterminacy and referred to self-organization. Since the middle of the nineteenth century, even the legal system has permitted itself to interpret contracts in the light of the will of the contracting parties.

Organizations have to adjust to the resulting constant reproduction of uncertainty. For this very reason, as we have seen, they require a hierarchical structure. The need for organizations in modern society is thus to be explained not by a proliferation of decision-making centers that depend on their decisions being carried out. Such centers develop only within organizations and do not explain the need for organization. The problem facing organizations is the uncertainty of the future that is constantly reproduced at a breath-taking pace, and they have to react by making decisions and by vertically integrating their own decision-making processes.

Notes

1. See Stanley H. Udy, Jr., *Work in Traditional and Modern Society*, Englewood Cliffs, NJ 1970.
2. It should be noted that this development primarily concerns male work, whereas women are expected to do the housework, raise the children, entertain, etc. owing to their gender role. To the extent that household staff are drained off to organized work, this becomes a problem, and, as far as possible, housework has to be shifted onto the market.
3. For more comprehensive criticism of this lack of awareness of social theory in recent organization research, too, see Michael T. Hannan and John Freeman, *Organizational Ecology*, Cambridge, MA 1989, chapters 1 and 2.
4. For more information see Chapter 1 note 68.
5. On this and the following remarks see Detlef Pollack, Das Ende einer Organisationsgesellschaft – Systemtheoretische Überlegungen zum gesellschaftlichen Umbruch in der DDR, *Zeitschrift für Soziologie* 19 (1991), 292–307. See also, with abundant material, idem, Kirche in der Organisationsgesellschaft: Zum Wandel in der gesellschaftlichen Lage der evangelischen Kirchen und der politisch alternativen Gruppen in der DDR, Habilitationsschrift Bielefeld 1993.
6. See in particular Niklas Luhmann, Selbstorganisation und Information im politischen System, *Selbstorganisation* 2 (1991), 11–26.
7. That sociology had not foreseen this has been much regretted and is to be attributed not least to a want of theory. On the other hand, as chaos theory and evolution theory show, concrete foresight would not have been possible anyway, but at best a description of the situation that indicated that now some accident, person, or event or other could suffice to trigger destabilization.
8. See Nicolas Hayoz, "*L'étreinte soviétique: Aspects sociologiques de l'effondrement programmé de l'URSS*, Geneva 1997.
9. The importance of trust based on recurrent cooperation and/or observation by third parties is often mentioned in the recent literature on interorganizational networks, but usually only in passing. But see also Edward H. Lorenz, Neither Friends nor Strangers: Informal Networks of Subcontracting in French Industry, in: Diego Gambetta (ed.), *Trust: Making and Breaking Cooperative Relations*, Oxford 1988, 194–210; Achim Loose and Jörg Sydow, Vertrauen und Ökonomie in Netzwerkbeziehungen – Strukturrationstheoretische Betrachtungen, in: Jörg Sydow and Arnold Windeler (eds.), *Management interorganisationaler Beziehungen*, Opladen 1994, 160–193; Christel Lane

and Reinhard Bachmann, The Social Construction of Trust: Supplier Relations in Britain and Germany, *Organization Studies* 17 (1996), 365–395.

10. See Michael Hutter and Gunther Teubner, The Parasitic Role of Hybrids, *Zeitschrift für die gesamte Staatswissenschaft* 149 (1993), 706–715.

11. See Niklas Luhmann, Kausalität im Süden, *Soziale Systeme* 1 (1995), 7–28.

12. See Richard von Weizsäcker im Gespräch mit Gunter Hofmann und Werner A. Perger, Frankfurt 1992. Many comments in the daily press. See also the subsequent publication Gunter Hofmann and Werner A. Perger (eds.), *Die Kontroverse: Weizsäckers Parteienkritik in der Diskussion*, Frankfurt 1992, as well as Siegfried Unseld (ed.), *Politik ohne Projekt? Nachdenken über Deutschland*, Frankfurt 1993.

13. See also Giancarlo Corsi, Die dunkle Seite der Karriere, in: Dirk Baecker (ed.), *Probleme der Form*, Frankfurt 1993, 252–265.

14. It should be noted that the old concepts of *oikos* or *familia* included not only spouses and their children but also other relatives living in the household, as well as dependent personnel and slaves, livestock, buildings, and land. In the case of the medieval court family, members of the court, for example, artists, were appointed "*familiares*" and thus rewarded. There was no name for what we now call family. Kinship was understood as clan structure.

15. Consider the well-known theses of Foucault on the beginning of new forms of social disciplining in the second half of the eighteenth century. See also S. Cohen, *Visions of Social Control*, Cambridge Engl. 1985.

16. See, in particular, Manfred Rühl, *Die Zeitungsredaktion als organisiertes soziales System*, Bielefeld 1969, as well as a series of subsequent studies with the same results. For an overview, see Frank Marcinkowski, *Publizistik als autopoietisches System*, Opladen 1993, esp. 98 ff.

17. See Adalbert Podlech, *Gehalt und Funktionen des allgemeinen verfassungsrechtlichen Gleichheitssatzes*, Berlin 1971, 50.

18. See W. Ross Ashby, *Design for a Brain: The Origin of Adaptive Behaviour*, 2nd ed. London 1954, 80 ff.; idem, *An Introduction to Cybernetics*, New York 1956, 82 ff.

19. An important discovery of Talcott Parsons concerning the general conditions of rationality. See, in particular, Talcott Parsons and Gerald M. Platt, *Die amerikanische Universität*, German translation Frankfurt 1990, 42, 409 ff. See also Rainer C. Baum, On Societal Media Dynamics, in: Jan J. Loubser et al. (eds.), *Explorations in General Theory in Social Sciences: Essays in Honor of Talcott Parsons*, New York 1976, 579–608.

20. See Humberto R. Maturana, *Erkennen: Die Organisation und Verkörperung von Wirklichkeit: Ausgewählte Arbeiten zur biologischen Epistemologie*, Braunschweig 1982, esp. 150 ff., 251 ff.

21. See for more detail Niklas Luhmann, Wie ist Bewußtsein an Kommunikation beteiligt?, in: Hans Ulrich Gumbrecht and K. Ludwig Pfeiffer (eds.), *Materialität der Kommunikation*, Frankfurt 1988, 884–905.

22. See, e.g., Edward O. Laumann and John P. Heinz et al., Washington Lawyers and Others: The Structure of Washington Representation, *Stanford Law Review* 37 (1985), 465–502; Robert L. Nelson and John P. Heinz, Lawyers and the Structure of Influence in Washington, *Law and Society Review* 22 (1988), 237–300.

23. On "discussion circles" that have to do with science, law, economics, and politics see Michael Hutter, *Die Produktion von Recht: Eine selbstreferentielle Theorie der Wirtschaft, angewandt auf den Fall des Arzneimittelpatentrechts*, Tübingen 1989.

24. See Gunther Teubner, *Organisationsdemokratie und Verbandsverfassung*, Tübingen 1978.

25. See Niklas Luhmann, *Das Recht der Gesellschaft*, Frankfurt 1993, 297 ff.

26. 1 Cranch (1803), 137 ff., esp. 176 ff. See also William E. Nelson, The Eighteenth-Century Background of John Marshall's Constitutional Jurisprudence, *Michigan Law Review* 76 (1978), 893–960.

27. See Marbury v. Madison loc. cit..

28. See Dieter Grimm, *Die Zukunft der Verfassung*, Frankfurt 1991.

29. See Gunther Teubner and Helmut Willke, Kontext und Autonomie: Gesellschaftliche Selbststeuerung durch reflexives Recht, *Zeitschrift für Rechtssoziologie* 11 (1984), 4–35; also Manfred Glagow and Helmut Willke (eds.), *Dezentrale Gesellschaftssteuerung: Probleme der Integration polyzentrischer Gesellschaft*, Pfaffenweiler 1987; Manfred Glagow, Helmut Willke, and Helmut Wiesenthal (eds.), *Gesellschaftliche Steuerung und partikulare Handlungsstrategien*, Pfaffenweiler 1989; Helmut Willke, *Ironie des Staates, Grundlinien einer Staatstheorie polyzentrischer Gesellschaft*, Frankfurt 1992; idem, *Systemtheorie III: Steuerungstheorie*, Stuttgart 1995. See also several contributions in: Roeland J. in't Veld, Linze Schaap, Catrien J.A.M. Termeer, and Mark J. W. van Twist (eds.), *Autopoiesis and Configuration Theory: New Approaches to Societal Steering*, Dordrecht 1991, and Volker Ronge, Politische Steuerung – innerhalb und außerhalb der Systemtheorie, in: Klaus Dammann et al. (eds.), *Die Verwaltung des politischen Systems: Neuere systemtheoretische Zugriffe auf ein altes Thema*, Opladen 1994, 53–64. Most of the literature on control justifies control on the grounds of rejection of the theory of autopoietic systems (e.g., as incompatible with the fact of control) turning instead to action theoretical concepts. See, e.g., Fritz W. Scharpf, Politische Steuerung und politische Institutionen, in: Hans-Hermann Hartwich (ed.), *Macht und Ohnmacht politischer Institutionen: 17. Wissenschaftlicher Kongress der DVPW 12. bis 16. September 1988*, Opladen 1989, 17–29. Here, too, however, is insight into obvious difficulties and likely setbacks.

30. See, e.g., F. Steier and K.K. Smith, Organizations and Second Order Cybernetics, *Journal of Strategic and Systemic Therapies* 4,4 (1985), 53–65.

31. See Chapter 2.

32. A similar argument, albeit with a differing distinction between meaning systems and organizations, is advanced by I. J. Koppen, Environmental Mediation: An Example of Applied Autopoiesis?, in: in't Veld et al. op. cit. 143–160.

33. This is stressed by Uwe Schimank, Politische Steuerung in der Organisationsgesellschaft – am Beispiel der Forschungspolitik, in: Wolfgang Zapf (ed.), *Die Modernisierung moderner Gesellschaften. Verhandlungen des 25. Deutschen Soziologentages in Frankfurt am Main 1990*, Frankfurt 1991, 505–516.

34. On this question there is more suspicion than serious empirical research. But see Dan Clawson, Alan Neustadtl, and Denise Scott, *Money Talks: Corporate PACs and Political Influence*, New York 1992. (PAC stands for: political action committee.)

35. It is worth noting that success is more likely if organizations manage to stage events that can interest the media, which, following their own logic, the media are more or less obliged to report on. This means that, whatever the motive behind them, operations have to take place already in another system. Think of the typical scene in which prominent politicians shake hands without looking at one another, exemplified by that captured by photographers of the first, demonstratively early meeting between prime minister Berlusconi and the pope. The pope tries to look at Berlusconi, who does not look at the pope but into the "public."

36. This could induce action theoreticians to consider the action to be an indispensable component of the concept of control (arguing that someone has to do it!). But then the concept of action would first have to be clarified, particularly in terms of the causal schema. Is the actor as the cause of the action part of the action? And what about other causes, for example, his education, his socialization, the situation that motivates him? And what effects of the action are part of the action. All? Only direct ones? Only intended ones? Such questions can lead to the exclusion of all causes and all effects from the concept of action. But then action would be nothing more than the bare difference between overall causes and overall effects – of what?

37. On the effect of organizations on the arising of turbulence in the environment of other organizations, see the early study by Shirley Terreberry, The Evolution of Organizational Environments, *Administrative Science Quarterly* 12, 1968, 590–613.

38. We leave the minor special case out of account in which public institutions such as museums and theaters can finance themselves fully from their own incomes. Hospitals, too, require special treatment in connection with the insurance system that is partly imposed by the state and partly co-financed.

39. A method by which, incidentally, empirical research too deserves the title of "empirical" by concretizing many of its variables by means of estimations.

40. See Erich Gutenberg, *Die Unternehmung als Gegenstand betriebswirtschaftlicher Theorie*, Berlin 1929.

41. See Gordon Donaldson and Jay W. Lorsch, *Decision Making at the Top: The Shaping of Strategic Direction*, New York 1983.

42. See Donaldson and Lorsch op. cit. 84.

43. A great deal of recent literature. See, e.g., Walter W. Powell, Neither Market nor Hierarchy: Network Forms of Organization, in: Barry M. Staw and L.L. Cummings (ed.), *Research in Organizational Behavior* 12 (1990), 295–336; Anne S. Milner, Terry L. Amburgey, and Timothy M. Stearns, Interorganizational Linkages and Population Dynamics: Buffering and Transformational Shields, *Administrative Science Quarterly* 35 (1990), 689–713; Adriana Signorelli, *Relazioni interorganizzative: Teorie e ricerche*, Milano 1991; Arman Avadikyan, Patrick Cohendet, and Patrick Llerena, Coherence, Diversity of Assets and Networks: Towards an Evolutionary Approach, *Revue internationale de systemique* 7 (1993), 305–331; Mark Lazerson, A New Phoenix?, Modern Putting Out in the Modena Knitwear Industry, *Administrative Science Quarterly* 40 (1995), 34–59 (with clear pointers to conditions in the societal environment). See also the literature mentioned in notes 9 and 11 above.

44. However, within the legal system illegality would be a clear and hence unproblematic case. The real problems these recent developments in the economic system

cause for the legal system are quite different in kind. They arise from the difficulty of attributing the classical categories of property and contract to either corporation law or contract law. With the aid of these categories, the legal system had in the past been able to accept structural coupling with the economy while preserving its independence. See Niklas Luhmann, Das Recht der Gesellschaft op. cit.. 448 ff. These forms are sabotaged by recent organizational developments in the economic system, with the legal system being able to accept the *economic* rationality of this development as *legally convincing argument*. See Gunther Teubner, Den Schleier des Vertrags zerreißen? Zur rechtlichen Verantwortung ökonomisch "effizienter" Vertragsnetzwerke, *Kritische Vierteljahresschrift für Gesetzgebung und Rechtswissenschaft* 76 (1993), 367–393.

45. For literature see note 9 above.
46. See Lane and Bachmann op. cit. (1996), 379.
47. See only Marc Granovetter, Economic Action and Social Structure: The Problem of Embeddedness, *American Journal of Sociology* 91 (1985), 481–510.
48. See as the result of case studies Andrea Larson, Network Dyads in Entrepreneurial Settings: A Study of the Governance of Exchange Relations, *Administrative Science Quarterly* 37 (1992), 76–104.
49. See Nathalie Lazaric, Organizational Learning and Combinative Capacity During Technological Agreements: Some Empirical Evidence in the Robotic Sector, *Revue Internationale de systemique* 10 (1996), 201–221.
50. See e.g., Avadikyan et al. op. cit.
51. Following Marc Granovetter, Economic Action and Social Structure: the Problem of Embeddedness, *American Journal of Sociology* 91 (1985), 481–510.
52. See Volker Wittke, Vertikale versus Horizontale Desintegration: Zu unterschiedlichen Erosionsdynamiken des Großunternehmens im Prozeß industrieller Restrukturierung, Mitteilungen 22/95 des Soziologischen Forschungsinstituts Göttingen with further pointers on the recent debate.
53. The research perspective had already been broadened once, under the heading of "political economy." See J. Kenneth Benson, The Interorganizational Network as a Political Economy, *Administrative Science Quarterly* 20 (1975), 229–249.
54. One could, following usage in Italian, consider distinguishing between organizations and corporations (impresa rete). See Federico Butera, *Il castello e la rete: Impresa, organizzazioni e professioni nell' Europa degli anni '90*, 2nd ed, Milano 1991. See also Dirk Baecker, *Die Form des Unternehmens*, Frankfurt 1993. Another name to be found for this is "virtual corporation." See William H. Davidow and Michael S. Malone, *The Virtual Corporation*, New York 1992; Nitin Nohria and James D. Berkeley, The Virtual Organization: Bureaucracy, Technology, and the Implosion of Control, in: Charles Heckscher and Anne Donnellon (eds.), *The Post-Bureaucratic Organization: New Perspectives on Organizational Change*, Thousand Oaks, CA 1994, 108–128. The name is misleading. It has nothing to do with virtual corporations that do not exist at all but with corporations for virtual products. But then it clearly becomes more difficult to speak of self-description or corporate culture at the level of the enterprise, and one would have to consider whether this can be an advantage in the sense of greater flexibility.

55. E.g., Wolf V. Heydebrand, New Organizational Forms, *Work and Occupation* 16 (1989), 323–357 (331): "dissolution of boundaries between organizations and their environments."

56. See James E. McNulty, Organizational Change in Growing Enterprises, *Administrative Science Quarterly* 7 (1962), 1–21.

57. See Chapter 1–6

58. This was, incidentally, a result (although not formulated as such) of Neo-Kantian analyses, which, via Rickert, influenced Max Weber and led to his tragic-conflictual value aphorism. We could therefore trace the analyses carried out above more or less directly to Max Weber.

59. See Niklas Luhmann, Konzeptkunst: Brent Spar oder Können Unternehmen von der Öffentlichkeit lernen?, *Frankfurter Allgemeine* Zeitung 19 July 1995, 27.

60. Ross Stagner, Corporate Decision Making: An Empirical Study, *Journal of Applied Psychology* 53 (1969), 1–13.

14   Self-Description

By "self-description" we mean the production of a text or a functional equivalent of a text (e.g., indexical expressions such as "we" or "here" or a proper name) with which and by which the organization identifies itself. Such texts do not need to be, as it were, biblical, canonic documents; but whatever fulfills the function of self-description has to meet certain requirements of self-reference at the level of the system. A wide variety of situations, occasions, and circumstances have to mesh and combine, have to indicate "the same" over time while remaining flexible in meaning content.[1]

Self-descriptions differ from the ongoing self-observations by which the system ensures reference to itself, the absorption of uncertainty, and the connectivity of decision-making. Self-observations constitute the medium, namely the memory material from which the forms of self-description can be extracted. At the level of self-observation, the organization remains intransparent to itself – and for this very reason operational. Every articulation of the self that includes the exclusion of everything else would have to take the paradoxical form of reentry; it would thus obstruct itself and provoke a permanent, inward looking search for meaning.[2] A self-description cannot eliminate the intransparency of the system for itself. It replaces and displaces it by a substitute, namely an encipherment that conceals (not eliminates, for no system can do what it is) the operational intransparency, which thus takes its place and guides operations by its text. Recently, especially in organization research,[3] there has been talk of ambiguities necessary for communication. A text can focus the attention of many communications in unpredictable situations, whereas it would be impossible to take note of everything that actually happens simultaneously or sequentially. A text can therefore fix ideas, which can then be spoken about without taking what actually happens at the operational level too much into consideration.[4]

Like all descriptions, self-descriptions are simplifications and hence sensitive to disturbance by circumstances left out of account. On the other side of its form (the side to which one cannot connect), the self-description text thus remains a witness to non-knowledge and can be described as such by an observer. To motivate such observations, a "critique of ideology" has been spoken of, and the corresponding deconstruction judged to be positive. It turns out, however, that crossing the boundary merely by observing and not by operating means that nothing can be done on the other side. What then happens is the constantly repeated expression of impulses for reform.

The function of texts, and hence of self-descriptions, is to coordinate memory performance, which otherwise has to rely on mental processes, namely on perceptions and on the recognition of perceptions.[5] In fact, texts are the memory of social systems, regardless of whether written down or passed on orally. In social systems they are therefore a functional equivalent for what perception does mentally, indeed for what makes perception possible in the first place.[6] The function of texts is not to adapt a system to its environment, nor to honor institutional values or duties symbolically. *Instead* they produce the distinction between conformity and deviation, so that the system can let itself be provoked into deviation by its own text if the circumstances provide enough backing.

Memory performance, whether by the brain, the consciousness, or social communication occurs only in the present time in which consistency checks take place. In the past nothing more can happen and in the future nothing can yet happen.[7] It can, but does not have to, use a time schema to resolve inconsistencies by distributing them across different points in time. With or without temporal recollection, memory performance takes the form of recognizing something already known; with regard to texts, this means recognizing written characters, words, single textual components, single texts, or even certain books, and only rarely recalling the situation when the relevant meaning content was first updated.[8] The memory thus assumes the function of giving shape to an operation as observation – in both social and psychic systems. In other words, it sows observational possibilities in the soil of autopoietic operation. Without memory, the difference between operation and observation would collapse; the system would not even be able to distinguish between past and future, because it could not fill the time horizons with content, and thus could not establish and distinguish between congruence (continuity) and diversity (discontinuity).

These general remarks on the memory function of texts have been necessary to indicate the framework in which self-descriptions perform their special function. They are texts of a special sort, characterized by their reference to the system as the unity of all its operations (= as the autopoietic context of reproduction). If explicitly formulated, they make the system the subject of predicates, even though this happens in the system itself, which implies self-predication. This ensures that every use of self-reference relates to one and the same invariant and that every use of this reference, even if only hinted at, indicates something that could be explained.

Even the normal text/memory structure is based on double closure,[9] containing several layers of operational guidelines. We had spoken of decision premises.[10] Decision premises, too, can be introduced in several stages. For example, personnel decisions can be programmed. Closer analysis soon shows that there is no underlying logical hierarchy of authorities or levels, but that prevailing points of view constantly change, depending on what the situation requires; and this also means that points of view can dominate only for a time (and not structurally).[11] No efficient memory can be hierarchically ordered; it must have at its disposition a multitude of generalizations varying in power, varying in how frequently they are called up, and which are not updated according to a predictable pattern but when the opportunity arises. The concept of double closure is then also set explicitly in contrast to the notion of a hierarchical order with the intention of replacing it.[12] A fortiori, self-description texts can therefore not be seen as the topmost level or topmost authority of the system one turns to when at a loss or when inconsistencies cannot be resolved. Self-descriptions are more likely to be necessary precisely because the operations of the system cannot be ordered hierarchically and another mode of coordination for highly complex and shifting quantities of updating has to be built in *instead*.

It is therefore perhaps useful to replace the concept of heterarchy with that of labyrinth, which intuitively corresponds better to what one finds in large organizations. With very few entrances and exits, a labyrinth offers a maximum of internal contact possibilities, which are actualized in basically unpredictable sequences. This produces a multitude of assessments that do not depend on (are not determined by) the quality of the input signals. Not only can the system receive irritations but also generate them and pass them on; and in its operations it can produce the necessary acceleration and deceleration. Such tempo regulation can then produce an impression of reiteration, of identity, of condensation by which the consciousness and then the communication system register the neurophysiological work to make its memory appear to be a world. For all this, an organizational system uses societal givens, above all the easily recognizable words of language; but also, and, recognizably a supplement of its own, the decision premises produced in the system itself for which everything applies that a memory does under the precondition of a labyrinthine order: recognition, identification, condensation, generalization, and above all the continuous forgetting of unused material. But a labyrinthine order does not stop hierarchies from also being formed in the system. However, the system must then be able to switch hierarchies on and off, for example, by separating formal from informal communications; and this can happen only through local decisions.

What could possibly be needed and what could be relied on if responsibility has to be claimed or relinquished is recorded and recalled in the form of decision premises – thus if higher or more competent authorities have to be made responsible. This function suffices unto itself, it does not have to be outdone. It requires no basic norm, no authority that generates and answers for everything, and also (which will be denied) no "legitimation."[13] It can be hierarchized in communication channels and decision-making powers, but, at the top of the resulting hierarchy, it necessarily remains a moot point whether business obeys the boss or the boss obeys business. It makes all the less sense to treat self-descriptions as directive texts.

The function of self-description texts appears rather to be to concentrate, bundle, and center the constantly occurring self-references in order to make it clear that always the "same," a system identical with itself, is at issue. The self-description serves the system as "official culture of remembrance,"[14] which can be communicated without any problem; and "without any problem" means without concern for whoever perceives it, in other words, whoever perceives it publicly. This requires only vague, unconceptualized notions of system identity.

A consciousness has its "own" body, which imposes an "I" on it.[15] The I is always where its body is, and from this standpoint can concern itself with all sorts of things without having to lose itself in the world outside itself. It always knows where it is and what place centers its perception and thinking. Social systems have no such guarantee. Where "are" they? They can identify with locations in space, with buildings, for example; but this gives them no "soul" that could survive the end of this relationship, just as the consciousness imagines a soul to transpose the inconceivability of an end to its autopoiesis into the form of an eternal I. Social systems can leave their locations without having to take their bodies with them (perhaps their debts instead).[16] They can make their communications outside their locations, extraterritorially, so to speak. So what stops them from losing themselves in the world of their topics and not finding their way back to themselves? Or what guarantees them the continuity of their constitutive difference between self-reference and other-reference? An organization has no body: it has a text.

It can be objected that communication still needs a material substratum to make it discernible, a medium such as sound, paper, or electricity, in which it can manifest its utterances. But this clearly does not suffice to give adequate consistency to the memory of the system through localization; for these media take up practically everything fed to them (whereas the body provides the consciousness with an unequivocal here and now, and in social contacts also ensures that the perception of being perceived restricts behavior). The communication that forms social systems, including organizations, requires additional assurance of consistency. In simple systems it may suffice to attribute utterances to persons, who as individuals may well have all sorts of objectionable thoughts, but who are expected to mean what they say and abide by it. For organizational systems, alone because of shifting relations between positions and persons, this does not suffice. They therefore reduce the genuine underdetermination (or overdetermination) of their self-reference through a conglomeration of additional, communicable indicators such as name and address; more specific and effectively differentiating functional information, such as type of product or service; reputational characteristics that indicate what one can be proud of; and, above all, a narratable history of the system. All this condenses into the assumption of a unity – consistent, if not in logical, then at least in practical terms – that one can cite; and this is the case even if disruptive events or open conflicts occur, or cynical or carnivalesque communications are forthcoming that undermine the "official" self-description. The basic paradox of the unity of all differences has to remain concealed, which can also happen by assigning mockery of the official cult or more or less open deviation to another level of communication, which takes over the paradox, fighting out the difference between earnestness and jest or between solemn and cynical communication *within itself*.[17]

In self-description, the system memory recalls itself. Its topology is both the location and the topic of memories. If meaning is to be concentrated across time in this fashion, self-description texts have to include themselves; they have to be autological. However, this is usually not said openly but hidden in categorical formulations or in simple statements of fact to prevent opposing opinions from arising at all. But also in the mode of categorical statements or statements of fact (on the lines of "human dignity is inviolable"), autological texts of this type always refer back to themselves – to the fact that they present themselves.

II

Every analysis of self-description or, in classical terminology, of "reflection" will have to assume that the system is operationally inaccessible to itself and thus remains intransparent even to its own operations.[18] Not a single operation can be or even indicate what takes place simultaneously or sequentially within the bounds of the system. No decision "is" the system, since every decision presupposes recursive networking in the system and can be a decision only on this condition. This might be why the classical theories of self-reflection, whether of the consciousness, or of the "mind" or "spirit," work with the determinate/indeterminate schema. This can be dissolved into the distinction between an ideal and its approximate realization, or, in aesthetics, characterized by the concept "noble,"[19] which defines the determinate as indication of the indeterminate. In Hegel's theory, this becomes a problem of transitions disciplined by dialectic. We shall not attempt to apply this grand pattern of the philosophical tradition directly to organization theory. We posit, however, that the self-description of organization systems also has to work with the basic determinate/indeterminate schema because it otherwise cannot indicate the inaccessibility of the system to itself (or only negatively, only paradoxically, and thus unproductively).

For organization theory it seems obvious to treat the determination of the indeterminate as decision. Classical organization theory did so by describing the organization as the framework condition for rational decision-making. An organization is as good as the decisions it produces. Factual limitations to the capacity for information processing were built into this idea without questioning that information contributes to solving problems in the decision process. Not until the 1970s and 1980s was more attention paid to the circumstance that finding and compiling knowledge is also undertaken for its own sake, regardless of whether and how it can contribute to solving problems.[20] There are clearly incentives for transforming what is not known into what is known, for investigating states of affairs and for writing reports that are not even read or assessed. Anyway, the usefulness of knowledge is difficult to appraise in advance; but it can at least be presented as the result of work, and this work gives rise to enough difficulties in obtaining information and coordinating descriptions to allow the product to be presented as a successful achievement.

Activities of this sort are based on the official self-description, according to which the organization is concerned with knowledge-based, rational decision-making. On the recommendation of economists, the metaphor of "equilibrium" is often used, and rational decision-making is understood as re-establishing equilibrium.[21] However, what actually happens can be far better understood if one assumes that it is about transforming an unknown world into a known one. But the organization must assume that indeterminacy is continuously renewed. Either indeterminacy penetrates the organization from the environment as chance disturbance, making itself felt as irritation and thus being ultimately attributable to the environment while the organization considers itself to be orderly; or the decision itself is seen as a source of continuous regeneration of indeterminacy, for instance, in the sense of the permanent problem of interpreting its meaning under constantly changing circumstances.

In this version, the problem of determining the indeterminate and the indeterminacy of the determinate takes on a form that can be further processed. The decision itself remains a mystery – but a known and familiar one, which can be experienced every day. It is charged to a *qualitas occulta*: to the person who decides. Further demystification makes use of the tools that we have come across repeatedly and that go by the name of classical organization theory, namely the restriction of decision-making to specific purposes and the hierarchization of personnel structures by which people are entitled and empowered to make decisions. Although it is now hardly contested that the classical organizational model is obsolete[22] – not only as a tool for scientific analysis but also as a form of self-description and self-presentation by organization, above all in the economy – no theoretical innovation commensurate with the changes has been forthcoming. Descriptions use the old schemata (e.g., structure/process, centralization/decentralization, constancy/innovation); they use concepts that need explaining – such as institution, culture, and networks – without clarifying the operational basis; and they concentrate essentially on economic organizations and not so much (except in the sectors of "tasks" and possibly technologies) on public administration or on universities, trade unions, hospitals, courts. Innovations are pursued under such headings as "group work" or "lean production" without the organization being able to keep up with the dismantling of hierarchical structures, let alone at the level of wage and salary structures.[23] At the level of ideas, the system oscillates more strongly than at the level of actual structures. For this reason a theoretical explanation is lacking for the widely accepted, "known" fact that the classical model is no longer convincing. Members of the organization who continue to see their real task in contributing to rational problem-solving react to prevailing conditions with disappointment, at times with cynicism.[24]

We therefore turn again to this model of means-end oriented hierarchy to ask how it is structured and what about it is no longer convincing. The classical model sets out from the mythology of deciding persons and sees the only problem in how to discipline their decisions to conform to the purposes of the organization. The mythology of deciding persons is thus compensated for by the fact that a greater or lesser degree of technical rationality is expected of them in their decisions. The organization now appears as a means-end oriented hierarchy. And now the determinate/indeterminate schema has a structure that, in accordance with the distinction between ends and means or between top and bottom, is determined or at least determinable on both sides of the distinction. The self-description of the organization concentrates on this form, and then treats everything that is not congruent with it as deviation – for example, as violation of norms to be tolerated or ignored, or if necessary as helpful "informal organization." The self-description finally assumes a new name; it appears as the rationality of decision-making and of the organization. In this every organization can lean on the "culture" of society, and thus on an expectation of rational work firmly established in its environment.[25] That the results are not always satisfying must and can be explained on top of this – by the insight that not everything "in this world" goes the way one wants it to; or by complexity[26]; or by the conditions of evolutionary changes determined by the environment.

For example, the classical theory, like the typical self-description concept of organizations, assumed that power and freedom are closely connected if not one. Later, freedom was visible only where someone had the power to push through their own decisions. Freedom and power increased on the way up through official channels and decreased on the way down the chain of command. If, by contrast, one switches the concept of freedom to the competent-interpretative construction of alternatives about which one can then decide rationally or irrationally, both freedom and power diminish with the increase of complexity.[27] And the previously assumed connection between freedom and power (or unfreedom and coercion) dissolves. The problem of the visible and attributable use of freedom shifts to the level of communication. Whoever has no power to push through his decisions can still communication riskily, whether as boss or subordinate, as expert, as advisor. It therefore becomes a question of what distinctions, what alternatives, what choices can be constructed and introduced into communication; and whether this is done to symbolize the part one plays in events, or whether one prefers not to run any "political" risk and wait in the wings to join the winning side when opportune. This order can be expected to leave open the choice of strategies and, in dependence on this choice, the selection of criteria. Communication will then, psychically and socially, serve essentially the intellectual self-gratification of systems without having to presuppose consensus.

To the extent that the best possible rationality is replaced by "culture," organizations will understandably no longer justify themselves solely by their product but adapt to societal expectations and thus to public opinion. On the occasion of the confrontation between Greenpeace and the Shell Group in the Brent Spar scandal, Shell placed full-page advertisements in a hundred daily newspapers, declaring it had learned that in the future it had to take account of public opinion (and not only internal rationalities). Whatever one might think of it, the self-description of the enterprise has become ambiguous and will, in the future, have to be guided primarily by the distinction between external and internal representation, which then have to be brought into balance.

These changes in the reality and self-presentation of complex organizations could also provide new opportunities for the theoretically inspired but local imagination. It is striking how persistently organization research has pursued this rationalistic-hierarchical self-description and that it had also derived the scientific definition of its object from this model. It had found a "self-description from above" in the object and had accepted this for itself – at least as requirement for the demands that organizations make of themselves. The self-reflection of the system then defines the object of scientific analysis. Such proximity to the object may, in some aspects, be advisable – for example, to facilitate agreement with members of the organizations under study or as a condition for understanding and accepting advice. However, an analysis of the logical and structural problems of each self-description drives a wedge into this agreement. If science, and especially sociology, exploits its theoretical possibilities to the full, it could produce descriptions with a great deal more contingency and of much greater structural complexity in which "praxis" would not recognize itself without further ado.

A decision between these two possibilities does not have to be made at this juncture. It can anyway not be demanded as correlate of an appropriate (e.g., "critical") concept of science. But classical organization theory having favored and elaborated a practical version, it seems advisable to try out others, too; all the more so because in many regards, above all in reflection on the conditions of successful intervention and in the problem-constructivism of therapists and organizational consultants, greater theory-driven distance has been called for and to some extent achieved. The suggestion that self-descriptions can be understood as products of texts that assume the functions of memory, thus regulating forgetting and remembering (and therefore sorting the indeterminate out from the determinate), points in this direction.

One of the consequences of abandoning the classical model is likely to be a change (long in the offing) in the assessment of personnel management. The classical model more or less explicitly assumed that the rationality of action by individual members is adequately determined by purpose and by hierarchical position and the scope of freedom. In other words, there was officially no problem of motivation unless it was in negotiating membership conditions. After that, no motivation problems were expected to turn up – unless they were problems of deviance, of norm violation, and thus of supervision.

But if the premises of hierarchically structured rationality have to be replaced by the premises of the paradox of decision-making and uncertainty absorption, these assumptions change. The classical division between motivation and cognition can no longer be maintained – any more than the division between intellect and will in anthropology.[28] It is replaced by the question of how the individual constructs one's own world (or, to be more precise, oneself in the world). For the social system this means switching to second-order observation: in the hierarchy both top-down and bottom-up. The consequence is not a return to the human relations approach, which had assumed that the well-being of the individual was the precondition for motivating him. The organization must rather manage without such underlying anthropological assumptions in handling its members and be guided instead by what can be observed. Because organizations are closed systems, they must be able to bear a great deal more openness than was provided for under the classical model. Structurally this means that all structures that determine decision-making must first be developed through the operations of the system in an environment that in principle remains unknown, but, given the experience of the organization with itself, can be constructed and remembered as construction.

Another consequence of self-description as rationally functioning hierarchy is that it inevitably leads to disappointment and, through disappointment, to resignation. Thus projects or reforms are logically expected to be "implemented." But on the part of both the initiating and the executing organization, there are good reasons why these expectations are in many regards illusory. The illusion may serve to bolster the self-gratification of the initiators or to muster reasons for the resistance for which there are motives anyway. Organizational science offers explanations for all of this, which show that it normally has to be expected[29]; and these explanations merely confirm what experienced members of organizations know in any case. One should and could thus prevent organizations from deceiving themselves with their self-descriptions. These considerations can show why it will be difficult to continue taking the classical text of organization theory as the basis for the self-description of organizations. Or if one does so, account will have to taken of its opposite, of its implausibility, of the constant threat of its deconstruction in the same system.

Given the current status of systems-theoretical research, all this may well appear cogent. Whether a self-description of individual organizational systems can follow this is quite another matter. It remains to be seen whether and how organizations manage with a more experimental attitude toward themselves and with the continuous restructuring of their own memory, and, in particular, to what extent they can retain or exchange persons as factors of the system memory.

Following the classical text, one would have to claim to have solved the "problem of the third person,"[30] either by irrevocably setting a goal or by assuming a final decision-making authority at the apex of the system's hierarchy, or, as is mostly the case, by accepting both solutions, which permits open problems to be shifted back and forth. Goals and final authority then serve as stop rules to avoid infinite regression. They provide a surrogate for the third value that cannot be calculated, or for the third subject that cannot appear.

At least at the level of self-descriptions, but often and very massively also at the level of the strategic planning of practical operations, these certainties prove to have lost credibility. Members of the system react with more or less cynical comments.[31] Communication recognizes that the issue is setting limits that are all too easy to transgress; and whoever, like Remus climbing over the walls of Rome, does overstep these limits, cannot be killed in the interests of sovereignty.[32] One has to reckon with the presence of the absent third person and allow for it. Organization is then pure positivity, and restrictions are to be had only through self-organization, hence only through operations of the organization itself. Identities are not given, they have to be formulated, and this holds true for framework conditions of all types. They have to be put in a form whose other side would be the communication of non-knowledge – of unobservability, of operational inaccessibility, of lacking information. In concrete terms, this means doubts being continually expressed about whether goals are still right and whether instructions are factually justified. Such a trite (and again cynical) way of putting things can of course be avoided, but given the present level of reflection, the two-sidedness of all forms must inevitably be taken into account. What would have to be formulated is therefore the boundary, which as boundary remains stable, stable precisely because referential regression would have to lead *ad infinitum* to unobservablity – on the inside of the form (what, for example, goals require) and on the outer side of the form (why these goals are pursued at all).

For this problem, the old European semantics had provided an either/or model, namely the distinction between a disturbing dogmatics and a restless skepticism, and everything pointed to peace in one dogmatic form or the other. This distinction dissolved in the seventeenth century. At the level of the individual organization (we are not speaking about the societal system here) it cannot be realized anyway. Not least because every dogmatic setting has to be continuously tested on the market or against other environmental conditions (professional acceptance, government financing, etc.). It will have to be replaced by constant oscillation between setting and cancellation, system loyalty and cynicism, constructive and deconstructive communication, with the system memory also remembering – or forgetting – the "crossing." What would then be at issue would be the communicative organization of this oscillation, indeed the ongoing parallelization of the two possibilities of communication, the avoidance of permanent hierarchical honors for what is "right," and the intensification of simultaneous trust and mistrust in the text.

Very typically in this difficult identity-fixing situation, two answers are found, which insiders can keep apart: one for external presentation and one for members.[33] Here, too, a distinction helps resolve the identity paradox. External presentation seeks to gain recognition and support. But internally it would be embarrassing to mistake this presentation for the reality of things (which is, however, no more than another, also conventional description).[34] In external presentation one will not be able to admit that the head office cannot effectively control events, that it is a labyrinth or a "garbage can," and that there can be no question of rational decision-making. On the other hand, it would, for internal purposes, seem curiously naïve to present the self-description intended for the environment as reality. The notion of a hierarchically guaranteed rationality can thus also be called a "script,"[35] intended above all for those who approach the organization from the outside. Although one must now know which communications belong in which context, one has to recognize system boundaries and be able to appraise discretion/indiscretion, but these are burdens that, as experience shows, can be borne, whereas it is quite inconceivable to capture and represent the entirety of the system's operations in an overall formula.

Whoever knows organizations from the inside will know that this is not so very difficult and has already been realized to a considerable degree in the everyday life of organizations. The question is only whether self-descriptions can catch up with this everyday life, or whether sham belief in fictional texts is unavoidable. The current apotheosis of culture and institution appears to be convinced that this is the case. A sociological theory of the organization could offer reasons why this question should at least be kept open.

III

A self-description can naturally only be produced in the system itself. A description of the system by systems of the environment remains an external description – for example, when scientists elaborate theories about organizations or describe specific organizations in "case studies." In such instances we speak of exogenous description. However, a particular sort of activity (and of organization), namely the activity of organizational consulting by external experts, cannot simply be ascribed to this clear distinction.

With the development of this sector and with the constant reflection on its experience in seminars, training courses, publications, and other forms of soliloquy, considerable modifications have been made to its original self-conception. In the framework of a concept of technical-rational organizations, it was mainly concerned with adapting the organization to different conditions. The consultant had to present himself with better knowledge and prescribe solutions – like a physician who can help when organisms are ill or like an engineer who can help with defective machines. The modified concept does not necessarily have to break with expectations of improved performance, but with the pretensions to better knowledge it no longer duplicates what would have been expected of the organization and, above all, of its management.

The older concept had related the task of advising to the planning of the system's decision premises. However, this becomes progressively more questionable (or at any rate less certain of succeeding) as it becomes clear that the stability of a dynamic system in a turbulent environment requires premises and decisions to be loosely (and not tightly) coupled. The consultant (like the manager) lacks intervention causality. Instead, he can offer benchmark knowledge[36]; and a theory of self-observation and self-description of organizations is accordingly needed to determine the function of advice coming from outside the organization.[37]

Consultants set out from the self-description available and see it as their task to deconstruct and reconstruct it. The main lever they use is the concept of problem. The first thing to be done is often to discover the problem that had inspired practice to date. The stated purposes often serve only to disguise problems whose solution had stabilized behavior. In other cases they have simply become obsolete without this being noticed. Sometimes it is a matter of developing ways to deal with badly defined and difficult to define problems.[38] Usual practices are often also considered useful without asking why they are the way they are and not otherwise. Habits and procedures often have a symbolic value; they show that everything is in order as always. Asking about the problem serves first of all to prepare the ground and to present accepted ways as contingent, as amenable to change. The question can be put "naïvely" as by an outsider who wants to understand something; or psycho-analytically on the suspicion that there is something unconscious or unmentionable behind things; or functionalistically in the search for functional equivalents. The question about the problem is abstract enough for the team of the organizational consultant to coordinate widely varying experience and preferences; and it is open enough to avoid pinning the consultant down to a specific solution of the problem. It can also be passed on as a question: What is the problem that you are trying to solve? At the same time, however, it involves a certain commitment to go into the problem. A problem implies the expectation that it can be solved (if one only knew how).

The supposition that there are problems is the point of departure for cooperation between consultants and organization. Why otherwise would the consultants have been engaged? On this basis one can attempt, with a new definition of the problem, to formulate a new way of looking at things and to work out the consequences – if only to undermine old conflict lines. The system can be given new hope: a new ball game, a new chance. But one can also increase the uncertainty content of problem-solving and establish reflection loops in which the system itself continuously transforms self-observations into self-descriptions.

Discussions about problems can therefore give the oscillation between exogenous descriptions and self-descriptions a form that remains sufficiently ambivalent. What remains ambivalent is who determines whose problem, how the problem can be solved, and finally, whether the problem named (rather than some other one) has to be solved at all and what state the system will find itself in if it addresses the problem and tries to solve it. Agreement can be reached on defining a problem without having to reach agreement on how to solve it – and vice versa. The distinction between problem and solution thus permits agreement with the reservation that disagreement is possible; or also provisional agreement without being able to foresee how far it will go.

After all this, talk about "problems" is a fall-back position that presents itself if the system finds itself confronted by inconsistent decision requirements.[39] One can then withdraw to a level of communication at which no effective action is expected but the autopoiesis of the system nevertheless continues. And no one will deny that there are problems that need clarification if possible solutions are to be assessed.

If this is a more or less accurate account of the reality that is developing, it is worth noting that no superordinate competence is developed for oscillation between internal and external perspectives but rather a subordinate competence. And it is not concerned with abstracting comprehensive principles that have to be agreed. It is not concerned with the diffusion of true knowledge, where contradiction could be treated as error. It rather has to do with forms of thought that, given the basic paradox of observation (the unity of a difference, the sameness of what is distinguished), can generate neither recursively stabilized identities nor "eigenvalues." And if this can succeed at all, science would have to be in a position to construct a suitable theory.

IV

Organizations and families can be distinguished and compared. There are evident differences between them in size, internal order, function, and appropriateness of behavior (not to say rationality). And families cannot be subsystems of other functional systems, which is possible, indeed typical, for organizations. But things tally in one regard: on their operational basis, neither families nor organizations constitute a uniform societal subsystem – "the" family of society or "the" organization of society just as there is an economic system or a legal system of society.[40] In relation to the societal system, families and organizations are directly segmentarily differentiated, whatever differences there are in the social position of families or the size, power, and financial strength of organizations. For this reason, self-descriptions of these systems cannot refer to a societal subsystem. They remain tied to a specific family (name, genealogy, often also old place of residence) or to a specific organization. In the environment of such a system within society, there are numerous other systems of the same type, whereas in the environment of the science system within society, for example, there are no other science systems with divergent truth qualifications.[41] What are the consequences for the self-descriptions of individual organizations, which have to take into account that there are other organizations with other self-descriptions?

Although for quite different theoretical reasons, Parsons had posited a special hierarchical level (institutional as opposed to managerial and executive) on which individual organizations could relate to the societal system and its symbols and norms.[42] Thus, as long ago as the 1950s, the view was expressed that it was not enough for organizations to define themselves and relate to society solely through their product, and hence through their market. At the time this was a belated reaction to the Great Depression of 1929, which had moved Parsons to criticize utilitarian theoretical assumptions.[43] This view is now widespread, albeit without any memory of its historical origins and without recalling Parsons. It bears the name of "new institutionalism" (without offering anything particularly new) and is proposed as a theoretical advance.[44] It is asserted that organizations need a cultural identity, which, however, they cannot procure themselves. It is claimed that they have to relate to the values of the societal environment in order to legitimate themselves; that, where this is usual or considered progressive, they have to draw up an eco-balance sheet and the like. It remains open whether this has to be sincere (but how is this to be established?) or whether it is a symbolic action that no one believes in. It also remains open how this disbelief can be communicated – for example, in cynical or carnivalesque guise. For all textual self-descriptions are highly vulnerable, they are very suggestive of second thoughts, and this vulnerability can be cushioned by differentiating between semi-official and cynical communication, by communication that marks and communication that sees through things.

The propositions of this institutional theory, which via Parsons takes us back to the early institutionalists of the first three decades of the twentieth century[45] and which had been elaborated mainly as a theory of law, are still followed today uncritically, although in many different interpretations. The theory posits that relations with the societal world are concerned with adequate consensus, mutual recognition, a common basis of lifeworld accord. This is not to be contested, not to be brought down by a counter-theory. While this is undoubtedly true, it stresses only one side of the problem of identity and fails to mention the other. This paints a conciliatory picture: the problem of constructing identities is suppressed, controversies are defused – ascribed either to persons or to situations that one wishes ultimately to bring under the roof of institutional peace. This, in turn, is in keeping with the classical assumption that the hierarchical order of authority, which the unity of the system puts into effect, can settle differences of opinion (nowadays hierarchy in often replaced or supplemented by dialogue, without noticing how often dialogues between opposing points of view exacerbate controversies rather than attenuating them).

The more fundamental problem is how the *uniqueness* of an individual system can be formulated and asserted as comprising the *same* values as the systems of the environment. To put it in question form: Does recognition not always have to be paid for somewhere or other with a renunciation of uniqueness?

We had already mentioned the paradox of uniqueness in connection with storytelling as a form of system memory.[46] Stories convince because of the concrete uniqueness of the events related, which are intended to be instructive. In the philosophical tradition and especially in aesthetics, this paradox is displaced by the distinction between general and particular or between the ideal and its material realizations; and the unique work of art is expected to give expression to something general. The same is expected of the educated person. There are thus tradition-forming resolutions of this paradox that we have become so accustomed to that the paradox is no longer apparent and must first be reconstructed by radicalizing the definition of the problem.

Organizations use their self-descriptions to present their individual particularity in a terminology that, it is hoped, will find general agreement. The most important way in which the paradox of uniqueness is resolved appears to consist in *excel strategies*. Older societies had made a morality of merit available for this purpose, which reached into the world of heroes and demigods, ascetics and saints – in pursuit of excellence, as we would now perhaps say. While consensus in the assessment dimensions was presupposed, there was no duty of emulation. Guidance was offered here, too, by the status order of the societal hierarchy, which excluded comparison across the barriers of rank. While admiring heroes, one could note with relief that aspiration levels were regulated and that one did not have to expect such top performance of oneself. In the double function of admiration and disburdenment we recognize from afar a background paradox, namely a permission to exempt oneself that is unusual in the moral sphere. To put it in reciprocity theoretical terms: one could pay for disburdenment with admiration.

Like social stratification, a morality of merit drew boundaries for meaningful comparisons. In modern society, such a morality would lack structural backing. Of course, there are still award rituals, art, literature, and other prizes, Nobel prizes and Oscars; but they are typically awarded in recognition of performance only by special juries (and hence through organization!) as awards that have to be proclaimed as consensual decisions. But these precautions alone, and the celebration of what are (with few exceptions) trifles, betray an artificial structure not embedded in society.

The old ethic of distinction on grounds of merit appears to have been replaced, as functional equivalent, by the principle of competition, and in its most general form, perhaps, by the principle of competition for attention and access to the media resources of *others* (like truth, love, money, power). This allows a person to distinguish oneself and, even in the absence of canonized evaluation rules, to judge by the conditions for success whether one is within the zone of concurring assessment or on the way to communicating one's individuality only by deviating from the norm (today this is likely to hold true to a considerable degree for religious organizations and, above all, for modern art).

Another identity strategy, which overlaps strongly with competition, is innovation. One reason for insisting on innovation could be that the temporal rhythm of internal switches is mostly no longer determined externally, for example, through product cycles imposed by the market or through changes in political leadership: the organization itself organizes its time, and to this end has to be constantly ready to innovate. In other words, what is at issue is relocating control over the extent to which past and future can be distinguished from outside to inside; and "innovation" is only a euphemism for the demand to provide the necessary flexibility – even if the environment does not impose it.

All the more, however, this raises the question of whether and how organizations can take self-imposed innovation.

There has been enough discussion about doubts in this regard to allow us to say that the unreservedly positive assessment of innovation applies only at the level of self-description, not at the level of the reality of structural changes and reforms either carried out or blocked. At the level of product innovations, what is often involved are only novel combinations of advantages and disadvantages (it is becoming more and more difficult to get into and out of the new streamlined automobiles). In the field of the organization itself, the positive assessment of innovation provides the preliminary legitimation for ever new attempts; or also for constantly forgetting why previous innovations failed. Here, too, one depends not so much on given consensus on values than on current tests of success. An organization that describes itself as innovative and motivates itself accordingly believes it is always a step ahead of the organizations in its environment. It has already earmarked a bit of future for itself, has risked something, and is accordingly in a position to gain both positive and negative experience to which other organizations have no access. This relegates other organizations to the role of observer and emulator, and thus to roles without opportunities for individuality.

Excel strategies of this sort can be on a very small scale, involving narrowly defined services or products ("swatch" being an example of a very successful innovation spilling over from the timepiece to the car). But more than isolated cases can be involved. If the facts justify it, organizations can write a success story and establish a reputation for leadership, for a partiality for experiment, or also for publicity, public recognition, fund-raising skills, devotion to charitable causes, etc.

Finally, it should once again be recalled that all text production also uses, enriches, and actualizes the memory of the system. But memory as the generation of the difference between forgetting and remembering is not a special skill, not a special achievement of the system; it is the obvious result of the autopoiesis of communication. For this very reason, an organizational system (unless very small and ephemeral) cannot simply be left to the care of some memory or other. Self-descriptions tighten up and link the self-reference components of what condenses as memory. They have a higher-level function, namely to reduce order through ordering to order. Inevitably, manipulative intervention occurs; but it is itself subject to contextual conditions, which keep arbitrariness within narrow bounds. The formation constraints typical of text production are therefore more characteristic. Self-descriptions fulfill their function by producing forms of paradox resolution against the background of a shadowy realm of the unmentionable, of the repressed, of the forgotten; and they thus make it possible to cross this boundary and bring back what has been excluded with the aid of special additional signals of wit, irony, and cynicism.

And this is why institutional theory is not enough. For the difference between semi-official and cynical, whose maintenance as distinction is essential, cannot be found in the environment, cannot be coordinated with the environment. It can be processed and maintained only in the system itself as a sort of equalization of burdens, or also as a possibility of carrying out reality tests in constant contradiction between the system and itself.

V

Let us assume that a different self-description could be prescribed for an organization for therapeutic reasons with the aim of replacing the model of the rational, purposive, hierarchically structured system. What would the consequences be?

We must remember that the system is and remains intransparent to itself. With the much more complex modus operandi of observing and describing, it can never keep up with the totality of actual operations that determine its state from one moment to the next. The daily forms of self-correction and learning can, therefore, not be reoriented to a different, better, more realistic model of the system in the system.[47] It is more likely that the system will abide by but repress the rational model and operate in the future with two different self-descriptions. A new *façon de parler* develops, superimposed on preceding interpretations without being able to replace them. The system thus uses two identifications simultaneously, and can schematize the distinction between them temporally – as, in analogy to the description of society, we speak of postmodern organizations, which of course have to be modern organizations, as well. In other words, a more complex architecture of differences develops; and it seems almost likely that the system no longer has to rely on a unanimously accepted identity, on a "self," but only has to be able to switch from one distinction to another as the need arises.

This would require reflection loops in the system that organize such switches in terminologies and distinctions, so that it neither depends completely on chance nor has to be negotiated from case to case whether purposes or decision premises, principles or paradoxes, products or culture are to be addressed. Problems could then be shifted from one language into another to find out what can be observed in this fashion. The system would then be "hypercomplex," in a strict sense of the term, insofar as its complexity itself (as expression of its unity) can be described in different ways.[48]

If one understands self-description as a sort of reproduction of the system memory, this has the advantage of shifting attention from normative to temporal problems. However, this presupposes a more up-to-date theory of memory according to which memory serves the always present, and thus always renewed, coordination of past and future.[49] It is not a question of merely preserving what has once been learned. In a turbulent world, such a memory would have little chance of surviving. It is rather a matter of constantly discriminating between forgetting and remembering, constantly freeing capacities, which, however, require ample redundancy and hence sufficient identities to be available to avoid sinking into total chaos. In more recent, environmentally aware organization theories, the conditions for keeping to and implementing what has been recognized as right accordingly shifts to problems of continuous modification; we could also say to problems of continuous reselection of decision premises. In every new situation, the past of the system would also have to be submitted to redescription.[50] It has to be remembered that this past, too, came into being through a decision, and is hence contingent and will remain so. The acute problem now lies in the question of the system level at which this memory, which is constantly renewing, constantly "re-impregnating" itself, comes to bear, and to what extent it can be connected with basal decision-making processes or whether it continues to be reserved to a more high-flown level of system description and system planning.[51] These are questions, among others, of the organization of corporate accounting and of dovetailing it more closely with day-to-day business.

If, however, hierarchy is temporalized in this manner and treated as a problem of synchronizing processes, must the old rationality concept be repressed, as therapists could assume? Or could it be modified and adapted so that the system can develop routines for switching description and for dealing with its top level, its consultants, and its therapists? For this question we need a further chapter.

Notes

1. A classical sociological monograph on this subject is Philip Selznick, *TVA and the Grass Roots: A Study in the Sociology of Formal Organizations, (1949)*, New York 1966.
2. It should be recalled that in Spencer-Brown's calculus of forms, the reentry of the form into the form leads to bistability and oscillation.
3. See James G. March and Johan P. Olsen, *Ambiguity and Choice in Organizations*, Bergen 1976 with the distinction between ambiguities of intention, understanding, history and organization. See also Martha S. Feldman, *Order Without Design: Information Production and Policy Making*, Stanford 1989.
4. See Nils Brunsson, Ideas and Actions: Justification and Hypocrisy as Alternatives to Control, *Accounting Organizations and Society* 18 (1993), 489–506.
5. That this psychic basis of memory performance (external to the organization) is important, indeed indispensable, is naturally not to be denied. But it also has to rely on psychic coordination mechanisms, especially the assumption confirmed by experience that others know what is what, understand it, and will do what is needed when the time comes. This does not permit greater complexity to be assessed; and, above all, structural changes cannot be planned and carried out on this basis.

6. On the latest literary research that focuses on this function of texts and in this sense addresses "intertexuality," see Renate Lachmann, *Gedächtnis und Literatur: Intertextualität in der russischen Moderne*, Frankfurt 1990.

7. In this regard the reader is referred to the chapter on time relations.

8. And every student knows that one of the most difficult, largely unconscious psychic achievements of memory is to pick out the few works in texts that really count.

9. On this concept of Heinz von Foerster see above p.

10. See Chapter 7.

11. Warren S. McCulloch, *The Embodiments of Mind*, Cambridge, MA 1965, had spoken of "heterarchy." But this is essentially only a counter-concept to hierarchy, and has to rely on more precise definition of operations in the systems in question.

12. See Heinz von Foerster, Für Niklas Luhmann: Wie rekursiv ist Kommunikation?, *Teoria Sociologica* 1/2 (1993), 61–85(84).

13. That legitimation can be demanded "critically" is quite another matter. It is typical presumption on the part of "critical" intellectuals to deem themselves legitimated, to demand legitimation in the way a policeman demands someone's papers. But the text is concerned only with operational necessities, and it will be difficult to find anyone who claims that the business has to be closed down and the staff dismissed if legitimation is lacking.

14. A formulation of Renate Lachmann op. cit. (1990), 10.

15. On this new, no longer unusual thesis, see Michel Serres, *Die fünf Sinne: Eine Philosophie der Gemenge und Gemische*, German translation Frankfurt 1993, especially the introductory chapter. One could also cite Bachtin or Bataille.

16. We know that the European tradition had drawn on the image of the city (*polis, civitas*) and later the country (*regnum*), had given it expression with phrases such as *civitas sive societas civilis*, postulating the unity of rule (*imperium*) on this basis. The social had thus been conceived of in this sense in "political" terms, and also in analogy to the human body. And this has had a lasting effect. Politics would probably have turned out quite differently had there been no printed, multi-colored maps and politics had therefore not known where it actually takes place.

17. Inevitably, see Michail Bachtin, *Rabelais und seine Welt: Volkskultur als Gegenkultur*, German transl. Frankfurt 1988.

18. For the psychic self, this is the undisputed starting point for all psychiatric theories interested in therapy. See, e.g., Jurgen Ruesch and Gregory Bateson, *Communication: The Social Matrix of Psychiatry*, New York 1951, 2nd ed. 1968, 199 ff.

19. See, following Kant and Lyotard, Gerhard Plumpe, *Ästhetische Kommunikation der Moderne*, Opladen 1993, 99 ff.

20. See e.g., Martha S. Feldman and James G. March, Information in Organizations as Signal and Symbol, *Administrative Science Quarterly* 26 (1981), 171–186, and Martha S. Feldman, *Order Without Design: Information Production and Policy Making*, Stanford 1989.

21. It has often been pointed out that such metaphors have little to do with reality. See Brian J. Loasby, *Choice, Complexity and Ignorance: An Enquiry into Economic Theory and the Practice of Decision-Making*, Cambridge 1976.

22. See, e.g., Federico Butera, *Il castello e la rete: Impresa, organizzazioni e professioni nell' Europa degli anni '90*, 2nd ed, Milan 1991.

23. See Mitteilungen Nr. 22/Juni 1995 des soziologischen Forschungsinstituts der Universität Göttingen.

24. See Feldman op. cit. (1989), esp. 106 ff.

25. See Virginia H. Ingersoll and Guy B. Adams, Beyond Organizational Boundaries: Exploring the Managerial Metamyth, *Administration and Society* 18 (1986), 360–381. However, it should be added that in many areas of world society, this does not apply or only to a limited extent or only for certain types of organization.

26. For example, by overloading interactions with extreme complexity. See Karl E. Weick, The Vulnerable System: An Analysis of the Tenerife Air Disaster, *Journal of Management* 16 (1990), 571–593, reprinted in: Peter J. Frost et al. (eds.), *Reframing Organizational Culture*, Newbury Park, CA 1991, 117–130.

27. See Larry M. Preston, *Freedom and the Organizational Republic*, Berlin 1992, 30 f.

28. See Gotthard Günther, *Cognition and Volition: A Contribution to a Cybernetic Theory of Subjectivity, in idem,* Beiträge zur Grundlegung einer operationsfähigen Dialektik vol. 2, Hamburg 1979, 203–240.

29. See, e.g., Vicki E. Baier, James G. March, and Harald Saetren, Implementation and Ambiguity, *Scandinavian Journal of Management* 2 (1986), 197–212.

30. In this we follow Michel Serres. See, e.g., *Le Parasite*, Paris 1980, or *Les cinq sens*, Paris 1985.

31. See, e.g., Martha S. Feldman, The Meanings of Ambiguity: Learning from Stories and Metaphors, in: Frost et al. (eds.), op. cit. 145–156; idem, *Order Without Design: Information Processing and Policy Making*, Palo Alto, CA 1989.

32. The early modern discussion of this case goes back to Machiavelli's *Discorsi*. See also Juan Pablo Mártir Rizo, *Vida de Rómulo (1633)*, Madrid 1945 and Virgilio Malvezzi, *Il Romulo, in: Opere des Marchese Malvezzi*, Mediolanum 1635, 11–131.

33. See, for one of many examples, Mayer N. Zald, Comparative Analysis and Measurement of Organizational Goals, *Sociological Quarterly* 4 (1963), 206–230; also Barry M. Staw, Pamela I. McKechnie, and Sheila M. Puffer, The Justification of Organizational Performance, *Administrative Science Quarterly* 28 (1983), 582–600. See also Gerald R. Salancik and James R. Meindl, Corporate Attributions as Strategic Illusions of Management Control, *Administrative Science Quarterly* 29 (1984), 238–254. Further literature is to be found under the heading latent/manifest function. See, e.g., Burton R. Clark, *The Open Door College: A Case Study*, New York 1960.

34. See Klaus A. Ziegert, Courts and the Self-concept of Law: The Mapping of the Environment by Courts of First Instance, *Sydney Law Review* 14 (1992), 196–229.

35. This concept is understood in the sense of cognitive psychology. See, e.g., Robert P. Abelson, Psychological Status of the Script Concept, *American Psychologist* 36 (1981), 715–729.

36. See Barbara Czarniawska-Joerges, Merchants of Meaning: Management Consulting in the Swedish Public Service, in: Barry A. Turner (ed.), *Organizational Symbolism*, Berlin 1990, 139–150.

37. With this we replace the assertion, which has recently been gaining popularity, that organizational management and organizational consulting have something to do with giving meaning. The claim itself makes no sense; it can be applied to every communication if it not defined more narrowly.

38. In such cases, the problem lies in bad (imprecise, ambiguous) definitions of the problem. See, e.g., Walter R. Reitman, *Cognition and Thought*, New York 1965; Herbert A. Simon, The Structure of Ill-structured Problems, *Artificial Intelligence* 4 (1973), 181–201; reprinted in idem, *Models of Discovery and Other Topics in the Methods of Science*, Dordrecht 1977, 304–325.

39. See Nils Brunsson, Managing Organizational Disorder, in: Massimo Warglien and Michael Masuch (eds.), *The Logic of Organizational Disorder*, Berlin 1996, 127–143 (131 f.).

40. We do not exclude that there can be self-descriptions of this sort – for instance, society as a big family (community), or society as organization that takes care of everything and is responsible for everything. But under present-day conditions, it is obvious that they can at best be tools for symbolic policy that no one really believes in.

41. Only if one takes a further stage of differentiation into account are there research institutes in the science system, states in the political system, newspapers, radio stations, etc. in the system of the mass media.

42. See Talcott Parsons, Some Ingredients of a General Theory of Formal Organizations, in idem, *Structure and Process in Modern Societies*, New York 1960, 59–96.

43. See also the parallel essay Some Reflections on the Institutional Framework of Economic Development in the same volume, 98–131, and above all the early work The Structure of Social Action, New York 1937.

44. For references see Chapter 1 note 68

45. See, e.g., Santi Romano, *L'ordinamento giuridico I, Pisa 1918*, reprint of the 2nd ed. Florence 1962; John R. Commons, *Legal Foundations of Capitalism*, New York 1924; idem, Institutional Economics: Its Place in Political Economy (1934), Madison, WI 1959; Maurice Hauriou, *Die Theorie der Institution und zwei andere Aufsätze (ed. Roman Schnur)*, German translation, Berlin 1965; Roman Schnur (ed.), *Institution und Recht*, Darmstadt 1968.

46. See above XXX f.

47. For instance, in the sense of Roger S. Conant and W. Ross Ashby, Every Good Regulator of a System Must be a Model of That System, *International Journal of Systems Science* 1 (1970), 89–97.

48. See Lars Löfgren, Complexity Descriptions of Systems: A Foundational Study, *International Journal of General Systems* 3 (1977), 197–214, and Robert Rosen, Complexity as a System Property, *International Journal of General Systems* 3 (1977), 227–232.

49. See Heinz Förster, *Das Gedächtnis: Eine quantenphysikalische Untersuchung*, Vienna 1948; Heinz von Foerster, What Is Memory that It May Have Hindsight and Foresight as Well?, in: Samuel Bogoch (ed.), *The Future of the Brain Sciences*, New York 1969, 19–64; German translation in idem, *Wissen und Gewissen: Versuch einer Brücke*, Frankfurt 1993, 299–336.

50. With regard to the theory of art see Michael Baldwin, Charles Harrison, and Mel Ramsden, On Conceptual Art and Painting, and Speaking and Seeing: Three Corrected Transcripts, *Art-Language NS* 1 (1994), 30–69.

51. See Bo L. T. Hedberg, Paul C. Nystrom, and William H. Starbuck, Camping on Seesaws: Prescriptions for a Self-Designing Organisation, *Administrative Science Quarterly* 21 (1976), 41–65.

15   Rationality

I

Any empirical investigation of what outsiders expect of organizations would probably show that they expect them to further their own interests or at least give due consideration to them. This is likely to be so for the individual outsider, whether applicant or affected party, customer or patient, school pupil or felon in prison. But it is also the case in relations between organizations – between firms and their banks, or between banks and firms seeking loans; or in relations between trade unions and companies or government; or in relations between hospitals and health insurance schemes. Since consideration of interests is difficult to specify, and since disappointing experience in individual cases cannot simply be generalized, a sort of trust develops on this basis; or at least mistrust strains relations to an almost unbearable degree, increasing the information and communication load – and is probably to be borne only when there is no alternative, and thus no market.

However, backcasting to interests leads to difficulties if, as is typical, the organization in question has to serve more than one interest. Interest in the given interest has to be extrapolated, so to speak, and a more general expression found. For example, the orientation on "interests" can be replaced by orientation on "problems." Only in rare cases will impartiality be the formula chosen. Impartiality may well be expected from the courts but not from the trade unions. Even government should not decide impartially; after all, the concept of the public interest was invented to avoid this. The problem is therefore to find a concept that, while not ignoring interests – because that is what is at issue – leaves them unmentioned and incorporates them under a more formal heading. The job is done by "rationality."[1]

Rationality abstracts from the evaluation of interests. It abstracts from *every* interest, for it would not be rational to give precedence to the public interest (or the common weal or the public good) over private interests. To express this, it suffices to stand up for the public interest with enthusiasm. But this is not an option for the state in the liberal understanding of the concept, let alone for organizations. Communicating at the level of the rationality concept requires all evaluation of interests to be left aside, which naturally does not exclude interests from being recognized, acknowledged, and differently appraised. That organizations ought to decide rationally is accordingly the flag by which everyone (including the organization itself) can drape their expectations without having to identify with a particular interest. It is, so to speak, an equivalent in decision-making to what epistemology calls "objectivity." But what can rationality mean?

Perhaps it means only a form of communication that keeps the interests that are really meant in reserve; or a form of communication that reserves itself the right to express dissatisfaction and comes out with it as soon as it is clear what has been decided or what will be decided. The assertion of rationality would thus be a rhetorical act[2] to lend certain positions an air of incontestability. Or the term "contextual rationality" is used to express that rationality can mean different things depending on the circumstances.[3] At any rate, if anything determinable is meant at all, something else has to be excluded.[4] A form with another side to it has to be involved. But the question remains whether the other side is only the unmarked space of the indeterminable (so that everything determined would be rational as in the case of Hegel's absolute spirit, which has the work of the concept behind it and can be satisfied with itself), or whether one can and must specify what is excluded as irrational in order to treat the rest as rational – just as one can argue for a long time about taste but at best establish what bad taste is.

Since judgments about irrationality are made using the same criteria as judgments about rationality, irrationality cannot very well be regarded as the other side of the rationality form; it is only the negative version of the same form. Rationality as form differs from what "ethnomethodology" has described as "taking for granted." This tempts one to see rationality and culture or rationality and institution as opposites and to react to clear rationality deficits by calling for culture. If matters are observed as to their rationality (whether they are judged rational or irrational), a form is activated that cancels the normal assumption that the world is the way it is. This may well be attributable to an interest in change or an interest in legitimation. Be that as it may, the decisive, formative difference is in the cancellation of the "taking for granted," which naturally can take place only in the world and only in specific regards, while the world itself must always be taken as given *and therefore* (in keeping with our conceptual proposal) *cannot be taken to be rational.*

Judgments about rationality have to include the future. But the future is and remains unknown. The problem therefore shifts to a need for information.[5] Although information, too, can be taken only from the past, it can be selected in such a way that it offers conclusions (however unreliable) about the future. But this simply transfers the problem of rationality to a problem of information, and in this context it not only takes the guise of information overload but is also more radical in that there is dependence on information at all.

As long as rationality remains indeterminable and recognizable only in the violation, this facilitates the self-description of the system as rational. The system calculates its identity by oscillating within the form of rationality. For sections of the world the assumption that things are the way they are is cancelled and replaced by schemata that enable oscillation between positive and negative. One does good by fighting evil and considers oneself healthy if no symptoms of illness manifest themselves. But as soon as structural characteristics are used as conditions or marks of rationality – and classical organization theory had attempted to do precisely this with characteristics like purposive orientation or hierarchy – oscillation shifts to other distinctions. For example, one can now ask about non-rational (informal, emotional, motivational) conditions of rationality; one can shift the problem of rationality to contextual conditions of rational action (trust, for instance), or move on to registering rationality damage. The organization theory of the twentieth century has trodden this path with great success, with the result that a distinction has to be drawn between the self-description of systems and the scientific analysis of the systems describing themselves. On the basis of this distinction and by means of second-order observation, one can recognize that even the mere *description* of structures and decisions as rational can be rational, *even if they deviate from reality and represent it highly selectively.*[6] The criteria of rationality thus take on a double meaning, depending on whether they relate to first-order observation or to second-order observation.

II

Various distinctions are drawn in the general discussion on the concept and forms of rationality. Depending on the distinction taken as point of departure, different types of rationality result.[7] If it is the difference between means and ends, we have instrumental rationality. If it is the difference between facts and values, we speak of value rationality. If the starting point is the difference between system and environment, this gives us the concept of system rationality. To judge rationality, a distinction has apparently to be presupposed that in itself is not yet rational. Otherwise the evaluation of rationality would stick to given conditions.

The same applies for organization research. The classical model of organizational rationality was based on externalizations. Disorder (uncertainty, risk, etc.) therefore found its way into the organization only in moderate form. The small but acute minds of calculated rationality then had their chance. Essentially, problems appeared to have been solved in advance or, at any rate, a structure found that enabled rational processing. Organizations were accordingly understood as instrumental, as purposive-rational, as tools serving the interests of those who had set them up for their own ends. This could be plausibly demonstrated by industrial enterprises or public authorities. Hierarchical super- and subordination was not an end in itself but a means to an end; and it was also the form in which difficult problems could be disposed of upwards and thus outwards. Public administration could define them as "political" problems and request its leadership to make decisions that were tenable or could at least be legitimated politically. Courts could clearly base unsatisfying decisions on the law and refer complainants to the lawmakers for a remedy. In the private sector, capital owners could be asked to decide in advance under what conditions and at what risk they were prepared to make capital available. And, vice versa, the organization assured those who provided needed help that it would make rational decisions. The difference between system and environment thus converged, at least in theory, with the difference between top and bottom and with that between problems that are easy and those that are difficult to define. Hierarchical control was considered an essential condition for the rationality of a broadly ramified operational context.

This was associated with implicit assumptions about the system of society that used organizations to perform specific tasks. Society had to be seen as a sufficiently ordered system if it was to answer the questions organizations addressed to it. This task had previously been assigned to the market or to the democratic processes of politics. It is now often described as a requirement of institutions, and in this regard we can think of the state, of property, of sufficient consensus about the educational canon in schools, or of the professional ethos of doctors, for instance, or of the limits to reasonable attention. Organizations could hope to hear nothing more about the matter if they "externalized" problems. And it was not only other organizations that stepped in with their own decisions, such as courts to settle legal matters or banks to provide additional loans; society itself was assumed to be so ordered that in organizations, too, a framework for determining decision premises could be taken as given.

This provision of support by an external order and by externally imposed restrictions has become progressively less plausible. For the self-description of societal functional systems and for the reconceptualization of the individual as subject, the relevant changes set in as long ago as the eighteenth century. The traditional supportive world formulas (harmony, the hierarchy of being, *analogia entis*, perfection in diversity, *concordia discors*, etc.) have lost their credibility. They have come to grief because of antinomies; they have produced a multiplicity of discrepant world descriptions, and finally an infinite concept of the world, which can be broached by various observers with various distinctions. As a result, every system has to distinguish and process self-reference and other-reference in its own way,[8] so that descriptions can no longer converge; instead, one is referred to the observation of observers if one wishes to discover what reality is and for whom.

If this has been European knowledge at the level of the concept of the world and theory of society for two hundred years, how was it possible at the level of organization theory for the notion of an exogenous instrumental rationality to persist until recently? How could the existence of a fixed environment be assumed in relation to which an organization could adapt? Or if the environment is taken to be turbulent, how could an instrumental concept of rationality persist? How can one, even now, assume that the solution to the rationality problem lies in contextual or institutional conditions? To put it still another way, how could one cling to an asymmetrical or market-type relationship between organizational systems and societal environments when it is perfectly clear that no functional system in society can maintain its level of performance without organization (government and political parties, manufacturing plants and banks; courts, hospitals, schools, and so forth)? In other words, circular relations between organizational systems and the societal environment have to be assumed. This is true even if the circle, for example, in the case of the many markets of the economic system, is so large that from the perspective of the individual organization it appears to be a straight line or a relationship between independent and dependent variables; or, as in so-called contingency theory, if one has to assume that the rationality of an organization lies precisely in being geared to an environment that does not operate rationally.

The classical theory of rationality had clearly survived so long because it succeeded in representing and satisfying an interest in *corrective critique*. Or this at least appeared to be the case, above all in the organization of production processes. The organization and the people employed in it were demanded to operate constantly at the limits of their possibilities or otherwise face criticism designed to improve matters.[9] Meanwhile, however, at least organizational sociology (but not the literature that recommends management concepts) has abandoned this notion. Leading figures are James March and Karl Weick or in decision theory, Daniel Kahneman and Amos Tversky. An empirical science cannot simply ignore the fact that decision-makers in general and managers in particular are not guided by the rules put forward by models of rational decision-making. There is simply not enough time in everyday working life. The notion of rationality continues to play a role; but more recent theory is interested rather in understanding why and how things can work without rationality. Older criticism of rationality weaknesses has been replaced by astonishment at how organizations put up with themselves and how this can preserve their own decision-making capacity without being able to guarantee it through rational decision-making. The subversion of rationality raises the question of intelligent behavior that can take account of these conditions.[10] The answer can be sought at the behaviorist level of describing actual behavior.[11] However, a theoretical framework for this purpose appears to be provided only by recent reflections on a general theory of self-referential systems, from which the preceding chapters have benefited.

Within rationalistic organization theories, too, there was room for counter-concepts, which, however, remained undefined. For example, experience and skill in handling conditions were appreciated, and this provided not least an argument for the older generation against the younger, or also a way to reject proposals that are "not acceptable here." Only if the temporal relations, recursivity, and uncertainty absorption in decision-making processes are taken more strongly into account can these requirements be described more exactly. What is at issue is the ability to adapt in experience and action to constantly changing situations with ever new pasts and ever new futures.[12] This includes adaptation to the social interdependence of preferences, thus also willingness to change one's own preferences. If rationality is to include these requirements, it can be seen neither as a long chain of means and ends nor as clinging to particular preferences. In day-to-day operations, ideologies then emerge that are honored in communication (also as ideologies of the other side) but that scarcely influence events. An observer intent on getting to the bottom of such behavior is left only the possibility of describing demands and behavior as paradoxical.[13]

Theoretical reflection now appears to react to such critical experience with rationality by taking the time dimension more strongly into account. The unknownness of the future continues to be a source of difficulty and of differences of opinion in the decision-making process. But it is naturally also a condition for making decisions at all. And if the wrong decision has been taken, it allows corrections to be made. And all planning of decisions can provide for further decisions to be necessary and possible at later points in time. From this point of view, time, and in particular the unknownness of the future, replaces fixed goals and premises, which more than ever before can be left to controversial assessment and provisional agreement.

How the theory of self-referential systems reacts to this challenge is traced out by the concept of autopoiesis. Autopoietic systems, and hence organizational systems, distinguish themselves from the environment by setting up and maintaining a recursive reproduction context. They themselves regulate relations between self-reference and other-reference in the observation of their operations. They generate new situations of restriction and opportunity, of certainty and uncertainty. But it naturally cannot be said that autopoiesis is itself rational. This would render a concept of rationality superfluous and reduce us to the idea that reality itself is rational. But if this answer is not accepted and one must also focus the concept of rationality on a given society, how are we to understand the rhetoric of the rationality of autopoietic organizations?

III

Before we go into this question, we must take a long detour in an attempt to explain the relationship between rationality and causality. Theory had distinguished between logical and empirical issues and been satisfied with this distinction. From a logical point of view, the issue was consistency as a logical requirement for connectivity. From an empirical point of view, it was causality as an empirical requirement for connectivity. However, this already takes us beyond the extant discussion, makes sense only in retrospect, and raises the question of why this distinction has to be made and not another.

With the paradox problem and with Gödel, logic has brought its own difficulties to light. Corresponding reflection on the concept of causality is still outstanding.

Causality can be said to present an infinite horizon of ever new causes and a second infinite horizon of ever new effects. In this horizon every cause is also an effect and vice versa. For this reason specific causes have to be ascribed to specific effects. This presupposes a logical separation of causes from effects and can take place only selectively, only by ignoring other causes and other effects. Every causal proposition therefore remains relative to an observer, who attributes thus and not otherwise, and this requires greater or lesser consensus and a greater or lesser guarantee for repeatability.[14]

It always has to do with reductions, with forms of simplified attribution. This has to be taken into consideration if the importance of the cybernetic revolutionization of systems theory is to be assessed. It is concerned with attribution to structures, not to events. Whereas attribution to constant characteristics (a knife cuts because it is sharp) had earlier been usual (and in an everyday understanding still is), cybernetics proposes attribution to circular, self-correcting mechanisms. To begin with, this looked like a return to teleological causality.[15] In fact, however, only a structure was presented that explains why it looks as if the system pursues purposes. There is therefore a switch from the attribution of purpose to the attribution of structure. This led to the suggestion of building such self-correcting reflection loops into systems (e.g., in computers) to enable states or performances to be attained under changeable environmental conditions. What is concerned is thus a form of attribution that can be set up, hence a use of causality in two steps. It is about simplifying attribution that abstracts from concrete events, and thus from time. And it is about handling a problem that presupposes the difference between system and environment. The "rationality" of cybernetic arrangements always refers to this difference, and is therefore always system rationality.

If the theory of autopoietic systems is also introduced, then it is obvious to posit that attribution takes place primarily with regard to the system's own autopoiesis. This depends on both internal and external causes.[16] The system will therefore orient its attribution on this difference and arrange the cause/effect constellation to which it pays heed primarily around its own operations, around the freely chosen, internally available employment of causes. Although this is not prescribed by the world as it is, decisions are imagined to be made through actions, and that this has effects that would not occur without decision/action. What is then important is discovering the causes that enable meaningful decision/action and what effects they will have. This consequently implies a minimum of self-attribution and corresponding risk, even if the system can always shift attribution to the environment (if, for example, blame is to be placed or accounts rendered). In the causal schema, as elsewhere, the system can oscillate between self-attribution and other-attribution. Some already call this autonomy and therefore speak of relative autonomy.

The conclusion is that the distinction between causes and effects cannot be brought into line with that between system and environment. The two distinctions are logically independent of one another, are at right angles to one another, even if each system tends to make itself particularly important, indeed indispensable in the causalities it has constructed. We could almost say that the difference between causes and effects neutralizes the distinction between system and environment. If systems are included, the causal schema can be applied only if both causes and effects can occur in both the system and its environment. This finds expression, for instance, in the concept of production or reproduction (production from products) – in contrast to what since theological times has been described as "creation" (creatio).

But this does not yet bring us to the heart of the problem. We have seen that the distinction between causes and effects separates *two* infinite horizons and thus produces an attribution problem. We can also say that, in the *medium* of causality, *forms* always have to be produced that reduce the endless variety of possible combinations to one; and we also understand that this requires *time*, so that the form passes and new forms become possible if the cause has had an effect. The medium itself remains invisible; but it regenerates itself in observation through a continuous change of forms in which it becomes reality and does its work.

Like every distinction, this raises the question of the unity of the difference. In other words, what is meant by the effectiveness that is posited in the production of effects by causes? This problem is normally put in the form of an explanatory question: How do we explain that certain causes produce certain effects? The explanation is then given in terms of empirically verified causal laws or, if one cannot proceed so strictly, then in terms of empirically tested, statistical probabilities. But this answer misses the point of our question. It presupposes switching the problem to the question of the form of causal explanation, tacitly adopting an ontological concept of the world: there is causality in the world, and cognition can form right or wrong ideas about it.

But such information has been rendered questionable by the attribution theory now held in high esteem. It can be saved only if one relativizes the importance of attribution. A certain scope is seen for system-specific attribution; but in many cases reality shows through. The choice is not between attributing water on the street to rain or not but only between ascribing an aquaplaning accident to excessive speed or to rain.

Once again we have lost sight of the unity of the difference and have instead discussed how to deal practically with causal problems in the life-world. What unites the distinction here, too, is only the observer himself, or, to be more exact, the operation of observing at the moment in which it is carried out. Causality is attribution, but attribution through a recursive system that needs indications and, above all, a memory if it is to cognize. Coupling certain causes with certain effects thus stabilizes distinctions to which one can return if need be.[17] And even if errors are realized and causal explanations or causal plans have to be modified, this requires resorting to distinctions that have partly proved their worth and partly not.

It amounts to the same if, using Gotthard Günther's terminology, we say that causality is based on a transjunctional operation, which in the given present selects one differentiation schema and not another to construct its own operations or calculate its own behavior. For organizational systems this would mean that causality is the decision that produces a connection between causes and effects, thus using the medium of causality to give it a form that leaves open how the decision observes for its part and is used to construct other causalities. The decision is a mystery to itself, at any rate not a cause that, like the old *mechane*, must cunningly penetrate a cosmological causal web to turn something to its advantage. It is the operation that couples, and only by doing so does it make causes into causes and effects into effects in the given infinite horizons of the "and-so-on." But this does not exclude another observer (who can be the decision-maker himself) construing the decision as a cause without which its effect would not occur. But it should not be forgotten that the causes of the decision, too, would not have become causes without the decision.[18] From the point of view of the causal schema (and not, for example, from an expressive or ethics of conviction perspective), the decision is curiously ambivalent: it can be seen as the cause for a causal relation existing at all between its causes and its effects. On the one side of the cause/effect distinction we then find it as both cause and actualization of this distinction. This ambivalence conceals a paradox, which would become apparent if one permitted the question whether attribution is not the real cause, the primal cause of what it construes as a relationship of cause and effect.

In the ambivalence of decision causality, we thus discover the paradox of time – in schematized and hence credible form. The decision brings infinite cause and effect relations together in one point, namely in itself. It lets causality take place simultaneously with itself, although the causal chains point back far into the past (but are only now rendered effective) and the effect chains lie in the future (but are already caused). This striking simultaneity of temporally distant (at the moment non-actual) causes and effects is a variant of the simultaneity of time itself, that is to say, of the observation that past and future can be distinguished only in relation to a present and ultimately (if the observation of observations is also taken into account) in the present. For practical purposes and for the practical concept of rationality, this means that a control illusion comes into play,[19] which gives the impression that a vast number of causal factors can now be drawn on in distribution to causes and effects. And indeed, it is up to the decision to produce causality without being able to produce the necessary causes and the ensuing effects; for only if the coupling succeeds do causes become causes and effects become effects. As long as notions about the quality of decisions under the "rationality" heading are oriented on the causal schema, interfering residues have to be reckoned with – like the "corruption" of natural perfection in the old world of teleology. But, as regards the state of the world resulting from historical determination, this is handled under the category of error, and, as regards the costs of allowed-for effects, with the concept of side effects or possibly that of risk. For the theory of economic decision-making, it then seems as if decisions can be made about revenue and expense, costs, benefits and risks, advantages and disadvantages *at the same time*. With the same control illusion, politics confirms to itself that it has the power to shape society and can justify the use of this power. It is the same with education science when it inculcates the courage to educate into the teachers it trains and provides the corresponding, professionally validated self-descriptions.

The logic of such control illusions (not to say their rationality) is easier to understand if we relate them to the demand of decision-making in organized positions. The traditional theories of the "prudentia" of the practitioner had drawn his attention more to favorable opportunities, to the right point in time, to good luck, to the favor of the gods.[20] And the problem here had been that unintelligible links between past and future events (forms of being remaining constant) had to be reckoned with and also with immoral behavior on the part of opponents (vice and virtue catalogues remaining constant). Modern society, however, has done away with the framework conditions for these recommendations, even though their practical reasonableness may now and again still be plausible. Although organized decision-making on the basis of decision premises can also be opportunistic, and is then described as "adhocracy," superstition, too, can be useful as a sort of random mechanism for preventing the worst. But when rationality is at issue, the answer cannot very well be: sometimes this way, sometimes that.

If one nevertheless insists on a concept of rationality that relies on causality that is aim-driven and instrumentalist, it will be increasingly contradicted by experience. The illusory components, which had hitherto been successfully suppressed or marginalized or simply ignored in normative models of rational decision-making, come to the fore and demand attention – increasingly so as the importance for modern society of the organization as a form of system becomes a subject of debate. Famous names in organization research such as James March or Karl Weick owe their reputation to their efforts to put head-standing classical rationality premises on their feet. James March appears to recommend a "technology of foolishness."[21] And Karl Weick lists the following criteria for effective organizations: they are (1) garrulous, (2) clumsy, (3) superstitious, (4) hypocritical, (5) monstrous, (6) octopoid, (7) wandering, and (8) grouchy.[22] Nils Brunsson calls for a distinction to be drawn between talk and action, between decision rationality and action rationality, thus dissolving the unity of classical rationality ambitions without replacing it.[23] Others stress that an organization can gear itself to change only through "self-designing," and this requires as little as possible of all things bright and beautiful: consensus needs to be minimized; rationality, consistence, faith in goals, etc. need to be kept at a low level; and only small surpluses should be run (in order to gain "more").[24] A recent habilitation thesis treats organization as the production of garbage,[25] and there is indeed much to be said for no longer measuring the organization in terms of its goals but in terms of its effects on its ecological and human environment. From a dynamic perspective, setting a decision premise would have to be treated as a debt owed to the world, which has to be paid back under unforeseeable conditions. Then, as the concept of autopoiesis teaches us, the relationship with the environment can no longer be described as "adaptation." However, it is striking that none of these attempts at re-orientation claim or could claim to formulate a new perspective for insiders. They therefore have nothing to do with a new concept of rationality able to take account of the insight level offered by the theory of self-referential systems. Although, like Tartarin de Tarascon in his cabin, one hears hectic and contradictory commands being given, aft, forward, and frantic running around on deck seeming to signal that the ship is sinking, the next chapter reveals that *"on ne sombrait pas, on arrivait."*[26]

IV

Setting out from the paradox of observation or the paradox of form offers a way out.[27] In organization theory itself, there are signs that forms of paradoxical communication are attracting increasing attention.[28] This branch of organization studies realizes that communication in organizations (as in families) often involves reference to contradictory matters and, above all, to opposing opinions, the articulation of which is effectively suppressed. From the point of view of participants, this looks like designed inconsistency, which, however, has to be treated consistently as incommunicable.[29] Controversies on theory are also treated as resolved paradoxes: one accepts the one side of the paradox as correct theory and denies any justification to the other side. But this theory of paradoxical communication then speaks for itself without reflection on the paradox it contains. It promises that paradoxical communication will trigger creativity and considers the promotion of creativity to be a good thing.[30] However, this is at best half the truth and lacks empirical underpinning. Thus, the alleged relationship between paradoxical communication and creative innovation is merely evidence of the still prevailing idea that an organization should and can operate rationally, and, should the need arise, can do so through the instrumental use of paradoxical communication. More radical problematization would require examining whether the assertion of rationality or creativity is not itself a paradoxical communication because it conceals and renders incommunicable the fact that an organization cannot operate rationally at all and that creativity can prove very harmful.

This is likely to be achieved only if theory switches in principle (!) from principles to paradoxes.[31] This has already been initiated with the switch from input/output models to autopoiesis. But the problem of paradox must correspondingly be formulated more radically, on the lines of: every beginning is paradoxical.

We had already referred to this as the paradox of observation or paradox of form. In order to indicate something, every observer has to distinguish what is indicated from what is not. He therefore relies on a distinction, but uses only one side of it, leaving the other unmarked. If he wishes to cross to the other side, he has to indicate it – once again in distinction to the other side. In such observation practices, the unity of the distinction – and thus also of the observer who draws the distinction – remains unobserved. One can also indicate a distinction. One then establishes a form – for instance, the form of the sign that is distinct from what is signified,[32] or the form of the system, which is distinct from its environment. If the observer indicates a form, and always a specific form and not another, he selects a unit with two sides to it. He knows that the operations of further observation have to set out from the inner side and not from the outer side of the form. The observation of a form is thus always observation of an asymmetry. In order to see the form, one must accordingly see a boundary and also observe the inclusion of exclusion. But then the observation of a form requires indication of a distinction determined by it – a specific distinction and not any other, for instance the form system (and not environment), or the form good (and not bad).

And if observation is involved (and how else could we approach the concept of rationality?), there is therefore always a paradox involved. This paradox can go under various names, depending on what one is concerned with – for example, identity of the difference; unity of differentiation; invisibility as the condition of visibility. But all observation gives the paradox an asymmetrical form, thus breaching symmetry or de-tautologizating matters. In other words, observing is the unfolding of a paradox, the substitution of an operational distinction, which (and "operational" means nothing else in this context) amount to a distinction between the inner side and the outer side or between positive and negative.

If one chooses this approach, one goes back beyond the traditional distinction between logical consistency and empirical-causal purposiveness, depriving it of the rank of a primary distinction that directs all others. Efforts to obtain logical consistency that necessarily excludes or ignores paradoxes are replaced by a calculus of forms that falls rather in the domain of mathematics.[33] It is about developing complexity in dependence on the choice of a distinction; and this is termed calculus because, owing to the formal structure of the arrangement, everyone who follows it has to agree (insofar as errors do not occur, which can be corrected). What appears to be a paradox and what can be resolved in the calculus depends on the complexity of the system state attained (e.g., on whether second-order functions, imaginary numbers, or imaginary spaces are permitted). In Spencer-Brown's calculus of forms, this problem focuses on the figure of the reentry of a form into itself, thus of a distinction into what is distinguished.[34]

In the field of empirical research that makes use of the causal schema, we have already discovered a corresponding figure, namely the question whether one can regard the attribution of effects to causes as a cause, and thus reenter it into the causal schema. At first glance this is a highly irritating procedure; but it could be that mathematics can offer us at least some ideas about what would happen if this happened, or how a system has to be equipped to afford such a reentry. The same thought comes to bear if we treat the concept of system as an empirical one and then ask how an actually operating system can reenter the difference between system and environment, which it produces itself and to whose reproduction it owes its existence, into this same system. This is a quite usual process. We had repeatedly noted that organizations, like other social systems, orient their own operations on the distinction between self-reference and other-reference. This is nothing other than a reentry of the difference between system and environment into the system. The function of this figure in paradox resolution is apparent in the fact that the system renders itself invisible in carrying out this function, and consequently does not distinguish between the environment that it indicates and the environment "out there" that could be observed by other observers. A fusion takes place.[35] The reentry also conceals the paradox that could be discovered if one asked whether a distinction remains *the same* if it reenters *into itself*.

This brings us to the heart of the problem. If rationality is to address demands to an observer, the problem of system rationality could lie in handling the distinction between self-reference and other-reference (this could then easily be transferred to other distinctions: in decision-making it would involve the distinction between the decision before the decision and the decision after the decision, thus the problem of risk; in observations oriented on causality, it would be about the problem of taking attribution into account; in the case of observing itself it would be a question of second-order observation, of the observations of observers, etc.). And it would always have to be remembered that the sole "substratum" of rationality is the only momentarily actual operation, which has to actualize demands made of itself through recursion.

When it is a question of system rationality, then, how can one assume indifference toward the environment while at the same time treating it as a variable? How can one maintain operational closure and nevertheless permit greater account to be taken of the environment; and not only of the environment as it is "out there" and "is" operationally inaccessible (whatever that means), but of the environment as construed in the system itself on the basis of operationally connective distinctions? How can the system organize its internal structures in such a way that it can generate more irritability without this ending in confusion, hence without the conversion of irritation into information being hampered or costing too much effort?

Normally, the system does not distinguish between what it calls the environment and the environment as it is. For the system, the two have a single cognitive status: reality. At best, second-order observers can say: "We can never be quite clear whether we are referring to the world as it is or to the world as we see it."[36] To get closer to what we want to call rationality in this context, the system has self-correction mechanisms at its disposition. It tries to recognize and avoid "errors." This is still within the classical realm of truth rationality and can be handled with the usual two-valued logic. More demanding procedures could try to recognize and avoid self-referential "projections." Self-correction mechanisms are developed into self-accusation mechanisms. The system then observes itself with the aid of the distinction between normal and pathological. As it were, it psychiatrizes itself, often with the help of advisers, to establish whether its own structures (programs, interests, and above all, naturally: organizational culture) lead to a distorted perception of reality. But even then, the assumption remains that one can gear oneself to the reality of the world as it really is. A "radical constructivism" may be convincing as theory, but in practical terms it is unattainable. Taken seriously, it would mean that other-reference, too, is only self-reference and would thus allow this distinction to collapse in its own paradox.

Nevertheless, this rationality concept of seen-through reentry may be useful, and precisely because it draws attention to a paradox. The distinction (in this case between system and environment) that reenters itself is the same and not the same. The "reality" is always given only as indicated reality, thus only thanks to referential observation, but it is not only reference. This at least implies that the system can carefully generalize its projection awareness, can normalize its self-psychiatrization, and can hence be self-critical in a strict sense of the term while keeping its feet on the ground of reality. It can use it to feel its way carefully ahead without the illusion that the right location, the natural telos of the movement can be reached.

That no boundaries set by nature or logic have to be respected – except the very remote material limits for information processing – permits open perspectives. Although, as we know,[37] evolution punishes almost every specification as restricting further evolutionary potential, there are exceptions. The invention of the system type organization, and thus, roughly, the procurement of flexible, both specifiable and modifiable motivation in return for remuneration is already an impressive example of the possibility for social systems to gain structural complexity in the relationship between self-reference and other-reference. This development does not have to be regarded as over. Although disappointment with the traditional expectations of rationality is currently predominant – no optimal solutions to problems, no consistency and no temporal stability of preferences, no reliability in linear, longer-term causal plans – this type of disappointment need not give rise to resignation; it could be countered by switching expectations to a different concept of rationality.

Above all, durable notions of rightness on the lines of "once right, always right" will have to be abandoned. Complexity at the level demanded requires complexity to be temporalized. Every later decision "redescribes" preceding decisions, thus remaining within the system while creating scope for its own contingency and thus for its own decidability.[38] If a reentry is to be made possible in such a redescriptive process (and it is always introduced, since no organization manages without self-reference and other-reference), time becomes the decisive variable, taken into account in all operations – in this case in all decisions. The operations of the system are structurally determined and autopoietic; it can only produce itself. However, it has no corresponding capacity for self-observation, for this would mean multiplying every operation by its distinctions; thus not only to let them happen but also to register what does not happen while it happens. It is therefore precisely complete self-determination that produces a discrepancy between operation and observation that increases with growing complexity. It now appears that the resulting "unresolvable indeterminacy"[39] is compensated for by the distinction between self-reference and other-reference and by the inclusion of time. In relation to the past, the system needs memory, that is to say, the capacity actualized in the present to remember *and to forget*. In relation to the future, the system has to gear itself to oscillation, for example, to oscillation between knowledge and non-knowledge, or between transparent and opaque objects, to oscillation between code values, thus between decisions judged good and bad; and not least to oscillation between focal points in the field of self-reference and in that of other-reference, which are both given only in infinite horizons of unceasingly possible exploration.

If one has to rely on memory, one can fall victim to self-created simplifications.[40] For example, one reckons with a situation, takes something to be unique and forgets it, and can then no longer recognize that it repeats itself. Or states of affairs one recalls are considered to be still relevant even though environmental conditions have changed.[41] Or adjustments have to be made to an oscillated future determined by various bifurcations, a future whose course cannot be foreseen or deduced from what one knows. In the social dimension, this gives rise to agreement without consensus, without strong commitment, without motivation to persevere. Willingness can then be expected only in the form of irrationality.[42]

Such a concept of rationality must breach the hitherto assumed link between rationality and forecastability. This applies for both external and internal forecasts. What is called forecast is then rather a tool that points out what has to be changed in the forecast if, as typically occurs, it proves inaccurate. Forecasts are, as it were, memoirs, which remind the system of how the future had looked and how it had been motivated by it – memoirs that have to be continually revised to take account of what one needs at the moment in the way of future in order to decide. In other words, they offer possibilities to observe problems and changes more closely (at the risk of failing to see other things) than would have been possible without memory.

V

There is no cosmological justification for such a concept of system rationality. It cannot be explained by the nature of things. And putting it under the heading of "reason" would be going too far, if by reason we mean that the individual potential for subjectively convincing sensemaking is to be exhausted and everything that does not satisfy this wish is to be disqualified as merely technical rationality.[43] Even if the "subject" is exchanged for society, such extrapolation from organizational rationality to societal rationality will not work. The systems differ too greatly in the nature of their autopoiesis. What can be achieved in the way of rationality by a system that communicates on the operational basis of decisions cannot, for this reason alone, claim the title of macro-societal rationality – not even if in both cases only system rationality is under consideration and the more far-reaching ambitions of Jürgen Habermas's theory of communicative action are left aside.

Instead of insisting on overall rationality and regarded it a norm to be prescribed and implemented, we ask how organizational rationality affects the societal system that relies on it but cannot identify with it. In adding to what has been said in Chapter 13, we limit ourselves to three aspects without claiming to exhaust the subject.

If all organizations owe their flexible specification to the payment of wages and salaries, this means that all organizations also operate in the economic system regardless of whether the focus of their function lies in this system or in other functional systems, for example, in the case of governmental organizations in the political system, in the case of schools in the education system, in that of courts in the legal system, or for research organizations in the science system. Every organization that spends money has to ensure that money comes in. This gives particular importance to the economic system, which alone can provide money and, especially, ensure the willingness to accept money;[44] and in this connection, since not all organizations can refinance themselves economically through their products, the state has to intervene by coercive means, using political resources. This leads to optical distortions, as it were, namely to the idea that in modern society the economy and, in conjunction with it, politics have functional primacy, with other functional systems playing at best a secondary role.[45] However, if one keeps in mind the importance of failure or malfunctioning, this view soon has to be corrected: politics without law and without mass media, economy without education in schools? This does not necessarily mean that all functional systems are equally important for the further evolution of society, but at any rate the relative prominence of systems cannot be judged solely at the level of the organization. Precisely the weak performance currently evident in politics as organized by the state and in an economy dependent on borrowing and steered by the financial markets should serve as a warning.

At least – and this is the next aspect – the extent to which modern society has made the distribution of access to the satisfaction of economic needs and, in this connection, the financing of the welfare state dependent on organized work and on nonwage labor costs gives food for thought. At the level of organizations, a trend would be expected toward rationalizing away costly work where possible or outsourcing to low-wage countries. On the other hand, society cannot do without the distribution tool of (organized) work. Under the name of "work," organization is one of the key problems of modern society. Worries about the "future of work" had been a first storm cloud to loom over the left-wing scene of the 1970s, and not there alone. However much the economy may impose economic management on organizations and however much organizations that are not primarily economic orient themselves on market-type demand, greater efforts have to be made to make more out of work by specifically organizational means.

Another remark follows from the assumption that organizational rationality in social relations requires agreement without consensus. All absorption of uncertainty is only temporarily valid, anyway; it involves remembering the guiding aspects of decisions, and can be called into question if things change. So why get worked up? The decisions that ultimately determine the course of events come about through collective thinking, even if certain contributions, ideas, and even obstructions can be attributed to individuals. Seen from the outside, the system works anonymously anyway, and if names are named, it is display for publicity purposes, allowing no conclusions about specific decisions – as at least insiders are aware.

If at all, society must therefore provide other terrain for the communication of individual identity. In the nineteenth century it had been assumed that this could be private life, love relations, and the family who share all burdens and appreciate the individual whatever the world grants or denies him.[46] Under present-day conditions, we find at best public rhetoric recommending the family as societal remedy, but hardly any reality that provides such service. This may well be because this solution had systematically disadvantaged women; or also because it could work only as long as the stratification of families came to bear as a supplementary factor. This cannot adequately satisfy the need for an identity that can be communicated as being voluntary and stubbornly upheld. The mass media supplement this by presenting heroes and heroines as identification figures.[47] But this has now been added to by quite different possibilities of public communicating resolute, not to be discouraged, uncompromising identity. Above all in prosperous parts of the world, there are protest movements pursuing widely differing, constantly updated causes;[48] and then there are ethnic, religious, and also thematic fundamentalisms of various sorts.[49]

It could be that opportunities or new sorts of organization arise – just as social work has to do with problems that other organizations leave unresolved behind them. What is striking about social movements is their fluctuating membership, their dependence on specific generations, and the tendency of their leadership to switch to other, more normal organizations when the opportunity arises. We merely note that society cannot be understood as the sum total of organizable work but that its dependence on rationally organized work is reflected in its reacting to problems to which organizations contribute as the other side of their form.

VI

An external observer, a sociologist, or an organizational consultant can observe that and how organizations observe themselves. He can analyze their explicit and implicit texts and draw conclusions about self-descriptions. The theory of autopoietic, operationally closed systems also says that that such self-observations and self-descriptions are to be expected. Since such systems are dynamic and react to themselves, it can also be expected that self-descriptions will not remain constant but will change, with or without the help of researchers. We had looked at such changes with regard to hierarchy and rationality. Although hierarchy continues to be used without dispute as a structure, it no longer appears to be the sensemaking center of organization descriptions. And even more clearly: although ends continue to be pursued, the optimization of ends/means relations no longer appears to be the ideal of self-description as rational; or where it is maintained, the supposedly irrational components of the organized decision-making process come more strongly to bear.

Although this analysis understands organizations as observers, it treats them as first-order observers. They relate to themselves as to objects. They measure themselves against the requirements that they presuppose. In all this, variability is built in and criteria of unconditional, *a priori* rightness are done without. The society often described as "postmodern" discourages abiding by such absolute criteria, describing this as "fundamentalist." In these cases, one cannot yet speak of second-order observation in the strict sense.[50]

We therefore have to distinguish between two concepts of autonomy. The *operational* closure of autopoietic systems does not imply a *cognitive* closure of such systems at the level of observation. This would presuppose that, with respect to everything that they observe in relation to themselves or in relation to their environment, the systems also observe that it is they (and only they) that choose and use the observation schema. This amounts to the practical acceptance of the radical-constructivist thesis. If, for example, a distinction is drawn between decision premises and decisions, it must remain open whether any discrepancies, errors, or deviations are attributable to decisions or to their premises. As far as the conditions of rationality are concerned, whether rationality deficits are to be attributed to decisions or to the way in which decisions are observed remains an open question if certain rationality requirements are taken as the basis for observation. However, this sort of well-considered (autological) second-order observation is hardly to be expected within the system and, above all, as a mode of everyday communication. Although second-order cybernetics may well postulate that all observations are to be observed as operations of observing systems, this does not impose the empirical assumption that the autological conclusion applies to all observations and that every observations says to itself: I am only the observation of an observer.

If crises in observation and growing uncertainty in decision-making arise, and if society itself has no remedy at hand, an obvious way out is to find "ethical" criteria that one can accept, however recklessly and provisionally, as in constructivist self-reflection in the sense of second-order cybernetics. But ethics are always directives for first-order observers. They do not ask who the observer is that distinguishes between ethical principles and behavior (at best they ask about the justification for these benchmarks), and attribute discrepancies between principles and behavior to behavior and not to the principles. Here, too, there may well be criticism and changes; but if ethics are involved and are to remain so, old values have to be replaced by new ones; otherwise the ethics in question would disintegrate.

Nevertheless, second-order cybernetics is not an "impractical" orientation, which one cannot seriously recommend let alone put into practice. Alone, the extent to which family therapists or organizational consultants apply this model suggests otherwise. But this constructivist attitude does not lead directly to principles, guidelines, or recipes, let alone to decisions. It leads directly to a paradox, namely to the question about the observer who cannot present himself in his distinctions and therefore remains invisible. Or to the paradox of undecidable decisions. But this need not remain so. It is an old wisdom of rhetorical paradoxization that this form serves to pose the question whether the conventional distinctions and indications can be abandoned for other forms of paradox resolution. In the schema of problem and problem-solving, the paradox then serves as insoluble problem, which can prompt reformation of the distinction between problem and problem-solving. This can obviously not take place in a rational fashion, since the basal meaning of the paradox has to be conceded, but perhaps in an intelligent fashion that manages to accommodate itself to existing conditions.

Notes

1. See Klaus P. Japp, Verwaltung und Rationalität, in: Klaus Dammann et al. (eds.), *Die Verwaltung des politischen Systems: Neuere systemtheoretische Zugriffe auf ein altes Thema*, Opladen 1994, 126–141.
2. In a broader context see Richard Harvey Brown, Rhetoric, Textuality, and the Postmodern Turn in Sociological Theory, in: Steven Seidman (ed.), *The Postmodern Turn: New Perspectives on Social Theory*, Cambridge 1994, 229–241. See also idem., *Society as Text: Essays on Rhetoric, Reason, and Reality*, Chicago 1987.
3. See Bernard Ancori, *Apprendre, se souvenir, décider: Une nouvelle rationalité de l'organisation*, Paris 1992, 25 ff.
4. This is the argument advanced by Japp loc. cit.
5. See Arthur L. Stinchcombe, *Information and Organizations*, Berkeley 1990.
6. See Barry M. Staw, Rationality and Justification in Organizational Life, in: Barry M. Staw and Larry L. Cummings (eds.), *Research in Organizational Behavior* 2 (1980), 45–80.
7. That differences have to be assumed is taken too little into account. But see Elena Esposito, Die Orientierung an Differenzen: Systemrationalität und kybernetische Rationalität, *Selbstorganisation* 6 (1995), 161–176.

8. See, for the development of poetry from Dryden to Shelley, Earl R. Wasserman, *The Subtler Language: Critical Readings of Neoclassic and Romantic Poems*, Baltimore 1959.

9. This is by no means the case only for production organizations but, to go by the abundant literature on reform in the education system, also for schools and universities. The general complaints about the leisurely pace prevailing in governmental bureaucracies follow this pattern.

10. See Massimo Warglien, Learning in a Garbage Can Situation: A Network Model, in: Massimo Warglien and Michael Masuch (eds.), *The Logic of Organizational Disorder*, Berlin 1996, 163–182: "one of the most radical and puzzling attempts to shape a theory of intelligent behavior when the main assumptions of rational (or quasi rational) decision making are violated" (163).

11. See above all the trail-blazing contribution by Richard M. Cyert and James G. March, *A Behavioral Theory of the Firm*, Englewood Cliffs, NJ 1963, 2nd ed. with an epilogue outlining subsequent developments, Oxford 1992.

12. Martha S. Feldman, *Order Without Design: Information Processing and Policy Making*, Stanford 1989, 123, defines: "A skill is a sequence of behavior in which each action is conditional upon the previous action or state."

13. On the search for excellence see also Robert E. Quinn, *Beyond Rational Management: Mastering the Paradoxes and Competing Demands of High Performance*, San Francisco 1989.

14. See also Niklas Luhmann, Das Risiko der Kausalität, *Zeitschrift für Wissenschaftsforschung* 9/10 (1995), 107–119.

15. See the trail-blazing contribution by Arthur Rosenblueth, Norbert Wiener, and Julian Bigelow, Behavior, Purpose, and Teleology, *Philosophy of Science* 10 (1943), 18–24; also Lawrence K. Frank et al., Teleological Mechanism, *Annals of the New York Academy of Sciences* 50 (1948), 189–196.

16. This had always been presupposed in systems theory and is not called into question by the concept of autopoiesis. For many similar views see, e.g., Jurgen Ruesch and Gregory Bateson, *Communication: The Social Matrix of Psychiatry*, New York 1951, S. 8, 75 f.; Ludwig von Bertalanffy, General Systems Theory: A Critical Review, *General Systems* 7 (1962), 1–20; F.E. Emery and E.L. Trist, The Causal Texture of Organizational Environments, *Human Relations* 18 (1965), 21–32. See also the important remarks by Chester I. Barnard, *The Functions of the Executive*, Cambridge, MA 1938 (reprinted 1951), 250 f., that no system can attribute success or failure to single causes (e.g., persons). "This is to say that no specific statement can be made significantly except it be in terms of *differential effect*. . . . Hence, the notion of cause and effect in an absolute sense is not pertinent."

17. See Francis Heylighen, Causality as Distinction Conservation: A Theory of Predictability, Reversibility, and Time Order, *Cybernetics and Systems* 20 (1989), 361–384.

18. The mythology of deciding tends to describe decisions as spontaneous, as causeless, and at best to concede the decision-maker needs "motives" to decide.

19. See J. D. Dermer and R. G. Lucas, The Illusion of Managerial Control, *Accounting Organizations and Society* 11 (1986), 471–482.

20. For the temporal reference of prudentia, which distinguishes humans from animals, which can react only sensorily, there was a long tradition of taking Cicero's De

officiis I,IV,11 (zit. nach Loeb Classical Library XXI, London 1968, S. 21) to be the decisive source: *"Sed inter hominem et beluam hoc maxime interest, quod haec tantum, quantum sensu movetur, ad id solum quod adest quodque praesens est se accomodat paulum admodum sentiens praeteritum aut futurum; homo autem quod rationis est particeps per quam consequentia cernit, causas rerum videt earumque praegressus et quasi antecessiones non ignorat."* On further effects, see Rodolfo de Mattei, Sapienza e Prudenza nel pensiero politico italiano dall Umanesimo al sec. XVII., in: Enrico Castelli (ed.), *Umanesimo e Scienza politica*, Milano 1951. The basic idea can be attributed via Aristotle to Anaxagoras. This tradition was upheld until well into the eighteenth century for as long as school instruction was guided by prudentia.

21. See James G. March and Johan P. Olsen, *Ambiguity and Choice in Organizations*, Bergen, Norwegen 1976.

22. See Karl E. Weick, Re-Punctuating the Problem, in: Paul S. Goodman, Johannes M. Pennings, et al., *New Perspectives on Organizational Effectiveness*, San Francisco 1977, 193–225 (193).

23. See: The Organization of Hypocrisy: Talk, *Decisions and Actions in Organizations*, Chichester 1989, and the critical review by M. Reed, Organizations and Rationality: The Odd Couple, *Journal of Management Studies* 28 (1991), 559–567.

24. See Bo L. T. Hedberg, Paul C. Nystrom, and William H. Starbuck, Camping on Seasaws: Prescription for a Self-Designing Organization, *Administrative Science Quarterly* 21 (1976), 41–65. However, the authors were unable to show that an organization that complies with these prescriptions will in fact be successful forever. It is therefore nothing more than a change in the self-description of the system. "A self-designing organization," to quote op. cit. 43, "functions most smoothly if its ideology cherishes impermanence."

25. See Theodor M. Bardmann, *Wenn aus Arbeit Abfall wird: Aufbau und Abbau organisatorischer Realitäten*, Frankfurt 1994.

26. Alphonse Daudet, *Aventures prodigieuses de Tartarin de Tarascon, Œuvres complètes* vol. 1, Paris 1899, 51 f. and 52.

27. See Niklas Luhmann, Die Paradoxie der Form, in: Dirk Baecker (ed.), *Kalkül der Form*, Frankfurt 1993, 197–212.

28. See Robert E. Quinn and Kim S. Cameron (eds.), *Paradox and Transformation: Toward a Theory of Change in Organization and Management*, Cambridge, MA 1988.

29. See Chris Argyris, Crafting a Theory of Practice: The Case of Organizational Paradoxes, in: Quinn and Cameron op. cit.. 255–278.

30. That family therapy argues the other way round, considering "double bind" to be a cause of pathological developments in families, may well be irritating but cannot necessarily be taken as a counterargument. Families and organizations, precisely from the point of view of the covert indication of personal attitudes, cannot simply be compared.

31. The much discussed Japanese methods of production could perhaps be analyzed in this way. The principle appears to be that perfection is possible (although it is not possible). The demands are reduced as directly as possible to situations that in various ways reflect a world of harmony and, in close communicative association, are successively developed from situation to situation. In this manner, it appears

possible to exclude the problems of Western thought that have to do with distinctions, demarcations, linearities, concatenations, etc. If under certain circumstances this proved successful, this is no reason to conclude that it is also rational.

32. See Niklas Luhmann, Zeichen als Form, in: Dirk Baecker (ed.), *Probleme der Form*, Frankfurt 1993, 45–69.

33. See George Spencer Brown, *Laws of Form*, reprint of the 2nd ed. New York 1979.

34. See op. cit. 56 ff.

35. It should be mentioned that Spencer-Brown (op. cit. p. XXX) interprets the central operator of mathematics, the equals sign, to mean "is confused with." One could also say that with this sign a boundary is formulated whose crossing must not produce any information.

36. Jurgen Ruesch and Gregory Bateson, *Communication: The Social Matrix of Psychiatry*, New York 1951, 2nd ed. 1968, 238, addressing the reality concept in psychiatry.

37. See above 357 ff.

38. A corresponding theory of the sequence of artistic-stylistic innovations is outlined in Michael Baldwin, Charles Harrison, and Mel Ramsden, On Conceptual Art and Painting, and Speaking and Seeing: Three Corrected Transcripts, *Art-Language NS* 1 (1994), 30–69 (esp. 31 f.) On "redescription" see also Mary Hesse, *Models and Analogies in Science*, Notre Dame 1966, 157 ff.

39. See Spencer Brown op. cit.. 57 with reference to the mathematical operations of arithmetic and algebra, which come up against their limits with the introduction of a reentry. And, it should be noted, it is not a matter of an indeterminacy that goes back to dependence on the environment, thus to independent variables, but an indeterminacy generated in the system itself.

40. Recent literature on the memory of organizations acknowledges this. See, e.g., James P. Walsh and Gerardo Rivera Ungson, Organizational Memory, *Academy of Management Review* 16 (1991), 57–91. But this means that memory is ambivalent in relation to rationality – sometimes helpful, sometimes disadvantageous.

41. This "error" is often noted in the literature and combated with demands for innovation, creativity, etc. See Walsh and Ungson op. cit. The problem can be more clearly defined if one accepts our thesis that a system can remember *only states of its own* and not states of the environment to which it has no access.

42. See Nils Brunsson, *The Irrational Organization: Irrationality as a Basis for Organizational Action and Change*, Chichester 1985. See also idem, *The Organization of Hypocrisy: Talk, Decisions and Actions in Organizations*, Chichester 1989.

43. Husserl had, of course, proposed such a concept of reason as the telos of Western philosophy as a way out of certain constrictions of European modernity. See Edmund Husserl, *Die Krisis der europäischen Wissenschaften und die transzendentale Phänomenologie, Husserliana* vol. VI, Den Haag 1954.

44. See Josef Wieland, Die Wirtschaft der Verwaltung und die Verwaltung der Wirtschaft, in: Klaus Dammann et al. (ed.), *Die Verwaltung des politischen Systems: Neuere systemtheoretische Zugriffe auf ein altes Thema*, Opladen 1994, 65–78 (74). Wieland calls the economy "the guidance system of modern societies."

45. As in a quartet, one could say, the second violin. But closer examination can show that precisely in this domain overall performance depends essentially on the tool that occupies the least space in the prominence scale.
46. See only Jules Michelet, *L'amour*, Paris 1858.
47. The alternative authentic love/*homme copie* had already been noted at the beginning of the nineteenth century; but with a clear preference for authentic love over merely adopted identification. See Stendhal (Henri Bleyle), De l'amour (1822), Paris 1959. And naturally novels like Madame Bovary and Effi Briest. *René Girard was then to resolutely reverse the weighting in Mensonge romantique de vérité romanesque*, Paris 1961.
48. See Niklas Luhmann, *Protest: Systemtheorie und soziale Bewegungen* (ed. Kai-Uwe Hellmann), Frankfurt 1996.
49. Recent research has demonstrated that the phenomena described as "fundamentalism" are new developments of the second half of the twentieth century, and that they are not the continuation of old traditions but a revival inspired by intellectuals. However, this tells us nothing about the extent to which this is in reaction to general globalization trends, for instance, in the money economy, in nationally (and not ethnically) oriented policy, in the dominant science that excludes "para" phenomena, or at least also in reaction to conditions in organized work. There will presumably be regional differences, and the historical speed of changes has to be taken into account.
50. See Frederick Steier and Kenwyn K. Smith, Organizations and Second Order Cybernetics, *Journal of Strategic and Systemic Therapies 4*, 4 (1985), 53–65.

Conclusion: Theory and Practice

When a theory is presented nowadays, the question follows – almost automatically and, at any rate, without reflection – of what use this theory is in practice. The theory of organization expounded here is also likely to face such interrogation. Rather than writhe in embarrassment, we shall conclude by asking whether such a question is justified in the first place.

At the outset, it should be noted that the confrontation between theory and practice is not rooted in history; it is relatively new, dating probably from the nineteenth century. Before then, theory and practice had been distinguished from different concepts: theory as remote knowledge from everyday knowledge and practice from poíesis, that is to say, from the production of works. What, then, needs to be established is the thinking behind opposing theory to practice. It is certainly a reaction to the science culture of the nineteenth century. This shows the sense of theory. Theory is a work program for the science system. But what is practice?

The science culture of the nineteenth century took it for granted that theory was the lead factor in the relationship. But how exactly is this to be understood? Hardly in the old hierarchical sense with theory taking precedence over practice in rank or essentiality. Theory will hardly be able to claim it is more important than practice for humankind, for culture, for society. The disequilibrium in the relationship between theory and practice finds expression rather in the circumstance that theory plays a role on both sides, on that of theory and on that of practice.[1] On the one hand, theory performs its function on its side of the distinction, on the side of theory. In so doing, it treats practice as the subject matter of theory under such headings as action or operation. It is therefore difficult to see why theory, as is often asserted,[2] ought to make an effort to be understandable for practitioners. Why should it accept the concomitant restrictions? On the other hand – and this is quite a different question – theory asks what effects it has on practice. It doubles itself, as it were, bringing itself into play as both observer and observed object. But such a maneuver sabotages the classical distinction between theory and practice (or between "subject" and "object"). The distinction reenters itself.[3] With such a reentry, the calculus goes beyond the scope of application of the classical modus operandi for cognition and, one could say, becomes non-computable. The question is then how continuing operation can still be steered with regard to objectivity or intersubjective congruence. Or how the now indispensable "imagination" can still be controlled.

Until this question has been answered, no path to meaningful critique will be opened by the initial question about the practical use of theory. Whoever poses this question therefore espouses the interests of practice. They are free to do so. But it is not clear what this could contribute to improving what a theory can be expected to provide. A theory contains its own amelioration program. Only in accordance with its own problem definitions can it be improved, possibly also by reformulating the problems it addresses on a different metaphorical basis, with the aid of different lead distinctions. For example, a successor can be sought for the concept of autopoiesis or an answer to the question of how reproducible differences – whether system/environment or structure/process – can arise from operations tied to a particular point in time. However, the question whether, at what cost, and with what side effects practice attains its ends with the help of theory cannot be answered (although this question can naturally be explicated theoretically). In other words, we have to be satisfied with a "loose coupling of cognition and action." And not least of all, it may be a practical advantage if one has to assume that loose coupling is a fundamental condition for system stability.

Notes

1. One can claim the same for practice, too, and speak of the practice of theory, the practice of theory design. But this reduces work on theory to a special case, as in the practice of brewing and pouring tea, and what counts above all is to avoid doing anything wrong.
2. See Barbara Czarniawska-Joerges, *Exploring Complex Organizations: A Cultural Perspective*, Newbury Park, CA 1992, 211 f.
3. In the sense of George Spencer Brown, *Laws of Form*, reprint New York 1979, 56 ff., 69. ff.

Index

accidents, 212
accountability
  defining, 156
  responsibility and, 156, 163
action
  attribution and, 98–99
  bodily, 115–116
  communicative, 115
  control and, 344
  decision-making and, 99
  defining, 99
  explanation of, 131
  motives and, 71
  theory, 317–318
  Weber on, 10
actuating factors, 221
adaptation, 49–50, 379
adaptive learning, 50
addresses, capabilities for, 263–264
adequate complexity, 253, 258
administrative organizations, 146
advancement, 238
aggregation ban, 122
agreement, 40
  boundaries and, 162
  in communication, 69, 162
  effective, 166
AIDS, 226
alarm signals, 168
all-inclusive social systems, 168–169
alternatives, 104–105
  extension of, 231–232
ambiguity, 202
  oral communication and, 202
  organizational culture and, 195
analogy, memory and, 123
animals, 87
anonymity, communication and, 167
antinomies, 372–373
apex, of political apparatus, 165
arbitrariness, in decision-making, 106
archetypes, 201–202

artificial intelligence, 308–309
Association of Chemical Industry, 322
attribution, 375
  action and, 98–99
  autopoiesis and, 375–376
  causality and, 140, 377
  decision-making and, 107–108
  of responsibility, 158
authority model, 64–65, 80
  communication and, 160
  traditional, 161
  uncertainty and, 160
autocompetence, 330
autological conclusions, 28, 160
automatic synchronization, 215
automatism, 240
autonomy, 213–214, 252–253, 375–376
  autopoiesis and, 33
autopoiesis, 32, 34, 56, 66, 113, 160, 285–286,
    325–326, 331–332, 374
  attribution and, 375–376
  autonomy and, 33
  basal unity, 29–30
  causality and, 226
  communication and, 46
  conservative ideology and, 57
  decision premises in, 186
  of decision-making, 132
  defining, 29
  operational closure and, 33
  operations and, 32
  organizations and, 148
  systems theory and, 43, 53
  uncertainty and, 132
auxiliary functions, 250

balance, 252–253
bank policy, 330, 369
Barel, Yves, 290–291
Barnard, Chester I., 5–6
Bateson, Gregory, 37, 275
behavior problems, 237

behaviorism, 373–374
binary codes, 192
biology, 34
bistability, 184, 251–252
bivalence, 191–192
blue-collar workers, 231
bodily action, 115–116
bodily perception, 66–67
bosses, 16–17
bottom-up communication, 266
boundary position, 165–166, 318–319,
    322–323, 338
bounded rationality, 10–11
Brunsson, Nils, 379
Brussels administration, 321
budget planning, 138, 139–140
bureaucracy, 129
    criticism of, 169
    defining, 4–5
    essence of, 12
    European, 5
    goals of, 5
    ideal, 10
    impersonal, 234
    objections to, 5
    theory of, 340
    Weber on, 4, 6, 7, 167
Burns, Tom, 267
business studies, 250
Butera, Federico, 307–308

calculus of forms, viii, 28, 85, 135, 381
    reentry in, 48–49
capabilities
    for addresses, 263–264
    negative, 278
career, 73 74, 79
    characteristics of, 74
    construction of, 243
    defining, 74
    identity and, 242–243
    incentives through, 243
    integration through, 245
    objective reality and, 244
    orientation, 74
    the present and, 243–244
    self-observation and, 244
    self-reinforcement and, 76
    uncertainty and, 75, 76–77
case studies, 358
causality, 136, 375
    attribution and, 140, 377
    autopoiesis and, 226
    conditional programs and, 225
    effects coupled with, 140–141

ends/means schema and, 218
establishing, 141
intrasystemic, 226
medium of, 141, 376–377
rationality and, 375
time and, 140
unexpected and, 218–219
values and, 196
centralization, 64–65
certainty, uncertainty and, 168, 169
ceteris paribus, 164
change. See also evolutionary models
    defining, 273–274
    in environment, 276–277
    inertial effects and, 197
    in organizational culture, 196–197
    planning and, 284–285
    structural, 274
Channel Tunnel, 221
charisma, 107
choice
    decision-making and, 99, 106
    defining, 98
circular self-reference, 53–54
civil servants, 248, 270, 281
class society, 319–320
clique formation, 250
closed contingency, 186
coercion, 77–78
cognition
    decision-making and, 214
    distinctions and, 213–214
    freedom and, 200–201, 214
cognitive maps, 11
cognitive psychology, 155
cognitive routines, 199
    construction of, 200–201
    decision premises and, 200
    defining, 199
    development of, 200
    organizational theory on, 201
    uncertainty and, 200
cognitive sciences, 47
cognitive training, 238
collaboration, 71
collective mind, 40
commodity market, 13–14
communicable forms, 85
communication, 6, 28, 114, 120, 141–142, 327
    agreement in, 69, 162
    anonymity and, 167
    authority and, 160
    autopoiesis and, 46
    bottom-up, 266
    channels, 182–183, 253, 260, 261–262, 268

command aspect of, 111
competence conveyed through,
    261–262, 263
components of, 68
computers and, 309
consensus and, 68–69
contradiction and, 69
decision premises and, 211, 259–260
decision-making and, 44, 45, 47–48,
    110–111, 150–151, 287
difficulties in, 151–152
experience in, 161
explicit, 157
formal, 8–9
forms of, 370
functions of, 39, 40
gestalt reference of, 148
hierarchies and, 220, 257, 266
informal, 8–9
information and, 100
interactional, 167
internal, 197
legal systems and, 322
medium of, 350–351
membership and, 323
memory and, 225
motives and, 69–70
non-linguistic, 168
open, 232
oral, 87–88, 167, 202
in organizational theory, 41
organizations and, 39, 41–42
paradoxes and, 83, 148
paradoxical, 84–85
perception and, 37, 86–87, 200
personal, 232
personhood and, 67–68
redundant, 195
report aspect of, 111
responsibilities developing, 260
sociable, 85
social systems and, 41, 81–82, 112,
    321–322
sociality and, 38–39
systems theory and, 84
time and, 123–124
topics of, 39
truth and, 83, 151–152
uncertainty and, 167
Weber on, 167
written, 87–88, 167
communicative action, 115
communicative irritation, 28
competence
    autocompetence, 330

communication conveyed through,
    261–262, 263
decision-making and, 266–266
differentiation of, 264–265
distribution of, 265, 266–266
hierarchical, 256, 257–258, 265
organization of, 267
professional, 256, 257–258
competition, 169, 362–363
complete information, 150
complexity, 49–50, 72–73, 191–192
adequate, 253, 258
costs of, 259
increases in, 258
information and, 260
other-reference and, 257–258
as paradox, 253
self-reference and, 257–258
time and, 383–384
computers, 88, 305–306, 307–308
communication and, 309
Comte, August, 2
conditional programs, 210–211, 221
actuating, 215
causality and, 225
defining, 213, 215
indeterminacy in, 215
purposive programs and, 217
risk and, 222–223
conditioned trustworthiness, 335–336
confusion, mitigation of, by decision
    premises, 192
congruence, 69
connectivity, 32–33, 110
information and, 36–37
consciousness systems, 34, 67, 115, 350
externalization of, 85–86
consensus, 72, 108–109, 305–306
communication and, 68–69
demand for, 108
fictions of, 88
for planning, 289
reform and, 278–279
consent, 162
consumer goods, market and, 80
contextual rationality, 370
contingency theory, 15, 65, 300
closed, 157, 186
criticism of, 15–16
decision-making and, 110
forms of, 134
open, 186
contractual ties, 256
contradiction, 40
communication and, 69

control, 74, 150, 332–333
  action and, 344
  illusions, 378
  judicial, 332
corporate culture, 232
corporate identity, 232
corporate management, 7
correlation, directive, 162–163
corruption, 241, 378
couplings
  loose, viii–ix
  tight, viii–ix
courts, 147
co-variation, 274
craft industries, 271
creativity, 289–290, 379–380
crises
  management, 287
  power and, 159
critical theory, 325
critique, 170
Crozier, Michel, 113, 275
curriculum vitae, 76
cybernetics, 14–15, 375
  operational closure and, 38

Darwinism, 29
data
  memory and, 224
  processing, 268–269, 309
dates
  decision-making and, 137–138
  expiration, 161
de Man, Paul, 28
deadlines
  decision-making and, 137–138
  defining, 138
  setting, 138
  time and, 138
  value-neutrality of, 139
death, 240
decentralization, vii–viii, 64–65, 250
decision premises, 349
  in autopoiesis, 186
  cognitive routines and, 200
  communication and, 211, 259–260
  confusion mitigated by, 192
  coordination of, 201–202
  decidable, 193
  decision-making and, 185
  defining, 181–182
  dependence on, 186
  distinguishing, 182
  in environment, 182
  as environment extension, 185–186

objectives and, 183
operational closure in, 185
organizational culture and, 182
orientation on, 193
as oscillators, 182
personnel management and, 235
planning, 187
rationality and, 183–184
reforms and, 277
roles and, 203
self-organization and, 185–186
self-reference and, 199
substitution of, 183
tasks and, 188–189
tests for, 186
uncertainty and, 181–182
undecidable, 194
decision programs, 182–183, 213
  defining, 210, 220–221
  management and, 211
  as memory, 223
  memory and, 224–225
  tasks and, 210–211
decision-making, 44, 131, 136–137, 285–286
  acceptance and, 108
  action and, 99
  arbitrariness in, 106
  attribution and, 107–108
  autopoiesis of, 132
  choice and, 99, 106
  classical theory of, 52
  cognition and, 214
  communication and, 42, 44, 45, 47–48,
    110–111, 150–151, 287
  competence and, 266–266
  contingency theory and, 110
  dates and, 137–138
  deadlines and, 137–138
  decision premises and, 185
  defining, 99
  discretionary power of, 156–157
  formal iteration of, 151
  future and, 129
  intentions and, 106
  as linear process, 132
  memory and, 123, 126, 133, 154
  monitoring, 182
  objectivity and, 106
  observation and, 104, 107, 387–388
  organizational culture and, 113
  in organizational theory, 49
  paradoxes and, 104
  personnel deployment, 241
  in personnel management, 233
  present and, 125–126

purposive programs and, 219
rational, 14–15, 52
rationality and, 217
reforms and, 279–280
responsibility and, 163–164
risky, 126
rules, 182–183
sequentiality in, 148
social systems and, 112
stories and, 132
time and, 127
at top, 266
uncertainty and, 150–151, 155
unity of, 104
world-time and, 142
deconstruction, 6, 83–84
deconstructivism, 112
degrees of freedom, 72–73
Gilles, 280–281
demystification, 352–353
dependent variables, 258
deregulation, vii–viii
Derrida, Jacques, ix, 28, 101–102
Descartes, Rene, 101–102
descriptions
    paradox and, 28
    of society, 28
    of world, 28
despotism, 171
determinate/indeterminate schema, 351–352
dialectic, viii, 351–352
    Hegel on, 27
difference, 27, 318
    future as, 129–130
    present and, 125
    purpose as, 130, 217–218
    unity of, 376–377
differential variation, 274
differentiation
    of competence, 264–265
    functional, 258, 330–331, 333–334
    horizontal, 251
    segmentary, 258, 327–328
    vertical, 251
directive correlation, 162–163,
    165–166
discrimination, 326
disembedding, 335–336
disorder, 371–372
distinctions, 124
    cognition and, 213–214
    combining, 105
    of decision premises, 182
    distinguishable, 105
    observation and, 100

reentry of, 103
    sides of, 130
division of labor, ix, 262
    specialization in, 256
double closure, 261, 349
    von Foerster on, 185
double framing, membership and, 81
double-entry accounting, 153–154
downsizing, 291
drug consumption, 211
Durkheim, Emile, 337–338

economic theory, 63, 340
    environment and, 373
    neoclassical, 142
economic utility calculation, 79
economies of scale, 253–254
    time and, 255
education system, 317
efficiency, 74
eigenvalues, 107, 359–360
elasticity, 210–211
    informal, 242
electronic data processing, 268–269, 309
embeddedness, 16, 335–336
employee assessments, 235
enactment, 33–34
ends/means schema, 9–10, 12, 299, 353
    causality and, 218
    maximum values in, 184
    nexus of, 219–220
    pathology of, 220
    purposive programs and, 220
    rationality and, 184
    suitability of, 200
enterprises, 210, 250, 334
entropy, 102
environment, 288–289, 382
    change in, 276–277
    decision premises as extension of,
        185–186
    decision premises in, 182
    defining, 15, 336–337
    economic theory and, 373
    inaccessibility of, 258
    internal, 90
    iteration in, 224
    reentry of, 189–190, 200
    as source of uncertainty, 164
    systems theory and, 17, 36, 46–47, 128, 376
    Weick on, 15
environmental complexity, 13
equality, 324, 326
equifinality, 69
equilibrium, 273, 352

error, 211–212, 378, 382
  in nature, 212
  normal, 212
esprit de corps, 40
essence, of organization, 26, 41
ethnomethodology, 161–162, 195, 370
Europe, 197, 321
evoked sets, 261
evolutionary models, 29, 49–50, 284,
    285–286, 287, 288
  planning and, 287–288, 289
  reforms and, 283–284
excel strategies, 362, 363
executives, 167
expectations
  in personnel management, 233
  rational, 126
experience, 50
  in communication, 161
  expiration date of, 161
  obsolescent, 176
expiration date, of experience, 161
explicit communication, 157
external boundaries, 192–193
external framing, 81
external recruitment, 238
externalizations, 371–372

face-to-face interaction, 167
facticity, 130
  of uncertainty, 161–162
failure
  learning and, 50
  of reforms, 276
  success and, 242–243, 280
false alarm, 221
family, 315
fate, 74–75, 77
feedback, 140
Fichte, Johann Gottlieb, 101–102, 144
fictional narrative, 63
financial market, 13–14
first-order observation, 387
fixed knowledge, 8
flexibility, 255, 385
flows, 122
forbearance, 154
forecastibility, rationality and, 384
forensics, 70
forgetting, 126
  memory and, 154
formal communication, 8–9
formal organization, 182–183
  visibility of, 267
formal/informal distinction, 7, 8–9

formalization, 211
formally free contract, 78–79
Frames, 3–4
free will, 77–78
freedom, 324
  cognition and, 200–201, 214
  individuals and, 77–78, 79
  Kant on, 99
  power and, 353–354
  programming and, 213–214
  psychic factors and, 79
  societal theory and, 78, 79
  symbolizing, 78
French Revolution, 2
Freud, Sigmund, 96
functional differentiation, 258, 330–331,
    333–334
functionalism, 11–12
functions
  of communication, 39, 40
  memory, 149, 224
fundamentalism, 387, 392
future, 279
  decision-making and, 129
  as difference, 129–130
  ignorance about, 132–133
  indeterminacy of, 237–238
  oscillations and, 130
  past and, 131–132, 135–136, 137, 154–155,
    213, 243, 278, 280–281
  personnel management and, 233
  planning and, 187
  in purposive programs, 218
  rationality and, 370–371
  reforms and, 279
  unknownness of, 374

Gehlen, Arnold, 227
genera, 26, 53–54, 155
general management, 231
general systems theory, 18
general theory, 40–41
Gergen, Kenneth, 28
Germany, 253–254, 281, 320–321, 336
Giddens, Anthony, 300
globalization, 291
goal-oriented organizations, 11
goal-seeking organizations, 11
Goffmann, Erving, 9, 203
gossip, 244
governance, uncertainty and, 172, 257
Great Depression, 360–361
Greenpeace, 354
group dynamics, 8
group formation, 250

Günther, Gotthard, 377
Gutenberg, Erich, 334

Habermas, Jürgen, 10–11, 384–385
Hawthorne experiments, 7
Hegel, G. W. F., viii, 36, 351–352
    on dialectic, 27
Heidegger, Martin, 28
Herbst, Philip G., 162–163
heteronomy, vii
hierarchical distinctions, 1–2
hierarchies, 251, 264, 337, 349
    alternatives to, 6
    communication and, 220, 257, 266
    competence and, 256, 257–258, 265
    market and, 5
    in organizational theory, 257
    planning and, 221–222
    rationality and, 355
    regulation by, 191
    self-description and, 355–356
    status, 244
    technology and, 306
    time and, 365
    uncertainty coping and, 6, 257
historical machine system, 131–132
history, 282
holism, 17
horizontal coordination, 257
horizontal differentiation, 251
how-questions, 53–54
human relations movement, 212, 299–300, 355
humanity, 66, 87
Husserl, Edmund, 314
hybrid formations, 336
hyperturbulence, 291

identity, 11–12
    career and, 242–243
    condensed, 224
    corporate, 232
    innovation and, 362–363
    paradox, 357
ideology, 347–348
ignorance
    knowledge and, 148, 149–150
    production of, 149
    uncertainty and, 149
imagination, 393–394
imperfect matching, 50–51
impersonal bureaucracy, 234
inclusion/exclusion, 324, 325
inconsistencies, observation of, 275
indeterminability, 184
    in present, 186

self-reference and, 189–190
indeterminacy, 125–126, 211
    in conditional programs, 215
    filling in, 216
    of future, 237–238
    structural, 340
    unresolvable, viii, 183–184, 383–384
indicators, 155
individual behavior, 44
individuals, 230
    freedom and, 77–78, 79
    understanding and, 86–87
inertial effects, change and, 197
informal communication, 8–9
informal organization, 8, 74, 108, 163, 212,
    267, 299–300, 353
information, 68
    assignment of, 160
    communication and, 100, 111
    complete, 150
    complexity and, 260
    connectivity and, 36–37
    growth of, 202
    micropolitics and, 157
    negative and, 38
    posts without, 188–189
    processing, 151
    transformation of, 147
    utterance and, 114
information processing, 10, 34
    negentropy and, 37
    organization and, 37
information theory, guidelines of, 156–157
innovation, 131, 274–275, 283
    identity and, 362–363
    improvement and, 170
    leadership and, 170
    rewarding, 224–225
    technology and, 300–301
innovations, within organizational culture, 198
input/output models, 51, 64–65, 212
inside, 1–2
institutional theory, 52, 65, 361, 364
    social systems and, 168–169
institutionalism, 78, 339–340, 360–361
institutions
    concept of, 16
    organizational theory and, 15–16
instrumental rationality, 10–11, 16
integration, 72
    characteristics of, 73
    defining, 72–73
    delayed, 73
    difference-oriented principle of, 76–77
    in technical systems, 73

intentions, 69–70
  decision-making and, 106
interaction, 53–54
  face-to-face, 167
  time and, 167
interactional communication, 167
interdependence interruption, 326, 327–328
interest, 369
  power and, 175–176
  schema, 116
internal communication, 197
internal environment, 90
interpersonal competence, 72
interpretant, 105–106
intersubjectivity, 72
intransparency, 161–162
intrasystemic causality, 226
irony, uncertainty and, 152
irrationality, 370
irritation, 30–31
  communicative, 28
  paradoxes of, 170–171
  uncertainty and, 170–171
Italy, 194, 320, 336

job cutting, 255
job descriptions, 259–260
job enlargement, 256
judicial control, 332
just-in-time, 46–47

Kahneman, Daniel, 373–374
Kant, Immanuel, 2, 27, 216
  on freedom, 99
kenograms, 189
knowledge, 17
  ignorance and, 148, 149–150
  uncertainty and, 149

labor
  division of, ix, 256, 262
  market, 13–14, 316
labyrinth, 349
Lamarck, Antoine de Monet de, 284
Lanzara, Giovan Francesco, 115–116, 278
large technical systems (LTS), 303–304
latent structures, 102–103
Lawrence, Paul R., 15, 65
leadership styles, 83
  innovation and, 170
leadership theory, 64, 107
lean management, 259
lean production, 352–353
learning, 49–50
  ability, 74

adaptive, 50
failure and, 50
memory and, 50
organizational, 216
success and, 50
legal systems
  communication and, 322
  in United States, 329
legality
  of means, 219
  written communication and, 167
linguistic analysis, 152
lobby organizations, 320
localization, of memory, 224
London Tavistock Institute, 63–64
long-term memory, 82
Lorsch, Jay W., 15, 65
LTS. See large technical systems
Lyotard, Jean-François, 91, 112

machine model, 46–47, 64–65
  critiques of, 165
machines
  broken, 200
  non-trivial, 49, 51, 198–199
  trivial, 49, 51
management, 2–3, 65. See also personnel
    management
  crises, 287
  decision programs and, 211
managerial revolution, 340
manifest structures, 102–103
Marbury v. Madison, 330
March, James, 50–51, 147–148, 261,
    373–374
  on organizations, 131, 379
marginal zones, 159
market
  commodity, 13–14
  consumer goods and, 80
  dependence on, 80
  financial, 13–14
  hierarchy and, 5
  labor, 13–14, 316
  product, 13–14
  regulation by, 191
Marquard, Odo, 281–282
Marx, Karl, 80, 113–114, 319–320
mass production, 301–302
Maturana, Humberto, 31, 258–259, 307–308,
    328–329
meaning, 34
  repetition and, 38
means
  legality of, 219

means-end rationality, 147
of production, 4
mechanical energy, 301–302
medical care, 340
membership, 77
  communication and, 323
  components of, 79
  double framing and, 81
  motivation and, 80
  rights to, 325
  self-realization and, 82–83
memory, 116, 307–308, 363
  analogy and, 123
  cells, 153
  communication and, 225
  data and, 224
  decision programs as, 223, 224–225
  decision-making and, 123, 126, 133, 154
  defining, 152
  evolved, 223
  forgetting and, 154
  function, 39, 149, 224
  as inventive mechanism, 154
  learning and, 50
  limitations of, 225
  localization of, 224
  long-term, 82
  mental, 153–154
  motives and, 65, 82
  observation and, 101–102
  in operations, 153
  in organizations, 154–155
  oscillation and, 130–131
  performance, 348
  psychic factors and, 133, 348
  reflections on, 225
  self-description and, 364–365
  short-term, 82
  social systems and, 133, 348
  time and, 123
  time-indexed, 152–153
  truth and, 224
  in uncertainty, 153–154
  writing and, 127
mergers, 256
merit, 362
Merton, Robert, 113–114
metaphor, 31
Meyer, Eva, 105
Meyer, John, 51–52
microdiversity, 203
  self-organization and, 203
micropolitics, 265–266, 267
  information and, 157
Middle Ages, 1

mixed programs, 214
mobile redundancies, posts as, 189
modernization, 321
motivation, 62–63
  membership and, 80
  psychic factors and, 69–70
  for reforms, 279
motives
  actions and, 71
  communication and, 69–70
  memory and, 65, 82
  time and, 70
mysticism, 16
mystification, 106

narratives, 234
  culture, 221–222
nature, ix–x
  errors in, 212
negative, information and, 38
negative capabilities, 278
negentropy, information processing and, 37
neoclassical economic theory, 142
nepotism, 241
New Age movement, 17
Nietzsche, Friedrich, 28
nobility, 351–352
non-linguistic communication, 168
non-trivial machines, 49, 51, 198–199
Norman invasion, 282
normative obligation, 79
normative validity, 214
norms, 211–212
nuclear missiles, 221

objective reality, career and, 244
objectives, decision premises and, 183
objectivity, 235–236
  decision-making and, 106
observation, 265
  conditions of, 100–101
  decision-making and, 104, 107, 387–388
  distinctions and, 100
  first-order, 387
  of inconsistencies, 275
  memory and, 101–102
  modes of, 8
  operation of, 130
  paradoxes of, ix–x, 103, 148, 380–381
  of personnel management, 242
  second-order, 140, 265
  third-order, 30
  time and, 124
obsolescent, experience, 176
official channels, 182–183

open communication, 232
open contingency, 186
openness, 13–14
operational closure, 33–35, 43, 50–51,
    189–190, 226, 258, 387
  autopoiesis and, 33
  cybernetics and, 38
  in decision premises, 185
  as structural drift, 258–259
operational separation, 66
operations
  autopoiesis and, 32
  memory in, 153
  modes of, 41
  of observation, 130
  systems theory and, 125
opponents, 169, 170
opportunities, recognition of, 231–232
oral communication, 167
  ambiguity and, 202
order, organization and, 2–3
organizational culture, 51–52, 127, 244,
    281–282, 288–289, 354
  ambiguity and, 195
  change in, 196–197
  decision premises and, 182
  decision-making and, 113
  defining, 194–195, 197
  development of, 195
  evolution of, 198
  formulation of, 198
  innovations within, 198
  positive connotations of, 194
  resistance in, 196–197
  Rodriguez on, 194
  values and, 195–196
organizational design, 201–202
organizational development, 8, 63–64
organizational learning, 216
organizational principles, 268
organizational symbolism, 232
organizational theory, 338–339
  abstraction of, 3
  classical, 3–4, 171, 252, 254, 352,
    353–354, 355
  on cognitive routines, 201
  communication in, 41
  decision-making in, 49
  in eighteenth century, 1–2
  hierarchy in, 257
  history of, 1
  institutional approach to, 15–16
  market and, 5
  in nineteenth century, 2
  rationality and, 9

organizations, 128
  administrative, 146
  aging, 234–235
  autopoiesis and, 148
  communication and, 39, 41–42
  competitors, 169
  defining, viii–ix
  as entities, vii
  essence of, 26, 41
  goal-oriented, 11
  goal-seeking, 11
  growth of, 255
  informal, 8, 74, 108, 267, 299–300,
    353
  information processing and, 37
  internal conflicts in, 53
  lobby, 320
  logic of, vii
  manual operations in, 42
  March on, 131, 379
  memory in, 154–155
  order and, 2–3
  as process, vii
  redescription of, 202
  risks managed by, 169
  size of, 253–254, 256
  size of, and posts, 190–191
  structural, 252
  uncertainty and, 42–43, 165
  Weick on, 379
oscillations, 359–360
  decision premises as, 182
  future and, 130
  memory and, 130–131
  primary, 231–232
other-reference, 48–49, 382
  complexity and, 257–258
other-selection, 74–75
  self-selection and, 77
outside, 1–2

paradoxes, 114, 379–380, 381
  communication and, 83, 148
  complexity as, 253
  decision-making and, 104
  descriptions and, 28
  form of, 103
  identity, 357
  of irritation, 170–171
  of observation, ix–x, 103, 148, 380–381
  reentry as, 135
  scientific theories and, 28
  self-referential systems and, 35–36
  of time, 377–378
  transformation, 273

unfolding, 102, 103, 135, 251–252
of uniqueness, 361
paradoxical communication, 84–85
reentry and, 85
Parsons, Talcott, 360–361
past
future and, 131–132, 135–136, 137,
154–155, 213, 243, 278, 280–281
posts and, 189
patronage, 241
Paul, Jean, 1, 29, 132
Peirce, Charles S., 105–106
perceivable, 86–87
perception
bodily, 66–67
communication and, 37, 86–87, 200
psychic factors and, 115
perfect competition, 10
performance assessment, 168–169
performative contradiction, 26, 83
Perrow, Charles, 193
personal communication, 232
personality, 68
personhood, 91
communication and, 67–68
roles and, 68
personnel deployment, 268
decision-making, 241
regulation of, 182–183
personnel development, 235
personnel dimension, 252
personnel management, 230, 244,
355
assignment criteria, 244–245
decision premises and, 235
decision-making in, 233
employee assessments, 235
expectations in, 233
future and, 233
multi-dimensionality in, 239–240
observation of, 242
responsibility in, 233
selection processes, 240
tasks of, 232–233
traditional, 231
uncertainty and, 234
upgrading, 251
vacancies, 236–237
physical violence, 158–159
planning, 202–203, 283
change and, 284–285
consensus for, 289
decision premises, 187
evolutionary models and, 287–288,
289

future and, 187
hierarchies and, 221–222
poiesis, 31–32
political apparatus, apex of, 165
political correctness, 152
political economy, 63
population, 1–2
ecology, 285
models, 284
positive law, 220–221
positivity, 2
postmodernism, 193–194, 387
posts
approval of, 190
assigning, 188
established, 190
half-time, 188
without information, 188–189
inventory of, 190
as mobile redundancies, 189
organization size and, 190–191
past and, 189
in private sector, 187
in public sector, 187
scope of, 188
structures, 188
symbolization of, 188
unity of, 201–202
vacant, 189
potentialization, 290–291
power, 241–242
crises and, 159
defining, 158
exercise of, 252
freedom and, 353–354
interest and, 175–176
threat, 158–159
uncertainty and, 159, 171, 175
power relations, 45
power-theoretical description, 158
practice, theory and, 393–394
praxis, 316
preferences, 217
premise control, 193
replacement of, 193
the present, 123–124, 152–153
career and, 243–244
decision-making and, 125–126
difference and, 125
indeterminability, 186
prevention rationality, 258–259
primary distinction, 118
principle, 204, 380
organizational, 268
right, 257

private sector, 46–47, 247
    posts in, 187
    promotion in, 160–161
privatization, 259
probability, 75
problem schema, 116–117, 359
    defining, 303
product markets, 13–14
production
    planning, 165
    plants, 18
proemial order, 189
professional competence, 256, 257–258
professional culture, 244
profit motive, 63
programming, freedom and, 213–214
programs, 223
    conditional, 210–211, 213, 215, 217, 221,
        222–223, 225
    interconnection of, 215
    mixed, 214
    purposive, 213, 216, 217, 218, 220, 225
prohibition, 228
promotion, 239
    in private sector, 160–161
psychiatry, 6
psychic factors, 65
    freedom and, 79
    memory and, 133, 348
    motivation and, 69–70
    perception and, 115
    social systems and, 71, 84
psychology, 63–64
public opinion, 354
public sector, posts in, 187
purpose, as difference, 130, 217–218
purposive programs
    causality and, 225
    conditional programs and, 217
    construction of, 216
    decision-making and, 219
    defining, 213
    ends/means schema and, 220
    future in, 218
    teleology of, 217

rational decision-making, 14–15
    classical theory of, 52
rational expectations, 126
rationality, 74, 230, 317–318, 382, 384–385
    attainability of, 11
    bounded, 10–11
    causality and, 375
    contextual, 370
    decision premises and, 183–184

decision-making and, 217
    defining, 369–370
    ends/means schema and, 184
    forecastibility and, 384
    future and, 370–371
    hierarchies and, 355
    instrumental, 10–11, 16
    irrationality, 370
    means-end, 147
    organizational theory and, 9
    prevention, 258–259
    through reentry, 382–383
    requirements, 261
    responsibility shift and, 136–137
    static, 240
    subversion of, 373–374
    system, 333
    technical, 353
    uncertainty and, 217
    understanding-oriented, 10–11
    value, 10–11
rationalization, 141
re-actualization, 134
reason, ix–x
recognition, 224
recruitment, 237, 238
    external, 238
recursions, 130–131, 374
    analysis of, 136
    non-programmed, 137
    programmed, 137
redeployment, 237, 239
reductions, 14
redundancies, 37
    in communication, 195
    mobile, 189
reentry, 381, 383–384
    in calculus of forms, 48–49
    consequences of, 183–184
    of distinctions, 103
    of environment, 189–190, 200
    generation of, 149
    as paradox unfolding, 135
    paradoxical communication and, 85
    rationality through, 382–383
    of time, 135, 142
reflection loops, 223, 253, 364
reforms, 261, 274–275, 278
    consensus and, 278–279
    decision premises and, 277
    decision-making and, 279–280
    defining, 277–278
    effects of, 276
    evolutionary models and, 283–284
    as experiments, 279

failed, 276
future and, 279
goals of, 281–283
marketing, 276
motivation for, 279
prompts for, 275
success of, 277, 278
regulation, of personnel deployment,
182–183
relativism, 53
relays, 138
religion, 198, 323
repetition, 136–137
fear of, 137
meaning and, 38
repression, 96
reproduction, 113, 285
of uncertainty, 341
requisitive variety, 14–15, 258
resource conservation, 11–12, 35
in technical systems, 306
responsibility, 261–262, 350
accountability and, 156, 163
attribution of, 158
communication developed from, 260
decision-making and, 163–164
defining, 156
in personnel management, 233
rationality and, 136–137
uncertainty and, 156
restructuring, 234–235
right principle, 257
rightness conditions, 211–212
risks, 133–134, 170, 222, 308
conditional programs and, 222–223
decision-making and, 126
organization management of, 169
Rodriguez, Dario, on organizational
culture, 194
roles, 316
decision premises and, 203
defining, 62
personhood and, 68
weaknesses of, 62–63
Rowan, Brian, 51–52
rule/exception schema, 216

Saint-Simon, Comte de, 2
Schiller, Friedrich, 197
schismogenesis, 275
schizophrenia, 83–84
Schlegel, Friedrich, viii
scientific management, 2–3
scientific theories, paradox and, 28
scientificity, 2

scripts, 357
second-order observation, 140, 265
segmentary differentiation, 258, 327–328
self, variability of, 30
self-conception, 358
self-contradiction, ix–x
self-description, 31, 348, 351, 353, 354–355,
356–357, 362, 371
consultants, 358–359
defining, 347–348
hierarchies and, 355–356
memory and, 364–365
official, 352
texts, 350
self-discipline, 231
self-evidences, 152
self-observation, 31, 48, 347
career and, 244
distinctions in, 48–49
self-organization, viii, 30, 202–203,
252–253
decision premises and, 185–186
microdiversity and, 203
self-preservation, 11–12
self-realization, 66
membership and, 82–83
self-reference, 327, 374, 382
complexity and, 257–258
decision premises and, 199
indeterminability and, 189–190
self-referential systems, 29, 31, 48–49
paradoxes and, 35–36
self-regulation, 156
self-reinforcement, careers and, 76
self-selection, 74–75
other-selection and, 77
self-symbolization, 78–79
self-transparency, ix
semantic forms, 133, 357
Serres, Michael, 107
Shackle, G. L. S., 132, 278
Shell Group, 354
short-term memory, 82
Simon, Herbert, 10–11, 14–15, 141, 147–148,
203, 261
simultaneity, 125
skepticism, 276
slavery, 316
sociable communication, 85
social, 18–19
social capital, 336
social stability, 62–63
social stratum, 160–161, 362
social systems, 62
all-inclusive, 168–169

social systems (cont.)
  communication and, 41, 81–82, 112,
    321–322
  decision-making and, 112
  institutional theory and, 168–169
  memory and, 133, 348
  psychic factors and, 71, 84
social work, 258, 386
sociality, communication and, 38–39
societal theory, 318, 334
  freedom and, 78, 79
  values and, 196
society, descriptions of, 28
sociology, 2, 62
socio-technical systems, 299–300, 301
software technology, 305
solidarity, 18–19
specialization, in division of labor, 256
species, 26, 53–54
Spencer-Brown, George, viii, 28, 48–49,
    85, 135, 191–192, 381
statements, 156
static rationality, 240
Stinchcombe, Arthur L., 276
storytelling, 361
stratification, 161, 265–266
structural changes, 274
structural coupling, 328–329, 330–331
structural diversification, 260
structural drift, 52, 328–329
  determination of, 157–158
  operational closure as, 258–259
structural indeterminacy, 340
structural organization, 252
structures, 274
sub-goals, 210
subjects, 46–47
sublation, 27
subsidiaries, 255
success, 344
  failure and, 242–243, 280
  learning and, 50
  of reforms, 277, 278
succession, 81–82
superstition, 378
supplements, ix
Sweden, welfare in, 5–6
symbolic force, 158
synchronization, 128–129
  automatic, 215
system boundaries, 53
  crossing of, 53
system rationality, 333
system reference, 58
  differentiation of, 205

system-oriented management, 23
systems theory, 16, 64–65
  autopoiesis and, 43, 53
  communication and, 84
  environment and, 17, 36, 46–47, 128, 376
  general, 18
  operations and, 125
  von Foerster on, 198–199

taboo, 198
tact, 71
Tarascon, Tartarin de, 379
tasks
  analysis of, 210
  decision premises and, 188–189
  decision programs and, 210–211
  defining, 188–189, 210
  elimination of, 210–211
  of personnel management, 232–233
Taylor, on work organization, 3
Taylorism, 3, 7, 230, 299
teamwork, 242–243
technical rationality, 353
technical systems, 308
  couplings in, 302, 305
  integration in, 73
  large, 303–304
  malfunctions in, 306
  resources in, 306
  socio-technical systems, 299–300, 301
technology, 299, 301, 310–311
  banning, 303
  defining, 300, 304–305, 307–308
  demands on, 304
  dependence on, 309–310, 319–320
  hierarchies and, 306
  innovation and, 300–301
  reliability of, 307
  software, 305
teleology, 378
  of purposive programs, 217
tempo, 191–192
temporal perspectives, 43
temporalization, 189–190
testing tools, 258
theory, practice and, 393–394
third man problem, 356
third-order observation, 30
thought, 115, 146
threat power, 158–159
time, 49, 72
  binding, 131–132
  causality and, 140
  communication and, 123–124
  complexity and, 383–384

deadlines and, 138
decision-making and, 127
economies of scale and, 255
hierarchies and, 365
interaction and, 167
memory and, 123
motives and, 70
observation and, 124
paradox of, 377–378
points in, 123
reentry of, 135, 142
scarcity of, 139
world, 109
time-indexed memory, 152–153
topics
of communication, 39
memory function and, 39
transformation paradox, 273
transition, 36–37
transversal values, 339–340
trivial machines, 49, 51
truth
communication and, 83, 151–152
memory and, 224
values, 154–155
turn-taking, 167
Tversky, Amos, 373–374
type, choice of, 155

Ulrich, Hans, 23
uncertainty, ix, 6, 75–76, 279,
337–338
absorption, 6, 30–31, 148–149, 150, 158,
159–160, 181, 267
authority and, 160
autopoiesis and, 132
career and, 75, 76–77
certainty and, 168, 169
cognitive routines and, 200
communication and, 167
coping with, 31
decision premises and, 181–182
decision-making and, 149, 150–151,
155
diffusion of, 166
environment as source of, 164
facticity of, 161–162
generation of, 149, 163, 257
governance and, 172, 257
hierarchies and coping with, 6, 257
ignorance and, 149
irony and, 152
irritation and, 170–171
knowledge and, 149
memory in, 153–154

organizations and, 42–43, 165
personnel management and, 234
power and, 159, 171, 175
rationality and, 217
recognition of, 150
reproduction of, 341
responsibility shift and, 156
self-generated, 81, 260
unconscious, 96
undecidability, 104
undecidable decision premises, 194
understandability, 116
understanding, 68
individuals and, 86–87
understanding-oriented rationality, 10–11
unexpected, causality and, 218–219
unhealthy working conditions, 196
uniqueness, 361
United States, 10
legal systems in, 329
unity, 140–141
of decision-making, 104
of difference, 376–377
of objects, 101
of posts, 201–202
University of Aston, 254
unmarked spaces, 192–193, 218–219,
261
unresolvable indeterminacy, viii, 183–184,
383–384
utterance, 68, 115
information and, 114

vacancies, 236–237
need for, 255
non-formalized criteria, 239
vacant posts, 189
value change, 64–65
value rationality, 10–11
values, 339
causality and, 196
organizational culture and, 195–196
societal theory and, 196
transversal, 339–340
validity of, 195–196
Varela, Francisco, 307–308
variability, of self, 30
variables, dependent, 258
variation, 286, 287, 288
vertical differentiation, 251
violence, physical, 158–159
virtual reality, 88
von Foerster, Heinz, 7, 49
on double closure, 185
on systems theory, 198–199

wages, 188, 385
Weber, Max, 7, 69–70, 80, 107, 165,
    172, 299
  on action, 10
  on bureaucracy, 4, 6, 7, 167
  on communication, 167
Weick, Karl, 23, 33–34, 284–285, 290,
    373–374
  on environment, 15
  on organizations, 379
welfare, 385
  in Sweden, 5–6
what-questions, 53–54
work, 302
  defining, 316

  social, 258, 386
  Taylor on, 3
  teamwork, 242–243
  unhealthy working conditions, 196
world, descriptions of, 28
world time, 109
Second World War, 3–4, 10
world-time, 128
  decision-making and, 142
writing, memory and, 127
written communication, 87–88, 127
  legality and, 167

zone of indifference, 5–6, 82–83
  limits of, 232